Walter B. Barbe

Associate Editor
HIGHLIGHTS FOR CHILDREN

PSYCHOLOGY and EDUCATION of the GIFTED: Selected Readings

New York

APPLETON-CENTURY-CROFTS

Division of Meredith Publishing Company

To my mother

Edith Barbe Jackson

PREFACE

This selection of readings on the psychology and education of the gifted includes philosophical presentations, discussions of particular points of view, reviews of literature on specific topics, and significant research reports. Although most of the material has been published in the past few years, inclusion was determined by importance in the field rather than recency of publication.

Much of the material is of an advanced level, being more suitable for the serious student than the casual reader. No claim is made that the book is all-inclusive, for the already voluminous professional literature on the gifted is ever increasing. Significant points of view are presented, some contradictory to one another, as are research reports, the results of which are not always in complete agreement. A conscientious effort has been made to include what the editor believes to be those materials that he would most want his students to read.

The intended purposes of the book are varied. As a collection of much of the outstanding literature on the psychology and education of the gifted, it serves as an overview of thinking and research either to supplement a text in the field or to serve as a text in a course on the gifted. Also, it is obvious that bringing together this many articles and research reports facilitates the serious student's search for particular material.

Included are materials on creativity, originality, and non-intellectual factors of giftedness. In addition to the historical development of the psychology and education of the gifted, concepts concerning the gifted and facets of giftedness are presented. The measurement of giftedness and the background of the gifted are treated. The section on developing and encouraging giftedness includes selections on the gifted in the elementary and high school. The book concludes with selections on issues and on research on the gifted.

Appreciation is expressed to the authors and publishers of the articles for permission to reprint their material in this book. The cause of the gifted is furthered today by the increased awareness and understanding of the problems of the gifted which is due in no small measure to the writings of those whose materials are reprinted here. The Author Index contains the name of virtually every person who has worked in the area of the gifted.

The editor expresses his sincere appreciation to those who aided him in the preparation of this manuscript. Mrs. Margaret Betzhold tended to the details, from the obtaining of permissions to the preparation of the index. Most certainly, the book would never have been completed without her assistance and support. Rev. Herbert Neff, of Tennessee Wesleyan College, aided greatly in the collection of the materials. Kent State University provided support through a released-time research grant. Numerous others aided in reading copy, typing, and providing encouragement, not least of which was my son, Fred, a freshman at Salem College, who has just discovered the excitement of his first course in psychology.

W. B. B.

CONTENTS

I

Introduction to the Study of the Gifted

THE PSYCHOLOGY OF gifted children has been too long neglected. Now that the social climate has changed so radically in attitudes toward gifted children, there is hope that more research on the psychology of the intellectually superior will aid teachers and administrators in assisting the gifted to realize their potential.

More and more is being learned about the physical characteristics, interests, attitudes, and mental abilities of all children—the retarded, average and gifted—but far less research has been done on the psychology of gifted children. If psychology is to be defined as the study of man in relation to his environment, there is definitely a need to devote more attention to the psychological problems involved both in the studying and education of the gifted individual. The study of the gifted is well underway; an understanding of the gifted will come about only from using what is known in an attempt to aid him in his adjustments.

The misconceptions concerning gifted individuals, widely believed before Terman disproved them, and to some extent still believed by many people today, probably come from the writings in the late nineteenth century of such men as Lombroso and Nisbet. In *The Man of Genius* (1), published in 1895 in London and New York, and widely read throughout the world, Lombroso attempted to show that insanity was closely related to genius. In *The Insanity of Genius* (2), Nisbet purports to prove this same theory.

While no intelligent person today believes that "genius and insanity go hand in hand," there is evidence that those individuals scoring in the highest ranges of the intelligence test (over 180) are characterized by different adjustment problems from those of the average child. Leta Hollingworth recognizes this in *Gifted Children* in which she states,

1

"Another generalization that can be made about these children (over 180 I.Q.) is that nearly all have been school problems (3)."

Perhaps the very existence of abilities so far superior to those of the average makes for this poorer adjustment. It must be remembered, however, that gifted children in general are better adjusted than the average. This does not mean that they have fewer adjustments to make, but rather that even though they may face more adjustments than do the average, they generally make such adjustments successfully.

CAUSES OF GIFTEDNESS

Since it was first realized that men differed from one another in mental capabilities, causes of giftedness have been the subject of much discussion. Whether giftedness is due entirely to heredity or entirely to environment, or to a combination of both, has been debated among psychologists for years. A general feeling exists today that, while heredity places certain limits upon one's intellectual range, environment provides the stimulus which makes it possible for one to function at the higher limit of this range.

Abraham states this in another manner, using actual I.Q. points as the way in which environment, be it good or bad, can influence a child's mental functioning. He states:

The authorities differ on the number of so-called I.Q. points that can be added by the richest kind of experiences, but some of them say as many as 10 to 20 points; on the other hand, an extremely restrictive environment might pull the child down that many points from his level of an early age. It would take an environment of almost complete deprivation to bring a child down to the lowest figure, however (4).

While there are not always explanations for the conflicting findings of different research reports on groups of gifted children, certain facts have nevertheless been well established. Consideration of these findings gives some enlightenment on the causes of giftedness.

1. *Are there more gifted boys than gifted girls?* For many years it was thought that the number of gifted boys was greater than the number of gifted girls. Hollingworth gives a detailed account of the sex ratio in each of Terman's groups which ultimately made up the group reported on in *Genetic Studies of Genius* (5). In the first group, consisting of 180 children with I.Q. of 140 and above, Terman found a sex ratio of 60:40, "boys preponderating." "Above 160 I.Q. the ratio was 65:35, and above 180 I.Q., it was 70:30." These data were collected in such a manner that there was the possibility of bias in the sample. With a more systematic selection of subjects, Terman reported a sex ratio of 55:45, in favor of boys. Hollingworth summarizes by saying:

The nearest approach we have to such a census is found in the recent investigations of Terman. In making the Stanford revision of the Binet-Simon tests, during the course of which the 905 school children . . . were tested, Terman found no difference in variability between boys and girls. The proportion of gifted and of marked inferior intellects was the same for both sexes (6).

Although psychologists generally concede that this is no longer an unanswered question, as late as 1947 Terman and Oden state, "In view of the contradictory nature of the evidence now available, any positive conclusions will have to await further investigation (7)."

Not all studies have favored boys, for in programs for gifted children which begin in the elementary grades there appears to be a preponderance of girls. Popular journals have plunged into the controversy with articles entitled, "Are Women Smarter Than Men?" which appeared in *McCall's* (8), and "Women Are Intellectually Inferior," which appeared in the *American Mercury* (9).

Perhaps the only answer which can be given to this question is a qualified one. When tested early in elementary grades, girls seem to receive higher scores on achievement and ability tests, but testing of high school seniors seems to favor boys. On the National Merit Scholarship Examinations there are twice as many winners who are boys. Undoubtedly, cultural factors, as well as factors involving maturation and even test construction, contribute to the cause for this. Of practical importance to school administrators, however, is that no program can be operated which, because of any mental factor, excludes all but a few boys or all but a few girls.

2. *Do gifted parents have gifted children?* While it is true that eminent men tend to come from eminent families, as Galton so well demonstrated in *Hereditary Genius* (10) in 1914, this does nothing more than add fuel to the nature-nurture controversy. Perhaps it is the influence of eminent parents which have made it possible for many individuals to become eminent, rather than any innate ability of their own.

There is a decided tendency for many, but certainly not all, gifted children to come from what might well be described as gifted homes. As Willard Abraham states, "The old law of filial regression expressed by Sir Francis Galton remains in the literature for our consideration. It maintains that parents in their physical and mental digressions will tend toward having children who digress in the same directions, but not to the same extent (11)."

This means that bright parents are most likely to have children who are also bright, but not so bright as themselves. If this were not so, the normal curve would soon become so skewed in favor of giftedness that the lower limit of I.Q. for "giftedness" would have to be moved upward.

3. *Do racial and religious background play any part in giftedness?* In a study by Witty (12), the "racial stock included a preponderance of

English, Scotch, German and Jewish ancestors." Ninety-six percent of the parents were American born. Terman and Oden (13) found a 100 percent excess (over that expected because of the percentage in the total population) of Jewish backgrounds, a 25 percent excess of native born parentage, but a deficiency of Italian, Portuguese, Mexican, and Negro ancestry.

A study (14) in Cleveland, Ohio, of 456 children found a much higher preponderance of German and Jewish ancestry than one would expect from their proportional share in the total population. In this same study, however, half of the subjects had one or both parents foreign born: a much higher percentage than expected and certainly contradictory to the findings of both Terman and Witty. The explanation might be in the small foreign element in California where Terman's study was made and in Kansas where Witty's studies were made. In the study in Cleveland, however, the percentage of gifted Negroes was less than that which would be expected by their proportional share in the total population. Examining the number of identified gifted Negro children over a period of years, however, did indicate a substantial increase.

The excess of Jewish children in any group of the gifted has come to be expected. Attempts to explain this by such factors as selective immigration do not seem to be plausible. The high premium placed upon education by Jewish families, combined with the strong family teaching among most Jewish groups, seem to be the only likely explanations. The smaller percentages of other minority groups can be somewhat explained by the penalties imposed by the test itself because of different cultural factors and by the deprivation, both environmentally and educationally, placed upon certain minority groups.

In answer to the question What causes giftedness? only a partial answer can be given. Certainly heredity plays a major role, but environment must also contribute a part. Sex differences appear to play only a minor role, if any role at all; racial factors appear to be important only when considered as either an environmental or hereditary factor. No list of factors causing giftedness can be actually isolated. This is one of the indefinite answers which must so often be given when attempting to explain human behavior in its many forms.

CHANGING ATTITUDES TOWARD THE GIFTED

No longer must the gifted child be ashamed of being different; afraid of social disapproval because of his mental superiority; withdrawn because he might not be understood. Instead there is new hope for the gifted—hope that he will be identified early, encouraged to develop to the limit of his ability, and recognized as a unique individual with a greatly needed potential. The pessimism of even recent years can now be viewed as something of the past. There is a bright future for the gifted child in today's world.

Probably no change in the attitude of the American public has been so great as that toward gifted children. At one time the gifted child was thought to be a physical weakling and a social misfit so parents' determination to have only an average child was to be expected. But long after the bespectacled introvert concept had been completely disproved, parents held on to the popular notion that "average" was really good enough. What they really meant, of course, was that they wanted a child potentially capable of achieving at a higher level than they did, but one who would have none of the negative traits that were supposed to go along with mental superiority. Being very unrealistic about the fact that "average" was not good enough to achieve near the level to which they aspired for their children, parents nevertheless felt that they must maintain the "average" label for their child. Fortunately, this universal worship of the average has changed. Today, for the first time in nearly a century, parents are saying that they hope they have a gifted child. The freedom that allows parents to make this statement is perhaps the greatest change since Terman's original studies which disproved the previously held notions about the eccentricity of giftedness. There is indeed hope for the gifted that was not present even a few years ago.

The beginning of the change in attitudes toward the gifted can be marked at the time Lewis Terman began to study gifted children in California. This was climaxed by the presentation in 1947 of Volume IV of *Genetic Studies of Genius,* entitled *The Gifted Child Grows Up* (15). To Lewis Terman must go the credit for having started us on the path toward a new era, one in which all children will be accepted for what they are and will be allowed to develop those innate abilities they possess without fear of ridicule from a society characterized by mediocrity.

The establishment of the American Association for Gifted Children in 1947 is another landmark in the increasing attention to children who are exceptional in a different way. The appearance, in 1951, of *The Gifted Child* (16), edited by Paul Witty, gave new impetus to the movement. The Educational Policies Commission booklet, *Education for the Gifted* (17), in 1950, drew still more attention to the gifted.

In 1953 the National Association for Gifted Children (18) was formed, with the purpose of providing an organization for both teachers and parents concerned with the problem of the gifted child. *The Gifted Child Quarterly* is a publication of this organization which provides valuable information to teachers and parents, bibliographies, and reviews of recent books on the gifted.

A definite shifting of attitudes was noticeable in this period but it was climaxed in the fall of 1957 when the United States entered the satellite age in second place. There was every reason for the American public to think that even though Russia was larger in land area, and had a larger population, in technology she would never be a serious threat. Without any warning, and in full view of the entire world, Russia displayed that superiority in any field lay with the nation which was most willing to strive for it. The myth of American superiority was exploded and the illusion was shattered that while we may have been neglecting our gifted children, the wealth of our nation was so great we could afford this waste. Suddenly the American public was forcibly made aware of the need for action.

Almost overnight there was a great change in attitude toward the potential scientist. Instead of his being somehow different, he was now recognized as our only hope. The race with Russia was recognized as a continuous, long range affair, with the full realization that not only was our position tenuous, but that there seemed every likelihood of our staying in this position for years to come.

The interest of the American public has shifted from mediocrity to achievement. For the first time the lay public is demanding more and harder courses for high school students, better trained teachers, identification of gifted children early, and many other things which Terman long ago pleaded for in vain.

REFERENCES

1. Lombroso, C., *The Man of Genius.* New York: Charles Scribner's Sons, 1895.
2. Nisbet, J. F., *The Insanity of Genius.* London: DeLaNore Press, 1895.
3. Hollingworth, Leta, *Gifted Children.* New York: The Macmillan Company, 1926, p. 265.
4. Abraham, Willard, *Common Sense About Gifted Children.* New York: Harper & Row, Publishers, 1958, pp. 61-62.
5. Terman, Lewis M., *Genetic Studies of Genius,* Vols. I-V, Stanford, Calif.: Stanford University Press.
6. Hollingworth, *Gifted Children, op. cit.,* p. 66.
7. Terman, Lewis M. and Oden, Melita, *The Gifted Child Grows Up,* Vol. IV, *Genetic Studies of Genius.* Stanford, Calif.: Stanford University Press, 1947, p. 14.
8. Gibson, J. E., "Are Women Smarter Than Men?" *McCall's,* Vol. 80 (April, 1953), p. 56.
9. Root, W., "Women Are Intellectually Inferior," *American Mercury,* Vol. 69 (October, 1949), pp. 407-414.
10. Galton, Francis, *Hereditary Genius.* London: Macmillan and Company, Ltd., 1914.
11. Abraham, *Common Sense About Gifted Children, op. cit.,* p. 63.
12. Witty, Paul, "A Study of One Hundred Gifted Children," Bulletin of Education, University of Kansas, Vol. 2, No. 7. Lawrence, Kansas: University of Kansas, February, 1930, p. 8.
13. Terman and Oden, *The Gifted Child Grows Up, op. cit.,* p. 14.
14. Barbe, Walter B., "A Follow-up Study of the Graduates of Special Classes

for Gifted Children." Unpublished Doctoral Dissertation, Northwestern University, August, 1963.

15. Terman and Oden, *The Gifted Child Grows Up, op. cit.*
16. Witty, Paul (editor), *The Gifted Child.* Boston: D. C. Heath & Company, 1951.
17. Educational Policies Commission, *Education of the Gifted.* Washington, D.C.: National Education Association, 1950.
18. National Association for Gifted Children (8080 Springvalley Drive, Cincinnati, Ohio).

1 | HISTORICAL DEVELOPMENT

The Discovery and Encouragement of Exceptional Talent

LEWIS M. TERMAN

I am deeply sensible of the honor of being invited by the American Psychological Association, through its special committee, to give the initial lecture in the Walter V. Bingham Lectureship series.

I am especially happy that Chancellor Kerr and the psychology department of the University of California graciously acceded to my request that the address be given here, where I have many friends and where so much notable research has been done on the mental, physical, and personality development of children; where such famous experiments have been made on the purposive behavior of rats, both gifted and dull; where authoritarian minds have been so exhaustively probed; and where the recently established Institute of Personality Assessment is engaged in such promising investigations.

Before beginning my lecture I should like to pay tribute to the life work of the late Walter Van Dyke Bingham, at whose request this lectureship was established by Mrs. Bingham. Born in Iowa in 1880, young Walter early demonstrated his exceptional gifts by skipping both the third and fourth grades and by graduating from high school at the age of 16. As a freshman in college he was the youngest in his class and the only one to make a straight A record. After graduating from Beloit College he taught in high schools for four years, then entered the graduate school of the University of Chicago and in 1908 won his doctorate in psychology with honors. From 1908 to 1910 he was instructor at Teachers College and assistant to Edward L. Thorndike. In 1910 he was appointed assistant professor at Dartmouth to teach all their classes in psychology, but when he left there five years later the staff included an instructor

Reprinted from *American Psychologist*, Vol. 9, No. 6 (June, 1954), pp. 221-230. By permission of the American Psychological Association.

and two full professors, all selected by Dr. Bingham. His rare ability to recognize exceptional talent is indicated by the fact that both of these professors became college presidents.

From 1915 to 1924 Dr. Bingham was professor of psychology and head of the division of applied psychology at the Carnegie Institute of Technology, and it was here that he found the opportunity he had long wanted to promote large-scale investigations in applied psychology. The faculty he assembled for that purpose was one of the most distinguished ever brought together anywhere in this country. Among them were J. B. Miner, L. L. Thurstone, Walter Dill Scott, Kate Gordon, and E. K. Strong. Three others appointed as consultants were F. L. Wells, G. M. Whipple, and Raymond Dodge. It was this faculty that, under the wise leadership of Dr. Bingham, laid the solid foundation for vocational and industrial psychology in America.

When our country entered the war in 1917, nearly all of the Carnegie group were soon engaged in psychological work either for the Surgeon General or for the War Department or for both. Dr. Bingham was a member of Yerkes' committee of seven that devised the army mental tests, in 1917–1918 was a member of the Committee on Classification of Personnel (the committee charged with devising and administering vocational tests in all the army camps), and in 1918–1919 was Lt. Colonel in the Personnel Branch of the Army General Staff.

During World War II even greater service was rendered by Dr. Bingham as chief psychologist for the Office of Adjutant General from 1940 to 1946. In this capacity he and his committee were responsible not only for the Army General Classification Test that was administered to the many millions of inductees, but also for advising on the entire program of psychological services in the armed forces. In this capacity too he was in position to influence the selection of men best qualified to head the various branches of military psychology. I have no doubt that the extraordinary success of the work accomplished by psychologists during the war was largely due to his leadership and to his judgment of men.

If time permitted, I should like to tell you about his more than 200 publications, about the great variety of problems they dealt with, and the contributions they made in several fields of psychology, but I am sure that if Dr. Bingham were here he would want me to get on with our scheduled program.

I have often been asked how I happened to become interested in mental tests and gifted children. My first introduction to the scientific problems posed by intellectual differences occurred well over a half-century ago when I was a senior in psychology at Indiana University and was asked to prepare two reports for a seminar, one on mental deficiency and one on genius. Up to that time, despite the fact that I had graduated from a normal college as a Bachelor of Pedagogy and had taught school for five years, I had never so much as heard of a mental test. The reading for those two reports opened up a new world to me, the world of Galton, Binet, and their contemporaries. The following year my MA thesis on leadership among children (10) was based in part on tests used by Binet in his studies of suggestibility.

Then I entered Clark University, where I spent considerable time during the first year in reading on mental tests and precocious children. Child prodigies, I soon learned, were at that time in bad repute because of the prevailing belief that they were usually psychotic or otherwise abnormal and almost sure to burn themselves out quickly or to develop postadolescent stupidity. "Early ripe, early rot" was a slogan frequently encountered. By the time I reached my last graduate year, I decided to find out for myself how precocious children differ from the mentally backward, and accordingly chose as my doctoral dissertation an experimental study of the intellectual processes of fourteen boys, seven of them picked as the brightest and seven as the dullest in a large city school (11). These subjects I put through a great variety of intelligence tests, some of them borrowed from Binet and others, many of them new. The tests were given individually and required a total of 40 or 50 hours for each subject. The experiment contributed little or nothing to science, but it contributed a lot to my future thinking. Besides "selling" me completely on the value of mental tests as a research method, it offered an ideal escape from the kinds of laboratory work which I disliked and in which I was more than ordinarily inept. (Edward Thorndike confessed to me once that *his* lack of mechanical skill was partly responsible for turning *him* to mental tests and to the kinds of experiments on learning that required no apparatus.)

However, it was not until I got to Stanford in 1910 that I was able to pick up with mental tests where I had left off at Clark University. By that time Binet's 1905 and 1908 scales had been published, and the first thing I undertook at Stanford was a tentative revision of his 1908 scale. This, after further revisions, was published in 1916. The standardization of the scale was based on tests of a thousand children whose IQ's ranged from 60 to 145. The contrast in intellectual performance between the dullest and the brightest of a given age so intensified my earlier interest in the gifted that I decided to launch an ambitious study of such children at the earliest opportunity.

My dream was realized in the spring of 1921 when I obtained a generous grant from the Commonwealth Fund of New York City for the purpose of locating a thousand subjects of IQ 140 or higher. More than that number were selected by Stanford-Binet tests from the kindergarten through the eighth grade, and a group mental test given in 95 high schools provided nearly 400 additional subjects. The latter, plus those I had located before 1921, brought the number close to 1,500. The average IQ was approximately 150, and 80 were 170 or higher (13).

The twofold purpose of the project was, first of all, to find what traits characterize children of high IQ, and secondly, to follow them for as many years as possible to see what kind of adults they might become. This meant that it was necessary to select a group representative of high-testing children in general. With the help of four field assistants, we canvassed a school population of nearly a quarter-million in the urban and semi-urban areas of California. Two careful checks on the methods used showed that not more than 10 or 12 per cent of the children who could have qualified for the group in the schools canvassed were missed. A sample of close to 90 per cent insured that whatever traits were typical of these children would be typical of high-testing children in any comparable school population.

Time does not permit me to describe the physical measurements, medical examinations, achievement tests, character and interest tests, or the trait ratings and other supplementary information obtained from parents and teachers. Nor can I here describe the comparative data we obtained for control groups of unselected children. The more important results, however, can be stated briefly: children of IQ 140 or higher are, in general, appreciably superior to unselected children in physique, health, and social adjustment; markedly superior in moral attitudes as measured either by character tests or by trait ratings; and vastly superior in their mastery of school subjects as shown by a three-hour battery of achievement tests. In fact, the typical child of the group had mastered the school subjects to a point about two grades beyond the one in which he was enrolled, some of them three or four grades beyond. Moreover, his ability as evidenced by achievement in the different school subjects is so general as to refute completely the traditional belief that gifted children are usually one-sided. I take some pride in the fact that not one of the major conclusions we drew in the early 1920's regarding the traits that are typical of gifted children has been overthrown in the three decades since then.

Results of thirty years' follow-up of these subjects by field studies in 1927–1928, 1939–1940, and 1951–1952, and by mail follow-up at other dates, show that the incidence of mortality, ill health, insanity, and alcoholism is in each case below that for the generality of corresponding age, that the great majority are still well adjusted socially, and that the delinquency rate is but a fraction of what it is in the general population. Two forms of our difficult Concept Mastery Test, devised especially to reach into the stratosphere of adult intelligence, have been administered to all members of the group who could be visited by the field assistants, including some 950 tested in 1939–1940 and more than 1,000 in 1951–1952. On both tests they scored on the average about as far above the generality of adults as they had scored above the generality of children when we selected them. Moreover, as Dr. Bayley and Mrs. Oden have shown, in the twelve-year interval between the two tests, 90 per cent increased their intellectual stature as measured by this test. "Early ripe, early rot" simply does not hold for these subjects. So far, no one has developed postadolescent stupidity!

As for schooling, close to 90 per cent entered college and 70 per cent graduated. Of those graduating, 30 per cent were awarded honors and about two-thirds remained for graduate work. The educational record would have been still better but for the fact that a majority reached college age during the great depression. In their undergraduate years 40 per cent of the men and 20 per cent of the women earned half or more of their college expenses, and the total of undergraduate and graduate expenses earned amounted to $670,000, not counting stipends from scholarships and fellowships, which amounted to $350,000.

The cooperation of the subjects is indicated by the fact that we have been able to keep track of more than 98 per cent of the original group, thanks to the rapport fostered by the incomparable field and office assistants I have had from the beginning of the study to the present. I dislike to think how differently things could have gone with helpers even a little less competent.

The achievement of the group to midlife is best illustrated by the case histories of the 800 men, since only a minority of the women have gone out for professional careers (15). By 1950, when the men had an average age of 40 years, they had published 67 books (including 46 in the fields of science, arts, and the humanities, and 21 books of fiction). They had published more than 1,400 scientific, technical, and professional articles; over 200 short stories, novelettes, and plays; and 236 miscellaneous articles on a great variety of subjects. They had also authored more than 150 patents. The figures on publications do not include the hundreds of publications by journalists that classify as news stories, editorials, or newspaper columns; nor do they include the hundreds, if not thousands of radio and TV scripts.

The 800 men include 78 who have taken a PhD degree or its equivalent, 48 with a medical degree, 85 with a law degree, 74 who are teaching or have taught in a four-year college or university, 51 who have done basic research in the physical sciences or engineering, and 104 who are engineers but have done only applied research or none. Of the scientists, 47 are listed in the 1949 edition of *American Men of Science*. Nearly all of these numbers are from 10 to 20 or 30 times as large as would be found for 800 men of corresponding age picked at random in the general population, and are sufficient answer to those who belittle the significance of IQ differences.

The follow-up of these gifted subjects has proved beyond question that tests of "general intelligence," given as early as six, eight, or ten years, tell a great deal about the ability to achieve either presently or 30 years hence. Such tests do not, however, enable us to predict what direction the achievement will take, and least of all do they tell us what personality factors or what accidents of fortune will affect the fruition of exceptional ability. Granting that both interest patterns and special aptitudes play important roles in the making of a gifted scientist, mathematician, mechanic, artist, poet, or musical composer, I am convinced that to achieve greatly in almost any field, the special talents have to be backed up by a lot of Spearman's g, by which is meant the kind of general intelligence that requires ability to form many sharply defined concepts, to manipulate them, and to perceive subtle relationships between them; in other words, the ability to engage in abstract thinking.

The study by Catharine Cox of the childhood traits of historical geniuses gives additional evidence regarding the role of general intelligence in exceptional achievement. That study was part of our original plan to investigate superior ability by two methods of approach: (*a*) by identifying and following living gifted subjects from childhood onward; and (*b*) by proceeding in the opposite direction and tracing the mature genius back to his childhood promise. With a second grant from the Commonwealth Fund, the latter approach got under way only a year later than the former and resulted in the magnum opus by Cox entitled *The Early Mental Traits of Three Hundred Geniuses* (1). Her subjects represented an unbiased selection from the top 510 in Cattell's objectively compiled list of the 1,000 most eminent men of history. Cox and two able assistants then scanned some 3,000 biographies in search of information that would throw light on the early mental development of these subjects. The information thus obtained filled more than 6,000 typed pages. Next, three psychologists familiar with mental age norms read the documentary evidence on all the subjects and estimated for each the IQ that presumably would be necessary to account for the intellectual behavior recorded for given chronological ages. Average of the three IQ estimates was used as the index of intelligence. In fact two IQ's were estimated for each subject, one based on the evidence to age 17, and the other on evidence to the mid-twenties. The recorded evidence on development to age 17 varied from very little to an amount that yielded about as valid an IQ as a good intelligence test would give. Examples of the latter are Goethe, John Stuart Mill, and Francis Galton. It was the documentary information on Galton, which I summarized and published in 1917 (12), that decided me to prepare plans for the kind of study that was carried out by Cox. The average of estimated IQ's for her 300 geniuses was 155, with many going as high as 175 and several as high as 200. Estimates below 120 occurred only when there was little biographical evidence about the early years.

It is easy to scoff at these post-mortem IQ's, but as one of the three psychologists who examined the evidence and made the IQ ratings, I think the author's main conclusion is fully warranted; namely, that "the genius who achieves highest eminence is one whom intelligence tests would have identified as gifted in childhood."

Special attention was given the geniuses who had sometime or other been labeled as backward in childhood, and in every one of these cases the facts clearly contradicted the legend. One of them was Oliver Goldsmith, of whom his childhood teacher is said to have said "Never was so dull a boy." The fact is that little Oliver was writing clever verse at 7 years and at 8 was reading Ovid and Horace. Another was Sir Walter Scott, who at 7 not only read widely in poetry but was using correctly in his written prose such words as "melancholy" and "exotic." Other alleged childhood dullards included a number who disliked the usual diet of Latin and Greek but had a natural talent for science. Among these were the celebrated German chemist Justus von Liebig, the great English anatomist John Hunter, and the naturalist Alexander von Humboldt, whose name is scattered so widely over the maps of the world.

In the cases just cited one notes a tendency for the direction of later achievement to be foreshadowed by the interests and preoccupations of childhood. I have tried to determine how frequently this was true of the 100 subjects in Cox's group whose childhood was best documented. Very marked foreshadowing was noted in the case of more than half of the group, none at all in less than a fourth. Macaulay, for example, began his career as historian at the age of 6 with what he called a "Compendium of Universal History," filling a quire of paper before he lost interest in the project. Ben Franklin before the age of 17 had displayed nearly all the traits that characterized him in middle life: scientific curiosity, religious heterodoxy, wit and buffoonery, political and business shrewdness, and ability to write. At 11 Pascal was so interested in mathematics that his father thought it best to deprive him of books on this subject until he had first mastered Latin and Greek. Pascal secretly proceeded to construct a geometry of his own and covered the ground as far as the 32nd proposition of Euclid. His father then relented. At 14 Leibnitz was writing on logic and philosophy and composing what he called "An Alphabet of Human Thought." He relates that at this age he took a walk one afternoon to consider whether he should accept the "doctrine of substantial forms."

Similar foreshadowing is disclosed by the case histories of my gifted subjects. A recent study of the scientists and nonscientists among our 800 gifted men (15) showed many highly significant differences between the early interests and social attitudes of those who became physical scientists and those who majored in the social sciences, law, or the humanities. Those in medical or biological sciences usually rated on such variables somewhere between the physical scientists and the nonscientists.

What I especially want to emphasize, however, is that both the evidence on early mental development of historical geniuses and that obtained by follow-up of gifted subjects selected in childhood by mental tests point to the conclusion that capacity to achieve far beyond the average can be detected early in life by a well-constructed ability test that is heavily weighted with the g factor. It remains to be seen how much the prediction of future achievement can be made more specific as to field by getting, in addition, measures of ability factors that are largely independent of g. It would seem that a 20-year follow-up of the thousands of school children who have been given Thurstone's test of seven "primary mental abilities" would help to provide the answer. At present the factor analysts don't agree on how many "primary" mental abilities there are, nor exactly on what they are. The experts in this field are divided into two schools. The British school, represented by Thomson, Vernon, and Burt, usually stop with the identification of at most three or four group factors in addition to g, while some representing the American school feed the scores of 40 or 50 kinds of tests into a hopper and manage to extract from them what they believe to be a dozen or fifteen separate factors. Members of the British school are as a rule very skeptical about the realities underlying the minor group factors. There are also American psychologists, highly skilled in psychometrics, who share this skepticism. It is to be hoped that further research will give us more information than we now have about the predictive value of the group factors. Until such information is available, the scores on group factors can contribute little to vocational guidance beyond what a good test of general intelligence will provide.

I have always stressed the importance of *early* discovery of exceptional abilities. Its importance is now highlighted by the facts Harvey Lehman has disclosed in his monumental studies of the relation between age and creative achievement (8). The striking thing about his age curves is how early in life the period of maximum creativity is reached. In nearly all fields of science, the best work is done between ages 25 and 35, and rarely later than 40. The peak productivity for works of lesser merit is usually reached 5 to 10 years later; this is true in some twenty fields of science, in philosophy, in most kinds of musical composition, in art, and in literature of many varieties. The lesson for us from Lehman's statistics is that the youth of high achievement potential should be well trained for his life work before too many of his most creative years have been passed.

This raises the issue of educational acceleration for the gifted. It seems that the schools are more opposed to acceleration now than they were thirty years ago. The lockstep seems to have become more and more the fashion, notwithstanding the fact that practically everyone who has investigated the subject is against it. Of my gifted group, 29 per cent managed to graduate from high school before the age of 16½ years (62 of these before 15½), but I doubt if so many would be allowed to do so now. The other 71 per cent graduated between 16½ and 18½. We have compared the accelerated with the nonaccelerated on numerous case-history variables. The two groups differed very little in childhood IQ, their health records are equally good, and as adults they are equally well adjusted socially. More of the accelerates graduated from college, and on the average nearly a year and a half earlier than the nonaccelerates; they averaged higher in college grades and more often remained for graduate work. Moreover, the accelerates on the average married .7 of a year earlier, have a trifle lower divorce rate, and score just a little higher on a test of marital happiness (14). So far as college records of accelerates and nonaccelerates are concerned, our data closely parallel those obtained by the late Noel Keys (3) at the University of California and those by Pressey (9) and his associates at Ohio State University.

The Ford Fund for the Advancement of Education has awarded annually since 1951 some 400 college scholarships to gifted students who are not over 16½ years old, are a year or even two years short of high school graduation, but show good evidence of ability to do college work. Three quarters of them are between 15½ and 16½ at the time of college entrance. A dozen colleges and universities accept these students and are keeping close track of their success. A summary of their records for the first year shows that they not only get higher grades than their classmates, who average about two years older, but that they are also equally well adjusted socially and participate in as many extra-curricular activities (17). The main problem the boys have is in finding girls to date who are not too old for them! Some of them have started a campaign to remedy the situation by urging that more of these scholarships be awarded to girls.

The facts I have given do not mean that all gifted children should be rushed through school just as rapidly as possible. If that were done, a majority with IQ of 140 could graduate from high school before the age of 15. I do believe, however, that such children should be promoted rapidly enough to permit college entrance by the age of 17 at least, and that a majority would be better off to enter at 16. The exceptionally bright student who is kept with his age group finds little to challenge his intelligence and all too often develops habits of laziness that later wreck his college career. I could give you some choice examples of this in my gifted group. In the case of a college student who is preparing for a profession in science, medicine, law, or any field of advanced scholarship, graduation at 20 instead of the usual 22 means two years added to his professional career; or the two years saved could be used for additional training beyond the doctorate, if that were deemed preferable.

Learned and Wood (7) have shown by objective achievement tests in some 40 Pennsylvania colleges how little correlation there is between the student's knowledge and the number of months or years of his college attendance. They found some beginning sophomores who had acquired more knowledge than some seniors near their graduation. They found similarly low correlations between the number of course units a student had in a given field and the amount he knew in that field. Some with only one year of Latin had learned more than others with three years. And, believe it or not, they even found boys just graduating from high school who had more knowledge of science than some college seniors who had majored in science and were about to begin teaching science in high schools! The sensible thing to do, it seems, would be to quit crediting the individual high school or the individual college and begin crediting the individual student. That, essentially, is what the Ford Fund scholarships are intended to encourage.

Instruments that permit the identification of gifted subjects are available in great variety and at nearly all levels from the primary grades to the graduate schools in universities. My rough guess is that at the present time tests of achievement in the school subjects are being given in this country to children below high school at a rate of perhaps ten or twelve million a year, and to high school students another million or two. In addition, perhaps two million tests of intelligence are given annually in the elementary and high schools. The testing of college students began in a small way only 30 years ago; now almost every college in the country requires applicants for admission to take some kind of aptitude test. This is usually a test of general aptitude, but subject-matter tests and tests of special aptitudes are sometimes given to supplement the tests of general aptitude.

The testing movement has also spread rapidly in other countries, especially in Britain and the Commonwealth countries. Godfrey Thomson devised what is now called the Moray House test of intelligence in 1921 to aid in selecting the more gifted 11-year-olds in the primary schools for the privilege of free secondary education. This test has been revised and is given annually to about a half million scholarship candidates. The Moray House tests now include tests of English, arithmetic, and history. In 1932 the Scottish Council for Research in Education (18) arranged to give the Moray House test of intelligence (a group test) to all the 90,000 children in Scotland who were born in 1921, and actually tested some 87,000 of them. The Stanford-Binet tests have been translated and adapted for use in nearly all the countries of Europe and in several countries of Asia and Latin America. Behind the Iron Curtain, however, mental tests are now banned.

I have discussed only tests of intelligence and of school achievement. There is time to mention only a few of the many kinds of personality tests that have been developed during the last thirty-five years: personality inventories, projective techniques by the dozen, attitude scales by the hundred, interest tests, tests of psychotic and predelinquent tendencies, tests of leadership, marital aptitude, masculinity-femininity, et cetera. The current output of research on personality tests probably equals or exceeds that on intelligence and achievement tests, and is even more exciting.

Along with the increasing use of tests, and perhaps largely as a result of it, there is a growing interest, both here and abroad, in improving educational methods for the gifted. Acceleration of a year or two or three, however desirable, is but a fraction of what is needed to keep the gifted child or youth working at his intellectual best. The method most often advocated is curriculum enrichment for the gifted without segregating them from the ordinary class. Under ideal conditions enrichment can accomplish much, but in these days of crowded schools, when so many teachers are overworked, underpaid, and inadequately trained, curriculum enrichment for a few gifted in a large mixed class cannot begin to solve the problem. The best survey of thought and action in this field of education is the book entitled *The Gifted Child*, written by many authors and published in 1951 (16). In planning for and sponsoring this book, The American Association for Gifted Children has rendered a great service to education.

But however efficient our tests may be in discovering exceptional talents, and whatever the school may do to foster those discovered, it is the prevailing *Zeitgeist* that will decide, by the rewards it gives or withholds, what talents will come to flower. In Western Europe of the Middle Ages, the favored talents were those that served the Church by providing its priests, the architects of its cathedrals, and the painters of religious themes. A few centuries later the same countries had a renaissance that included science and literature as well as the arts. Although presumably there are as many potential composers of great music as there ever were, and as many potentially great artists as in the days of Leonardo da Vinci and Michaelangelo, I am reliably informed that in this country today it is almost impossible for a composer of *serious* music to earn his living except by teaching, and that the situation is much the same, though somewhat less critical, with respect to artists.

The talents most favored by the current *Zeitgeist* are those that can contribute to science and technology. If intelligence and achievement tests don't discover the potential scientist, there is a good chance that the annual Science Talent Search will, though not until the high school years. Since Westinghouse inaugurated in 1942 this annual search for the high school seniors most likely to become creative scientists, nearly 4,000 boys and girls have been picked for honors by Science Service out of the many thousands who have competed. As a result, "Science Clubs of America" now number 15,000 with a third of a million members—a twentyfold increase in a dozen years (2). As our need for more and better scientists is real and urgent, one can rejoice at what the talent search and the science clubs are accomplishing. One may regret, however, that the spirit of the times is not equally favorable to the discovery and encouragement of potential poets, prose writers, artists, statesmen, and social leaders.

But in addition to the over-all climates that reflect the *Zeitgeist*, there are localized climates that favor or hinder the encouragement of given talents in particular colleges and universities. I have in mind especially two recent investigations of the differences among colleges in the later achievement of their graduates. One by Knapp and Goodrich (4) dealt with the undergraduate origin of 18,000 scientists who got the bachelor's degree between 1924 and 1934 and were listed in the 1944 edition of *American Men of Science*. The list of 18,000 was composed chiefly of men who had taken a PhD degree, but included a few without a PhD who were starred scientists. The IBM cards for these men were then sorted according to the college from which they obtained the bachelor's degree, and an index of productivity was computed for each college in terms of the proportion of its male graduates who were in the list of 18,000. Some of the results were surprising, not to say sensational. The institutions that were most productive of future scientists between 1924 and 1934 were not the great universities, but the small liberal arts colleges. Reed College topped the list with an index of 132 per thousand male graduates. The California Institute of Technology was second with an index of 70. Kalamazoo College was third with 66, Earlham fourth with 57, and Oberlin fifth with 56. Only a half-dozen of the great universities were in the top fifty with a productivy index of 25 or more.

The second study referred to was by Knapp and Greenbaum (5), who rated educational institutions according to the proportion of their graduates who received certain awards at the graduate level in the six-year period from 1946 to 1951. Three kinds of awards were considered: a PhD degree, a graduate scholarship or fellowship paying at least $400 a year, or a prize at the graduate level won in open competition. The roster of awardees they compiled included 7,000 students who had graduated from 377 colleges and universities. This study differs from the former in three respects: (a) it deals with recent graduates, who had not had time to become distinguished but who could be regarded as good bets for the future; (b) these good bets were classified according to whether the major field was science, social science, or the humanities; and (c) data were obtained for both sexes, though what I shall report here relates only to men. In this study the great universities make a better showing than in the other, but still only a dozen of them are in the top fifty institutions in the production of men who are good bets. In the top ten, the University of Chicago is third, Princeton is

eighth, and Harvard is tenth; the other seven in order of rank are Swarthmore 1, Reed 2, Oberlin 4, Haverford 5, California Institute of Technology 6, Carleton 7, and Antioch 9. When the schools were listed
separately for production of men who were good bets in science, social
science, and the humanities, there were eight that rated in the top twenty
on all three lists. These were Swarthmore, Reed, Chicago, Harvard,
Oberlin, Antioch, Carleton, and Princeton.

The causes of these differences are not entirely clear. Scores on
aptitude tests show that the intelligence of students in a given institution is by no means the sole factor, though it is an important one. Other
important factors are the quality of the school's intellectual climate, the
proportion of able and inspiring teachers on its faculty, and the amount
of conscious effort that is made not only to discover but also to motivate
the most highly gifted. The influence of motivation can hardly be
exaggerated.

In this address I have twice alluded to the fact that achievement in
school is influenced by many things other than the sum total of intellectual abilities. The same is true of success in life. In closing I will tell
you briefly about an attempt we made a dozen years ago to identify
some of the nonintellectual factors that have influenced life success
among the men in my gifted group. Three judges, working independently,
examined the records (to 1940) of the 730 men who were then 25 years
old or older, and rated each on life success. The criterion of "success"
was the extent to which a subject had made use of his superior intellectual ability, little weight being given to earned income. The 150
men rated highest for success and the 150 rated lowest were then compared on some 200 items of information obtained from childhood
onward (14). How did the two groups differ?

During the elementary school years, the A's and C's (as we call
them) were almost equally successful. The average grades were about
the same, and average scores on achievement tests were only a trifle
higher for the A's. Early in high school the groups began to draw apart
in scholarship, and by the end of high school the slump of the C's was
quite marked. The slump could not be blamed on extracurricular activities, for these were almost twice as common among the A's. Nor was
much of it due to difference in intelligence. Although the A's tested on
the average a little higher than the C's both in 1922 and 1940, the
average score made by the C's in 1940 was high enough to permit
brilliant college work, in fact was equaled by only 15 per cent of our
highly selected Stanford students. Of the A's, 97 per cent entered
college and 90 per cent graduated; of the C's, 68 per cent entered but
only 37 per cent graduated. Of those who graduated, 52 per cent of the
A's but only 14 per cent of the C's graduated with honors. The A's were
also more accelerated in school; on the average they were six months

younger on completing the eighth grade, 10 months younger at high school graduation, and 15 months younger at graduation from college.

The differences between the educational histories of the A's and C's reflect to some degree the differences in their family backgrounds. Half of the A fathers but only 15 per cent of the C fathers were college graduates, and twice as many of A siblings as of C siblings graduated. The estimated number of books in the A homes was nearly 50 per cent greater than in the C homes. As of 1928, when the average age of the subjects was about 16 years, more than twice as many of the C parents as of A parents had been divorced.

Interesting differences between the groups were found in the child-hood data on emotional stability, social adjustments, and various traits of personality. Of the 25 traits on which each child was rated by parent and teacher in 1922 (18 years before the A and C groups were made up), the only trait on which the C's averaged as high as the A's was general health. The superiority of the A's was especially marked in four volitional traits: prudence, self-confidence, perseverance, and desire to excel. The A's also rated significantly higher in 1922 on leadership, popularity, and sensitiveness to approval or disapproval. By 1940 the difference between the groups in social adjustment and all-round mental stability had greatly increased and showed itself in many ways. By that time four-fifths of the A's had married, but only two-thirds of the C's, and the divorce rate for those who had married was twice as high for the C's as for the A's. Moreover, the A's made better marriages; their wives on the average came from better homes, were better educated, and scored higher on intelligence tests.

But the most spectacular differences between the two groups came from three sets of ratings, made in 1940, on a dozen personality traits. Each man rated himself on all the traits, was rated on them by his wife if he had a wife, and by a parent if a parent was still living. Although the three sets of ratings were made independently, they agreed unani-mously on the four traits in which the A and C groups differed most widely. These were "persistence in the accomplishment of ends," "integration toward goals, as contrasted with drifting," "self-confidence," and "freedom from inferiority feelings." For each trait three critical ratios were computed showing, respectively, the reliability of the A-C dif-ferences in average of self-ratings, ratings by wives, and ratings by parents. The average of the three critical ratios was 5.5 for perseverance, 5.6 for integration toward goals, 3.7 for self-confidence, and 3.1 for freedom from inferiority feelings. These closely parallel the traits that Cox found to be especially characteristic of the 100 leading geniuses in her group whom she rated on many aspects of personality; their three outstanding traits she defined as "persistence of motive and effort," "confidence in their abilities," and "strength or force of character."

There was one trait on which only the parents of our A and C men were asked to rate them; that trait was designated "common sense." As judged by parents, the A's are again reliably superior, the A-C difference in average rating having a critical ratio of 3.9. We are still wondering what self-ratings by the subjects and ratings of them by their wives on common sense would have shown if we had been impudent enough to ask for them!

Everything considered, there is nothing in which our A and C groups present a greater contrast than in drive to achieve and in all-round mental and social adjustment. Our data do not support the theory of Lange-Eichbaum (6) that great achievement usually stems from emotional tensions that border on the abnormal. In our gifted group, success is associated with stability rather than instability, with absence rather than with presence of disturbing conflicts—in short with well-balanced temperament and with freedom from excessive frustrations. The Lange-Eichbaum theory may explain a Hitler, but hardly a Churchill; the junior senator from Wisconsin, possibly, but not a Jefferson or a Washington.

At any rate, we have seen that intellect and achievement are far from perfectly correlated. To identify the internal and external factors that help or hinder the fruition of exceptional talent, and to measure the extent of their influences, are surely among the major problems of our time. These problems are not new; their existence has been recognized by countless men from Plato to Francis Galton. What is new is the general awareness of them caused by the manpower shortage of scientists, engineers, moral leaders, statesmen, scholars, and teachers that the country must have if it is to survive in a threatened world. These problems are now being investigated on a scale never before approached, and by a new generation of workers in several related fields. Within a couple of decades vastly more should be known than we know today about our resources of potential genius, the environmental circumstances that favor its expression, the emotional compulsions that give it dynamic quality, and the personality distortions that can make it dangerous.

REFERENCES

1. Cox, Catharine C., *The Early Mental Traits of Three Hundred Geniuses.* Vol. II of *Genetic Studies of Genius*, Terman, L. M. (ed.). Stanford: Stanford Univer. Press, 1926.
2. Davis, W., Communicating Science. *J. Atomic Scientists*, 1953, 337-340.
3. Keys, N., The Underage Student in High School and College. *Univ. Calif. Publ. Educ.*, 1938, 7, 145-272.
4. Knapp, R. H., & Goodrich, H. B., *Origins of American Scientists.* Chicago: Univer. of Chicago Press, 1952.
5. Knapp, R. H., & Greenbaum, J. J., *The Younger American Scholar: His Collegiate Origins.* Chicago: Univ. of Chicago Press, 1953.

6. Lange-Eichbaum, W., *The Problem of Genius.* New York: Macmillan, 1932.
7. Learned, W. S., & Wood, B. D., The Student and His Knowledge. *Carnegie Found. Adv. Teaching Bull.*, 1938, No. 29.
8. Lehman, H. C., *Age and Achievement.* Princeton: Princeton Univer. Press, 1953.
9. Pressey, S. L., *Educational Acceleration: Appraisals and Basic Problems.* Columbus: Ohio State Univer. Press, 1949.
10. Terman, L. M., A Preliminary Study in the Psychology and Pedagogy of Leadership. *Pedag. Sem.*, 1904, 11, 413-451.
11. Terman, L. M., Genius and Stupidity: A Study of Some of the Intellectual Processes of Seven "Bright" and Seven "Dull" Boys. *Pedag. Sem.*, 1906, 13, 307-373.
12. Terman, L. M., The Intelligence Quotient of Francis Galton in Childhood. *Amer. J. Psychol.*, 1917, 28, 209-215.
13. Terman, L. M. (ed.), *et al. Mental and Physical Traits of a Thousand Gifted Children.* Vol. I of *Genetic Studies of Genius*, Terman, L. M. (ed.). Stanford: Stanford Univer. Press, 1925.
14. Terman, L. M., & Oden, M. H., *The Gifted Child Grows Up.* Vol. IV of *Genetic Studies of Genius*, Terman, L. M. (ed.). Stanford: Stanford Univer. Press, 1947.
15. Terman, L. M., Scientists and Nonscientists in a Group of 800 Gifted Men. *Psychol. Monogr.*, 1954, 68, in press.
16. Witty, P. (ed)., *The Gifted Child.* Boston: Heath, 1951.
17. *Bridging the Gap Between School and College.* New York: The Fund for the Advancement of Education, 1953.
18. *The Intelligence of Scottish Children.* Scottish Council for Research in Education. London: Univer. of London Press, 1933.

The Gifted Child in the American Culture of Today

MARGARET MEAD

The gifted child, in school, at home, and among peers has to deal with American attitudes towards success and failure, towards luck and happiness, towards inalienable and irreversible hereditary traits versus those that can be modified by environment, and towards continuities versus discontinuities in ability.

American culture combines a Puritan attitude towards success—"making good," the reward of hard work, postponement of pleasure, and exercise of virtue—with a belief that if success is excessive and con-

Reprinted from *Journal of Teacher Education*, Vol. 5, No. 3 (September, 1954), pp. 211-214. By permission of the author and publisher.

spicuous, it is the result of luck. Success that is the reward of application and hard work is approved fairly ungrudingly, although there is a persistent preference for recognizing success in another field rather than one's own.

This grudging willingness to recognize success within one's own field—of sport, scholarship, business, the arts—is congruent with the narrowness of the American competitive range; fourth graders compete with other fourth graders from the same kind of school, members of minor leagues with members of other minor leagues, television actors with television actors, etc. Within this narrow range, competition is keen and the rewards are regarded as limited, so that one person's gain is another's loss. Outside the narrow field of direct competition, Americans enjoy and reward success, but continue to make a distinction, on the one hand, between the Horatio Alger type of success in which a proper amount of time is spent selling newspapers in the cold dawn, grinding out the arithmetic examples in grade after grade, feeding the rats for the chemistry professor, suffering on every approved stage of the ladder—and, on the other hand, startling rises to stardom in which no such hard work is involved. Wherever the rise to success cannot be equated with preliminary effort, abstinence, and suffering, it tends to be attributed to "luck," which relieves the spectator from according the specially successful person any merit.

Then, although happiness and success are often used interchangeably there is an increasing emphasis in American life on happiness, defined as "enjoying life, living among friends who live the same way I do," contrasted with success which takes too much out of you, kills you at forty, or "being a brain and missing all the fun." Any degree of outstanding success is represented as cutting one off from the group so that it becomes fashionable not to get better grades than the others, not to be too good, not to go up too fast. These pressures for keeping on all fours with one's classmates, neighbors, business associates, which are increasing in American life, tend to be particularly felt in the school age groups, especially in the case of the child who shows intellectual or artistic gifts.

Athletic abilities, more conspicuously due to physique which to some extent is recognized as "natural," i.e. hereditary, is less difficult to handle. But even here complications may arise, for the boy who takes his success for granted may be punished for always winning by both teachers and peers and in turn become self conscious, unsure of himself, or intolerably boastful as a form of reassurance.

OUR HISTORICAL HERITAGE

A second difficulty in handling giftedness comes from our democratic American preference for recognizing only those elements in a situation about which something can be done. This attitude reflects two important historical situations, the empty landscape which our forefathers found here—a landscape which could be built on, farmed, landscaped, in any way the new settlers pleased—and the extent to which adults came to America so that their children could have a different life. So, as a people, we have learned to "fix" anything we don't like, rather than to "cope" as the British do—"fix" being defined as changing the environment, "cope" as changing one's character so as to deal with the environment. Americans think coping is dull, unenterprising, old-fashioned. If something is wrong, fix it! If you have a birthmark, no chin or an unfortunately prominent nose, don't groan, go to a plastic surgeon. If you are shy, learn how to make friends; if you are a slow reader, improve your reading speed; if you have a poor memory, take up a system! The homely girl today is no longer expected to be a wall flower, sing in the choir, and do the dishes after parties. She is expected to "make something of herself," sometimes euphemistically defined by beauty culture schools, as "learning to be the way nature meant you to be," thus combining a premium on the natural with an insistence on the hard work which will finally produce a natural effect. Americans' persistent bad conscience about types of race relations which have condemned part of the population to characteristics that are inalienable and irreversible, and not their own fault, is an example of the same set of values.

Still another part of our historical heritage as a culture built by adults who came from many different cultures, is our tendency to level any disparate set of values, or discontinuous set of gifts, down to one series so that they can be compared in the same units, dollars, grades, size of neon lights, number of inches of newsprint, etc. This national habit which has often misled foreigners into thinking that everytime we mention the dollar value of something we are grossly materialistic, is understandable enough in the light of our history. As immigrants from all over the world, many illiterate, many from ancient and exotic cultures, jostled each other in the market place and sent their children to the same schools, the need for some new currency of conversational exchange and comparison was very great. So mothers who could not understand what their children were learning at school, learned readily to discuss A's and B's over the back fences, and jobs and careers intrinsically unintelligible came to be evaluated in terms of the salaries they paid.

By using grades or dollars or ratings, neon lights or inches, people can grasp and compare disparate things, but use of such methods also tends to wipe out the kinds of incomparabilities and discontinuities between different realms of life, between athletics and scholarship, business, the arts and religion. Brawn, brains, business acumen, the ability to write a sonnet, paint a landscape or compose a symphony, or arouse a congregation to a sense of their sins, are all placed on the same scale.

This desire to compare also leads to looking at one or two attributes at a time, so cities are compared as to size, rate of growth, juvenile delinquency rate, or number of new businesses and only occasionally is it recognized that cities have composite personalities of their own which cannot be placed so easily on single scales.

THE GIFTED STUDENT

This then is part of the cultural background with which we have to come to terms in dealing with the problem of the gifted child. In American education, we have tended to reduce gift to a "higher I. Q.",—thus making it a matter of merely a little more on a continuity scale, to insist on putting more money and effort in bringing the handicapped child "up to par" as an expression of fair play and "giving everyone a break"— and to disallow special gifts. At present there are many large high schools where no effort is made to encourage the gifted student to go on to college or for special training because "it isn't democratic to emphasize such things when most of the students won't be able to go." By this refusal to recognize special gifts, we have wasted and dissipated, driven into apathy or schizophrenia uncounted numbers of gifted children. If they learn easily, they are penalized for being bored when they have nothing to do; if they excel in some outstanding way, they are penalized as being conspicuously better than the peer group, and teachers warn the gifted child, "Yes, you can do that, it's much more interesting than what the others are doing. But remember, the rest of the class will dislike you for it." And there is in America today an appalling waste of first-rate talents, while the slightly superior people just because they do have to work hard to get straight A's, are forgiven.

Meanwhile the parents of gifted children are terrorized with behests to bring their children up to be normal happy human beings, and told horror stories about infant prodigies who go mad at twenty. In American psychology the theory of "special gifts" competes and loses before two more congenial theories, (1) the theory of a general superiority factor, which makes you into an all-round superior person, in sports as well as in scholarship, in business or in music, or, (2) the specially gifted who are penalized by accusations of neuroses, and interpretations which make all special interests in childhood and adolescence into symptoms of trauma or psychological morbidity. Under these conditions it is not surprising that, as an English critic has acutely remarked, "The United States has more promising young people who fizzle out than any other country." First efforts, if they are recognized at all, are tailored into normal success terms, given prizes, published, exhibited prematurely, and forgotten.

This is admittedly a grim picture—a startlingly grim picture especially when one realizes that parents all over the world dream of making it possible for their children to be born in America, the country where there are the resources and the freedoms necessary for the good life.

WHAT CAN WE DO?

What as educators can we do about the situation, about recognizing and fostering those special, hereditary, discontinuous, incredible gifts which once in many centuries produce a Shakespeare, an Einstein, or a Leonardo da Vinci, an Abraham Lincoln or a St. Thomas Aquinas, and without whom a society, no matter how rich and industrious will stagnate in the end?

In the first place, we have the culture with us the minute we have stated the difficulty, for as Americans, "the possible we do at once; the impossible takes a little bit longer." Furthermore as Americans, we feel a moral obligation to remedy our defect. If it is true that we are at present lamentably poor in fostering genius, then it is obvious that we had better recognize what the obstacles are and proceed to clear them away. So that the clearer the facing of the number of culturally regular myths about the desirability of normalcy, the undesirability of skipping stages—especially if those stages are places where one can be miserable as one's predecessors have been miserable—the better.

But such recognition is only a first step, because most of what a wise teacher or counselor tells the parents of a gifted child is true, culturally speaking. The culture tries to make the child with a gift into a one-sided person, to penalize him at every turn, to cause him trouble in making friends, and to create conditions conducive to the development of a neurosis. Neither teachers, the parents of other children, nor the child's peers will tolerate the *Wunderkind*. The task for the school becomes then a redesigning of the school situation in such a way as to both protect and foster the gifted child. The device of having special science high schools or music and arts high schools is one such solution. The gifted are placed among their near peers—when chosen from a large enough area—and the school is represented to the outside world as requiring tremendous work to get into. But the little child, equally in need of fostering, can not be represented as having had to work, and suffer, for any special education. In the school where the gifted child must be educated among other children—which has many advantages for social adjustment—perhaps one of the best answers is such diversified, socially approved activities, that a gift is highly used but still not too conspicuous in the school setting. The school orchestra, with a large number of members who play instruments demanding different skill levels is one kind of model, within which the musically gifted can fit, "contribute to the group," "be a member of a group," "work" and conceivably get some access to music.

The more diversified, the more complex the activities within which children are encouraged to play a role, the better chance for the superlatively, discontinuously gifted child to exercise his or her special talent. Any activity where comparison on a single scale disappears, where the gifted is given a spot in which he can put his incomparably greater energy, imagination, drive into an activity without coming into destructive competition with his classmates, the better. School evaluation programs which included the idea of the conservation of precious resources so that ability to spot, protect and cherish the gifted became a matter of pride among educators, would also help.

But most of all, more than protection from active discouragement, much more than rewards and praise, the gifted child needs scope, material on which his imagination can feed, and opportunities to exercise it. He needs inconspicuous access to books, museums, instruments, paints, ideas, a chance to feed himself with the accumulated heritage from the genius of other ages. He needs a chance for contact, however, fleeting, perhaps only on television or in a special movie, with those who are masters in the abilities with which he has been specially endowed. And within our sternly Puritan tradition, he may well need also, a special sense of stewardship for the talents which he has been given, an explicit moral sanction against selling his birthright for a mess of pottage.

A New Approach to the Study of Genius

LEWIS M. TERMAN

Three stages may be noted in the study of genius during the last century. The first of these is typified by the work of Moreau de Tours, Lombroso, and Grasset. Its methods were impressionistic and anecdotal. Its characteristic procedure was the search for striking cases which would lend support to a preconceived theory.

The second stage is represented by the researches of Galton, de Candolle, Odin, Ellis and Castle. Here the method is inductive, the selection of cases is based upon objective criteria, and the data are sub-

Reprinted from *Psychological Review*, Vol. 29, No. 4 (July, 1922), pp. 310-318. By permission of the American Psychological Association.

jected to statistical treatment. Although the studies of this period marked a tremendous advance, they were limited by the nature of the biographical material upon which they were based. In the first place, the genius of biographical encyclopædias represents a selected type, namely, the socially successful. Extraneous factors doubtless operate to influence the personnel of such encyclopædias and the amount of space given to individual cases. In the second place, the biographical data are so incomplete and, what is worse, often so unreliable, that only an extremely limited number of facts can be assembled for as many as 75 per cent of any objectively selected group. Information regarding early life and training is likely to be especially scanty and untrustworthy.

A third and very significant advance is marked by Cattell's study of living American men of science. Here the selection of cases is accomplished by vastly improved methods, the desired data are obtainable from practically 100 per cent of his subjects, and the facts treated can be accepted as really facts. It is to be regretted, however, that it has not been possible in Cattell's study to secure the data which would be necessary to give a reliable picture of the juvenile traits and early mental development of his subjects. Those of us who have envied Professor Cattell his opportunity to witness the dramatic rise of his subjects from the mid-forenoon of their careers to their zenith, and their later subsidence or replacement by other luminaries, naturally regret that the author has not been able to extend his observations back to the period of childhood.

The logical next step is the study of genius in the making, that is, the investigation of gifted children. This approach has the great advantage that the number of obtainable facts is limited only by the time, patience and resources of the investigator. It opens the way to a more thoroughgoing study of the genetic aspects of the problem, of the environmental factors which affect genius, and of the exact nature of its deviation from the average. Tests and measurements in unlimited number can be made, and norms can readily be secured for the interpretation of data so collected. Moreover, follow-up work with large numbers of gifted children will throw light upon genius which aborts or deteriorates, as well as upon that which fulfills its promise. By this method we may even hope to learn something in time about the pedagogy of genius. We shall be able to test the theories of Witte, Berle, Wiener, Sidis, and others who believe that it is possible to make any child a prodigy. We shall find out to what extent, if at all, nature tends to even up the score of gifts by taking from him who has more than his fair share of one desirable quality some other advantage. We shall find out what truth there is in the widespread view that gifted children are usually conceited, freakish, socially eccentric, and prone either to illness and early death or to nervousness and insanity.

Perhaps a brief personal note in this historical sketch will be pardoned. My own interest in gifted children dates back to a master's thesis on leadership in 1903, to a review in 1904 of the literature on precocity, and to an experimental study of bright and dull children for the doctorate in 1905. It is unnecessary to recount the scanty results of these juvenile studies. By the time it became possible for me to return to the problem, in 1910, the progress which has been made in mental testing had created a new situation. For certain ages, at least, it was now possible to determine with some degree of approximation the relative brightness of a given child as compared with unselected children of his age.

It was in 1911 that we began more or less systematically to collect data at Stanford on children who had made exceptionally good records in a mental test. In 1913 three schools in San Francisco were sifted for bright children, and the following year certain data were published on 35 cases testing above 120 I.Q. Ratings on several traits were secured and a brief information schedule was filled out by the teacher. The results of this explorative study were considerably out of line with my own expectations and in contradiction to earlier views which I had published on the dangers of precocity. In passing it may be noted that one of the bright children tested in 1911 is now a teaching assistant in Stanford University, that another was recently awarded a scholarship for meritorious record, and that a third had just received his Ph.D. degree and been awarded an $1,800 research fellowship by the National Research Council. Not one has yet become insane or developed symptoms of post-adolescent stupidity!

In 1916 the methods were considerably revised. The teacher's information schedule was enlarged, a similar information schedule was prepared for the parent to fill out, and ratings on twenty traits were secured both from parents and teachers. Data were collected on 59 cases testing for the most part above 140 I.Q. The results have been summarized elsewhere and need not be reported here.

The establishment by the university of a special research fellowship in 1919 was the occasion for further revision of method and a stimulus to renewed search for cases. Unwisely, as it now appears, the number of traits to be rated was increased from 20 to 46. However, the information schedules were materially improved and an interest blank was arranged for the child. By the spring of 1921 approximately 180 cases testing for the most part above 140 I.Q. had been located, and for 121 of these fairly complete supplementary data had been secured. Some of the outstanding results for this "first group" are as follows:

1. The number of very high cases is larger than the standard deviation of the I.Q. distribution for unselected children would lead one to expect.

It is doubtful therefore whether the incidence of superior intelligence follows the normal probability curve.

2. The sex ratio for all the cases together is 60 to 40 in favor of boys. Above 160 I.Q. it is 65 to 35, and above 180 it is 70 to 30. These figures are not conclusive, however, owing to the fact that only a minority of the cases were discovered by a systematic canvass of the sexes.

3. As regards physical traits, it may be tentatively stated that these children, as a group, are above the average in height and weight, that they were precocious in learning to walk and talk, that they show no apparent excess of nervous symptoms, and that their general health conditions appear to be at least as good as the average for unselected children.

4. As regards school progress, the average acceleration is about two grades beyond the standard for their life ages; but as compared with the standard for their mental ages, there is an average retardation of more than two years. All but four have skipped one or more grades, and there are no genuine cases of grade repetition. According to the statements of their parents, about one sixth have been mildly encouraged to make rapid school progress, one sixth have been deliberately held back, and the remaining two thirds have been allowed to 'go their own pace.' Possibly three or four have been more or less systematically 'stuffed' but only one of these is near the top of the list.

5. Family data show strikingly superior heredity. On the Taussig five-fold classification of occupations about 50 per cent of the fathers belong to class 1 (the professional group), as compared with 4 or 5 per cent of the general population, while 37 per cent belong to class 2 and 13 per cent to class 3. Neither class 4 nor class 5 (the semi-skilled and unskilled occupations) is represented at all (in this 'first group'), unless we rate a barber as belonging to class 4. Fifteen of the 121 cases belong to seven families. More than a third of the parents are known to have one or more relatives who have attained a considerable degree of prominence. About 20 per cent of the father's and mother's sibs belong to one or another of the learned professions.

6. The parents whose families are reckoned complete have an average of only 2.53 children. The average age of fathers at the birth of the gifted child was 36.2 years; that of the mothers, 31.4 years.

7. As regards racial differences, there are two outstanding facts: there is a noteworthy excess of Jewish cases and a still more striking deficiency among Italians, Portuguese, Mexicans and Spanish, all of whom are numerous in the vicinity of Stanford.

8. The trait ratings, owing to the usual halo effects, have yielded data of only limited value. The halo largely invalidates any comparison of our group with normal children on the traits in question, although it

does permit a comparison of parents' and teachers' ratings with each other, also a comparison of average ratings on different types of traits. Classifying the traits under the five headings, intellectual, volitional, social, emotional, and psychophysical, we have the following average ratings by parents and teachers for the traits of each group, where the rating 1 is highest, 3 is average and 5 is lowest.

	Intellectual	Volitional	Social	Emotional	Psycho-physical
Parents	1.67	1.98	2.13	2.18	2.28
Teachers ..	1.64	1.99	2.08	2.04	2.27

It is seen that both parents and teachers tend to rate these children high on all types of traits; but especially high on those which are classed as intellectual and volitional. Teachers tend to rate rather consistently higher than parents, but the rank order of the traits based upon the ratings accorded by parents correlates .76 with a similar rank order based upon ratings by teachers.

9. The data on social adaptability and allied traits have been examined with special care, with the result that approximately two thirds of our cases have been classified as entirely normal or superior in this respect. A case study of the remaining one third shows that only three or four are seriously maladjusted. The difficulties of the large majority in social adjustment are readily accounted for by the natural tendency to jealousy and resentfulness on the part of their older classmates whom they almost invariably surpass, a form of reaction to which even teachers do not seem to be entirely immune.

The above conclusions are tentative only. The data on which they are based are faulty in more ways than we can here enumerate. What had been learned thus far, was, largely, what not to do; also, that what needed doing would be too costly for the little budget available. Fortunately at this time the directors of the Commonwealth Fund came to the rescue with a grant of $20,300. This subvention is being devoted to the search of 1,000 cases and to the immediate collection of psychological, educational, and social data concerning them. The expense of follow-up work will be borne for an indefinite period by Stanford University. Four full-time assistants began field work in September, 1921. The plan is to secure the following data from as many as possible of the 1,000 cases:

1. At least two intelligence tests;
2. Achievement tests in all the main school subjects; involving altogether three hours of testing;
3. A general information test of about an hour's duration;

4. A two-hour test of certain moral and emotional traits (for at least a part of the subjects);
5. About 20 anthropometric measurements;
6. A record of all the books read during two months, together with the child's rating of each book;
7. A test of interest in and knowledge of 90 typical plays, games, and amusements permitting the computation of deviations from age and sex standards;
8. Ratings from parents and teachers on 25 traits, by a much better method than we had formerly used;
9. Data to be supplied by the parents in a 16-page Home Information blank, by the teachers in an 8-page School Information blank, and by the child himself in a 4-page Interest blank;
10. Home and neighborhood ratings on the Whittier scale;
11. Of a small number of the highest cases more intensive studies will be made, especially with reference to heredity.

All of the tests and information schedules will be used with 500 or more unselected children from 8 to 16 years of age, in order to secure the necessary background of comparative norms.

A report of salient findings will be made in 1923 but the detailed treatment of data may occupy several years and the follow-up work an additional decade or two. Naturally the value of the data will be greater twenty or thirty years hence than at present.

A word about the selection of cases. For many reasons it did not seem feasible to attempt to locate *the* 1,000 brightest children in the state. The effort is simply being made to locate that number having a Binet I.Q. above 140 (also, by methods we cannot here describe, children of very exceptional special ability). The search is being confined in the main to the grades from 3 to 8 inclusive. Entire cities and counties are being taken in order to avoid, as far as possible, undesirable selection. A certain amount of arbitrary selection is, however, unavoidable. This would be true even if it were possible to give a mental test to all the children in the territory covered, for the test itself is of course an arbitrary criterion. Since it is not possible to test all, additional selection is necessary. At present we are testing in each classroom (by the National Intelligence Tests) the three children who are rated by the teacher as the brightest, second brightest, and third brightest, respectively, and in addition the child who is youngest. Those who test in the top 5 per cent for their ages by the National are then given either an abbreviated or a complete Binet, according to the promise shown. Of our cases to date who test above 140, about one third were not nominated as brightest, second brightest, or third brightest, and were caught only by virtue of being youngest.

Notwithstanding the use of such an inclusive drag-net method we have found by sheer accident a number of high I.Q.'s which it had failed to catch. In one case, the youngest child was at home, because of broken glasses, and the teacher substituted the second youngest, not otherwise nominated. This was the only pupil in the room who tested above 140. Another pupil brought to the test by mistake, by a child messenger, tested 149. Another, who was the only child to qualify in a school of 500, was erroneously named by the teacher as youngest as a result of his name appearing alphabetically adjacent to that of the youngest and being confused with it. Of four cases above 170 I.Q. located by one assistant, not one was named as first choice by the teacher. Two of the four were not named as first, second, or third choice and would have been missed but for the fact that they were youngest. It is no wonder that in the old-time school with its narrow curriculum and untrained teachers, the genius often escaped notice as completely as if he had worn an invisible cap. A pupil nominated by one of our teachers as brightest, was a ten-year-old in the first grade with I.Q. considerably below 100. By testing all the children in certain of the smaller cities, after the nominations have been regularly made, we are now trying to get a line on the number who are missed by the usual method of selection.

No results have been worked up, but the following miscellaneous facts may be of interest.

1. The ratio of boys to girls is now only about 55 to 45, and, as before, is slightly higher in the upper I.Q. ranges.
2. The individual schools of a given city differ enormously in the proportion of children who are gifted to the required degree. The average number with I.Q. above 140 is, in the larger cities of California, about 1 pupil in 250.
3. The proportion of Jewish children is even larger than in our earlier data.
4. Several of our new cases are of very inferior social status and a few are living in extreme poverty. Several have grown up with a minimum of home supervision and training. C. M., for example (I.Q. 141), is the son of a common Mexican laborer. B. S., who tests at 154, has lived most of his life with his mother, who is feeble-minded by test. One of his sisters is insane, another is feeble-minded, and two others are decidedly subnormal.

Our present undertaking, laborious as it is, will at best only help to open the field. Minute studies will have to be made of a large variety of individual cases. More searching and detailed information will have to be collected on health and heredity. The non-intellectual traits will have to be explored by methods which do not yet exist. Special intellectual abilities will have to be investigated. The pedagogy of genius offers unknown worlds to explore. The science of biography, as a special branch of psychology, is still to be created.

Until our knowledge of the social significance of genius has been made more exact, our conception of democracy will remain an illogical patch-work. Until an appreciation of the extent and meaning of individual differences has become more general, the eugenics movement will remain a futile hobby of a handful of enthusiasts, the present unfavorable differential birth rate will continue, and for want of creative thinkers and doers, the struggle of civilization will be, not to advance, but to hold its own against a relatively increasing spawn of inferior mentality.

A Decade of Progress in the Study of the Gifted and Creative Pupil

PAUL WITTY

The past ten years have encompassed a most important and productive decade in the education of gifted children and youth. Foremost among the developments of this period is the increased acceptance of a broader concept of giftedness. For many years, most educators and psychologists regarded a child as gifted if he earned an extraordinarily high IQ.

Over a period of many years, the writer of this article has repeatedly criticized this restricting concept. As early as 1927 to 1930, he published a number of articles in which he discussed the neglect of factors such as drive, motivation, and special opportunities which determine the nature and extent of achievement by gifted pupils. During the following ten years, he emphasized again and again the limitations of intelligence tests in identifying the creative pupil.

If by gifted children we mean those youngsters who give promise of creativity of a high order, it appears that the typical intelligence test is unsuitable for use in identifying them. For creativity posits originality, and originality implies successful management, control, and organization of new materials or experiences.

A high degree of creativity necessitates learning during the process of living—not the displayal of success in standard nonvariable situations. Moreover, creativity implies original, unique behavior in many forms of variable human responses—in human relations as well as in all art forms (1).

He pointed out that the intelligence test disregarded largely the role of feeling since it called for largely habitual or learned responses. Moreover, a low correlation between IQ and test results in music and art also

Reprinted from *Attention to the Gifted—A Decade Later* (Columbus, Ohio: State Department of Education, 1962), pp. 3-7. By permission of the author and publisher.

supported the hypothesis that high IQ's were undependable indicators of giftedness.

In 1940, the writer cited emphatically his conviction that evidence of creative ability should be sought from observation of the child's performance: "It is well to reiterate that 'giftedness' should be estimated by observation of a child's behavior. The child whose performance is consistently remarkable in any potentially valuable area might well be considered gifted."

In spite of such considerations, the tendency persisted to select the gifted largely in terms of IQ. Moreover, the gifted were infrequently differentiated from the creative.

Corroborative evidence concerning the unjustifiability "of equating IQ with creativity" was offered recently by J. W. Getzels and P. W. Jackson, whose work has awakened widespread interest and has stimulated research (2).

BROADER CONCEPTS INCREASINGLY ENDORSED

Broader concepts of the gifted have been increasingly endorsed by writers during the past ten years. For example, in *Education for the Gifted,* published in 1958, the chairman stated:

. . . The talented or gifted child is one who shows consistently remarkable performance in any worthwhile line of endeavor. Thus, we shall include not only the intellectually gifted but also those who show promise in music, the graphic arts, creative writing, dramatics, mechanical skills, and social leadership. Although most of the attention of educators has been directed toward the intellectually gifted . . . we think of such special attention to the intellectually gifted as a weakness or shortcoming in the kind of program for gifted children that we should like to see in existence (3).

It is important too that during the past ten years estimates of the number of pupils considered to be potentially gifted have been greatly expanded. Thus, Louis A. Fliegler and Charles E. Bish state:

For purposes of this review the term *gifted* encompasses those children who possess a superior intellectual potential and functional ability to achieve academically in the top 15 to 20 per cent of the school population; and/or talent of a high order in such special areas as mathematics, mechanics, science, expressive arts, creative writing, music, and social leadership; and a unique creative ability to deal with their environment (4).

It is clear, then, that during the past decade, we have witnessed a somewhat widespread adoption of a broader concept of the gifted student. Today, the potentially gifted pupil is considered by many scholars as any child whose performance in a worthwhile type of human endeavor is consistently or repeatedly remarkable. We have, of course, various suggestions and statements concerning the areas of endeavor that should be included as highly worthwhile. Following are some that have been proposed: (a) verbal ability and abstract intelligence, (b) science and mathematics, (c) art, (d) creative writing, (e) creative drama, (f) music, (g) social leadership, and (h) mechanical ability.

SEARCH FOR MEASURES OF CREATIVITY

Another significant development during the past decade is found in the search for measures of creativity. The pioneer work of men such as Viktor Lowenfeld and J. P. Guilford paved the way for establishing criteria which have been utilized by Jacob W. Getzels and Philip W. Jackson in the construction of tests. The tests have been used in a number of provocative investigations of creativity.

Current investigations of creativity offer promise for the early development of more valid measures. However, few dependable measures are now available for classroom use. Nevertheless, observation and subjective judgment may now be employed effectively in efforts to identify the creative pupil. From performance, the possession of a gift may be inferred. Ruth Strang comments on this approach which she designates "work sample" technique:

Creativity is probably best appraised by the "work sample" technique; the individual is given a task involving inventiveness and imagination. His production is then judged by experts in the field. This is a more direct way of appraising creativity than the elaborate inventories that have been developed (5).

Several such techniques are being used successfully to detect consistently remarkable performance in the arts. For example, the symbolic and imaginative film, *The Hunter in the Forest*, photographed by the distinguished cameraman, Arne Sucksdorff, was shown in about 80 classrooms in 34 cities (6).

More than two thousand compositions written by the children who viewed the film, were appraised according to the extent to which the writing disclosed creativity. About 10 per cent of the total number were judged to suggest potential creativity ability.

One phase of creativity, creative thinking in the early years, is being explored by E. P. Torrance, who has also compared the characteristics of "gifted" and creative pupils, and has suggested ways to stimulate creative thinking in the classroom (7).

The reawakening of interest in creativity may be noted in the comparatively large number of studies cited in summaries. Evidence of the present concern for creativity is found also in conferences devoted to this topic.

Far-reaching results have attended the study of creativity. For example, J. L. Holland has concluded that "the negligible relationships found between academic aptitude and creative performance at a high aptitude level suggests that we need to use non-intellectual criteria in the selection of students for scholarships and fellowships (8)."

HEIGHTENED INTEREST IN THE ACADEMICALLY GIFTED

The past ten years have brought an heightened interest in verbally gifted pupils and the number of books, articles, and monographs dealing with their education is almost overwhelming. A large number of bibliographies have also appeared. In 1959, Fliegler and Bish prepared an extensive bibliography which included 251 references (9). James J. Gallagher published in 1960 an analysis of research which contains a most comprehensive bibliography (10).

Most of the articles referred to in the bibliographies are concerned with the verbally gifted or academically talented student, although creativity is treated in the more recent publications.

CONCLUDING STATEMENT

The past decade has brought an unprecedented interest in the gifted pupil which has fostered the making of large numbers of studies and investigations as well as in more widespread efforts to enrich and extend opportunities for superior and talented students. Perhaps the most outstanding development of this period is in the emphasis on creativity. Criteria are being sought for creativity, and tests are being devised and improved. Moreover, large numbers of schools are initiating programs to promote creativity. The promise for the future is indeed great.

REFERENCES

1. Witty, Paul, "Some Considerations in the Education of Gifted Children," *Educational Administration and Supervision*, Vol. 26 (October, 1940), pp. 512-21.
2. Getzels, Jacob W. and Jackson, Philip W., "The Meaning of Giftedness," *Phi Delta Kappan*, November, 1958. *Education*, April, 1962. See also Getzels, Jacob W. and Jackson, Philip W., *Creativity and Intelligence*. New York: John Wiley and Sons, 1962.
3. Havighurst, Robert, chairman, *Education for the Gifted*. Fifty-seventh Yearbook of the National Society for the Study of Education, Part II. Chicago: University of Chicago Press, 1958, p. 19.
4. Fliegler, Louis A. and Bish, Charles E., "The Gifted and Talented," *Review of Educational Research*, Vol. 29 (December, 1959), p. 409.
5. Strang, Ruth, "Developing Creative Powers of Gifted Children," in *Creativity* by Paul Witty, James B. Conant and Ruth Strang. New York: Bureau of Publications, Teachers College, Columbia University, 1959.

6. Witty, Paul, "The Use of Films in Stimulating Creative Expression and in Identifying Talented Pupils," *Elementary English*, Vol. 33 (October, 1956).

7. Torrance, E. P. and Staff, "Rewarding Creative Thinking." Minneapolis, Minn.: University of Minnesota Press, 1960 (mimeographed). See also Torrance, E. P., *Guiding Creative Talent*. Englewood Cliffs, N.J.: Prentice-Hall, Inc., 1962.

8. Holland, John L., "Creative and Academic Performance Among Talented Adolescents," *Journal of Educational Psychology*, June, 1961.

9. Fliegler and Bish, *op. cit.*

10. Gallagher, James J., *Analysis of Research on the Education of Gifted Children*. Springfield, Ill.: Office of the Superintendent of Public Instruction, 1960.

2 | CONCEPTS AND CONCERNS ABOUT GIFTEDNESS

The Meaning of 'Giftedness'–An Examination of an Expanding Concept

J. W. GETZELS

P. W. JACKSON

When a concept becomes the focus of critical concern it is almost inevitable that its original meaning will simultaneously be expanded and differentiated. The concept of "giftedness" is, of course, of critical concern at this time, and the purpose of this paper is to examine the transformations this concept is presently undergoing and to suggest some additional modifications in its application.

"Giftedness" as related to children has most frequently been defined as a score on an intelligence test, and typically the study of the so-called gifted child has been equated with the study of the single I.Q. variable. Involved in this unidimensional definition of giftedness are several types of confusion, if not outright error. First, there is the limitation of the single metric itself, which not only restricts our perspective of the more general phenomenon, but places on the one concept a greater theoretical and predictive burden than it was intended to carry. For all practical school purposes, the term "gifted child" has become synonymous with the expression "child with a high I.Q.," thus blinding us to other forms of excellence. Second, within the universe of intellectual functions themselves, we have behaved as if the intelligence test represented an adequate sampling of *all* these functions. For example, despite the growing body of literature concerning intellectual processes which seem closely allied to the general concept of "creativity," we tend to treat the latter concept as applicable only to performance in one or more of the *arts*. In effect,

Reprinted from *Phi Delta Kappan*, Vol. 40, No. 2 (November, 1958), pp. 75-77. By permission of the senior author and publisher.

the term "creative child" has become synonymous with the expression "child with artistic talents," thus limiting our attempts to identify and foster cognitive abilities related to creative functioning in areas other than the arts. Third, there has been a failure to attend sufficiently to the difference between the *definition* of giftedness as given by the I.Q. and the variations in the *value* placed upon giftedness as so defined. It is often taken for granted, for example, that the gifted child is equally valued by teachers and by parents, in the classroom and at home; that he is held an equally good prospect by teachers and by parents to succeed as an adult; and that children themselves *want* to be gifted. It can be demonstrated that none of these assumptions regarding the value of the gifted child can be held without question. Empirical data related to these assumptions indicate that the gifted child is *not* equally valued by teachers and by parents, in the classroom and at home; he is *not* held to be an equally good prospect by teachers and parents to succeed as an adult; and children themselves do *not* necessarily want to be gifted, at least not in the traditional sense of the word.

Despite its longevity, there is nothing inevitable about the use of the I.Q. in defining giftedness. Indeed, it may be argued that in many ways this definition is only an historical happenstance—a consequence of the fact that early inquiries in this field had as their context the classroom and its attendant concern with academic progress. If we moved the focus of our inquiry from the classroom setting, we might identify qualities defining giftedness for other situations just as the I.Q. did for the classroom. Indeed, *without* shifting our focus of inquiry, if we only changed the original criteria of learning, we might change the qualities defining giftedness even in the classroom. For example, if we recognize that learning involves the production of novelty as well as the remembrance of course content, then measures of creativity as well as the I.Q. might become appropriate in defining characteristics of giftedness.

A research project, under the direction of the authors, is now being conducted at the University of Chicago in order to provide empirical data related to the considerations outlined above. As subjects of our research we have used a group of approximately 500 adolescents attending a Midwestern private school. The grade range covered by our group extends from the end of the sixth grade to the end of the senior year in high school. Because of the broad purpose of the research, we have inaugurated an extensive testing program involving the assessment of traditional qualities, such as intelligence and psychological health, and including attempts to assess less conventional dimensions such as creativity, morality, and the like. The study to be discussed here is but one small aspect of the larger investigation and concerns specifically a description of two of our experimental groups: one which we shall label the "highly intelligent" group, and the other the "highly creative" group.

TWO GROUPS MUTUALLY EXCLUSIVE

Our "highly intelligent" subjects were defined as those who were in the top 20 per cent of the sample population on conventional I.Q. measures, but who were *not* in the top 20 per cent on measures of creativity. Our "highly creative" subjects were defined as those who were in the top 20 per cent of our sample population on measures of creativity, but who were *not* in the top 20 per cent in I.Q. The groups comprised twenty-eight and twenty-four subjects respectively, with approximately an equal proportion of boys and girls in each.

Limitation of space does not permit a complete description of the instruments included in the creativity battery. However, an adequate understanding of the way in which the term "creative" is used in the material to follow requires at least passing comment concerning these tests. Most briefly, all of the tests in the creative battery involved facility in dealing with verbal and numerical symbol systems, and object-space relationships. Some instruments called for rapid verbal associations to stimulus words; others called for the ability to structure quickly an incomplete or distorted perceptual stimulus; still others required remote, or clever, or original responses to complex verbal situations (e.g., supplying last lines to a fable). In one test the subject was to respond to a complex paragraph involving numerical values by suggesting all of the mathematical problems which could be solved with the information in the paragraph.

It should be noted that we did not include in our experimental groups those children who were high in *both* creativity and intelligence, and there were many such individuals. Our attempt was to isolate the two qualities under study from each other as much as possible in order to examine the relative contribution of each to the functioning of the child. Those individuals who excelled in both areas are the objects of further investigation still in progress.

Having identified our two experimental groups, we compared them to each other and to the population from which they were drawn on a number of relevant variables, including: school performance as measured by standardized verbal and numerical achievement tests appropriate to each grade level; teacher preferences as measured by teacher ratings of the pupils on how much they "liked to have them in class"; the preferences of the children themselves for personal qualities they would like to possess; the children's perception of the personal qualities they believed would lead to success in adult life and those they felt teachers would most prefer in children. In addition, the children were asked to write four-minute stories in response to six pictures flashed on a screen for twenty seconds each. An examination was made of the differences in the writing "style" of the two groups.

EXPERIMENT SUBJECTS EQUAL IN ACHIEVEMENT

The results of these comparisons may be summarized as follows:

First, with respect to school achievement, despite a difference of twenty-three points between the *mean* I.Q.'s of the two groups, they were *equally* superior in school achievement to the student population as a whole.

Second, when asked to rate the children on the degree to which they would like to have them in class, the teachers exhibited a clear-cut preference for the high I.Q. child. The ratings given the high I.Q. group were significantly higher than those of the total student body; the ratings given the high creativity group did not differ significantly from those of the total student body. This occurred despite the fact, as we have seen, that *both* the high I.Q. and the high creative groups were *equally superior* to the other students in school achievement.

Third, comparing the personal aspirations of the children as reflected in the personal qualities they would like to possess, we find that the creative child himself rates high marks, I.Q., pep and energy, character, and goal-directedness *lower* than do members of the highly intelligent group, and that he rates wide range of interests, emotional stability, and sense of humor *higher* than do members of the highly intelligent group. The last item, sense of humor, is particularly noteworthy since the value which the creative child puts upon this quality so far exceeds the ranking it receives from high I.Q. children as to make it one of the outstanding differences between the two groups, and indeed sets the creativity group apart most sharply from *all* our other groups.

Fourth, the groups show distinct differences in the degree to which they aspire for "success" in adult life. The high I.Q. child desires to possess those qualities *now* which he believes will lead to success in adult life; the creative child does not seem to use this remote goal as criterion in the selection of his present aspirations.

Fifth, the relationship between the child's own personal aspirations and those qualities which he believes teachers prefer is quite different for the two groups. The high I.Q. child holds to a self-ideal which is consonant with the one he believes teachers will most readily approve; the self-ideal of the creative child is not only *not* consonant with what he believes to be the teacher approved model but shows a slight *negative* correlation with such model.

Sixth and finally, in their written responses to our six stimulus pictures, the creative students exhibited a degree of imagination and originality (not by any means the same as correct grammatical construction) unmatched by the high I.Q. students. Compared to the latter group, the creative students produced stories which seemed to "spring from" the stimulus rather than appeared to be "tied down" by it. Their stories made abundant use of humor, novel situations, and unexpected endings. They seemed to "play with" the picture stimulus for the pleasure of invention rather than "labor" the stimulus in order to find the "correct" theme.

SOME IMPORTANT IMPLICATIONS

There is, it seems to us, a consistency and unity even in these preliminary findings which may have important implications for defining and identifying so-called gifted children in the educational setting. We believe the high academic performance of our creative children coupled with the related lack of recognition which they may receive from teachers points to the core of the problem of expanding the present conception of "giftedness," and of breaking the bonds that the I.Q. has on this concept in the school situation. The personal qualities of such presently neglected groups as our creatives which tend to estrange teachers from them may very well derive from the very neglect which these children suffer in the educational setting. With respect to our creative students, for example, the quality of "disillusionment" which appears to be reflected in the discrepancies between their personal aspirations and the aspirations they believe to be valued by teachers and by society in general may be a function of just the neglect to which we have been pointing. Despite their exceptional talents, they may miss identification by the usual I.Q. instrument; and despite their superior achievement, they may fail to gain the same personal preference from teachers that the high I.Q. children seem to have. We venture to suggest that a consideration of these discrepancies may deepen our appreciation at once of the need for expanding the concept of giftedness in the school setting and of the very real difficulties involved in such expansion.

A CHALLENGE FOR EDUCATORS, RESEARCHERS

Once we set a precedent by allowing an exception to the practice of labeling only high I.Q. children as "gifted," the possibility of expanding the concept to include other potentially productive groups becomes a genuine challenge to both educators and research workers. The not inconsiderable dangers inherent in the possibility of expanding the concept to a point where it becomes meaningless seem to us to be compensated by the possibility of increasing the effectiveness of our education for *all* children.

Basic Concepts

VIRGIL S. WARD

The development of those phases of the total school program which comprise proper education for the gifted demands intelligent thought and skillful development. In this section of the *Manual*, some fundamental concepts which will be needed by all who engage in any part of these endeavors are introduced. The intention is not necessarily to provide definitions in the exact form to which every local school should subscribe, but rather to provide certain educational and psychological concepts from which as a point of departure, each responsible educational group can think through its own needs, problems, policies, and practices. Close consideration of these concepts should aid substantially in the understanding of the various discussions of curriculum and programmatic arrangements in the sections which follow.

Some basic considerations pertaining to the nature of human abilities are presented first; a limited number of generally applicable concepts which pertain both to psychological abilities and to educational provisions designed to bring them to fruition, next; and finally, some general features—"cardinal principles"—which the SRPEG participants observed to characterize the more excellent of the programs observed in the various sections of the nation, and hence to be essential to any serious or ambitious program.

THE NATURE OF GIFTEDNESS

The rationale of differential education for the gifted, as has been indicated, involves the belief that identifiable groups of children with high abilities exist for whom different kinds of educational provisions are necessary to equality of educational opportunity. Such groups of children, endowed with various kinds of superior abilities, have been diversely termed "superior and talented," "the able and ambitious," "the academically talented" and other familiar designations. For convenience, all these may be and are in this *Manual* referred to as "the gifted."

Reprinted from *The Gifted Student: A Manual For Program Improvement*. A Report of the Southern Regional Project For Education of the Gifted, 1962, pp. 25-30. By permission of the author and publisher.

The behavioral sciences recognize certain definable qualities around which subgroups of individuals with superior potential may be categorized with varying degrees of reliability for the purpose of special education. Clearest among these qualities are giftedness in:

1. *General Intelligence*, usually manifest in high I.Q. scores and
2. *Specific Aptitudes* (or talents), as measured by valid tests appropriately designated, or as evidenced through remarkable insights and skills in particular areas of knowledge or human endeavor.

Aptitudes are regarded as specific behavioral efficiencies, usually accompanied by above average general intelligence. These special abilities may be inferred through superior performance in subject areas such as mathematics and foreign languages, in skilled interpersonal relations which make for social leadership, in various forms of artistic expression such as music, dance or painting and in still other particular kinds of behavior.

Within both of these categories of giftedness, general intelligence and specific aptitude, it is practicable to recognize that *degrees* of superiority exist, such that school provisions may be devised respectively to meet the needs of those small numbers singularly exceptional in ability (e.g. one per cent or less), and the broader numbers (e.g. two, five, or ten per cent as variously suggested) still sufficiently above average to justify substantially modified educational procedures. In 1950 the Educational Policies Commission recognized two such levels of intellectual giftedness and identified these in terms of given intelligence quotients. Other organizations and individuals have similarly recognized varying degrees of giftedness in terms of I.Q., specific cutoff points beginning sometimes essentially where the usual demarcation for the upper limit of the "normal" or "average" group occurs. This recognition of levels of variation, of course, applies in substance also to the various aptitudes and to other recognizable clusters of abilities.

What is important to recognize is that any cutoff point on any measured psychological trait is by its nature arbitrary, and that no given demarcation can be defended on grounds of biological or psychological science. The search is for that degree of deviation in behavioral characteristics, comprising a potential for productive learning and thinking, which is so far above average that the graded materials and normal procedures devised for the education of children in the majority are less suited than curricular arrangements that can be deliberately devised to develop the exceptional qualities.

At the present time behavioral scientists are making significant efforts to distinguish other behavioral attributes worthy of special educational attention. Creativity, productive thinking as distinct from reproductive, and divergent thinking as opposed to convergent, are concepts representing attempts to isolate, define, and measure additional significant qualities of mind which relate to giftedness. The development of creativity is now being seen increasingly as a worthy educational objective. As these important behavioral characteristics become sufficiently well established at the levels of behavioral science, educators can and should devote particular thought to their appropriate development.

Finally, it must be recognized that certain aspects of personality, such as motivation, value orientation and cultural background weigh heavily in identifying particular individuals whose present behavioral patterns seem to promise superior performance in the future. Constructive combinations of these aspects of personality in persons of lesser relative ability may lead to higher ultimate attainment. On the other hand, even among youth of high ability-potential, aspects of personality arising from unfortunate experience may combine to hamper present performance, leading to *underachievement* or *emotional instability*. In the case of these gifted children, remediation should be undertaken as an initial phase of differential education in order subsequently to allow fuller operation of the natural potential. What is patently inexcusable is to exclude such children from developed provisions which promise to remove the obstacles to their "self actualization."

Remarkable demonstrations on the part of children in contemporary schools have been noted during the present wave of interest in the problems of the gifted. Reading, self-taught, prior to the age permitting entry into school; successful learning of higher mathematics on the part of elementary school youngsters; brilliant examples of children's insights into social and philosophical issues, and other striking manifestations of remarkable ability have occurred too consistently and too frequently to ignore. Such behavior suggests a potential for learning and thought hitherto undreamed of and defiant of management within the standard patterns and processes of education which serve children of ordinary abilities. Reliable studies indicate further that prodigious childhood accomplishments tend, on the whole, to be followed in adulthood by similarly constructive behavior through which creative inventions in the arts and sciences occur, and advances in human welfare are made by gifted statesmen and leaders in social thought. These facts and realizations suggest further the absolute urgency that persons in possession of such priceless human assets be identified early and treated with every resource available to the educator.

Specific expressive behaviors which characterize the gifted may be detailed in lists that number into the dozens. These particular behavioral traits, however, derive from a more manageable number of broader psychological variables which serve typically to distinguish the group. The following categories embrace most of the educationally significant behaviors of gifted individuals as they are presently recognized.

Capacity for Learning: Accurate perception of social and natural situations; independent, rapid, efficient learning of fact and principle; fast, meaningful reading, with superior retention and recall.

Power and Sensitivity of Thought: Ready grasp of principles underlying things as they are; sensitivity to inference in fact, consequence of proposition, application of idea; spontaneous elevation of immediate observations to higher planes of abstraction; imagination; meaningful association of ideas; forceful reasoning; original interpretations and conclusions; discriminatory power, quick detection of similarities and differences among things and ideas; able in analysis; synthesis, and organization of elements; critical of situations, self, and other people.

Curiosity and Drive: Mental endurance; tenacity of purpose; stubbornness, sometimes contrarily expressed as reluctance to do as directed; capacity for follow-through with extensive, but meaningful plans; curiosity about things and ideas; intrinsic interest in the challenging and difficult; versatile and vital interests; varied, numerous and penetrating inquiries; boredom with routine and sameness.

From these basic considerations as to the nature of giftedness, the local school may devise serviceable definitions for those groups of youngsters in whose interest they intend to develop specifically applicable school procedures. Starting efforts will perhaps wisely center upon the most clearly known deviant characteristics, i.e., general intellectual superiority, and those for which the clearest educational processes pertain. The identification of groups may be expanded as the program matures to include other kinds of abilities and larger numbers of children. A fair understanding of these concepts on the nature of giftedness will be essential to the establishment of adequate screening and identification procedures in the process of selecting and placing children, and to the broader and more nearly ultimate search for educational provisions exactingly geared to each group distinguishable through deviant characteristics.

A GLOSSARY OF FUNCTIONAL TERMINOLOGY

Terminology can both facilitate and deter progress. The following concepts have been selected for their functional value in thinking through the various problems arising in the accomplishment of a recognizable pattern of provisions for fortunately atypical youth. As with all the "basic concepts" in this section, it is not intended that given school personnel should accept verbatim the definitions offered. The fine arguments necessary for obtaining agreements at such a level of particularity would quite possibly tend rather to impede than to propel the changes integral to a good program. On the other hand, careful study of these deliberated descriptions and explanations on the part of every staff member to be involved in discussions about or responsibilities in the program, should assure some communality of sound understanding around which both thought and action may proceed. Reasoned departures from what is here suggested by way of definitions should be, and quite possibly can be, defensible in terms of more refined insights into educational or psychological processes, or in terms of practical contingencies governing a school's initial efforts to establish or to improve upon its differential provisions for youth of superior abilities. Such departures should not, however, reflect simple bias of person or of locality.

Ability Grouping: Also sometimes called "segregation." The practice of assembling or deploying students for instructional purposes who are somewhat nearer together in general capacity for learning, or in given specific aptitudes, so that instruction and learning may proceed at a pace and in terms of qualities suited to this (these) capacities. Contrasts with those forms of grouping which utilize chronological age or alphabet as criteria for homogeneity and developmental readiness. May take the form of special classes, special schools, multiple track curricula, etc., and may be arranged for part or for all of the school curriculum. Specific capacities for differing areas of knowledge or skill, with interests related thereto, are recognized as superior criteria for grouping, as opposed to general indices (e.g. composite I.Q.) applied across the range of school activities.

Acceleration: Any administrative practice designed to move the student through school more rapidly than usual. Includes such practices as early admission, grade-skipping, advanced placement, telescoping of grade levels, credit by examination, etc.

Articulation: The sequential arrangement of studies through the total school program so as to avoid undesirable repetition or duplication at various grade levels. Problems of articulation often arise when programs for the gifted are planned to affect given school years but not to encompass the entire graded sequence.

Differential Education (for the gifted): Educational experiences uniquely or predominantly suited to the distinguishing behavioral processes of intellectually superior people and to the adult roles that they typically assume as leaders and innovators. Then successfully arranged to involve the capacities and needs of the gifted, the experience (concepts, studies, activities, courses) by definition is beyond the reach of and not appropriate to the capacities and needs of persons *not* exceptionally endowed with potential for learning and productive or creative behavior.

Enrichment (for the gifted): Practices which are intended to increase the depth or breadth of the gifted student's learning experiences. May include special assignments, independent study, individual projects, small group work, and other adaptations of routine school processes. This purported form of provision for the gifted often in fact merely camouflages do-nothingness.

Identification: The process of finding those students who meet the criteria of giftedness adopted in a given school or system. Identification should begin as early as possible, should be systematic, i.e., follow a defensible plan, and should be continuous, so as to improve the chances of discovering larger numbers of youth qualified for differential education. A variety of techniques exist for screening the pupil population, most of which have some virtue, and no one of which—particularly a single measure of intelligence—is sufficient alone.

Mental Ability: An inclusive term, more properly referred to as "capacity," and including such conceptions as intelligence and aptitude (talent) and related processes such as creativity, productive thinking, divergent thinking, etc.

Mental Tests: Devices such as intelligence, aptitude, achievement, and personality tests, or rating scales for various skills, which are designed to provide relatively objective means of assessing or comparing certain of the capacities of characteristics of individuals.

Motivation: The basic psychological process involved in both under- and over-achievement in school. A subtle and complex literature on this aspect of personality exists in the behavioral sciences. As concerns the gifted, *underachievement* is recognized as a critical problem, and is thought of as a failure to perform as well as might be expected from scores on tests of aptitude or intelligence. No agreement exists as to how poorly a student must do, for how long, or in what activities, in order to be called an underachiever. Poor performance by gifted youngsters is not infrequently paralleled by singular out-of-school activities which possess intrinsic appeal to the child.

Program (of special education): A *pattern* of provisions within the total range of school activities which is designed to meet the distinguishable needs and abilities of intellectually superior and talented children. Single or scattered provisions such as advanced placement or early admission to first grade do not alone constitute a *program*.

The Conservation of Intellectual Talent

DONALD L. THISTLETHWAITE

Estimates of the number of highly talented students who fail to go to college are alarming. Even if we take the most conservative of the available estimates (1), about 34,000, or 28 percent, of the highest-ranking tenth of the nation's high school graduates do not enter college as full-time students. For students in the highest 30 percent in respect to ability, the estimated number not going to college increases fourfold. In 1955 one study (2) reported that some 150,000 students in the top 30 percent of ability failed to go to college, but would have gone if scholarships had been available.

These figures suggest the need for more financial aid. Certainly existing funds are small compared with available estimates of the number of drop-outs among students of high ability, and who could be induced to go to college by financial aid. Fortunately, a national scholarship competition has features which tend to reduce the number of students who drop out after high school (3). Public recognition of the excellent performance of high-scoring students seems to motivate both the students and scholarship donors. Holland and Stalnaker (4) report that 98.7 percent of a group of near winners in the first National Merit Scholarship program went to college, and that approximately 65 percent of these students obtained scholarships from other sources. Students who rank high in any nationwide testing program become highly visible; as a consequence, they are stimulated to go to college and they frequently attract offers of scholarships from colleges and other sources. Thus loss is reduced.

Previous appraisals of talent loss were made before the initiation of the large-scale Merit Scholarship program. Under present conditions, the number of drop-outs among students of high ability is only half as large as the lowest figure estimated in earlier studies. The second annual Merit Scholarship program included a greatly enlarged sample of very able students. Over 166,500 high-school seniors in some 12,500 secondary schools took the initial qualifying test, and the top-scoring 15,000 students from this group were surveyed in respect to their college-going behavior. This population provides the best available means for appraising the cur-

Reprinted from *Science,* Vol. 128, No. 3327 (October 3, 1958), pp. 822-826. By permission of the author and publisher.

rent talent loss and for identifying the social and psychological factors which contribute to it (5).

In the present study, the amount of talent loss which occurs under existing conditions was estimated from the number of near winners in the 1957 program who failed to enroll in college. The study also sought to estimate the number of drop-outs who might attend college if additional scholarships were available.

Students ranking in the top 5 or 10 percent of the nation's youth cannot be expected to make full use of their talents without further specialized training. The loss of these students to higher education is an undeniable waste of the nation's intellectual talent. To throw light on the factors underlying this waste, the present sample was studied to ascertain those attributes which differentiate drop-outs from college-attenders. A knowledge of the environmental and personal factors contributing to withdrawal from higher education is necessary if we are to devise effective methods for reducing talent loss.

SAMPLE

The results reported in this study are based on a survey of a stratified random sample of 14,945 top-scoring students who took the qualifying test (Scholastic Qualifying Test) in the 1957 Merit program (6). The total group was composed of three classes of students: 7690 high-ranking students who received a letter of commendation; 6428 finalists, who received a Certificate of Merit; and 827 Merit Scholars, who received monetary stipends. These groups are mutually exclusive. The designated stratum samples included 47 percent of the commended group, and 100 percent of the finalists and Scholar groups. Returns were received from 80, 80, and 94 percent, respectively, of the designated stratum samples. Though some bias resulting from nonresponse can be expected, no exact estimate of it can be made since a follow-up survey among nonrespondents has not been attempted.

It is important to note that the population of 15,000 students surveyed here represents the students scoring highest within each of the states and territories. Students from each state were ranked on the basis of their scores in the scholastic Qualifying Test, and the number designated for recognition in each state was arbitrarily made proportionate to the number of seniors in the public high schools of that state. A national scholarship program designed to help students throughout the nation must almost of necessity distribute recognition and awards to students in proportion to the state's population of high-school seniors. This feature of the program makes it difficult to estimate the number of recoverable dropouts from test score distributions which disregard state differences. On the other hand, the present sample is admirably suited for estimating the

TABLE 1. Estimates of Talent Loss Among Students
of High Ability

SOURCE	Population	Date of Graduation from High School	Estimated Percentage not Attending College
National Merit Scholarship program	Merit scholars $(N = 827)$	1957	0.2*
	Finalists $(N = 6428)$	1957	3.1
	Semifinalists $(N = 7690)$	1957	5.1
	Total $(N = 14,945)$	1957	3.9
Terman and Oden (9)	Highest 1 or 2 percent, by IQ, in California schools	1928	12
Phearman (10)	Highest 2 percent, by achievement tests, among Iowa high-school graduates	1947	8
Wolfle (11)	Highest 2.8 percent of high-school graduates on intelligence test	1953	39
Phearman (10)	Highest 9 percent of Iowa's high-school graduates	1947	36
Iffert (1)	Highest 10 percent in high-school graduating class	1950	28
Corcoran and Keller (12)	Highest 15 percent by IQ, of Minnesota high-school seniors	1950	33†
Wolfle (11)	Highest 8.8 percent of high-school graduates	1953	45
Educational Testing Service (2)	Highest 10 percent, by aptitude test, of public high-school seniors	1955	30
Iffert (1)	Highest 30 percent in high-school graduating class	1950	30
Wolfle (11)	Highest 31 percent of high-school graduates	1953	53
Educational Testing Service (2)	Highest scoring 30 percent of public high-school seniors	1955	47

* Two students awarded scholarships are having their scholarships held for 1 year.
† Percentage attending college within 4 years of graduation.

number of talented students salvageable under conditions likely to obtain in any federal scholarship program.

Despite the variations introduced by the principle of identifying excellence within each state, it is estimated that over 97 percent of the population of 15,000 students are in the top 6 percent of the nation's high-school seniors in respect to verbal ability. The group is less highly selected in respect to mathematical ability, since the test scores used to rank students were composites which weighted verbal scores twice as heavily as mathematical scores. Nevertheless, it is estimated that about three-quarters of this population of very able students fall in the top 9 percent, by mathematical ability, of the nation's high-school seniors.

ESTIMATES OF TALENT LOSS

Table 1 presents estimates of talent loss among students of high ability. The first estimates in the table are those of drop-out rates for winners and near winners in the 1957 Merit program; the other estimates in the table are previous estimates of talent loss, which were based upon knowledge of the college-going behavior of students not participating in a national scholarship competition. The previous estimates vary considerably: for the top 2 or 3 percent, estimates of the drop-out rate vary from 8 to 39 percent; for the top tenth of the nation's high-school graduates, it has been estimated that between 28 and 45 percent do not go to college.

Most noteworthy is the fact that the drop-out rate of approximately 4 percent among the 15,000 very able students in the Merit program is half the figure given in the most conservative previous estimate. Among boys the estimated drop-out rate is 3.5 percent; among girls, 4.8 percent. In the present study a student was considered a drop-out if he failed to enroll as a full-time student in an accredited college in the quarter or semester immediately following high school graduation. About 66 percent of the drop-outs plan to get at least a bachelor's degree, so that if we were to follow these students for a longer period after their graduation from high school, we would find that the talent loss is even smaller.

It is believed that the extremely low drop-out rate among these students is a consequence of the public recognition that the near winners attain through their participation in the Merit program. An estimated 58 percent of the near winners who enrolled in college immediately held freshman scholarships with an average stipend of $602. Furthermore, it is estimated that 70 percent of the 14,118 near winners received at least one offer of scholarship aid from other sources. In a previous survey (4), about 30 percent of the 1956 near winners reported that they either received direct offers of scholarships or were aided in securing scholarships on their own initiative because of recognition received in the Merit program. In addition, some 11 percent of this group indicated that the recognition provided them with considerable emotional support; in many cases the students believed the honorary award had stimulated them to attend college. It is expected that any national scholarship program will similarly affect near winners. Runners-up who receive recognition will not

TABLE 2.   Estimated Percentage, by State, of 14,118 Near-winners
in the 1957 Merit Program Who Did Not Enroll
in College Immediately

PERCENT	State *	PERCENT	State *
0	District of Columbia (6.5)	4	Mississippi (49.0)
0	New Hampshire (1.0)	4	Oregon (19.0)
0	Nevada (23.0)	4	Pennsylvania (12.5)
1	New Jersey (6.5)	4	Texas (40.5)
2	Alabama (46.0)	4	Vermont (30.5)
2	Massachusetts (2.5)	4	Virginia (37.0)
2	Missouri (27.5)	5	California (17.0)
2	Montana (27.5)	5	Connecticut (2.5)
2	New York (5.0)	5	Georgia (43.5)
2	North Carolina (40.5)	5	Idaho (33.5)
2	North Dakota (30.5)	5	Iowa (12.5)
2	Rhode Island (30.5)	5	New Mexico (35.5)
2	Tennessee (38.5)	5	Oklahoma (38.5)
2	Territories (Alaska,	6	Indiana (12.5)
	Hawaii, Puerto Rico,	6	Kansas (25.5)
	Canal Zone)	6	Michigan (8.5)
3	Colorado (20.5)	6	West Virginia (45.0)
3	Nebraska (25.5)	8	Arizona (23.0)
3	Ohio (17.0)	8	South Dakota (30.5)
3	South Carolina (48.0)	9	Minnesota (4.0)
3	Wisconsin (8.5)	9	Utah (33.5)
4	Florida (35.5)	11	Arkansas (47.0)
4	Illinois (17.0)	11	Washington (12.5)
4	Kentucky (43.5)	14	Maine (12.5)
4	Louisiana (42.0)	15	Delaware (12.5)
4	Maryland (23.0)	17	Wyoming (20.5)

* Numbers in parentheses represent order of rank in regard to talent supply. The
states and the District of Columbia were ranked 1 to 49, according to the percentage
of registrants scoring 70 or above on the Selective Service Qualification Test given
May through July, 1951 (13). A low number indicates a relatively high supply of
talent.

only be more highly motivated to go to college, but they will also tend to
attract offers of scholarships from private scholarship donors.

Table 2 shows that the drop-out rate varies considerably from state to
state. The District of Columbia, New Hampshire, and Nevada are at one
extreme, with an estimated zero percent of near winners dropping out,
while at the other extreme are Maine, Delaware, and Wyoming, with an
estimated 14 to 17 percent drop-out rate among near winners. The relatively high drop-out rates for Delaware, Maine, Washington, and Minnesota are of special interest since students in these states tend to rank high
in ability level.

ROLE OF SCHOLARSHIPS
IN REDUCING TALENT LOSS

Most drop-outs indicate that the problem of financing a college education was a major factor in their decision not to enter college immediately.
Over half (52 percent) of the near winners who did not go to college
mentioned as one of their most important reasons, "It would cost more
than my family could afford." Eighty percent replied "Yes" to the question, "Would you go to college if you had more money?" Some 84 percent
of the drop-outs say they would certainly or probably accept a scholarship paying all their college expenses.

Although finances are a problem for these students, very few have resolved *not* to enter college. It is estimated that 84 percent of the drop-outs
plan to do at least some college work. Sixteen percent plan to get Ph.D.
or M.D. degrees, and an additional 20 percent plan to do at least one year
of graduate work. It appears that the majority of the drop-outs have de-
layed, rather than definitely decided against, entering college.

In other words, of an estimated 600 drop-outs among the top 15,000
students in the 1957 Merit program, some 500 would have gone to college
immediately if scholarships had been available. But 500 of these students
who are now without prospects of scholarship assistance say that they are
still planning to do at least some college work. To be sure, the delay between high school and college will be critical for some, who will never
actually enroll. In 1955 an Educational Testing Service follow-up (2) of
the top-scoring 10 percent of a sample of high-school seniors showed that
of some 530 students planning to go to college, 15 percent failed to enroll
the following fall. But even if we assume that of the 500 drop-outs now
planning to attend college a quarter will not go, the drop-out rate would
be only about one percent of the near winners.

Considerably more than 500 scholarships would have been required to
send all the drop-outs who want further education to college immediately. This paradox arises because at present it is not possible to differentiate between the student who will not enroll immediately if he does
not get a scholarship and the student with comparable financial resources
who will manage to go to college without assistance. If it were possible
to differentiate these two groups of students in the selection stage, scholarship funds could be used more efficiently to forestall delay in entering
college.

The chief contribution of an augmented scholarship program for the
present population of students of high ability, it appears, would be to
hasten, rather than increase, college enrollment. On the other hand, new
scholarship funds could materially reduce talent loss if awards were of-

fered to *less* highly talented students. The most important reservoir of wasted talent is found among students who rank between the 70th and 95th percentile in the distribution of ability. Above this level the loss is, as we have seen, relatively small. The 70th percentile in ability is suggested because various authorities have estimated that students above this level of ability are the students who profit most from a college education.

FACTORS CONTRIBUTING TO TALENT LOSS

Table 3 compares drop-outs and college-attenders with respect to 17 attributes which previous research had found to differentiate drop-outs at lower ability levels. The most striking differences are found in the vocational and educational aspirations of the different classes of near-winners. Only about a third of the drop-outs plan to do postgraduate study, whereas about two-thirds of the college-attenders plan such study. About a third of the students not enrolling in college immediately have selected vocations which do not require the bachelor's degree; only 10 percent of the college-attenders have selected such vocations. Contrary to expectations, drop-outs are no more undecided in their vocational choices than are college-attenders.

The second feature which stands out in Table 3 is the difference in cultural stimulation between the homes of drop-outs and the homes of college-attenders. For the most part, the parents of drop-outs have not attended college and have fewer books in the home. The fathers of students not going to college tend to be employed in middle- or low-income occupations.

Talent loss among the near-winners does not appear to be the result of a lack of counseling or guidance in the schools. Drop-outs report receiving relatively more encouragement from their teachers and guidance counselors than do college-attenders. On the other hand, the parents of drop-outs—who presumably must assume the financial burdens—encouraged college attendance less frequently than did the parents of college-goers. Drop-outs also tend to have more close friends who are not going to college. In general, however, nine out of every ten drop-outs among the near winners received some encouragement to attend college.

As might be expected, drop-outs tend to have slightly lower aptitude test scores than do the near-winners who enrolled in college with scholarships. On the other hand, the large proportion of drop-outs whose aptitude test scores place them in the top two percent of the national ability continuum attests to the seriousness of losing such promising students.

At least part of the talent loss may be attributed to lack of initiative among drop-outs. Only 44 percent of the drop-outs made two or more applications for scholarships, whereas 74 percent of the near-winners enrolling with scholarships made this many applications. Mollenkopf and Dear (7) have previously shown that the likelihood of receiving a scholarship offer increases rather dramatically with the number of applications made.

The results confirm previous findings (2) that the drop-out rate is higher for girls than boys, and that drop-outs tend to have had less mathematics in high school. However, very few, if any, lack the prerequisites for college. Eighty-four percent of the drop-outs took high-school courses preparing them for college.

DISCUSSION

Although the present analysis demonstrates that the current loss of talent among the top 5 percent of the high-school-senior population is less than previous studies have estimated, these results do not justify complacence. There is clearly a need for the continuation of all current scholarship programs and for additional financial aid. True, the need probably will not be critical among students who receive recognition in existing scholarship programs, provided such programs are continued. Most of these students will go to college, many of them with scholarships. But there remains a large number of talented students who drop out of school because of their inability to finance a college education. There is particularly a need for additional funds to recover those students who rank between the 70th and 95th percentiles on the ability continuum. Talented drop-outs who are only "second best" are at present the most promising population in which governmental financial aid programs can effect a reduction in talent loss. Special effort may be required to dispel the notion that only the valedictorian deserves assistance. Particularly deserving of consideration are those needy students who are highly motivated to pursue higher education but who rank slightly below the top decile on the usual measures of college aptitude. Scholarship funds for the large number of potential drop-outs among the "second best" are in short supply.

Further research is also required. What impact, if any, does a national scholarship competition have upon students who compete but fail to win recognition? Are these students stimulated to develop their talents, or are they diverted into occupations less commensurate with their ability level? How can we devise better methods for identifying the potential drop-out while he is still in high school? What resources can be marshaled to lessen the talent loss arising from parental attitudes and cultural deficits? (8).

TABLE 3.   Differences Between Drop-outs and Near-winners Who
Attended College, Among 14,118 Participants
in the 1957 Merit Program

ATTRIBUTE	Estimated Percent of Near-winners Having Indicated Attribute		
	Enrolled in College Without Scholarship	Enrolled in College With Scholarship	Drop-out
Cultural stimulation			
200 or more books in home	69	58	51
Mother had at least some college	62	52	33
Father had at least some college	71	57	38
Father in professional or managerial occupation	72	54	37
Encouragement to attend college			
Mother encouraged student to attend	99	98	89
Father encouraged student to attend	99	97	85
Teachers gave "quite a lot" of encouragement	76	80	88
All of student's closely associated peers going to college	48	38	21
Scholastic Qualifying Test score			
Verbal score in top 2 percent of national senior norms	76	79	72
Quantitative score in top 2 percent of national senior norms	45	52	44
High-school preparation			
Took college preparatory curriculum	93	92	84
Took 8 or more semesters of mathematics	61	61	46
Vocational and educational aspirations			
Planning to enter vocation requiring bachelor's degree	86	90	66
Student's vocational plans are tentative or undecided	60	56	56
Planning to do at least 1 year of post-college graduate study	61	69	36
Personal characteristics			
Male	64	66	56
Applied for two or more scholarships (exclusive of NMS program)	41	74	44

REFERENCES AND NOTES

1. R. E. Iffert, *Coll. and Univ.* **31**, 435 (1956).
2. Educational Testing Service, *Background Factors Relating to College Plans and College Enrollment among Public High School Students* (Educational Testing Service, Princeton, N.J., 1957).
3. In this paper the term *drop-out* generally refers to a high-school graduate who does not enroll in college. In the discussion of drop-outs among participants in the Merit program, the term refers to high-school graduates who failed to enroll in an accredited college in the quarter or semester *immediately* following graduation from high school, or to students who enrolled but withdrew before completing a full quarter or semester.
4. J. L. Holland and J. M. Stalnaker, *J. Higher Educ.* **28**, 361 (1957).
5. The top-ranking 5 percent of the senior class in each participating high school was tested without charge. Further, the second annual program allowed additional seniors to take the qualifying test by paying a fee of $1; this provision in part accounts for a threefold increase in the number of participants in the second year. Since an estimated 88 percent of the 1956 senior population attended one of the 10,388 high schools in the first year's program, it is estimated that a minimum of nine out of every ten senior students were screened in the 1957 talent search.
6. The ability levels of 241 students were difficult to estimate (because of incomplete aptitude test scores or follow-up test performance incommensurate with performance on the initial test); these students were not surveyed and are not considered a part of the top 15,000 students referred to.
7. W. G. Mollenkopf and R. E. Dear, *An Analysis of Factors Affecting Financial Aid-Offers and Awards* (Educational Testing Service, Princeton, N.J., 1957).
8. I am indebted to John M. Stalnaker, John L. Holland and Laura Kent for their critical reading of the manuscript. This study was partially supported by research grants from the National Science Foundation and the Old Dominion Foundation.
9. L. M. Terman and M. H. Oden, *The Gifted Child Grows Up* (Stanford Univ. Press, Stanford, Calif., 1957).
10. L. I. Phearman, *J. Educ. Psychol.* **40**, 405 (1949).
11. D. Wolfle, *America's Resources of Specialized Talent* (Harper, New York, 1954).
12. M. Corcoran and R. J. Keller, *College Attendance of Minnesota High School Seniors* (Bureau of Institutional Research, Univ. of Minnesota, 1957).
13. C. C. Cole, Jr., *Encouraging Scientific Talent* (College Entrance Examination Board, New York, 1956), p. 83.

Concerning the Nature and Nurture of Genius

SIDNEY L. PRESSEY

It has been well said that "in the present international tug of war, survival itself may depend upon making the most effective use of the nation's intellectual resources" (1, p. 4). Means of better identifying young people of superior intellectual capacities, and of getting more of them into present programs of advanced training, have been widely discussed. However, there has been relatively little consideration of whether present educational programs are best suited to the needs of our most brilliant young pople. Superior abilities are now generally considered so predominantly a product of innate constitution that certain "educational" factors, possibly of very great importance in the growth of such abilities, are overlooked. It is sometimes well to get outside of current habits of thought and try to look at a topic in a reappraising way. This paper attempts so to do. It focuses attention on that most extraordinary type of very superior intellect—the precocious genius—as possibly exhibiting especially clearly both innate capacities and developmental influences involved in extraordinary accomplishment. It presumes to suggest that there may be ways by which many more "geniuses" might be not only discovered but even, to a substantial degree, *made* and brought to fruition.

MAJOR FACTORS MAKING FOR PRECOCIOUS MARKED SUPERIORITY

An informal search for instances of marked precocity suggests that such cases have been especially frequent (or, at least, especially noted and featured) in certain fields and in certain localities at certain times. In the Europe of 100 to 200 years ago there were outstanding musicians of whom most were precocious. Handel played on the clavichord "when but an infant" and was composing by the age of 11. Haydn "played and composed at the age of 6." Mozart played the harpsichord at 3, was composing at 4, and was on a tour at 6. Chopin played in public at the age

Reprinted from *Scientific Monthly*, Vol. 81, No. 3 (September, 1955), pp. 123-129. By permission of the author and publisher.

of 8; Liszt, at 9; Verdi, at 10; Schubert, at 12; and Rossini, at 14. Mendelssohn was playing publicly and also composing by the age of 9, as was Debussy at 11, Dvorak at 12, and Berlioz at 14. Wagner conducted one of his own compositions in public when he was 17 (2, 3, 4).

Recently, and especially in this country, there have been many precocious athletes. Thus, Bobby Jones was state golf champion at 14 (5). Marlene Bauer was playing notable golf at 13 (6). Sonja Henie was figure-skating champion of Norway at 10 and world champion at 15. Barbara Anne Scott was Canadian figure-skating champion at 15 (7). Vincent Richards was national tennis singles champion at 15, and Maureen Connolly was woman's singles champion at 16. Mel Ott was in big league baseball at 16; Feller, at 18. Eddie Lebaron was an intercollegiate football star at 16. Bob Mathias won an Olympic gold medal in track and field events at 17 (5). The reader may doubt whether athletic champions are relevant to the topic of this paper but he can hardly question that they are very competent in their fields. Moreover, precocity in athletics and in musical performance might seem especially extraordinary because finger reach and dexterity on a musical instrument and strength, as well as skill and endurance, in athletic competition would seem especially to call for physical maturity.

An especially remarkable type of athlete must also be noted: the champion whose superiority emerged after great and persistent efforts to overcome a crippling handicap. Walt Davis, holder of a world's record in the high jump, was a former polio victim (8). Glenn Cunningham, the Olympic runner, was burned so severely in the legs when he was 8 years old that it was doubted that he would ever walk again. At the age of 8, Nancy Merki had polio and at 10 was more paralyzed, but at 13 she was high-point scorer in a national swimming meet (5). Other well-known athletes have had polio. In all these instances, the athletic prowess was the final result of very persistent (and usually expertly guided) efforts to overcome the handicap. There was no evidence before the injury or illness of notable athletic potential.

The first question, then, is why there should have been a rash of notable precocious musicians in the Europe of a century and more ago and a spate of youthful athletic champions in this country now. Certain major factors seem evident. In the Europe of that time, music was the major popular interest, reaching practically all social classes and all ages, and offering even to underprivileged youngsters the possibility of wide popular acclaim. Athletics is a similar interest in this country now. The second question is more specifically how, in such favorable total situations, have these prodigies come about. A study of their careers suggests that the following factors are important.

1. Precocious musicians and athletes usually had excellent early opportunities for the ability to develop and encouragement from family and

friends. Mozart's father was a musician; his older sister was his companion in music; family and friends admired and encouraged the boy. Schubert's father was musical and fostered Franz's musical aptitude; soon Franz became a member of a string quartet with his father and two brothers. Of the athletes, Bobby Jones lived next to a golf course. When he was still a little boy, he was given small clubs and followed his father around the links. From early childhood, Barbara Anne Scott's skating was fostered by her father, and soon her whole life was so centered.

2. Usually individuals who developed precocious excellence had superior early and continuing individual guidance and instruction. From the age of 3, Mozart was taught, guided, and managed in his career by his father, who sought practically from the beginning to make his son an outstanding musician. Mendelssohn, also from the age of 3, was taught by his mother and other good musicians. Marlene Bauer's father, a golf professional, began to teach her the game when she was 3. Nancy Merki had an expert swimming coach.

3. Precocious individuals have had the opportunity frequently and continuingly to practice and extend their special ability and to progress as they were able. From the age of 3, Mozart practiced with his older sister; he had the opportunity to play the violin, the harpsichord, and the organ, to perform frequently in public, and a little later to conduct. From the age of 11, Maureen Connolly practiced tennis at least 3 hours a day. The climate of southern California made this possible at all seasons. She took on more able opponents and entered more important tournaments, as she was able. Nancy Merki was "in the water for hours at a time, just trying to master the trick of fluttering her legs." Under the guidance of her coach she moved forward in her aquatic accomplishments as she was ready.

4. The special precocious ability usually brought a close association with others in the field, which greatly fostered the abilities of all concerned, and led to a still wider stimulating acquaintance. Mozart lived from early childhood in a world of musicians who listened to and watched one another, played together, cooperated, competed, raised levels of aspiration, and were keen in criticism and encouragement. His musicianship brought acquaintance with the great all over Europe, including the Austrian emperor. Bobby Jones lived largely in a golfers' world, which developed his skills at the same time that he raised golfing standards and increased the popularity of the sport. His friendships have indeed been wide, including President Eisenhower.

5. As a result of many opportunities for real accomplishment, within his possibilities but of increasing challenge, the precocious musician or athlete has had the stimulation of many and increasingly strong success experiences—and his world acclaimed these successes. It is well recognized that frequent failure and continued frustration may debilitate per-

sonality and competency, just as a disease does. But the opposite also seems true, although it is not generally appreciated: frequent, much-admired successes increase effort, build up psychosomatic vigor, make attempts more vigorous, and adequate, and better integrated, and build ability. The opinion is ventured that such "furtherance" is as important a phenomenon as frustration, and that systematic research regarding furtherance might well be as profitable as research on frustration has been.

At any age, development of any ability is fostered by a favorable immediate environment, expert instruction, frequent and progressive opportunities for the exercise of the ability, social facilitation, and frequent success experiences. Important advantages would seem to accrue from having these factors begin operation early. The physique may grow and adapt in congruence. As the young musician stretches out his hands and exercises needed muscles and coordinations, his skills may be not only learned but somewhat made part of his growth. This might be true, not for mechanical skills alone, but also for related integrations in the central nervous system, and for related percepts and concepts. So the precocious musicians played not only with skill but also with understanding, and they composed, notably and early. Possibly some integration of learning and growth might occur with abilities less closely related to a skill. Any ability, developing early, might benefit by having the great energies of childhood and youth devoted to it. Also, the child in the grip of a strong interest (as a hobby) seems often single-mindedly absorbed in it to an extent less common later, when problems of social status, economic responsibility, or the other sex may distract. If an interest is already well established when adolescence comes, the energies of that period may pour into it.

The thesis thus is that, in attempting to account for notable precocity in such fields as music and athletics, too much stress has been put on presumed extreme constitutional genius and too little on a concomitance of favorable factors, operating in the growth years. Instances of great athletic skill emerging from efforts to overcome a seemingly crippling handicap seem to emphasize the potency of these last factors. Presumably, the original physical potentials of these individuals were good, although not manifest, before the handicap struck; but the great potential of favoring circumstances seems especially evident. In this connection, Wechsler's argument (9) may well be recalled—that the range of human physical traits, as in height, strength, and quickness, is really not great, and that the range in mental capacities may be less extreme than is usually supposed. Rather, superior original capacity, *growing under a favorable concomitance of circumstances*, develops into genius.

So far, the discussion has dealt primarily with outstanding precocious skills, in athletics and music. May the youthful organism not be capable of outstanding accomplishments more intellectual in nature? Here it should again be mentioned that notable musical performance would seem to involve keen musical understanding as well as dexterity (and outstanding athletic performance perhaps often involves more intelligence than is usually conceded). In youth, the famous precocious musicians not only performed but composed notably; and composing music is surely a highly intellectual activity.

But precocity has appeared in sundry other and clearly intellectual fields. John Stuart Mill began the study of Greek at 3. By the age of 8 he had read Xenophon, Herodotus, and Plato and had begun to study geometry and algebra. At 12 he began logic, reading Aristotle in the original. The next year he began the study of political economy; at 16 he was publishing controversial articles in that field (10). When he was 6 years old, John Ruskin wrote verse. Macaulay compiled a "universal history" at the age of 7. Published poems of William Blake, Thomas Chatterton, and Alexander Pope go back to their 12th years; poems of Robert Burns go back to his 14th year, and of Milton to his 15th year. Pascal wrote a treatise on acoustics when he was 12. Galileo made his famous observations of the swinging cathedral lamp when he was 17. Perkin discovered the first synthetic dye when he was 18 (11, pp. 198-219). Farnsworth, at 15, "evolved an electronic means of sending pictures through the air" (12). Recently, 11-year-old Italian Severino Guidi, 10-year-old Turkish Hasan Kaptan, and 11-year-old French Thierry Vaubourgoin have been mentioned (13) as precocious painters. Norbert Wiener has written his sensitive account of his own precocity: college entrance at 11, Harvard doctorate at 18 (14). However, as compared with music and athletics (15), precocity seems more rare in art, literature, and science, and especially so in this country. Why?

INFLUENCES HAMPERING THE PRECOCIOUS

There is a general belief, fostered in this country by most child psychologists and "progressive" educators during the past 25 years, that intellectual precocity is somehow not quite healthy, is almost always a hazard to good social adjustment, and should be slowed down rather than facilitated. In the home the early-reading precocious child causes anxiety, in spite of the usualness of such precocity in Terman's gifted group and in biographies of famous men (16, 17). The schools oppose entrance before the standard age of 6, in spite of the evidence, from some half-dozen experiments, that gifted tots admitted earlier have done well, both academically and adjustment-wise (18). The general public tends to regard the intellectually gifted small child as a freak. In short, there is usually none of the initial encouragement in the family, early fostering, and favorable general social climate that got many musical and athletic prodigies off to a flying start.

As a result of mass education and indifference to the needs of the gifted, there is almost none of the individualized guidance and instruction for excellence that was mentioned as an important element in the rapid development of precocity in music and athletics. A good music teacher is usually especially interested in finding and training pupils who are gifted musically. The athletic coach tries to find and bring to peak performance the ablest young athletes in his school. But the usual public school teacher does not have the time, the attitude, or the methods to do much, if anything, for another young Macaulay or Farnsworth in his classes.

In contrast to possibilities of continuing intensive practice and rapid progress in music or athletics, opportunities often are entirely lacking for a youngster to indulge intensively and continuingly an aptitude in such a field as a science, advancing as he is capable. A boy precociously interested in chemistry may have to await schoolwork in that subject until the regular course in his high-school junior year. He must then start and progress with his classmates, and in his senior year must take other subjects (intensive work in one field is frowned upon as interfering with a broad program) and not "hang around" the chemistry laboratory (19). Nor can the broadly gifted and precocious youngster advance in his total school program more rapidly than the average; acceleration is, in most schools, considered unwise.

Whereas the precocious young musician or athlete soon has an acceptance and a mounting status that is tremendously stimulating and educative for him, in musical or athletic groups—and these groups have status in school and community—the budding young scientist or scholar may be isolated or may associate only with a friend who is also considered "odd" or may belong only to an anemic subject club of no prestige in the community.

In contrast to the early and continuing successes of the young athlete or musician, possibly mounting to international acclaim, the young scholar or scientist may have no opportunities to make good except in class assignments and may obtain no evidence of success other than good marks. The teacher (perhaps made uncomfortable by keen questions) may even criticize his intense interest, and the other youngsters may call him sissy or odd. For him there is frustration, *not* the furtherance of cumulative success.

Suppose that Mozart or Bobby Jones had not been allowed to begin his music or his golf until the other children did, or to practice more or progress faster, or had had only the instruction of a school class in music or physical education. Suppose that they had been kept from playing with older children or adults in the fear that they might become socially maladjusted, kept from associating much with other musicians or golfers because that would be narrowing and undemocratic, kept from public performances or tournaments because that would be exploiting the poor child! It surely may be questioned whether they would then have reached the preeminence they did. Abuses in the afore-mentioned directions are, of course, possible. But it is also an abuse to withhold opportunities from precocious youngsters who are eager to advance and excel. The opinion is ventured that the last type of abuse is now, in this country, the more common one.

TOWARD MORE AND BETTER AMERICAN GENIUSES

The hypothesis thus is that a practicing genius is produced by giving a precocious able youngster early encouragement, intensive instruction, continuing opportunity as he advances, a congruent stimulating social life, and cumulative success experiences. In the instances given however, the circumstances have all been so superior as to seem somewhat out of reach. Moreover, there was sometimes imbalance or exploitation. In the average college or school, what steps might be possible that would move with reasonable caution and good sense in the directions indicated here and perhaps somewhat benefit a great many youngsters as well as occasionally help toward the production of a "genius"? Two steps would seem feasible and of great possible fruitfulness.

The first proposal is that there should be, in a college or a school system, a person who might be given the somewhat colorless title of coordinator of special programs, lest the more precise label of personnel specialist for superior students cause them embarrassment and antagonize parents of students not selected or served by him. Such a person in a college should scan each entering student's record to find high-school valedictorians, science-fair winners, and others with evidence of superior ability. He should watch for such evidence especially among students in the freshman year. He might even follow reports on high-school science fairs and the like and recruit promising youngsters for his college in the manner of a football coach. (If other colleges object to this, maybe competition among colleges for the intellectually superior might be a good thing! As he locates such cases he should seek them out, encourage them, and bring them to the attention of appropriate faculty members. He should try to help these students in any problems they have, find opportunities for them on campus, and perhaps arrange summer work or travel opportunities. He should make a special effort to bring congenial members of his group together and to foster stimulating companionship and morale. He should see to it that his program receives publicity and that his youngsters receive recognition. He should guide and further any plans they have for professional or graduate training and for careers.

In a secondary school or school superintendent's office, a person similarly designated to find and foster the most able students would try to keep the elementary schools alert to discover especially bright children there. As these move on to high school, he could watch for them. He would have the high-school teachers inform him of outstanding students in their classes and keep alert for other evidences of talent, as in hobbies. He would become acquainted with all such youngsters, encourage them, and bring them into contact with appropriate teachers and into appropriate subject clubs or other groups. Educative trips with other youngsters might be arranged and perhaps summer work that would be both financially and educationally profitable. A local business or professional man might be enlisted to sponsor an outstanding youngster who needed such support. Contacts might be readied with a college or university.

If such guidance or personnel specialists for the most able were generally available in colleges and high schools or public school systems, it is believed that they could greatly increase the number of young people going into advanced training, select them better, and greatly improve the effectiveness of their education (20, 21). Such a position might be only half time, for a student counselor or assistant principal, but it should be seen as his distinctive opportunity. If in a college, he would work with the ablest students, the best teachers on the faculty, and the best professional and graduate schools. If in a secondary school, he would deal with the finest students and the community leaders most interested in young people. He would try cumulatively to build community interest in and opportunities for these ablest young people, as through the local papers and service clubs. He would have mutually profitable relationships with the best colleges and universities. At regional and national meetings, as of guidance associations, these personnel workers at all levels would meet with others doing like work. Slowly, they might change public attitudes to interest in the intellectually, as well as the athletically, able. Surely no position could be more finely rewarding.

It is not enough, however, to provide special student personnel or guidance service for superior students. *In proportion as they are very able and especially as they have special talents, special adaptations of the usual curriculums are likely to be desirable.* The able youngster not yet sure of his special interests may wish to explore very widely. Once he has found that interest he may, legitimately, wish to push it hard. Before long, his accomplishments may warrant his admission into courses ahead of his status. (The sophomore may desire some course not usually available before the junior year.) Soon, he may be ready for an independent project under supervision of one of the ablest teachers, for an honors seminar, perhaps a project off campus or work experience in the field of his interest—first attempts at real accomplishment in that field.

There should be readily usable administrative machinery—it might be called an honors program—making it possible for an able student, perhaps under the guidance of a person as mentioned in the previous paragraphs, and under the general direction of a faculty committee, to have certain curricular freedoms and special opportunities to foster best his potentialities (22, 23).

It should be possible to adapt school and college programs to the needs of superior youngsters with regard to not only the nature of these programs but also their length. Occasionally a late start or an added year in school or college may be warranted. Far more often, an early start and rapid progress are desirable. Not only the occasional prodigy but most people of superior abilities show their superiority early and develop more rapidly than the average person (17, 24). Moreover, impressive evidence indicates that intellectual creativity reaches its peak relatively early in adult life (11). The practically universal American educational policy, nevertheless, is the lockstep: every child must enter school at 6 (none more than a month or so earlier), progress a grade a year, and, if he seeks advanced training, continue his schooling often till around 30, which was the median age of receiving the doctorate in this country just before World War II. Now, military service may delay even more the completion of education. Yet numerous studies are practically unanimous in showing that able children can enter earlier and progress more rapidly than the average child, without harm and often with gain in regard to realized abilities and social adjustment (18, 24, 25). Outcomes have been thus favorable in spite of most common use of the *worst* methods for "acceleration"—grade-skipping in school and a lengthened year in college. Better methods—admission to the first grade on the basis of readiness for school rather than chronological age, replacement of the first three grades by a "primary pool" out of which children would move early or late depending on when they finish primary work, rapid-progress sections doing 3 years' work in 2 in junior and senior high school, and credit by examination in college—should permit each youngster to move through educational programs at his own pace, without being conspicuous if his rate is not that of the average.

Not only are accelerates usually successful and happy in school, but they are more likely to complete collegiate and advanced training. At Ohio State University, 50 percent of the students entering when they were 16 years old graduated, but only 38 percent of the 18-year-old entrants paired with them according to tested general ability at entrance and type of program. With selection for acceleration and guidance therein, outcomes should be even better. Of a group of students selected in their freshman year as capable of finishing a 4-year program in less time and guided in so doing 63 percent graduated. Further, accelerates seem more often successful in their careers than individuals proceeding through their education at the usual pace. From 1880 to 1900, 29 percent of those graduating from Amherst at 19 became nationally known, as compared with 12 percent of those graduating at 22 (18). Of those in Terman's gifted group who graduated from high school under the age of 15 years and 6 months, 16 percent more graduated from college and 19 percent more took one or more years of graduate work than did those who finished high school when they were 16 years and 6 months or older, although there was little difference between the two groups in general ability when they were tested in childhood. (The average IQ's of the two groups at that time were 158 and 149, respectively.) Moreover, twice as many of the first group (42 percent as compared with 19 percent) were very superior in respect to career (17, pp. 265-279).

In short, simply to increase the number of bright American youngsters who "accelerate" should substantially increase the number obtaining technologic or other advanced training and make it easier for precocious genius to emerge. If it were possible for bright youngsters not only to move through school more rapidly but also in other ways to have their programs adjusted to their special needs, still more might be expected to complete such training, still more successfully, and with still more notable careers following. Moreover, they would finish their training and get into their productive careers sooner. And educational costs would probably be reduced! Thus it seems a reasonable estimate that every year there remain in the secondary schools around 300,000 students whom a reasonable program of acceleration would have graduated. Such a reduction in enrollment would involve substantial savings, which might more than provide for the suggested special counselors for the gifted.

To meet the needs for trained manpower mentioned at the beginning of this paper, greater efforts to interest bright students in collegiate and advanced training programs (as they are now), better guidance of students in those programs, and more scholarship or other financial aid, have been suggested. The suggestion is here ventured that special facilitated programs adapted to the needs of the gifted would be the best means of interesting them, that special guidance in such programs (as suggested here) would best keep these students in school, and that such facilitated and early-completed programs (often including paid work experience) would substantially reduce the need for financial aid to students. Finally, the proposed special measures should produce more "geniuses." To produce persons of notable accomplishment, educational efforts should be directed straight toward that goal, in the light of all that can be found out about such persons and their upbringing. Simply to increase the number of students in physical education classes would probably *not* very much increase the number of athletic champions!

REFERENCES AND NOTES

1. D. Wolfle, *America's Resources of Specialized Talent* (Harper, New York, 1954).
2. F. Barlow, *Mental Prodigies* (Philosophical Library, New York, 1952).
3. M. Davenport, *Mozart* (Scribner, New York, 1942).
4. F. Schwrimmer, *Great Musicians as Children* (Doubleday, New York, 1930).
5. A. J. Stump, *Champions Against Odds* (Macrae Smith, Philadelphia, 1952).
6. *Life*, 20 Mar. 1950, p. 95.
7. *Time*, 2 Feb., 1948.
8. *Time*, 6 July 1953.
9. D. Wechsler, *Range of Human Capacities* (Williams and Wilkins, Baltimore, rev. ed., 1952).
10. M. St. J. Packe, *The Life of John Stuart Mill* (Macmillan, New York, 1954).
11. H. C. Lehman, *Age and Achievement* (Princeton Univ. Press, Princeton, N.J., 1953).
12. *Newsweek*, 28 Mar. 1949.
13. *Time*, 14 Jan. 1952; 10 Nov. 1952; 14 Feb. 1955.
14. N. Wiener, *Ex-prodigy* (Simon and Schuster, New York, 1953).
15. And the entertainment world in general; stars of the stage, screen, radio, and television have not been mentioned because physical attractiveness and luck in promotion, rather than ability, have often been of major importance. But the ablest seem usually precocious, as a result of circumstances such as those mentioned here.
16. C. M. Cox, *The Early Mental Traits of 300 Geniuses* (Stanford Univ. Press, Stanford, Calif., 1926).
17. L. M. Terman, *The Gifted Child Grows Up* (Stanford Univ. Press, Stanford, Calif., 1947).
18. S. L. Pressey, *Educational Acceleration: Appraisals and Basic Problems* (Ohio State Univ., Columbus, 1949), p. 11.
19. Subjects that might arouse early interest often cannot be started in high school. Thus, a youngster may have no opportunity to study psychology until his junior year of college. But trial of group discussion of social adjustment in junior-high-school and secondary-school home economics courses on "family life" have demonstrated the possibility of early beginning of a colloquial psychology. Children may be very shrewd in human relations. The opinion is ventured that precocity in psychology *should* be especially feasible. Such a youngster, entering adolescence with extensive relevant knowledge, might make distinctive contributions to knowledge of that period.
20. Wolfle (1, p. 251) has reported a study showing a substantial increase in the number of high-school students going to college as a result of a general school guidance program. A recent account (*21*) dramatizes possibilities of finding and furthering talent in even a small and isolated school.
21. F. V. Rummell and C. M. Johnson, "Bill Lane's Students Win the Prizes," *Reader's Digest*, Jan. 1955, p. 29.

22. A program of this general type was for some years in effect at Ohio State University, but unfortunately it was dropped at the beginning of World War II, primarily because of lack of any such personnel specialist as has been urged in the preceding paragraphs. Many of the undergraduates in this program did research or service projects worthy of publication (23). The conventional honors program lacks the opportunities for work experience and for the research or service project (as distinct from a paper or library reading) that were found most distinctively valuable in the Ohio State University program.

23. S. L. Pressey, "The New Program for the Degree with Distinction at Ohio State University," *School and Society*, 36, 280 (1932).

24. L. M. Terman, "The Discovery and Encouragement of Exceptional Talent," *Am. Psychologist* 9, 221 (1954).

Intellectual Resources

DAEL WOLFLE

The scientific and intellectual advances of a nation are generated by a comparatively small number of people. These few—the inventors, scientists, thinkers and scholars who have given us the Declaration of Independence and atomic energy, railroads and radar, antibiotics and masterpieces of music and literature—have contributed to civilization out of all proportion to their numbers. In the U. S. we think immediately of such giants as Thomas Jefferson, Benjamin Franklin, Josiah Willard Gibbs, Thomas Hunt Morgan, Alexander Graham Bell, John Dewey, Mark Twain and Walt Whitman. But the geniuses represent only a part of a nation's intellectual resources; for every genius there are hundreds of less eminent but highly competent men and women who also contribute significantly to the nation's intellectual progress.

The first step in appraising the intellectual resources of the U. S., therefore, is to try to define just what group we are talking about. We cannot define it simply in terms of education, for our intellectual manpower certainly does not include all of the six million college graduates in the U. S. Some of them have retired from work; some are in nonintellectual occupations; some, though they have obtained degrees, can hardly be classed as capable of high-level mental work. Conversely, there are many people making important intellectual contributions who never went to college.

From *Scientific American*, Vol. 185, No. 3 (September, 1951), pp. 42-46. Reprinted with permission. Copyright © 1951, 1952 by Scientific American, Inc. All rights reserved.

As a rough definition of our intellectual manpower let us say that it comprises all those who work primarily with their brains. We do not know how large this number is, because no exact census of them has ever been taken. Efforts are now being made to do so: the Federal government, professional societies and other agencies have been compiling rosters of specialists in the sciences, humanities and various professions, and the 1950 Census made a number of new tabulations of scientific specialties.

It is estimated that we have about 400,000 engineers, 209,000 doctors, 200,000 college teachers and 175,000 scientists. If we add the architects, editors, lawyers, social scientists and persons in other high-level fields, the total number of brainworkers is perhaps a million and a half. Even if the actual number is twice that, we are still considering only two per cent of the total population and five per cent of the nation's labor force.

Individually the members of this group vary greatly in their intellectual contributions to society. But in general these are the people who have ideas, develop new inventions, processes and products, manage the nation's social, intellectual and administrative machinery, run its industry and commerce and train others for these complex tasks. They are a growing resource. Through their work they have greatly increased the demand for people like themselves. Their scientific discoveries, inventions and social improvements have created new demands for engineers, scientists, social scientists, historians, scholars and other men of ability and training who can manage our ever-more-complex society.

Our problem is: Where are we to find the resources to meet these additional demands? How many people have we who are capable of making creative contributions? How effectively are we discovering and utilizing our intellectual potential? Can we increase our intellectual manpower?

To answer these questions we must have some reliable measure of intellectual ability. No one will pretend that this can be determined by a simple formula. Intelligence alone is not enough for effective intellectual work; to make creative contributions in a scientific or scholarly field one must also be endowed with interest in it, industry, persistence, strength of character, confidence and some spark of originality.

Twenty-five years ago the U. S. psychologist Catharine Cox Miles made an attempt to estimate the intelligence quotients of 300 of the most eminent men of history. Her estimates were based upon studies of their early writings, school progress and other evidences of achievement in comparison with the records of average children. She concluded that the average I.Q. of these 300 geniuses was above 160, that few fell below 140 and that many were above 180. An I.Q. of 160 is so rare that theoretically only one person in a million ranks that high. But not everyone—in fact, scarcely anyone—who has an I.Q. of 160 goes down in history as a genius; the other traits also are necessary. There are 152 million people in the U. S., but not 152 of the eminence of the group studied by Dr. Miles.

On the other hand, the psychologist Anne Roe recently studied 60 of the most eminent research scientists in the U. S. and found that they varied considerably in intelligence. What the 60 had in common was an intense driving interest in their chosen fields of science. They had become America's most eminent scientists despite the fact that they would not all make the very highest scores on an intelligence test. As for the little-understood gift of creative talent, it is apparently not restricted to geniuses; it exists in lesser amounts in many people—the people who develop short-cuts, who put ingenious new ideas into the suggestion box, who think up improvements on old routines. No one knows for sure, but it is quite possible that creative talent is qualitatively the same sort of thing in such people as in geniuses, the only difference being that the latter have more of it.

If intelligence is not a sufficient condition for creative intellectual work, at least it is a necessary one. Some minimum level of intelligence is necessary to master the basic concepts, problems and techniques of a specialized field. The minimum level varies, of course, with the difficulty of the field. It turns out, for example, that people who go into work in the pure sciences score higher in intelligence tests, on the average, than those in applied fields; within the field of the basic sciences the physical scientists average a little higher than the biologists. Remember, however, that we are speaking only of averages; there are very high I.Q.'s in all fields.

On the whole, we must depend upon intelligence tests, for want of a better measure, as the basis for estimating our potential intellectual resources. Such tests can measure a number of different kinds of ability, but for our general purpose a composite measure of academic aptitude, scored by the method used during World War II for the Army General Classification Test (AGCT) will suffice. The Army scale has an average score of 100 and a standard deviation of 20. These figures are quite arbitrary. They do not mean that the average man answered correctly exactly 100 of the test items. Rather, the raw score of the average man, regardless of what it actually was, was converted to a score of 100 points. Other raw scores were converted to arbitrary scores higher or lower than 100 so that the total distribution had a standard deviation of 20 points (*i.e.*, so that 68 per cent of the population would have scores between 80 and 120).

Now what do the AGCT scores show as to our intellectual potential and how much of that potential we are actually training for intellectual work? Suppose we take graduation from college as a standard of training for such workers. This is not a perfect criterion, because we need brains in many fields for which college is not always the best preparation, but colleges train most of the high-level specialists, and college graduation will serve as a rough measure of the extent to which we are exploiting our intellectual resources.

About 10 per cent of the total population in each age group in the U. S. now graduates from college. The median score of these graduates on the AGCT is about 120; that is, half of them score 120 or higher. This means that the youths with an I.Q. of 120 or above who graduate from college represent 5 per cent of the total population in an age group. But in the whole population 16 per cent are at that level of intelligence or above. In other words, of those youths with intelligence equal to or better than that of the median college graduate, only about one in three graduates from college. Actually it would be better to take the score surpassed by three quarters of the college graduates, rather than the median score, as the measure of the ability to do college work. On the AGCT scale this score is 109. About 33 per cent of the total population in an age group exceed this score, but less than a fourth of them go to college and receive a bachelor's degree.

The story is even less favorable when we examine what proportion of able people obtain the Ph.D. degree—today a requirement for many of our top-level intellectual occupations. During the 10 years from 1941 through 1950 U. S. universities conferred an average of about 3,300 Ph.D.'s a year. According to the best available information, the median score of Ph.D.'s on the AGCT is probably in the neighborhood of 134, and the score exceeded by 75 per cent is approximately 123. About 12.5 per cent of the total population scores above 123. Of this group, who possess the intelligence to earn a Ph.D., only about 1.5 per cent actually do so. The proportion will probably increase during the next 10 years; perhaps the figure will be 2 per cent instead of 1.5 per cent. But even so only a fiftieth of the young men and women with AGCT scores over 123 will earn Ph.D.'s.

This is not to imply that everyone with an AGCT score above 109 should graduate from college or that everyone with a score above 123 should get a Ph.D. Bright people are needed in some fields, *e.g.*, in business and the highly skilled crafts, where college training is not necessarily the most effective preparation, and the Ph.D. is not generally needed in such high-level fields as medicine, law, engineering, schoolteaching, business administration or social work. Nonetheless, we have serious shortages of people in many specialties that do require college or Ph.D. training. Consequently we need to give serious attention to the large potential of intellectual resources that we fail to use to full capacity because of lack of the necessary education.

Clearly the raw material is available for training more engineers, more scientists, more people in other important fields. Just how many more we might realistically expect is hard to estimate. It is easy to see, however, how the numbers could be increased substantially; we need only look at the reasons why so many bright youngsters fail to go to college.

We could not add greatly to the number of potential intellectual workers by attempting to keep in school those who drop out before finishing high school; the great majority of these drop-outs are only of average or less than average ability. It is at the point of high-school graduation that the biggest single loss of bright students occurs. Only a third of the high-school graduates enter college, and of the two-thirds who do not, a large proportion are above average in ability. The attrition among bright students continues in college, for half of the people who enter fail to graduate. Most of the drop-outs, to be sure, are in the lower-ability brackets, but many are brilliant students; even among that rare company who score above 150 on the AGCT more than 20 per cent leave college before graduating.

There are two main reasons why bright students fail to go to college or quit before graduation if they do go: lack of interest and lack of money. Of these, lack of interest is the more common one. A great many able students forego college because their parents do not expect them to go, because they decide early on a vocation that does not require college, because they prefer to marry or because their friends are not planning to go to college.

If the country wants to use the abilities of its ablest youngsters at the highest possible level, it must somehow encourage more of them to go on with their education. The first step, of course, is to identify these best brains. Fortunately this is not too difficult. The people who possess the talent for academic work and scholarship of a high order can be picked out at a fairly early age. Dr. Miles pointed out that the eminent people she studied gave evidence of their unusually high I.Q.'s in early childhood. Voltaire wrote verses "from his cradle." Coleridge could read a chapter from the Bible at the age of 3. Mozart composed a minuet at 5. Goethe produced grown-up literary work at 8. Nowadays intelligence-test scores and school-achievement records make possible reliable early selection of the able children. Indeed, whether a youngster will be successful in college can be predicted about as well by tests given at the ninth-grade level as at the time of college admission.

The next step is to give active encouragement to those who show the greatest promise. In some cases it is necessary to offer financial help. At the highest levels of training considerable help is becoming available. The Federal government, concerned about shortages of scientists and engineers, has started several new scholarship programs. The Atomic Energy Commission grants fellowships to graduate students in the sciences related to atomic developments. The Veterans Administration gives subsidies to college graduates interested in careers in clinical psychology. The new National Science Foundation plans to make a scholarship and fellowship program one of its chief activities. But I suspect that graduate fellowship programs will be less effective in increasing our intellectual manpower than their supporters hope. To qualify for a fellowship one must first finish college. If the goal is to enlarge the total pool of highly trained talents, money offered as scholarships to help bright youngsters start to college would probably be more effective than fellowships awarded to graduate students. There is no doubt that we need a great many more scholarships at the undergraduate level.

We have an even greater need, however, to improve our efforts to interest the brightest youngsters in pursuing an advanced education. In this task our schools frequently fall down. Despite the widespread school use of intelligence tests, too frequently the results are not used as a basis for encouraging the most promising. More school systems should follow the example of that in the State of Iowa. Each Iowa child is given the Iowa Test of Educational Development at several points during his school career. The most promising are actively encouraged by their teachers to continue their education, and their parents are notified of their promise. The Iowa psychologist Leo Phearman found that 92 per cent of the Iowa high-school seniors who scored in the top 2 per cent on these tests, and 75 per cent of those in the top 10 per cent, continued their educational careers into college.

Probably one of the reasons why so many bright students lack interest in going on to higher education is the poverty of stimulation in the school program to which they have been exposed. Elementary and secondary schools all over the country have gone in for "how-to-study" courses, remedial reading, sight-saving classes, opportunity rooms and other commendable special provisions for the handicapped and the slow, but very few devote as much effort to special handling of their most brilliant students. One of the outstanding exceptions is the Bronx High School of Science in New York. This school each year selects a freshman class high in ability and eager for scientific careers. It then gives these students a high-school training and experience so effective that practically all of them graduate from high school and practically all of the graduates go to college. A widely influential effort to encourage bright students is the annual Westinghouse Science Talent Search. The Jackson Memorial Laboratory in Maine each summer uses as research assistants a small selected group of high-school students who show interest and outstanding promise in biology. This approach—giving young students an opportunity to engage in research—seems to be an effective method of starting people on careers in science or scholarship.

The colleges themselves could do a good deal more to promote the development of superior students. One change that would cost little or nothing and would probably have good results would be to let the brightest students go ahead at their own pace. Youngsters of high I.Q.'s are capable of very rapid learning and early productive contributions. The Ohio psychologist Harvey Lehman, who has made a special study of this subject, cites many examples of great achievements by young thinkers. The grain binder was invented by John F. Appleby at the age of 18. Jane Austen finished *Pride and Prejudice* when she was 21. Louis Braille, blind since the age of 3, developed the Braille alphabet at 20. William Cullen Bryant wrote *Thanatopsis* at 18. Samuel Colt was 16 when he conceived the idea of the revolver. Sir Humphrey Davy was 20 when he discovered the anesthetic properties of nitrous oxide gas. Galileo at 17 discovered the isochronism of the pendulum. Marconi was 21 when he transmitted the first radio signals. The first synthetic dye was discovered by William Henry Perkin at 18. Lord Kelvin had established a reputation in mathematical physics by the time he was 21 years old. And in general, according to Lehman's study, the great scientists and scholars who contributed the most in total creative output were the ones who started earliest.

We can find similar examples of early achievement in the current crop of youngsters in this country. An important new method for releasing archaeological specimens from the limestone in which they are imbedded was developed just this year by a 21-year-old college student. An 18-year-old student at the University of Minnesota holds several patents on electronic equipment and serves as a consultant to a large electronic manufacturing company. One of the stellar contributors to the Los Alamos project during the war was a youth not old enough to vote.

No one knows how much is lost to science and creative scholarship by holding brilliant youngsters back to the pedestrian pace of the typical school and college. They can develop faster. As S. L. Pressey has effectively demonstrated at Ohio State University, they can do so without damage to health, without appreciable loss of opportunity to participate in extracurricular activities, without loss in quality of work and with the very positive benefit that a larger percentage of these accelerated students graduate from college than is true of equally bright but non-accelerated students. They can start graduate work earlier and can begin contributing sooner to society and to their chosen fields of work.

From every standpoint it is clear that we are not exploiting the intellectual resources of the U. S. to anywhere near their full potential. We can have more engineers, more scientists, more doctors, more scholars and more specialists of all types if we need them. To obtain them, however, we must do better than we have done in the past to identify the brightest youngsters, encourage them to plan on higher education, offer them a chance to work in their chosen fields, give them financial assistance when necessary and give them the kind of education that will allow them to go ahead rapidly to take their places among America's intellectual leaders.

3 | FACETS OR TRAITS OF MENTAL GIFTEDNESS

Three Faces of Intellect

J. P. GUILFORD

My subject is in the area of human intelligence, in connection with which the names of Terman and Stanford have become known the world over. The Stanford Revision of the Binet intelligence scale has been the standard against which all other instruments for the measurement of intelligence have been compared. The term IQ or intelligence quotient has become a household word in this country. This is illustrated by two brief stories.

A few years ago, one of my neighbors came home from a PTA meeting, remarking: "That Mrs. So-And-So, thinks she knows so much. She kept talking about the 'intelligence *quota*' of the children; 'intelligence *quota*'; imagine. Why, everybody knows that IQ stands for 'intelligence *quiz.*'"

The other story comes from a little comic strip in a Los Angeles morning newspaper, called "Junior Grade." In the first picture a little boy meets a little girl, both apparently about the first-grade level. The little girl remarks, "I have a high IQ." The little boy, puzzled, said, "You have a what?" The little girl repeated, "I have a high IQ," then went on her way. The little boy, looking thoughtful, said, "And she looks like such a nice little girl, too."

It is my purpose to speak about the analysis of this thing called human intelligence into its components. I do not believe that either Binet or Terman, if they were still with us, would object to the idea of a searching and detailed study of intelligence, aimed toward a better understanding of its nature. Preceding the development of his intelligence scale, Binet had done much research on different kinds of thinking activities and apparently recognized that intelligence has a number of aspects. It is to the lasting credit of both Binet and Terman that they introduced such a great variety of tasks into their intelligence scales.

Two related events of very recent history make it imperative that

Reprinted from *American Psychologist*, Vol. 14, No. 8 (August, 1959), pp. 469-479. By permission of the American Psychological Association.

we learn all we can regarding the nature of intelligence. I am referring
to the advent of the artificial satellites and planets and to the crisis in
education that has arisen in part as a consequence. The preservation of
our way of life and our future security depend upon our most important
national resources: our intellectual abilities and, more particularly, our
creative abilities. It is time, then, that we learn all we can about those
resources.

Our knowledge of the components of human intelligence has come
about mostly within the last 25 years. The major sources of this information in this country have been L. L. Thurstone and his associates,
the wartime research of psychologists in the United States Air Forces,
and more recently the Aptitudes Project at the University of Southern
California, now in its tenth year of research on cognitive and thinking
abilities. The results from the Aptitudes Project that have gained perhaps the most attention have pertained to creative-thinking abilities.
These are mostly novel findings. But to me, the most significant outcome has been the development of a unified theory of human intellect,
which organizes the known, unique or primary intellectual abilities into
a single system called the "structure of intellect." It is to this system that
I shall devote the major part of my remarks, with very brief mentions
of some of the implications for the psychology of thinking and problem
solving, for vocational testing, and for education.

The discovery of the components of intelligence has been by means of
the experimental application of the method of factor analysis. It is not
necessary for you to know anything about the theory or method of factor analysis in order to follow the discussion of the components. I
should like to say, however, that factor analysis has no connection with
or resemblance to psychoanalysis. A positive statement would be more
helpful, so I will say that each intellectual component or factor is a
unique ability that is needed to do well in a certain class of tasks or
tests. As a general principle we find that certain individuals do well in
the tests of a certain class, but they may do poorly in the tests of another
class. We conclude that a factor has certain properties from the features
that the tests of a class have in common. I shall give you very soon a
number of examples of tests, each representing a factor.

THE STRUCTURE OF INTELLECT

Although each factor is sufficiently distinct to be detected by factor
analysis, in very recent years it has become apparent that the factors
themselves can be classified because they resemble one another in certain ways. One basis of classification is according to the basic kind of
process or operation performed. This kind of classification gives us five

major groups of intellectual abilities: factors of cognition, memory, convergent thinking, divergent thinking, and evaluation.

Cognition means discovery or rediscovery or recognition. Memory means retention of what is cognized. Two kinds of productive-thinking operations generate new information from known information and remembered information. In divergent-thinking operations we think in different directions, sometimes searching, sometimes seeking variety. In convergent thinking the information leads to one right answer or to a recognized best or conventional answer. In evaluation we reach decisions as to goodness, correctness, suitability, or adequacy of what we know, what we remember, and what we produce in productive thinking.

A second way of classifying the intellectual factors is according to the kind of material or content involved. The factors known thus far involve three kinds of material or content: the content may be figural, symbolic, or semantic. Figural content is concrete material such as is perceived through the senses. It does not represent anything except itself. Visual material has properties such as size, form, color, location, or texture. Things we hear or feel provide other examples of figural material. Symbolic content is composed of letters, digits, and other conventional signs, usually organized in general systems, such as the alphabet or the number system. Semantic content is in the form of verbal meanings or ideas, for which no examples are necessary.

When a certain operation is applied to a certain kind of content, as many as six general kinds of products may be involved. There is enough evidence available to suggest that, regardless of the combinations of operations and content, the same six kinds of products may be found associated. The six kinds of products are: units, classes, relations, systems, transformations, and implications. So far as we have determined from factor analysis, these are the only fundamental kinds of products that we can know. As such, they may serve as basic classes into which one might fit all kinds of information psychologically.

The three kinds of classifications of the factors of intellect can be represented by means of a single solid model, shown in Figure 1. In this model, which we call the "structure of intellect," each dimension represents one of the modes of variation of the factors (2). Along one dimension are found the various kinds of operations, along a second one are the various kinds of products, and along the third are various kinds of content. Along the dimension of content a fourth category has been added, its kind of content being designated as "behavioral." This category has been added on a purely theoretical basis to represent the general area sometimes called "social intelligence." More will be said about this section of the model later.

In order to provide a better basis for understanding the model and a better basis for accepting it as a picture of human intellect, I shall do

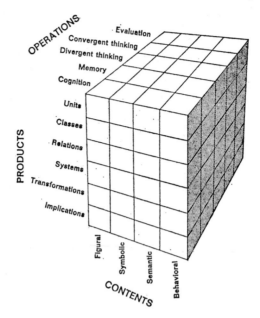

FIG. 1.   *A Cubical Model Representing the Structure of Intellect*

some exploring of it with you systematically, giving some examples of tests. Each cell in the model calls for a certain kind of ability that can be described in terms of operation, content, and product, for each cell is at the intersection of a unique combination of kinds of operation, content, and product. A test for that ability would have the same three properties. In our exploration of the model, we shall take one vertical layer at a time, beginning with the front face. The first layer provides us with a matrix of 18 cells (if we ignore the behavioral column for which there are as yet no known factors) each of which should contain a cognitive ability.

The Cognitive Abilities. We know at present the unique abilities that fit logically into 15 of the 18 cells for cognitive abilities. Each row presents a triad of similar abilities, having a single kind of product in common. The factors of the first row are concerned with the knowing of units. A good test of the ability to cognize figural units is the Street Gestalt Completion Test. In this test, the recognition of familiar pictured objects in silhouette form is made difficult for testing purposes by blocking out parts of those objects. There is another factor that is known to involve the perception of auditory figures—in the form of melodies, rhythms, and speech sounds—and still another factor involving kinesthetic forms. The presence of three factors in one cell (they are conceivably distinct abilities, although this has not been tested) suggests that more generally, in the figural column, at least, we should expect to find more than one ability. A fourth dimension pertaining to variations in sense modality may thus apply in connection with figural content. The model could be extended in this manner if the facts call for such an extension.

The ability to cognize symbolic units is measured by tests like the following:

Put vowels in the following blanks to make real words:

P__W__R

M__RV__L

C__RT__N

Rearrange the letters to make real words:

R A C I H

T V O E S

K L C C O

The first of these two tests is called Disemvoweled Words, and the second Scrambled Words.

The ability to cognize semantic units is the well-known factor of verbal comprehension, which is best measured by means of a vocabulary test, with items such as:

GRAVITY means _____

CIRCUS means _____

VIRTUE means _____

From the comparison of these two factors it is obvious that recognizing familiar words as letter structures and knowing what words mean depend upon quite different abilities.

For testing the abilities to know classes of units, we may present the following kinds of items, one with symbolic content and one with semantic content:

Which letter group does not belong?

XECM PVAA QXIN VTRO

Which object does not belong?

clam tree oven rose

A figural test is constructed in a completely parallel form, presenting in each item four figures, three of which have a property in common and the fourth lacking that property.

The three abilities to see relationships are also readily measured by a common kind of test, differing only in terms of content. The well-known analogies test is applicable, two items in symbolic and semantic form being:

JIRE   :   KIRE   : :   FORA   :   KORE   KORA   LIRE   GORA   GIRE
poetry : prose : : dance : music   walk   sing   talk   jump

Such tests usually involve more than the ability to cognize relations, but we are not concerned with this problem at this point.

The three factors for cognizing systems do not at present appear in tests so closely resembling one another as in the case of the examples just given. There is nevertheless an underlying common core of logical similarity. Ordinary space tests, such as Thurstone's Flags, Figures, and Cards or Part V (Spatial Orientation) of the Guilford-Zimmerman Aptitude Survey (GZAS), serve in the figural column. The system involved is an order or arrangement of objects in space. A system that uses symbolic elements is illustrated by the Letter Triangle Test, a sample item of which is:

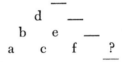

What letter belongs at the place of the question mark?

The ability to understand a semantic system has been known for some time as the factor called general reasoning. One of its most faithful indicators is a test composed of arithmetic-reasoning items. That the phase of understanding only is important for measuring this ability is shown by the fact that such a test works even if the examinee is not asked to give a complete solution; he need only show that he structures the problem properly. For example, an item from the test Necessary Arithmetical Operations simply asks what operations are needed to solve the problem:

A city lot 48 feet wide and 149   A. add and multiply
feet deep costs $79,432. What is   B. multiply and divide
the cost per square foot?   C. subtract and divide
                                       D. add and subtract
                                       E. divide and add

Placing the factor of general reasoning in this cell of the structure of intellect gives us some new conceptions of its nature. It should be a broad ability to grasp all kinds of systems that are conceived in terms of verbal concepts, not restricted to the understanding of problems of an arithmetical type.

Transformations are changes of various kinds, including modifications in arrangement, organization, or meaning. In the figural column for the transformations row, we find the factor known as visualization. Common measuring instruments for this factor are the surface-development tests, and an example of a different kind is Part VI (Spatial Visualization) of the GZAS. A test of the ability to make transformations of meaning, for the factor in the semantic column, is called Similarities. The examinee is asked to state several ways in which two objects, such as an apple and an orange, are alike. Only by shifting the meanings of both is the examinee able to give many responses to such an item.

In the set of abilities having to do with the cognition of implications, we find that the individual goes beyond the information given, but not to the extent of what might be called drawing conclusions. We may say that he extrapolates. From the given information he expects or foresees certain consequences, for example. The two factors found in this row of the cognition matrix were first called "foresight" factors. Foresight in connection with figural material can be tested by means of paper-and-pencil mazes. Foresight in connection with ideas, those pertaining to events, for example, is indicated by a test such as Pertinent Questions:

> In planning to open a new hamburger stand in a certain community, what four questions should be considered in deciding upon its location?

The more questions the examinee asks in response to a list of such problems, the more he evidently foresees contingencies.

The Memory Abilities. The area of memory abilities has been explored less than some of the other areas of operation, and only seven of the potential cells of the memory matrix have known factors in them. These cells are restricted to three rows: for units, relations, and systems. The first cell in the memory matrix is now occupied by two factors, parallel to two in the corresponding cognition matrix: visual memory and auditory memory. Memory for series of letters or numbers, as in memory span tests, conforms to the conception of memory for symbolic units. Memory for the ideas in a paragraph conforms to the conception of memory for semantic units.

The formation of associations between units, such as visual forms, syllables, and meaningful words, as in the method of paired associates, would seem to represent three abilities to remember relationships involving three kinds of content. We know of two such abilities, for the symbolic and semantic columns. The memory for known systems is represented by two abilities very recently discovered (1). Remembering the arrangement of objects in space is the nature of an ability in the figural column, and remembering a sequence of events is the nature of a corresponding ability in the semantic column. The differentiation between these two abilities implies that a person may be able to say where he saw an object on a page, but he might not be able to say on which of several pages he saw it after leafing through several pages that included the right one. Considering the blank rows in the memory matrix, we should expect to find abilities also to remember classes, transformations, and implications, as well as units, relations, and systems.

The Divergent-Thinking Abilities. The unique feature of divergent production is that a *variety* of responses is produced. The product is not completely determined by the given information. This is not to say that divergent thinking does not come into play in the total process of reaching a unique conclusion, for it comes into play wherever there is trial-and-error thinking.

The well-known ability of word fluency is tested by asking the examinee to list words satisfying a specified letter requirement, such as words beginning with the letter "s" or words ending in "-tion." This ability is now regarded as a facility in divergent production of symbolic units. The parallel semantic ability has been known as ideational fluency. A typical test item calls for listing objects that are round and edible. Winston Churchill must have possessed this ability to a high degree. Clement Attlee is reported to have said about him recently that, no matter what problem came up, Churchill always seemed to have about ten ideas. The trouble was, Attlee continued, he did not know which was the good one. The last comment implies some weakness in one or more of the evaluative abilities.

The divergent production of class ideas is believed to be the unique feature of a factor called "spontaneous flexibility." A typical test instructs the examinee to list all the uses he can think of for a common brick, and he is given eight minutes. If his responses are: build a house, build a barn, build a garage, build a school, build a church, build a chimney, build a walk, and build a barbecue, he would earn a fairly high score for ideational fluency but a very low score for spontaneous flexibility, because all these uses fall into the same class. If another person said: make a door stop, make a paper weight, throw it at a dog, make a bookcase, drown a cat, drive a nail, make a red powder, and use for baseball bases, he would also receive a high score for flexibility. He has gone frequently from one class to another.

A current study of unknown but predicted divergent-production abilities includes testing whether there are also figural and symbolic abilities to produce multiple classes. An experimental figural test presents a number of figures that can be classified in groups of three in various ways, each figure being usable in more than one class. An experimental symbolic test presents a few numbers that are also to be classified in multiple ways.

A unique ability involving relations is called "associational fluency." It calls for the production of a variety of things related in a specified way to a given thing. For example, the examinee is asked to list words meaning about the same as "good" or to list words meaning about the opposite of "hard." In these instances the response produced is to complete a relationship, and semantic content is involved. Some of our present experimental tests call for the production of varieties of relations, as such, and involve figural and symbolic content also. For example, given four small digits, in how many ways can they be related in order to produce a sum of eight?

One factor pertaining to the production of systems is known as expressional fluency. The rapid formation of phrases or sentences is the essence of certain tests of this factor. For example, given the initial letters:

W____ c____ e____ n____

with different sentences to be produced, the examinee might write "We can eat nuts" or "Whence came Eve Newton?" In interpreting the factor, we regard the sentence as a symbolic system. By analogy, a figural system would be some kind of organization of lines and other elements, and a semantic system would be in the form of a verbally stated problem or perhaps something as complex as a theory.

In the row of the divergent-production matrix devoted to transformations, we find some very interesting factors. The one called "adaptive flexibility" is now recognized as belonging in the figural column. A faithful test of it has been Match Problems. This is based upon the common game that uses squares, the sides of which are formed by match sticks. The examinee is told to take away a given number of matches to leave a stated number of squares with nothing left over. Nothing is said about the sizes of the squares to be left. If the examinee imposes upon himself the restriction that the squares that he leaves must be of the same size, he will fail. Other odd kinds of solutions are introduced in other items, such as overlapping squares and squares within squares, and so on. In another variation of Match Problems the examinee is told to produce two or more solutions for each problem.

A factor that has been called "originality" is now recognized as adaptive flexibility with semantic material, where there must be a shifting of meanings. The examinee must produce the shifts or changes in meaning and so come up with novel, unusual, clever, or farfetched ideas. The Plot Titles Test presents a short story, the examinee being told to list as many appropriate titles as he can to head the story. One story is about a missionary who has been captured by cannibals in Africa. He is in the pot and about to be boiled when a princess of the tribe obtains a promise for his release if he will become her mate. He refuses and is boiled to death.

In scoring the test, we separate the responses into two categories, clever and nonclever. Examples of nonclever responses are: African Death, Defeat of a Princess, Eaten by Savages, The Princess, The African Missionary, In Darkest Africa, and Boiled by Savages. These titles are appropriate but commonplace. The number of such responses serves as a score for ideational fluency. Examples of clever responses are: Pot's Plot, Potluck Dinner, Stewed Parson, Goil or Boil, A Mate Worse Than Death, He Left a Dish for a Pot, Chaste in Haste, and A Hot Price for Freedom. The number of clever responses given by an examinee is his score for originality, or the divergent production of semantic transformations.

Another test of originality presents a very novel task so that any acceptable response is unusual for the individual. In the Symbol Production Test the examinee is to produce a simple symbol to stand for a noun or a verb in each short sentence, in other words to invent something like pictographic symbols. Still another test of originality asks for writing the "punch lines" for cartoons, a task that almost automatically challenges the examinee to be clever. Thus, quite a variety of tests offer approaches to the measurement of originality, including one or two others that I have not mentioned.

Abilities to produce a variety of implications are assessed by tests calling for elaboration of given information. A figural test of this type provides the examinee with a line or two, to which he is to add other lines to produce an object. The more lines he adds, the greater his score. A semantic test gives the examinee the outlines of a plan to which he is to respond by stating all the details he can think of to make the plan work. A new test we are trying out in the symbolic area presents two simple equations such as $B - C = D$ and $z = A + D$. The examinee is to make as many other equations as he can from this information.

The Convergent-Production Abilities. Of the 18 convergent-production abilities expected in the three content columns, 12 are now recognized. In the first row, pertaining to units, we have an ability to name figural properties (forms or colors) and an ability to name abstractions (classes, relations, and so on). It may be that the ability in common to the speed of naming forms and the speed of naming colors is not appropriately placed in the convergent-thinking matrix. One might expect that the thing to be produced in a test of the convergent production of figural units would be in the form of figures rather than words. A better test of such an ability might somehow specify the need for one particular object, the examinee to furnish the object.

A test for the convergent production of classes (Word Grouping) presents a list of 12 words that are to be classified in four, and only four, meaningful groups, no word to appear in more than one group. A parallel test (Figure Concepts Test) presents 20 pictured real objects that are to be grouped in meaningful classes of two or more each.

Convergent production having to do with relationships is represented by three known factors, all involving the "eduction of correlates," as Spearman called it. The given information includes one unit and a stated relation, the examinee to supply the other unit. Analogies tests that call for completion rather than a choice between alternative answers emphasize this kind of ability. With symbolic content such an item might read:

pots   stop   bard   drab   rats   <u>?</u>

A semantic item that measures eduction of correlates is:

The absence of sound is _____ .

Incidentally, the latter item is from a vocabulary-completion test, and its relation to the factor of ability to produce correlates indicates how, by change of form, a vocabulary test may indicate an ability other than that for which vocabulary tests are usually intended, namely, the factor of verbal comprehension.

Only one factor for convergent production of systems is known, and it is in the semantic column. It is measured by a class of tests that may be called ordering tests. The examinee may be presented with a number of events that ordinarily have a best or most logical order, the events being presented in scrambled order. The presentation may be pictorial, as in the Picture Arrangement Test, or verbal. The pictures may be taken from a cartoon strip. The verbally presented events may be in the form of the various steps needed to plant a new lawn. There are undoubtedly other kinds of systems than temporal order that could be utilized for testing abilities in this row of the convergent-production matrix.

In the way of producing transformations of a unique variety, we have three recognized factors, known as redefinition abilities. In each case, redefinition involves the changing of functions or uses of parts of one unit and giving them new functions or uses in some new unit. For testing the ability of figural redefinition, a task based upon the Gottschaldt figures is suitable. In recognizing the simpler figure within the structure of a more complex figure, certain lines must take on new roles.

In terms of symbolic material, the following sample items will illustrate how groups of letters in given words must be readapted to use in other words. In the test Camouflaged Words, each sentence contains the name of a sport or game:

I did not know that he was ailing.
To beat the Hun, tin goes a long way.

For the factor of semantic redefinition, the Gestalt Transformation Test may be used. A sample item reads:

From which object could you most likely make a needle?

> A. a cabbage
> B. a splice
> C. a steak
> D. a paper box
> E. a fish

The convergent production of implications means the drawing of fully determined conclusions from given information. The well-known factor of numerical facility belongs in the symbolic column. For the parallel ability in the figural column, we have a test known as Form Reasoning, in which rigorously defined operations with figures are used. For the parallel ability in the semantic column, the factor sometimes called "deduction" probably qualifies. Items of the following type are sometimes used.

> Charles is younger than Robert
> Charles is older than Frank
> Who is older: Robert or Frank?

Evaluative Abilities. The evaluative area has had the least investigation of all the operational categories. In fact, only one systematic analytical study has been devoted to this area. Only eight evaluative abilities are recognized as fitting into the evaluation matrix. But at least five rows have one or more factors each, and also three of the usual columns or content categories. In each case, evaluation involves reaching decisions as to the accuracy, goodness, suitability, or workability of information. In each row, for the particular kind of product of that row, some kind of criterion or standard of judgment is involved.

In the first row, for the evaluation of units, the important decision to be made pertains to the identity of a unit. Is this unit identical with that one? In the figural column we find the factor long known as "perceptual speed." Tests of this factor invariably call for decisions of identity, for example, Part IV (Perceptual Speed) of the GZAS or Thurstone's Identical Forms. I think it has been generally wrongly thought that the ability involved is that of cognition of visual forms. But we have seen that another factor is a more suitable candidate for this definition and for being in the very first cell of the cognitive matrix. It is parallel to this evaluative ability but does not require the judgment of identity as one of its properties.

In the symbolic column is an ability to judge identity of symbolic units, in the form of series of letters or numbers or of names of individuals.

Are members of the following pairs identical or not:

825170493_____825176493
dkeltvmpa_____dkeltvmpa
C. S. Meyerson_____C. E. Meyerson

Such items are common in tests of clerical aptitude.

There should be a parallel ability to decide whether two ideas are identical or different. Is the idea expressed in this sentence the same as the idea expressed in that one? Do these two proverbs express essentially the same idea? Such tests exist and will be used to test the hypothesis that such an ability can be demonstrated.

No evaluative abilities pertaining to classes have as yet been recognized. The abilities having to do with evaluation where relations are concerned must meet the criterion of logical consistency. Syllogistic-type tests involving letter symbols indicate a different ability than the same type of test involving verbal statements. In the figural column we might expect that tests incorporating geometric reasoning or proof would indicate a parallel ability to sense the soundness of conclusions regarding figural relationships.

The evaluation of systems seems to be concerned with the internal consistency of those systems, so far as we can tell from the knowledge of one such factor. The factor has been called "experiential evaluation," and its representative test presents items asking "What is wrong with this picture?" The things wrong are often internal inconsistencies.

A semantic ability for evaluating transformations is thought to be that known for some time as "judgment." In typical judgment tests, the examinee is asked to tell which of five solutions to a practical problem is most adequate or wise. The solutions frequently involve improvisations, in other words, adaptations of familiar objects to unusual uses. In this way the items present redefinitions to be evaluated.

A factor known first as "sensitivity to problems" has become recognized as an evaluative ability having to do with implications. One test of the factor, the Apparatus Test, asks for two needed improvements with respect to each of several common devices, such as the telephone or the toaster. The Social Institutions Test, a measure of the same factor, asks what things are wrong with each of several institutions, such as tipping or national elections. We may say that defects or deficiencies are implications of an evaluative kind. Another interpretation would be that seeing defects and deficiencies are evaluations of implications to the effect that the various aspects of something are all right (3).

SOME IMPLICATIONS OF THE STRUCTURE OF INTELLECT

For Psychological Theory. Although factor analysis as generally employed is best designed to investigate ways in which individuals differ from one another, in other words, to discover traits, the results also tell us much about how individuals are alike. Consequently, information regarding the factors and their interrelationships gives us understanding of functioning individuals. The five kinds of intellectual abilities in terms of operations may be said to represent five ways of functioning. The kinds of intellectual abilities distinguished according to varieties of test content and the kinds of abilities distinguished according to varieties of products suggest a classification of basic forms of information or knowledge. The kind of organism suggested by this way of looking at intellect is that of an agency for dealing with information of various kinds in various ways. The concepts provided by the distinctions among the intellectual abilities and by their classifications may be very useful in our future investigations of learning, memory, problem solving, invention, and decision making, by whatever method we choose to approach those problems.

For Vocational Testing. With about 50 intellectual factors already known, we may say that there are at least 50 ways of being intelligent. It has been facetiously suggested that there seem to be a great many more ways of being stupid, unfortunately. The structure of intellect is a theoretical model that predicts as many as 120 distinct abilities, if every cell of the model contains a factor. Already we know that two cells contain two or more factors each, and there probably are actually other cells of this type. Since the model was first conceived, 12 factors predicted by it have found places in it. There is consequently hope of filling many of the other vacancies, and we may eventually end up with more than 120 abilities.

The major implication for the assessment of intelligence is that to know an individual's intellectual resources thoroughly we shall need a surprisingly large number of scores. It is expected that many of the factors are intercorrelated, so there is some possibility that by appropriate sampling we shall be able to cover the important abilities with a more limited number of tests. At any rate, a multiple-score approach to the assessment of intelligence is definitely indicated in connection with future vocational operations.

Considering the kinds of abilities classified as to content, we may speak roughly of four kinds of intelligence. The abilities involving the use of figural information may be regarded as "concrete" intelligence. The people who depend most upon these abilities deal with concrete things and their properties. Among these people are mechanics, operators of machines, engineers (in some aspects of their work), artists, and musicians.

In the abilities pertaining to symbolic and semantic content, we have two kinds of "abstract" intelligence. Symbolic abilities should be important in learning to recognize words, to spell, and to operate with numbers. Language and mathematics should depend very much upon them, except that in mathematics some aspects, such as geometry, have strong figural involvement. Semantic intelligence is important for understanding things in terms of verbal concepts and hence is important in all courses where the learning of facts and ideas is essential.

In the hypothesized behavioral column of the structure of intellect, which may be roughly described as "social" intelligence, we have some of the most interesting possibilities. Understanding the behavior of others and of ourselves is largely nonverbal in character. The theory suggests as many as 30 abilities in this area, some having to do with understanding, some with productive thinking about behavior, and some with the evaluation of behavior. The theory also suggests that information regarding behavior is also in the form of the six kinds of products that apply elsewhere in the structure of intellect, including units, relations, systems, and so on. The abilities in the area of social intelligence, whatever they prove to be, will possess considerable importance in connection with all those individuals who deal most with other people: teachers, law officials, social workers, therapists, politicians, statesmen, and leaders of other kinds.

For Education. The implications for education are numerous, and I have time just to mention a very few. The most fundamental implication is that we might well undergo transformations with respect to our conception of the learner and of the process of learning. Under the prevailing conception, the learner is a kind of stimulus-response device, much on the order of a vending machine. You put in a coin, and something comes out. The machine learns what reaction to put out when a certain coin is put in. If, instead, we think of the learner as an agent for dealing with information, where information is defined very broadly, we have something more analogous to an electronic computor. We feed a computor information; it stores that information; it uses that information for generating new information, either by way of divergent or convergent thinking; and it evaluates its own results. Advantages that a human learner has over a computor include the step of seeking and discovering new information from sources outside itself and the step of programming itself. Perhaps even these steps will be added to computors, if this has not already been done in some cases.

At any rate, this conception of the learner leads us to the idea that learning is discovery of information, not merely the formation of associations, particularly associations in the form of stimulus-response connections. I am aware of the fact that my proposal is rank heresy. But if we are to make significant progress in our understanding of human learning and particularly our understanding of the so-called higher mental processes of thinking, problem solving, and creative thinking, some drastic modifications are due in our theory.

The idea that education is a matter of training the mind or of training the intellect has been rather unpopular, wherever the prevailing psychological doctrines have been followed. In theory, at least, the emphasis has been upon the learning of rather specific habits or skills. If we take our cue from factor theory, however, we recognize that most learning probably has both specific and general aspects or components. The general aspects may be along the lines of the factors of intellect. This is not to say that the individual's status in each factor is entirely determined by learning. We do not know to what extent each factor is determined by heredity and to what extent by learning. The best position for educators to take is that possibly every intellectual factor can be developed in individuals at least to some extent by learning.

If education has the general objective of developing the intellects of students, it can be suggested that each intellectual factor provides a particular goal at which to aim. Defined by a certain combination of content, operation, and product, each goal ability then calls for certain kinds of practice in order to achieve improvement in it. This implies choice of curriculum and the choice or invention of teaching methods that will most likely accomplish the desired results.

Considering the very great variety of abilities revealed by the factorial exploration of intellect, we are in a better position to ask whether any general intellectual skills are now being neglected in education and whether appropriate balances are being observed. It is often observed these days that we have fallen down in the way of producing resourceful, creative graduates. How true this is, in comparison with other times, I do not know. Perhaps the deficit is noticed because the demands for inventiveness are so much greater at this time. At any rate, realization that the more conspicuously creative abilities appear to be concentrated in the divergent-thinking category, and also to some extent in the transformation category, we now ask whether we have been giving these skills appropriate exercise. It is probable that we need a better balance of training in the divergent-thinking area as compared with training in convergent thinking and in critical thinking or evaluation.

The structure of intellect as I have presented it to you may or may not stand the test of time. Even if the general form persists, there are likely to be some modifications. Possibly some different kind of model will be invented. Be that as it may, the fact of a multiplicity of intellectual abilities seems well established.

There are many individuals who long for the good old days of simplicity, when we got along with one unanalyzed intelligence. Simplicity certainly has its appeal. But human nature is exceedingly complex, and we may as well face that fact. The rapidly moving events of the world in which we live have forced upon us the need for knowing human intelligence thoroughly. Humanity's peaceful pursuit of happiness depends upon our control of nature and of our own behavior; and this, in turn, depends upon understanding ourselves, including our intellectual resources.

REFERENCES

1. Christal, R. E., Factor Analytic Study of Visual Memory. *Psychol. Monogr.*, 1958, 72, No. 13 (Whole No. 466).
2. Guilford, J. P., The Structure of Intellect. *Psychol. Bull.*, 1956, 53, 267-293.
3. Guilford, J. P., *Personality*. New York: McGraw-Hill, 1959.

Primary Mental Abilities of Children

THELMA G. THURSTONE

For many years psychologists have been accustomed to the problems of special abilities and disabilities. These are, in fact, the principal concern of the school psychologists who deal with children who cannot read, have a blind spot for numbers, or do one thing remarkably well and other things poorly. It seems strange with all this experience in differential psychology that we have clung so long to the practice of summarizing a child's mental endowment by a single index, such as the mental age, the intelligence quotient, the percentile rank in general intelligence, and other single average measures. An average index of mental endowment should be useful for many educational purposes, but it should not be regarded as more than the average of several tests. Two children with the same mental age can be entirely different persons, as is well known. There is nothing wrong about using a mental age or an intelligence quotient if it is understood as an average of several tests. The error that is frequently made is interpreting it as measuring

Reprinted from *Educational and Psychological Measurements*, Vol. 1, No. 12 (1941), pp. 105-116. By permission of the author and publisher.

some basic functional unity when it is known to be nothing more than a composite of many functional unities.

The researches on the primary mental abilities which have been in progress for several years have had as their first purposes the identification and definition of the independent factors of mind. As the nature of the abilities became more clearly indicated by successive studies, a second purpose of a more practical nature has been involved in some of the studies. This purpose has been to prepare a set of tests of psychological significance and practicable adaptability to the school testing and guidance program. The series of studies will be summarized in this paper, the battery of tests soon to be available will be described, and some of the problems now being investigated will be discussed briefly.

PREVIOUS STUDIES

The first study in this series involved the use of 56 psychological examinations that were given to a group of about 250 college students. That study revealed a number of primary abilities, some of which were clearly defined by the configuration of test vectors while others were indicated by the configuration but less clearly defined. All of these factors have been studied in subsequent test batteries in which each primary factor has been represented by new tests specially designed to feature the primary factors in the purest possible form. The object has been to construct tests in which there is a heavy saturation of a primary factor and in which other factors are minimized. This is the purification of tests by reducing their complexity.

These latter studies of the separate abilities were in each case made in the Chicago high schools—one study emphasizing the perceptual factor at the Lane Technical High School, one study of the inductive factor at the Hyde Park High School, an intensive study of the memory factor or factors in four high schools, and a study of numerical ability by Coombs in six high schools. In each series of tests, one factor was represented by a large number of tests, but all factors were well represented. In all of these studies the same primary abilities were identified as had been found in the experiment with college students. These studies led to the publication by the American Council on Education of an experimental battery of tests for the primary mental abilities, adaptable for use with students of high school or college age.

The identification of the same primary mental abilities among high school students as we had previously found among college students encouraged us to look for differentiation among the abilities of younger children. In the Chicago Public Schools, group mental tests are made of all 1B, 4B, and 8B children in the elementary schools and of 10B students in the high schools. The demand for a series of tests to be used in the guidance program for high school entrants and the advisability of not making too broad a leap in age led us to select an eighth-grade population for the next study.

THE EIGHTH-GRADE EXPERIMENT

In view of the purpose of investigating whether or not primary mental abilities could be isolated for children at the fourteen-year age level, the construction of the tests consisted essentially in the adaptation for the younger children of tests previously used with high school students. In some of the tests little or no alteration was necessary, while for other tests it was considered advisable to revise vocabulary and other aspects of the tests to suit the younger age level. A number of new tests were added to those selected from previous experimental batteries. Sixty tests constituted the final battery.

When the tests had been designed and printed, they were given in a trial form to children in grades 7A and 8A in several schools. Groups of from 50 to 100 children in these two grades were used for the purpose of standardizing procedures and, especially, for setting time limits.

Fifteen Chicago elementary schools were selected by Miss Minnie L. Fallon, Assistant Superintendent in charge of elementary education, and by Dr. Grace E. Munson, Director of the Bureau of Child Study, as experimental schools for this study. The tests in the main investigation were administered in the schools by the adjustment teachers. These adjustment teachers had had special training in testing procedures with the Bureau of Child Study and also had had considerable experience in giving psychological and educational tests. Special instructions in the procedures for these tests were given to the adjustment teachers, as well as written instructions for each day's testing program.

Eleven hundred and fifty-four children participated in this study. The complete battery of 60 tests was given in 11 one-hour sessions to the children in the 8B grades in each of the 15 schools. The children enjoyed the tests and, with very few exceptions, the sustained interest and effort were quite evident. One thing which a psychologist might fear in such a long series of tests would be fluctuating motivation on the part of the students. Although the adjustment teachers administered the tests, every session was observed by a member of our staff, and we were highly gratified by the sustained interest and effort of the pupils.

In addition to the 60 tests we used three more variables: chronological age, mental age, and sex. The latter test data were available in school records. They were determined by the Kuhlmann-Anderson tests which had been given previously to the same children. Therefore, the battery to be analyzed factorially contained 63 variables.

The total population in this study consisted of 1,154 eighth-grade children. When all the records had been assembled, it was found that 710 of these subjects had complete records for all of the 63 variables. We decided to base our correlations on this population of complete records rather than to use the large population with varying numbers of cases for the correlation coefficients. For convenience of handling with the tabulating-machine methods, the raw scores were transmuted into single digit scores from which the Pearson product-moment correlation coefficients were computed. With 63 variables there were 1,935 Pearson correlation coefficients.

This table of intercorrelations was factored to 10 factors by the centroid method on the tabulating machines by means of punched cards. Successive rotations made by the method of extended vectors yielded an oblique factorial matrix which is a simple structure.

Inspection of the rotated factorial matrix showed seven of the factors previously indicated: Memory, Induction, Verbal Comprehension, Word Fluency, Number, Space, Perceptual Speed, and three less easily identifiable factors. One of these is another Verbal factor; one is involved in ability to solve pencil mazes; and one is present in the three dot-counting tests which were used.

We have computed the intercorrelations between the 10 primary factors. Our main interest centers on the seven primary factors that can be given interpretation and, especially, on the first six of these factors for which the interpretation is rather more definite. Among the high correlations we note that the Number factor is correlated with the two Verbal factors. The Word Fluency factor has high correlation with the Verbal Comprehension factor and with Induction. The Rote Memory factor seems to be independent of the other factors. These correlations are higher than the correlations between primary factors for adults.

Because of the psychological interest in the correlations of the primary mental abilities, we have made a separate analysis of the correlations for those factors which seem to have reasonably certain interpretation. If these six primary mental abilities are correlated because of some general intellective factor, then the rank of the correlation matrix should be one. Upon examination, this actually proves to be the case. A single factor accounts for most of the correlations between the primary factors.

The single factor loadings show that the inductive factor has the highest loading and the Rote Memory factor the lowest loading on the common general factor in the primary abilities. This general factor is what we have called a second-order general factor. It makes its appearance not as a separate factor, but as a factor inherent in the primaries and their correlations. If further studies of the primary mental abilities of children should reveal this general factor, it may sustain Spearman's contention that there exists a general intellective factor. Instead of depending on the averages or centroids of arbitrary test batteries for its determination, the present method should enable us to identify it uniquely.

We have not been able to find in these data a general factor that is distinct from the primary factors, but the second-order general factor should be of as much psychological interest as the more frequently postulated, independent general factor of Spearman. It would be our judgment that the second-order general factor found here is probably the general factor which Spearman has so long defended, but we cannot say whether he would accept the present findings as sustaining his contentions about the general factor. We have not found any occasion to debate the existence of a general intellective factor. The factorial methods we have been using are adequate for finding such a factor, either as a factor independent of the primaries or as a factor operating through correlated primaries. We have reported on primary mental abilities in adults, which seem to show only low positive correlations except for the two verbal factors. In the present study we have found higher correlations among the primary factors for eighth-grade children. It is now an interesting question to determine whether the correlations among primary abilities of still younger children will reveal, perhaps even more strongly, a second-order general factor.

INTERPRETATION OF FACTORS

The analysis of this battery of 60 tests revealed essentially the same set of primary factors which had been found in previous factorial studies. Six of the factors seemed to have sufficient stability for the several age levels that have been investigated to justify an extension of the tests for these factors into practical test work in the schools. In making this extension we have been obliged to consider carefully the difference between research on the nature of the primary factors and the construction of tests for practical use. Several of the primary factors are not yet sufficiently clear as regards psychological interpretation to justify an attempt to appraise them generally among school children. The primary factors that do seem to be clear enough for such purposes are the following: Verbal Comprehension V, Word Fluency W, Number N, Space S, Rote Memory M, and Induction or Reasoning R. The factors which in several studies are not yet sufficiently clear for general application are the Perceptual factor P and the Deductive factor D.

The Verbal factor V is found in tests involving verbal comprehension, for example, tests of vocabulary, opposites and synonyms, completion tests, and various reading comprehension tests.

The Word Fluency factor W is involved whenever the subject is asked to think of isolated words at a rapid rate. It is for this reason that we have called the factor a Word Fluency factor. It can be expected in such tests as anagrams, rhyming, and producing words with a given initial letter, prefix, or suffix.

The Space factor S is involved in any task in which the subject manipulates an object imaginally in two or three dimensions. The ability is involved in many mechanical tasks and in the understanding of mechanical drawings. Such material cannot be used conveniently in testing situations, so we have used a large number of tasks which are psychologically similar, such as Flags, Cards, and Figures.

The Number factor N is involved in the ability to do numerical calculations rapidly and accurately. It is not dependent upon the reasoning factors in problem-solving, but seems to be restricted to the simpler processes, such as addition and multiplication.

A Memory factor M has been clearly present in all test batteries. The tests for memory which are now being used depend upon the ability to memorize quickly. It is quite possible that the Memory factor will be broken down into more specific factors.

The Reasoning factor R is involved in tasks that require the subject to discover a rule or principle covering the material of the test. The Letter Series and Letter Grouping tests are good examples of the task. In all these experimental studies two separate Reasoning factors have been indicated. They are perhaps Induction and Deduction, but we have not succeeded in constructing pure tests of either factor. The tests which we are now using are more heavily saturated with the Inductive factor, but for the present we are simply calling the ability R, Reasoning.

In presenting for general use a differential psychological examination which appraises the mental endowment of children, it should not be assumed that there is anything final about six primary factors. No one knows how many primary mental abilities there may be. It is hoped that future factorial studies will reveal many other important primary abilities so that the mental profiles of students may eventually be adequate for appraising educational and vocational potentialities. In such a program the present studies are only a starting point in substituting for the description of mental endowment by a single intelligence index the description of mental endowment by a profile of fundamental traits.

THE FINAL TEST BATTERY

In adapting the tests for practical use in the schools for the appraisal of six primary mental abilities, we must recognize that the new test program has for its object the production of a profile for each child, as distinguished from the description of a child's mental endowment in terms of a single intelligence index. For many educational purposes it is still of value to appraise a child's mental endowment roughly by a single measure, but the composite nature of such single indices must be recognized.

The factorial matrix of the battery of sixty tests was inspected to find the three best tests for each of seven primary factors. In making the selection of tests for each primary factor we considered not only the factorial saturations of the tests, which are, of course, the most important consideration, but also the availability of parallel forms which may be needed in case the tests should come into general use. Ease of administration and ease in understanding of the instructions are also important considerations.

The three tests for each primary factor were printed in a separate booklet and the material was so arranged that the three tests for any factor could be given easily within a 40-minute school period. The main purpose of the larger test battery was to determine whether or not the primary factors could be found for eighth-grade children, but the purpose of the present shorter battery was to produce a practical, useful test battery and to check its factorial composition. The selected tests were edited and revised so that they could be used for either hand-scoring or machine-scoring. The Word Fluency tests constitute an exception in that none of the tests now known to be saturated with this factor seems to be suitable for machine-scoring.

In order to check the factorial analysis at the present age level, we arranged to give the selected list of 21 tests to a second population of eighth-grade children. The resulting data were factored independently of the larger battery of tests. There were 437 subjects in this population who took all of the 21 tests. This population was used for a new factor analysis. The results of this analysis clearly confirmed the previous study. The simple structure in the present battery is sharp, with only one primary factor conspicuously present in each test, so that the structure could be determined by inspection for clusters.

A battery of 17 tests has been assembled into a series of test booklets for use in the Chicago schools. An experimental edition of 25,000 copies has been printed, and the plan for securing norms on these tests includes their administration to 1,000 children at each half-year grade level from grade 5B through the senior year in high school. These records have been obtained during the school year 1940 to 1941. The use of such a wide age range in standardizing the test is at first thought, perhaps, rather strange. The effort was made in order to secure age norms throughout the entire range of abilities found among eighth-grade children since the tests are to become a part of the testing procedure for all 8B children in the Chicago schools. Separate age norms will be derived for each of the six primary abilities. If a single index of a student's mental ability is desired, it is recommended that the average of his six ability scores be used.

As soon as the norms are established, the tests will be published by the American Council on Education under the title "Chicago Primary Mental Abilities Tests." It is expected that the tests will be ready for distribution during the summer of 1941. The norms provided with the tests will be of a wide enough range to make the tests useful at the high school and upper grade levels.

The complete test program consists of 17 tests, all of which have been reduced to machine-scoring form except the three tests for the Word Fluency factor W. In the nature of the case there seem to be difficulties in reducing this test to machine-scoring form, and hence it has been retained in hand-scoring form. It should be said, however, that the W tests can be scored almost as fast, if not as fast, as the tests which are machine-scored. Since all of the tests can be hand-scored, their use is not limited to schools large enough to avail themselves of the scoring machine. The hand-scoring of all the tests is very easily accomplished by the use of perforated stencils to be provided with the tests. Hand-scoring is facilitated by the use of the scoring board distributed by the Stoelting Company.

The new battery represents six primary mental abilities, namely, Verbal Comprehension V, Space S, Number N, Memory M, Word Fluency W, and Reasoning R. They enable the skilled psychologist to tabulate a profile of six linearly independent scores instead of a single measure, such as the intelligence quotient.

Principals, teachers, adjustment teachers, and school psychologists have expressed their satisfaction with the profile of abilities plotted for each child. Probably the children themselves have found the profiles most interesting and have profited most from an examination of their own profiles. In the school year 1941–1942, these tests will be installed as a part of the educational guidance program in the Chicago schools by administering them regularly to 8B elementary school pupils and 10B high school pupils.

Some of the features of the tests should be mentioned. The tests are so arranged that machine-scoring and hand-scoring tests are directly comparable and will have the same norms. The child's task does not vary with the type of scoring; only the scorer's job is changed. Another feature is the use of fore-exercise booklets printed on yellow paper. The time limits for the practice exercises are approximate. When a test proper is started, the student places his white test booklet on top of his yellow practice booklet, and the examiners and proctors can check at a glance that every child is working in the right place. The tests proper are to be timed exactly. The three tests of each of the six abilities are arranged in a booklet for administration within a 40-minute school period. It is recommended that the successive booklets be given on successive school days.

FURTHER PROBLEMS

One of our principal research interests at the present time is to determine whether primary abilities can be identified in children of kindergarten or first-grade age. A series of about 50 tests is well under way, and some of them are now being tried with young children. If we succeed in isolating primary abilities among these young children, our next step will be to prepare a practical battery of tests for that age. A subsequent problem will be to make experimental studies of paper-and-pencil tests for appraising the primary abilities of children in the intermediate grades, approximately at the fourth-grade level. We are fairly confident that such tests can be prepared for use in the intermediate grades.

It is a long way in the future, but it is interesting to speculate on the possibility of using the tests of the primary mental abilities as the tool with which to study fundamental psychological problems of mental growth and mental inheritance. Absolute scaling of the tests at the different age levels will make possible studies on the rates of development of the separate abilities at various age levels. Modifiability of the abilities will be another problem to which we shall later turn attention.

Some Special Ability Test Scores of Gifted Children

FRANK T. WILSON

A. THE PROBLEM

The pupils of the Hunter College Elementary School have, for the past 10 years, been admitted on the basis of *IQ* scores in the upper one per cent of their age groups. The average *IQ* for the 1947–1948 year, according to the entering Binets of the children in the year of their admittance, was about 151.

It was of interest to know something of their abilities in special areas and therefore, insofar as it was practicable within rather severe limita-

Reprinted from *The Pedagogical Seminary* and *Journal of Genetic Psychology*, Vol. 82, First Half (March, 1953), pp. 59-68. By permission of the author and publisher.

tion of research possibilities, a variety of special abilities was measured by standardized instruments. The testing was limited to 11-year-old groups and took place during various years from 1947 to 1950.

The age range of the Hunter College Elementary School pupils is from 3 to 11 years. "Promotion" is chronological and enrichment in a regimen of informal and interest-motivated activities is the underlying approach to meeting their growth needs.

Findings from tests in five special ability areas given to children during their last year in the school are reported herewith. Validity of administration was high. Directions were carefully followed with ease and clarity and the response by the children was excellent in terms of effort and interest. They characteristically were cooperative, accepted the tests as challenges, exhibited poise, and worked with unhurried care and dispatch. Only occasionally did any individual show any resistance or lack of seriousness.

In connection with some of the analyses of these findings use has been made of results of the Wechsler-Bellevue Scale I (8), which was given to the children within a year of the time the special ability tests were administered. The Wechsler provides both a verbal and a performance *IQ* as well as a full scale score, which adds some interest to the study. As shown elsewhere, the Wechsler clearly taps other abilities as well as some of the same that enter into the Binet scores, on which the children were admitted to the school, or they do so in different proportions, since they characteristically ran 20-25 points lower than the Binets and since correlation of the Binet and Wechsler-Bellevue scores has been found to be .49 ± .04 for 153 cases of these children.

B. ART

The Meier Art Judgment Test was given to 59 children. This test is based upon "the general assumption—that aesthetic judgment is one of the most important, if not the most important, single factor in artisic competence" (5, p. 4). The task set the subject is to choose, between two almost identical versions, the better one, so keyed because therein an artistic "principle functions to make for a greater aesthetic value." The alternate version presents the same picture except that in it "the functioning of the principle has been impaired." The answer sheet on which the subject marks his judgment informs him "regarding what aspect of the composition change has affected some principle, but the principle is not named." "The subject is to respond to the separate versions as to a whole." The "materials have been devised on the basis of works of established merit." All are in black and white only.

The test was given to 40 boys and 49 girls of the sixth grade and results are presented in Tables 1 and 2.

TABLE 1. The Frequency Distributions, Medians, and Quartile Deviations of the Meier Test

	Boys	Girls	TOTAL
107.5	1		1
103.5	1	1	2
99.5		6	6
91.5	7	6	13
87.5	5	7	12
83.5	5	11	16
79.5	6	8	14
75.5	8	5	13
71.5	3	2	5
67.5	1	2	3
63.5		1	1
59.5	2		2
N	40	49	89
Mdn	83.5	85.9	85.0
Q	± 7.25	± 5.25	± 8.86
Q3			93.86
Norms for grades 7, 8, 9 (N = 1145)			
Mdn			88.3
Q3			95.5

TABLE 2. Correlations of the Meier Art Judgment Tests and the W-B I *IQ* Scores

			W-B	
	N	Verbal	Performance	Full Scale
Boys	40	.41	.26	.36
Girls	49	.39	.34	.41
TOTAL	89	*	.30	.39

* Not computed.

Table 1 indicates very similar median scores for boys and girls, but a considerably wider variability among the boys. Norms are not given in the manual for Grade 6. Norms for 1,445 junior high school pupils, Grades 7, 8, and 9 are provided, however, and are about 88.3 for the median score and 95.5 for the upper quartile of scores. The upper quartile score for the Hunter Grade 6 children, obtained by adding one quartile deviation, 8.86, to the median score of the group, 85.0, is 93.86.

This level in the norms is considered critical in that, the manual says, "Individuals falling into this range should, other things being equal, find almost certain success in an art career." A large proportion of the upper quartile of these sixth grade children fell within the range of the upper quartile of the junior high school pupils on whom the norms were established. That fact seems to support the conclusion that there was a strong trend toward superior art judgment ability in this group of sixth grade children.

Table 2 is given to indicate whether or not the superior general ability of these children may have markedly affected their art scores. The coefficients for the total group of 89 children are presumably more indicative of trends than the coefficients for the smaller sex groups. These coefficients are fairly high and seem to indicate that general intelligence had perhaps some effect on art scores, but other factors were more largely determinant of art scores.

C. MUSIC

1. *Drake Musical Memory Test.* The Drake Musical Memory Test was devised to measure "*capacity* for musical achievement" (2, p. 2). "Discovery of innate talent is the chief aim" of the test according to the author. It is made up of 12 series of 2-bar melodies, increasing in difficulty and in span of memory, which are played on the piano. In each series the first melody is repeated one or more times with slight changes in either key, time or notes, or is played without change. The pupils indicate for each repetition what change is made, or if it is the same. The score is the number of errors made.

Form A was given to several 11-year-old groups, a total of 144 children being tested.

Table 3 shows scores by sex and for total boys and girls. Compared with the norms both the boys and the girls scored in the average age group of 22 years "based on 1,979 cases from the third grade through college," for Form A. By percentile rank for average 11-year-olds the group average is at the 87.5 percentile for boys and girls 11-13 years of age, averaging 12 years old.

In order to indicate whether or not general intelligence contributed markedly to this superior rating of musical memory ability, Table 4 is presented. It shows small negative coefficients throughout. Since the scores of the music test are error scores the relationship is an inverse one by definition. The table needs to be inversely interpreted, therefore, to express the relationships between the music abilities discriminated by the test and mental abilities measured by the Wechsler test. So interpreted, the relationships are in the main quite small in degree, and somewhat varied in respect to parts of the test and to sex differences. The relatively low figures for both the number of cases and the size of the coefficients

TABLE 3. Distribution, Means, and *SD*'s of Drake Musical Memory Error Scores, Form *A* (Large Numbers Are Low Scores)

	Boys	Girls	TOTAL
87-89	1		1
51-53	1		1
48-50		1	1
45-47			
42-44	1		1
39-41	1	2	3
36-38	2	2	4
33-35	8	4	12
30-32	4	8	12
27-29	9	6	15
24-26	12	6	18
21-23	14	7	21
18-20	8	13	21
15-17	6	10	16
12-14	3	5	8
9-11	5	4	9
6- 8		1	1
N	75	69	144
Mn	25.18	22.42	24.07
SD	10.89	9.42	9.87
Norm Average Age Equivalent	22	22	

TABLE 4. Correlations of the Drake Music Memory Test Error Scores and the W-B I *IQ* Scores

	N	Verbal	Performance	Full Scale
Boys	69	−.03	−.27	−.20
Girls	61	−.27	−.01	−.22
TOTAL	130	−.08	−.23	−.16

probably means that the differences obtained were of uncertain significance.

2. *Kwalwasser-Ruch Test of Musical Accomplishment for Grades IV-XII.* This test "is designed to measure the achievement of pupils in the typical public school music course" (3, p. 1), validated against "specifications adopted by the Music Supervisors' National Conference," 1921. Thus the content was not especially suited to use in this school where enrichment and adaptability of experiences are major principles determining young children's activities. The median scored by 45 chil-

dren on this test of formal music knowledge, was 92.5, 3.5 points below
that of the norm for Grade VI.

Variability was quite large, reflecting what was known to be true
regarding learnings from private music lessons taken by many of the
children. Boys seemed less accomplished on the whole than girls, although a boy made the highest score in the group.

D. SCIENCE

The elementary form of the Calvert Science Information Test was
given to three 11-year-old groups in the spring of 1947. This test was
standardized for use in Grades 4-6, but it was entirely inadequate to
measure these children, since 59 of the 72 who took it scored above the
top grade equivalent of 8.5+.

Accordingly, in the spring of 1949 Form A of the Ruch-Popenoe General Science Test, "primarily for Grades 8 and 9" was given to 19 boys
and 23 girls of two 11-year groups. The test was "designed primarily
to measure the accomplishment of pupils in general and elementary
science courses in either the 8th or 9th grade" (6, p. 1).

The general reaction of the children to this test was unusual. Most of
them were completely at a loss in regard to many of the exercises and
omitted a great many altogether. There seemed to be an emotional
element best described as frustration for many of the children who
squirmed, groaned, and mumbled about their situation. However, they
made scores on both parts of the test and the medians for boys and for
the total group of boys and girls were not far below the norms for the
children who had had one semester of science in Grade 8 or 9. This is
all the more significant in view of the fact that no special teacher of
science has been provided in the school and what work the children
had was under the direction of their regular classroom teacher with no
special materials. The findings bear out opinions that gifted children
tend to be especially interested in science and acquire unusual understanding in that area.

There were 41 cases for whom *W-B* scores were available. A rho correlation of .45 indicates that general mental ability had a fair degree of
relationship to the science abilities, but probably did not have a marked
effect on scores.

E. MECHANICAL ABILITY

The Stenquist Mechanical Aptitude Test II was given to 76 eleven-
year-olds. Thirty-seven of the group were children in a special class of
gifted children in a New York City public school whose *IQ* scores were
similar in range and median to those of the *HCES* children. The Stenquist
scores were also similar to those of the Hunter pupils and so in order to

TABLE 5.   Distributions, Medians, and Range of Kwalwasser-Ruch
Test of Musical Accomplishment

	Boys	Girls	TOTAL
220	1		1
210		3	3
200		1	1
190		1	1
180	1		1
170			
160		1	1
150		2	2
140		2	2
130	1	2	3
120	3		3
110		3	3
100		1	1
90	1	1	2
80	1	1	2
70	1	3	4
60		4	4
50		1	1
40	1	2	3
30	1	4	5
20			
10			
0	3		3
N	14	31	45
Mdn	85	95	92.5
Range	1-221	31-215	1-221
Norm Grade VI			96

TABLE 6.   Distributions, Medians, and Range of Scores on Ruch-
Popenoe General Science Test

	Boys	Girls	TOTAL
35	3	1	4
30	2	1	3
25	8	3	11
20	2	6	8
15	3	8	11
10	1	4	5
N	19	23	43
Mdn	27.2	19.9	23.1
Range	12.5-37.5	12.5-37.5	12.5-37.5
Norms Mid-Year Gr. 8 or 9			28.1
Rho Science: W-B $N = 41$		.45	

have a larger sampling for purposes of comparing sexes the two groups
were combined.

Table 7 shows eight points difference in medians between the sexes—
a finding consistent with well-substantiated fact that boys tend to surpass

TABLE 7.   Distributions, Medians, and Quartiles of Stenquist
Mechanical Aptitude Test II

	Boys	Girls	TOTAL
60	1		1
55	4	1	5
50	5	1	6
45	4	6	10
40	5	11	16
35	3	5	8
30	3	12	15
25	3	6	9
20	1	3	4
15		2	2
N	29	47	76
Mdn	44	36	40
Q	8.67	6.36	7.59
Norm for 11-yr.-old Children			28
Percentile Position			
of Medians	91	77	85
T Score Equiv.	±1.2 *SD*	+.5 *SD*	+.9 *SD*

girls in achievement in mechanical ability. The variability was also
greater for the boys. However, one girl scored at the interval next to the
highest interval reached by the boys, and one boy scored at the interval
just above that of the lowest girl.

The median score for each sex was much above the Stenquist norm for
1,087 children reported in 1922. The manual is not clear as to the sex
of the standardization group as the words "children," "pupils," and
"boys" are used in various connections. The score of one of the illustrative cases, a 14-year-old boy, was interpreted as being "exceeded by 97
per cent of boys of *his own age*" (7, p. 17). If the norms are for boys
only then the 47 girls of this study presumably surpass the abilities of
girls in general, even more than is shown by the comparison in the
table.

The percentile positions and *T*-Scores used in the Stenquist norms
show, of course, similar evidence of superiority of these pupils, the boys
scoring at the 91 percentile and the girls at the 77 percentile of the

TABLE 8. Correlations of Stenquist Scores and
W-B Full Scale *IQ* *

Boys and Girls $N = 39$			
Part I	.41±.13	Part III	.43±.13
Part II	.51±.12	Total	.57±.11

* Only 39 of the children who took the Stenquist had also taken the W-B I.

standardization group, equivalent to about ± 1.2 *SD* and ± .5 *SD* respectively, of the distribution of scores of that group.

In order to see what relationship to general intelligence might be indicated correlations of the 39 *HCES* children and *W-B* scores is shown in Table 8 for the total Stenquist score and three component parts of it. All coefficients are fairly high, and even within the limits of their *PE's* would indicate considerable, but far from major, overlap of abilities. Stenquist reported a Pearson *r* of .21 ± .04, and that of 275 seventh and eighth grade boys in a NYC school who "were above average in general abstract intelligence 52 per cent were also above average in general mechanical aptitude." The standardization group was, presumably, more nearly representative of seventh and eighth grade boys, than the group herein reported.

The Detroit Mechanical Aptitude Examination, Form *A*, was also given to a group of 22 *HCES* boys and girls. The median score was 160.6, *Q* ± 15, total range 109 to 202. According to Baker's Table 1, this is in the upper 8 per cent of scores for 11-year-old children, which includes scores 149-337. He suggests that *A* and *B* scores, according to "approximately 200 Detroit counselors and teachers" indicate promise as "artist, civil engineer, dentist, laboratory teacher, osteopath, shop teacher, and surgeon" (1, p. 15)—an interesting selection, and names of occupations numerously represented in the parental vocations of parents of the *HCES* children.

The Revised Minnesota Paper Form Board Tests were given to 20 children in January, 1948. The 1948 manual says that the tests appear "to measure the ability to perceive spatial relationships" (4, p. 2). "Scores have predictive value for achievement in mechanical fields and shopwork. . . ." The test is designed for use in high schools, colleges, and for industrial purposes. Although for this reason it was very difficult for 11-year-old children it was administered to a small group of 11-year-old pupils of the school to see what these gifted children could do with it.

Table 9 shows considerable variability for both the boys and the girls, the range for both running from 16-55. A girl made the highest score and a boy the lowest one, although the boys' median was some

TABLE 9. Distributions, Medians, and Ranges of Scores on the
Revised Minnesota Form Board Test

	Boys	Girls	TOTAL
55		1	1
50			
45			
40	1		1
35	2	1	3
30	3		3
25	2	5	7
20	1	3	4
15	1		1
N	10	10	20
Mdn	33.3	27.0	30.4
Range	16-41.2	20.6-55	16-55
Mdn Norm Grade 9 & 10			39

six points above that of the girls. The norm on the group nearest these
children in age was for boys and girls in Grades 9 and 10 who scored
a median of 39. Compared with that older group the Hunter children
scored a median of 30.4, equivalent to the 28th percentile for the 9th
and 10th graders.

F. SUMMARY

Gifted 11-year-old children who had spent most of their school life
in the Hunter College Elementary School for young gifted children
showed, in general, superiority in abilities in art judgment, music memory, science, and mechanical abilities, as measured by seven different
standardized tests. The degree of superiority was most marked, apparently, in music memory, and least in music accomplishment as
measured by the 1921 Kwalwasser-Ruch test.

The distribution of scores approached more closely to the normal
curve in all of these measures, than did the *IQ* scores on which the children had been admitted to the school. Variability in the measures was
also very marked.

Correlations of scores on these tests with recent Wechsler-Bellevue *IQ*
scores of the children were from near zero to moderate in degree.

The findings corroborate other reports of trends toward excellence in
abilities of various kinds among gifted children together with relatively
unimpressive correlations with *IQ*. They also indicate pronounced individual variability among young gifted children in terms of their various
individual abilities and in comparison with one another.

REFERENCES

1. Baker, H. J., Voelker, P. H., & Crockett, A. C., Detroit Mechanical Aptitudes Examination, Form *A*, Manual. Bloomington, Ill.: Public School Publishing.
2. Drake, R. M., Musical Memory Test, Forms *A* and *B*. A Test of Musical Talent, Manual. Bloomington, Ill.: Public School Publishing, 1934.
3. Kwalwasser, J., & Ruch, G. M., Kwalwasser-Ruch Test of Musical Accomplishment for Grades IV-XII, Manual. Iowa City: State Univ. Iowa, 1942.
4. Likert, R., & Quasha, W. H., The Revised Minnesota Paper Form Board Test, Manual. New York: Psychological Corporation, 1948.
5. Meier, N. C., The Meier Art Test: I. Art Judgment, Manual. Iowa City: State Univ. Iowa, 1942.
6. Ruch, G. M., & Popenoe, H. F., Ruch-Popenoe General Science Test, Manual. New York: World Book, 1926.
7. Stenquist, J. L., Stenquist Mechanical Aptitude Tests, Manual. New York: World Book, 1922.
8. Wechsler, D., The Measurement of Adult Intelligence. (Third ed.). Baltimore: Williams & Wilkins, 1944.

The Psychology of Gifted Children

RUTH STRANG

The purpose of psychology is to help people to understand themselves and others. To achieve this aim in the case of the gifted, we must find out, "how they got that way," ascertain their common characteristics and how they learn, become aware of their special problems of adjustment, and understand how they cope with them. Psychology is concerned with the individual as a whole, with the complex interrelation of physical, intellectual, social, and emotional factors.

GENESIS OF GIFTEDNESS

Gifted children are lucky. Theirs has been a particularly fortunate combination of heredity and early childhood experience. According to the French psychiatrist, Piaget, they are endowed with a certain organizing quality of mind that is able to see relations and to make deductions and generalizations. This quality of mind influences their development

Reprinted from *Journal of Teacher Education*, Vol. 5, No. 3 (September, 1954), pp. 215-217. By permission of the author and publisher.

from the first week of life. It enables them to select from their environment the experiences they need for their physical, intellectual, and social development.

The ordinary environment supplies the intellectual experiences they need in the early years. Only extreme deprivation can prevent the early development of the gifted child's native ability. However, a certain minimum of experience is essential, for intelligence is not something given at birth; it constantly creates itself through life experiences which it selects, relates, and organizes. In this sense, intelligence is learned. The gifted child becomes increasingly able to use his environment to good advantage.

But even a "lush environment" of material things is not enough. Lack of love may inhibit a young child's use of his exploring, relating, organizing quality of mind. Convincing evidence of this has been presented in motion pictures and research reports. An infant who receives the best physical and medical care, but is deprived of normal human contacts may become apathetic—unable to put forth effort or use his native endowment.

In later years also, lack of suitable experiences may prevent the gifted child from attaining full intellectual and social stature. Among these inhibiting conditions are extremes of parental pressure or neglect in the preschool years; a boring or disappointing first school experience; a curriculum that has no meaning, use, or purpose for the child; or a high school environment which causes the gifted adolescent to suppress his real intellectual interests and avoid getting high marks in order to be accepted by his classmates. After high school, the fullest development of some highly gifted individuals is limited by lack of opportunities for appropriate further education. Dr. Leta S. Hollingworth has reported studying several young people with very high IQ's who were not able to finance the graduate study which they needed to make their greatest contribution to society.

How do gifted children "get that way"? Giftedness is a product of the interaction of native ability and life experiences. If a child has native ability, his environment determines the use he makes of his gifts and special talents. Every stage of life is important, for intelligence unfolds in response to experience; "intelligence elaborates itself."

HOW GIFTED CHILDREN LEARN

We know that gifted children learn to read by various methods at an early stage. About half of them know how to read when they enter school. Some of them have just picked up this ability by themselves, they do not know how. Others have parents who have read to them a great deal, and have helped them recognize words in which they were interested. Still others have received some systematic instruction at home. Quite a few mention phonics as being helpful, and it is reasonable to suppose that gifted children would profit more than others from this analytical type of reading instruction. Once they have mastered the basic reading skills, they tend to read widely.

We also know that gifted children are bored and disappointed by many of their school experiences. One little girl, who had dutifully read aloud several pages of an inane primer, looked up at her teacher and said, "Boring, isn't it?" Many have expressed their dissatisfaction with the practice of taking turns around the class, reading aloud. They read ahead of the others and don't know the place when they are called on; thus they get into trouble. Sometimes they are so bored with the repetitive routine of class recitations that they talk with their neighbors or get into other kinds of mischief.

They have definite ideas about the kind of teachers they want. One youngster described her favorite teacher as follows:

The best teacher I ever had was W. A. He was good, because we got our work done and were interested in it. We did things to learn our social studies by doing other things besides reading and writing. We had projects of all sorts on the Revolution, the Civil, and all other wars. When we were studying the Industrial Revolution, we all pretended that we were inventors and picked an invention. We looked up information on this and gave an oral report explaining how it worked. He not only was interesting but he had a quiet but firm way of conducting the classroom. Unlike most teachers he did not yell when reprimanding someone. He spoke in a quiet tone that made you feel ashamed in a way but also kept you quiet for the rest of the period. He did not have any pets. You could look upon him as a friend and not as one who gives you tests to "catch" or to "trick" you. You could tell in his teaching that he was trying to help you. He tried to get the most learning out of one year, pleasantly. If you had a problem or a question he would give suggestions that might help you, but he never gave you the answer. He made you do that work yourself! As a whole, I think that most students who had him looked upon him as a friend. He used the honor system and stressed the point that if you cheated you were hurting no one but yourself.

The gifted tend to learn by complex associative methods rather than by rote drill; they look for generalizations, are interested in abstract aspects of school subjects, and are able to work independently. Yet they do want and need instruction in effective methods of reading and study, and they appreciate teachers who "hold us up to standards of achievement appropriate for us." They love to talk, and participate in group discussions with enthusiasm. They want to be able to take an additional subject in which they are interested, to do creative work, to learn to speak before an audience, to apply principles to the solution of life problems, to match wits with equally gifted persons.

We do not know whether gifted children employ learning procedures similar to those of the average pupil. Probably basic learning theory is common to all: learning starts with a need; the need, either physiological or environmental, arouses an emotional drive of some kind; this poses a problem to be solved, and leads eventually to action. Gifted children have an advantage in this problem-solving type of learning. They perceive the situation more clearly than the average; a slight clue may give them an understanding of what needs to be done.

Gifted children from middle- or upper-class homes are usually expected to succeed in academic work. Their parents set high levels of aspiration for them, and they compare themselves with the famous people they read about in their favorite biographies and autobiographies. This is why so many able students feel inadequate and inferior. In some cases the anxiety is so intense, the threat of failure so great, as to have a disorganizing effect on the child's performance. Moreover, competition to get the highest mark in the class, or to be on the honor roll, results in many instances in bitter rivalry between individuals. In schools in which the curriculum is not vital or challenging, some gifted pupils feel that this kind of competition and extrinsic incentive is necessary to make them work up to capacity.

Certain methods of teaching may be especially effective with gifted children. They like to take initiative in planning what they will learn and how they will learn it. Like other pupils, they need guidance at the beginning stages of the learning process. They learn more quickly when they are helped to find some organizing principle, rather than being subjected to rote methods and sheer memorization. In differing degrees, these methods may be equally important for all learners. We need to know more about the learning methods most appropriate for different pupils.

PROBLEMS OF ADJUSTMENT

Although the gifted show, on the average, a smaller proportion of serious maladjustments, such as mental disorders, suicidal tendencies, and delinquency, than the general population, such deviations do occasionally occur. But the gifted also have greater inner resources for coping with their problems, and treatment is more likely to be successful. It is possible that an intense creativity may cause nervous strain and tension, and that a supersensitive nervous system (or some other underlying condition) may be conducive to both emotional instability and creative intelligence.

Some social maladjustment may occur, especially in those rare individuals with IQ's above 170. It is difficult for them to relate themselves to people who have such different abilities and backgrounds and to find some communality of interests. Yet it is important for the gifted to learn to do this, since most of the vocations which they will enter require skill in human relations. The social adjustment of gifted pupils who are accelerated varies with a number of factors.

The psychology of gifted children is still to be written. And some of the most authentic information, significant insights, and practical suggestions for their education will come from the gifted youngsters themselves.

II

Measurement of Giftedness

THE CONCEPT OF giftedness, as of intelligence itself, is today a much broader one than earlier in this century. The purpose of measurement of giftedness is to identify as many individuals as possible who possess mental abilities significantly above the average, as well as to understand giftedness.

FACTORS IN MENTAL SUPERIORITY

There is reason to believe that the truly creative "genius" operates mentally in some manner different from that of one who is merely far above the average in intellectual powers. In such cases, Thorne points out in *Principles of Psychological Examining,* "an entirely different orientation of examining is necessary (1)." But the great concern with which we are faced today, in an attempt to realize better the potentialities of our children of superior intelligence, is not so much concern for the *one-in-a-million genius* as it is for the much more common *one-in-a-hundred gifted child.* The differences of these children, then, is not so much a difference of kind as it is a difference of degree, although both differences need much further study.

Thorne has presented both the classic mental functions and the factors in intelligence which have been statistically derived. Following this pattern allows us to view systematically those abilities that are measurable, and clearly indicates the complexity of the problem of distinguishing between the child who is gifted and the one who is not.

The classic mental functions are (2):

1. Sensation
2. Perception

3. Memory
4. Symbolic or language function
5. Association and learning
6. Reasoning
7. Psychomotor ability
8. Mechanical ability
9. General intelligence

Recognizing that there are many different factors of intelligence may come as a surprise to those who have preferred the earlier idea of one factor, the "general intelligence" factor, alone. Certainly both identification of and special provisions for gifted children would be easier to provide if there were only a single intelligence factor. The numerous factors of intelligence, however, make it apparent that even among those children who manage to score high on an intelligence test, there will still be great homogeneity of mental abilities.

It would be impossible to state in which of these areas gifted children excel. By definition, they would excel in all of them. Because of the highly verbal nature of most intelligence tests, however, it would seem likely that those children who are superior in symbolic or language function are the ones who are most frequently being identified as gifted.

PROBLEMS IN MEASURING MENTAL SUPERIORITY

The basic problem in measuring mental superiority is not that those identified as gifted are not. The problem is instead that many of the gifted remain unidentified. The Educational Policies Commission states:

. . . the evidence is overwhelming that (a) the level at which an individual is able to score on an intelligence test (in relation to the scores of other individuals of comparable age) remains fairly constant throughout later childhood and youth and probably in adult life, too; (b) ability to score on an intelligence test is related to success in school and college; and (c) individuals who make high scores on intelligence tests in youth are much more likely than others to attain distinction in adult life (3).

With the ever increasing popularity of the school of thought which would like to see I.Q. tests discarded, an examination of some testing concepts is needed.

Intelligence tests do not measure all aspects of intelligence, but only a small part of it. Those taking the tests and scoring high are truly gifted, but those making a lower score may or may not be gifted, or they may be gifted but not in the areas which that particular test attempted to measure. Although this happens, it does not mean that the intelligence test is wrong. It suggests that in locating gifted children we should not rely on any single test or type of test.

Intelligence tests are based on the assumption that all children have the same cultural background. It is well known that this is not true, but attempts to make tests which were *culture free* (free of cultural influences) or *culture fair* have met with no great degree of acceptance. Culture-free tests are confronted with the problem that perhaps adjustment to one's cultural environment, or to the cultural environment of the middle-class citizen, is a part of one's ability to succeed. If this is so, and culturally influenced factors are removed from the test, the test loses much of its predictive value. The sensible approach would be to recognize that children from culturally deprived backgrounds cannot be adequately measured by existing tests, and special provisions must be made to identify giftedness among these children in other ways. The most likely way is, of course, through observation over a prolonged period of time.

Intelligence tests are not so reliable at the upper limits as they are at either the average or the lower levels. The authors of the tests themselves readily admit this, but the opponents of I.Q. tests point to the many instances of changes in I.Q. of 10, 20, and even 30 and 40 points as proof that the tests are of no value. If such changes were for children who had scored at the average range (90-110), they would indeed be significant evidence in the argument against the I.Q. test. Most often this is not the case, however. The changes will be for the child whose I.Q. was found to be 175 at the age of six and only 140 at the age of thirteen. Actually, such changes can and do occur frequently at the higher ranges. The major factor being overlooked, however, is that almost all intelligence tests have a low ceiling. As children grow older, they reach the top of the test and cannot possibly score above a certain point. There are merely no items any higher. For this reason, the test may indicate a lower I.Q. than that previously obtained, but in no way indicates lower intelligence.

There is also the ever-present chance that the child's environment has changed radically, or that the testing conditions were radically different, and that the score had actually changed. There is no reason for being particularly alarmed at such a change, for the child still is scoring in the gifted range, and to find the approximate range was the only reason for administering the test in the first place.

Group intelligence tests are particularly poor in identifying superior children. The extremely low ceiling on the group test, plus the dependency for a score upon the measurement of so few items, makes it possible that gifted students will not be identified by a group test. Gifted students will usually score over 110 on a group test, but many times will not come even close to the score which they will receive on an individual test.

It must be recognized that many problems exist in measuring mental superiority, and constant attention must be given by workers in the field to avoid overlooking the potentially gifted child who has not been identified by means of an intelligence test. But to discard I.Q. tests, merely because they do not identify every gifted child, would be as foolish as doing away with all schools because they do not adequately provide for all children.

In order that the I.Q. may be used effectively, classroom teachers need to know more about the test itself. The I.Q. score alone is not of enough value to warrant either the time required of the examiner and the child or the expense. The valuable part of an individual test must be things other than the I.Q. score.

Of utmost importance to the teacher of a bright child is the Basal Age, which must be obtained on every child who is administered a Stanford-Binet Intelligence Test Form L-M. This indicates the highest age level at which the child can perform all the mental tasks without making any mistakes. The teacher should also know the range and the highest level at which the child is able to perform successfully some of the tasks. In addition to the Basal Age and the range, it is assumed that the teacher will be told the quality of the responses and the particular areas of strengths and weaknesses. If such information is not provided, the time necessary to administer the Stanford-Binet I.Q. test cannot be justified. Particularly for gifted children is such information necessary. Assignment to special classes should be done with particular concern for the Basal Age, for even though the child may have a high I.Q., if he has a much lower Basal Age he may have difficulty in the special class.

All of these problems are ones which must be considered in measuring mental superiority. Considering these factors and remembering that no test is any better than the person who interprets it, will assure a sounder identification program.

REFERENCES

1. Thorne, Frederick C., *Principles of Psychological Examining*. Brandon, Vt.: Journal of Clinical Psychology, 1955, p. 302.
2. Adapted from a table in Thorne's *Principles of Psychological Examining, ibid.*, pp. 284-285.
3. Educational Policies Commission, *Education of the Gifted*. Washington, D.C.: National Education Association, 1950, p. 39.

4 | IDENTIFICATION AND TESTING

Contributions to the IQ Controversy From the Study of Superior Deviates

PAUL WITTY

More than two decades have now elapsed since the advent of the Stanford-Binet test. The intervening time has encompassed enormous advance and continuous progress in the scientific study of education. Experimentation has been deeply influenced and appreciably enriched by the intelligence-testing movement. Perhaps the most notable contribution of the movement has been the recognition and understanding of individual differences which it has engendered. In this area, the studies of gifted children by L. M. Terman, L. S. Hollingworth and others have proved illuminating.

As early as 1924, a Yearbook of the National Society for the Study of Education contained reports of many studies which led to the formulation of certain widely accepted theories concerning the nature and needs of gifted children. In the intervening period (1924–1940) our knowledge has been extended and deepened by contributions from other areas and by the supplementary evidence accumulating from genetic studies of the gifted. In this Yearbook, much relevant material is presented for the first time. The writer will present some basic premises the validity of which has been affected by these recent findings.

MEANING OF A HIGH IQ

About 1920, the concept was advanced that an extraordinarily high IQ was associated with genius. L. M. Terman designated his volume, which described 643 children having IQ's of 140 plus, "Genetic Studies of Genius." Moreover, he stated that "from the ranks of gifted children [IQ 140 plus] and from nowhere else our geniuses in every line are

Reprinted from *School and Society*, Vol. 51, No. 1321 (April 20, 1940), pp. 503-508. By permission of the author and publisher.

recruited." L. S. Hollingworth also made similar prognostications; she asserted "only the gifted can create," and "individuals of surpassing intelligence create national wealth, determine the state of industry, advance science and make general culture possible." It is now possible to appraise the validity of these optimistic claims. Investigations by Terman, Hollingworth and Witty have shown the gifted to be healthy, well-rounded, socially adequate and generally successful as children, youth and young adults. Yet, no investigation discloses any justification for the synonymous use of the terms "IQ 140 plus" and "genius." Terman's follow-up studies reported in the present Yearbook lead him to conclude (1):

> Although a considerable proportion of the subjects have not lived up to their ability, the accomplishments of the group as a whole have been as good as could reasonably have been expected, considering that most of its members are still under thirty years of age. At least half the boys are launched upon promising careers and several are already nationally or internationally known. The group includes novelists, short-story writers, poets, a sculptor, a gifted musical composer and several scientists who have published important researches. With few exceptions, creative intellectual productivity is confined to the males.

Hollingworth displays greater caution in writing now; however, she advances a new hypothesis concerning IQ and "genius" (2):

> It has now become clear from follow-up studies that children who test at 140 IQ are far from genius in any accepted meaning of that term. . . . It is necessary, therefore, to revise the idea that 140 IQ delimits genius. From subsequent observation of the mental products of tested persons, it seems reasonable to suggest that the degree of mental ability involved in producing works of genius falls as far above 140 IQ as the latter falls above the generality. At and above 180 IQ, performance begins to appear that corresponds to the lexicographer's idea of genius.

This interesting new hypothesis is not substantiated by the work of other contributors to the present Yearbook. In fact, Terman states (3): "Our conclusion is that *for subjects brought up under present-day educational regimes, excess in IQ above 140 or 150 adds little to one's achievement in the early adult years.*" Moreover, he expands his concept to this degree: "The data reviewed indicate that, *above the IQ level of 140, adult success is largely determined by such factors as social adjustment, emotional stability, and drive to accomplish.*"

It is abundantly clear that an extraordinarily high IQ in childhood is not an indicator of later attainment that may be regarded as highly or significantly creative; nor do the most remarkable test ratings in childhood warrant expectancies of adult performance which may be characterized as the work of genius. The promise of youth in so far as creativity and the work of genius are concerned seems not to have been fulfilled by the gifted youngsters identified and studied during the past two decades.

Why is it that high IQ's have proved so generally disappointing in ful-filling the promise some investigators held for them? An answer to this recurring question should be of interest to teachers in their attempts to reorient their thinking concerning the role of intelligence in modern life.

If by gifted children we mean those youngsters who give promise of creativity of a high order, it is doubtful if the typical intelligence test is suitable for use in identifying them. For creativity posits originality, and originality implies successful management, control and organization of new materials or experiences. Intelligence tests contain over-learned ma-terials which, as Rockwell (4) states, call for stable predictable response, not original creative reaction. It is evident, then, that an acceptable criterion for giftedness must be sought primarily outside the provinces covered by the intelligence test. For the content of the intelligence test is patently lacking in situations which disclose originality or creativity.

Another criticism of the intelligence test which may help explain its failure in the identification of creative ability lies in its makers' disavowal of concern for the motive or drive which actuates high attainment. The intelligence test neglects the role of feeling and motive and requires only the habituated response of the child to situations which are "set" and which are "low in feeling-tone (5)."

Over-learned material is low in "feeling tone" as well as in potentiality to deviate. Such being the case, no surprise should be experienced at the rela-tive stability of intelligence as we measure it. But the intelligence in which everyone is interested is the responsive kind of action capable of being mo-bilized to meet a sudden and unusual demand. In such unusual demands, survival or annihilation is imminent.

Hence it may be that the very character of the test has doomed it to failure for the high services which it came to be expected to render in locating society's leaders, creators and geniuses.

INHERITANCE OF HIGH IQ's

The work of the investigators who contributed to the 27th Yearbook of the N.S.S.E. led in general to the conclusion that by the side of heredity all other factors which determine intelligence are "dwarfed in compari-son." Moreover, the mental test was thought to yield a reliable IQ which reflected a heritable, stable intelligence. From Hollingworth's volume (6) on "Gifted Children" the following statements illustrate the some-what general tendency at that time to accept and use the results of intel-ligence tests as reliable measures of inborn ability: (*a*) "From data so far collected, we can only say that the IQ is certainly constant within narrow margins. . . ." (*b*) "Psychologists no longer doubt that it is now possible

to predict, when a child is six years old, what his relative position will be
in the total range of intellects when he is sixteen."

The investigations reported in the 39th Yearbook show that the IQ is
variable in early childhood and alterable in later years. Even the follow-
up studies of L. M. Terman have forced a modification in these early
claims for the inheritance of a stable IQ. For Terman now gives greater
weight to environmental factors. However, he states: "There is certainly
nothing in our data to warrant giving all or most of the credit for the
superior achievement of the A subjects (7) to their vastly superior family
environment. The facts themselves are as amenable to interpretation in
terms of heredity as in terms of environment (8)."

The foregoing admission that heredity or environment (or both) may
account for superior achievement reveals an alteration in point of view.
Indeed, in 1927, Terman and Burks assigned much higher percentages
of influence to heredity than to environment in attempting to account for
differences in intelligence. Hollingworth in the present Yearbook now
admits the complexity of motivation in intelligent or successful performance, but stresses the general stability of the IQ (9).

Follow-up studies of the past decade show that children selected at and
after seven years of age as rating in the top centile of the distribution of
Stanford-Binet IQ's maintain their centile status on mental tests with a very
high degree of reliability. . . .

In other words, intelligence is maintained, as shown by tests, but intelligence alone is not enough for "success."

Three trends are at once discernible in these recent studies and interpretations of the gifted: (*a*) an abandonment of the claim for creativity
or genius predicated upon high IQ; (*b*) a tendency to be cautious in
assigning percentages of influence to heredity and environment respectively (10); and (*c*) a willingness to acknowledge the complexity of
"giftedness" and its motivation.

Yet the specter of determinism is still present in several discussions in
the 39th Yearbook. It is clearly revealed in two sections dealing with the
gifted: in the presentation of the relationship of socio-economic status to
high IQ and in the treatment accorded the frequencies of high IQ's
among racial groups.

SOCIO-ECONOMIC STATUS AND HIGH IQ

After a review of selected studies of the socio-economic groups that
produce the gifted, Hollingworth concludes (11):

All surveys have agreed in finding that a large majority of children testing at or above 140 IQ have been fathered by persons in classes I to III on
occupational scales devised by economists; and that classes IV, V and VI yield

very few of such children. . . . However, it is necessary to emphasize the fact that a substantial and important minority of superior deviates originate in poverty, in families where all means are lacking for appropriate development.

This position is reinforced by the following analysis: "The professional group of fathers yielded 1003 per cent. of their quota [number of off-spring to be expected if all occupational groups were alike] (12)."

Such statements may prove misleading; they have sometimes been made the basis for gross misrepresentations (13). Gifted children, according to any definition, will often be found in average and inferior socio-economic groups because of the overwhelming frequencies of human beings who make up these classifications. That gifted children have not been located often in these classes is simply because they have been sought primarily in other groups. The studies of gifted children reported in this volume have typically been made among the white population in urban centers. That gifted children are present in large numbers in *all* groups may be readily demonstrated. For example, Stoke and Lehman made an analysis of the anticipated number of gifted children in unselected populations; they then ascertained the number to be expected in different occupational categories. Census figures were consulted; and these investigators concluded that if *all* gifted children were identified, the majority would come from the ranks of skilled, semi-skilled and unskilled laborers—the masses. These authors conclude: "The great majority of superior children (IQ 120–140) and the great majority of gifted children (IQ 140 and above) come from the non-professional classes (15)." The data give unequivocal support to the following authoritative statements of H. S. Jennings (16):

Examination shows that in man a very large proportion of the individuals recognized as superior come from parents that give no evidence of superiority. The few children coming from the small class of superior parents do indeed show a larger proportion of superior individuals than those from mediocre or inferior parents. *But owing to the fact that the latter classes contain many more individuals, the absolute number of superior offspring produced by them is much greater than the number produced by the superior parents.* [Italics not in the original.]

RACE AND INTELLIGENCE

In attempts to identify gifted children, we have neglected to explore the possibilities in several other rather large segments of our population. The present Yearbook includes the following statements which may lead to unwarranted generalizations concerning racial differences and intelligence (16): "According to mental surveys so far made, the American Indian, the Negro, the Mexican and the Sicilian yield few superior deviates. To this may be added that the Portuguese in California contributed few or no children who tested above 140 IQ to Terman's sample."

It is demonstrable that when gifted children are sought in some of these groups, they may be found (as is shown in the writer's report on gifted Negroes). A bias or prejudice in this area should not prevent us from carrying out the research suggested in Chapter IX of the 24th Yearbook of the National Society for the Study of Education in a sincere effort to provide the educational opportunities which individual differences in every racial group justify and merit.

CONCLUDING STATEMENT

We have witnessed, during the period 1927 to 1939, a change in our basic concept of the nature of "giftedness." No longer can we use a high IQ to posit creativity, genius or near-genius. Nor are we justified in assuming that hereditary factors are the primary determiners of high test ratings. Moreover, physical, emotional and social drives are now receiving increased attention as factors of significance in successful and intelligent behavior.

The writer has cited certain current interpretations of the nature of gifted children which disclose a gratifying change in attitude among the pioneers in this important field. However, a consideration of another character needs now to be recognized and emphasized. Perhaps we should concede frankly that the intelligence test can no longer be looked upon as a valid instrument for identifying gifted children. It will be useful, as significant studies in the Yearbook show, in identifying one group of children whose superior attainment requires further stimulation, study and guidance. But evidence of giftedness should be sought outside the area covered by intelligence tests. For it appears that "giftedness" can be estimated only by observation of a child's behavior. The child whose performance is consistently remarkable in any potentially valuable area might well be considered gifted; he should be given the opportunity which his attainment demands for nurture and continuous growth, but his development should not be predicted nor his future attainment prescribed except as increased growth necessitates adaptations and changes. And certainly he should not be placed in a special group alleged to be homogeneous. There can be no justification for homogeneous grouping of gifted children, since scientific studies reveal variability, not constancy within the human organism; and since there has been no evidence advanced to show the validity of employing any mental test in effecting homogeneity. Moreover, homogeneous grouping violates the basic premises on which democratic institutions are founded; it conceals or minimizes differences arising from exchange of opinion and interpretation; it encourages the development of a "class" education; it rewards or puts a premium on fortunate *social* heritage and penalizes the less fortunate, and it fails to envisage the potentialities of the masses for becoming competent, critical, productive and even creative citizens. It fails, therefore, to recognize the very essence of democratic doctrine and faith.

In any event, recent disclosures call for re-evaluation of mental tests and revision of certain educational practices which have been based upon its acceptance as a measure of inborn, unchanging ability. As Rockwell has said (17): "An atomistic, predetermined, rigidly stable intelligence may fit the current theories of psychology. It is out of place in the rest of the biological world."

REFERENCES AND NOTES

1. Terman, L. M. and Oden, M., 39th Yearbook of the National Society for the Study of Education, Part I, p. 73.
2. Hollingworth, L. S., 39th Yearbook of the National Society for the Study of Education, Part I, p. 62.
3. Terman and Oden, *op. cit.*, pp. 83-84.
4. Rockwell, John L., *Educational Method*, Vol. 19 (November, 1939), pp. 80-92.
5. *Ibid.*, p. 92.
6. Hollingworth, L. S., *Gifted Children.* New York: Macmillan, 1926, pp. 156, 158.
7. In their follow-up study reported in the 39th Yearbook, Terman and Oden have designated the successful group as A and the non-successful group as C.
8. Terman, L. M. and Oden, M., *op. cit.*, p. 84.
9. Hollingworth, L. S., *op. cit.*, pp. 61-62.
10. The unfortunate practice followed by Terman and Burks in the 27th Yearbook has not entirely disappeared. Despite the caution urged in this practice by biologists and anthropologists, one finds Raymond Cattell stating that Burks, in assigning 20 per cent of IQ variance to environment, "assigns too much to environment. . . ." (39th Yearbook of the National Society for the Study of Education, Part I, p. 225.)
11. Hollingworth, L. S., *op. cit.*, pp. 58-59.
12. *Ibid.*
13. The following quotations are examples: ". . . the operation of the social ladder tends to concentrate the valuable qualities of the whole nation in the upper strata, and to leave the lowest stratum depleted of the finer qualities." (W. McDougall, "Is America Safe for Democracy?" New York: Scribner's, 1921, p. 155.) "Evidence is constantly accumulating that the more successful economic and social classes have far the largest share of the nation's brains." (A. E. Wiggan, *World's Work*, Vol. 52, 1926, p. 687.)
14. Stoke, S. M. and Lehman, H. C., *School and Society*, Vol. 31, 1930, pp. 372-77. Stoke, S. M. and Lehman, H. C., *The American Journal of Sociology*, Vol. 36, 1930, pp. 221-32. Stoke, S. M., *Harvard Educational Monographs*, No. 8. Cambridge, Mass.: Harvard University Press, 1927. Lehman, H. C. and Stoke, S. M., *The American Journal of Sociology*, Vol. 36, 1930, pp. 15-27.
15. Jennings, H. S., *The Biological Basis of Human Nature.* New York: W. W. Norton Company, 1930, pp. 219-20.

16. Hollingworth, L. S., *op. cit.*, p. 56. Similar data were used as the basis for the following statements: "Several surveys have been made to test the mentality of Negro children. These surveys unexceptionally show a low average of intellect among children having Negro blood. Comparatively few of these children are found within the range which includes the best one per cent of white children. *It is, however, possible by prolonged search to find an occasional Negro or mulatto child testing above 130 IQ.*" [Italics not in original.] Hollingworth, L. S., *Gifted Children.* New York: Macmillan, 1926, pp. 69-70.

17. Rockwell, *op. cit.*

Locating Gifted Children in Junior High Schools: A Comparison of Methods

CARL W. PEGNATO

JACK W. BIRCH

This is a report on a study of the relative efficiency and effectiveness of seven different means of locating gifted children in junior high schools. The major purpose of the investigation was to discover which procedure or which combination of commonly used procedures would prove best.

The importance of finding gifted children has long been acknowledged (2). Only in the last quarter-century have the individual intelligence testing tools been shaped and sharpened sufficiently to allow psychologists to identify gifted children with a very high degree of certainty (4). The international events of recent years have heightened the urgency for the prompt and early discovery of all gifted children—those who show their capacity through exceptional achievements and those in whom great potentialities are latent—in order that they may be given the best possible guidance toward self-realization through education and training (1).

The gifted children in a junior high school could be discovered if every child in the school were individually examined by a psychologist (3). While some few schools in this nation have access to sufficient psychological service to provide for individual examination for all children, and while that amount of psychological service should ideally be available to all school districts, it is very rarely the case. In fact, it is the very shortage of psychological staff which makes it so necessary to find ways of

Reprinted from *Exceptional Children*, Vol. 25, No. 7 (March, 1959), pp. 300-304. By permission of the senior author and publisher.

choosing some small group of children from the total student body to refer for individual evaluation.

Several questions relating to locating children who might be gifted for referral to a psychologist seemed to need answers based on direct investigation.

1. Do teachers recognize the mentally gifted children in their classes?
2. Are the children who win Honor Roll status the gifted children of each class?
3. Are some gifted children to be found only through the interest and achievement they display in music or arts?
4. Are some gifted children identifiable primarily through the interest and ability they show in social, political, and other extra-curricular activities?
5. Does outstanding performance in mathematics call children to teachers' attention as gifted?
6. Can group intelligence tests be relied upon in the identification of gifted children?
7. Are group achievement test scores useful in selecting gifted children?
8. Are some gifted children overlooked even though all the criteria suggested above are employed in searching for them?
9. What screening method or combination of methods is most effective and efficient?
10. What is the magnitude of the problem of under-achievement among gifted children?

For the purposes of this inquiry, mental giftedness was defined in terms of a Stanford-Binet Intelligence Quotient of 136 or higher as determined from an examination by a school psychologist. This definition includes the most intelligent one percent of the general population, and, to that extent, is consistent with a number of current and widely used definitions.

As a setting in which to seek answers to these and other closely related questions, the junior division of a junior-senior high school in a large city (Pittsburgh, Pa.) was chosen. The school, in grades seven through 12, had 3600 students. The junior division enrolled 1400 students in grades seven through nine. In order to improve the prospect that a fairly large proportion of gifted children would be available for the study the school chosen was not only a large one, but it was situated in and drew upon a very favored group or neighborhood from a socio-economic standpoint.

METHODS OF SCREENING FOR REFERRAL

Teacher Judgment. The first step in the investigation was to find which pupils the teachers considered mentally gifted. This was accomplished by circulating a simple inquiry form which read as follows:

We are in process of identifying mentally gifted children at the junior high school level. We feel that teachers have recognized most of these children in their classes. It would be helpful to have a basic and general list that we can share and use in program planning. Will you please, therefore, use the attached form to name the children you consider mentally gifted in your home room and in any of your classes. Make a statement for each child as to why you judge the child to be mentally gifted.

The form referred to in the directions simply provided blanks for the child's name, grade, and room, as well as space for any statement the teacher wished to make. No definition was given; each teacher was free to interpret the term "gifted" in his own way. No limitation was placed on the teachers' access to records on the children. Except that the teachers had been informed in a general faculty meeting that their help would be enlisted in finding all the gifted children in the schools, no further orientation was furnished. The forms returned by the teachers contained 154 different names.

Honor Roll Listing. A second step was to collect the names of children on the Honor Rolls for the different grades in the junior high school. An all-subject average of "B" or higher on an "A-B-C-D-E" scale of relative excellence of achievement was necessary for placement on the honor roll. The letter-grades used in arriving at the average were assigned by the teachers, and each teacher was free to use his own judgment in determining the child's letter-grade. At the close of the report period from which this list of names was taken, the 39 teachers involved had placed 371 children on the honor roll.

Creative Ability in Art or Music. A third step in the investigation was aimed at locating mentally gifted children who might be displaying creative ability through art or music. The art and music teachers were asked to consider their students in terms of creativity and talent, and to submit the names of outstanding children. Teachers of vocal music, instrumental music, and arts contributed to a list of 137 children, 71 from music and 66 from art.

Student Council Membership. Social and political leadership might prove a special field of achievement for children who show mental giftedness in few or no other ways. It was felt that students selected in each home room to represent their peers in the Student Council would be classifiable as social and political leaders. A review of records on this point yielded 82 names.

Superiority in Mathematics. Because mathematical skill is considered closely associated with mental giftedness, a fifth screening method was used. Arithmetic teachers were asked to name children who were outstanding. This was done about a month subsequent to the time all teachers were asked for the more general referrals. Again, there were no limitations placed on the teachers with respect to what information they might use in making their selections. The arithmetic teachers suggested 179 children's names.

Group Intelligence Test Results. The investigation then turned to two somewhat more objective screening procedures which depended less upon professional judgment of teachers. These were group intelligence test scores and group achievement test scores.

The sixth step, then, was the review of cumulative records and the listing of children with group test intelligence quotients of 115 or higher. In the Pittsburgh school system the Otis Quick-Scoring Mental Ability Test, Beta Form, is administered at the end of the sixth grade and again at the end of the eighth grade. Scores were available on all the children at the school. The latest results were used. An IQ of 115 was chosen as the cut-off point for referrals for individual examination. This screening procedure produced 450 children with Otis IQ's 115 or higher.

Group Achievement Test Results. The final screening procedure used the results of standardized achievement tests. Metropolitan Achievement Tests are administered at the close of each school year in Pittsburgh. The latest scores available were used. Sub-test scores in two basic skill subjects, reading and arithmetic, were averaged. A list was compiled of the children with average scores at least three grade levels above grade placement. (Since the ceiling of the Metropolitan was 11th grade, the ninth graders who scored at the test ceiling were included.) This list contained 334 names.

PROCEDURE

When the lists from all of the seven screening methods were combined and analyzed, 781 different names appeared (394 boys and 387 girls). More than half of the total population of the junior high school grades (1400) had been recommended, by one or more screening method, for referral for individual examination to determine if they were actually mentally gifted.

At this point, the counselor and the vice-principal of the junior high school were asked to list the names of all children known to them to be emotionally or socially maladjusted and who might also be mentally gifted. When the names of those children were checked against the master list of 781, it was found that all had been included through some other screening procedure.

After the necessary individual psychological examinations were completed, the Stanford-Binet Intelligence Quotients of the 781 children were tabulated. The effectiveness and efficiency of the various screening procedures can be evaluated by reference to the material in Table 1, Effectiveness and Efficiency of Screening Procedures.

Effectiveness of a screening procedure is defined by the percentage of gifted children it locates. A screening procedure which includes all the gifted children among those it selects for referral to a psychologist is 100 percent effective. If it allows half of the gifted children to slip through its net and fails to refer them to the psychologist, it is 50 percent effective.

Efficiency of a screening procedure is defined by the ratio between the total number of children it refers for individual examination and the number of gifted children found among those referred. If the screening procedure refers 10 children and nine of them are found, upon individual examination, to be gifted, its efficiency is 90 percent.

The best screening method is one which combines high effectiveness and high efficiency, for that would result in most of the gifted being found with a minimum amount of wasted motion. Of course, if the main objective is to find as many of the mentally gifted children as possible, it may be necessary to use a highly effective screening method with less importance being placed on its efficiency.

TABLE 1. Effectiveness and Efficiency of Screening Procedures

SCREENING METHODS	No. Selected by Screening Method	No. Identified as Gifted by Stanford-Binet IQ	Effectiveness (Percent of Gifted Located; Total Gifted N = 91)	Efficiency (Ratio of No. Selected by Screening to No. Identified as Gifted, in Percent)
Teacher judgment	154	41	45.1	26.6
Honor roll	371	67	73.6	18.0
Creativity	137	14	15.5	10.2
Art ability	(66)	(6)	6.6	9.1
Music ability	(71)	(8)	9.9	11.2
Student Council	82	13	14.3	15.8
Mathematics achievement	179	50	56.0	27.9
Group intelligence tests				
Cut-off IQ 115	450	84	92.3	18.7
Cut-off IQ 120	(240)	(65)	71.4	27.1
Cut-off IQ 125	(105)	(40)	43.9	38.1
Cut-off IQ 130	(36)	(20)	21.9	55.5
Group achievement tests	335	72	79.2	21.5
TOTAL	781			

RESULTS

Of the 781 children selected by screening methods, 91 had Stanford-Binet IQ's of 136 or higher. To find 6.5 percent of the population of a junior high school with Stanford-Binet IQ's of 136 or above is quite unusual. However, the school was selected in part because other information had suggested that an extraordinarily large number of gifted children attended. While individual psychological examinations on the other 619 students might have uncovered more children who would rank among the most intelligent one percent of the population, it is doubtful if many were missed. Since the findings are to be interpreted largely in relative terms, it was not essential that every gifted child be located.

Some of the questions which prompted this investigation can now be answered in quantitative terms.

1. Teachers do not locate gifted children effectively or efficiently enough to place much reliance on them for screening. The category *Teacher Judgment* in Table 1 indicates that only 45.1 percent of the gifted children actually present were included in the teachers' lists. Not only were more than half of the gifted missing, but a breakdown of those children referred as gifted by the teachers revealed that almost a third (31.4 percent) of those chosen by the teachers were *not in the gifted or superior* range but in the *average* intelligence range on the Binet.

2. Almost three-fourths (73.6 percent) of the 91 gifted children were on the Honor Roll. However 304 other children were rated Honor Roll status; therefore, the Honor Roll is among the less efficient screening methods.

3. Some gifted children do display unusual interest and achievement in music or art. However, these same children are noteworthy in other aspects of school work, too. All of the 14 gifted children among the 137 called outstanding in music or art were also screened for referral in at least two other ways.

4. The Student Council membership list contained no gifted children who were not among those already included by the group intelligence test screening. All of the gifted children on Student Council appeared on at least two other lists, also.

5. When mathematics achievement alone was the criterion used by teachers, the gifted children did not fare well. Almost half of them were overlooked, and for every mentally gifted child referred, more than two who were not mentally gifted were on the referral list.

6. Group intelligence tests like the one used in this study cannot be relied upon in the identification of gifted children in the junior high school grades. Reference to Table 1 indicates, when a cut-off point of IQ 130 is used that the group test located only 21.9 percent of the gifted children. Almost four out of five were missed. Even if the cut-off point of IQ 125 were used, more than half of the gifted children would be missed. The important point seems to be that the group test does not discriminate well between

children who are a little above and those who are a great deal above average in learning capacity. The group intelligence test does seem to possess the best combination of efficiency and effectiveness as a screen. Using IQ 115 as the cut-off point a little better than nine out of 10 of the gifted will be found among the group so chosen when they are examined by a psychologist.

7. Group achievement test scores run a fairly close second to group intelligence test scores in combined efficiency and effectiveness when used as they were in this situation.

8. Three gifted children were found who apparently did not make favorable showings in either group tests of intelligence or group achievement tests. One of these was located through the Honor Roll, and the other two were overlooked by all the screening procedures. The latter two were found because their cumulative records indicated that they had been examined by a school psychologist in the elementary grades and proved to be gifted.

9. By combining the group intelligence test list and the group achievement test list into one screening procedure, 88 of the 91 gifted children, or 96.7 percent of them, were found. Taken together the two group tests resulted in the most effective screening procedure.

10. This investigation did not set out to obtain detailed information on under-achievement among gifted children. However, analysis of the records of the 91 children with Binet IQ's 136 or higher showed six of them appearing on no list other than that of children with Otis IQ's 115 or higher. In addition, four others were on neither the Honor Roll or the list of children with achievement test scores three years above grade placement. There is good reason to think, therefore, that 10 of the 92 gifted children might be under-achievers. The implication is strong that perhaps more than one out of 10 gifted children (10.8 percent in this study) is achieving markedly below an optimum level. Certainly the screening based on group intelligence test scores is helpful in locating gifted children who are not showing their potentialities either in letter-grades given by teachers or on group achievement tests.

SUMMARY

A major concern of our educational system is the identification and education of mentally gifted children. With reasonable certainty the identification of intellectually gifted students is now possible in the junior high school years through the use of individual intelligence tests administered by school psychologists. This identification procedure, though quite accurate, is both expensive and time consuming. Effective and efficient screening methods are necessary for choosing the children to be referred to the psychologist. Effective and efficient screening methods are those which make possible the identification of all the gifted children in a school while minimizing the total number of children who must be examined individually by the psychologist.

Seven kinds of screening procedures are considered. The use of group intelligence test results for screening is found to have advantages over other methods both in effectiveness and efficiency; they are of little value, however, for actual identification. The latter should be left to psychologists employing individual examination methods if measures of intelligence are to be the criteria used.

REFERENCES

1. Educational Policies Commission, *Education of the Gifted*. Washington, D.C.: National Education Association, 1950.
2. Hollingworth, Leta S., *Gifted Children, Their Nature and Nurture*. New York: The Macmillan Company, 1927.
3. Pegnato, Carl, *An Evaluation of Various Initial Methods of Selecting Intellectually Gifted Children at the Junior High School Level*. Doctoral Thesis, Pennsylvania State College, 1958.
4. Terman, Lewis M., and others, *Genetic Studies of Genius, Volumes I-II-III-IV*. Stanford, California: Stanford University Press, 1925 through 1947.

Are There Tops in Our Cages?

E. PAUL TORRANCE

The dropout problem in high school and college has always been a serious one. In recent years it has become even more serious. A substantial percentage of all children in the United States drop out of high school before graduation. Many talented young people choose not to enter college. Those of you who have talked with these youngsters frankly know that many of them feel that "they are in a cage," that they "are trapped" as long as they remain in the educational situation. They see dropping out as the only way of escaping from this "trap" or "cage."

There is indeed an urgent need to appraise and discover how we can utilize better our educational resources. I am sure that your professional training and experience have given you many tested procedures for "appraising and utilizing educational resources." I would like to suggest that we approach this problem by thinking how we can appraise and utilize our *creative* resources.

WHO ARE THE CREATIVE PEOPLE?

These are people able to produce a large number of ideas, exhibit a high degree of flexibility in their responses, produce ideas that are un-

Reprinted from *American Vocational Journal*, Vol. 38, No. 3 (March, 1963), pp. 20-22. By permission of the author and publisher.

usual or off-the-beaten-track, or are able to develop these ideas in detail. We call these qualities fluency, flexibility, originality and elaboration.

We believe that they are capable of a high degree of creative achievement. Although many of these individuals feel they are in cages, and frequently their parents, teachers, and counselors feel they are in cages, I am convinced that almost always there are "tops in these cages."

IS IDENTIFICATION NECESSARY?

Many argue that it is unnecessary and unfruitful to attempt to identify creative talent. They contend that if one possesses a real spark of creativity, it will somehow flourish and manifest itself miraculously despite neglect and repressive or coercive forces which inhibit it. They maintain that creative persons have always met opposition, ridicule and scorn, and that they always will.

I believe this is a dangerous fallacy. We see children in the process of sacrificing needlessly what promised to be great creative talents. It is true that some of them will sacrifice their creativity only for a time and will regain it, when they learn better how to cope with coercive pressures.

The truly creative person, some say, may be the first to give in but the last to give up. I am afraid however, that some never regain the creativity they showed so richly in the 3rd grade. Instead, they choose a life of unrealized possibilities.

Others have contended that the best way to identify individuals who will make creative contributions is by tests of intelligence or scholastic aptitude. Still others would identify them on the basis of teachers' grades or measures of scholastic achievement of the individual.

I believe that the history of creative achievement proves all of these arguments to be false—or at best to have serious weaknesses. I also would argue that under existing conditions there is even a conflict between scholarly achievement, as usually defined and measured, and creative achievement. Throughout history there have been outstanding creative and inventive people whose scholastic performance has been poor.

Some have objected, "Measures of I.Q. or scholastic aptitude also identify creative individuals. Measures of creativity and measures of I.Q. are inseparable and measure the same thing." This contention is simply not true. For 70 years, investigators have consistently found little or no correlation between these two types of measures.

Abilities measured by tests of intelligence and scholastic aptitude emphasize logical reasoning, memory and convergence. Tests of creative thinking emphasize divergent kinds of thinking—ideational fluency, flexibility, originality, and elaboration, sensitivity to defects and missing elements, and ability to redefine and restructure.

Traditional measures of intelligence emphasize conformity and getting the "correct" answer. Measures of creative thinking abilities call for the unconventional response, breaking away from the beaten, safe pathway. The type of response required is also different, especially from the group forms of intelligence tests in the multiple-choice format.

Creative individuals can be identified without tests. Most teachers, however, have to redefine their concepts and values before they can do this successfully. I recently asked two teachers of gifted 6th graders to name the five most and the five least creative children in their classrooms. To help them in this redefinition process, we used Wallace and Ethel Maw's (1961) criteria of curiosity.

Both teachers said they had never before thought of their pupils in this way and admitted they were forced to place in the low group some children whom they valued most as pupils because they were so good in arithmetic computation, spelling, etc. Quite interestingly, we obtained excellent differentiations on all of our measures of creativity between the two groups of children nominated as most and least curious.

WHY CAN'T CREATIVE PERSONS
SEE THE TOPS IN THEIR CAGES?

We know that one of the marks of the creative person is his ability to see where others cannot see. Why is he unable to see his way out of some of the predicaments in which he finds himself? Most of the successful ones can.

Even some of our dropouts might be credited with seeing the tops of their cages. They are willing to take their chances without the benefit of diplomas. They are so absorbed in developing some idea and believe so strongly in this idea that they are willing to take their chances. The trouble is that many of them become bogged down later on and are unable to achieve their potentialities.

DOES THE CURRICULUM PROVIDE
FOR CREATIVE ACHIEVEMENT?

Even though there are many tops in their cages which creative individuals do not use, I think we ought to accept responsibility for creating more tops by providing a curriculum which gives opportunities for creative kinds of achievement and for learning through creative ways. In other words, create more tops in the cages.

There are many ways in which this can be done. It can be done by making assignments which call for this kind of performance. It can be done by the kinds of questions we ask in class or by the kinds of problems which we set for class discussion.

In a recent study in Wisconsin, arrangements were made for one pupil each day to record all of the questions asked by the teacher in junior high school social studies classes. When these questions were analyzed over a period of time for several teachers and classes, it was found that 90 per cent of the questions called only for recall. Few questions called for thinking of any kind—creative thinking, critical thinking, convergent thinking, evaluative thinking, etc.

Although the situation may not be this bad in your class, there probably is room for improvement in asking questions, using problems and materials which require creative problem-solving and making other changes in the curriculum which supply more tops for your creativity students.

DO WE REWARD CREATIVITY?

There are, as I see it, two major obstacles to valuing creative thinking. The first is the difficulty of recognizing and appreciating the student's creative productions. It is hard for a conventional teacher to see and appreciate the contribution of an unconventional or an unloved and unlovely student.

Despite average differences in I.Q. as high as 26 points, we have found that highly creative but less intelligent students achieve as well as the highly intelligent but less creative ones. Teachers, however, rate the highly intelligent ones as more desirable students, more ambitious and hard-working, less unruly, and more friendly. Teachers also say that they know and understand the highly intelligent pupils better than the highly creative ones.

A second obstacle to valuing creativity is our tendency to overrate the finished product—the completed poem, the masterpiece of music or art, or in home economics, the well-dressed person or smoothly running household. We are too easily deceived by the comparative perfection and smoothness of these masterpieces and evaluate them as if they were the immediate deliveries of a creative act.

We reward or punish creative behavior, as the case may be, in many ways other than by the way we grade. (I should add, however, that I think our testing and evaluation procedures should be revised to include the evaluation of creative kinds of achievement.) I would like to offer five simple, but rather powerful suggestions, I believe, for rewarding creative behavior.

1. Be respectful of the student's unusual questions.
2. Be respectful of the unusual ideas of students.
3. Show students that their ideas have value.
4. Provide opportunities for self-initiated learning and give credit for it.
5. Provide for periods of non-evaluated practice or discovery.

MAKE CREATIVE STUDENTS FEEL
YOU ARE ON THEIR SIDE

I would like to leave you one more idea capable of transforming your relationships with creative students: the necessity for making creative individuals feel confident that you are on their side. This is always important in helping people find the tops in their cages. In fashioning your relationship to the highly creative student, I would like to suggest seven ways in which you can play this important role for such persons:

1. Provide a model of creative behavior. Perhaps one of the most fundamental roles any adult can play in helping creative individuals is to provide a model of creative behavior in whatever ways is appropriate to him. This does not mean that he must possess outstanding abilities in art, music, writing, science or invention.

It is far more important that he maintain his curiosity, his openness and aliveness, his excitement in learning and thinking, his courage, and independence in thinking. If he does this, he will provide a model whereby others will learn how to behave in creative ways.

2. Provide a "refuge." We know that highly creative adolescents are often estranged from their teachers and peers. Thus, the highly creative person needs encouragement. The adult must recognize, however, that the estrangement exists and that he will have to create a relationship in which creative individuals feel safe.

3. Be a sponsor or patron. Someone has observed that almost always wherever independence and creativity occur and persist, there is some individual or agent who plays the role of sponsor or patron. This role is played by someone who is not a member of the peer group, but who possesses prestige and power in the same social system.

He does several things. Regardless of his own views, the sponsor encourages and supports the other in expressing and testing his ideas and in thinking through things for himself. He protects the individual from reactions of his peers long enough for him to try out some of his ideas and modify them. He can keep the structure of the situation open enough so that originality can occur.

4. Help him understand his divergence. A high degree of sensitivity, a capacity to be disturbed, and divergent thinking are essentials of the creative personality. Frequently, creative young people are puzzled by their own behavior. They desperately need to understand themselves, particularly their divergence, the ways in which they are different from others. There are crucial times in the lives of creative persons when being understood is all that is needed to help them cope with the crisis and maintain their creativity.

5. *Let him communicate his ideas.* The highly creative person has an unusually strong urge to explore and to create. When he thinks up ideas, or tests them and modifies them he has an unusually strong desire to communicate his ideas and tell others what he has discovered.

Yet both peers and teachers named some of the most creative pupils in our studies as ones who do not speak out their ideas. When we see what happens when they do speak out their ideas, there is little wonder they are reluctant to communicate their ideas. Frequently, their ideas are so far ahead of those of their classmates and even their teachers that they have given up hopes of communicating.

6. *See that his creative talent is recognized.* Information from many sources indicates that much creative talent goes unrecognized. In our own studies at all educational levels, about 70 per cent of those in the upper 20 per cent on tests of creative thinking would be eliminated if only an intelligence or scholastic aptitude test had been used.

Frequently, the top can be lifted from a highly creative individual's cage by having someone call attention to his talent at the opportune time and finding someone who can create the proper kind of opportunity for the utilization of his talent. Such talent may be overlooked, if judgments are made only on the basis of course grades.

7. *Help parents understand the creative student.* When teachers or parents fail to understand highly creative individuals, refusal to learn or withdrawal may be a consequence. In some cases, the quiet and unobtrusive intervention of a responsible person offers about the only possibility whereby teachers and parents may come to understand them and thus salvage outstanding talent.

5 | NON-INTELLECTUAL FACTORS AND GIFTEDNESS

Cognitive, Conative, and Non-Intellective Intelligence

DAVID WECHSLER

It is always a good omen for science when different men in different places make independent discoveries or arrive at similar conclusions. In the last two decades psychologists in their efforts to define the nature of general intelligence seem to have arrived at the threshold of such a situation. In this paper I wish to present to you what appears to me to be the germ of the impending re-orientation: it is this, that general intelligence cannot be equated with intellectual ability however broadly defined, but must be regarded as a manifestation of the personality as a whole.

From an historical point of view, the first one to argue against the identification of general intelligence with intellectual ability was Henri Bergson. Already in his *"Donees Immediate de la Conscience,"* and more emphatically in his *"Evolution Creatrice,"* he pointed out the insufficiencies of the human intellect or, what was for him the same, normative logic, in dealing effectively with man's total environment.

I shall not here restate Bergson's arguments nor his attempted solution of endowing the human mind with a new faculty, creative intuition, and its generating force, the "elan vital." I wish only to call your attention to the fact that in our attempts at measuring intelligence we have persisted in treating intelligence as if it consisted exclusively of intellectual elements or factors. What, in fact, are these intellectual elements which we have continued to use and to posit in appraising intelligence? They are abstract reasoning, verbal, spatial, numerical, and a few other specified factors, all of which in some particularized manner deal with man's cognitive ability. Shades of Bergson, are we confirming his claim that

Reprinted from *American Psychologist,* Vol. 5, No. 3 (March, 1950), pp. 78-83. By permission of the author and the American Psychological Association.

human intelligence, as the psychologist conceives it, can only deal with geometric and logical symbols?

Now, the remarkable thing is that while this is what we are saying in our tests of intelligence, most of us don't believe it. What is more important, it isn't true! Our contemporary definitions of intelligence assert as much: intelligence according to these is not only the ability to learn, to abstract, to profit from experience, but also to adjust and to achieve. Everyone with clinical experience knows that the latter involve other capacities besides eductive, verbal, numerical, spatial, and the other intellective factors that have been demonstrated. Yes, but what are they? The answer is: they are *not* intellective. They are capacities and traits dependent upon temperament and personality which are not restricted to logical and abstract perception: they are, in my opinion, factors of personality itself. It is this point of view, independently sensed or suggested, at times only tangentially, by a number of investigators including Goldstein, Alexander, Wechsler, and more recently by Halstead and Eysenck, which I presented six years ago for the first time under the term *"Non-intellective Factors of Intelligence."* I wish now to present to you more fully the evidence in its support and to justify what appears to be not only the need for a re-orientation in our concept of general intelligence, but of a new psychometric that will, in fact, measure what is purported in our definition of intelligence.

Let me begin by restating the issue in terms of the actual psychometric problem. The crux of this problem, as we have already noted, is the discrepancy between what the clinical psychologist does and what he says he does in clinical practice. If we examine any of the current psychological tests of intelligence, we shall find them to consist of sample tasks measuring, by definition, a variety of mental abilities. One would imagine that any summary of the results obtained with such tests would be essentially a report of the degree to which an individual possesses these abilities and the manner in which they vary. However, it will be found that once a summative score is obtained from them, whether in terms of MA, IQ, or whatnot, the clinical psychologist proceeds to enlarge his summary to include not only specific psychologic interpretations but broad social and biological implications as well.

An IQ is thus used, not only to determine comparative mental endowment, capacity to learn, presence of special abilities and disabilities, and evaluation of degree of mental deficiency, but also as a basis for school placement, for vocational guidance, for psychiatric diagnosis, and for the prediction of adjustment potentials in a variety of situations from infancy to old age, including such areas as child adoption, juvenile delinquency, fitness for military service, college success, and old age counseling.

Assuming that intelligence tests may be used in all these situations, and within limits I believe they may, the question arises how this is possible under the concept that general intelligence is a matter of a single basic or even a combination of a number of intellectual abilities. It is this question which I shall try to answer this evening. But I must first call your attention to the fact you are all aware of, that this is not the usual criticism of intelligence tests. The historic and continued objection to intelligence tests is not that they measure too much, but that they do not measure enough, or at least, not well enough.

You are all acquainted with the arguments against intelligence tests, and I shall not repeat them; the damaging criticism pertains, not as is generally emphasized, to the question of reliability, but to one of basic validity. Even such studies as those of Wellman, Goldfarb and others, showing changes in IQ produced by a variety of social and environmental factors, though relevant, are not crucial. The crucial instances are those where individuals obtain identical IQs (say an IQ of 65) but, on overall appraisal, must nevertheless be rated differently, say, one as a defective and the other as not defective. Such instances are not necessarily common, but neither are they rare exceptions. Here is a situation which needs explaining and cannot be by-passed.

The first to attack this problem was E. L. Thorndike. His answer, as always characteristic of his approach, was straightforward and to the point. Our tests measure intelligence to be sure, he said, but there is not just one unique, but several different kinds of intelligence, namely, abstract, social and practical. The first is manifested by the individual's ablity to work with symbols, the second by his ability to deal with people, and the third by his ability to manipulate objects. Thorndike, himself, seems to have been primarily interested in the first kind of intelligence and, having made the above trichotomy, and along with it the distinction between tests which measure breadth, as against those which measure altitude, left the working out of these concepts to others. But relatively little has been done to verify or refute the hypothesis.

In the 1920's Moss published a test of social intelligence which consisted essentially of items involving memory and recognition of names and faces, and a series of multiple-choice questions involving social situations, in which the correct answer seemed to have been based on the notion that "the customer is always right." Although Moss's test for a time had some vogue among business firms, clinical psychologists, as far as I have been able to discover, seldom if ever make use of it.

The other important effort at producing a test of social intelligence is Doll's Vineland Social Maturity Scale. This Scale, as you know, consists of a series of questions listing a variety of social acquisitions, that is, of approved and useful acts and achievements, which a child may be expected to have learned from infancy to adolescence. The Scale is hardly a test in the ordinary sense of the term, since it involves no test performance or response by the subject, and can be completed, as it usually is, by other persons. But it does correlate fairly well with other tests of intelligence and has been shown by Doll and others to correlate positively and significantly with a number of practical criteria of social adjustment.

Clinical psychologists appear to have accepted performance tests, almost from the start, as a measure of practical intelligence. Only they seem to have regarded practical intelligence, as measured by these tests, as a kind of special aptitude rather than as a kind of intelligence. For many years the situation in clinical practice was something like this: a child would be given routinely a Binet test. Then, if his Binet MA did not seem to do justice to him, he would be given a Pintner-Paterson or similar performance battery as a supplementary test. But the child's score on the performance test, except in instances of language handicaps, would seldom be integrated with, or serve to alter, his Binet intelligence rating. Instead, it would usually be used as evidence of a compensatory useful special ability. Thus, if a child attained an IQ of 85 on the Binet, and one of 110 on the Pintner-Paterson, the reporting psychologist would ordinarily give the rating as "dull normal" intelligence with good practical or manipulative ability. It was not until the publication of the Bellevue Scales that any consistent attempt was made to integrate performance and verbal tests into a single measure of intelligence. The Bellevue tests have had increasingly wider use, but I regret to report that their popularity seems to derive, not from the fact that they make possible a single global rating, but because they enable the examiner to obtain separate verbal and performance IQs with one test.

The Aristotelian hierarchical white-collar concept of intelligence dies hard. This, in spite of the fact, that performance tests often can and do contain a larger amount of *g* than do the verbal tests. Thus, in his differential study of *"Abstract and Concrete Intelligence,"* W. P. Alexander, after correcting for communality, specific factors, and chance errors of measurement, found the theoretical *g* loadings for verbal and practical ability to be .60 and .81, respectively. Alexander concludes that "a perfect performance battery would be a better measure of *g* than a perfect verbal battery."

This and other findings by Alexander bring me to what constitutes the most compelling evidence for the reorientation in our concept of intelligence mentioned at the onset of this paper. I refer to the findings contributed by factor analysis. Here two important names appear on the horizon: Carl Spearman and L. L. Thurstone. I believe that the answers which they have given to the problem of the nature of general intelligence are incorrect. But I am sure that without the inspiration and without the tools which they furnished us, the solution of the problem would be altogether impossible.

Such a statement before a gathering of clinical psychologists may be unorthodox, because to many, factor analysis is almost anathema. But I can assure you, on the authority of expert consultants, that the mathematics of factor analysis is quite elementary, and on the basis of my own experience with it, extremely practical; and, with due apologies to Freud, even "sexy." For with what, in effect, does factor analysis concern itself, but with the bedfellowship of psychometric tests. For, mind you, it embraces matrices, correlational to be sure, and then tells you what test stays close to what other tests when axes are rotated. Now that, I submit, is what clinical psychologists want to know: what test, what factor, or, if you will, what function or what trait goes with what other factor, or function, or trait. And when the findings are examined, some very interesting and unsuspected relationships come to light. For example, some tests of intelligence, like some human beings, are extremely promiscuous. Thus, vocabulary, the paragon of verbal tests, correlates very frequently, and to a considerable measure, with Block Designs, the perfect example of a performance test. But to return to a more serious vein, the importance of factor analysis is, of course, that it enables us to discover what our tests measure and the extent to which they measure the things they purport.

What are the elements which factor analysis has shown our intelligence tests to measure? The first is abstract reasoning. This is Spearman's g of eduction. Spearman argued that g was the only independent factor, and while he hesitated to identify g with general intelligence, his actual applications are tantamount to it. In equating g with general intelligence Spearman was in error, not because the tetrad equation is incorrect but because in point of fact, it is not satisfied as he claimed. Spearman's answer to this finding was that we can not expect the tetrad equation to be satisfied by all the tests of general intelligence but only by "good" tests of intelligence, like analogies and mathematical reasoning which require eduction. But of course, if you select your tests, you can choose them so highly saturated with a single factor that the residuals vanish. This is all that the tetrad equation says, and it was the perceptive insight of Thurstone which recognized the tetrad equation for what it was, namely, a mathematically special case of a more general solution of the factorial problem. What was needed was a statistical analysis which would permit the emergence of other factors when present. By the use of his expanded technique, it has now been shown that intelligence tests, such as they are, contain not one but several independent factors. Some five or six have been definitely identified; they are, to repeat, induction, verbal, spatial, numerical, and one or two other factors. Notice, however, that these factors, like Spearman's eduction, are all cognitive.

At this point it is important to bear in mind what a factor stands for in factor analysis. Basically, it is an identifiable independent variable which accounts for a certain portion of the total test variance in a correlational matrix. The amount of variance it accounts for in any given test is called the test's factor loading. In a perfectly factorialized correlation matrix, the sum of the factorial loadings of the extracted factors should be 100 per cent, that is, account for the total test variance.

Now, it is a remarkable finding that when matrices of intelligence tests are factored, the amount of variance accounted for is seldom more than 60 per cent of the total, and, what is perhaps of equal significance, the greater the number of different tests included, the smaller, generally, the total per cent of variance accounted for; and this is seemingly independent of the number of factors extracted. In the case of our present intelligence test batteries, factors beyond the first 3 or 4 usually contribute so little to the already accounted-for variance that it is generally not profitable to extract them. It is the observation of this important finding that in the factorialization of batteries of intelligence tests, there always remained a considerable per cent of unaccounted-for variance, which began to arouse my interest some years ago. It seemed to hold the key to our problem.

If after successive attempts at factoring out all the components of intelligence, there always remained a large residue of these unknown elements, the obvious inference to be made was that our intelligence tests measured other things than those accounted for by the extracted factors. The second inference was that those other factors were numerous and occurred in relatively small amounts, because it was impossible to extract single additional factors which would account for any considerable portion of the residual variance. I assumed that the principal reason for this was that the test batteries usually factored did not include tests which contained sufficient amounts of these other factors, to enable some of the remaining tests to cluster about them. Provisionally I called these residual components the non-intellective factors of intelligence. But in terms of more recent findings, I believe they can be more justly designated as the personality components of general intelligence, which in fact they are.

The evidence for this conclusion comes from a number of sources. As early as 1913, Webb (8), in factoring a battery of tests, along with a number of ratings which attempted to appraise traits of character, was able to extract a factor "W." "W" in a broad sense seemed to relate to a moral and conative propensity, which he called conscientiousness or purposeful consistency. A few years later, in Spearman's own laboratory, Lankes and Wynn Jones (7) demonstrated the existence of another non-intellective factor, "p," or perseveration, which characterized their subjects' tendency to resist changes in set, and which Spearman related to his law of inertia. In 1921, W. M. Brown (2) discussed character traits as factors in intelligence tests, and in 1933, R. B. Cattell (3) reported correlations between tests of temperament and ratings in intelligence. But perhaps the most crucial findings are those of W. P. Alexander (1) who, in an extensive factor analysis of a large series of verbal and performance tests, supplemented by tests of achievement and academic marks, showed that in addition to the now familiar g, V (verbal ability), and P (practical ability), a considerable portion of variance had to be ascribed to two other extracted factors, namely, X and Z. X was a factor which determined the individual's interests and "concerns," in Alexander's words, "temperament rather than ability"; while Z was "an aspect of temperament related to achievement," in the case of Alexander's subjects, to school achievement.

The factor loadings of X and Z varied greatly from test to test, but even some of Spearman's ostensibly pure tests of g contained some Z and nearly all the performance tests showed considerable X or Z loadings. As might be expected, these factors played an even greater role in academic or technical achievement. For success in science, for example, the X factor loading was .74, as against only .36 for g, and for English .48 as against .43 for the g loading. From these findings one might even infer that lack of intellectual ability, beyond a certain point, accounts for relatively little of school failures. Indeed Dorothea McCarthy (6) recently offered the "hypothesis," and I quote, "that emotional insecurity . . . is the basic cause of most educational disabilities and learning failures, which are not due to mental defect."

What are we to make of these two findings? First, that factors other than intellectual contribute to achievement in areas where, as in the case of learning, intellectual factors have until recently been considered uniquely determinate, and, second, that these other factors have to do with functions and abilities hitherto considered traits of personality. Among those partially identified so far are factors relating primarily to the conative functions like drive, persistence, will, and perseveration, or in some instances, to aspects of temperament that pertain to interests and achievement. This, to be sure, is just the beginning, but one of the reasons that not much more has been done is that psychologists have continued to assume that personality has little to do with intelligence. To Thurstone as well as to Spearman, general intelligence seems to be first and foremost a cognitive function, by Spearman to be accounted for by a single pervasive factor, by Thurstone by a number of factors.

It is curious that the clinical psychologist, so little impressed by or, at least, so little conversant with factor analysis, has almost from the start dealt with intelligence test findings as if the personality components in intelligence were already an established fact. For what does psychological diagnosis on the basis of intelligence test findings consist of but inferring adjustive capacities of the subject as a persona? It appears that the clinician, like the character in Moliere's *"Malade Imaginaire,"* has been speaking prose all his life without knowing it.

One might add that diagnosing personality and personality disorder, at the level it is being done, is not very difficult. Practically every good individual test of intelligence lends itself to such application to a greater or lesser degree, the Bellevue Scales and the new Children's Test of Intelligence perhaps a little more readily. This does not mean that they are tests of personality, but they do suggest that our intelligence tests contain elements which are essentially factors of the personality as a whole rather than of specific cognitive abilities. When the neurotic does poorly on the Digit Span Test, it is not because of defective memory, but generally because of a basic anxiety mobilized by the test, as by any other situation, in which he is seemingly on trial. Conversely, when a mental defective does relatively well on the Maze Test, it is generally not because he has better planning ability, but because he is less impulsive. Similarly, a large variety of traits and personality factors may be inferred from test performance—for example, energy level from a subject's performance on the Digit Symbol, asocial tendencies from general comprehension, masculinity-femininity from the picture completion test. These are only a few of the traits and diagnostic constellations with which every clinician who has done psychological diagnosis is familiar.

The point here is not that personality traits can be discovered in psychometric performance, or, what needs no special argument, that personality and abnormal conditions influence intelligence test findings, but that personality traits *enter into* the effectiveness of intelligent behavior, and, hence, into any global concept of intelligence itself. It is one thing if a child does poorly on an intelligence test because he is disinterested or upset and quite another if he is congenitively impulsive or emotionally unstable.

One would naturally suppose that if intelligence is a function of the personality as a whole, one should find significant positive or negative correlations with measures of personality itself. Such, indeed, are the findings, but the results are extremely hard to evaluate. This is in part due to the fact that the studies in this area have been done primarily with the intent of discovering the extent to which intelligence accounts for variance in personality. In an article which appeared in 1940, Irving Lorge reviews the studies published to that date on the general relationship between measures of intelligence and various measures or estimates of personality. The personality tests included most of the current and older inventories (Woodworth, Laird, Thurstone, Bernreuter, Allport, et al.), as well as the association experiment and the personality measures of Hartshorn, May, and Maller. Some 200 correlation coefficients were analyzed. The range of coefficients was from +.70 to —.49 with a median of +.04. Disregarding the signs, half of the ratios were between .00 and .15, and one quarter of them .30 and above. Lorge's general feeling about the findings is that the range is so "extraordinary that anybody can make any statement." Nevertheless, his conclusion is "that some correlation between intelligence and personality exists" (5).

All this is rather meager fare, but the findings are perhaps as satisfactory as could be expected. Apart from the known unreliability of paper-and-pencil inventories, there is the more disturbing fact of their uncertain validity and relevance. At times they do not measure the traits claimed for them, at others they measure only small segments of the personality, although in different ways; and at still other times, traits which are purely nominal. The latter, for example, was shown by Flanagan (4) to be the case with the Bernreuter Inventory dichotomies. In the original publication the test was scored for six different traits, which by factorization were then reduced to two.

Flanagan's study is a good example of how factor analysis aids us in getting at basic components. Mere evidence of concomitant variation is not enough; in fact, it is often misleading. For example, defective hearing may have a measurable effect on both learning arithmetic and size of vocabulary, but, obviously, has no basic relation to either arithmetical reasoning or verbal ability. A variable to be basic and scientifically significant must be independent. In the case of man's cognitive functions, these independent variables, in so far as they are relevant to general intelligence, have been pretty well identified. It may be possible to add one or two to Thurstone's list, but not many more. Those of personality are yet to be discovered. We have some knowledge of what the factors to be measured are likely to be, some on the basis of researches like those of Webb, Alexander, Guilford, Cattell, and Eysenck, others on the basis of general observation and clinical experience. The latter have thus far gone unrecognized, not only because we have no tests for them but because clinicians, like their more academic colleagues, still think of intelligence as consisting primarily of cognitive abilities. Any bit of behavior that seems concerned with or related to instinct, impulse, or temperament is ipso facto considered as having no direct relation to general intelligence.

Such, for example, is curiosity. This was one of the traits which Terman in his studies of genius found most frequently among his gifted children. But he did not have, nor do we as yet have, any test of curiosity. No attempt has been made to extract curiosity as a factor of intelligence. We all know how important curiosity is for biologic adaptation as well as scientific achievement. It is, to quote McDougall, "at the basis of many of man's most splendid achievements, for rooted in it are his speculative and scientific tendencies," and ". . . in men in whom curiosity is innately strong, it may become the main source of intellectual energy and effort." But what is curiosity? "It is the impulse to approach and examine more closely the object which attracts it," that is an instinct, and according to McDougall, one of the basic instincts.

One need not be afraid or ashamed to acknowledge impulse, instinct and temperament as basic factors in general intelligence. It is indeed because I believe they are that I have brought before you the arguments and evidence presented. My main point has been that general intelligence cannot be equated with intellectual ability, but must be regarded as a manifestation of the personality as a whole. I have tried to show that factors other than intellectual enter into our concept of general intelligence, and that in everyday practice, we make use of them knowingly or not.

What is needed is that these factors be rigorously appraised. Factor analysis has been emphasized because, at present, it is the only method which enables us to demonstrate and discover independent variables. We already have some clues as to what the non-intellective but relevant factors of intelligence may be. What we now need are tests which not only identify but measure them. This in effect demands broadening our concept of general intelligence and calls for a revised psychometric to measure these added variables as sub-tests of all general intelligence scales.

To say that general intelligence can be social and practical, as well as abstract, was just a beginning. We had to know what basic components of the mind were responsible for making an individual effective in one rather than in another area.

To realize that general intelligence is the function of the personality as a whole and is determined by emotion and conative factors is also just a beginning. We now need to know what non-intellective factors are relevant and to what degree. This is the task which lies immediately before us.

REFERENCES

1. Alexander, W. P., Intelligence, Concrete and Abstract. *Brit. J. Psychol. Monogr. Suppl.*, 1935, 6, No. 19.
2. Brown, W. M., Character Traits as Factors in Intelligence Test Performance. *Arch. Psychol.*, 1923.
3. Cattell, R. B., Temperament Tests. I. Temperament. *Brit. J. Psychol.*, 1933, 23, 308-29.
4. Flanagan, J. C., Factor Analysis in the Study of Personality. Stanford Univ. Press, 1935.
5. Lorge, I., *Intelligence: Its Nature and Nurture.* 39th Yearbook. National Society for Study of Education, 1940, Part I, 275-81.
6. McCarthy, Dorothea, Personality and Learning. Amer. Coun. Educ. Studies, 1948, Series I, No. 35.
7. Spearman, C., *The Abilities of Man.* New York: Macmillan, 1927.
8. Webb, E., Character and Intelligence. *Brit. J. Psychol. Monogr. Suppl.*, 1915, III.

Identification of the Socially Gifted

ROY K. JARECKY

There has been slow but perceptible progress towards a liberalized interpretation of the concept of giftedness. A review of the literature suggested that probably it was not until after 1940 that serious attention was given to forms of gifted behavior other than intellectual. Wesman's comment expressed what appears to be the currently accepted view of giftedness: ". . . the concept of giftedness has been broadened to include not only such areas as music and art, but areas such as mechanics and social maturity and personal relations as well. The child who displays unusual understanding of the physical forces in his world, and the child who exhibits unusual understanding and leadership of his peers, have been taking their place alongside the child who excels in performance on a test of mental ability (10, p. 4)."

Specifically, this paper summarizes a study with focus on the problem of identifying adolescent boys and girls possessed of an exceptional capacity for mature productive relationships with others—both peers and adults (5). This capacity was termed social giftedness.

IMPORTANCE OF THE SOCIALLY GIFTED

The important contribution that the socially gifted adolescent can make, especially in the area of cooperative peer endeavor, cannot be over-estimated. The young person who is highly skilled in relating to others and whose behavior is tempered by a mature social conscience acts as a sort of leavening agent among his fellows. For instance, he may help a group to integrate its efforts to achieve a common goal by forging new psychological channels of communication which in turn help group members to form more realistic and sympathetic perceptions of each other. Or he may, through a combination of warm good humor and gentle emphasis on ethical concerns, stimulate his peers to positive productive type behavior when the direction that the group behavior might take hangs in the balance. Socially gifted behavior is in fact a vital and hitherto neglected human resource.

The socially gifted person has an important function to perform in

Reprinted from *Exceptional Children,* Vol. 25, No. 8 (May, 1959), pp. 415-419. By permission of the author and publisher.

our society. His particular skills are as badly needed as those of the skilled technician and the scientist. The error that we are liable to make is to assume that somehow such skilled practitioners of human relations will always be available when needed. It should be abundantly clear that such is not the case. We can no more depend on a rich periodic harvest of socially gifted adults without special techniques of early identification and appropriate education than we can of biochemists. In all likelihood the socially gifted adolescent has benefited from a highly fortunate combination of heredity and environment. The socialization process of which he has been a part has instilled in him the psychological basis for effectiveness in interpersonal relationships. But, this potential must first be recognized and then nurtured to full maturity. Pritchard made this point with vigor and clarity:

It should go without saying that the greatest need existing today is to find those who can lead in establishing the bases and means of wise living with our fellow men. It is of utmost importance to discover at an early age patterns of behavior which will predict unusual strength in the positive factors of emotional maturity, perseverance, social insight, and drive to accomplish. We need to discover those who excel in these attributes of "social intelligence" early in childhood in order that their unique gifts may be developed to the highest potential (7, p. 82).

CHARACTERISTICS OF THE SOCIALLY GIFTED ADOLESCENT

Prior to discussing the instruments that were used in the classroom to identify socially gifted adolescents the primary characteristics of socially gifted behavior as derived from the study will be presented. The social behavior of 76 fourteen-year-old boys and girls, members of two freshman classes of a large metropolitan high school, was observed and evaluated for a period of 15 weeks. Those young people finally designated as socially gifted appeared to have the following characteristics:

1. They were generally physically attractive and neat in appearance.
2. They were clearly accepted by an overwhelming majority of the people whom they knew, peers and adults alike.
3. They were generally involved in some sort of social enterprise to which they made positive, constructive contributions.
4. They were generally looked to as arbiters or as "policy makers" in their own group.
5. They related to peers and adults on an egalitarian basis, resisting insincere, artificial or patronizing relationships.
6. They maintained no facades. Their behavior was non-defensive in character.

7. They appeared free of emotional tension; that is, they were unafraid to express themselves emotionally, but their demonstrations of emotion were always relevant.
8. They maintained enduring relationships with peers and adults. Socially gifted adolescents did not experience rapid turnovers in friendship.
9. They stimulated positive productive behavior in others.
10. They were gay young people who, in general, seemed to personify an unusual capacity for coping with any social situation. They managed to do so with a delightful mixture of intelligence, humor, and insight (5).

In short, these characteristics represent a life style peculiar to the socially gifted adolescent. These young people are to be recognized not by something specific that they can produce in the usual sense but by the extraordinary effectiveness of their social behavior.

DESIGN OF THE STUDY

In order to identify the socially gifted it was first necessary to devise a battery of differential tests of social behavior appropriate for use in a classroom situation. These instruments provided quantified assessments of the social behavior of the students and brought to light those patterns of overt behavior most closely associated with each individual by his peers, teacher, student teachers, and by himself. The behavior of those students with highest scores on the assessment instruments was then evaluated with reference to anecdotal records developed by the investigator over a three-month-observational period. Restated, the problem of evaluation was to determine whether certain students would consistently register high scores on the various tests and whether these scores would be supported by the evidence included in the anecdotal reports. High scores coupled with supportive anecdotal evidence then warranted careful comparison of the behavior patterns they represented with the characteristics of social giftedness derived from the literature and from questionnaire responses submitted by members of the American Association for Gifted Children.

Two freshman classes (referred to in the study as Class A and Class B) of a large metropolitan high school were selected as subjects for the research. These co-educational classes of 38 students each were part of an experimental program in which material in the social sciences, natural sciences, and communicative skills were integrated and presented in the form of projects to be mastered by individual study and small group discussion and review. Much time was spent at the beginning of each term teaching the students how to work together effectively in units of five or six. Emphasis was placed on the importance of individual responsibility for the total success of any group project. Thus, these two classes afforded a wealth of material relative to the social behavior of young adolescents in daily cooperative contact with each other.

The 76 students observed were all 13 to 15 years of age with the majority a few months past their 14th birthday. The group represented the middle-to-upper-middle socio-economic bracket in practically all cases. For the most part, fathers of the students were professional men, business men, merchants, or highly skilled workers. An administration of the American Council on Education Psychological Examination resulted in scores indicative of the high intellectual ability of the group. The mean score stood at the 80th percentile of ninth grade norms. Seventy-eight percent of the group had total scores at or above the 50th percentile. Only two students had total scores standing below the 25th percentile.

DESCRIPTION OF THE INSTRUMENTS

The students assessed each other by means of groupmate selection questionnaires and *Guess-Who?* questionnaires. The groupmate selection questionnaire is a type of sociometric device in which a group member is given the opportunity to indicate those members of his class with whom he particularly prefers to associate in dealing with some part of the term's work. The choosing of three fellow students as most desired groupmates represented a gross sort of evaluation of social acceptance and competence on the part of the class members for each other. The individual whose social ability was such that his influence was classwide tended to be chosen not only by the immediate members of his own subgroup but by members of other class subgroups as well. In general, the greater the number of choices cast for a particular individual the more certain that the class or group attitudes were uniformly positive toward that person. Groupmate choices were made on three separate occasions about one month apart when new project groups were to be formed. The scoring procedure was as follows. First, second, and third choices were weighted 5, 3, and 1 respectively. A student's score for a given selection period was the sum of the weighted choices cast for him. The mean of these selection period scores was considered the overall acceptance score for the total three month period.

The *Guess-Who?* type of questionnaire was first used in the Hartshorne and May studies of deceit and honesty among school children (3). It continues to be used as an effective technique in determining how young people in a relatively stable group perceive each other as well as themselves. The technique involved in constructing a *Guess-Who?* questionnaire centers on the development of short descriptive statements about social behavior. Generally the statements are developed in couplet form. One statement of the couplet is a positive or socially "good" type statement while its mate represents the negative side of the same social value. Thirty-one such statements were utilized in this study. Twenty-one were adopted from Tryon's monograph on the "Evaluation of Adolescent Personality by Adolescents," (9) while 10 others were devised by the investigator to reflect more specifically the characteristics of social giftedness as suggested by members of the American Association for Gifted Children and articles in the professional literature dealing with the behavior patterns of socially successful adolescents. The directions presented at the administration of the *Guess-Who?* questionnaire were as follows:

Below are some word pictures of members of your class. Read each statement and write down the names of the persons whom you think the descriptions fit. One description may fit several persons. You may write as many names as you think belong under each. The same person may be mentioned for more than one description. Write "myself" if you think the description fits you. If you cannot think of anyone to match a particular description, go on to the next one.

Scoring of the *Guess-Who?* questionnaire was accomplished by algebraically summing "plus" and "minus" votes for each student.

The second group of evaluative instruments were those used by appropriate adults to assess the social behavior of the students. These methods of assessment included a rating scale, a ranking procedure, and the Vineland Social Maturity Scale.

Two student teachers assigned to each class and the investigator rated the social behavior of the students using a modified version of the Integral Scale adapted from a study by Newman and Jones (6). As finally utilized, the scale incorporated eight items with ratings of 1-to-7 for each item. A rating of 1 represented complete concurrence with the positive aspect of the item whereas a rating of 7 represented complete concurrence with the negative aspect of the item. Scale items rated such aspects of behavior as sociability, social prestige, social self-confidence, attention seeking, stability in interpersonal relationships, and so forth. A total rating scale score was derived by averaging the eight subscores ascribed by each of the three raters and then summing the three averages. Thus 3 represented the most positive rating and 21 the most negative. If, for instance, each of the three raters assigned ratings of 1 for every item on the scale, the hypothetical student would receive three average ratings of 1. His total score would then be 3, the sum of the averages.

The ranking procedure represented an overall estimate of the social ability of each of the students by the classroom teacher. Each student was judged with reference to the proposed characteristics of social giftedness and then ranked accordingly. The individual considered to be the most socially gifted was ranked first, the next most socially gifted was ranked second, and so on.

The Vineland Social Maturity Scale was administered to each student by the investigator. The Scale was utilized since, in Doll's words, it "seeks to quantify the evaluation of social competence as a global aspect of individual maturation at successive age levels" (1, p. 81). The Scale measures social development in the areas of self-help, self-direction, locomotion, occupation, communication, and social relations. Doll believes that the value of the Scale lies in its synthesis of these six competencies into one total assessment which can be expressed in the form of a social quotient.

The student's perception of himself was obtained from a composition entitled "The Sort of Person I Am." This self-concept sketch was employed so that the adolescent could evaluate the adequacy of his relationships with others as he himself felt about it. A clinical psychologist, a social psychologist, and a college student personnel dean were asked to rate each of the 76 compositions on a 1 to 5 basis. A rating of 1 labeled a composition as devoid of any reference to criteria considered reflective of social giftedness whereas a rating of 5 represented a demonstration of much concern on the part of the writer for attitudes considered to play an important role in the complex of superior social behavior.

Besides keeping records of apparently socially gifted behavior, an attempt was also made to record examples of highly negative and/or ineffectual social behavior. This was done in order to accumulate evidence about students who otherwise appeared to be possible candidates for the characterization of socially gifted on the basis of the test scores they achieved. Anecdotal records were secured in as many different types of social situations as possible. The investigator spent time with the students outside of the classroom as well as in it. He visited with them in their homes, went to their parties, ate lunch with them, and accompanied them on various field trips.

INTERCORRELATIONS AMONG TEST SCORES

The intercorrelations among test scores are presented in Table 1. The levels of significance of the correlation coefficients were derived from reference to Table 49 in Garrett (2, p. 299).

Reference to the table of intercorrelations indicates that the most substantial relationships were found among those instruments whose scores reflected actual behavior in interpersonal relationships. Thus, there appeared to be general agreement among the students and adults regarding the quality and effectiveness of the social behavior of the students. Scores derived from the Vineland Social Maturity Scale, the self-

TABLE 1.   Intercorrelations

1—Groupmate Choice   4—Teacher Rankings
2—Guess-Who? Questionnaire   5—Self-concept Composition
3—Rating Scale   6—Vineland Social Maturity Scale
7—ACE Psychological Examination

	2		3		4		5	6	7
	A	B	A	B	A	B			
1	.69	.71	.66	.61	.71	.67	.40	.24*	.38
2			.74	.78	.67	.74	.42	.45	.41
3					.72	.71	.30	.37	.52
4							.31	.45	.45
5								.10**	.21**
6									.26*

NOTE: Separate coefficients of correlation were calculated for class A and class B when both sets of scores being correlated were derived from intraclass assessments. Where one or both sets of scores represented a total assessment of both classes as one group, one coefficient and correlation was calculated. All correlations are positive and significant at the .01 level except as otherwise noted.
* Significant at the .05 level.
** Not significant.

concept compositions and the ACE Psychological Examination seemed to contribute less to an assessment of social ability than had been anticipated. For example, the investigator's experience with the Vineland Scale suggested that it may provide a better estimate of the young person's capacity for independent action than for finesse in interpersonal relationships. The self-concept compositions although affording important insights about their authors do not necessarily represent what the adolescents will do in a given social situation. Finally, the ACE Psychological Examination scores suggest that although social ability and intellectual ability are interrelated, the correspondence is certainly not a perfect one. As has often been noted, high intelligence does not guarantee social giftedness although obviously the socially gifted tend to be of above average intelligence.

SELECTION OF ADOLESCENTS AS SOCIALLY GIFTED

The selection of adolescents as most probably socially gifted was accomplished by utilizing the scores of the groupmate choice questionnaire, the *Guess-Who?* questionnaire, the rating scale, and the teacher ranking procedure to evolve a composite rank for each one of the students. The social behavior of the three highest ranked students in classes A and B as described in their anecdotal records was then reviewed. The pattern of social behavior delineated by these records agreed with the implications of the composite ranks. That is, the behavioral patterns of the highest ranked students were similar to what had been hypothesized as socially gifted behavior whereas the records of average and low scoring students contained practically no evidence of such behavior.

CONCLUDING STATEMENT

The study indicates that social giftedness in adolescence can be ascertained and described. The groupmate choice questionnaire, the *Guess-Who?* questionnaire, the rating scale, and the teacher ranking procedure proved to be assessment techniques easy to administer and minimally disruptive of classroom routine. These instruments possess another advantage in that they are multifunctional. The data they provide can be used for purposes other than the identification of the socially gifted.

Finally, it is important to keep in mind that the testing procedures utilized in this study were administered to a group of middle-class, urban, academically oriented adolescents. Until the results of further research are available, the teacher interested in the socially gifted will have to experiment to determine how these instruments might best be modified if the students under consideration are considerably different in background from the subjects of this study.

REFERENCES

1. Doll, Edgar A., *The Measurement of Social Competence.* Minneapolis: Educational Publishers, Inc., 1953. 664 p.
2. Garrett, Henry E., *Statistics in Psychology and Education.* Third edition. New York: Longmans, Green and Company, 1947. 487 p.
3. Hartshorne, M. and M. A. May, *Studies in Deceit.* New York: The Macmillan Company, 1928. 414 p.
4. Hollingworth, Leta S., *Gifted Children: Their Nature and Nurture.* New York: The Macmillan Company, 1926. 374 p.
5. Jarecky, Roy K., "The Identification of Socially Gifted Adolescents." Unpublished Doctor's Thesis. Teachers College, Columbia University, New York, 1958. 118 p.
6. Newman, Frances Burks, and Harold E. Jones, "The Adolescent in Social Groups; Studies in the Observation of Personality," *Psychology Monographs* No. 9. Berkeley: Stanford University Press, 1946. 94 p.
7. Pritchard, Miriam C., "The Contributions of Leta S. Hollingworth to the Study of Gifted Children," *The Gifted Child,* pp. 47-85. Edited by Paul Witty. Boston: D. C. Heath and Company, 1951. 388 p.
8. Terman, Lewis M. and Melita Oden, *The Gifted Child Grows Up; Twenty-Five Years' Follow-Up of a Superior Group.* Vol. IV of *Genetic Studies of Genius.* Edited by Lewis M. Terman. Stanford, California: Stanford University Press, 1947. 448 p.
9. Tryon, Carolyn, "Evaluation of Adolescent Personality by Adolescents,"

Monographs of the Society for Research in Child Development. Vol. IV, No. 4, 1939. 83 p.

10. Wesman, Alexander G., "Methods of Identifying Gifted Students," *Guidance News*, 9:4-5, October, 1956.

The Measurement of Individual Differences in Originality

R. C. WILSON

J. P. GUILFORD

P. R. CHRISTENSEN

One of the most important aspects of creative thinking is originality. This article discusses the problem of developing methods for measuring individual differences in originality. The problem arose in connection with a factor-analytic study of creative thinking conducted at the University of Southern California.

In that investigation various definitions of originality were considered in the light of their implications for measurement. Three definitions and corresponding methods of measuring originality were finally adopted and applied to specially constructed tests. The methods are based upon: (*a*) uncommonness of responses as measured by weighting the responses of an individual according to the statistical infrequency of those responses in the group as a whole; (*b*) the production of remote, unusual, or unconventional associations in specially prepared association tests; and (*c*) cleverness of responses, as evaluated by ratings of degrees of cleverness exhibited in titles suggested for short-story plots.

These three methods permit the operations of measurement of individual differences and, while recasting the definition of originality, they preserve much of the essential meaning usually assigned to the concept. In the following sections, some of the nonmeasurable aspects of originality are pointed out and each of the three proposed methods is discussed in conjunction with a description of tests developed to utilize the method. Since the tests were included in a factor analysis along with other tests of creative thinking, the three methods are evaluated in the light of the loadings of scores from these tests on a factor which has been called originality.

Reprinted from *Psychological Bulletin*, Vol. 50, No. 5 (September, 1953), pp. 362-370. By permission of the senior author and the American Psychological Association.

DEFINITION OF ORIGINALITY

In developing methods for measuring individual differences in originality, the meaning to be assigned to the term *originality* and the operations for measurement must be clearly specified. The term originality has several distinct meanings. We wish to use it as the name for a psychological property, the ability to produce original ideas. What we mean by an original idea will be further specified in relation to each of the proposed methods of measuring originality.

Many writers define an original idea as a "new" idea; that is, an idea that "did not exist before." They are frequently not in agreement, however, in their interpretation of "new," since they use it with different connotations. We shall point out the inadequacy of two of these connotations for the measurement of individual differences in originality.

In one connotation, a "new" idea is an idea that "has never previously been thought of by anyone who has ever lived." In practice, of course, it would be impossible to verify whether or not an idea meets these requirements of newness since one could never examine all the ideas of everyone who ever existed to determine whether the idea has been thought of before. This conception also presents a problem in the case of independent productions of the same idea. Two or more scientists may produce the same idea independently in different parts of the world. One of them may precede the others by a matter of months or weeks, or even hours or minutes. In trying to find creative scientists, we would probably not wish to regard the scientists who produced the idea later as unoriginal merely for having been preceded by someone unknown to them.

On the other hand, we find that "new," while meaning that which did not exist before, is sometimes interpreted, at least by implication, as including all human behavior that is not repetitive. That is, not only poetry, science, and inventions, but dreams, hallucinations, purposive behavior, and all perceptions are regarded as new. They are "new" in the sense that they are never duplicated exactly, even by the individual himself. Such a conception of "new" also fails to be fruitful, since it does not supply us with a basis for differentiating between more original and less original individuals.

For measurement purposes, we have found it useful to regard originality as a continuum. We have further assumed that everyone is original to some degree and that the amount of ability to produce original ideas characteristic of the individual may be inferred from his performance on tests. Rather than define original as "new" or "did not exist before" we have investigated three alternative definitions. We have regarded originality in turn as meaning "uncommon," "remote," and "clever." It was felt that these three definitions include significant aspects of what is commonly meant by the term original. Tests and scoring methods were developed for each of these approaches to originality.

THE UNCOMMONNESS-OF-RESPONSE METHOD

Our first approach to the measurement of originality assumes a continuum of uncommonness of response. For this purpose originality is defined operationally as the ability to produce ideas that are statistically infrequent for the population of which the individual is a member. "Population" may here be regarded as any cultural group, professional group, or other aggregation of individuals having significant characteristics in common.

This definition of originality was utilized by constructing completion or open-end tests, which require the examinee to produce responses. The tests were administered to the group of individuals whose relative degrees of originality were to be determined. The responses of all the members of the group were tallied to determine their frequency of occurrence within the group. Weights were assigned to the various responses, the higher weights being given to the statistically more infrequent responses. A score was derived for each individual either by summing the weights assigned to his responses or by counting only the responses having high weights. On the basis of the score thus derived, those individuals with the highest scores were the individuals who had given the most infrequently mentioned responses.

This procedure may be clarified by an example. The items in the Unusual Uses test are six common objects. Each object has a common use, which is stated. The examinee is asked to list six other uses for which the object or parts of the object could serve. For example, given the item "A newspaper," and its common use, "for reading," one might think of the following other uses for a newspaper: (*a*) to start a fire, (*b*) to wrap garbage, (*c*) to swat flies, (*d*) stuffing to pack boxes, (*e*) to line drawers or shelves, (*f*) to make up a kidnap note. The test is given in two separately timed parts of five minutes each. Each part gives the names of three objects and their common use with spaces for listing six other uses per object.

All the responses given by a group of 410 Air Cadets and Student Officers to each object were classified, tallied, and weighted. A system of five weights was used. A weight of 5 was assigned for the (approximately) $\frac{1}{5}$ most infrequently mentioned responses, a weight of 4 for the $\frac{1}{5}$ next most infrequently mentioned responses, and so on down to a weight of 1 for the $\frac{1}{5}$ most frequently mentioned responses. This gave a possible range of scores for each object (six responses) of 0 to 30 and a possible range of scores for the total test (six objects) of 0 to 180. The total scores actually obtained ranged from 5 to 129.

Let us consider the actual frequencies obtained for one of the objects. The 1,767 responses to the object given by the group of 410 Air Cadets and Student Officers were tabulated. One hundred and eighty-two different uses were mentioned. Eighty of these 182 uses were unique in that they were mentioned by only one member of the group. At the other extreme, one of the uses was mentioned by 173 individuals. The three most common uses mentioned, with frequencies of 173, 94, and 90, accounted for 357 responses and were assigned weights of one. The next six most common uses, with frequencies from 89 to 48, were assigned weights of two. Nine uses with frequencies from 45 to 29 received weights of three, 24 uses with frequencies from 23 to 9 received weights of four, and the 139 most uncommon uses, with frequencies from 8 to 1, received weights of five. It should be noted that there were not exactly $\frac{1}{5}$ of the total number of responses in each weight category. Because of the way in which the responses distribute themselves it is usually not possible to designate an exactly equal number of responses for each weight. It is possible, however, to achieve a close approximation.

After the weight for each response had been determined for all six objects, each examinee's paper was scored by assigning the appropriate weights to his responses and summing them. By definition, those individuals who tended to produce the most infrequently given ideas were the ones with the highest total scores and were regarded as the most original members of the group. The mean score on the Unusual Uses test was 64.0, its standard deviation was 23.5, and its alternate-forms reliability was .74.

The same procedure was applied to the Quick Responses test and the Figure Concepts test (1). The Quick Responses test is similar to the conventional word-association test. It consists of a list of 50 stimulus words, derived principally from the Kent-Rosanoff list and a more recent list developed by D. P. Wilson (4). The 50 words were read to the examinees at the rate of one every five seconds, the examinee being instructed to respond with the first word that came to mind. Responses of 410 individuals were tabulated for each of the 50 stimulus words. Frequencies of occurrence for each response were determined, weights were assigned, and scores derived in a manner similar to that for the Unusual Uses test. The mean score on the Quick Responses test was 99.8 with a standard deviation of 18.7. The reliability estimate was .81 as computed for odd and even items and corrected for length.

The Figure Concepts test consists of 20 simple pen-and-ink drawings of objects and individuals. Each picture is identified by a letter. The examinee's task is to find qualities or features that are suggested by two or more drawings and to list the features and the letter designations of two drawings which possess them. For example, picture A might be a sketch of a child wearing a hat, picture B might be a sketch of a woman wearing a hat, picture C might be a sketch of young birds in a nest. The examinee might give such responses as "wearing a hat (a, b)"; "young (a, c)"; "family (a, b)"; etc.

All responses of all individuals were tabulated and classified according to frequency of mention. A further breakdown was made for each response mentioned in terms of the combinations of drawings used in identifying the feature. It was noted that while there were 190 possible pairs of drawings available, certain ones were rarely used, while others were used as a source of more than one feature. Weighting of responses was thus based on both the infrequency of the response itself and the infrequency of the drawing combination used as a source of that response.

How this dual classification affected an individual's score may be seen in the situation where two individuals gave the same response (feature name), but cited different combinations of drawings. If one individual's response was derived from a drawing combination that was frequently mentioned by others in connection with that feature, the weight assigned was low. The other individual's response, if derived from a drawing combination infrequently mentioned for that feature, was assigned a high weight.

As with the Unusual Uses test, weights were assigned so that an approximately equal number of all the responses given by the group received each weight. Each examinee's responses were then assigned their appropriate weights and the weights were summed to derive the individual's total score for the test. The mean score on this test was 29.9 with a standard deviation of 12.9. Since the format of this test did not permit the direct computation of a reliability estimate, the communality of the test (.41) found in the factor analysis is offered as an estimate of a lower bound of its reliability.

In the Number Associations test the examinee is given, in turn, four different numbers (digits) and for each is allowed two minutes in which to list as many synonyms, uses, and things associated with the number as he can. For example, for the number 4 he might list coach-and-four, for, fore, foursome, quartet, etc.

The associations listed by the group were tabulated and weights were assigned in a manner similar to that described for the Unusual Uses test. In order to try out a further variation of the uncommonness method, however, the individual's total score was derived in a slightly different manner from that previously described. Instead of summing the weights for all the responses given by the individual, his total score was derived by counting the number of responses with weights of 4 and 5. The mean score for this test was 12.5 with a standard deviation of 3.6 and an alternate-forms reliability of .57.

In the approach described in this section, we have chosen to define original as meaning "uncommon." An original idea or response is one that is uncommon or statistically infrequent, and an individual's degree of originality, as inferred from his scores on the tests described, is characterized by the degree of uncommonness of his responses.*

THE REMOTENESS-OF-ASSOCIATION METHOD

The second approach is in terms of remoteness of association. Originality is here defined as the ability to make remote or indirect associations. To measure originality from this point of view, tests were constructed that required the examinee to make remote associations if he responded at all. Remoteness of association was imposed by the task. Three tests of this type were constructed. The degree of originality of an individual, according to this definition, would be manifested in terms of the number of remote associations he made.

The Associations I test presents 25 pairs of words. The associative connection between the two words is not immediately apparent. The examinee's task in each item is to call up a third word that serves as a link between them. For example:

> Given:
> Indian_____money
> Write on the line between these words a word that associates the two.

There are several possible words that could be used such as penny, nickel, copper, and wampum, each of which is related to both Indian and money.

The examinee's score was the number of responses given to the 25 items in four minutes. The mean score for this test was 14.0 with a standard deviation of 4.9. The odd-even reliability estimate was .87, corrected for length.

The Associations II test is similar to the Associations I except that there is more emphasis on the correct response word having two different meanings in its relationship to the two stimulus words. It is also a multiple-choice test in which the examinee must indicate which one of five letters is the first letter of the correct association.

---

* The reader may recall that an uncommonness or idiosyncrasy score has previously been used in connection with word-association tests in the assessment of abnormalities of behavior in clinical practice, particularly of the schizoid type. The fact that such a score measures an originality factor, as we shall show later, might be regarded as support for the popular idea expressed in the words of Seneca, "There is no great genius without some touch of madness."

For example:

    tree   *a b g m s*   dog

Which of the five letters is the first letter of a word that is associated with both tree and dog and has a different meaning in relation to each?

The word "bark" is the correct answer. It means the external covering of a tree and it also means the noise made by a dog. It also begins with *b* which is one of the choices, so the examinee circles the letter *b*.

The examinee's score was the number of correct responses given to 25 items in 12 minutes. The mean score was 14.0 with a standard deviation of 3.9. The odd-even reliability estimate was .62, corrected for length.

The Unusual Uses test, previously described, was also regarded as a test requiring the examinee to respond with remote associations. Since the six items composing the test were common objects, each with one well-known use, which was given, the examinee was compelled to utilize remote associations in seeking six additional uses for each object. Both a statistical-infrequency score and a simple-enumeration score were derived for this test. The correlation between these two scores was .94. There is, of course, much spurious overlap of the two scores. In view of the high correlation between the two scores and the similarity of their correlations with other tests in the creative-thinking battery, the simpler score was chosen for inclusion in the factor analysis. The mean for this score on this test was 22.1 with a standard deviation of 6.7 and an alternate-forms reliability of .80.

In the approach described in this section we have chosen to define original as meaning "remote." An original idea or response is "remote" to the extent that the individual is required to bridge an unusually wide gap in making associative responses. An individual's relative originality, as inferred from his scores on these tests, is characterized by the number of remote responses given in limited time.

CLEVERNESS

According to the third approach, originality is defined as the ability to produce responses that are rated as clever by judges. This definition requires a test that calls forth responses showing variation on a continuum of cleverness. Weights are assigned to an individual's responses in proportion to their degrees of rated cleverness.

The Plot Titles test used to measure this type of originality presents two brief stories. For each story the examinee is allowed three minutes in which to write as many appropriate titles as he can. Although relevancy rather than cleverness is stressed in the instructions, an examination of the responses of the group revealed considerable variation in the ingenuity, cleverness, or striking quality of the titles suggested.

In an attempt to develop a reliable scoring procedure for evaluating cleverness, a sample of 50 individuals was selected from the total group of 410. These 50 individuals averaged approximately six responses for each plot. The approximately 300 titles for each plot were typed on separate slips of paper. Three judges, working independently, sorted the titles into six successive piles on the basis of their judgments of the relative cleverness of the titles. Weights from 0 through 5 were assigned to the titles in the successive piles, with the high weights being assigned to the more clever titles. Agreement among the judges is indicated by the interjudge correlations (of ratings) ranging from .53 to .76. Reliabilities of test scores derived from individual judges ranged from .69 to .77. These reliabilities were computed from the two cleverness scores, one from each story, for each of the 50 individuals. The reliability computed from the composite ratings of the three judges (.76) was not higher than that for the best individual judge. Since the most reliable judge was also the one who agreed best with the other two judges, it was decided to have this one judge do the scoring of the test for all examinees, with one of the other judges serving as a check scorer.

In an effort to simplify scoring, a study was made of total scores derived from the weights 0 through 5. That is, each test paper was scored by the number of responses at each of the cleverness levels of 0, 1, 2, 3, 4, and 5. Intercorrelations among the six scores were computed for the sample of 50 individuals. It was found that scores based on weights 0 and 1 intercorrelated well, and scores based on weights 2, 3, 4, and 5 intercorrelated well. A combination of scores based on weights 0 and 1 had a low correlation with a combination of scores based on weights 2, 3, 4, and 5. It was decided to reduce the scale to two intervals, clever and nonclever. That is, responses receiving weights 0 and 1 would be called nonclever. This greatly reduced the fineness of discrimination required of the scorer. Utilizing the titles already rated as a standard, the remainder of the tests were scored on this simple dichotomy. Two scores were recorded for each individual: the number of clever titles and the number of nonclever titles. It was decided to include both scores in the computation of the intercorrelation matrix and to determine, prior to the factor analysis, whether the cleverness and noncleverness scores were sufficiently independent to warrant including both of them in the factor analysis. The correlation between the two scores was −.031 and their patterns of intercorrelations with other tests in the battery were quite different; consequently, both scores were included in the factor analysis. The cleverness score (based on weights 2 to 5) emerged with a loading of .55 on the originality factor. The noncleverness scores (weights 0 to 1) had a loading of −.05 on this factor and had its highest loading (.59) on a factor identified as ideational fluency. The cleverness score had a loading of .07 on the ideational-fluency factor.

In the approach described in this section, we have chosen to define original as meaning "clever." An original idea or response is one that is rated as clever by judges. An individual's degree of originality, as inferred from this kind of test score, would be characterized by the number of clever responses given in limited time.

DISCUSSION

The seven test scores representing the three scoring methods described were included with 46 other test scores in a battery designed to explore the domain of creative thinking. The test battery was administered to 410 Air Cadets and Student Officers. The scores were intercorrelated and 16 factors were extracted. Orthogonal rotations resulted in 14 readily identifiable factors, a doublet, and a residual. Five of the seven originality test scores emerged with loadings regarded as significant (.30 and above) on one of the factors obtained. Following is a list of the tests, their scoring principles, and their loadings on the factor.

Plot Titles (cleverness)	.55
Quick Responses (uncommonness)	.49
Figure Concepts (uncommonness)	.32
Unusual Uses (remoteness)	.31
Associations I (remoteness)	.30
Number Associations (uncommonness)	.25
Associations II (remoteness)	.09

We have tentatively named this factor originality (3). Another test from the creative thinking battery which should be discussed in relation to this factor is the Consequences test. This test requires the examinee to list the consequences of certain unexpected events such as the sudden abolition of all national and local laws. Two scores were derived from this test on the basis of the degree of remoteness of ideas indicated by the individual's responses. The number of remote consequences was counted for one score and the number of immediate or direct consequences for the other. It was hypothesized that the remoteness of ideas represented by the remote-consequences score might refer to something different from the remoteness of ideas required by the originality tests already mentioned. A separate factor of penetration or the ability to see remote consequences in space, in time, or in a causal chain of circumstances was therefore hypothesized. No such factor emerged in the factor analysis. The remote-consequences score of the Consequences test came out with its highest loading (.42) on the originality factor. Evidently, the remoteness of ideas represented by this test score is not different from the remoteness of ideas required by the test scores hypothesized for originality. This finding lends additional support to the generality of the obtained originality factor.

Inasmuch as test scores representing all three methods of measuring originality have significant loadings on this factor, we may have some confidence in its generality. Had test scores of only one method emerged on the factor, we might wonder whether the factor were specific to the particular kind of scoring method.

It should be mentioned that this factor has some appearance of bi-polarity since there were a few small negative loadings of other test scores in the battery on this factor. Those test scores with negative loadings are of the kind whose "right" responses are keyed on an arbitrary, conventional basis by the test constructor. The examinee who engages in an unusual line of thought is likely to be penalized for his originality in such tests. In this connection, the essentially zero loading for originality in Associations II (as contrasted with the significant loading in Associations I) is worth mentioning. In this test, too, one "correct" answer is given credit. It may be that the original examinees think of other appropriate responses whose initial letters appear among the alternatives, and for which they receive no credit.

The fact that five of our tests designed to measure originality have in common a single factor is regarded as evidence for the potential fruitfulness of the scoring methods described for the measurement of individual differences in originality. Further work is necessary in refining the tests and in validating them against objective criteria of originality. It is felt that considerable progress has been made toward the development of objectively scored tests of originality, with promise of satisfactory reliability.

As to the relative merits of the three approaches suggested, the uncommonness and cleverness methods have the greatest amount of the originality-factor variance but are the least economical in time and energy required to determine the scores.

In an exploratory study such as this one, expenditure of time and energy in scoring by the less economical methods may be justified in terms of the insights to be gained. In later studies, however, it is desirable to use more economical procedures. The remoteness principle is a more economical procedure, but does not yield factor loadings as high as the less economical cleverness and uncommonness procedures. The next steps will be to revise the remoteness tests in an attempt to increase their originality variance and to seek methods of simplifying further the cleverness and uncommonness scoring procedures without decreasing their originality variance.

REFERENCES

1. Guilford, J. P., Wilson, R. C., Christensen, P. R., & Lewis, D. J., A Factor-Analytic Study of Creative Thinking, I. Hypotheses and Description of Tests. *Reports from the Psychological Laboratory*, No. 4 Los Angeles: Univer. of Southern California, 1951.
2. Guilford, J. P., Wilson, R. C., & Christensen, P. R., A Factor-Analytic Study of Creative Thinking, II. Administration of Tests and Analysis of Results. *Reports from the Psychological Laboratory*, No. 8. Los Angeles: Univer. of Southern California, 1952.
3. Hargreaves, H. L., The "Faculty" of Imagination. *Brit. J. Psychol. Monogr. Suppl.*, 1927, **3**, No. 10.
4. Wilson, D. P., An Extension and Evaluation of Association Word Lists. Unpublished doctor's dissertation. Univer. of Southern California, 1942.

III

Background of the Gifted

ONLY A FEW YEARS ago the purpose of a section on background of the gifted would be to report concomitant superiority in all areas. Terman's studies clearly indicated such superiority in virtually all areas. Today, however, greater understanding of the gifted exists. More is known about his background, what he is like, how he adjusts, and how he learns. All of the research on the gifted has resulted in a better understanding of the gifted individual.

HOW GIFTED CHILDREN LEARN

Gifted children, by definition, learn differently from other children. It is this difference, and it is one primarily of learning rate, that makes regular classroom instruction often inadequate for the gifted child.

Although Terman has shown that the gifted child is approximately two years beyond his grade placement in achievement, the gifted child still likes school and prefers the hard subjects to the easy ones. It is a serious indictment of our schools when the statement can be made that ". . . children with an I.Q. of 140 waste half their time in the average classroom—and those with 160 waste all their time (1)!" Just how gifted children acquire the phenomenal backlog of information has never been fully explained.

The importance of interest can never be overlooked. One writer maintained that a child prodigy's phenomenal ability in mathematics was nothing more than an unusually strong interest in numbers. He believed that the proof of this was demonstrated by the fact that the "ability weakens as the individual becomes interested in something else (2)."

While it must be recognized that this is an oversimplification of the problem, undoubtedly interest does exert a great influence.

Some attempt has been made to explain the phenomenal background of information of many gifted children by the term *eidetic imagery* or the ability to reproduce a picture in one's mind of anything that had been previously seen. It is undoubtedly true that eidetic imagery is stronger in young children than it is in adults, and that it is stronger in some children than in others.

Eidetic imagery and memory are perhaps closely related. Gifted children are characterized by a retentive memory, and in many instances this memory may actually be eidetic imagery without the child always being aware of just how he does remember.

The most useful mental process to the gifted child is reasoning and association. One cannot possibly remember everything in an unrelated fashion and so, through association, related items are remembered. The popular Dale Carnegie courses on memory operate on the principle of association. The expressed aim is to teach the individual to relate items, even if the relationship is an artificial one, for more things can be remembered in this way.

The sideshow type of stunt in which the magician remembers many things is usually nothing more than a practical application of this same device. Mnemonic aids, or memory crutches, assist him to remember. The piano student remembers "Every Good Boy Does Fine," and many of us still say "Thirty days hath September, April, June and November, . . ." That gifted children use this same device in order to remember is undoubtedly true.

This discussion is not intended to imply that the gifted child merely has a stunt, or trick, which makes it possible for him to remember things that others do not. Gifted children, often without realizing it, resort to association and memory devices, but the very fact that their minds are able to do this without the necessity of formal instruction along these lines is proof again of their mental superiority. When given the same type of memory training, the brighter individuals learn more quickly and are able to make more application of certain basic principles than the average individual.

Interestingly enough, a clue to the way in which gifted children learn may have been touched upon in an article about William James Sidis, an identified child prodigy of the early 1900's. "His most notable trait," according to one editor of that day, "was that he could not be turned aside from any purpose or deviated as children are (3)."

The gifted child learns best by associative methods and poorest by methods involving the use of rote memory. This is the explanation of the fact that gifted children excel in language, but not in spelling; and in arithmetic reasoning, but not in arithmetic fundamentals. Gifted children do not do well in handwriting and spelling because of the necessity for meaningless repetition.

The gifted child finds opportunities to learn even when his environment seems totally against him, according to Warren A. Ketcham, professor of education, University of Michigan. The gifted child's superior achievement is due primarily to his ability to make the maximum use of his opportunities to learn. "Research shows these children have an insatiable hunger for knowledge, and an almost mysterious way of learning. They frequently learn before they are taught." The gifted make up the brightest two per cent of children. "The achievement of these children is not adversely affected unless their entire environment—home, school, and community—is seriously limited in opportunities in the home, but in an equal number of cases the home successfully compensates for what the school does not provide."

Parents and teachers sometimes are disturbed because some gifted children exhibit marked inconsistencies in their learning pattern. "At one time the gifted child is completely absorbed in the mastery of a single skill or a narrow field of knowledge to the exclusion of all others. The parents and teachers of this child wonder when he will do his 'required work' or whether he will 'miss something.' At another time the gifted child dabbles in many areas and tries many skills without trying to master any of them. Parents and teachers then describe him as 'careless' or 'irresponsible.' These alternating periods of concentration and exploration may persist through the secondary school years. Research shows, however, that the promise of childhood and youth is fulfilled at adulthood for the gifted to a far greater degree than for the less able," says Professor Ketcham (4).

A valuable list of learning characteristics and concomitant problems is to be found in a report by Martinson (5) to the California Legislature. Power of observation, liking for structure, questioning attitude, and persistence are some of the characteristics listed.

ADJUSTMENTS OF GIFTED CHILDREN

Studies of the gifted have repeatedly emphasized the superiority of the adjustments of the gifted as compared with the average. This does not mean that the gifted have fewer adjustment problems than the average, for, if the total picture were known, it is likely that the gifted would be found to be faced with more adjustment problems. It is clearly indicated by research data, however, that the gifted do as well, or perhaps even better, in facing these problems and finding adequate solutions to them.

It is important to realize that although gifted children may be mentally advanced, they are still children, and their advanced mentality does little to help them through many of the problems of growing up.

While it is true that many gifted children are able to use their gift in order to make an adequate adjustment to life, too often this adjustment is made at the expense of the child's ability. Three distinct unfortunate patterns seem to stand out among some gifted children in their effort to adjust to a society which places little value on mental precocity (6).

1. They may withdraw from the group rather than attempt to compete in a situation which offers no challenge and therefore no reward.
2. They may become a show-off in an effort to gain attention from both the teacher and their own peer group.
3. They may pretend not to know answers in an effort to cover up their superior intellect.

Withdrawal. This is a common enough adjustment of mentally superior children. Such children retain their self respect, but pay dearly by not having friends of their own age group. This is the type of adjustment which led to the stereotyped attitude that gifted children are shy, withdrawing and unable to operate as social beings. There seems to be reason to believe that this is not so commonly found as an adjustment for gifted children today as it once was. This may be due to the change in emphasis in modern schools; where once the primary purpose of the school was to provide the child with skills and knowledge, the primary purpose today is to develop the child into an effective social being.

Show-Offishness. In the school situation of today, in which such a high premium is placed upon social aplomb, there is probably not so much withdrawing from the group as there was in earlier days. Unfortunately, however, the gifted child has come to another type of adjustment which is even less favorable. This type of adjustment is manifested by show-offishness, silliness, and clowning. It is an effective manner in which to gain the attention and approval of the group. Intelligence used in this way, for the entertainment of the group, is too often socially acceptable. The gifted child cannot be expected to realize that he is making a fool of himself at the expense of the development of his abilities. In a democratic society which is so dependent upon the development of its leaders it is inconceivable that such behavior would ever be tolerated.

Pretending Ignorance. A third method of adjustment often used is for the gifted child to pretend ignorance. This is probably the result of the child's realizing he is rejected because of his superior intellectual ability. Gifted children soon become aware of the fact that the school curriculum does not demand any great amount of effort from them. Once this realization has occurred, and it most likely comes about early in the primary grades, the gifted child must decide if he is willing to be labeled as a "brain." Since intellectual superiority is sometimes scorned, the gifted child realizes that this intelligence is not actually gaining him those things which the school is teaching him are so important. The child learns that always to hold his hand up first or always to be the one who knows the correct answer is not an admirable trait in the eyes of his fellow students. Rather than be the best pupil in the class, he begins doing less well than he is capable of doing. In this way he is not rejected by the group. Pretending ignorance can be the beginning of a method of adjustment which will last throughout life.

If the gifted child is expected to develop to the limit of his potentialities and to use his capability to produce for society, poor school adjustment must be prevented. The result of poor school adjustment is constant frustration, for not only is society losing the benefits which this individual might have contributed, but the person himself can never be well adjusted without the opportunity for any true self-expression.

In an article entitled, "Adjustment Through Partial Segregation," Pregler discusses the adjustment pattern of gifted children in the early elementary grades in a highly informative manner:

Gifted children are normal, happy children with few problems until they reach the point where they recognize the need for group approval. In the early stages of growth they receive much admiration. Their outstanding accomplishments are appreciated by their parents, relatives and by other adults with whom they come in contact. This continues in the early grades at school. Teachers frequently are lavish with their praise. If other children resent it, they don't know exactly what to do about it, so for one or two years they, too, add to the court of praise by choosing the bright child for a partner in their games and by forming other school attachments.

In about the third or fourth year of school, however, the picture changes. Those who have enjoyed a smaller measure of success and the resulting approbation of the adult world but who also need praise both at home and at school, gang up on him and begin to deny him that which he soon discovers he needs most, social approval.

The mentally superior child soon unravels this mystery and it doesn't take him long to discover that if he fails to display all of his knowledge, if he pretends *not to be* the smartest boy in the class, he can have that which he wants most, the acceptance and the approval of his classmates. Thus, he no longer works up to his capacity, and not being challenged, he becomes mentally lazy.

Sometimes the mentally superior child makes another choice. He may decide to maintain his academic standing in class and to win approval of classmates in other ways. He either has to depend on his wit and become the class clown, or to become belligerent and by physical prowess fight his way into acceptability (7).

Writing in *Exceptional Children,* Gallagher and Crowder (8) report on "The Adjustment of Gifted Children in the Regular Classroom." The purpose of the study was to "discover to what extent highly intelligent children are having difficulty in adjusting to a regular classroom situation academically, intellectually, socially, and emotionally." The subjects were twenty boys and fifteen girls, all of whom had received a Stanford-Binet I.Q. of 150 or more. As a result of a sociometric device used with the children's peers, it appeared as though those in the gifted group were quite popular socially. The judges of the Rorschach Ink Blot Test were not impressed with the creative aspects of the records, however. "Most unusual was the composite judgment that seventeen of the cases revealed no originality or creativity in their records." The teachers rated the gifted children very high in all areas except creativity and leadership. The two areas that presented the difficulty were "motivational problems" and "intellectual flexibility," and "the older children in the study had more problems of intellectual rigidity." Gallagher and Crowder state:

> One of the more striking observations to be made was that the problems that exist in these children were generally of the non-irritating variety. They were not anti-socially aggressive. They were not academic problems. They did not generally have emotional problems of sufficient magnitude to disturb their teacher, parents, or peer group (9).

This report of Gallagher and Crowder suggests, as does Pregler's report, that while gifted children often are not the problem cases within a class, they too may have problems. The very effort which they must make to conform to a world of mediocrity may make for poor adjustments.

REFERENCES

1. Cited in Abraham, Willard, *Common Sense About Gifted Children*. New York: Harper & Row, Publishers, 1958, p. 6.
2. Editorial, *Literary Digest*, Vol. 45 (September 28, 1912), p. 514.
3. Harvey, George, "The Editor's Diary," *North American Review*, Vol. 184 (April 19, 1907), p. 888.
4. Editorial, "Learning Patterns Among the Gifted," William W. Brickman, editor, *School and Society*, Vol. 91, No. 2220 (January 26, 1963), p. 30.
5. Martinson, Ruth A., *Educational Programs for Gifted Pupils*. Sacramento, Calif.: California State Department of Education, 1961, pp. 171-172.
6. Barbe, Walter, "Differentiated Guidance for the Gifted," *Education*, Vol. 74 (January, 1954), pp. 306-311.
7. Pregler, Hedwig, "Adjustment Through Partial Segregation," *National Elementary Principal*, Vol. 32 (September, 1952), pp. 241-246.
8. Gallagher, James and Crowder, Thora, "The Adjustment of Gifted Children in the Regular Classroom," *Exceptional Children*, Vol. 23, No. 7 (April, 1957), pp. 306-312, 317-319.
9. *Ibid.*, p. 318.

6 | HEREDITARY FACTORS AND FAMILY BACKGROUND

The Inheritance of Mental Ability

CYRIL BURT

THE PROBLEM OF INDIVIDUAL DIFFERENCES

In Britain as in America, the earliest applications of the new techniques of mental testing were concerned chiefly with the lower end of the intellectual scale. They were readily accepted as practical aids to the doctor in diagnosing the mentally deficient, and to the teacher in discriminating the temporarily retarded from the irremediably dull. It was Bingham's firm belief that: "in the long run it would be even more profitable to discover and aid the bright and the supernormal than to ascertain and provide for the dull and defective."

In this country the traditional method of dealing with the problem was by means of what was popularly known as "the scholarship system." British teachers and parents were apt in those days to think of scholarships rather as a means for rewarding hard work than as a device for detecting and assisting impecunious talent. But considerable misgiving was felt over the erratic local distribution not only of scholarship winners but also of defectives. It was indeed widely affirmed that these variations in the numbers were "largely the result of the injustice of the ordinary methods of examination." Accordingly, in 1913 the London County Council took the unprecedented step of appointing an official psychologist. His chief duties were to act as referee for what were sometimes known as "problem children"—particularly in disputed cases of feeblemindedness and of scholarship ability.

In the surveys that I carried out in this capacity I found that, in the poorer districts of the East End, there were three times as many certified defectives, eight times as many backward pupils, but only one-tenth the number of scholarship winners as were reported in the well-to-do areas of London. Who or what was to blame: the teachers, the homes,

Reprinted from *The American Psychologist*, Vol. 13, No. 1 (January, 1958), pp. 1-15. By permission of the author and the American Psychological Association.

the traditional examination in arithmetic and English? Or the fact that the varying modicum of ability bestowed on each child was irretrievably fixed at birth? Environment or heredity, those seemed to be the alternative explanations; and each had its own enthusiastic advocates. As a rule the social reformers gave one answer and the psychologists the opposite.

During the nineteenth century the main champions of social reform were the philosophical radicals: Bentham, James and John Mill, and their various followers. Their motto was the maxim of Helvétius: *l'éducation peut tout;* or, as James Mill put it, "if education cannot do everything, there is hardly anything it cannot do." In psychology, their one basic law was the law of association; and the wide differences between one individual and another they attributed solely to the cumulative effects of association, through the operation of "habit, custom, training, and environmental opportunity or deprivation."

By the beginning of the twentieth century, however, most British psychologists had abandoned this simple creed. Impressed by the novel doctrines of the evolutionary school, they began to follow Darwin, Spencer, Huxley, and Galton in holding that the laws of heredity and individual variation applied to men as well as to animals, to mind as well as to body. "It is not so much," said Karl Pearson, "that the slums create the dullards, but rather that the duller stocks gravitate automatically to the slums." It followed that the only cure would be to start breeding citizens as we bred race horses, prize rabbits, or pedigree pups. Huxley's celebrated essay on the "Natural Inequality of Man" won over the few who still wavered. Most teachers were already converted by firsthand experience under the new scheme of universal education.

However, during the last few decades psychologists have been gradually discovering that the problem is far more complicated than either side had originally assumed. And, largely as a result, there has been yet another swing of the polemical pendulum. In part this is due to a reluctance to support what G. K. Chesterton once described as "the modernized dogma of predestination—a dogma calculated to paralyse all progress towards a welfare state"; in part it has been due to a fuller appreciation of the possibilities of experience and learning, which in turn has involved a reversion to something like a rejuvenated belief in the fundamental law of association.

To the British psychologist the experimental work on "conditioning" seemed to offer a more precise interpretation, on a more adequate basis, of the traditional doctrine of association as preached by Hartley and Mill; and the behaviourist school was widely welcomed as substituting a more profitable line of practical research for inconclusive speculations about heredity and innate endowment. As a result, we find contemporary educationists reminding each other of Bagley's well known dictum that, "except for a few cases of pathological deficiency, the factor of heredity plays a very small part in human life, as compared with the factor of environment" (1); while several of their psychological colleagues quote with approval the pronouncements of Watson: "there are inheritable differences in structure, but we no longer believe in inherited capacities." "Give me," he adds, "a dozen healthy infants, and my own world to bring them up in, and I'll guarantee to train any one of them to become any type of specialist I might select—doctor, lawyer, artist, merchant-chief, and even beggar-man or thief" (43, p. 104).

A glance through the current literature will show that, for the most part, the hypotheses which our younger psychologists desire to challenge are the two propositions which, at the beginning of the century, were accepted almost without question as justifying the organization of our system of education: first, the hypothesis of general ability, i.e., the view that "up to adolescence the chief differences distinguishing individual pupils are differences in 'general intelligence' "—a view which led the Chief Inspector of Schools to declare that, "with a few exceptions, each pupil may be taught in the same class for every subject, or, if mentally defective, sent to a special school on the ground that he is defective all round"; secondly, the hypothesis of mental inheritance, i.e., the view that the wide differences in the degree of general ability exhibited by various pupils were due mainly to genetic endowment.

THE HYPOTHESIS OF GENERAL ABILITY

Of these two hypotheses the first was firmly rejected by the report of the "Norwood Committee"—a report which strongly influenced the reorganization of our national education as envisaged in the Education Act of 1944. The committee maintained that children differed far more in quality of ability than in amount; and recommended a tripartite classification of "secondary" schools, based on the doctrine that pupils fall into three main types: a literary or abstract type, to be educated at "grammar schools"; a mechanical or technical type, to be educated at "technical schools"; and a concrete or practical type to be educated at "modern schools." This conception was supported by several leading psychologists who argued that "the statistical analyses of Thurstone disclose no evidence for Spearman's factor of general ability, but only a number of 'primary abilities,' each more or less specialized" (8 and refs.).

The scheme has not worked out in actual practice so successfully as was hoped; and the proposal itself at once stimulated a large number of new inquiries. Those who still defend the tripartite theory seem to overlook the vast and varied character of the evidence that has since become available on the issue thus raised. As a rule they content themselves with citing one particular line of reasoning—usually the statistical. If, however, we take a wider view, we shall find that there are three or four independent chains of converging arguments, none perhaps irrefragable by itself, but all of them tending to rehabilitate the older view. The evidence on which these inferences rest is drawn from many different fields: introspection, observation, biology and neurology, as well as statistical research.

In point of fact, the distinction between "general ability" and "special abilities" was due, not (as is so widely supposed) to Spearman but rather to Francis Galton, from whom Spearman, as he expressly states in his earlier papers, originally borrowed it. Spearman, however, went on to deny the existence of "special abilities" which Galton had supported, on the ground that they were "just relics or revivals of the obsolete theory of faculties" (35). It is this aspect of the Spearman doctrine that the modern educationist repudiates, and with it he is a little too ready to discard "general intelligence" as well.

However, even Galton had been partly anticipated by previous writers who, in a vague and inchoate fashion, had inculcated a somewhat similar doctrine on the basis of speculative arguments, partly introspective, partly biological. Introspection, so the faculty school had claimed, revealed a sharp distinction between intellectual or cognitive qualities on the one hand and emotional or orectic qualities on the other. Spencer and his followers accepted this distinction, and supplemented it with biological arguments, which in those days were almost equally conjectural. During the evolution of the animal kingdom, and again during the development of each individual, the fundamental capacity which Spencer termed intelligence ". . . becomes [so he tells us] progressively differentiated into a hierarchy of more specialized cognitive capacities—sensory, perceptual, associative, and ratiocinative, much as the trunk of a growing tree ramifies into boughs and twigs" (36, Part iv). Later writers were not so sure that the term cognition really furnished the best differentia: for them the real distinction was between directive or adaptive processes on the one hand and valuative or dynamic processes on the other: "intelligence," said Sully, "steers like a rudder; emotion and interest supply the steam." A similar reinterpretation has more recently been proposed by Piaget in his book on *The Psychology of Intelligence* (30, pp. 4ff.).

Far more convincing to my mind is the neurological evidence. The alternative doctrine of distinct and independent abilities drew much of its support from early experiments on cerebral localization. These, it was claimed, ". . . appear to indicate that distinct functions—motor, sensory, perceptual, associative, linguistic, and the like—can be assigned to distinct and definite centres or areas within the brain." And this conclusion was apparently corroborated by the maps of cell structure subsequently produced by histologists like Campbell, Brodmann, and von Economo. Their inferences, however, have been severely criticized by more recent workers, like Bok, Lorente de Nò, and, at University College, by D. A.

Sholl (34). Few of the older map makers (he says) realized "the enormous amount of variability that exists between individual human brains." In their studies of comparable cortical areas from different specimens of *Ateles* Lashley and Clark have shown that the differences between different individuals are at least as large as the differences upon which the distinction of "architectonic areas" was based (26). Hence it now seems clear that the charts that used to figure in popular textbooks "greatly exaggerated the amount and the definiteness of the alleged localization, both as regards structure and as regards function."

After all, as Sherrington so frequently pointed out, in any one individual each anatomical tissue—skin, bone, hair, or muscle—tends to be of the same general character all over the body: minor local variations are often discernible; but in the same individual the variations are much slighter than those between one individual and another; and we should naturally expect the same to hold good of nerve tissue. Bolton's studies of the cerebral cortex, both in normal and defective persons, suggest that the quality of the nervous tissue in any given individual tends to be predominantly the same throughout: in low-grade defectives, for example, the nerve cells tend to be "visibly deficient in number, in branching, and in regularity of arrangement in every part of the cortex." The clinical work of Hughlings Jackson, the experimental researches of Sherrington, and the microscopical studies of the infant brain carried out more recently by Conel and de Crinis, seem in many ways to provide increasing confirmation for Spencer's theory of a "hierarchy of neural functions," developing stage by stage out of a simpler basic activity into higher and more specialized forms. Even if we cannot wholly accept Lashley's doctrine of the "mass action" of the brain, nevertheless the actual facts that he has reported are far more in keeping with a theory of general ability (and minor special abilities) than with a theory of major "special abilities" and no general factor. And Sholl himself concludes that "intelligence," like retentivity, is a "general attribute of all cortical tissue" (34, p. 111).

Each of the foregoing arguments—from introspection, from biology, and from neurology—is admittedly inconclusive. The most we could so far claim is that, when taken in combination, the evidence from each of these separate fields sets up a fairly strong a priori probability in favor of Galton's twofold theory of general abilities plus special. It is at this point, therefore, that the psychologist is tempted to invoke the aid of statistical analysis. In my view, the function of statistics, at any rate in psychological research, is simply to provide a more rigorous method of testing alternative hypotheses. How then do the various hypotheses that confront us stand up to this ordeal?

Each of the three main suggestions leads to distinctive corollaries which are open to statistical verification. First of all, if, as Thorndike held, there was no such thing as a general factor, but only a set of independent abilities, then the cross-correlation between the tests or assessments for those abilities should be zero, or at least nonsignificant. They are not: they are always both significant and positive. Secondly, if, as Spearman maintained, there were no such thing as special abilities but only a single general factor, the intercorrelations for every test should diminish proportionately in the same descending order (except, of course, for nonsignificant deviations due to sampling and the like): in technical language, the table of intercorrelations should constitute a matrix of rank one. It does not.

The third hypothesis assumes the presence of both general and special abilities. In the early article (3) to which I have already referred,[1] I endeavored to apply to the correlations between mental tests the procedure which Karl Pearson had already elaborated for use with measurements of bodily characteristics. In this way I sought to compare each of my various tables of observed coefficients with the best fitting set of theoretical values deduced from the hypothesis of a single "general ability" only; this hypothetical ability was redefined as the "highest common factor" entering into all the processes measured in any given table.[2] The fit was moderately good, but by no means perfect. The differences between the observed and the theoretical values were accordingly tested for statistical significance; and the result was to disclose small but significant clusters of residual correlations, common to certain limited groups of tests only, thus plainly indicating the presence of certain supplementary abilities. This seemed definitely to clinch the double hypothesis put forward by Galton. Precisely the same conclusion was reached in many later analyses carried out both by myself and by other workers with larger numbers of pupils and a greater variety of tests (5, 6, and refs.).

---

[1] Those to whom this earlier (1909) paper is inaccessible will find the essential figures from one of the tables reproduced in books by Freeman (22) and Thorndike (41); Garnett (24) reprints not only the observed values, but, beneath them, the theoretical values, the discrepancies, and the probable errors, as I myself had done. It should be noted that the procedure subsequently developed by Spearman (35) was rather different. He preferred to secure independent assessments for intelligence, based on teachers' ratings, examination results, or, in later inquiries, the results of one or two accredited tests, and use them as "reference values." In other words, he used an *external* criterion; whereas I have used an *internal* criterion or "factor" derived from the intercorrelations themselves. My reasons were that both examination results and teachers' assessments were commonly influenced by the child's capacity to learn, i.e., by his memory, rather than by his sheer intelligence, and thus often reflected what the child had actually acquired rather than his innate capacity.

[2] The simplified formula used for this purpose in most of these earlier researches (6, p. 53) was the same as that subsequently adopted by Thurstone under the name of the centroid formula (42, p. 94, Equation 13). When in addition "special abilities" were studied as well as "general ability," they were regarded as "group factors" obtainable by an arithmetical rotation of the "bipolar" factor matrix. I may add that we encountered a certain amount of evidence indicating that several of these special abilities were also largely dependent on heredity, but space does not permit me to deal with them here.

The factorization of correlations between persons and between successive occasions (with the same persons and tests) revealed, or at least very plainly confirmed, the constant presence of a random factor, which appeared to be due, not merely to sampling as ordinarily understood, but to something essentially characteristic of the working of the mind or brain. A somewhat similar conclusion has been independently reached by neurologists like Beurle, Cragg and Temperley, and Uttley and Sholl. Thus the type of "neuronal connectivity" suggested by the histological study of dendritic fibres strongly suggests "the semi-random arrangement of a machine working largely in accordance with the principles of probability" (34 and refs.).[3] This partly agrees with, though it is by no means identical with, the doctrine of "equipotentiality" put forward by Lashley; and thus further supports the value of factorial procedures as a means of investigating variations in mental ability.

However, what is far more important from the practical standpoint of educational guidance is this: in nearly every factorial study of cognitive ability, the general factor commonly accounts for quite 50% of the variance (rather more in the case of the young child, rather less with older age groups) while each of the minor factors accounts for only 10% or less. With increasing age, the "group factors," which represent special abilities, contribute increasing amounts to the total variance; and this fact lends further support to the view that, as a result of maturation, cognitive ability progressively differentiates and tends to become more and more specialized (10 and refs.).

Be that as it may, whatever be our views on the various biological or neurological issues, we may, I think, safely say this: for purposes of prediction—forecasting what this or that individual child is likely to do in school or in after-life—the general factor is by far the most important, though admittedly not our only, guide. For all practical purposes, almost every psychologist—even former opponents of the concept of general intelligence, like Thorndike, Brown, Thomson, and Thurstone—seems in the

---

[3] This is not the same as the "sampling theory" of Thomson, which maintains that the apparent emergence of "factors" is "a result of the laws of chance and not of any psychological laws": like all simplified theories, it seems to amplify just one aspect of mental process, at the expense of denying all the rest. What is needed is a model which will combine the "integrative action" of the nervous system with its "stochastic action." As I have suggested elsewhere (*Psychometrika*, 3, p. 160), the mathematical model which most effectively does this is a classificatory model derived from Pearson's method of principal axes. The mechanical model would resemble, not the homeostat of Ashby or the mechanical tortoise of Grey Walter, but rather a classification machine like that proposed by Uttley and Sholl. Similarly a stochastical induction machine would seem to reproduce the results of human learning far better than the model adopted by Hull and his followers. It is therefore tempting to suggest that what has been called the A/S ratio—i.e., the proportionate amount of "association cortex" with which either a species or an organism is endowed at birth—would form an index primarily of the amount of its intelligence and only incidentally of its capacity to learn.

end to have come round to much the same conclusion, even though, for theoretical purposes, each tends to reword it in a modified terminology of his own. And thus today, save for one or two occasional attacks, current psychological criticism is not so much concerned with the problem of "general intelligence," but is directed rather against the second of our two initial propositions: the assumption, namely, that individual differences in intelligence are hereditary or innate.

THE GENETIC COMPONENT

Here three distinct questions seem to be involved: (a) what evidence is there for the *fact* of inheritance, (b) what precisely is the *mode* in which intelligence is inherited, and (c) what is the *relative importance* of the genetic factor as compared with the environmental?

TABLE 1. Correlations Between Mental and Scholastic Assessments

	Identical Twins Reared Together	Identical Twins Reared Apart	Nonidentical Twins Reared Together	Siblings Reared Together	Siblings Reared Apart	Unrelated Children Reared Together
Mental "Intelligence"						
Group test	.944	.771	.542	.515	.441	.281
Individual test	.921	.843	.526	.491	.463	.252
Final assessment	.925	.876	.551	.538	.517	.269
Scholastic General attainments	.898	.681	.831	.814	.526	.535
Reading and spelling	.944	.647	.915	.853	.490	.548
Arithmetic	.862	.723	.748	.769	.563	.476

The Fact. In controversies about the facts of mental heredity most critics have tended to assume that the two causal agencies commonly discussed—heredity and environment—are not merely antithetical but mutually exclusive. The environmentalists apparently suppose that, once they have shown that intelligence tests are affected by environment, it follows that all differences in intelligence are due to nothing but environment. Similarly the thoroughgoing hereditarian is apt to talk as though he believed that differences in intelligence were due to nothing but genetic constitution. This is the old familiar fallacy which I am tempted to label "nothing-buttery." In point of fact, with a few rare exceptions, like eye colour or serological differences in the blood, every observable characteristic that geneticists have studied has proved to be the product of the joint action of both heredity and environment. There are, in short, no such things as hereditary characters: there are only hereditary tendencies.

Now, where two contributory factors, such as heredity and environment, are likely to be involved, the obvious procedure will be to keep first one and then the other as constant as possible, and observe the results in either case.

1. *Uniform environment.* As psychological consultant to the London County Council, I had free access to orphanages and other residential institutions, and to the private files of case records giving the history of the various inmates. My co-workers and I were thus able to study large numbers of children who had been transferred thither during the earliest weeks of infancy, and had been brought up in an environment that was much the same for all. To our surprise we found that individual differences in intelligence, so far from being diminished, varied over an unusually wide range. In the majority of cases, they appeared to be correlated with differences in the intelligence of one or both of the parents. Some of the most striking instances were those of illegitimate children of high ability: often the father (so the case records showed) had been a casual acquaintance, of a social and intellectual status well above that of the mother, and had taken no further interest in the child. In such cases it is out of the question to attribute the high intelligence of the child to the special cultural opportunities furnished by the home environment, since his only home has been the institution.[4]

2. *Uniform heredity.* To secure cases in which the children's genetic endowment is the same, we may turn to assessments obtained from monozygotic or "identical" twins. The mother is not infrequently unable or unwilling to bring up two children at the same time, and one twin is consequently sent to a relative or to a foster home. Owing to the strong popular prejudice against separating twins, she not unnaturally tries, as a rule, to keep these arrangements secret. But patient and tactful inquiries show that cases of twins brought up in different environments almost from birth are in fact much commoner than is usually believed. We have now collected over 30 such cases (9, 11). I reproduce the more

---

[4] Details are given in the various *Annual Reports of the Psychologist to the London County Council* (5) and are summarized in (9). In the recent symposium on *Quantitative Inheritance* (31), Woolf, quoting a later paper of mine, regrets that I have "based such far reaching conclusions on the study by Barbara Burks . . . covering only 214 foster children" (2). But the principal basis for my own conclusion was a series of investigations in residential schools under the LCC covering in the course of years over 600 cases. I cited Burks' inquiry merely to show how an independent investigator in a different country had arrived at much the same figures as my own.

important correlations for the twins in Table 1 and have added for comparison corresponding coefficients obtained from other pairs, both related and unrelated. As regards intelligence the outstanding feature is the high correlation between the final assessments for the monozygotic twins, even when reared apart: it is almost as high as the correlation between two successive testings for the same individuals. On the other hand, with school attainments the correlations are much lower for twins reared separately than for twins reared together in the same home.

Several of our critics—Heim and Maddox, for example—have cited the account of analogous cases (described by Newman and others) as proving that intelligence is dependent on environment. Thus, to take an oft-quoted pair, "Helen," who had been trained as a teacher, scored with the Stanford-Binet tests an I.Q. of 116; whereas her twin sister, "Gladys," brought up for much of her childhood in an isolated district of the Canadian Rockies, scored only 92. But, says Newman, her score ". . . was higher than we might expect considering her scant education; and . . . it seems certain that the great deficiency in education had inhibited the development of the rather high grade of mental ability with which she was *endowed by heredity* (28, pp. 136-144)." Thus Newman's interpretation in no way conflicts with ours.

It is sometimes alleged (27) that, since twins are born at the same time, the intrauterine environment must have been the same for both before birth, even if later on their environments differ widely, and that quite conceivably it is the former that is crucial. As it happens, however, this rather gratuitous assumption reverses the actual facts. Embryological and obstetric records show that, particularly with twins developed from split ova, the position of each in the uterus, and the subsequent development, is liable to differ widely (12, pp. 123ff. and refs.).

I think, therefore, that it may be safely said that, apart from the influence of some preconceived theory, few psychologists nowadays would be inclined to contest the mere fact of mental inheritance: the most that can be plausibly alleged is that its influence is comparatively slight and distinctly elusive.

The Mode of Inheritance. The majority of those who still question the importance of mental inheritance, and many of those who support it, seem by preference to adopt entirely antiquated notions of the way in which inheritable characteristics are transmitted. If, as I have maintained, mental capacities are dependent on the physical characteristics of the brain (or, to speak a little more precisely, on the structural and biochemical qualities of the nervous system), then we should expect those capacities to be inherited in accordance with the same principles that govern the inheritance of physical characteristics; and these principles (except for obscure and apparently exceptional instances of extra-nuclear heredity) are essentially those commonly associated with the name of Mendel. Many British psychologists, however, feel a strong and not unreasonable prejudice against applying "atomistic theories like Mendel's" to explain the facts of mental life, and consequently, so far as they admit the possibility of mental inheritance at all, still cling to the old Darwinian principle of blended inheritance. On this view heredity means "the tendency of like to beget like" (the definition quoted by one of them from the *Oxford English Dictionary*). As a result, they commonly assume that the arguments for inheritance must consist in demonstrating resemblances between the parent and his children by means of correlations. When the two parents differ, then the child is still expected to consist in an intermediate blend of both.

The approach of the modern geneticist is the reverse of all this. As he views it, the real problem is rather to explain why in so many instances "like begets unlike." Both for the environmentalist and for the believer in blended inheritance, one of the most puzzling phenomena is the appearance, not merely of extremely dull children in the families of the well-to-do professional classes, but also of extremely bright children in families where both the cultural and the economic conditions of the parents would, one might imagine, condemn every child to hopeless failure. With the Mendelian hypothesis these anomalies are just what we should anticipate. However, the few critics who are familiar with the Mendelian explanation appear, as a rule, to suppose that it can apply only to discontinuous variations; and point out that intelligence, like stature, exhibits not discontinuous but continuous or graded variation. Hence, so they contend (sometimes citing the experiments of De Vries on "pure lines"), the apparent differences in intelligence between one individual and another must be due almost entirely to differences in environmental conditions.

Mendel himself was the first to indicate how his theory could be extended to account for this particular difficulty. When supplementing his experiments on the hybridization of peas by hybridizing beans, and (as before) crossing white flowered plants with purple, he found, that, whereas with peas the two types always sorted out with no hint of any intermediate color, with beans the offspring displayed "a whole range of hues from white to deep purple." This, he suggested, might be explained by postulating that with beans the color was determined, not by a single pair of alternative factors, but by a *number* of such pairs, each positive factor, when present, contributing a small additional amount of color. And if, as before, the recombinations are the effects of chance unions, then the resulting frequencies would obviously approximate to those of the normal curve.

However, in our early surveys of London children (5, 6), we found that, when complete age groups were tested, the distribution of intelligence departed significantly from that of a perfect normal curve: there was a swollen tail at the lower end, due to an excess of mental defectives, and a smaller enlargement at the upper end. This and other considerations led me to put forward the tentative hypothesis that innate variations in intelligence are due partly to unifactor and partly to multifactor inheritance: i.e., they result from Mendelian factors of two main kinds (no doubt overlapping), viz., (*a*) major genes responsible for comparatively *large* deviations, usually of an abnormal type, and (*b*) multiple genes whose effects are *small, similar,* and *cumulative.*

Karl Pearson (29) endeavoured to test the Mendelian theory in its multifactorial form by comparing its implications with actual figures obtained for height, arm length, and similar physical measurements, collected by himself and Alice Lee, from over 2,000 students and their relatives. The expected correlations which he deduced for various degrees of kinship were in every case far smaller than the observed coefficients. He therefore emphatically rejected the hypothesis of Mendelian inheritance, and fell back on the older theory of blending. However, in deriving his formulae and his expected values, Pearson relied on an oversimplified model. Contrary to what we now know to be the case, he assumed that the effect of assortative mating—the tendency of like to marry like—could be ignored as negligible, and that dominance would in every case be perfect. Ronald Fisher has since undertaken the rather formidable task of deducing more appropriate formulae, which allow for these and other complicating factors (18). And with these refinements the calculated correlations fit Pearson's own figures as well as could be wished.

My colleagues and I have applied Fisher's methods (suitably modified) to assessments for intelligence (12). The data were secured in the course of surveys of the entire school population in a representative London borough, and covered nearly 1,000 pairs of siblings, together with ratings for parents, and (so far as they were accessible) grandparents, uncles and aunts, and first cousins. The final assessments for the children were obtained by submitting the marks from the group tests to the judgment of the teachers who knew the children best: where the teacher disagreed with the verdict of the marks, the child was interviewed personally and subjected to further tests, often on several successive occasions. The assessments for the adult members of the family were naturally far less accurate. Nevertheless, in almost every case the correlations computed from the actual data agreed with the theoretical values deduced from the multifactorial hypothesis far better than with the values deduced from any other hypothesis hitherto put forward. The only appreciable discrepancy occurred in the case of first cousins. Here, as for stature, the observed correlation for intelligence is larger than the theoretical; but the difference is not statistically significant, and could readily be explained if (as has been suggested above) variations in intelligence are affected by a few major genes as well as by numerous minor genes. I may add that on sorting out figures for cousins of maternal, paternal, and mixed kinship there is also some slight evidence suggestive of sex linkage.

The Relative Influence of Heredity and Environment. In practical work, however, the question most frequently raised is, not whether differences in intelligence are inherited, nor even how they are inherited, but rather what is the relative influence of heredity as compared with environment. To an omnibus inquiry like this there can be no single answer. We can only try to determine, for this or that type of environment, for this or that population, and for this or that type of assessment, how far the observable results appear to be influenced by each of the two main groups of factors.

As Fisher's analysis has shown, formulae analogous to those used to deduce the expected correlations from the theoretical variances can also be devised for deducing the amount of the constituent variances from the observed correlations. I have ventured to amplify Fisher's methods (mainly on the lines of later work by Mather and Sewall Wright) so as to allow for unreliability and for the systematic effects of environment, i.e., of environmental influences which are correlated with those of heredity, as well as for random effects. The genetic contribution may be regarded as comprising two distinguishable portions: that due to the "fixable" component (or, as Fisher expresses it, to the "essential genotypes") and that due to the "nonfixable" (i.e., deviations due to dominance and similar influences). The data analysed consist of (*a*) the marks obtained from intelligence tests of the ordinary type taken just as they stand and (*b*) adjusted assessments obtained by the supplementary methods already described (12).

TABLE 2. Analysis of Variance for Assessments of Intelligence

SOURCE	Unadjusted Test Scores	Adjusted Assessments
Genetic component:		
fixable	40.51	47.92
nonfixable	16.65	21.73
Assortative mating	19.90	17.91
Environment:		
systematic	10.60	1.43
random	5.91	5.77
Unreliability	6.43	5.24
TOTAL	100.00	100.00

From Table 2 it will be seen that, with crude test results, taken just as they stand, nearly 23% of the total variance appears due to nongenetic influences, i.e., to environment or to unreliability, and about 77% to genetic factors; with the adjusted assessments only about 12% (or slightly more) is apparently due to nongenetic influences and 88% to genetic factors. This of course means that the common practice of relying on tests alone—usually a group test applied once only—is by no means a satisfactory method of assessing a child's innate ability. Better assessments are obtained by submitting the test scores to the teachers for criticism or correction, and where necessary adjusting them by the methods described above. But such intensive inquiries would be too costly for routine use except in borderline cases.

Environment appears to influence the test results chiefly in three ways: (*a*) the cultural amenities of the home and the educational opportunities provided by the school can undoubtedly affect a child's performance in intelligence tests of the ordinary type, since so often they demand an acquired facility with abstract and verbal modes of expression; (*b*) quite apart from what the child may learn, the constant presence of an intellectual background may stimulate (or seem to stimulate) his latent powers by inculcating a keener motivation, a stronger interest in intellectual things, and a habit of accurate, speedy, and diligent work; (*c*) in a few rare cases illness or malnutrition during the prenatal or early postnatal stages may, almost from the very start, permanently impair the development of the child's central nervous system. The adjusted assessments may do much towards eliminating the irrelevant effects of the first two conditions; but it is doubtful whether they can adequately allow for the last.

LIMITATIONS INVOLVED IN THESE CONCLUSIONS

As in almost all scientific investigations, the hypothetical model which has formed the basis of our inquiry involves of necessity certain minor simplifications. In particular we have assumed, for purposes of calculation, a sharp distinction between the "major genes" of unifactor inheritance and the "polygenes" of multifactor inheritance, and have treated the latter as contributing equal and additive doses to the sum total of each child's innate intelligence. We have then supposed that the effects of the former would on the whole be excluded if the few obviously pathological cases (mostly found in special schools or institutions) were omitted from our final calculations. However, these assumptions have led several critics to accuse us of

. . . disrupting the individual personality into atomic bits and discrete pieces which have subsequently to be joined together like a mosaic. . . . Personality [it is argued] is not a mosaic but a seamless whole, and hence the entire Mendelian hypothesis with its particulate genes, each producing a unit-character or adding another unit to the same character, is quite inapplicable to the facts of conscious behavior, and therefore to the study of mental capacity.

Objections of this kind could of course be used just as well to prove that a neuronic theory of the central nervous system is incompatible with the facts of conscious behaviour or of individual variations in ability, since nerve cells or "neural bonds" are equally "particulate." Nevertheless, even those neurologists who prefer to start from a "field theory" do not wholly reject the neuronic hypothesis (cf. 34). In both cases the difficulties raised owe their force chiefly to the fact that there is a vast series of elusive processes intervening between theory and observable results which the critic is exceedingly apt to forget. Moreover, criticisms like those just cited plainly rest on an obsolete version of the Mendelian doctrine. No geneticist today, I imagine, accepts the hypothesis of the autonomous corpuscular gene; and the genotypic endowment of the individual can only affect the phenotypic resultant through the mediation of innumerable obscure biochemical steps.

In our original papers Howard and I tried carefully to guard against recurrent objections of this type. As we pointed out, the phrase "multiple factors" may be used to cover either (*a*) relatively numerous loci each with only two allelomorphs or (*b*) a single locus (or relatively few loci) each with numerous allelomorphs, or possibly (*c*) some combination of the two. Hypothesis *b* by itself would hardly seem to fit the facts. We are inclined to think that factors of all the various types may be operative in varying degrees, and that the attempt to classify factors or genes should not be too severely pressed.

We further assumed that in all probability the influence of such factors on the individual's observable intelligence was mainly the indirect result of their influence on the development of his central nervous system, and was presumably effected by modifying growth rates. And we expressly stated that the ultimate influence of any one "gene" upon intelligence might be but one of its multifarious consequences, and possibly a comparatively remote consequence at that. Some genes may have a larger share in the final result; others a smaller; and the rough classification of genes into "major" genes and "minor" was adopted primarily with a view to simplifying our general discussion.[5] We ourselves find the "theory of chromosomal hierarchy," advanced by Goldschmidt (25), especially attractive as a basis for the ultimate hierarchical differentiation of mental ability.

---

[5] If Mather's view that "the major genes occur only in euchromatin, while heterochromatin contains only polygenes" (15, p. 151 and refs.) is eventually confirmed, there would be more adequate grounds for retaining a sharp distinction between the two modes of inheritance. However, this view is not universally accepted. For an alternative interpretation of the experimental results on which Mather largely relies, see the papers by Reeve and Robertson quoted in our article (12, p. 116). These writers incline more to what in the text I have called hypothesis *b*. But, as Howard and I contended, their alternative interpretation would affect only the method, not the results, of our statistical deductions.

However, this is not the place to enlarge on these speculative interpretations. We fully admit that the simplifications involved in our hypothetical model mean that the figures finally deduced can be no more than approximations. But we maintain that the error of approximation, however large, will nevertheless be smaller than the amount of "unreliability" inevitably involved in all such measurements.

In any case we must repeat that the conclusions reached are at best only valid in reference to the particular conditions under which they were obtained. They would not necessarily hold good (*a*) of other mental traits, (*b*) of different methods of assessment, (*c*) of a population of a different genetic composition, or (*d*) of a population at a different cultural level: much less would they hold good if there were any subsequent change (*e*) in the present distribution of environmental and genetic characteristics, or (*f*) in the influences affecting their mutual interaction.

THE INHERITANCE OF OTHER MENTAL QUALITIES

The mental trait in which we have been chiefly interested is the general factor of "intelligence." This, we readily concede, is but one psychological ingredient in ordinary everyday behavior. Our critics are accustomed to reproach us for apparently ignoring the rest. There are several obvious reasons why we have dealt less fully with other determinants. The first and the most conclusive is that comparatively little evidence is as yet available in regard to the genetic composition of other mental factors. We have, however, in the course of our surveys, met with an appreciable number of cases which strongly suggest the inheritability of certain specific abilities and disabilities, or rather of certain ill-defined tendencies that presumably underlie such disabilities—particularly in our studies of memory, of visual, auditory, and kinaesthetic imagery, and of verbal, numerical, artistic, and musical aptitudes (5). We have encountered other cases which suggest the inheritability of general emotional instability, of temperamental qualities like introversion and extraversion, and of certain quasi-instinctive tendencies like sex and bad temper (or "pugnacity," as McDougall would have termed it). But emotional tendencies are always much more liable to be influenced and altered by postnatal experiences, and in any case undergo considerable changes during the developmental stages, so that all attempts at assessment are apt to be precarious. The most convincing evidence is afforded by the family histories of children brought up in orphanages or residential institutions (7, especially p. 14 and refs.). In all these instances the evidence, such as it is, appears to indicate that each of the characteristics mentioned, cognitive and temperamental alike, are influenced both by unifactor and by multifactor modes of inheritance—the latter tending on the whole to predominate, but in varying degrees. This after all is what is commonly found in investiga-

tions on physical characteristics. Characteristics depending mainly
(though not entirely) on the development of the long bones—such as arm
length, leg length, stature, and perhaps the longer dimensions of the face
and head—yield correlations of much the same magnitude as those obtained for general intelligence. Others, like cephalic index, breadth at
hips, and particularly facial characteristics, seem to be rather more subject to the influence of single (or relatively few) genes, which often appear to exhibit almost perfect dominance. Variations in the cartilaginous
features, and particularly those depending on flesh and fat, are far more
readily affected by environmental influences (for data, see 38 and refs.).

But secondly there is a practical reason for concentrating attention first
of all, and chiefly, on the inheritability of general intelligence. General
intelligence, as we have seen, accounts for four times as much of the
variance as any other identifiable factor. Galton's pronouncement is thus
fully borne out by our own results: ". . . general ability appears far more
important than special gifts; and, where the allowance granted by nature
is inadequate, the keenest will and the stoutest industry must strive in
vain." Moreover, the child's innate endowment of intelligence sets an
upper limit to the best he can possibly attain. No one would expect a
mongolian imbecile, with the most skilful coaching in the world, to
achieve the scholastic knowledge of an average child. In the same way,
no one should expect a child who is innately dull to gain a scholarship to
a grammar school, or one whose inborn ability is merely average to win
first class honors at Oxford or Cambridge. No doubt, in any individual
case the ascertainment of this upper limit can never be a matter of absolute certainty: an I.Q. derived from tests alone falls far short of a trustworthy indication. Hence education authorities, like life insurance
companies, have to follow Butler's maxim, and take probability for their
guide. They cannot, however, afford to risk a lavish expenditure on cases
where there are fairly heavy odds against success.

Nevertheless, it must be owned that, in Britain at any rate, the existing

TABLE 3. Estimates for Grammar School Entries

	General Population[*]	Proportions Over +0.85 SD	Expected Entries		Actual Entries
Middle class	20%	.40	.08	(40%)	55%
Manual class	80%	.15	.12	(60%)	45%
TOTAL	100%		.20	(100%)	100%

[*] The *Census of Great Britain* (1951) gives an estimate of 81.7 for males over 15, occupied or retired, falling into the classes of "Skilled," "Mixed," and "Unskilled" workers: these I have pooled in a single broad group.

administrative machinery is far less efficient than it might be. In an inquiry made just before the introduction of the Education Act of 1944 we found that "approximately 40 per cent of those whose innate abilities are of university standard are failing to reach the university" (9). The new arrangements proposed by the act, and the postwar changes in the economic circumstances of the various social classes, have appreciably altered the entries to "grammar schools"; but it is too early to say how far they have affected the composition of the universities. For grammar schools the entries vary considerably from one area to another and even from year to year. The general aim is apparently to provide a grammar school education for the brightest 20% of each age group; this corresponds to a borderline of about 113 IQ. On this basis the round figures in Table 3 represent estimates deduced from the information so far available.

A more intensive survey of two contrasted areas ("industrial" and "prosperous") has just been published by J. E. Floud and her colleagues. Briefly their conclusion is that, in both areas, gross material handicaps have been greatly lessened, though not entirely eliminated. Nevertheless, in their view, the "problem of social wastage" is by no means overcome. The fact that, even today, a large proportion of the children from the working classes fail to reach the higher levels of scholastic instruction Floud herself attributes to the way in which the "educational ladder" is still widely regarded as a "middle class prerogative," to be anxiously watched and jealously preserved (21).

I myself should be inclined to look rather to a difference in the aims and aspirations which are traditional in the different classes. The consequences seemed clearly revealed by the differences in the after-careers of LCC scholarship winners from the lower and the middle classes respectively whom my colleagues and I have been able to follow up (cf. 5, 9, and refs.)[6] The figures show that the abler children from the working classes, even when they have obtained free places or scholarships at secondary schools of the "grammar" type, frequently fail to stay the course: by the time they are sixteen the attractions of high wages and of

---

[6] Additional evidence is furnished by the recent report of the Central Advisory Council for Education (England) on *Early Leaving*. In 1953, at the age of entry to the grammar school (11 plus), 66% of the top intelligence group were the children of manual workers; at the end of the grammar school period the proportion had fallen to 47%. Of those who drop out, some are "premature leavers," i.e., they leave voluntarily, as soon as they are legally able to do so; others fail to reach the top form and so leave at 16; of these many even fail to secure a school leaving certificate. In such cases, the award of a special place in the grammar school would seem itself to have been a wasted effort. Nevertheless, in the long run there may be certain compensating advantages to the community as a whole: even the early leavers may have gained something from the higher education to which they have been for a while subjected, and it would surely be a misfortune were all the brightest youngsters to forsake the social class into which they were born. Their continued presence there must help, not only to elevate its tone, but also (a point too often overlooked) to prevent its genetic constitution from being wholly depleted of its better elements.

cheap entertainment during leisure hours prove stronger than their desire for further knowledge and skill, and easily overcome their original resolve to face a long prospect of hard sedentary work *in statu pupillari*. As a headmaster of a secondary school which receives both types of boy has put it: "The working class parent wants his boy to be 'selected' chiefly to prove that 'his child is as good as anybody else's'; having done so, he will withdraw him at the earliest possible opportunity: I do not press them, for the presence of those whose chief interest in life is television, Hollywood films, football pools, 'the dogs,' and 'the girls' has not improved the tone of my school. And too often these 'ignobler attitudes and crude ambitions' are shared by, and encouraged by, both parents and friends." On the other hand, if I may quote the report of an experienced university teacher: "That section of the middle class which seeks, by paying fees that it can ill afford, to assist its children to climb, *via* a 'public school' or an independent 'grammar school,' to a University education and a good honours degree in the humaner subjects, is animated by a tradi-tional morale which is comparatively rare in children and parents from the other classes: those who nowadays come here on grants, at no cost to themselves or their parents, are, on the whole, most irregular attend-ants, and the least satisfactory students." Or, to quote a still more recent pronouncement of the High Master of St. Paul's:[7] "The parents are themselves imbued with four tradtional ideals which they hand on to their posterity: self-discipline, a community spirit, the Christian religion, and a readiness to accept social responsibility even at the sacrifice of material enjoyments—a genuine *noblesse oblige.*"

Underlying all these differences in outlook I myself am tempted to suspect an innate and transmissible difference in temperamental stability and in character, or in the neurophysiological basis on which such tem-peramental and moral differences tend to be built up. Tradition may explain much, it can hardly account for all. However, it would be idle to pursue such speculations here in the absence of more adequate data.[8]

[7] A. N. Gilkes, *Independence in Education,* 1957.

[8] Since my lecture was written and delivered, some further information has be-come available in the data published by the Association of Universities of the British Commonwealth (*Report of an Inquiry into Applications for Admissions to Universi-ties,* 1957). It appears that at Oxford and Cambridge only 12% of the men and 7% of the women had fathers in manual occupations; at other universities the proportions were somewhat higher, namely 31% and 19%, respectively. Among the general popu-lation 72% of the population would fall into the manual category. The report points out that to a large extent the decline must occur during the school period, and the real reason, it is suggested, is more often lack of zeal than lack of the requisite ability. "Differing environmental influences and aspirations seem mainly responsible for the fall from 66% at the point of entry to the non-fee-paying grammar school and 36% at the point of university entry. . . . Discrimination against those of humble social origin can be virtually ruled out."

Most education authorities nowadays tend to use what are misleadingly termed "intelligence tests" as tests of suitability for a grammar school. (Such tests, as I have

NEED FOR FURTHER RESEARCH

To my mind the most pressing need at the moment is for more extensive research. Hitherto the most active investigators have been research-students, with little or no experience of the ways of children or the conditions of the classroom. For the requisite facilities, and for any supplementary information they may want, they have to rely on the goodwill of the busy teacher. And one important factor is still more often overlooked: the motivation of the children themselves. This takes two obvious forms. There is first what may be called direct or short distance motivation. As actual trial has repeatedly shown, neither pupils nor students are likely to exert their full powers in a test conducted merely in the interests of someone else's research; but when the examinees' entrance to a grammar school or university depends on their performances, the average score may rise 5 to 10 IQ points higher. Secondly, there are the effects of indirect or long distance motivation: the influence of parental attitudes, of teachers' exhortations, and (most of all perhaps with British lads) of the social pressure that arises from the opinions and the comments of their school fellows, and from the tone and atmosphere of the school or class to which the pupil belongs. It is therefore hardly surprising if the results obtained in mere academic researches are at times disappointing, and evince a comparatively low reliability.

I myself had the good fortune to be appointed a member of the school inspectorate, and so not only acquired a firsthand knowledge of the schools, teachers, and pupils, but enjoyed full authority to interrupt the timetable, examine private records, and requisition whatever information might be wanted. Here therefore I must again record my indebtedness both to the London County Council for facilitating these inquiries and financing their publication, and to the teachers, social workers, and school medical officers, who rendered such wholehearted cooperation in all our investigations. It is to be hoped that other education authorities will in the near future perceive the practical value of systematically organized inquiries of this kind, conducted on an official basis by those who know the schools from inside.

The basic researches must be carried out on children rather than on students or adults. With adults, it is much harder to achieve accurate

---

argued elsewhere, should rather be termed "tests of scholastic aptitude.") The original intention was that the "intelligence test" should, so far as possible, assess innate ability. Bright children with special verbal or literary abilities and interests were then to be allocated to grammar schools; and those with practical or mechanical abilities and interests, to technical schools. But for the majority the age of 11 plus is too early to make a satisfactory distinction. Hence the brightest still seem likely to be sent to secondary schools of the grammar type rather than to a technical school, even if more suited to the latter.

assessments; innate tendencies are already obscured and overlaid; and detailed family histories difficult to obtain. In allocating adults to appropriate occupations, whether in civil life or in the fighting services, innate capacities are of little consequence, and accordingly tend to be ignored. As a result the severest critics of researches on heredity are generally those whose experience of mental testing has been gained in the adult field. This was manifest during the symposium recently arranged by the Psychological Section of the British Association. Several contributors, for instance, echoed remarks like those of H. E. Jones that "potential investigators should now be advised that the nature-nurture controversy has been shown to be an unproductive field of research" (14); and similar conclusions have more recently been voiced by writers like Maddox, Renshaw, and others, who deplore what they call "the resurrection of the nature-nurture controversy" as "wholly anachronistic" (27, 32).

But whether or not this is now the prevailing view among psychologists, it is not the opinion of leading geneticists. Goldschmidt, Snyder, Calvin Hall, and Calvin Stone all deplore the neglect of genetic inquiries by psychologists of the present day. Goldschmidt in particular has criticized "the extreme belief of contemporary psychologists in the power of environment"—a belief which he ascribes to the "doctrine of universal conditioning, which has, until lately, dominated the behaviourist school" (17). In this country eminent authorities like R. A. Fisher (19, 20) and Fraser Roberts (33) have not only argued the importance of genetic studies for psychology, but have made noteworthy contributions of their own.

Mere statistical inquiries, however, can never suffice. In this country one of the most obvious needs is a series of intensive studies of able boys and girls similar to those already carried out on the backward, the defective, the neurotic, and the delinquent. The brilliant investigation of 1,000 gifted children, started by Terman and his colleagues over 30 years ago, and so assiduously followed up, furnishes an admirable model (37, 38). But nothing like conclusive answers can be given to the questions here raised until far more extensive research has been undertaken on the fundamental problems of psychogenetics. An adequate understanding of the basic processes can be secured only if we start with carefully planned experiments on lowlier creatures, where pure strains can be obtained, breeding controlled, and successive generations more speedily raised. When we know more about the genetics of intelligence in animals, we may be able to construct with greater confidence a more exact hypothesis regarding the transmission of intelligence in man.

SOCIAL IMPLICATIONS

After all, the practical importance of the issues involved is so profound and so far-reaching that it would be fatal to dismiss the problem as "unproductive" or "anachronistic" without attempting to settle it one way or the other. No democratic state can afford to pass it by. If in the end the views of the early pioneers should turn out to have been approximately correct—if "innate intelligence varies between limits at least as wide as IQ's of 50 and 150," and if too "the average intelligence of the general population at maturity is little if at all above that of an average child of thirteen or thirteen-and-a-half"—then the bearing of genetic variation on the national and social questions of the present day would be all too obvious.

In our laudable eagerness to improve the lot of our own generation, we have been tempted to close our eyes to the effects of present policy on the generations to come. The over-all efficiency of the citizens who make up a nation or a state must in the last resort depend on what has been called its "chromosomal pool." Improved environmental amenities can of themselves ensure no lasting results; but the changes in a nation's genetic constitution are likely to prove irreversible. Throughout almost the entire Western world, and to a less extent in other areas as well, the last half-century or so has witnessed radical modifications in the conditions that previously governed marriage and fertility. Increased mobility, enhanced freedom, new means of production, new methods of government, the progressive reduction of the traditional barriers separating different peoples and different social groups, and, in our own country, the recent extensions of the educational ladder, all these transformations are visibly disturbing the stability alike of classes and of races. Almost inevitably they must alter the genetic constitution of what have hitherto been the dominant nations and the dominant stocks within those nations.

From history and from past experience we know full well how changes in the balance between inbreeding and outbreeding [9] can affect the later destinies of populations, remoulding them sometimes for good, sometimes for ill. Geneticists have repeatedly drawn attention to the processes at work, and indicated the need for studying the possible effects of contemporary trends (cf., e.g., 16, pp. 49ff. and 20, pp. 170ff.). Yet current sociological textbooks seem almost wholly to ignore them. Surely it is high time that the social psychologist should now take up the question and plan a systematic series of investigations on the intricate but highly

---

[9] British readers will find it instructive to compare current copies of such works as *Who's Who* with those of (say) 60 years ago, and note the changes in the pedigrees of the British clergy (who in the nineteenth century were probably the most inbred profession in the country) and in the ancestry of members of the British cabinet and Civil Service during that period. The recent work of Ginsberg, Glass, and Moss has shown very plainly how the extension of the educational ladder is altering the composition of the different social groups, though none of the writers has considered the possible genetic consequences. The most illuminating discussion is still that contained in the concluding chapters of Fisher's book on *The Genetical Theory of Natural Selection* (1930), especially Chap. X, "Reproduction in Relation to Social Class."

important issues involved. May I therefore conclude by endorsing, in the strongest possible terms, the verdict of Stone (17), quoted by Bingham in the last letter he wrote to me: "It is a matter of shame and regret that only an amateurish beginning has been made by psychologists in applying modern genetic methods to fundamental study in the nature-nurture area." And may we hope that in the near future Bingham's "deepest wish" may be fulfilled, and that "a small band of enthusiasts will come forward to explore afresh this urgent and many-sided field of research."

REFERENCES

1. Bagley, W. C., *The Educational Process*. New York: Macmillan, 1912.
2. Burks, Barbara, *27th Yearbook National Society for the Study of Education*, 1928, 1, 219.
3. Burt, C., Experimental Tests of General Intelligence. *Brit. J. Psychol.*, 1909 3, 94-177.
4. Burt C., The Inheritance of Mental Characteristics. *Eugen. Rev.*, 1912, **4**, 168-200.
5. Burt, C., *Annual Reports of the Psychologist to the London County Council*. London: London County Council, 1914-1931.
6. Burt, C., *The Distribution and Relations of Educational Abilities*. London: P. S. King & Son, 1917.
7. Burt, C., Is the Doctrine of Instincts Dead? *Brit. J. Educ. Psychol.*, 1941, 11, 155-172; 1943, 13, 1-16.
8. Burt, C., The Education of the Adolescent: The Psychological Implications of the Norwood Report. *Brit. J. Educ. Psychol.*, 1943, 13, 126-140.
9. Burt, C., Ability and Income. *Brit. J. Educ. Psychol.*, 1943, 13, 83-98.
10. Burt, C., The Differentiation of Intellectual Ability. *Brit. J. Educ. Psychol.*, 1954, **24**, 76-90.
11. Burt, C., The Evidence for the Concept of Intelligence. *Brit. J. Educ. Psychol.*, 1955, **25**, 158-177.
12. Burt, C., & Howard, M., The Multifactorial Theory of Inheritance and Its Application to Intelligence. *Brit. J. Statist. Psychol.*, 1956, 9, 95-131.
13. Campbell, F., *Eleven Plus and All That*. London: Watts, 1956.
14. Carmichael, L. (Ed.), *Manual of Child Psychology*. New York: Wiley, 1946.
15. Darlington, C. D., & Mather, K., *The Elements of Genetics*. London: Allen & Unwin, 1949.
16. Darlington, C. D., & Mather, K., *Genes, Plants, and People*. London: Allen & Unwin, 1950.
17. Dunn, L. C. (Ed.), *Eugenics in the Twentieth Century*. New York: Macmillan, 1921.
18. Fisher, R. A., Correlation Between Relatives on the Supposition of Mendelian Inheritance. *Trans. Roy. Soc., Edin.*, 1918, **52**, 399-433.
19. Fisher, R. A., The Causes of Human Variability. *Eugen. Rev.*, 1919, **11**, 213-220.
20. Fisher, R. A., *The Genetical Theory of Natural Selection*. Oxford: Clarendon Press, 1950.
21. Floud, J. E., Halsey, A. H., & Martin, F. M., *Social Class and Educational Opportunity*. London: Heinemann, 1956.
22. Freeman, F. N., *Mental Tests*. New York: Houghton Mifflin, 1926.

23. Galton, F., *Hereditary Genius*. London: Macmillan, 1869.
24. Garnett, M., *Education and World Citizenship*. Cambridge: Cambridge Univer. Press, 1921.
25. Goldschmidt, R. B., *Theoretical Genetics*. Univer. California Press, 1955.
26. Lashley, K. S., & Clark, G., The Cytoarchitecture of the Cerebral Cortex of *Ateles:* A Critical Examination of Architectonic Studies. *J. Comp. Neurol.*, 1946, **85**, 223-305.
27. Maddox, H., Nature-Nurture Balance Sheets. *Brit. J. Educ. Psychol.*, 1957, **27**, 166-175.
28. Newman, H. H., *Twins and Super-Twins*. London: Hutchinson, 1942.
29. Pearson, K., On a Generalized Theory of Alternative Inheritance with Special Reference to Mendel's Laws. *Phil. Trans.* 1904, **203**, 53-87.
30. Piaget, J., *The Psychology of Intelligence*. London: Kegan Paul, 1950.
31. Reeve, F. C. R., & Waddington, C. H. (Ed.), *Quantitative Inheritance*. London: H. M. Stationery Office, 1952.
32. Renshaw, T., Burt's Concept of Intelligence. *Brit. Psychol. Soc. Bull.*, 1957.
33. Roberts, J. A. F., *An Introduction to Medical Genetics*. Oxford: Oxford Univer. Press, 1940.
34. Sholl, D. A., *The Organization of the Cerebral Cortex*. London: Methuen, 1956.
35. Spearman, C., *Abilities of Man*. London: Macmillan, 1927.
36. Spencer, H., *Principles of Psychology*. London: Williams & Norgate, 1870.
37. Stone, C. P. Methodological Resources for the Experimental Study of Innate Behaviour as Related to Environmental Factors. *Psychol. Rev.*, 1947, **54**, 342-347.
38. Tanner, J. M., The Inheritance of Morphological and Physiological Traits. *Ap.* Sorsby, A. *Clinical Genetics*. London: Butterworth, 1953.
39. Terman, L. M. (Ed.), *Genetic Studies of Genius*. Stanford: Stanford Univer. Press, 1925, 1947.
40. Terman, L. M., The Discovery and Encouragement of Exceptional Talent. *Amer. Psychologist,* 1954, **9**, 221-230.
41. Thorndike, E. L., *Educational Psychology*. New York: Teachers College, Columbia University, 1914.
42. Thurstone, L. L., *The Vectors of Mind*. Chicago: Univer. Chicago Press, 1935.
43. Watson, J. B., *Behaviourism*. London: Paul, Trench Trubner, 1931.

A Study of the Family Background of the Gifted

WALTER B. BARBE

Of what influence has heredity and environment been in the development of the gifted child? Specifically, how does the family background of the gifted child differ from that of the child who is average in intelligence? Unfortunately, it is not possible to determine from such a study as this whether heredity or environment played a larger part in the development of the superior intellect of the subject. But by means of such a study, factors in the development of the gifted may be revealed. In a follow-up study of a group of gifted Negro subjects, Jenkins concluded:

. . . desirable as it would be to know which of these factors (heredity or environment) has been most potent in the development of our subjects, the writer is unable to present any crucial data on the question. The data relative to heredity are meager, and to some extent, superficial; and while the picture of the cultural background is more complete, even here there are intangible factors which elude objective evaluation (1).

The 456 subjects in this study received an I.Q. of 120 or above on the 1917 Form of the Stanford-Binet. These data were taken from the records of the Psychological Clinic of the Cleveland Board of Education. The range of I.Q. is from 120 to 164, with a mean I.Q. of 130.2. The largest number of subjects were in the 125-129 range (37.3 per cent), while almost sixty-two per cent were between 125 and 135. This placed all of the subjects in about the upper ten per cent (2) of the population of the United States at the time they were tested. A large percentage of the group (forty-four per cent) were in the upper one per cent of the population in intellectual ability as measured by this particular test.

All of the subjects were graduates of the Major Work Program of special classes for public school children in Cleveland, Ohio. The data for this study were obtained from information reported on a five-page printed questionnaire which was distributed to the graduates of the program over the last fifteen years. Of those who received the questionnaire, a return of seventy-seven per cent was received.

Reprinted from *Journal of Educational Psychology*, Vol. 47, No. 5 (May, 1956), pp. 302-309. By permission of the publisher.

RACIAL AND RELIGIOUS BACKGROUND

It is difficult to determine the racial background of a group of subjects. The question arises just how far back the subject should trace his ancestry. With regard to the ancestry of gifted subjects, Hollingworth states: "So few data have been gathered to show the proportion of gifted children in relation to race, that it is perhaps scarcely worth while to discuss the topic except to say that we are ignorant of the facts. We have, however, a few studies of the proportion of gifted in samplings of the various races found at present in the United States (3, pp. 68-69)."

In a study by Witty (4), the "racial stock included a preponderance of English, Scotch, German, and Jewish ancestors." Ninety-six per cent of the parents were American-born. These findings are similar to those of Terman and Oden: "The reports on racial origin indicate that, in comparison with the general populations of the cities concerned, there is about a one hundred per cent excess of native-born parentage, a probable excess of Scottish parentage and a deficiency of Italian, Portuguese, Mexican, and Negro ancestry (5)."

The racial stock of the subjects in the present study is predominantly German, nearly half (47.6 per cent) of the subjects reported having some degree of German ancestry. The next highest group mentioned, twenty-three per cent, was English. The next most frequent were: Hungarian, 14.7 per cent; Russian, 14.4 per cent; and Polish, 10.2 per cent. Hardly any European country was not at least mentioned.

The fact that the population of Cleveland consists of such a diverse foreign element would tend to make the racial background of the subjects different from the subjects in both Terman and Witty's studies. According to the 1940 Census (6) of the City of Cleveland, the largest foreign-born element, about thirteen per cent, was Polish. Czech, Hungarian and Italian each made up about twelve per cent of the foreign-born population. German, Yugoslavian, English and Russian each represented about seven per cent.

Slightly more than two and one-half per cent of the total sample are Negroes. The percentage of Negroes has risen from less than one per cent in 1938 to nearly five per cent in 1952. According to the census, the per cent of Negroes in Cleveland has risen from eight per cent in 1930 to 9.5 per cent in 1940 (6).

About 11.3 per cent of the group was Catholic, 46.3 Protestant, and 38.8 per cent Jewish. Other groups make up the remaining 3.8 per cent. As Hollingworth reports of New York City (3), children of Catholic parents, many of whom are gifted, are commonly being educated in parochial schools. This explains the rather low percentage of Catholic subjects in Major Work classes. The Jewish group appears to be represented in far greater numbers than its proportional share. This is also true of the gifted in the public schools of New York where Hollingworth reports there is "a marked excess of Jewish parentage (3, p. 70)."

ECONOMIC BACKGROUND

An important phase of a study of the gifted which has not received adequate attention is their socio-economic background. This is difficult to determine and, when done in retrospect, is subject to many errors. The procedure followed in this study was to locate the economic tenth of the census tract in which the subject had lived while he was in public school (7). This gave an indication of the rent and property value of the neighborhood in which the gifted subject had been reared. The results of this phase of the study are presented in Table 1.

The economic tenth from which the greatest number of subjects came was the seventh, while the sixth and seventh economic tenths included more than fifty-eight per cent of the subjects. This indicates that the background of the majority of the subjects in the study may accurately be described as "upper middle-class."

TABLE 1. The Economic Status of 456 Gifted Subjects

Economic Tenths	PER CENT
Highest	1.1
Ninth	7.9
Eighth	10.3
Seventh	37.1
Sixth	21.3
Fifth	11.0
Fourth	5.0
Third	3.5
Second	2.2
Lowest	0.7

ORDER OF BIRTH AND SIZE OF FAMILY

It has long been a popular belief that the gifted child is an only child, or, perhaps, has one sibling. In a study of 253 subjects (8), Goddard reported half as being first-born and three-fourths as being either first- or second-born. Of the first-born, forty-five (about eighteen per cent) were only children.

Hollingworth reported that the gifted child had few siblings. In a study by Cobb and Hollingworth, fifty-seven gifted children averaged less than one sibling each (3). With respect to the order of birth, they found that more than one-half of their subjects were first-born.

In 1940, Terman reported that "the parents of the gifted subjects had produced . . . an average of 3.09 (children) per family." He states that this rate would more than maintain the stock, but "it appears likely that the subjects themselves will not equal the fertility rate of their parents" (5, p. 18).

In the present study two questions were asked to determine the size of the family and the order of birth of the gifted child. About 21.8 per cent of the subjects had no siblings, while 42.6 per cent had only one. Almost twenty per cent had two siblings, and seven per cent three.

About twenty-two per cent of the subjects in this study are only children. This is not as large a number as that found by Cobb and Hollingworth, although their finding that "more than half were first-born" (3, p. 180) is substantiated by the fact that 52.5 per cent of the subjects in this study were first-born. About twenty-nine per cent are second-born, and only 9.3 third-born. The data indicate that in this group the gifted child was the first-born in a family of two children.

PARENT OR GUARDIAN OF GIFTED SUBJECTS

Eighty-seven and a half per cent of the gifted subjects were reared by their own parents. The next largest group, 7.2 per cent, were reared by only their mothers. Two per cent were reared by their own mother and a step-father, and 1.5 per cent by their own father and a stepmother. The father or foster parents each reared 0.9 per cent of the total number of subjects.

Witty (9), in studying one hundred gifted children in Kansas, found that most of their parents were American-born. This was not true of the subjects in this study. Slightly less than fifty per cent of the subjects had one or both parents who were foreign-born. This is partially due to the large foreign element in the population of Cleveland.[1] It emphasizes the contribution of the immigrant to the mentally superior groups of the country. Table 2 presents these data.

TABLE 2.   Percentage of Parents of Gifted Subjects Who Were Born Outside the United States

Both parents U.S.-born	51.3
One parent foreign-born	21.1
Both parents foreign-born	27.5

[1] About 20 per cent of the population of Cleveland were foreign-born.

Even though more rigid government controls have been placed on immigration, no trend is noted which would indicate that fewer of the subjects have parents who are foreign-born.

EDUCATION OF PARENTS

Hollingworth states (3) that the educational level of the parents of gifted subjects is far above the average for their generation. "In the majority of the cases where the gifted child has been born since 1915, both parents are graduates of high school, and in far more cases than in the population at large both parents are college graduates (3, p. 180)." Since all of the subjects in the present study were born after 1915, it is interesting to compare Hollingworth's statements with the data obtained for this group.

Of the fathers of the subjects, 38.4 per cent had a grammar school education or less; 33.6 per cent had a high school education; 8.8 per cent trade or business school; and 19.2 per cent had some college. Of the mothers of the subjects, 32.5 per cent had a grammar school education or less; 42.2 per cent had a high school education; 12.3 per cent trade or business school; and 13.0 per cent had some college. The mothers of the gifted subjects on the average appeared to be slightly better educated than the fathers through the high school and business school levels. However, there were more fathers than mothers who attended college.

MARITAL STATUS OF PARENTS

Terman reported (5) that until 1922, 5.2 per cent of the parents of his gifted group had been divorced and 1.9 per cent were separated. By 1940, the percentage of divorced and separated parents had risen to 13.9.

The data in the present study are not exactly comparable to the results of Terman's study. The information obtained in this study deals with the marital status of the parents while the subject was in public school. It is perhaps comparable to Terman's 1922 data but is definitely not comparable to his 1940 data.

Eighty-eight per cent of the parents of the subjects were living together while the subject was in public school. About 6.3 per cent were either divorced or separated. This is only slightly higher than the report for Terman's 1922 group and is certainly lower than that of the general population. The remaining five per cent consists of cases where one or both of the parents were deceased.

OCCUPATIONAL LEVEL OF PARENTS OF GIFTED SUBJECTS

The occupations of the parents were listed according to the U. S. census classification. The *Dictionary of Occupational Titles* (10) was used to classify the occupations into seven distinct groups: professional and managerial; clerical and sales; service; agriculture, fishery, forestry, etc.; skilled; semi-skilled; and unskilled. The subjects were asked the title and description of the father's occupation. It was possible to classify all but a few of the occupations listed. Where descriptions were not given and two classifications were possible, the data were omitted. Classifications of the parent's occupation were made for four hundred and thirty-seven subjects. Three of the remaining nineteen were on government pensions, while the rest gave no response to the question at all. The data are presented in Table 3.

TABLE 3.   Occupational Level of Parents of Gifted Subjects

	PER CENT
Professional and managerial	40.3
Clerical and sales	22.4
Service	3.7
Agriculture, fishery, forestry, etc.	0.2
Skilled	21.5
Semi-skilled	8.2
Unskilled	3.7

Hollingworth reports (3) that more than fifty per cent of the children testing above 140 I.Q. have fathers who are professional men or proprietors. The I.Q.'s of the subjects in the present study are not this high, which may partly explain why only about forty per cent of the parents fall into the professional and managerial group. Hollingworth also states (3) that half of the remaining fathers are in semi-professional and clerical occupations. This corresponds to the clerical and sales group of the U. S. Census Bureau, and the data for this group agree with the data in Hollingworth's study.

The fact that over thirty per cent of the parents are in the laboring class, and about forty per cent of these are semi-skilled or unskilled, is noteworthy. It indicates that while the majority of gifted children do come from parents of higher occupational status, the laboring class also contributes a sizeable number.

SUMMARY

In this study data were presented concerning the composition of the group being studied and their family background.

1. The range in I.Q. of the four hundred and fifty-six subjects was from 120 to 164 with a mean I.Q. of 130.2. Almost sixty-two per cent of the group were within the 125–135 range.

2. Slightly less than fifty-two per cent of the subjects are females; slightly more than forty-eight per cent are males.

3. Of the total samples, only 2.6 per cent are Negroes.

4. About thirty-nine per cent of the subjects are Jewish. The Jewish group is represented in far greater numbers than the size of this group in the total population would lead one to expect.

5. The economic tenth of the census tract in which the subjects lived while in public schools was most frequently the sixth and seventh. This would characterize the gifted child as being upper middle-class.

6. The gifted child appears to be either an only child or firstborn in a family of two.

7. Eighty-seven and one-half per cent of the gifted subjects were reared by their own parents.

8. Almost fifty per cent of the subjects had one or both parents who were foreign-born. These data indicate that the group studied is quite unlike other studies of gifted groups. Previously, the gifted child was found to have American parentage. The high percentage of foreign-born in Cleveland (approximately twenty per cent) partially explains these data.

9. The education of the mothers of gifted subjects is slightly higher than that of the fathers, even though more of the fathers went to college.

10. Forty per cent of the parents were in the professional and managerial group, 22.5 per cent in the clerical and sales, and thirty per cent in the laboring class.

The subjects in this study come from about average backgrounds with respect to occupational level, educational level and marital adjustment of their parents. Economically the majority of them come from an upper middle-class group.

REFERENCES

1. Martin David Jenkins, "A Socio-Psychological Study of Negro Children of Superior Intelligence." Unpublished Doctoral Dissertation. Graduate School, Northwestern University, Evanston, Illinois, p. 53, June, 1935.

2. Merle R. Sumption, *Three Hundred Gifted Children*, p. 6. Yonkers-on-Hudson, New York: World Book Co., 1941.

3. Leta A. Hollingworth, *Gifted Children*. New York: The Macmillan Co., 1926.

4. Paul A. Witty, "A Study of One Hundred Gifted Children." *Bulletin of Education, University of Kansas*, 2:8, February, 1930.

5. Lewis M. Terman and Melita H. Oden, *The Gifted Child Grows Up*. Stanford, California: Stanford University Press, 1947.

6. U. S. Department of Commerce, Bureau of the Census, Sixteenth Census of the United States, 1940, *Population*, 11:712, Part 5, Washington, D. C.: U. S. Government Printing Office, 1943.

7. Howard Whipple Green, *Census Tract Street Index for Cuyahoga County*, fifth edition. Cleveland Health Council, 1951.
8. Henry H. Goddard, *School Training of Gifted Children*, p. 129. Yonkers-on-Hudson, New York: World Book Co., 1928.
9. Paul A. Witty, "A Genetic Study of Fifty Gifted Children," In *Intelligence: Its Nature and Nurture*. Thirty-Ninth Yearbook, Part II, National Society for the Study of Education. Chicago: University of Chicago Press, 1940.
10. Job Analysis and Information Section, Division of Standards and Research, United States Department of Labor, *Dictionary of Occupational Titles*, *Part I*, second edition. Washington, D. C.: United States Government Printing Office, 1949.

Resources of Mental Ability: How Can the Supply of Superior Ability Be Conserved and Perhaps Increased?

LEE R. DICE

As modern civilization grows in complexity the demand for mental ability is increasing in something like a geometrical progression. Needed are able and inspiring teachers, imaginative engineers and architects, resourceful investigators, broad-minded administrators, competent physicians and lawyers, and a host of other types of professional workers. In the past 50 years, for example, the number of scientists in the United States has increased ten times as rapidly as the whole population (Wolfle, 1954), but the demand still exceeds the supply.

Craftsmen, technologists, and many other types of workers with above-average ability also are required in increasing numbers. To build and to maintain the complicated machines of modern industry requires a high degree of competence. Business also is demanding increasingly higher levels of ability. The farm manager now requires a long process of education and experience added to a large degree of natural talent. The successful housewife and mother, furthermore, must have many special abilities. Men with muscular power and physical endurance are still needed for many operations, but machines are taking over an increasing proportion of their duties.

The maintenance and further evolution of the complicated human

Reprinted from *Eugenics Quarterly*, Vol. 7, No. 1 (March, 1960), pp. 9-12. By permission of the author and publisher.

communities that now dominate the earth requires not only that all our resources of mental ability be fully utilized and conserved but also that these resources be, if possible, further expanded.

Facilities are consequently required in every society for discovering which of its young men and young women possess potential mental ability of any type. Means must then be found for encouraging each of these young people to prepare for the field of activity best suited to his talents and interests. Each should be educated and trained so that the best possible use is made of his capabilities. The full exploitation of potential ability of every useful kind will benefit not only the individuals concerned, but will promote also the welfare of the whole common-wealth.

SUPPLY OF TALENT IS LIMITED

Even if every capable student is identified and given the best possible education and training, however, this will at best permit only the full utilization of those talents that already exist in the population. The sup-ply of potentially able young men and women in the present world population, unfortunately, is limited. Even if all promising young people can be located and trained, their number will certainly be less than can profitably be used by the increasingly complex civilizations which are in process of evolution.

Students with high mental capacities are rare, as every teacher knows. A good education added to strong incentive has enabled many a below-average student to become a useful worker. More than education and incentive are needed, however, to produce an individual who ranks high in any special field of effort.

Some of the qualities that may enable a person to be outstanding in one type of work may contribute to his possible success in a different field of effort. The mathematician, physician, engineer, research scientist, artist, and musician, however, must each have talents of a special kind (Dorn, 1947), as well as training in his own particular field. The demand for specialists of many diverse kinds can be expected to increase for many years in the future.

Success in any kind of career undoubtedly is based on a complex of factors. These factors include not only the various elements of intelli-gence and training but also involve attributes of personality, such as may be called imagination, perseverance, dependability, curiosity, and social cooperativeness (Cattell, 1957: Table A-3). The state of physical health also may sometimes affect the expression of the mental qualities. At the present time, unfortunately, the numerous elements of intelligence, per-sonality, education, and physical well-being that together may create a predisposition for any special type of ability cannot be successfully measured or classified.

IMPORTANCE OF HEREDITY

Heredity is known, however, to be an important factor in the production of many features of superior intelligence. Some important factors of personality also have a strong hereditary component (Cattell, 1950). By comparing sets of identical twins with sets of non-identical but same-sexed twins, for example, it has been demonstrated that many of the measurable psychological characters that might contribute to mental ability are dependent to a considerable degree on heredity (Vandenberg, 1956; and unpublished data). Those persons who have a special talent of any kind may fail to use it effectively unless they are given sufficient encouragement and unless they receive a suitable education. No amount of encouragement or education, however, can transform a stupid student into one who is intellectually superior.

The precise mode of heredity of the several factors that in proper combination may provide the potentiality for any human special ability, or for excellence in overall ability, is not known with certainty. The available evidence, however, strongly suggests that the several factors which underlie intelligence, personality, and physical health and are basic to the expression of superior ability are each inherited through the combined action of numerous genes (Fuller, 1954; Neel and Schull, 1954). This is the multiple-factor or polygene type of heredity.

A special feature of multifactorial heredity is that the genes concerned are additive in their effects. A character that is controlled by genes of this type will in general be only slightly affected by the presence or absence of any one gene. The identification of the precise genes that may influence mental superiority, consequently, is not essential as a basis for considering the level of hereditary talent in any given population. Those individuals who exhibit superiority in any character can be assumed to be the carriers of more than an average number of those genes which may contribute to the production of that character.

Those multiple genes that control the heredity of mental capacities must be widely distributed in every human population. Due to the recombination of these genes in each generation, considerable variation is to be expected among the children in each family, but there also will be certain family resemblances. The children of a person with a certain outstanding ability may not equal their parent in this character. The expectation, nevertheless, is that from parents who both exhibit a talent of any particular kind, the children will for that talent average above the general level of the population of which they form a part.

Long before there was any precise knowledge of genetic laws, the plant and animal breeders had demonstrated how to improve traits that are controlled by multiple genes. By selecting as parents those individuals who exhibited in highest degree the particular trait desired, such wonders have been developed as high milk productivity by cows, high egg productivity by hens, and swift running by race horses. Breeds of dogs have been developed which have the capacity to be trained for various special types of behavior.

No such rigorous selection could be applied to a human population, nor would we wish it to be. The selection which would result from a wholly voluntary increase in family size by those persons who possess a particular character, such as a special mental ability, however, would be expected to produce in just a few generations an appreciable improvement in the character selected for. We are not here concerned with developing a new kind of human race but only with raising the general level of ability.

The increase of potential mental ability in human populations actually is basically not a genetic problem at all. Although it is desirable to learn as much as possible about the mode of inheritance of all kinds of human traits, including special mental abilities, it is not necessary to know the precise mode of heredity of a trait controlled by multiple genes in order to plan for the increase of that trait in a population. The knowledge we really need is how the several social factors operate among persons with differing mental capacities to determine their mate selection, age at marriage, and size of family.

DIFFERENTIAL FERTILITY IN RESPECT TO ABILITY

For as far back as we have any records, there appear to have been differences in fertility between the several economic, educational, occupational, and social classes and between rural and urban groups, in almost every case the higher birth rates being found in the lower class and in the rural groups (Osborn, 1951; Kiser, 1952; Grabill and others, 1958; Westoff, 1954). These differences increased with the introduction of birth control and have declined somewhat as contraception has come into wider use. At the present time these differentials appear to be directly related to the extent of the use of contraceptives.

Standing alone, these differentials would appear to make for a decrease in each generation of those genetic factors favorable to high intelligence, character, and drive. But there may be offsetting factors of which at present we have no knowledge. Indeed we do not know the extent to which the social classes differ in genetic capacities, nor whether differences in size of family within social groups may offset differences between groups.

In general, scientific opinion today favors the more pessimistic interpretation. But these differences are due to social causes, and we believe that acceptable and relatively slight changes in social, psychological, and economic conditions could result in differentials of a favorable sort. Some of these possible changes will be suggested in a later section of this paper.

OTHER MECHANISMS THAT MAY AFFECT ABILITY

In addition to differential reproduction the most important of the mechanisms which may conceivably affect changes in mental capacity from one generation to another are assortative mating, sexual selection, natural selection, heterosis, and mutation.

Positive assortative mating, the tendency for like to mate with like, should result in the production of some families with above-average mental ability. On the other hand, some families with below-average ability also will be produced. Assortative mating offers the possibility of producing some individuals with exceptionally high mental capacity, but this is balanced by the equal probability of producing some individuals with exceptionally low capacity. Assortative mating by itself, consequently, will neither raise nor lower the average intellectual level of a population, but it may be an important mechanism in the evolution of special abilities.

Sexual selection (preferential mating) may be presumed to have been important in early human societies in promoting the evolution of certain special abilities (Holmes, 1936; Dice, 1955). In a hunting tribe, for instance, ability in hunting may give a man a preferred rating as a marriage partner (Holmberg, 1950). In many preliterate societies not only did those persons who exhibited preferred types of abilities have priority in the marriage market, but the most able men often had more than one wife. In such societies sexual selection must often have resulted in differential reproduction which favored the particular abilities which were locally esteemed.

Reliable information about the operation of sexual selection for or against mental abilities, unfortunately, is almost completely lacking in modern societies. In the United States, however, sexual selection seems in general not to favor intellectual capacity. On the contrary, overemphasis on female physical beauty probably results in some degree of selection against intellectual capacity, at least in women. This is indicated by the fact that 15 per cent or more of women college graduates never marry (Population Reference Bureau, 1956). In this country there also is overemphasis on athletic ability and on economic success in men. In intellectual circles, intelligence is probably of some advantage, both to men and to women, in securing a desirable mate. It may be doubted, however, if this is true for most classes in the population. In the United States, therefore, sexual selection may be contributing to adverse differential reproduction in respect to mental capacity.

Natural selection (differential mortality) is another agency that may affect the frequency in the population of those genes that contribute to mental superiority of any kind. Any hereditary factor that results in involuntary sterility or in death before the end of the reproductive period may be considered to be subject to natural selection. In spite of statements sometimes made that natural selection is ineffective in modern populations, it is still a powerful force (Holmes, 1936; Dobzhansky and Allen, 1956; Noel, 1958). It operates especially to remove those hereditary defects which cause death before or soon after birth or which results in infertility. Idiots and imbeciles generally have no offspring, and consequently a portion of the genes that produce these severe mental defects will be eliminated from each generation. One type of low-grade mental defect associated with phenylketonuria is produced by a recessive gene. Several other types of mental defects likewise are inherited through simple genetic mechanisms (Kallmann, 1953). Mutations that produce mental defects such as these may be presumed to occur at a low but persistent rate. If these genes were not removed by natural selection, they would accumulate to form a heavy load of unfortunate heredity. On the other hand, there is no evidence that in modern populations natural selection in any way affects the frequency of those multiple genes that control superior mental capacity.

Differential mortality produced by cultural rather than by biological factors might also affect the supply of inherited ability. In some populations mortality may be at a higher rate for children who are low in intelligence than for those who have greater inborn intellect (Holmes, 1933). Such differential mortality might result from inadequate care of their children by parents who are themselves of relatively low intelligence. The families of incompetent parents, moreover, will likely be reared under conditions of poverty which predispose to malnutrition and disease. The economic condition and health of all classes in the United States, fortunately, are steadily being improved. The current amount of differential mortality in the United States due to inadequate child care or other cultural features is unknown, but may be presumed to be small.

That heterosis (hybrid vigor) may cause differential fertility in respect to intelligence has been suggested by Penrose (1955). According to this hypothesis, those genes that control intelligence are assumed also to affect fertility. It is postulated that when these genes are in homozygous combinations they may produce either low intelligence combined with low fertility or high intelligence, also combined with low fertility.

When, on the contrary, these genes are in heterozygous combinations, they are assumed to produce not only an intermediate level of intelligence, but also, through hybrid vigor, an increase in fertility.

There is no good evidence, however, that those genes which in the homozygous combination produce both mental defects and infertility, occur at the same loci as any of those multiple genes that may contribute to mental superiority. In modern populations, furthermore, family size is mostly controlled by economic and social factors, rather than by inability to produce children. In the early years of the United States family size averaged much greater than now. This was true of families in which the parents presumably had high intelligence as well as of those whose parents were less well endowed. This indicates that high intelligence is not directly related to biological infertility. Heterosis among the genes responsible for intelligence consequently seems not to be an important factor in producing differential fertility among the classes in our society.

Mutation undoubtedly occurs in those genes that control mental ability. Little information is available about the mutation rates of those multiple genes that underlie superior talent, but each of these can be expected to mutate at approximately the same slow rate as other human genes. Further, it can be expected that most such mutations will result in a decrease, rather than in an increase of potential ability. Even those mutations that may produce some improvement in mental capacity will not spread in a large population except as a result of favorable selection. Mutation, consequently, may be expected in general to produce deterioration rather than improvement.

That the intelligence requirements for marriage are currently being pushed upwards in modern societies has been suggested by Neel (1958). If this is occurring and if it is not accompanied by an increase of children born out of wedlock, it might offset to some degree any adverse effects of differential fertility. Evidence in support of this hypothesis, however, seems not to be available.

Differential mortality due to war undoubtedly affects to some degree the frequency of those genes that underlie ability (Hunt, 1930). So also does the celibacy which is obligatory in certain religious orders (Holmes, 1921: 361). Both these agencies, however, are believed to decrease, rather than to increase the supply of inherited ability.

The number of generations per century differs according to amount of schooling. Those persons who prepare themselves for intellectual careers by attending college, and especially those who go on to graduate school or professional school, marry on the average later in life and begin their families at an older age than those who do not have to spend so much time in special training (Wrong, 1958). This differential among the educational classes in the number of generations produced per century must be added to the other factors making for a decline in intelligence.

DECREASE IN GENES FOR SUPERIOR ABILITY

None of the genetic mechanisms or other agencies known to be operating in human societies, consequently, seem to be of a sort likely to increase the frequency of the genes underlying mental ability. It seems likely that in the United States at least some decrease in each generation must be taking place in the frequencies of those genes that produce superior mental capacity.

The seriousness of the decline per generation and per century of potential mental ability, however, is in much dispute. Some authors, taking into account not only genetic factors but also the effect on development of different home environments have estimated that present rates of differential fertility would, if no other factors were involved, make for a decline at the rate of from 0.9 to as much as 4.0 or more I.Q. points per generation, when both hereditary and environmental factors are taken into account. Reliable methods for measuring this loss of intelligence, unfortunately, do not now exist (Dorn, 1947). Consequently, it is impossible to estimate the effects of current trends on the future supply of children who will have the capacity to become skilled workers or to profit by advanced training. The trend, however, is probably in the wrong direction. The world of the future will need a greater rather than a lesser percentage of persons who possess superior ability.

REQUIREMENTS FOR AN INCREASE
IN HEREDITARY TALENT

Increase in the supply of hereditary mental capacity in any population evidently requires that those persons who possess an above-average level of ability must have more children than those persons who are below average. The reservoir of hereditary talent in any community resides in all those individuals who rank above average in any type of ability. Included in this category are technicians, craftsmen, businessmen, farm and factory managers and supervisors, professional workers, and numerous other types of workers who exhibit special competence in some particular line of endeavor. Women who rate above average in home making and child rearing must also be included. If the resources of mental ability of the country are to be increased, the fertility of these persons must exceed that of the less competent members of society.

Fear of overpopulation in the nation or world should not deter talented persons from rearing as many children as they can afford. Should overpopulation come in time to any country, the more able persons should have the best chance for survival. On the other hand, should the more talented members of any society continue for long to be less fertile than the less able members, then the average level of mental capacity of that society must inevitably decline.

A high diversity of those genes that underlie the production of superior mental abilities of various types undoubtedly is carried by every human population. In other words, every population carries a large supply of genetic material on which selection in the form of differential fertility can act. The genes for ability, however, are not distributed evenly throughout each population but are most concentrated in those individuals who exhibit any type of superior ability. The greater the endowment of talent enjoyed by any person, therefore, the more important it is that he or she should have a greater number of children than the average for the population.

HEREDITY COUNSELING CENTERS

Some talented persons remain childless because of the fear of transmitting to their children certain physical or mental defects which are known to occur in their ancestors or relatives. Every person, however, even though presumably "normal," carries in his heredity a number of more or less serious defects (Muller, 1950). Should it be certainly known that there is a high probability of transmitting a serious defect of any kind, then of course no considerate person will take the risk of afflicting a child. In every case, however, the probability of transmitting a defect should be balanced against the probabilities for the transmission of superior characters, both mental and physical.

The heredity counseling centers which are being organized in many parts of the nation (Hammons, 1959) can aid prospective parents in assessing the probabilities for transmitting their good as well as their bad heredity. More of these centers are needed so that advice about their heredity will be available to all our citizens. Each such counseling center, moreover, should possess facilities for evaluating intelligence and personality as well as for the diagnosis of medical defects.

INCREASE IN THE FERTILITY OF
INTELLECTUAL WORKERS

The current lesser fertility of intellectual workers than of other occupational classes undoubtedly is in part due to the longer period during their early life that such workers must spend in education and training. When they are financially able to begin their families, they are consequently older than other types of workers.

For most kinds of professional work graduate training, in addition to a college degree, is a necessary prerequisite. The master's degree, which is recommended for high-school teaching and for a number of other intellectual occupations, requires at the present time an average of about one and one-half years of graduate study. The Ph.D., or equivalent degree, which usually is required for university teaching or for research, requires an average of about four years in graduate school. Professional training in such subjects as medicine or law may require from two to as many as eight or more years after the bachelor's degree.

The period of graduate study is an expensive one, no matter what the field of specialization. Not only is there tuition and living expenses to pay but also books to buy and frequently travel or other special expenses. All this expense comes at the age when most other young people are getting married and starting their families. Unless the graduate student defers marriage, however, his wife probably will have to work to help support the pair. To care properly for children then is difficult or impossible. The young scientist who marries must consequently usually defer having children until he has completed his training and has secured a more or less permanent position. The salary of a young scientist after graduation, moreover, usually is low. The paying off of debts incurred during the training years may impose additional burdens upon the young family. Parents who are wealthy can aid their children during these difficult years, but not all the parents of gifted children are financially able to supply such aid. The proportion of graduate students who are married has increased in recent years, but it still is difficult to combine post-graduate study with marriage and the rearing of a family.

In order to ease to some degree the financial burden of graduate study, I recommend that every competent graduate student who has been accepted as a candidate for the master's or Ph.D. or equivalent degree by any reputable institution be provided with a tuition scholarship. These scholarships should not be competetive. Instead, a sufficient number should be available so that one can be granted to each qualified student. The qualifications should of course be sufficiently high to select only those students who truly have superior talents.

The number of teaching and research assistantships available to graduate students also should be increased, so that all competent students can be provided for. Such assistantships not only help in recruiting able students for intellectual careers but incidentally provide teaching and research aid to the presently overburdened universities. A student learns much from serving as an assistant. An additional advantage of the assistantship is that the student works for the financial help he receives and is not given something for nothing.

Graduate students in the social sciences and humanities should in my opinion be eligible for scholarships and graduate assistantships on the same basis as students in the natural sciences, and graduate students who are candidates for degrees in medicine, dentistry, law, and other professions should also be considered. Ability of every kind is needed by our society.

A dependency allowance for a wife and for each child should be provided in each graduate assistantship. Such allowances now are provided in many fellowships. The extension to include assistantships is highly desirable, because of the added inducement this would give talented young married persons to prepare for intellectual careers.

These proposed graduate scholarships and assistantships should, in my opinion, be provided through the Department of Health, Education, and Welfare or through some other federal agency. Graduate students regularly cross state lines to attend those universities which provide the best instruction in their chosen field of specialization. Intellectual achievements, furthermore, are the property of the whole nation and world. The support of advanced training is consequently a national rather than merely a local or state obligation.

A program for loan funds for prospective teachers and college and graduate students has recently been organized by the federal government. Sufficient funds for this purpose should be made available so that every qualified student can obtain such assistance.

The availability to graduate students of tuition scholarships, assistantships, dependency allowances, and loan funds, as recommended above, can be expected to encourage graduate students to marry and to begin their families at a younger age than the present average. With such financial help these talented individuals will probably have larger families than otherwise they might have had. This is highly desirable, because the children of such intellectually superior parents have a better than average chance of being also talented. Osborn (1956) and others have urged that early marriage be made economically possible for gifted young people. Intellectual workers, however, comprise only a relatively small proportion of the population. Although an increase in their fertility will be valuable, no improvement in their fertility which can reasonably be anticipated will suffice alone to provide the desired amount of increase in the supply of talent.

ECONOMIC STATUS AND FERTILITY

Within certain social and occupational groups, fertility is known to be positively related to income level, at least in countries where birth control is widely practiced. We may also note that birth rates in the United States average higher during years of prosperity than during years of adverse economic conditions (Population Reference Bureau, 1958). Further study should reveal ways in which economic forces could be harnessed to bring about desirable changes in fertility differentials.

Natural fertility decreases with age. Especial care, therefore, should be taken to make it economically possible for those workers who are above average in ability to start their families early in life. The current difference in salary between the beginning professional worker and the older, well-established worker in the same field is probably too great.

PROGRAMS OF NEGATIVE EUGENICS

Certain past proposals have been designed to increase the level of intelligence in the population through limiting the reproduction of the least intelligent members of society.

One such program of negative eugenics has been directed toward the sterilization of persons who are mentally deficient. This program has been only slightly successful. Some persons have objected to sterilization on religious grounds. Others have objected to the compulsory aspects of the program. In some states there has been confusion between sterilization and punishment. A total of 60,926 individuals are reported by the Human Betterment Association of America to have been sterilized in the United States over the 52-year period from 1907 through 1958. Of this total, 31,500 were sterilized because of mental deficiency. In 1958 the number sterilized was 747. Compared to the size of the national population, these figures are relatively small. The number of unfavorable genes eliminated so far as a result of this program of sterilization must be too few to have produced any important increase in the level of intelligence of the nation as a whole (Neel and Schull, 1954: 344-346).

The segregation in mental institutions of persons with severe mental disorders, including mental deficiencies, undoubtedly operates to decrease the frequency in following generations of the genes that adversely affect mental competence. The shortage of hospital space to care for persons with subnormal mentality, however, limits the number who can be confined. No estimates seem to have been made of the actual genetic effects of the current amount of segregation of such persons.

The elimination of as many as possible of those genes that contribute to the production either of physical defects or of mental disorders certainly is highly desirable. The production of children by persons who carry hereditary defects of any serious kind or who are mentally, temperamentally, or financially not qualified to rear children properly, therefore, should be discouraged. Those individuals who for sufficient genetic or social reasons voluntarily request to be sterilized should be given this permission. The probate court or some other local authority should have the power to authorize the surgeon to perform the necessary operation. The parents or legal guardians of mentally incompetent individuals should be permitted to petition for the sterilization of their wards.

Relatively few individuals in any generation, however, are likely to be sterilized under any program suitable to a democracy. No considerable increase from such a program can be expected, consequently, in the frequency of those multiple genes that are believed to produce superior intellectual capacity.

BIRTH CONTROL

Birth-control methods have in recent years become of increasing importance for the voluntary limitation of family size. Unfortunately, birth control seems to have been more effective in limiting the number of children per family in the professional and skilled-labor classes than in the unskilled-labor class. Those individuals who have ambition to raise their own economic and social position and those desirous of giving their children the best possible education and other advantages have presumably restricted the number of their children to a greater degree than those individuals who have less ambition for themselves or for their children. The result has been that in past years birth control probably has increased the fertility differentials among the economic classes in the United States. With the spread of contraceptive methods throughout the whole society, some decrease may be expected in the fertility of the lower occupational and educational classes. It may be doubted, however, that birth control will ever by itself operate to reverse the adverse differentials in fertility in respect to mental ability among these classes.

Birth-control methods, nevertheless, provide opportunity for parents to adjust the size of their families to their own particular economic and social conditions and also to their own hereditary endowments. Those legal and religious barriers that now obstruct the dissemination and use of birth-control methods should consequently be removed.

INADEQUACY OF PRESENT KNOWLEDGE

The organization of any effective program designed to increase the supply of inherited ability is hampered by lack of information about the distribution and frequency in the population of those persons who possess the various desired types of intelligence and personality. No satisfactory classification now exists of those special abilities which are needed by a modern society, such as ours. Nor are fully reliable methods available for identifying the persons who exhibit the desired qualities. The accuracy of the current estimates of differential fertility among the several occupational, economic, educational, and social classes leaves much to be desired. It is impossible with our present meager knowledge to estimate the current rate of decrease in the frequencies of those genes that affect intellectual capacity or to plan effectively for their increase.

The inadequacy of our information about these important matters has been noted by numerous psychologists, sociologists, and biologists. Research in this field, unfortunately, is not receiving nearly as much attention as its importance demands. The major reason for this neglect undoubtedly is the complexity of the problems involved. The isolated research worker on some university campus can at best make only slow progress in this difficult field of investigation. For their solution these complex problems will require the concentrated efforts of research teams composed of persons trained in the several special disciplines which are directly concerned (Snyder, 1951; Scheinfeld, 1958). Only a permanent research institute with an adequate staff can effectively investigate concurrently the numerous interrelated psychologic, economic, social, and genetic problems which are involved in the production of superior intellectual capacity.

PROPOSAL FOR A RESEARCH INSTITUTE

A research institute dedicated to investigations in the field of human abilities should be organized immediately. To be successful such an institute must have strong and permanent financial backing. Any large foundation which has uncommitted funds might well consider this opportunity. Another possibility would be the organization of such a research institute in the Department of Health, Education, and Welfare. The National Institute of Mental Health, under the Public Health Service, currently is supporting some investigations of the genetics of mental traits. The comprehensive attack which is needed, however, demands the organization of a new institute with its own permanent staff.

In addition to investigations of the numerous genetic and environmental factors that control or affect the development of human abilities, the proposed institute could profitably make surveys of the distribution and frequency of occurrence of the various types of special talent among the people of the nation. Another desirable activity would be to secure reliable information about the magnitude of the differences in reproductive rate which currently are exhibited by the several occupational, economic, social, and educational classes in our society. Studies designed to improve the identification of potential ability early in school life also would be highly useful. By conducting investigations and surveys such as these, and others of a related kind, an institute dedicated to research on human abilities could be of incalculable value.

HOPE FOR THE FUTURE

When reliable information becomes available about the degree to which each type of special ability is inherited, about those environmental factors which may affect the development of the talents which each individual may possess, and about the distribution of mental capabilities in the population, then I am confident that our citizens can be depended upon to take the necessary steps to conserve and to increase the total supply of talent.

Mental ability and character are the most valuable resources that the world possesses (Wolfle, 1954). These resources should be utilized to the highest possible degree. The total supply of ability also should be increased. Any steps which will induce an increased proportion of capable young people to devote themselves to the types of work for which they are individually best suited or which will provide them with better training will be of immediate value to society. Any steps which will result in an increase in the proportion of mentally superior persons in the population will be of inestimable value to the world of the future.

SUMMARY

As civilization grows in complexity, the demand for mental abilities of many diverse kinds steadily increases. Mental ability is based in considerable part on the various elements of intelligence and is influenced by many items of personality. In its development mental ability is shaped by training and education and is affected by health and by other environmental factors. Many or perhaps all the hereditary factors involved in the production of superior intelligence and personality are believed to be based on multiple genes.

An adverse differential fertility in respect to mental capacity is probably now occurring in all Western countries and this presumably tends to decrease in each generation and in each century the frequencies of those genes that underlie superior ability. Practically no scientific knowledge, however, is available as to the actual rate of such deterioration.

The only known way for increasing the proportion in the population of persons with superior mental capacity is to provide conditions under which those individuals who are above average in ability will have larger families than those who are below average. Those persons who rate above average in mental ability and personality should be encouraged to have as many children as they can properly rear and educate. This encouragement may be economic, social, or psychological. It should be based on an ever-increasing fund of knowledge. To this end, sound genetic advice should be made available in every part of the nation. The number of heredity counseling centers should be increased. Each of these centers should have facilities for giving advice about mental superiorities as well as about physical and mental defects.

Part of the lesser fertility of intellectual workers compared to other types of workers is due to the older average age at which they marry and start their families. To enable advanced students to marry and to start their families while in graduate or professional school, it is here recommended that (1) a tuition scholarship be granted to every graduate student who has been accepted by a competent university as a candidate for the master's or Ph.D. degree or equivalent; (2) the number of teaching and research assistantships available to graduate students be increased; (3) dependency allowances for a wife and for children be provided in each graduate assistantship and fellowship; and (4) long-term loans on liberal terms be made available to every student who is engaged in graduate or professional training.

The organization of a national institute dedicated to research on the factors that produce or affect superior mental ability is strongly recommended.

REFERENCES

Cattell, R. B. 1950. *Personality: A Systematic, Theoretical and Factual Study.* New York: McGraw-Hill.

———. 1957. *Personality and Motivation; Structure and Measurement.* Yonkers-on-Hudson: World Book Co.

Dice, Lee R. 1955. *Man's Nature and Nature's Man: The Ecology of Human Communities.* Ann Arbor: University of Michigan Press.

Dobzhansky, Th., and G. Allen. 1956. Does Natural Selection Continue to Operate in Modern Mankind? *Amer. Anthrop.* 58: 591-604.

Dorn, Harold F. 1947. Present Knowledge Concerning the Effects of Differential Fertility in the United States. *Milbank Memorial Fund Quarterly,* 25: 359-366.

Fuller, J. L. 1954. *Nature and Nurture: A Modern Synthesis.* New York: Doubleday.

Grabill, W. H., C. V. Kiser, and P. K. Whelpton. 1958. *The Fertility of American Women.* New York: John Wiley and Son.

Hammons, Helen G., Ed. 1959. *Heredity Counseling.* New York: Paul B. Hoeber.

Holmberg, Allan R. 1950. Nomads of the Long Bow: the Siriono of Eastern Bolivia. *Publ. Inst. Soc. Anthrop.,* Smithson. Inst., 10: 1-104.

Holmes, S. J. 1921. *The Trend of the Race.* New York: Harcourt, Brace, and Co.

———. 1933. *The Eugenic Predicament.* New York: Harcourt, Brace, and Co.

———. 1936. *Human Genetics and Its Social Import.* New York: McGraw-Hill.

Hunt, Harrison R. 1930. *Some Biological Aspects of War.* New York: Galton Publishing Co.

Kallmann, Franz J. 1953. *Heredity in Health and Mental Disorder.* New York: W. W. Norton and Co.

Kiser, Clyde V. 1952. Fertility Trends and Differentials in the United States. *J. Amer. Statistical Assoc.,* 47: 25-48.

Muller, H. J. 1950. Our Load of Mutations. *Amer. J. Human Genetics,* 2: 111-176.

Neel, James V. 1958. The Study of Natural Selection in Primitive and Civilized Human Populations. *Human Biol.*, 30: 43-72.

Neel, James V., and William J. Schull. 1954. *Human Heredity*. Chicago: University of Chicago Press.

Osborn, Frederick. 1951. *Preface to Eugenics*. Rev. ed. New York: Harper and Bros.

————. 1956. Galton and Mid-Century Eugenics. *Eugenics Rev.*, 48: 15-22.

Penrose, L. S. 1955. Evidence of Heterosis in Man. *Proc. Roy. Soc. London*, B, 144: 203-213.

Population Reference Bureau. 1956. The College Study Report—1956. *Population Bull.*, 12: 89-105.

————. 1958. Recession in Births? *Population Bull.*, 14: 109-123.

Scheinfeld, Amram. 1958. Changing Attitudes Toward Human Genetics and Eugenics. *Eugenics Quart.*, 5: 145-153.

Snyder, Laurence H. 1951. Old and New Pathways in Human Genetics. *Amer. J. Human Genetics*, 3: 1-16.

Vandenberg, Steven G. 1956. The Hereditary Abilities Study: The University of Michigan. *Eugenics Quart.* 3: 94-99.

Westoff, Charles F. 1954. Differential Fertility in the United States. *Amer. Sociological Review*, 19: 549-561.

Wolfle, Dael. 1954. *America's Resources of Specialized Talent*. New York: Harper and Bros.

Wrong, Dennis H. 1958. Trends in Class Fertility in Western Nations. *Canadian J. Econ. and Pol. Sci.*, 24: 216-229.

Characteristics of the Gifted: A Case for a Sequel to Terman's Study

HERBERT H. HUGHES
HAROLD D. CONVERSE

The many issues in the area of education for the gifted typically focus on three questions. What criteria should be used to identify the gifted? What are the characteristics of the gifted? How should the gifted be educated? With the widespread increase of interest in creative dimensions of talent, all of these questions need renewed investigation. In this paper attention will be focused on a reexamination of Terman's attempt to answer the second question.

Reprinted from *Exceptional Children*, Vol. 29, No. 4 (December, 1962), pp. 179-183. By permission of the senior author and publisher.

Other studies have been concerned with the characteristics of the gifted, but a relatively large proportion of the information disseminated on characteristics of gifted children has been derived from *one* major study, Terman's study of 1000 gifted children. School systems throughout the nation have often made decisions on identification, programs, and policies for gifted children on the basis of his findings. Terman gained well deserved praise and wide acclaim for what was in his time a monumental study: there is no doubt that he should stand high on the list of great men in psychology. But research techniques and theory are more sophisticated now, and his study should be given careful consideration in the light of present criteria for rigor in research. Terman himself stated in the summary chapter of his classic *Genetic Studies of Genius*, "If the methods that have been employed have at times led to erroneous conclusions, these in time will be discovered and corrected. One who suspects error at any point has only to apply the same or demonstrably better objective methods to test the justness of his suspicions. It is to be hoped that sooner or later all our conclusions will thus be put to trial. The ultimate value of our study will be measured more by the investigations which it stimulates or provokes others to make than by the amount of its factual data that later experiments may verify" (Terman, 1925, p. 633).

Many have criticized Terman's methodology, but few have questioned the validity of his portrait of the gifted. The authors contend that in this respect modern techniques will allow us to make considerable improvement over his findings and that a reevaluation is dictated by the evidence available. Unfortunately, it is sometimes necessary to emphasize weaknesses of an otherwise highly significant contribution in order to stimulate further research in an area. In this paper past evaluations of Terman's study are merged with a critique by the present authors in an effort to convince the reader that a new large scale study on the characteristics of the gifted is sorely needed.

Apparently few researchers have been concerned with the contrast between the number with IQs of 140 or above (approximately .4 percent) located in Terman's search for the gifted and the number with IQs of 140 or more (1.1 percent) in the 1937 revision of the Stanford-Binet. The main experimental group of 643 (*not* 1000 as seems to be commonly believed) in Terman's study was obtained from a canvass of a school population of 159,812 students. Another group, drawn from a second population not clearly specified in his report, composed the remainder of the group typically known as the 1000 gifted children. This second group was tested by volunteers and drawn from cities both in California and outside the state. Based upon the percentage (1.1 percent) of the 1937 standardization group of the Stanford-Binet with IQs above 140, Terman should have located approximately 1758 cases with

IQs above 140 from the 159,812. (More should have been located if the second population—from which the remaining members of the 1000 gifted were drawn—is included, but information on this group is too inadequate to permit any projections.) By lowering the cut-off point to 135 there should have been an additional 1600 cases for a total of 3358 from the 159,812. This is over five times the 643 Terman actually located.

SELECTION WEAKNESSES

Evidence in the literature on low and underachievement leads the present authors to suggest that an interaction between selection methods and personality factors in achievement causes proportionately too few children to be identified as gifted in many of the populations under study.

Selection Methods. Fliegler and Bish, summarizing 251 studies in a recent review, were concerned about the narrow definition of giftedness (typically by tests of intelligence), but they gave little evidence of concern over the sampling methods and procedures generally used for selecting gifted subjects. They did comment, however, that "The conglomerate characteristics extensively illustrated and described by Terman and Oden need still further definition and clarification if the potentially gifted are to be described" (1959, p. 410). Barbe (1956) found evidence of a skewed distribution in a sample of 456 gifted due to a disproportionate representation of certain racial groups. In addition, his sample differed somewhat from Terman's with respect to father's occupational status. In a study reported by Lewis (1940), in which he also questioned Terman's method of selection, approximately 50,000 children were canvassed in grades four to eight. The teachers were asked to rate any child as extremely mentally retarded, genius, or as a distinct problem; they selected 341 children as geniuses. Of this group only 57 percent fell within the top 10 percent in mental ability on the Kuhlmann-Anderson Test. Levinson (1956) has pointed out inconsistencies in identification procedures which tend to favor children from the middle socio-economic level. He proposed that separate norms for different socio-economic levels be established at the 98th percentile. In an attempt to discover what procedures or combination of procedures would prove most reliable for locating gifted children, Pegnato and Birch (1959) chose as subjects approximately 1400 children from grades seven through nine. They compared the efficiency and effectiveness of seven different means of locating gifted children using the test criterion of a Stanford-Binet IQ of 136 or higher. Significantly, the teachers missed, by ratings, more than half of the gifted as measured by the intelligence test score of 136 on the Stanford-Binet while 31.4 percent of those named by them as gifted were of average intelligence on the Stanford-Binet.

Personality Factors in Achievement. Recent research on underachievement and low achievement has pointed consistently to the important role of personality factors in achievement at all levels of schooling (Anderson, 1961; Miller, 1961). Only some of the projects will be mentioned here. In a study of scholastic underachievement made by Shaw and Grubb (1958) on bright college students, it was concluded that a personality trait called "hostility" was characteristic of bright underachieving students in comparison with bright achieving students. A similar finding was reported by Gough in a study made on high school sophomores (1949). Barrett (1957), from an intensive study of 32 gifted children chosen on the basis of intelligence test scores over 130 on the Henmon-Nelson Advanced Test, found that the underachievers exhibited a negative attitude toward school. In his study children with weak performance in the elementary school did even more poorly in the secondary school. Gowan (1960) summarized the findings of a dozen research studies in an effort to formulate a comprehensive picture of the various factors contributing to underachievement or fostering achievement. He reported 19 factors accounting for achievement and eight for underachievement, most of which were either personality or environmental factors.

In the Talent Preservation Project of New York City (Krugman, 1960, p. 461), which is concerned with gifted underachievers, almost 5000 ninth and tenth grade students out of 50,000 in 39 high schools scored in the 90th percentile or higher on the Iowa Tests of Educational Development and registered an IQ of 130 or better. (The IQ score was obtained from the group test of intelligence regularly administered in each of the participating schools. The schools are permitted to use one of several group tests, such as the Henmon-Nelson and Lorge-Thorndike, which are appropriate for the ninth and tenth grade level.) Of these it was found that considerably more than half were not achieving at an arbitrarily agreed upon standard and thus might not have been chosen by teachers as "gifted."

TERMAN'S STUDY

An analysis of Terman's study in the light of the research reported above strongly suggests that through his method of selecting his 1000 gifted children a minimum number of under or low achievers with high test scores were chosen. Secondly, certain racial and socio-economic groups may not have been adequately represented in his sample of gifted children because of the sampling procedures used. In addition, it should also be noted that Terman listed as one of his problems the fact that his group contained an unexpectedly large proportion of cases in the upper intelligence score ranges (Terman, 1925, p. 633). His method of selection and sampling techniques could well have resulted in the selection of a relatively skewed sample which had proportionately too many subjects in the 160-and-above intelligence score range.

Sampling Techniques. The plan of research directed by Terman was continually changed to provide convenience of sampling. In the population defined only about one half of grades one and two were covered. This sampling was based upon the rationale that only in the *best* schools would the examiners test grades one and two, but if a large school had netted no cases in grades three to eight it was arbitrarily deemed safe to omit grades one and two. Furthermore, the field assistants were left to adapt the method of selection somewhat according to the *type* of school in which they were working in order to save time and ". . . make the search more effective" (Ibid, p. 29).

In subsequent studies the sampling and testing procedures will need to be defined more carefully than in Terman's study. For example, Terman states "It is *probable* that the number of different children nominated was in the neighborhood of 10,000. *Practically* all these were given some kind of intelligence tests, *probably* 8000 of them the National" (Ibid, p. 34). (The italicizing above is by the present writers.) Moreover, the data on Group II were not even summarized due to inadequate information, yet some of this group are included in the group more popularly known as the "1000 gifted children."

There is confusion when one attempts to determine the cut-off point for inclusion in Terman's final sample. At different points in his report one can find 140, 135, or 130 all mentioned as cut-off points. The initial purpose of his search was to locate subjects to a degree of brightness that would rate them well within the top one percent of the school population (by Terman's definition, over 140 IQ). Yet in the "main experimental group" of 643 pupils, 21 cases were included whose corrected IQs are in the interval 135-139 and one in the interval 130-134. These cases were included because of indications that the Binet score, due to conditions of examination, was lower than it should have been. Several cases were included because they were siblings of children who had already qualified; a few were included because of special interest of an investigator in a particular child (Ibid, p. 43). Although their inclusion *may not* have affected the general character of the group, it *could have,* and moreover, rigorous designs should require consistent criteria for the selection of cases and exact specifications of the number of pupils tested.

Method of Selecting Nominees. Two crucial steps in Terman's selection and elimination process were teacher ratings and performance on *group* tests of intelligence. It should be emphasized that almost his entire sample was required to survive screening first by teacher ratings and then by scores on group tests of intelligence, *before* they were admitted to the final group to be tested by the individual test of intelligence. Terman estimated that from 10 to 25 percent of cases may have been missed by this method (although his field assistants estimated only 10 percent). It is here that a disproportionately large number of scholastically and emotionally maladjusted cases could have been missed and thus led Terman to an unduly optimistic picture of the gifted child. Factors (mentioned in the research cited previously) such as hostility, rebellious attitudes, goals set by others, intense personal problems, study habit problems, cultural aggression, race, and socio-economic status could be expected to affect both teacher ratings and successful performance on group tests of intelligence.

Group Test Used for Screening. An analysis of the National Intelligence Tests (National B) reveals that their reliability and validity for screening gifted children is questionable. In addition, original norms for this test were discounted by Terman, and for the purposes of his study, he used norms established on the school population in Vallejo, California. Regardless of the basis of his logic, in the light of his later generalizations this arbitrary decision does not seem justified.

Ballard (1922, p. 7) criticized the reliability of the National B on the basis that it has to be worked at break-neck speed, it picks out the rapid thinkers, and it leaves the profound thinkers. Highsmith (1925) also made a detailed study of the test and concluded that the rate of response (of which the National B is more nearly a measure) to material in a test such as the National B is by no means an adequate measure of intelligence. Poor readers, slow starters, and test-anxious children could be severely handicapped on such a test. On the one hand, Terman did not feel that such children would be missed, but on the other hand, he was concerned that the slightly less accelerated, excessively shy, or lazy child might be overlooked by his selection method. From the evidence available, however, it appears that shortcomings of the instrument used for the group testing could have unduly limited the composition of the group which was selected.

DESIGN FOR A NEW STUDY

In the light of the conclusions reached herein a new investigation might overcome the shortcomings of Terman's study by requiring a consistent and rigorous sampling plan and devoting careful attention to procedural controls. The present emphasis on dimensions of talent other than that measured by intelligence tests would also make it desirable to include several "gifted" groups in the new study, each chosen on the basis of different measures. A general outline for such a study is presented below.

1. Define a representative sample of school children at each grade level considering the variables of sex, race, socio-economic level, geographical location, size of school enrollment, and type of school (public, parochial, or private).
2. Screen the sample for gifted children by replicating Terman's method of selection.
3. Screen the sample for gifted children by testing all the children in the sample with an individual test of intelligence; this is the only alternative guaranteeing an accurate evaluation of the number of high scorers in the sample and thus permitting a rigorous comparison with Terman's method.
4. Identify control groups whose test scores fall below the score used as the criterion for giftedness.
5. In addition, obtain scores from all children in the sample on measures of creativity, curiosity, and achievement using standard procedures and identical measures throughout.
6. Identify high scorers and appropriate control groups on each of the measures.
7. Analyze the degree of overlap among the methods and measures.
8. Compare the characteristics of the different groups chosen, and prepare a composite description of each group.

SUMMARY

Basing their arguments on an analysis of Terman's study of 1000 gifted children, the authors have pressed for a new study of the characteristics of the gifted. The major point made in support of these arguments is the failure of the particular selection methods to take into account the underachiever or low achiever (with a high test score) who may have been almost entirely excluded from his sample. No reference was made in this paper to the control group with which Terman compared his gifted group, a matter which may deserve more careful attention in future studies of the gifted. Crucial methodological weaknesses were also pointed out in a rather hard look at Terman's study. In answer to critics who may frown upon the need for such an analysis the authors would counter: Have you ever heard anyone reflect upon characteristics of the gifted without reference to Terman's study?—The authors haven't.

REFERENCES

Anderson, K. E. (Ed.), *Research on the Academically Talented Student.* Washington, D. C.: National Education Association, 1961.

Ballard, P. B., *Group Tests of Intelligence.* New York: Hadder and Stoughton, 1922.

Barbe, W. B., A Study of the Family Background of the Gifted. *J. Educ. Psychol.,* 1956, **46**, 302-309.

Barrett, H. O., An Intensive Study of 32 Gifted Children. *Personnel Guid. J.,* 1957, **36**, 192-194.

Fliegler, L. A., & Bish, C. E., The Gifted and Talented. *Rev. ed. Res.*, 1959, **29**, 408-450.

Gough, H. G., Factors Related to Academic Achievement of High School Students. *J. Educ. Psychol.*, 1949, **40**, 65-78.

Gowan, J. C., Factors of Achievement in High School and College. *J. Counsel. Psychol.*, 1960, **7**, 91-95.

Highsmith, J. A., Relation of the Rate of Response to Intelligence. *Psychol. Rev. Monogr.*, 1925, **34**, 1-33.

Krugman, M., Identifying and Preservation of Talent. *Teachers Coll. Rec.*, 1960, **61**, 459-463.

Levinson, B. M., Rethinking the Selection of Intellectually Gifted Children. *Psychol. Rep.*, 1956, **2**, 127-130.

Lewis, W. D., *A Study of Superior Children in the Elementary School*. Nashville: Cullom and Ghertner, 1940.

Miller, L. M. (Ed.), *Guidance for the Underachiever With Superior Ability*. Washington, D. C.: U. S. Government Printing Office, 1961.

Pegnato, C. W., & Birch, J. W., Locating Gifted Children in Junior High Schools; a Comparison of Methods. *Except. Child.*, 1959, **25**, 300-304.

Shaw, M. C., & Grubb, J., Hostility and Able High School Underachievers. *J. Counsel. Psychol.*, 1958, **26**, 46-66.

Terman, L. M., *Genetic Studies of Genius*. Palo Alto: Stanford Univer. Press, 1925.

7 | WHAT IS THE GIFTED INDIVIDUAL LIKE?

A Psychologist Examines 64 Eminent Scientists

ANNE ROE

What elements enter into the making of a scientist? Are there special qualities of personality, mind, intelligence, background or upbringing that mark a person for this calling? Besides the natural interest in these questions, they have a practical importance, because the recruitment of qualified young people into science is a growing problem in our society. Where and how shall we find them?

During the past five years I have been making a study of the attributes of a group of scientists and the reasons why they chose this field of work. The most eminent scientists in the U. S. were selected as subjects, since they are most likely to exemplify the special qualities, if any, that are associated with success in research science. They were selected by panels of experts in each field of science. The study finally settled on a group of 64 eminent men who agreed to participate—20 biologists, 22 physicists and 22 social scientists (psychologists and anthropologists). A high percentage of them are members of the National Academy of Sciences or the American Philosophical Society or both, and among them they have received a staggering number of honorary degrees, prizes and other awards.

Each of the 64 individuals was then examined exhaustively by long personal interviews and tests: his life history, family background, professional and recreational interests, intelligence, achievements, personality, ways of thinking—any information that might have a bearing on the subject's choice of his vocation and his success in it. Each was given an intelligence test and was examined by two of the modern techniques for the study of personality: the Rorschach and the Thematic Apperception

From *Scientific American*, Vol. 187, No. 5 (November, 1952), pp. 21-25. Reprinted with permission. Copyright © 1951, 1952 by Scientific American Inc. All rights reserved.

Test (TAT). The Rorschach, popularly known as the inkblot test, gives information about such things as the way the subject deals with problems, his manner of approach to them, the extent and efficiency of his use of rational controls, his inner preoccupations, his responsiveness to outside stimuli. The TAT gives information about attitudes toward family and society and self, about expectations and needs and desires, and something about the development of these.

My study was financed during the first four years by grants from the National Institute of Mental Health and is being continued this year under a Guggenheim Fellowship. It has developed a great deal of material, much of which has been published in technical detail in special journals. In this brief article it is possible only to recapitulate the high points.

There is no such thing, of course, as a "typical" scientist. Eminent scientists differ greatly as individuals, and there are well-marked group differences between the biologists and the physicists, and between the natural scientists and the social scientists. Certain common patterns do appear, however, in the group as a whole, and the most convenient way to summarize these generalizations is to try to draw a picture of what might be called the "average" eminent scientist.

He was the first-born child of a middle-class family, the son of a professional man. He is likely to have been a sickly child or to have lost a parent at an early age. He has a very high I.Q. and in boyhood began to do a great deal of reading. He tended to feel lonely and "different" and to be shy and aloof from his classmates. He had only a moderate interest in girls and did not begin dating them until college. He married late (at 27), has two children and finds security in family life; his marriage is more stable than the average. Not until his junior or senior year in college did he decide on his vocation as a scientist. What decided him (almost invariably) was a college project in which he had occasion to do some independent research—to find out things for himself. Once he discovered the pleasures of this kind of work, he never turned back. He is completely satisfied with his chosen vocation. (Only one of the 64 eminent scientists—a Nobel prize winner—says he would have preferred to do something else: he wanted to be a farmer, but could not make a living at it.) He works hard and devotedly in his laboratory, often seven days a week. He says his work is his life, and he has few recreations, those being restricted to fishing, sailing, walking or some other individualistic activity. The movies bore him. He avoids social affairs and political activity, and religion plays no part in his life or thinking. Better than any other interest or activity, scientific research seems to meet the inner need of his nature.

This generalized picture represents only majority traits; there are, of course, many exceptions to it, not only in individual cases but by groups;

the social scientists, for instance, tend to be by no means shy but highly gregarious and social. Let us now consider the differences between groups. I have separated the physicists into the theorists (12) and the experimentalists (10), because these two groups differ sharply. The biologists (physiologists, botanists, geneticists, biochemists and so on) are sufficiently alike to be grouped together, and so are the social scientists.

FIELD	Age at Time of Study		Average Age at Time of Receiving College Degrees	
	Average	Range	B.A.	Ph.D., Sc.D., M.D.
Biologists	51.2	38-58	21.8	26.0
Physical scientists	44.7	31-56	20.9	24.6
Social scientists	47.7	35-60	21.8	26.8

AVERAGE AGE of the subjects at the time of the study and at the time they received their degrees is given in this table. The upper age limit was set at 60; the lower limit was determined by the eminence of the subjects.

No standardized intelligence test was sufficiently difficult for these eminent scientists; hence a special test was constructed by the Educational Testing Service. To provide ratings on particular intellectual factors, the test was divided into three parts: verbal (79 items), spatial (24 items) and mathematical (39). (The mathematical test used was not difficult enough for the physicists, and several of them did not take it.)

While the group as a whole is characterized by very high average intelligence, as would be expected, the range is wide (*see table on page 239*). Among the biologists, the geneticists and biochemists do relatively better on the nonverbal tests than on the verbal, and the other biologists tend to do relatively better on the verbal. Among the physicists there is some tendency for theorists to do relatively better on the verbal and for the experimentalists to do relatively better on the spatial test. Among the social scientists the experimental psychologists do relatively better on the spatial or mathematical than on the verbal test, and the reverse is true of the other psychologists and the anthropologists.

On the TAT the social scientists tended to give much longer stories than the other groups did—verbal fluency is characteristic of them. The biologists were inclined to be much more factual, less interested in feelings and, in general, unwilling to commit themselves. This was true to a lesser extent of the physical scientists. The biologists and physical scientists manifested a quite remarkable independence of parental relations and were without guilt feelings about it, while the social scientists showed many dependent attitudes, much rebelliousness and considerable helplessness, along with intense concern over interpersonal relations generally. The biologists were the least aggressive (but rather stubborn) and the social scientists the most aggressive. The most striking thing about the TAT results for the total group, however, is the rarity of any indication of the drive for achievement that all of these subjects have actually shown in their lives.

On the Rorschach the social scientists show themselves to be enormously productive and intensely concerned with human beings; the biologists are deeply concerned with form, and rely strongly upon a nonemotional approach to problems; the physicists show a good deal of free anxiety and concern with space and inanimate motion. Again the social scientists, particularly the anthropologists, are the most freely aggressive.

FIELD	Visual	Verbal	Imageless	TOTALS
Biologists	10	4	3	17
Physicists	10	4	4	18
Psychologists and anthropologists	2	11	6	19
TOTALS	22	19	13	54

IMAGERY OF THE SCIENTISTS was correlated with specialty. The natural scientists were strong in visual imagery; the social scientists, in verbal.

PROFESSION OF FATHER	Visual	Verbal	Imageless	TOTALS
Verbal	5	10	3	18
Non-verbal	8	2	2	12
TOTALS	13	12	5	30

IMAGERY OF THE FATHER'S Profession was strongly influential. The numbers on the right side of this table refer to the imagery of the sons.

Early in the course of the work it became apparent that there were some differences in habits of thinking, and a special inquiry was instituted along these lines. The data are unsatisfactory from many standpoints —there are no objective tests for such material, and I had to ask many leading questions in order to convey any idea of what I was after. Nevertheless rather definite and meaningful patterns did appear. The biologists and the experimental physicists tend strongly to dependence upon visual imagery in their thinking—images of concrete objects or elaborate diagrams or the like. The theoretical physicists and social scientists tend to verbalization in their thinking—a kind of talking to themselves. All groups report a considerable amount of imageless thinking, particularly at cru-

	Biologists	Experimental physicists	Theoretical physicists	Psychologists	Anthropologists	TOTALS
PROFESSIONS	9	5	10	7	3	34
Research Science	0	1	0	0	0	1
Physician	0	2	1	2	0	5
Lawyer	0	0	1	1	3	5
Engineer	0	0	3	2	0	5
Clergyman	2	0	1	0	0	3
Editor	0	2	0	0	0	2
College teacher	4	0	3	2	0	9
School teacher	2	0	0	0	0	2
School superintendent	1	0	0	0	0	1
Pharmacist	0	0	1	0	0	1
BUSINESS	8	1	2	4	5	20
Own business	4	0	2	2	4	12
Clerk, agent, salesman	4	1	0	2	1	8
FARMER	2	4	0	2	0	8
SKILLED LABOR	1	0	0	1	0	2
TOTALS	20	10	12	14	8	64
PER CENT PROFESSIONAL	45	50	84	50	38	53

OCCUPATIONS OF THE FATHERS of the 64 eminent scientists showed a strong bias in favor of the professions. This was especially true of the 12 theoretical physicists, 10 of whose fathers had been professionals. The anthropologists were an exception: five out of eight came from business backgrounds. Four of the 10 experimental physicists were the sons of farmers. None of the scientists were the sons of unskilled laborers.

	Number	Verbal Test		Spatial Test		Mathematical Test	
		Average	Range	Average	Range	Average	Range
Biologists	19	56.6	28-73	9.4	3-20	16.8	6-27
Experimental physicists	7	46.6	8-71	11.7	3-22		
Theoretical physicists	11	64.2	52-75	13.8	5-19		
Psychologists	14	57.7	23-73	11.3	5-19	15.6	8-27
Anthropologists	8	61.1	43-72	8.2	3-15	9.2	4-13
TOTAL	59	57.7	8-75	10.9	3-22	15.9	4-27
APPROXIMATE IQ EQUIVALENTS		163	121-177	140	123-164	160	128-194

INTELLIGENCE TEST RESULTS revealed minor variations among the specialties of the scientists. The theoretical physicists did best in the verbal test; the experimental physicists rated lowest. Both theoretical and experimental physicists did not take the mathematical test because it was not sufficiently difficult. Two anthropologists who took the verbal test did not take the other tests on the ground that they could not do them.

cial points. Men whose fathers followed talkative occupations (law, ministry, teaching) are more likely to think in words.

The life histories of these 64 men show some general similarities, and there are patterns characterizing some of the subgroups. Geographical factors seem not to be particularly significant, except that only a few came from the South. The economic level was varied, ranging from very poor to well-to-do; among the anthropologists and the theoretical physicists a somewhat higher percentage came from well-to-do homes.

In several respects the scientists' backgrounds differ very much from the population at large. There are no Catholics among this group of eminent scientists; five come from Jewish homes and the rest had Protestant backgrounds. Only three of the 64 now have a serious interest in any church; only a few even maintain church memberships.

Another striking fact is that 53 percent of the scientists were the sons of professional men; not one was the son of an unskilled laborer and only two were sons of skilled workmen. Why do more than half of our leading scientists come from the families of professional men? It seems to me most probable, from more knowledge of the family situations of these men than I can summarize here, that the operative factor is the value placed by these families and their associates on learning—learning for its own sake. Most of the scientists developed intellectual interests at an early age.

Another remarkable finding is how many of them were their parents' first children. This proportion is higher than chance expectancy in all of the subgroups. Thirty-nine were first born; of the rest five were eldest sons and two who were second born were effectively the eldest because of the early death of the first child. For most of the others there is a considerable difference in age between the subject and the next older brother (averaging five years). It seems probable that all this may point to the most important single factor in the making of a scientist—the need and ability to develop personal independence to a high degree. The independence factor is emphasized by many other findings: the subjects' preference for teachers who let them alone, their attitudes toward religion, their attitudes toward personal relations, their satisfaction in a career in which, for the most part, they follow their own interests without direction or interference. It is possible that oldest sons in our culture have a greater amount of independence or more indulgence in the pursuit of their own interests than other children have. On the other hand, there is some psychological evidence that first-born tend to be more dependent, on the average, than other children, and a good case could be made out for a hypothesis that reaction to this overdependence produced the scientists' strong drive to independence.

The early extracurricular interests of these men were varied, but here, too, there are some general patterns. More of the physicists than of the other groups showed early interests directly related to their later occupations, but this seems quite clearly to be due to the common small-boy preoccupation in this country with physical gadgets—radio, Meccano sets and so on. The theoretical physicists were omnivorous readers, the experimentalists much less so. Among the social scientists many went through a stage of considering or even working toward a literary career. Half of the biologists showed some early interest in natural history, but for only five was it of an intense and serious sort, involving keeping field records of birds and flowers, and so on. Many of the biologists did not know during childhood of the possibility of a career in biology. This was even more true of the psychologists and anthropologists, since there are almost no boyhood activities related to professional social science.

It is of considerable interest that over half of these men did not decide upon their vocations until they were juniors or seniors in college. More important, perhaps, than when they decided, is why they decided. It certainly was not just a matter of always following an early bent. From fiddling with gadgets to becoming a physicist may be no great leap, but the attractions of theoretical physics are not so obvious or well known, nor are those of the social sciences or advanced biology. In the stories of the social scientists and of the biologists it becomes clear that the most important factor in the final decision to become a scientist is the discovery of the joys of research. In physics the discovery may come so gradually as not to be noticed as such, but in the other sciences it often came as a revelation of unique moment, and many of these men know just when and how they found it out. A couple of quotations will illustrate this:

"I had no course in biology until my senior year in college. It was a small college and the teacher was about the first on the faculty with a Ph.D. It was about my first contact with the idea that not everything was known, my first contact with research. In that course I think my final decision was really taken. It was mainly that I wanted to do something in the way of research though I didn't know just what, but working out something new."

"One of the professors took a group of us and thought if we wanted to learn about things, the way to do it was to do research. My senior year I carried through some research. That really sent me, that was the thing that trapped me. After that there was no getting out."

That research experience is so often decisive is a fact of very considerable importance for educational practice. The discovery of the possibility of finding things out for oneself usually came through experience in school with a teacher who put the students pretty much on their own.

There are other things in the general process of growing up that may have influenced the choice of career in subtle ways. One fourth of the biologists lost a parent by death or divorce at an early age. This may have tended to shove them to greater independence. Among the theoretical physicists there was a high incidence of serious illness or physical handicaps during childhood, which certainly contributed to the feelings of isolation characteristic of them. Among the social scientists there is an unusually intense concern with personal relationships, which often goes back to family conflicts during childhood. A relatively large proportion of them seem to have come from homes in which the mother was dominant and the father inadequate in some way. The divorce rate among the social scientists in this study was remarkably high—41 per cent.

Whereas the characteristic pattern among the biologists and physicists is that of the shy, lonely, over-intellectualized boy, among the social scientists the characteristic picture is very different. They got into social activity and intensive and extensive dating at an early age. They were often presidents of their classes, editors of yearbooks and literary magazines, frequently big shots in college. This contrast between the natural and social scientists was still evident after they grew up. It is true only in general, of course; even among the theoretical physicists there are some ardent party-goers.

The one thing that all of these 64 scientists have in common is their driving absorption in their work. They have worked long hours for many years, frequently with no vacations to speak of, because they would rather be doing their work than anything else.

Analyzing the Superior College Student
RUTH E. ECKERT

In any scientific approach to the problems raised by the superior student, careful description of individuals of high scholastic promise must precede the attempt to provide a suitable instructional situation for them. The question as to who the superior student is must first be answered. What characteristics serve to identify him most accurately? Are the differences between gifted students and those who do less acceptable work confined to scholastic activities or do they vary significantly in other respects?

Reprinted from *School and Society*, Vol. 41, No. 1046 (January 12, 1935), pp. 69-72. By permission of the author and publisher.

I

The present report, which is based on an analysis of superior students at the University of Buffalo, furnishes at least tentative answers to these questions. The aim has been not only to determine the more salient characteristics of students who have established their superiority in college, in contrast to those who have clustered near the failure line, but also to test the effectiveness of various types of academic and personnel data in prognosticating college success.

Cases were selected for this investigation on the basis of the junior college grade-point average, a quality index to work taken in the first two years of the arts college, and the study was also limited to men students. Those who entered college between 1926 and 1930 and were in the upper or lower quartiles of the grade-point distribution for this period (120 in each case) constituted the subjects for this analysis. The typical student in the superior group had approximately a straight B record, whereas a D record was characteristic of the lower-grade student. The superior students have also taken a significantly greater amount of work (10.32 S.E.)[1] during their freshman and sophomore years, especially in the social studies and languages.

II

The first group of comparisons, which were concerned with the high-school background of these students, disclosed a number of interesting and reliable differences. The superior students spent less time in high school, with almost a fifth of the group completing the course in less than the usual four years. They also graduated at a younger age, and tended to be drawn more largely from Buffalo public high schools rather than from the smaller suburban or rural schools.

The subjects which entered into their high-school programs were studied to determine whether extent of work influenced later achievement and whether acquaintance with certain areas of thought constituted more effective preparation for college than did other fields. While the superior group completed more units in high school (3.09 S.E.), the difference is not as pronounced as might be expected and is probably due to the fact that many superior students spent less than four years in high school. It is interesting to contrast these results with those for the college period where the time factor was held constant (two years) and where extensity of work proved to be a major differentiating factor.

---

[1] A difference may be classed as significant—greater than zero and favoring the group that now shows superiority—if it is at least three times the standard error of the difference. A ratio stated as 1 S.E. or greater indicates that the chances of a real difference are over 84 in 100, 2 S.E. or greater—over 98 chances in 100, and 3 S.E. or greater—practical certainty of a genuine difference.

The only significant variation in the subjects elected was the greater proportion of able students taking Latin III (3.57 S.E.). Modern European history and economics were taken somewhat more frequently by inferior students, and differences of about the same size occurred in advanced mathematics courses where superior students predominated.[2] Taken as a whole, the data on high-school elections indicate very little concerning the quality of subsequent work in college, and do not lend any substantial support to the theory that certain subjects prepare students for college better than others.

Two general measures of high-school achievement—the fifth of class in which the student graduated and his Regents' average—revealed how much the two groups varied in the quality of their preparatory work. The disparity in high-school quintile ranking was striking, with 81.7 per cent. of the superior group in the upper two fifths of their class as contrasted with 29.1 per cent. of the lower-grade students. High-school Regents' average, which reflects achievement in a number of subjects taken over several years, showed a difference in means amounting to 14.69 S.E. and the smallest degree of overlapping obtained for any measure considered in this study.

Among individual subjects, English literature and chemistry showed the greatest difference between the two groups in average achievement. The number of students taking these subjects was rather small, however, so that the most reliable differences were found in other fields—American history and English. The least differentiation was found for Spanish II, which, interestingly enough, was the only subject where the variation between the two groups can not be considered as statistically significant. These results show rather definitely that it is the student's reaction to the subject, the degree to which he can demonstrate his mastery of the field, rather than the character or number of subjects he has pursued in high school, which is intimately related to differential achievement in college.

Due possibly to more careful grading standards in Buffalo high schools the data did not reveal the wide difference in the predictive value of high-school classroom and Regents marks found by other investigators. Another question which may be answered in a tentative fashion is whether the gaps perceptibly widen between these groups as they progress through high school. While there was a slight increase in mathematics, science and languages, there was no observable trend in the social studies and somewhat negative evidence in English. The constancy of these differences in central tendencies from year to year, as well as from sub-

---

[2] The subject itself may merely function as a highly selective device, so that students who have already established their superiority elect it. It makes little practical difference, however, whether the subject stands in a causal or concomitant relationship, so long as the presence of the subject in an applicant's program indicates high probability that he will do superior work in college.

ject to subject, apparently indicates that the grades are measuring some enduring quality in the students themselves, so that as far back as the analysis might be pushed, significant differences would be found in the achievement of these two groups. Other factors, such as personality differences in teachers and variations in subject-matter and instructional methods, would seem to be of minor importance as compared with the potentialities which the student brings to the course.

III

The American Council on Education Psychological Examination, given to these students at the time of entrance to college, ranks somewhat lower than the Iowa High School Content Examination in differentiating power, while both are inferior to the Regents' average. The extent of overlapping, as measured by the percentage of the inferior group who exceed the median score for superior students, was 21.2 for the A.C.E., as contrasted with 6.9 per cent. for the Iowa Examination and 2.3 per cent. for Regents' average. When separate sections of each test were analyzed, the mathematics division on both the A.C.E., and the Iowa Content Examination showed considerably more overlapping than other sections, apparently indicating that tests of mathematical abilities are of much less predictive power than other types for the highly verbal character of our present college courses.

IV

The University of Buffalo Personnel Blank, a six-page questionnaire filled out at the time of entrance, affords information on a number of non-scholastic factors which might be related to marked academic ability or disability. Judging from the results of other studies, very substantial reliability coefficients should be obtained for a blank as comprehensive as that used at Buffalo, and while the validity of certain items, such as self-ratings on emotional control and social attitudes, is undetermined, it is at least interesting to see what kinds of individuals superior and inferior students wish others to believe them to be.

A number of items concerned the parents and the home background of the student, and the trend on these points—showing a greater number of foreign-born parents among superior students, with the correlated factors of less formal schooling, lower socio-economic status and less use of English in the home—runs contrary to the findings of studies made at other colleges. The present results undoubtedly reflect local conditions, for not only do many of the best high-school students from American-born families go to the larger Eastern universities, but there is also a greater degree of selection among the children of immigrant parents because of the high tuition rate at Buffalo.

On self-ratings on emotional control the able students credited themselves with more persistence in problem-solving, greater disturbance after unkind remarks, and less ability in meeting new people and in participating in social activities. These points coincide with the studies of Thurstone and others who have found that the academically superior student tends to be somewhat more introverted than the average or inferior student. In an estimation of skills three differences exceeded 2 S.E.—on ability to write interestingly and on clerical aptitude, in both cases suggesting greater proficiency on the part of the superior group, and on athletic ability, where the inferior students show a higher rating.

Subject interests, as measured by best-liked subjects, other favorite subjects and courses especially disliked, revealed that interest in a field and quality of performance are not closely related factors. Except for a slightly greater interest in languages on the part of superior students, the elections of the two groups coincided to a remarkable degree. A rather extensive list of items on reading skills, study techniques and provisions for study in the home also yielded only a few differences worth noting, such as the more rapid reading rate of the better student, his keener memory and the greater amount of time he devotes to study. On several items covering various approved study techniques the replies tended to favor the inferior group, so that differences in achievement can hardly be attributed to the possession of certain types of study habits, if these replies can be taken as a valid indication of how students actually study.

The most striking individual difference among vocational choices was the interest in teaching on the part of the superior group (5.35 S.E.). Research in science also elicited more interest from superior students, as did the legal profession and journalism. On medicine and dentistry the larger endorsement came from those doing low-grade college work. The average time of vocational decision was the same for both groups (about second-year high school), so that an early professional objective did not necessarily motivate students to higher scholastic attainment. Also uncertainty in choice did not militate against superior achievement in college, for gifted students listed a somewhat greater number of vocational interests. The able student attached greater importance to community service as a reason for entering a vocation, and also attributed more weight to the influence of teachers or advisers at schools, whereas the inferior student placed greater emphasis on the fact that his father or a close relative was engaged in the profession.

Studies of the recreational activities of these students showed more interest on the part of inferior students in fraternities, Scouts or Y. M. C. A. clubs and glee clubs, both in respect to membership and to leadership, as measured by the number of offices held, while the superior student more frequently engaged in publication staff activities, debate clubs and chess and scientific organizations. Parties and theaters appeared to have much less attraction for the able students. In enumerating hobbies, they revealed a keener interest in reading, nature study and the solution of mathematical problems or puzzles, in contrast to the lower achievement group which more frequently endorsed organized games, such as football and basketball, movies and cards. Not only did more students in the inferior group engage in athletics during the high-school period, but there was a reliably greater number of activities per student reported in this group.

A final section of the blank contained twenty-five statements on social, economic and religious problems, and the student was asked to express his own attitude on a five-point scale. Eight statements showed differences greater than 2 S.E., while ten others exceeded 1 S.E. Of these eighteen statements which tended to differentiate the groups, all but four indicated a greater degree of liberalism for the superior achievement group. There was also evidence that poorer students were more suggestible, tending to agree with the statement whether it was worded to favor the conservative or radical view.

V

Taken as a whole, the present study shows clearly that the superior college student has been the superior high-school student, so that adequate provision for his needs may well begin with advisement and guidance of individuals of marked ability on the high-school level. The trends found as to family background of these superior students would apparently indicate that, for the University of Buffalo population at least, academic superiority can not be attributed to a very favorable socio-economic situation, thus opening up an interesting problem as to the motivational factors involved in superior high-school and college performance. Finally, while the largest distinctions were found in factors closely allied to college work, enough differences were discovered in personality traits, social attitudes, recreational interests and vocational objectives to warrant the statement that the superior student has a different outlook upon life and organizes his thinking and activities to somewhat different ends than does the student of limited scholastic ability.

Characteristics of Gifted Children

WALTER B. BARBE

It has long been known that certain individuals are intellectually superior, but only since about 1920 has there been an attempt to study the gifted child scientifically. In a report to the American Psychological Association, Lewis Terman (1) describes three stages in the study of what he unfortunately chose to call genius instead of giftedness. The report, "A New Approach to the Study of Genius," is more valid if the term 'gifted' is used in place of 'genius.'

The first stage which Terman describes is exemplified by the work of Nordau and Lombroso. The methods used in this stage were, according to Terman, 'impressionalistic and anecdotal.' The objection which Terman makes to this type of research is that it was based upon proving a preconceived theory by locating cases which would support it.

The second stage is represented by such investigators as Galton and Ellis. This was, according to Terman, a much more scientific method for the selection of cases and was based upon objective criteria. The method used was called inductive and the data collected were treated statistically. The major disadvantage of this method was the limitation of biographical data about the subjects.

The third stage is represented by Cattell's study of living American men of science. Terman said that this was a "very significant advance" in the study of giftedness.

Following these three steps, Terman says that the logical next step is the study of gifted children. The development of intelligence tests early in the Twentieth Century made possible the early identification of intellectually superior children and this new approach to the study of the gifted.

PHYSICAL CHARACTERISTICS OF GIFTED CHILDREN

It was believed for many years that the gifted child was physically weak, immature and less attractive than the average child. Evidence has been collected since that time, however, which indicates that not only was

Reprinted from *Educational Administration and Supervision*, Vol. 41, No. 4 (April, 1955), pp. 207-217. By permission of the publisher.

this belief incorrect, but that exactly the opposite is true. Elise Martens in answering the question, "Gifted Children: What Do We Know About Them?" summarizes research findings on the physical status of intellectually gifted children by saying that they "show on the average high level of physical development, health and mental and social adjustment (2). . . ."

Hollingworth, in a study of children with IQ's above 180, found that general health was always considered good and that the development of these children was ahead of schedule in all respects (3). Thom and Newell report that a child with a high IQ is at his own age level in physical skills and not above it (4). While there is some controversy about whether the child is at, or above, his age level in physical development, writers in the field are definite in stating that he is not below his age level. In a report by Olson on the growth patterns of exceptional children, it is stated that the gifted child is not only superior in intellectual ability but that his entire growth pattern is accelerated (5). He is taller, weighs more and is stronger than the average child.

In a study of gifted children whose IQ's were above 130, Hollingworth found that the gifted exceed those of lesser mental ability in height, weight and other physical traits, but that the range within each group overlaps (6). Supporting this, Bentley states that the gifted child is usually large and strong for his age and healthier than the average child. He states that: "There is a positive correlation between size and health of body and intellect, in the majority of cases. . . . This correlation is not so close, however, that one factor can be inferred from the other in individual cases chosen at random (7)."

In a study by Witty, similar findings are reported: "The physical status and general growth of the group are undoubtedly above average. Typically the gifted child is not a physical weakling. He is somewhat above normal in his physical development when compared with unselected children of the same chronological age. . . . He approaches the normal for the average child more closely in physical traits and motor ability than in mental ability (8)."

It is important to realize, as Witty states, that even though the gifted child is superior in physical development, this superiority is not as great as is his mental superiority.

In the study by Terman and Oden, it was concluded that: "The gifted children as a group were above the best standards for American-born children in growth status as indicated by both height and weight. . . . In all respects the results of the measurements showed that the gifted group was slightly superior physically to the various groups used for comparison (9)."

These conclusions, based on the study of one thousand five hundred gifted children, certainly do not picture the gifted child as a physical weakling, unable to compete with his classmates in any area other than intelligence.

The relative superiority in physical health of gifted children has been determined by numerous studies, but little attention has been given to the influence of the superior home environment of gifted children. In every study of unselected gifted children the home environment has been found to be above average, but the effect of the superior environment on the physical health of gifted children has not been investigated. Both Terman and Theman state the importance of the environment on physical health. Theman states that the health data which she presents reveal the superior socio-economic status of the families of gifted Negro children (10). Terman and Oden state: "We now know that in physique and general health, children of high IQ are on the average superior to the general child population . . . but we do not yet know how much of this is to be credited to superiority of home environment (11)."

The gifted child is superior not only in physical characteristics, but also, by definition, is superior in mental ability. The specific mental characteristics in which gifted children differ are not as easily measured as the differences in physical characteristics.

MENTAL CHARACTERISTICS OF GIFTED CHILDREN

Since the gifted children being studied are those who are intellectually superior, it is obvious that they would possess superior mental abilities. The question can well be asked as to how these gifted children differ from average children in their everyday performance.

Baker emphasizes that two important areas need to be considered, the quantitative and qualitative characteristics of mental superiority.

"*Quantitative differences in intelligence:*—The superior learner has a surplus of mental age beyond his chronological life age. This surplus begins as soon as he is born, and, by the time he reaches six years of age, his increased ratio of mental growth has produced at least one year of mental maturity above his age . . .

"*Qualitative differences in intelligence:*—(a) Superior learners tend to learn by complex associative methods rather than by simple, direct rote drill. By such associative processes, they are able to make many connections or to use many mental facets upon which they may draw when putting meaning into learning . . . (b) A second qualitative characteristic is that superior children look for the abstract or generalized rules underlying all school subjects . . . (12)."

Recognition of these two distinct areas in intellectual ability is important when studying the education of the gifted child. However, data reveal that the gifted child is superior in both quantitative and qualitative intelligence.

The gifted child has certain mental characteristics which may be observed without the use of an intelligence test. Terman and Oden, Witty, Hollingworth and Carroll state some of the characteristics which may be observed very early in the life of the child. Terman and Oden report that early indications of superior intelligence noted by parents include quick understanding, curiosity, extensive information, retentive memory, large vocabulary and unusual interest in such things as number relations, atlases and encyclopedias (13). Hollingworth states that very early interest and ability in reading are signs of superior intelligence (14). She reports that, in the opinion of their teachers, pupils selected as bright are more inquisitive, more imaginative, more courteous and have a keener sense of humor than the average child (15).

Carroll says that gifted children are characterized by early development of self-criticism, initiative and independence in thinking, ability to see relationships, make associations, adapt abstract principles to concrete situations, and observe and remember details (16). He also says that the gifted child is superior in such traits as desire to know, desire to excel, originality, and power to learn (17).

A similar list of intellectual abilities of the gifted is given by Goodhart and Schmidt. They state that the gifted have great curiosity, wide range of divergent interests, a large, fluid vocabulary, good memory, the ability to generalize, interpret and recognize relationships, the ability to use economy in work methods, and a strong sense of responsibility (18).

The abilities possessed by mentally superior children which are measured by intelligence tests are summarized by William Bristow, et al., as follows:

"Mentally gifted children have a high degree of general intelligence in the sense of the ability to do abstract thinking and other types of relational thinking. These children rate high in respect to the general intelligence factor which Spearman designated by the letter 'G.' In terms of Thurstone's theory they possess to a high degree most, if not all, of the eight primary mental abilities. According to Thorndike, they excel in the abilities involved in 'abstract' intelligence.

"The mentally gifted are characterized by 'power'—that is, they are able to do mental tasks of a high degree of difficulty. . . . The mentally gifted are alert and quick. . . . The mentally gifted are also characterized by broad attention-span, by a high degree of insight into problems, and by the ability to generalize (19)."

Correlations between achievement test scores and scores on IQ tests have been found to be very high. It would therefore be expected that intellectually superior children would also be superior in achievement. The achievement quotients of the gifted subjects in Terman and Oden's study were not equally high in all subjects. They found that the superiority of gifted over unselected children was greatest in reading, language usage, arithmetical reasoning, and information in science, literature and the arts. Their superiority was less marked in arithmetical computation, spelling, and factual information about history and civics. In such subjects as penmanship, manual training, sewing and cooking, gifted subjects did not perform much better than did unselected children (20).

Goodhart and Schmidt also point out the areas in which the gifted child is not superior. These include carelessness in the mechanics of spelling, punctuation and computation (21).

There were minor achievement differences between gifted boys and girls in the various subjects, but these sex differences were trifling when compared with the great superiority of gifted over unselected children (22). Terman and Oden conclude that: "The amount of unevenness in the subject-matter profiles of gifted children does not differ significantly from that shown in the profiles of unselected children. . . . The unevenness of the gifted child occurred on a high level of achievement, that of the normal child on a much lower level (23)."

The belief that the superior mental ability of gifted children is not maintained throughout life has been proved to be false. Follow-up studies in which children were retested later in life have been made by several educators. Terman and Oden found that: "The intellectual status of the average member of the group at the mean age of thirty years was close to the 98th or 99th percentile of the general adult population, and was far above the average level of ability of graduates from superior colleges and universities (24)." Similar results were obtained by Witty and Lorge and Hollingworth.

In summarizing the literature on the mental characteristics of gifted children, it is evident that they are superior in both the quantitative and qualitative characteristics of mental ability. Many of the mental characteristics of gifted children, such as curiosity, interest and ability to generalize, may be observed in the child's everyday behavior. Other characteristics, such as the extent of mental capacity, may be determined by intelligence and achievement tests. While gifted children are characterized by superior over-all mental ability, there is, nevertheless, a variation in their abilities. Follow-up studies have shown that they maintain their superiority throughout life.

EMOTIONAL AND SOCIAL CHARACTERISTICS
OF GIFTED CHILDREN

In an article entitled "The Gifted Child—Facts and Fallacies," Witty states that "the idea that bright and gifted children are eccentric, queer, or emotionally unstable has been expressed again and again (25)." The basis for this belief can be found in reports by writers of the late Nineteenth Century who believed that great over-development of certain traits was always accompanied by other defects. This belief was even carried to the point where it was stated that the amount of instability was in direct proportion to the amount of genius.

In the early stages of Terman's research upon gifted children, he concluded that the "eccentricity of genius is a myth." Protesting this conclusion, Witty and Lehman said that they were "reluctant to accept these hasty conclusions (26)." Witty and Lehman explain their objection to Terman's statement: "It may be that the assumption of early writers to the effect that the ways of genius was a manifestation of instability was a hasty generalization and one that was not founded on fact. However, the recent assumption that the eccentricity of genius is largely a myth is probably also an example of hasty generalization. Certainly, this more recent assumption is not proved by the test results obtained by examining gifted children, since it has not been proved that every gifted child is necessarily a genius. Neither has it been proved that every recognized genius was a gifted child (27)."

It was perhaps unfortunate that Terman chose to call his research *Genetic Study of Genius,* for his study was of children found to be intellectually superior. There was no justification in assuming that merely because his subjects were intellectually superior, they would become geniuses. In another article, Witty and Lehman indicate that this is the crux of the problem. "The term nervous instability, like the term genius, is difficult to describe and delimit (28)." Hollingworth believed that "the term genius was a definite misnomer for a child or youth." She believed that the term genius "should be reserved to describe individuals who have already made original contributions of outstanding and lasting worth (29)."

There is general agreement among authorities that gifted children show superior personality and character traits. Terman gave his subjects a battery of seven character tests. Terman found that gifted children show superior personality and character traits. They are less inclined than average children to boast or to overstate their knowledge, are more trustworthy when under temptation to cheat, have more wholesome reading preferences, character preferences and social attitudes and score higher in emotional stability. The typical gifted child of nine years tested as high as the average child of twelve (30).

Hollingworth says that "children selected wholly by intelligence tests, without consideration of other factors, show desirable traits of character and temperament, in superior degree," and that they are more cooperative (31). She also says that the gifted may be disciplined more readily than ordinary children by appeals to reason, hero-worship, presenting another point of view, and consistently rewarding merit (32).

According to Hollingworth, gifted children are rated above average in nervous stability and neurotics are few among them (33). Terman and

Oden conclude their composite portrait of the gifted child as follows: "One can find within the group individual examples of almost every type of personality defect, social maladjustment, behavior problems, and physical frailty; the only difference is that among gifted children the incidence of these deviations is, in varying degrees, lower than in the general population (34)."

Terman also points out that there is no certainty that the relationship between intelligence and character present during childhood persists throughout life, although a majority of psychologists believe that it does (35).

Unfortunately, even among gifted groups there is not complete absence of emotional maladjustment. Elise Martens recognized this fact and reports that: "Research also shows the danger of emotional maladjustment in individual cases within an unfavorable environment. Prison records tragically reveal those whose giftedness is turned into paths of crime because some one . . . failed in guidance (36)."

According to the data from the Wyman Interest Test given by Terman to his subjects, ninety per cent of the gifted scored above the average of unselected children in intellectual interests and eighty-four per cent scored above the average in social interests. In activity interests, the gifted differed little from the average (37).

The gifted are greatly interested in play and tend strongly to choose playmates of their own mental age. This often results in social grouping with older children (38). Terman and Oden found that the gifted acquire far more knowledge of plays and games than the average child of their age. Their preferences among plays, games, and amusements follows the normal sex trends fairly closely, but gifted girls tend to be more masculine in play interest than average girls. The play preferences of the gifted are two or three years beyond their age norm in interest maturity (39).

Nearly half of the children in Terman and Oden's study learned to read before starting to school. They learned to read easily, read more and better books than the average child, and largely educated themselves (40). They read over a considerably wider range than average children. They particularly read more science, history, biography, travel books, folk tales, informational fiction, poetry, and drama, and proportionately fewer books of adventure or mystery and far less emotional fiction (41). Hollingworth states that the gifted have characteristic reading preferences. They are more interested in dictionaries, encyclopedias and atlases before they are ten years old than most people ever are (42).

Terman and Oden report that the vast majority of gifted children like school (43). They are more interested than unselected children in the more abstract subjects and somewhat less interested in the more practical subjects. The scholastic interests of gifted girls resemble those of gifted boys much more than they resemble those of average girls (44).

Even though gifted children do make high scores on tests of personal adjustment and appear to be better adjusted than the average, there is still a definite need for guidance. Ruth Strang, in *The Gifted Child*, in a section on the Mental Hygiene of Gifted Children, emphasizes this need (45).

The reasons for maintaining good mental health among gifted groups differ only in degree from the reasons for maintaining mental health in the average population. In a democratic society which depends upon the continued development of intelligent leaders, the mental health of future leaders is most important. Failure to develop talent represents a loss of potential wealth which society can not afford.

Another important reason for the maintenance of good mental health among gifted children is the potential threat they offer to society if their ability is misdirected.

Strang states the following reasons for the maintenance of mental health among the gifted: "First, undeveloped talent is expensive to society: it represents a lost contribution. Second, misdirected ability or talent, as in the case of the criminal or mentally disturbed leader, constitutes a social menace: intelligence and talent can be misused for aggressive, destructive purposes. Third, the maladjusted individual himself fails to attain the deep satisfaction that accompanies self-fulfillment and service (46)."

Perhaps the most important reason for early recognition and guidance of the gifted child is to aid him in attaining "the deep satisfaction that accompanies self-fulfillment and service (47)" of which Strang writes.

Research has clearly indicated that the gifted child, instead of being the social and emotional misfit that he was once thought to be, is superior in personal adjustment. The incidence of nervous instability and maladjustment is slight, although there is not complete absence of emotional maladjustment in the gifted group. The interests of gifted children are normal, but the extent to which they pursue these interests is much greater. In spite of better emotional and social adjustment, however, there is a need for guidance and understanding of this child if he is to fulfill his potentialities in later life.

REFERENCES

1. Lewis Terman, "A New Approach to the Study of Genius," *Psychological Review*, Vol. 29, No. 4, July, 1922, pp. 310-318.
2. Elise H. Martens, "Gifted Children: What Do We Know About Them? What Shall We Do About Them?", *The Nation's Schools*, June, 1951, p. 33.
3. Leta S. Hollingworth, *Children Above 180 IQ*. Yonkers-on-Hudson, New York: World Book Co., 1942, pp. 61-62.

4. D. A. Thom and N. Newell, "Hazards of the High IQ," *Mental Hygiene,* January, 1945, pp. 61-77.
5. Willard C. Olson and B. W. Hughes, "Growth Patterns of Exceptional Children," *Forty-Ninth Yearbook,* National Society for the Study of Education, Part II, p. 63.
6. Leta S. Hollingworth, *Gifted Children.* New York: The Macmillan Co., 1926, p. 87.
7. John Bentley, *Superior Children.* New York: W. W. Norton Co., 1937, pp. 15-16.
8. Paul A. Witty, "A Study of One Hundred Gifted Children," *Bulletin of Education,* University of Kansas, Vol. 2, No. 7. Lawrence, Kansas: University of Kansas, February, 1930, p. 38.
9. Lewis M. Terman and Melita H. Oden, *The Gifted Child Grows Up.* Stanford, California: Stanford University Press, 1947.
10. Viola Theman, "A Follow-Up Study of Negro Youth of Superior Intelligence." Unpublished Doctoral Dissertation, Northwestern University, Evanston, Illinois, August, 1942, p. 94.
11. Terman and Oden, *op. cit.,* p. 377.
12. Harry J. Baker, *Characteristics of Superior Learners and the Relative Merits of Enrichment and Acceleration for Them.* Supplementary Educational Monograph, No. 69. Chicago: University of Chicago Press, October, 1949, pp. 153-154.
13. Terman and Oden, *op. cit.,* p. 25.
14. Hollingworth, *Gifted Children, op. cit.,* p. 139.
15. *Ibid.,* p. 122.
16. Herbert Carroll, *Genius in the Making.* New York: McGraw-Hill Book Co., Inc., 1940, pp. 115-121.
17. *Ibid.,* p. 112.
18. B. F. Goodhart and S. D. Schmidt, "Educational Characteristics of Superior Children," *Baltimore Bulletin of Education,* Vol. 18, September, 1940, pp. 14-17.
19. William H. Bristow, et al., "Identifying Gifted Children." *The Gifted Child.* Edited by Paul A. Witty. Boston: D. C. Heath and Co., 1951, p. 14.
20. Terman and Oden, *op. cit.,* p. 28.
21. Goodhart and Schmidt, *op. cit.*
22. Terman and Oden, *op. cit.,* p. 28.
23. *Ibid.,* p. 29.
24. *Ibid.,* p. 378.
25. Paul A. Witty, "The Gifted Child—Facts and Fallacies," *National Parent Teacher,* Vol. 42, June, 1948, p. 4.
26. Paul A. Witty and Harvey C. Lehman, "Religious Leadership and Stability," *The Psychological Review,* Vol. 36, No. 1, January, 1929, p. 80.
27. *Ibid.,* p. 82.
28. Paul A. Witty and Harvey C. Lehman, "Nervous Instability and Genius," *Journal of Abnormal and Social Psychology,* April–June, 1929, p. 78.
29. Hollingworth, *Gifted Children, op. cit.,* p. 73.
30. Terman and Oden, *op. cit.,* p. 28.
31. Hollingworth, *Gifted Children, op. cit.,* p. 56.
32. *Ibid.,* p. 123.
33. *Ibid.,* p. 150.
34. Terman and Oden, *op. cit.,* p. 57.
35. *Ibid.,* p. 44.
36. Martens, *op. cit.,* p. 33.

37. Terman and Oden, *op. cit.*, p. 56.
38. Hollingworth, *Gifted Children, op. cit.*, p. 147.
39. Terman and Oden, *op. cit.*
40. *Ibid.*
41. *Ibid.*, p. 39.
42. Hollingworth, *Gifted Children, op. cit.*, p. 139.
43. Terman and Oden, *op. cit.*, p. 56.
44. *Ibid.*, p. 31.
45. Ruth Strang, "Mental Hygiene of Gifted Children," *The Gifted Child, op. cit.*, pp. 131-162.
46. *Ibid.*, p. 131.
47. *Ibid.*

8 | SOCIAL AND EMOTIONAL CHARACTERISTICS

Nervous Instability and Genius: Poetry and Fiction

PAUL A. WITTY
HARVEY C. LEHMAN

The writers have stressed in previous articles the convictions set forth by various scholars in reference to the nature of genius (1) (4). A present-day attitude that is gaining rather general credence is exemplified by Terman who has stated that the eccentricity of genius is largely a myth, and that from the ranks of the gifted (I.Q. 140 and above) *and from nowhere else* our geniuses in every line of endeavor are recruited.

The data show that the physical and mental traits which characterize typical gifted children appear to warrant the belief that more intense educational effort in their behalf on the part of the school would not involve the risks which various writers have feared. The 'eccentricity of genius' is largely a myth (2).

One reason for the general neglect of this field of pedagogy has been the widespread belief that the apparently gifted child is merely precocious, and usually pathologically so. However, recent experimental studies have shown *conclusively* that this belief has little or no foundation in fact. All the scientific evidence at hand points to the conclusion that gifted children are superior to unselected children in physical and nonintellectual mental traits as well as intelligence and that they carry this advantage into adult life. *We are coming to recognize that from their ranks and from nowhere else, our leaders in every line are recruited* (3). (Italics ours.)

In the above quotation we have the extreme point of view set forth. From the gifted (children of I.Q. 140 and above) and from nowhere else our leaders in every line are recruited. Here we have over-simplification in the extreme—leadership in every line of endeavor reduced to a magical formula—I.Q. 140 and above.

Reprinted from *Journal of Abnormal and Social Psychology*, Vol. 24, No. 1 (April-June, 1929). By permission of the senior author and the American Psychological Association.

In a preceding paper the writers have adduced evidence which shows that in so far as the religious genius is concerned the eccentricity of genius is hardly a myth (4). As is indicated by its title, this paper will discuss the problem of the stability of certain other types of genius.

The writers recognize the importance of no less than three variables in effecting genius, namely, ability, drive, and opportunity. They have shown that numerous factors effect the drive which directs the inordinate ability of many men to a fortunate culmination (15). The thwarting of certain strong desires often results in a redirection of energy and sometimes to conspicuous attainment.

The thwarting of desires is of course only one of numerous elements which create drive or intensity of effort concentrated upon a desired end. The writers have shown that instinctive urges actuate drive for some, that habits, once acquired, become the impetus for drive in the case of others and that the malfunctioning of glands may be responsible in some instances for intensity of effort (15). They have shown also that, in numerous instances of so-called greatness, there are apparent unmistakable evidences of the desire to compensate for thwarted wants. Some thwarted individuals find satisfyingness in religious frenzy. Others turn to music for substitute gratification; some find vicarious gratification in creating imaginative products in which the sublimated wish is to some degree fulfilled. It is apparent that the forms of substitute activity are numerous and diverse.

In men of literary ability the direction of effort undoubtedly is determined in many instances by the nature and the intensity of the thwarting of fundamental desires. Literary production of an imaginative sort offers one intensely satisfying mode of substitute activity through which vicarious gratification is achieved and adjustment facilitated. Since the unstable person is more emotional and hence less able to endure thwarting than the normal individual he is more often seriously disturbed and harassed by the inevitable thwarting which life brings. Consequently, ability plus nervous instability seems to furnish a propitious background for literary eminence, for when a capable but nevertheless unstable individual is thwarted he is likely to seek satisfyingness through an easily accessible and intensely satisfying channel, namely, imaginative writing. This is particularly true if the environment is such as to encourage literary endeavor.

The term nervous instability, like the term genius, is difficult to describe and delimit. Nervous instability is of course a relative term. The writers are using the term as Mateer employs the word psychopathy to denote irregularities in the functioning of mentality (5). In their most extreme forms, irregularities in function produce insanity; in lesser degrees all the conduct disorders which man exhibits. Individuals differ greatly in their emotional responsiveness and consequently in their ability to withstand thwarting. At one extreme of the distribution surface are the stolid, apathetic individuals; at the other, the excitable, hypersensitive ones; and from one extreme to the other every degree of sensitivity is to be found. It is obvious that the extremely emotional person is one likely to be unstable. Life abounds with conflicts for such a person; he is driven often to seek indirect gratification. Such an individual, if he possess unusual ability, is likely to be driven through maladjustment to creative endeavor which the world calls the work of genius.

The statistical method is employed often to determine the relationship between nervous instability and genius. Hirsch summarizes some of the results obtained by such attempts (6). In commenting upon a long list of names of men of eminence who displayed nervous instability Hirsch asks: Of what possible use can such a list of names be? (6) p. 113. He insists that even if the number of names were multiplied by ten it would be of little value. The question is not whether there have been great men who were insane but whether the proportion of those who at some period of their lives have been attacked by insanity of different types has been markedly greater among famous personages than among the general run of mankind (6).

Hirsch is correct in his assertion that the statistical method proves little in a scientific way regarding this question for the degrees of nervous instability are not easily amenable to quantitative expression. In some instances the evidences of nervous instability are numerous and subtle. Yet the blanket term insane has been used by some writers to include all individuals who are unstable to any degree. There is no generally accepted method at the present time which delimits the degrees of nervous instability. Because of the failure to describe nervous instability precisely, two types of errors result when attempts are made to ascertain the frequency of instability among men of genius. First, there is the tendency to exaggerate the presence of certain symptoms and to catalogue relatively stable people as "insane," and, second, there is encountered the tendency to overlook the presence of symptoms of instability when the subjects deviate *only slightly* from the average. Those who start with the preconception that genius is relatively stable would be more likely to manifest the second tendency, *i.e.*, that of overlooking slight deviations from the average. The slight deviation may have been, however, an important agent in determining the genius of a given individual. On the other hand those who believe at the outset that genius is relatively unstable find it easy to prove their point by exaggerating the presence of minor symptoms.

Of the first tendency, numerous examples are found in the writings of Nisbet, Nordau *et al.* Certain biographical accounts of Goethe exemplify the second trend. Very few writers have cited the peculiarities of Wolfgang Goethe; Goethe is commonly thought to have led an entirely normal and happy life. Indeed, Goethe is sometimes cited as an example of a genius who was conspicuously normal. Hirsch, however, calls attention to the fact that Goethe once experienced the hallucination of seeing his own counterpart riding toward him. Goethe's own testimony is as follows:

'I saw myself coming along the same path on horseback toward me, dressed, as I had never been, in pike-gray and gold. I shook myself out of the dream, and the figure was gone. But it is singular that eight years later, not at all by choice but only by chance, I found myself riding over the same path in the very direction my visionary self took and clad in just those clothes, being again on my way to Frederica. Whatever the explanation of these things may be, the wonderful phantom gave me at that moment of separation some alleviation.' Quoted by Hirsch (6).

Corroborative evidence of the instability of Goethe is given by William James who declared that Goethe is a conspicuous example of a great man who had a sick soul. If Goethe were not, how is the following statement to be explained? " 'I will say nothing,' writes Goethe in 1824, 'against the course of my existence. But at bottom it has been nothing but pain and burden, and I can affirm that during the whole of my 75 years, I have not had four weeks of genuine well-being. It is but the perpetual rolling of a rock that must be raised up again forever' " (7).

Although in a casual examination, Goethe may appear to have been a well-balanced man, detailed study reveals significant symptoms of nervous instability. Detailed studies of other men of proven genius reveal mental conflicts and maladjustments which would be overlooked by the unwary observer or by the statistician whose purpose is to compile data, not analyze them. The writers will not attempt to tabulate the frequency with which instability is found among men of literary genius. They propose merely to cite certain instances of a linkage between eminence in literary work and nervous instability *where the nervous instability appears to have been an important factor* in creating the drive of the subject.

EDGAR ALLAN POE

In a recent biography of Edgar Allan Poe, Krutch points out that Poe was driven to literary eminence by a desire to compensate for a precluded social position, denied sexual craving, and a knowledge of mental instability. The three factors are thought collectively to have effected a strong and persistent drive. "Just as his whole life was a struggle, conducted with all the cunning of the unconscious, against a realization of the psychic impotence of his sexual nature, so was it a struggle also against a realization of the mental instability to which the first gave rise" (8).

Mr. Krutch asserts that if what he says of Poe be true, it is plausible to assume that *all* imaginative work is the result of attempts to compensate for human maladjustments to life. This hypothesis in reference to the actuating of *all* works of genius in imaginative fields of course needs validation. Other writers than Krutch have insisted that Poe's work was the product of his abnormality. Marks asserts that *The Fall of the House of Usher* was autobiographical (9).

There are allusions to opium in his stories. *The Fall of the House of Usher* is a good illustration. We are not a page into this story before there is reference to opium and to the "bitter lapse into everyday life," which Poe himself knew better than his heroes. Every paragraph of *The Fall of the House of Usher* writes itself down as drug work, not alone in its study of the morbid in character, but also in other ways. Take, for example, the somatic distress due to opium, the tortured sensitiveness to light, to odors and to sounds. All this preoccupation with disease is characteristic of the narcotized mind. In another study, what but a drugged imagination would have thought of "Dark-eyed violets that writhe"? Where, but in drug work, with its diseased auditory nerves, would we get so many explosive maniacal screams and cries and groans? Where, but in drug work, do we get such broken structures, such inconsistent and unlooked-for endings? Take, for example, *Eleanor*. Where such rioting phantasmagoria of colors, lights, sounds and kaleidoscopic manias of one sort or another? (9).

The following statement by Poe indicates that he may have had knowledge of his own mental instability: "I am come of a race noted for vigor of fancy and ardor of passion. Men have called me mad; but the question is not yet settled, whether much that is glorious, whether all that is profound, does not spring from disease of thought, from moods of mind enacted at the expense of general intellect" (9).

In view of the preceding statements, including Poe's own testimony, it seems quite possible that Poe's instability may have been an important determiner of his drive and therefore essential to his genius.

LORD BYRON

Among English writers Lord Byron is often pointed out as an example of an unusual man afflicted with nervous instability. Cassity has summarized some of the attempts to account for Byron's unusual behavior (10). Thus Woods naïvely stresses what Byron accomplished in spite of epilepsy (11). In the light of Cassity's conception of epilepsy it would have been much wiser to have emphasized what heights Byron attained by virtue of the epileptoid seizures which may have afforded an outlet for "his vicious psychic accumulations." Hughes also errs in attributing Byron's baser tendencies to "Brain-fag," thus ignoring the fact that Byron displayed gross disorders of conduct before he was of sufficient age to have thought "exhaustively" (12). Knott is another theorist who fixes the blame for Byron's neuroses on alcoholic excesses, apparently unaware of markedly neuropathic manifestations in the poet before he had so much as tasted alcohol (13).

Cassity holds that alcoholism was not the cause of Byron's instability but a symptom of it (10). The tendency to assign the cause of maladjustment to a symptom of the actual maladjustment occurs with great frequency in the writings of eugenicists and moralizers. It is unjustifiable to attribute his excesses and peculiarities to alcoholism for Byron's whole life discloses a series of erratic gestures. The accounts of Byron's early years give undeniable evidence of neural instability. It is of course unknown whether Byron's instability was affected by hereditary forces or by environmental obstacles and issues. Certainly, the Byron clan shows numerous symptoms of gross maladjustment and instability. One is led inevitably to the conclusion that Byron was handicapped from the start by hereditary predispositions to neural disorder. There is, however, no way to ascertain the relative forces of environment and heredity in producing the maladjustment. Certainly, Byron was seriously handicapped in both regards from the start.

That Byron was nervously unstable is generally accepted. The force of this instability in determining the nature of his work is unknown but clear evidence of its potency is present in his writings. When Byron started to school at Aberdeen, he was doomed to an unfortunate plight. His schoolmates mercilessly called attention to and ridiculed his deformed cloven foot. Unbearable torturing ridicule to a sensitive nature! Again and again this ridicule was forced upon him and an audacious insolence developed to offset his ever-present feeling of inferiority.

Byron was an exceedingly vain person. Witness his strict diet and torturing exercise to preserve his physical beauty. He has been rightly accused of narcissism which probably resulted from his desire to compensate for awareness of his physical anomaly.

Several writers have emphasized Byron's amours and have sentimentalized upon his burning affection for Mary Chatworth. They dote at length on the love sonnets dedicated to her (10). Byron once asserted as follows: "I have taken all my fables about the celestial nature of women from the perfection my imagination created in her (Mary Chatworth), I say created, for I found her, like the rest of the sex, anything but angelic" (10).

Once Byron heard Mary remark to her maid, "Do you think I could ever marry that lame boy?" and he later admitted to Moore that the speech was like a shot through his heart. Byron chafed immeasurably at this direct affront and there resulted poems of beauty and intensity dedicated to Mary, not however to the real Mary but to an ideal who exemplified the traits lacking in the human Mary. When Byron was only sixteen years of age he wrote several poems in which he created celestial women who personified the type he most desired. Thus Byron's early poems may have been means by which he escaped the unpleasant feelings of inferiority attending forced realization of his deformity.

Byron's deformity led to a number of exaggerated attempts at adjustment. No one can trace with certainty Byron's narcissism to this source. It seems logical however to assume that his deformity exercised a tremendous influence upon determining the direction of his energy. His attempts and his success in modifying his physical appearance are well-known to the student of biography. The results were so successful as to win him the title Apollo. It seems plausible that Byron's early literary work afforded balm also to his wounded pride and dominating feelings of inferiority.

That Byron developed his literary ability to satisfy personal animosities is obvious. A defiant spirit appears to have developed as a compensation for his feelings of inferiority. Byron's first ambitious work, *English Bards and Scotch Reviewers,* was a bitter satire upon English writers and their audacious Scotch reviewers. The vitriolic invectives were directed particularly toward Lord Carlyle, Byron's uncle, who had refused properly to recognize him. The *Childe Harold,* in beautiful verse, Byron achieves his greatest work,[1] chanting the poetic music of sorrow and ecstasy, but always defiant and audacious. The mockery and the dalliance of the wit are present always and always too, an arrogance arising from a sense of defiant inferiority. Byron writes of the third Canto of *Childe Harold,*

It is a fine piece of poetical desolation, and my favorite. I was half mad, during the time of its composition, between metaphysics, mountains, lakes, love inextinguishable, thoughts unutterable, and the nightmare of my own delinquencies. I should, many a good day, have blown my brains out but for the recollection that it would have given pleasure to my mother-in-law. Quoted by Hirsch (6).

In *Childe Harold,* Byron achieved another triumph. Although *Childe Harold* is characteristically different from Byron's earlier work, there is exemplified in it again the strange ingredients so conspicuous in his earlier writing. There is evident always the relentless driving power of wounded feelings and deep-rooted antagonism. It seems reasonable therefore that Byron's unbalanced nature furnished the drive for the expression of an ability so unusual that genius of a rare order was consummated. Throughout Byron's entire literary career it is possible to trace the bitterness and defiance born from deep-seated feelings of inferiority.

It is of interest that Byron produced his most famous work[2] at a time

---

[1] In the opinion of one of the writers.
[2] Not necessarily his best.

when he was working under the most adverse circumstances. Cassity gives the following account.

Due to Byron's infidelity and rumors of his incestuous relationship with his half-sister, Augusta Leigh, Byron was dethroned overnight and received, from then on, the appellation of "Monster" in all respectable households in London. . . . But here we observe an important factor in Byron's personality, namely, his decidedly compensatory fashion of coping with adverse situations. As has been shown, he reacted viciously to derogatory comment. Now all comment was not only derogatory, but maiming to his character, but he more than withstood the assault. He retired to Italy and produced his most famous works, viz., his plays and "Don Juan" (10).

OTHER CREATIVE ARTISTS

There are numerous other poets whose nervous instability seems to have been a decisive factor in determining their genius. The two cited thus far, Poe and Byron, are conspicuous examples of unstable persons driven to escape from the persistent harasses of the real world. The writers recognize that both Byron and Poe possessed unusual ability. These poets possessed also extremely sensitive natures and because they were repeatedly thwarted they sought in poetry satisfying avenues of escape from reality.

Ernest Dowson is one to whom nature, caprice—whatever one chooses to call it—presented an insurmountable burden. He desired the expression and the joy of free sense gratification. Most of all he desired the daughter of a keeper of a humble restaurant in a foreign quarter of London. She listened to his verses, smiled indulgently, and ultimately married a waiter. All his life, he clamored for the impossible. Not only was he thwarted by the whims of fate in the object of his affection, but his weak physical nature also precluded satisfaction of certain basic human desires.

The result was the development of a strange dual personality. At one time, Dowson was a naïve boy, unspoiled by contact with the gross indulgences of the world. At another, he was the drunken inebriate seeking to forget the devastating fate assigned to him. His indulgences were always more imaginary than real and his most important contributions to literature were the songs chanted to the girl whom he could not possess. The futility of his life is epitomized in his poem, *Num sum qualis eram bonae sub regno cynarae,* one of the immortal lyrics. Stronger characters than he might have met fate, realized more, and produced more. It is doubtful, however, that any could have produced so lovely and appealing a tribute to unfulfilled desire as he in his poem to the girl whom he could not possess.[3]

[3] This sketch of Dowson is based in part upon A. Symon's excellent introduction to Dowson's work. This book is one of the *Modern Library* series.

Another poet whose work reveals always the domination of defiant feelings of inferiority is Heinrich Heine. His life was filled with denials and disappointments. Browne has recently treated ably and fully the conflicts in the development of this man (14). Sprung from a lowly cobbler, Heine desired to demonstrate to the world that he was a superior individual entitled to recognition and social prestige. While Dowson succumbed to the obstacles presented by an unsympathetic world and produced little, Heine was driven persistently to written expression by the obstacles in his life. He has been characterized as a libertine and sensualist. His Paris life offered certain obstacles to attainment of physical contact with those of high rank and enviable social caste. Instead of creating imagery situations as did Dowson, Heine wrote exquisite poems to the Isabellas, the Roses, and the Arabellas whom he found on the streets. The carnal pleasures were consummated and the effigies of the ladies of uneasy virtue were subsequently glorified. Strange potency— this thing compensation! Bawdy, lewd, and ignorant coquettes transformed and immortalized in poetry into the very types Heine so greatly desired but failed to secure! In this phase of Heine's writing, one sees the mechanism of compensation affording an adjustment for physical wants.

Another interesting phase of Heine's development was in connection with his attacks upon politics. The polemics upon politics were the result of his dominating feelings of inferiority. Exile and persecution followed. Disease and poverty faced him too. Weak men would have succumbed. Not so with Heine. Until the very last, even when he was partly paralyzed and physically incompetent, he continued to write—always writing with the desire either to attain precluded desires vicariously or to force the world to acknowledge his superiority. The strange ingredients of his personality reacted to the continual thwarting by prolific writing. Today our literature is enriched greatly by the reactions of this unstable man to an unkind, unsympathetic and ununderstanding world.

Miss Marks insists that it is questionable whether the man who is perfectly equipped to enjoy life would write poetry. She suggests that suffering, disease, and disaster produce the desire to create poetry (9). Much emphasis is placed upon the fact that in writing poetry one may create imaginary situations which satisfy desires which society or nature thwart. Certainly it is debatable whether all poetry is actuated by conflict. Nevertheless reason must grant that the element of mental conflict is an important one in effecting the genius of many poets. The sonnets which are the most beautiful in the world's literature have been created in many instances by individuals who were congenitally abnormal or socially maladjusted. The sonnets of Sappho and Shakespeare are excellent examples of such work. Sappho was probably a Lesbian and the love life of a Lesbian must be thwarted and scorned by a society which little understands or sympathizes with the deviation. Consequently, avenues of escape often are sought by such deviates. When ability is present and environment propitious the writing of poetry offers an intensely satisfying means of escape. Not only are the sonnets of Sappho probably a result of homosexual conflicts but those of Shakespeare may have had a similar impetus. Certainly, it is not a normal reaction for a male to dedicate sonnets to another of the same sex. The dedication by Shakespeare of his sonnet to Mr. W. H. is much discussed by the professors of English.[4]

The case of Oscar Wilde of course is a much bruited one. Although some critics dismiss him with a gesture, his importance as a writer must be granted. Throughout all his writing, there is revealed a brilliant wit and epigram which reflect his abnormality.

One could assemble a list of homosexual or bisexual individuals who have produced poetry and of course have little valid proof of the relationship between abnormality and genius. The list would be long and conspicuous (6). Although such a statistical procedure would have little value, it is reasonable to asume that the sexual anomaly of homosexual geniuses played a decisive rôle in effecting their work as exemplified in the work of Oscar Wilde. The work of the homosexual reveals direct or indirect evidence of the abnormality in many instances. An unbalanced and thwarted sex life leads of course to desire to escape and it is questionable whether Wilde and Sappho would have had the desire to write if normal well-adjusted life had characterized them. Certainly, the work would have taken quite a different form of expression in the lack of the sexual anomaly. The strange magic of poetry and other forms of aesthetics in satisfying vicariously sexual desires is little understood. Certain psychologists, however, have traced the origin of aesthetics primarily to sexual manifestations and drives. Shakespeare's unsurpassed sonnets, Sappho's lovely writing, Walt Whitman's beautiful and sagacious poems written to certain men and Wilde's brilliant and ebullient poetry—all these must have been intensely satisfying products. Surely, the normal person with well-regulated sex life would not have found expression and satisfyingness through the channels used by these writers.

The particular direction of the energy of these characters must have been occasioned in part by the potency of abnormality and conflict. Not only in the case of homosexuals does conflict cause the thwarted individual to seek vicarious gratification through creating poetry but many thwarted individuals who are not homosexuals find outlet for precluded desires by this agency. The cases of Poe, Dowson, Heine, and Byron were cited previously. Many others could be added without difficulty.

[4] The dedication of Shakespeare's sonnets as well as the character of Whitman are matters of speculation only.

The relative influence of disease, maladjustment, unconscious conflict, etc., in creating or fostering genius are unknown. Here we have a complex situation impossible to analyze. Marks attributes genius in some instances to the driving force effected by disease. It is likely that the disease as well as the creative endeavor in many instances spring from a common source, nervous instability. It would be more logical to attribute the physical ailment so frequently encountered in men of genius to the physical reaction attendant upon emotional thwarting. Miss Marks, however, feels that available data offer another explanation for genius. She attributes much of the drive of great poets to the speeding of metabolic rate associated with certain diseases.

The significance of the *spes phthisica*—the psychical quickening—found in poets and writers of known tuberculous taint requires more than a second thought to comprehend. It would not do, for example, to conclude that the invariable effect of a disease of the body shows itself in mental ways that are equally diseased. With the tuberculous at least such is not the case. In Shelley's *Ode to the West Wind* it is doubtful whether the flight of his song and the tumult of wind and leaves would have been so swift without the quickening which Shelley had from tuberculosis. In the case of Emily Brontë, life may have been shortened physically by consumption, but study convinces the reader that psychically in *Wuthering Heights* and in her poems power and passion were made the greater by the *spes phthisica*.

Nature is a wise economist and has in view her own disease compensations. Keats' mother died of tuberculosis as did also his brother Tom who was nursed by the poet. In two years Keats produced many poems—enough to fill a bulky volume—which will make his name known and loved as long as English poetry is read. *Spes phthisica?* Elizabeth Barrett Browning had trouble with the lungs and at the age of thirty-one a hemorrhage. For a long period Robert Louis Stevenson fought tuberculosis. In his search for health he made the world his debtor by many volumes of the most delightful travels ever written. But biographical study of Stevenson's life shows that when he was in improved condition his literary output was least. Only one conclusion is possible: that he missed the psychical excitation of disease. In American literary annals Poe, Thoreau, Emerson, Lanier, are four famous illustrations of the tuberculous taint. Here are but a few of those many special studies which might be made. The closer the study of the illustrations the firmer grows the conviction that however much the physical life may be shortened by tuberculosis, there is acceleration, speeding-up of the mental processes (9).

The hypothesis set forth by Miss Marks in reference to the stimulus for poetry of course needs validation. That disease is a single or a predominant factor in determining literary output is yet to be demonstrated. The assumption, however, seems warranted that the psychical excitation accompanying certain kinds of disease may be one factor of considerable importance.

Among present-day fiction writers, the list of the unstable is long and among the realists, the psychiatrist might find a fertile field for analysis. Some of the most noteworthy of modern American books are the volumes written as reactions to the deadly routine of primitive life or as protests against the rigorous Puritanism of the Middle-West. Noticeable also is it that, in many contemporary novels dealing with the modern business man, one finds revolt against bigotry and chauvinism. Almost every institution of American life has been attacked by writers of fiction and the bitterness and defiance of the writers give evidence of the desire to compensate for dominant feelings of inferiority evolved by numerous and bitter youthful thwarting.

Therefore one finds the anguish and the torture of suppression and the revolt of sensitive natures in many modern novels and short stories. Of course not all writers of fiction are unstable. But certainly the average stable man would not be annoyed so intensely by the banalities and stupidities of life as are those who produce realistic fiction. The unstable nature revolts and the result in many instances brings literature of merit.

It is clear of course that numerous factors produce the drive essential to creative endeavor. In poets and in certain fiction writers one factor of importance is the conflict produced by nervous instability; another is the conflict arising from physical anomalies or abnormal nature (as in the case of homosexuality); another is the desire to escape from the ravages of disease. Things rarely go happily for sensitive natures. If ability be present, a way out is sought in the songs of the poet. Thus the store of human contributions is augmented by the product of unhappy or sick souls who seek an indirect mode of expression through poetry.

It is well-known that things rarely go well with the poets. Few reach a conventional happy ending. Some are of strong intellect, of great understanding. They sin superbly, they repent sublimely. And when desires are thwarted, as they must be constantly for such people, they create divine imaginative situations. They find, in the delightful labor of writing, balm for unfulfilled desires. The beautiful songs of all ages, the really immortal verses, have come from those harassed natures who seek avenues of escape from the conflicts of a world exacting impossible tasks from unusually sensitive natures.

REFERENCES

1. Witty, P. A., and Lehman, H. C., "Nervous Instability and Genius: Some Conflicting Opinions." Jour. of Abn. and Soc. Psy. (Forthcoming).
2. Terman, L. M., The Twenty-third Yearbook of the National Society for the Study of Education. Part I. "The Education of Gifted Children." Bloomington, Ind., Public School Publishing Co., 1924, p. 184.
3. Terman, L. M., Editor's introduction to "Gifted Children: Their Nature and Nurture," by Lulu M. Stedman. Yonkers-on-the-Hudson, New York: The World Book Co., 1924, p. vii.

4. Witty, P. A., and Lehman, H. C., "Religious Leadership and Stability." Psychol. Rev., 1929, 36, 56-82.
5. Mateer, Florence, The Unstable Child. New York: D. Appleton & Co., 1924, pp. xii-471.
6. Hirsch, Wm., Genius and Degeneration. New York: D. Appleton & Co., 1896 (translated from the second edition of the German work), pp. xi-333.
7. Quoted by James, Wm., in The Varieties of Religious Experience. New York: Longmans, Green and Co., 1925, pp. xii-435.
8. Krutch, J. W., Edgar Allan Poe, A Study in Genius. New York: Alfred A. Knopf, 1926, pp. x-245.
9. Marks, Jeannette, Genius and Disaster: Studies in Drugs and Genius. New York: Adelphi Company, 1925, pp. viii-185.
10. Cassity, J. H., "Psychopathological Glimpses of Lord Byron." The Psychoan. Rev., 1925, 12, 397-413.
11. Woods, Matthem: "In Spite of Epilepsy." Cosmopolitan Press, 1913.
12. Hughes, C. H., "A Neurologist's Plea for Lord Byron." Alien & Neurol., St. Louis, 1926, 23, 349-351.
13. Knott, John, "Last Illness of Byron: A Study in the Borderland of Genius and Madness." St. Paul Med. Jour., 1912, 14, 1-43.
14. Browne, Lewis, That Man Heine. The Macmillan Co., 1927.
15. Witty, P. A., and Lehman, H. C., "Ability versus Effective Ability." Psychol. Rev., 1928, 35, 67-86.

Adjustment Problems of the Gifted

EDITH H. GROTBERG

Scientific approaches to the study of the gifted, which followed the development and use of mental tests, yielded results inconsistent with beliefs held forty or fifty years earlier. The early works of Terman (10), Witty (12), and Hollingworth (4, 5) dispelled the beliefs that the gifted are "the products of supernatural causes of human behavior," and that "intellectual precocity is pathological" (10). Indeed, Terman, Witty, and Hollingworth found the gifted to be physically superior, attractive, and generally well-adjusted.

Although these authors recognized that adjustment problems existed among the gifted, relatively little effort was made to investigate problem behavior until recently. It should be recalled, however, that Hollingworth (4) found that pupils of IQ's 180 plus had more adjustment problems than pupils whose IQ's fell between 130 and 180.

Recently a number of studies have appeared which tend to sub-

Reprinted from the April, 1962, issue of *Education*. Copyright 1962 by The Bobbs-Merrill Co., Inc., Indianapolis, Indiana.

stantiate the findings of the early research endeavors as far as the generally superior adjustment of the gifted is concerned. But recent studies have attempted to determine the factors correlated with maladjustment.

Some of these studies have dealt with identifying the characteristics of underachievers, i.e., verbally gifted students who are not earning grades commensurate with IQ or test score expectancy. Haggard (3) found that by third grade high achievers responded to socialization pressures and accepted adult values readily. They co-operated, had good work habits, and maintained satisfactory relationships with parents, peers, and teachers. They were also highly competitive.

Gowan (2) reported that the underachiever experienced parental rejection and hostility frequently. Roesslein (8) found among high school male underachievers a pattern involving oversolicitous parents and resultant feelings of inadequacy. Armstrong (1), who studied the adjustment of underachievers in the ninth and eleventh grades, found that they were more influenced by the desires of others rather than their own wishes and were regarded by their teachers as unco-operative, undependable, and poor in judgment.

Further, O'Leary (7) found the underachievers in the ninth grade to have poor work habits. Patterns of maladjustment found among underachievers at the college level by Wedemeyer (11) and Horrall (6) were similar to those noted in the elementary and high school pupils. And Shaw and Brown (9) found a high degree of hostility and hypercritical attitudes among underachieving college students.

INSTITUTIONALIZED GIFTED

Clearly the verbally gifted have adjustment problems, although their incidence is lower than that found in less intelligent individuals. A frequently used method for identifying the maladjusted gifted, as we have already indicated, has been in association with underachievement in elementary, high school, and college.

Another method of identifying the problems of the maladjusted gifted is to study gifted adults who have been institutionalized and whose conditions have been diagnosed. These individuals are to a large extent the underachievers or failures as adults. An examination of their records reveals a number of factors which should be of interest to educators. The remainder of this article is based on a study of institutionalized gifted in the Elgin, Illinois, State Hospital. This study was made by the writer in 1961.

TEST GROUPS AND TESTS

Forty gifted and forty non-gifted institutionalized patients comprised the experimental and control groups. Each group contained twenty male and twenty female patients. Psychological tests, consisting of a Wechsler-Bellevue or Adult Intelligence Scale, the Rorschach Test, a Thematic Apperception Test, and a Sentence Completion Examination, were given to ascertain the characteristics which differentiated the gifted population from the non-gifted population.

The gifted population was selected on the basis of high IQ. An IQ of 120 was set as the base, and the range was from 120 to 137. An IQ between 80 and 110 was used to designate the non-gifted population.

A SUMMARY OF CHARACTERISTICS

A summary of the findings concerning the characteristics of the gifted as compared to the non-gifted institutionalized population is organized around (1) age, (2) education, (3) occupation, (4) psychological controls, and (5) general diagnosis, frequency of paranoid tendencies, and incidence of obsessive-compulsive features.

1. *Age:* The institutionalized gifted and non-gifted had a median age of 33.5 to 34 years. The age differences are not significant. The gifted enter mental hospitals with the same relative frequency as the non-gifted. Another way of stating this fact is that the percentage of gifted in mental hospitals is the same as the percentage of gifted in the total population. Mental hospital populations represent the total population in terms of IQ distribution. The adjustment advantage of the gifted in childhood and youth apparently is lost in adulthood.

2. *Education:* The gifted have obtained on the average from three to five years more education than the non-gifted. The gifted male has continued his higher education more frequently and for more advanced degrees than the gifted female. Nine of the twenty gifted males were college graduates; two of these had master's degrees, three had doctor's degrees. Four gifted females, by contrast, were college graduates; two of these had master's degrees; none had a doctor's degree. Apparently the male is encouraged to pursue higher education more frequently and for more advanced degrees than the female.

3. *Occupation:* In spite of more education, the gifted female attained no higher occupational status than the non-gifted population. The gifted male holds the occupations associated with higher education, such as physician, teacher, publisher, pilot, and engineer.

4. *Psychological Controls:* The F score of the Rorschach was used to determine the degree of control that the patients indicated as they interact with their environment. No significant differences in control were found between the gifted and non-gifted populations. Further, the gifted demonstrated no greater control than that which would be expected by chance.

5. *Diagnosis:* The most frequently occurring diagnosis for the gifted male and the non-gifted population was schizophrenia or schizophrenic reaction. No significant differences existed. The gifted female was significantly more

psychoneurotic than the non-gifted male (.01 level of significance) and the gifted male (.05 level of significance).

Statistically significant differences in incidence of paranoid tendencies did not appear between the gifted and the non-gifted. However, the gifted male showed the highest frequency of such characteristics. Over half of the gifted males could be so designated.

The gifted male also showed the highest incidence of obsessive-compulsive tendencies, although differences were not statistically significant.

FEELINGS AND ATTITUDES

Factors which may further contribute to an understanding of differences between the gifted and non-gifted institutionalized population are organized around (1) feelings of superiority, (2) perceptions of failure, (3) attitudes toward work, and (4) attitudes toward parental pressures in terms of parental expectations.

1. *Feelings of superiority:* At times, the gifted male tended to perceive himself as superior to others. The gifted female and the non-gifted populations did not perceive themselves so often in this way. The feelings of superiority of the gifted male were significantly higher than the gifted female.

2. *Perceptions of failure:* Half of the gifted female population perceived themselves as failures while three-fourths of the gifted males so perceived themselves. The gifted female resembled more closely the non-gifted population. The gifted male felt significantly more of a failure than the non-gifted population. He felt more of a failure than the gifted female, but the difference was not significant.

3. *Attitudes toward work:* Negative attitudes toward work were held most frequently by both male and female gifted, while positive attitudes were held most frequently by the non-gifted. The gifted female had more negative attitudes toward work than the gifted male. She also had the least positive attitudes toward work. All of the relationships were significant at the .01 level.

4. *Attitudes toward parental pressures:* More male and female gifted resisted parental pressures than non-gifted, but the gifted submitted to parental pressure with about the same frequency as the non-gifted. The gifted showed a similar frequency of ambivalence toward parental pressures as the non-gifted. Both the male and female gifted showed a higher frequency of striving beyond parental standards than the non-gifted. All of the relationships were significant at the .01 or .05 levels.

DISCUSSION OF FINDINGS

The discussion is organized around two foci: (1) the characteristics and perceptions that distinguish the institutionalized gifted from the institutionalized non-gifted, and (2) educational implications of the findings.

The institutionalized gifted resembled the age groups of the institutionalized non-gifted and have developed no higher set of controls to ward off or postpone a psychotic or psychoneurotic disorder. The adjustment advantage found among gifted children and youth is apparently lost in adulthood.

The institutionalized gifted was better educated than the non-gifted. The gifted male continued higher education more frequently than the gifted female at a rate of more than 2 to 1. The gifted male also continued higher education for more advanced degrees than the gifted female. Gifted males held the better occupational positions and had the highest socio-economic status. Gifted females attained no higher socio-economic status than the non-gifted.

The institutionalized gifted male tended to become schizophrenic and to display paranoid or obsessive-compulsive features. He was more likely to project the blame for his failure onto others. He was not so likely to assume responsibility for his own failures. The gifted female more frequently developed psychoneurotic disorders.

The gifted male was more frequently aware of his superiority and also of his own sense of failure. Neither the gifted male nor female had marked positive attitudes toward work; indeed their attitudes were highly negative. Both the gifted male and female tended to reject pressure in terms of parental expectations. Yet as a group, they submitted to parental pressures about as frequently as did the non-gifted population. However, they more frequently attempted to surpass the expectations and achievements of their parents.

IMPLICATIONS

Assuming that growth and development are continuous, and that adult adjustments are to a large extent contingent upon earlier experiences, a number of implications for education may be derived from the findings on institutionalized gifted. These findings may be suggested by the following questions:

1. What are the schools doing to determine and influence the gifted student's attitude toward work?
2. How does the school help gifted students deal with failure?
3. What are schools doing to help the gifted student develop a self-concept and ideal consonant with his promise?
4. How do the schools work with parents to foster achievement of a high order?
5. Are teachers and parents working together in efforts to stimulate more gifted girls to continue their education and make greater contribution in accord with their promise?

The institutionalized gifted have poor attitudes toward work. Is it possible that too many gifted meet school requirements without much effort? Perhaps these students acquire knowledge and information with a minimum of effort and therefore do not find it necessary to develop positive attitudes and desirable work habits.

The institutionalized gifted, especially the male, experience pervasive feelings of failure. Has academic work been so easy in the elementary school and high school that the gifted seldom experience failure and therefore do not learn to deal with it constructively? Does the gifted male's pattern of blaming others for his failures need to be examined and altered?

The institutionalized gifted male appears to feel superior to others. Have the schools contributed to the feelings of superiority on the part of the male? Similarly, have schools attempted to help girls develop a realistic appreciation of their abilities?

The institutionalized gifted report excessive conflict with their parents. Is the school helping parents to formulate realistic expectations for their gifted children? Are teachers helping the gifted relate effectively to those in authority?

The institutionalized gifted male is better educated and is higher in the occupational hierarchy than is the female. Do present programs for the gifted provide sufficient incentive for the full development of gifted girls?

Answers to these questions seem to be worthy of consideration by schools in their efforts to provide more adequately for gifted pupils.

REFERENCES

1. Armstrong, Marion E., *A Comparison of the Interests and Social Adjustments of Under Achievers and Normal Achievers at the Secondary School Level,* doctoral dissertation (Storrs, Connecticut: University of Connecticut, 1955). Abstract in *Dissertation Abstracts* 15, 1955, pp. 1349-1350.
2. Gowan, John C., "The Underachieving Gifted Child—A Problem for Everyone," *Exceptional Children,* Vol. 21 (April, 1955), pp. 247-249, 270-271.
3. Haggard, Ernest A., "Socialization, Personality, and Academic Achievement in Gifted Children," *School Review,* Vol. 65 (December, 1957), pp. 388-414.
4. Hollingworth, L. S., *Children Above 180 IQ* (Yonkers-on-Hudson, N.Y.: World Book Company, 1942).
5. Hollingworth, L. S., *Gifted Children: Their Nature and Nurture* (New York: Macmillan, 1926).
6. Horrall, Bernice M., "Academic Performance and Personality Adjustments of Highly Intelligent College Students," *Genetic Psychology Monographs,* Vol. 55 (February, 1957), pp. 3-83.
7. O'Leary, Maurice J., *The Measurement and Evaluation of the Work Habits of Overachievers and Underachievers to Determine the Relationship of These Habits to Achievement,* doctoral dissertation (Boston: Bos-

ton University, 1955). Abstract in *Dissertation Abstracts* 15, 1955, pp. 2104-2105.

8. Roesslein, Charles G., *Differential Patterns of Intelligence Traits between High Achieving and Low Achieving High School Boys* (Washington, D.C.: Catholic University of America Press, 1953).
9. Shaw, Merville, C., II, and Brown, Donald J., "Scholastic Underachievement of Bright College Students," *Personnel and Guidance Journal*, Vol. 36 (November, 1957), pp. 195-199.
10. Terman, L. M., and Oden, M., *Mental and Physical Traits of a Thousand Gifted Students*, Vol. I of *Genetic Studies of Genius* (Stanford, California: Stanford University Press, 1925).
11. Wedemeyer, Charles A., "Gifted Achievers and Non-Achievers," *Journal of Higher Education*, Vol. 24 (January, 1953), pp. 25-30.
12. Witty, Paul, *A Study of One Hundred Gifted Children*, University of Kansas Bulletin in Education, Vol. II, No. 7 (Lawrence, Kansas: University of Kansas Press, 1930).

Problems of Highly Creative Children

E. PAUL TORRANCE

Inescapably, the individual who thinks of a new idea is in the very beginning a minority of one. Even when matters of demonstrable fact are involved, as in the Asch experiments, there are very few people who can tolerate being a minority of one. Since creativity involves independence of mind, nonconformity to group pressures, or breaking out of the mould, it is inevitable that highly creative children experience some unusual problems of adjustment. Thus, the highly creative child must either repress his creativity or learn to cope with the tensions which arise from being frequently a minority of one. Repression of creative needs may lead to actual personality breakdown. Their expression frequently leads to loneliness, conflicts, and other problems of adjustment. Educators of gifted children need to understand both types of problems.

1. SANCTIONS AGAINST DIVERGENCY

In one of our studies, we have asked approximately 5,000 children in grades three through six to write imaginative stories concerning animals or persons with some divergent characteristic. These have given us many insights concerning the way children see the operation of their society's

Reprinted from *Gifted Child Quarterly*, Vol. 5, No. 2 (Summer, 1961), pp. 31-34. By permission of the author and publisher.

sanctions against being different. The following story by ↗ girl illustrates many of these sanctions:

Far into the jungle of Africa lived a flying monkey named ╌ was a well-educated monkey and very cute . . . Pepper was unusual too. was not like all of the other flying monkeys. You see, Pepper didn't eat ba- nanas like everybody else. He wanted to be different. He ate peppers!

No one ever went out of the jungle so Pepper, being different, decided to go to America! . . . When the people saw him, they began to laugh and then others began to scream. Then out of nowhere a man from a zoo came and took Pepper by surprise. . . .

Now Pepper was sad. He didn't like the cage they put him in. He made a vow that if he ever got out he would never be different again and ten minutes later he saw some bent bars big enough to fly through. All of a sudden he flew out and in two days was back in the jungle. He kept his promise too. He was never different again. He was a good little flying monkey.

I suppose *he ate his bananas!*

About two-thirds of the stories about flying monkeys tell similar tales of conformity or of destruction. Some cultures, however, are more in- dulgent of divergency than others. Stories written by gifted children in special classes are far more hopeful in outlook than those of gifted chil- dren in regular classes. In about 70 per cent of the stories of pupils in classes for high achieving children, the flying monkey is in some way able to persist in his flying. The stories written by children in a small Oklahoma town composed of Indians, whites, and a few Negroes also reflect this tolerance of divergency. In 74 per cent of their stories, the flying monkey succeeds.

2. CREATIVE CHILDREN MAY NOT BE WELL ROUNDED

The highly creative child is likely to have lagged in some phase of his development. Many investigators in a variety of fields have been dis- appointed to find that outstanding individuals in the field under study are not well-rounded, "all-American" boys. Verbal abilities frequently will be below some of their other abilities. Perhaps the most inventive and imaginative child we have tested is a boy who has had unusual dif- ficulty in learning to read, yet his store of information and his ability to use it imaginatively in solving problems and developing ideas is fantastic.

This problem is particularly acute at the fourth-grade level. In a num- ber of cases, fourth graders identified by our tests as highly creative have been reevaluated by teachers. Teachers then discover that these children are far more knowledgeable and thoughtful than they had imagined. One examiner after testing orally a certain fourth grade boy remarked: "This boy impresses me as the kind of individual who will become a top executive who can dictate to five secretaries at the same time without becoming confused." The boy's responses gave evidence of high inventive level, flexibility, and originality. This boy, however, has a serious reading disability and ranked near the bottom of his class on the written test of creative thinking.

Because verbal skills are highly valued in our society, tremendous pressures are placed on children to be "well-rounded" in this respect. The relentlessness of these pressures is symbolized in the following story by a sixth-grade girl:

"Quack! Quack! They were after him again—the Ladies Duck Aid Society, with their hair up in pin curls and their screaming, fat ducklings swimming and holding onto their skirts. They never failed. Alas! It was getting too much for little Glob-Blob. Every day there would be quacking and screaming of ducklings while poor Glob-Blob would run as fast as he could to get away from the vicious ducks.

"The reason for this was because poor Glob-Blob could not quack. So every day the Ladies Duck Aid Society would chase Glob-Blob, for they said it was for the good of the ducks, and it was not only right but they were doing a good turn.

"It was lucky for Glob-Blob that the ducks were fat and flabby, for if they were limber, I will not mention what would happen. But one day, these lazy ducks did reduce, and when chasing Glob-Blob dealt him a good many hard blows. And the next day, poor Glob-Blob was at last doomed. The vicious quackers had come and the chase was on. Glob-Blob was failing. It is a shame that so noble a duck should be doomed, but 'That's life,' said Glob-Blob to himself as, slowly but surely, failing, he dropped to the ground. The quackers, very pleased with themselves, sat down for a chat.

"But I shall always remember Glob-Blob and his death. So I shall let him finish his journey, where there will be no more quackers and chasers, and where at last, he may have passionless peace forever."

Many children must consider their counselors, teachers, and parents as "quackers and chasers" when we work so hard to make them become "better rounded personalities." They might contribute far more to society and be far happier and more successful by capitalizing upon their unique strengths rather than spending fruitless energy trying hopelessly to compensate for some divergent characteristic or behavior. I would not, of course, deny that it is necessary for some of our highly creative youngsters to achieve basic skills necessary for success in their chosen areas of specialization.

3. CREATIVE CHILDREN PREFER TO LEARN ON THEIR OWN

Many creative children prefer to learn on their own and schools have been slow in providing such opportunities. Last year we conducted an exciting study in which we found that children would do a great deal of writing on their own, if properly motivated. In another it was found that gifted children in a split-shift school showed more growth in language development, science, and social studies than under a full-day schedule. Only in spelling was there significantly less growth among the split-shift children (seventh graders).

Since we have generally assumed that children do not learn on their own, we have seldom provided them with opportunities to do so. I have seen learning situations "accidentally" left "open" a sufficient number of times to have become quite excited about what would happen, if we should do so more frequently. The following story by an Oklahoma sixth grader, symbolizes this situation:

"Once there were some monkeys sitting in a group. They were all alike except three monkeys. They were very different because they could fly.

"One day some men from a park zoo were looking for some monkeys because theirs had died. They came upon the three that flew. So they took them in a cage. The cage didn't have a top to it. They were in the sun one day and the monkey said to the other, 'I wish we could get out of here.'

"'Then, why don't we fly out of here?' said the other.

"They started to fly out. When they got about half a mile, some men came to feed them. When they couldn't find the three monkeys, they saw them flying away. One of them said, 'If we would have put them in a cage with a top, we would have had a real good thing here in the zoo.'"

One function of the school counselor might be to help highly creative children recognize or discover the "openings" in their cages to which they might be blinded.

4. CREATIVE CHILDREN LIKE TO ATTEMPT DIFFICULT TASKS

Frequently highly creative children strongly desire to move far ahead of their classmates in some areas. They always make us afraid that they are not "ready." Fortunately, however, educators of gifted children are rapidly revising many of their concepts about what can be taught at various levels of education. This terrifies many. The following recent headlines reflect such a fear:

"Caution Urged in Changing Primary into High Schools"
"Can We Rush Primary Education?"
"Don't Turn Grade Schools into High Schools, Educators Warn at Parley"
"Reading for Kindergarten, Language Too Soon Attacked."

Some of the panic may have been eased by a recent report of the Educational Policies Commission of the NEA and the American Association of School Administrators (*Contemporary Issues in Elementary Education, 1960*).

A very frequent theme in our imaginative stories is related to this problem. The young animal or fowl asks, "When can I roar? When can I crow? When can I quack? When can I fly?" Almost always, the answer is, "When you are a little older." We are always afraid that the young one might not be ready to learn and that he would be forever scarred by even the most temporary failure.

A common experience in the lives of many highly outstanding individuals has been their ability to cope with failure and frustration. Certainly, almost all highly creative scientists, inventors, artists, and writers attempt tasks which are too difficult for them. Had they not attempted such tasks, it is quite unlikely that their great ideas would have been born.

5. CREATIVE CHILDREN ARE SEARCHING FOR A PURPOSE

It has been said of most outstanding creative achievers that they seemed to be possessed by a purpose and to be "men of destiny." Creative children need some purpose which is worthy of the enthusiastic devotion they seem capable of giving. Some of this need is symbolized in the following story by a sixth-grade boy:

"There once was a South American monkey that didn't know what he was, who he was, or why he was even alive. He decided that he didn't know even the way to figure it out, so he thought he would make up a reason.

"He had seen many airplanes fly overhead. He had seen many ferocious animals, many nice animals, and many machines. He had always thought that it would be nice to fly, so he pretended he was an airplane.

"He had also heard that buzzing sound of the engines, so he called himself 'Buzz.' He also decided that he was a real fast flyer so that this was the reason he was alive.

"Now, we all know that monkeys can't fly, but he didn't know this. Why he didn't even know that he was a monkey, so he kept trying and trying— and you know what? He flew!"

Perhaps this has some implications not only concerning the need for helping children discover their potentialities but for helping them achieve their self-concepts creatively rather than by authority.

6. CREATIVE CHILDREN SEARCH FOR THEIR UNIQUENESS

Counselors and teachers may become irritated with creative children who seem to create problems for themselves by trying consciously to be different—searching for their uniqueness. Barron maintains that creative individuals reject the demands of their society to surrender their individuality because "they want to own themselves totally and because they perceive a shortsightedness in the claim of society that all its members should adapt themselves to a norm for a given time and place."

One way in which the creative individual searches for his uniqueness is through his vocational choice. Getzels and Jackson, for example, found that their highly creative compared with their highly intelligent subjects gave a greater number of different occupations and more "unusual" or rare occupations. Their attitudes toward adult success were also different, the high creatives being less concerned with conventional standards.

7. THE PSYCHOLOGICAL ESTRANGEMENT OF CREATIVE CHILDREN

In no group thus far studied have we failed to find relatively clear evidence of the operation of pressures against the most creative members of the group, though they are far more severe in some classes than in others.

When we select the most creative members of each sex in each classroom and match them for sex and Intelligence Quotient with other children in the same classroom, three characteristics stand out as differentiating the highly creative children from the less creative ones. First, there is a tendency for them to gain a reputation for having wild or silly ideas. Their teachers and their peers agree on this. Second, their work is characterized by its productivity of ideas "off the beaten track." This explains one of the difficulties of teachers and peers in evaluating their ideas and perhaps why they show up no better than they do on traditional intelligence tests. Their ideas simply do not conform to the standardized dimensions, the behavioral norms, on which responses are judged. Third, they are characterized by humor and playfulness. All of these characteristics help explain both the estrangement and the creativity.

In the next issue, I shall discuss some of the problems which arise when highly creative children repress their creative needs and abilities.

Friendship and the Intellectually Gifted Child

HARRIET E. O'SHEA

Few areas in social psychology, in critical psychology, and in developmental psychology are more confused semantically and more difficult ones in which to establish clear-cut measurement—than the area of friendship. Further difficulties attendant upon the original one lie in appraising the effect of friendship or of the lack of friendship upon the individual.

Close friendship involves in some fashion a personal, mutual awareness, a liking and confidence, and a secure satisfaction in interchange, which seem to be recognized introspectively by psychologists and sociologists. However, it is exactly here that measurement becomes so difficult. Presumably, there is a genuine difference between friendship, as such, and what has sometimes been called "popularity" in various sociometric and other studies. Presumably also, genuine close friendship has an effect upon the individuals involved which is different from the condition and experience of being "popular."

This paper reaffirms the assumption made by Lippitt (1) that "the power fields of friends strengthen each other." To the extent that this is true, it is manifestly important for developing human beings, for gifted children as well as others, to have friends. Maslow's (2) "self-actualizing people," in his observation, are those who seem to be especially at home in this life. One wonders whether the experience of constructive, close friendships may not be a contributing factor in reaching the condition of being self-actualizing.

If one looks for identities within the two experiences, it seems possible that the favorable relation of security with adults demonstrated by Spitz and Ribble and others to be so exceedingly important for infants, may, at its core, be something like the experience in the later preschool years, in the primary school years, and in the elementary school years of close friendships with peers. The possibility exists, in other words, that there is a central area of similarity, if not of identity, in the two experiences, with the attendant probability that the experience is comparably nourishing in both instances.

Reprinted from *Exceptional Children*, Vol. 26, No. 6 (February, 1960), pp. 327-335. By permission of the author and publisher.

FRIENDSHIP—A POTENT SOCIAL FORCE

If the relationship of friendship is a potent force in the development of human beings, then this issue together with all other aspects of programs for gifted children should be taken into account as a major issue when educators and others are endeavoring to see how to meet the needs of gifted children. This issue becomes important if we are to insure their performing academically at top levels in order that they may, presumably, become especially productive for the benefit of society when they leave school and in order that they may have satisfying lives for themselves. All educational and clinical evidence shows that the individual must be complete and contented and "self-actualizing" within himself in order to be of maximum benefit to society. In other words, what is good for the individual gifted child will also be good for him as a social contributor. The question then becomes urgent: "Who are potential friends for gifted children? With whom can they establish relationships of friendship?"

Before we undertake a tentative answer to this question, it may be well to note further that there is a genuine need for the gifted child, as for all other human beings, to become a socialized person, both, again, for his own mental health and for his functioning in society. Undoubtedly relationships of friendship can be, and perhaps are, the most significant way to achieve socialization. The concept of making the intellectually gifted child "get along" with the child of the same chronological age in the center of the distribution of intelligence "because the world is full of such people and you have to get along with everyone" seems to the writer to be a thoroughly bankrupt concept. The contrary hypothesis is that it is only those persons who have experienced closeness and mutual trust and have thus achieved understanding of others throughout the years of childhood who can display sympathy and understanding and can achieve closeness to anyone as adults.

FACTORS OF SOCIAL LIMITATION

In the welter of studies of relationships between children, which frequently have probably been only "popularity studies," the choices in any case have almost always been strictly limited by geographical boundaries (friends are within a few blocks of each other) and by the child's most frequent contacts being within a narrow chronological age range imposed by the schools. Obviously, in such circumstances, the child with a higher mental age than his chronological age group has very little chance to find anyone of like mental age, even if he would take greater pleasure in such a relationship.

Even so, nothing correlates higher with mutual choices than mental age, and in various studies it stands considerably above any other factor. At the junior high school level, presidents of self-government groups typically are at about the 55th percentile of the group in mental age, and so on.

MENTAL AGE FACTORS

It is instructive to compare performances of different mental ages on various tasks and to think how completely communication must fail between children of two widely separated mental ages in the light of these radically different performances. Convenient examples of these phenomena for illustrative purposes can be seen in the Terman-Merrill Stanford-Binet Test Forms L and M. The tests for *comprehension* and for recognition of *similarities* show some clear mental age differences.

At the three-year mental age level, the simplest sort of answer to the following questions is acceptable:

a. What must you do when you are hungry?
b. What must you do when you are sleepy?

It is apparent that the questions at the five-year mental age level involve more coordination of different items, and more selection amongst material that should not be used for the answers, and more dealing with organized patterns:

a. What do we do with our eyes?
b. What do we do with our ears?

A child who has not yet reached the five-year mental age level would give answers that utilize simple associations to the objects mentioned without selection of what is appropriate and what is inappropriate. He does not see that the patterns imbedded in the questions make certain associations relevant and others totally irrelevant. A failing answer to "What do we do with our eyes?" would be *Sleep,* and to "What do we do with our ears?" would be *Wash them with soap,* or *Put hair over them.* It is apparent that the failing answers (below the five-year mental age level) have not been controlled by the abstract part of the questions, "What do we do with . . . ?" The main functions of eyes and ears have not been located by these respondents, and associations which are ruled out by the total pattern of the question have not been discarded.

At the eight-year mental age level, the requirement is to answer two of the following three questions satisfactorily:

a. What should a man do if he comes home and finds that a burglar has robbed his house?

b. Why is a train harder to stop than an automobile?

c. What should a man do if he finds that he is earning less money than it takes to live on?

It is apparent that much more material must be held together to answer any of these three questions than to answer the question, "What do we do with our eyes?" Not only must more material be brought together at once, but also many random, spontaneous reactions to each of the elements of the questions must be discarded under the control of the total pattern. Some satisfactory eight-year mental age reactions and some failing below-eight-year mental age reactions are the following:

1. (BURGLAR) "He would send down the police." This satisfactorily takes into account the problem, what the individual can do, and the facilities for dealing with it. Failing reactions are such as, "Find out who it was," or "Put it in the paper."

These two answers have not been controlled by the necessary steps for identifying the burglar or the possible results if one put an announcement in the paper, as contrasted with the series of actions necessary to meet the special conditions of a robbery in a house.

2. Similarly, in considering why a train is harder to stop than an automobile, a true eight-year mental age answer would be, "Trains are heavy and are hard to turn off" as contrasted with lower-mental age response such as: "Because a train has more things to stop—and in the automobile, you just have to push down the brakes."

It is apparent that this under-eight-year mental age answer has not seen the issue of weight and kinetic energy and has not been able to reject some immediate associations such as the one, "A train has more things," if that answer means more complicated machinery in the cab, as it appears to mean, in relation to the rest of the answer.

3. Finally, to the question of the man earning too little money, a satisfactory answer for an eight-year-old is: "He should go into another business." A below-eight-year mental age response could be, "Shouldn't spend so much money to live on" or "Borrow some." The response "Spend less money to live on" has not been ruled out by the specification in the question that, in effect, the man is already spending beyond his income for the minimum necessities of life. The less-than-eight-year-old answer which recommends borrowing has not been cancelled by the overall specification that the man is already on the way to being in debt.

As one considers the characteristics of these mental age levels, it becomes apparent that the five-year or the three-year mental age cannot respond to or interact with the eight-year mental age. The first two groups are unable to keep track of all the items or perceive the abstract patterns that the eight-year mental age does automatically. The other way around, the three-year-old and five-year-old mental age levels would be exasperating and probably seemingly intentionally obstructive to the eight-year mental age level, because of omission of factual issues.

MATURING PERCEPTUAL CONTRASTS

In the area of recognizing similarities, the contrast between the seven-year mental age level and the eleven-year mental age level shows up clearly how much more material is organized in one grasp of the situation at the eleven-year level, way beyond what the seven-year-old level can do. It is apparent also that more subtle abstract patterns are perceived by the eleven-year-old mind than by the seven-year-old mind.

The seven-year-old mind can give two satisfactory similarities from the list below:

Seven year mental age

(a) Wood and coal
(b) Apple and peach
(c) Ship and automobile
(d) Brass and silver

The eleven-year-old mind can give three satisfactory similarities from the list below:

Eleven year mental age

(a) Snake, cow, sparrow
(b) Rose, potato, tree
(c) Wool, cotton, leather
(d) Book, teacher, newspaper
(e) Knife-blade, penny, piece of wire

In the reactions of under-eleven-year mental ages to the above items, it is apparent that the lower mental age mind does not compare each entry with each other entry (snake, cow, sparrow) discarding in the similarities reported between two of them (taken two by two) all characteristics that would not include the third. In other words, the lower mental age uses without selections, or with very little selection, the first association that comes to mind for two of the stimuli, and it happily relaxes with no feeling of discrepancy even though the full pattern has not been met. For instance, for snake-cow-sparrow, some under-eleven-year answers are, "They can all hurt you" (ignoring the sparrow) and "All can walk" (ignoring the snake).

An under-eleven response for rose-potato-tree might be, "Rose grows like a tree, potato grows under ground." Here the under-eleven mind is not troubled by the fact that it has failed to unite the three ("Potato grows under ground") and is not troubled by differences between a rose bush and a tree, even in comparing those two. Perhaps there is a foggy feeling that there is some similarity between a rose bush and a tree but the under-eleven mind cannot cast out the inappropriate associations that come to mind and penetrate through to those characteristics that are identical for a rose and a tree.

In wool-cotton-leather, an under-eleven answer might be, "Comes from animals." Here the under-eleven mind is not troubled by cotton being nonanimal. Again, first, early associations cannot be resisted to satisfy a controlling selector pattern.

A foggy perception of *something* similar in book-teacher-newspaper without the ability to penetrate through to the central characteristic shared by the three (giving information) is displayed by the under-eleven answer, "They belong to schools—newspaper has reading on it and we use it sometimes in school." Here, "belongs to school" may be moving in towards recognizing the information-giving characteristics of the three items but this reaction, among other things, fails to rule out many other aspects of a school such as having chairs, a furnace, and so on. This under-eleven reaction also fails to perceive the characteristic that both teacher and newspaper can give you information no matter where they may be, in school, on subways, in a living room, or wherever it may be.

Under-eleven reactions to knife-blade-penny-piece of wire are such as the following: "They are both strong." Among other things, this fails to utilize any scale of strength by which a usual piece of wire would be low in the scale and ignores the fact that a penny would be of very little use for leverage and so on. Another under-eleven reaction might be, "All made of the same metal" which is not controlled by the fact that a penny is never made of steel, which would be the almost invariable metal for a knife-blade, and does not take into account the fact that wire might be made of one of any number of different metals. The under-eleven mind cannot get to the more abstract, general category "All made of metal."

An eleven-year-old mind endeavoring to deal with a mind around seven would be bored or exasperated by the uninterestingness or the apparently obstructive action of the lower mental age. In the same way, the seven-year mental age which can only just manage to get two comparisons out of: wood and coal (fuel), apple and peach (fruit), ship and automobile (transportation), brass and silver (metal) would be completely bewildered in trying to deal with the ordinary, complicated, abstract thinking of the eleven-year-old mind illustrated by its ease of recognizing the similar element in three objects.

One can guess the discouragement of the higher mental age level child when he tries to talk and to play with the younger mental age level child who keeps missing the point and confusing issues and requiring endless explanations to get him into action at all, whereas it can be seen what a joy it is (all other things being equal) when one's companion sees instantly what one is talking about and says things that seem interesting, clear and important to one, even when he disagrees.

In the examples of reactions to similarities that have been quoted one might be seeing two seven-year-old children, one with an IQ of 100 and a mental age of seven, the other with an IQ of 157 and a mental age of eleven. In many school systems, or perhaps one has to say, in most school systems, these two seven-year-olds would be in the second grade together. The mental ages around seven would predominate in the class, perhaps 27 or 28 such children to only one or two with mental ages anywhere near our child of the IQ of 157. It then develops that day after day the eleven-year mental age confuses the majority, who usually protect themselves by cold shouldering him or even attacking him. He not only is starved for friendly interactions with equal minds but often, perhaps most of the time, the recipient of social exclusion or even hostility.

In Terman's (3) studies of "genius," although the gifted children were rated higher in personality traits than other children, there were no direct measures of friendship included in the data. However, in connection with these favorable personality ratings, it should be remembered that, typically, the gifted child in the study was the youngest in his classroom, which indicates that the gap between his mental age and that of the group was a little reduced. Also, it is interesting to note that, in the follow-up studies, the most successful group of these gifted children graduated from college younger than the least successful group, again suggesting less isolation from their classmates in mental age.

At the three-year-old level, there are data concerning who can be friends with whom. In a too-little-known study of spontaneous group formations in the nursery school, Hubbard (4) established what many would consider an extraordinary fact. In these little spontaneous groups, which averaged two or three children, which lasted perhaps six minutes, and which were engaged in twice in every 15 minutes, the question was: who played with whom? Hubbard investigated the occurrence of three factors in the choices made: chronological age, the general amount of social participation by the individual, and mental age. She measured her groups both in terms of the number of times that children joined each other and in terms of the length of time that they spent together in a group. The correlations between general amount of social participation or chronological age and the personnel of the little groups ran between −.22 and +.19. When, however, Hubbard calculated the relationships between mental age and spontaneous group participation, she found that those who played together most often showed a correlation of +.41 in mental age; in the case of those who played longest together in groups the correlation was +.62 for mental age. In other words, in these early years, an age when one is certain that the child is not standing around asking himself which is the appropriate child to play with, the most powerful factor pulling the membership of a group together appears to be similarity in mental age.

A direct comparison of the sociometric choices of gifted children within a gifted group and within their homeroom group assigned by chronological age has been reported by Mann (5). From a population of 1000 children, from kindergarten through sixth grade, he studied 67 intellectually gifted children who were taken for half of each day into a special workshop. The other half day, they were with their chronological age homeroom group. He utilized a sociometric technique in which each child chose those whom he would want to have with him at a school party, or whom he would want to have help him catch up with his work if he had been absent, or whom he would like to have on his side on a team. Mann also utilized the same factors in reverse, "Whom would you *least* like to have for . . ." Remembering that the gifted children spent an equal amount of time with the other gifted workshop children and with their chronological age homeroom children, the positive choices were found to be overwhelmingly for other workshop children. Also, the rejections were overwhelmingly for other workshop children. In other words, there seems to be revealed here a perfectly clear-cut difference in the lack of awareness of, and undoubtedly the lack of interest in, the lower mental-age children (of the same chronological age) and a greatly heightened awareness of and interest in the children of the same high mental ages.

In other words, the contention that keeping a gifted child with others of his own chronological age will help him have friendships with this group appears to be strongly refuted by Mann's findings. Insofar as a sociometric technique is measuring friendships (it is at least measuring "awareness of" and "interest in"), it is shown that friendships occur with those of like mental age, rather than with those of like chronological age.

"LIKE ATTRACTS LIKE"

Long ago, Hollingworth (6) reported many striking cases of the radical change in the life experience of highly gifted children, originally lonely, ineffectual, shunned non-participators who, when they were later moved into groups of comparable mental age, began to function richly in the new group, were well-liked, and frequently became some of the most valuable contributors to the life of the group, and, in each case, changed from a shy, lonely person into a happy, friendly, socialized individual.

The dynamics of the choice of like mental ages revealed by Hubbard amongst three-year-olds and of choices (and rejections) of like mental ages in the elementary school years as measured by Mann, and of the resuscitation of individuals placed among equals as reported by Hollingworth may be partly suggested by formulations of Lewin (7). He has stated that differences in mental age are closely related to the degree of differentiation of the person, and that increasing mental age means increasing flexibility, that is to say, increasing richness of behavior. It would seem highly likely that the three-year-old in the nursery school discovers those other children who provide him with appropriate richness of behavior, and who, in turn, are pleased by his richness of behavior. Less differentiation of the person presumably is unsatisfying and, in that sense, boring, and undoubtedly involves frustration of the higher mental age personality when some of his behavior and some of his advances are left hanging in mid-air or are rejected by the less rich and less flexible person who cannot deal with the higher mental age manifestations. Undoubtedly, the same dynamics exist in the elementary school years. It seems clearly apparent that those who are more differentiated as persons find the less differentiated, less rich personalities dull and uninteresting, and undoubtedly frustrating because there is no "comeback" to the gifted child's advances. On the other hand, the person of equal differentiation as a person, the one with greater flexibility and richness of behavior, provides interesting material to observe and to respond to and gives satisfying reactions to one's own behavior.

Assuming that close friendship, that genuine interaction with other persons does many favorable things—such as increasing the socialization of the individual, making his life more satisfying, widening and deepening his "power field," establishing and maintaining general mental health —then it is urgent that arrangements be made for intellectually gifted children (in school, on playgrounds, in community activities) which will offer them appropriate social contacts to enable them to build friendships. It seems highly probable that when the gifted child is externally bound to persons of lower mental age, who are less flexible and less rich in personality differentiation of the person, he is then, in effect, an isolated individual for whom activities tend to drop dead, and for whom there is malnutrition in the area of rich, constructive, developing, rewarding experience of close friendship.

REFERENCES

1. Lippitt, Ronald, "Studies In Topological and Vector Psychology: I. An experimental study of the effect of democratic and authoritarian group atmospheres," *University of Iowa Studies in Child Welfare*, 1940, *16*, p. 45-195.
2. Maslow, A. H., "Cognition of Being in the Peak Experiences," *The Journal of Genetic Psychology*, 1959, 94, p. 43-66.
3. Terman, Lewis, *Genetic Studies of Genius*. Stanford University Press, California, 1925, 1926, 1930, 1947, 1959.

4. Hubbard, Ruth, "A Method of Studying Spontaneous Group Formation in: Thomas, Dorothy and associates," *Some New Techniques for Studying Social Behavior.*
5. Chapter IV, New York, 1929. Child Development Monograph, I, Bureau of Publications, Teachers College, Columbia University.
6. Mann, Horace, "How Real are Friendships of Gifted and Typical Children in a Program of Partial Segregation?" *Exceptional Children*, 1957, *23*, p. 199-201.
7. Hollingworth, Leta, *Gifted Children: Their Nature and Nurture*. Macmillan, New York, 1926.
8. Lewin, K., *Dynamic Theory of Personality*. McGraw-Hill, New York, 1935.

IV

Developing and Encouraging Giftedness

RECOGNITION OF THE gifted immediately implies the need for guidance. Giftedness by definition means more awareness of what is happening in the world around one. It is true that "ignorance is bliss," if one's goal is to escape from as many of the problems of adjustment as possible. Giftedness itself is sensitivity—or awareness of the problems in one's environment. The presence of adjustments which must be made does not mean that the gifted child fails to make good adjustments. The contrary is actually true. In spite of more adjustments, and certainly a more complex type of adjustment, most gifted children nevertheless emerge better adjusted than any other intellectual group.

It is not known how the gifted child has managed to be better adjusted with the attitudes of other children and adults often hostile to his particular needs. Society has left to chance the possibility that gifted children will adjust to a world characterized by normalcy and mediocrity. Instead of relenting, once the gifted child has proved his value to society by actually producing for the benefit of mankind, we have instead done everything possible even then to brand him a misfit. In a democratic society, so dependent for its very existence upon intelligent leadership which will come from the people, we must be certain that we are not leaving to chance the development of what has been labeled "our most valuable natural resource."

While identification of the gifted is a vital first step, any provision that does not go beyond this is of little value. If the progress we have made since Sputnik could be measured, it would be that we have moved beyond the stage of talking about the gifted and are now trying to do something for him. Identification alone is not the answer; but from proper identification can come the type of guidance program which is an essential part of the gifted child's school program, irrespective of the administrative educational provisions which are made for him.

CAN GIFTEDNESS BE DEVELOPED?

Since the modern concept of giftedness was first developed parents have been avid readers of the "how to develop a gifted child" type of article. Irrespective of the fact that psychologists maintain that the I.Q. is relatively constant, popular journals persist in publishing what parents want to believe. The public, not so gullible as it once was, will no longer accept an article merely stating that the I.Q. can be raised. Instead, they must be told "how" it can be done. With what could be justified only by the expression "literary license," articles regularly appear on the development of "genius."

Perhaps the outstanding example of this type of article is one which appeared a few years ago in *Coronet* entitled, "How to Raise Your Child's I.Q." This article, given feature billing, contained no information that was not readily available to parents in child-rearing books. The suggestions were all sound ones for providing a child with a good environmental background, but could hardly be guaranteed to develop giftedness. The article states:

Your child's—and your own—I.Q. can be raised. Here are four ways to do it:
1. *Improve the emotional climate in your home.* Many low I.Q. children are emotionally, not mentally, stunted. . . .
2. *Check the physical condition of your child.* Sometimes low I.Q.'s are caused by a physical ailment. . . .
3. *Improve your child's cultural life.* Frequently a child with a poor I.Q. is handicapped because he hasn't had the opportunity to see or hear about things his classmates have. . . .
4. *Stimulate mental ability of your child to a maximum.* Many children do not work up to their mental capacities. Because of lack of stimulation at home, they become lazy, or just don't care (1).

The article ends with the statement, "No child yet has been born who does not respond to love and affection, to good food and a happy home, to proper supervision and warm friends." And to all of this must be given complete agreement. Instead of informing the public that there is a difference between I.Q. and intelligence, too often authors capitalize on the misunderstanding.

It must be recognized that for many reasons children sometimes do not do as well as they are able on an intelligence test and are actually penalized. But if I.Q. is recognized as a measure of status attained, likely to be changed when environmental conditions change radically, then there can be no excuse for such hoodwinking of the public by such titles as, "How to Raise Your Child's I.Q." Parents reading such an article readily confuse the terms *I.Q.* and *intelligence.*

Popular treatment of the idea of developing giftedness brings back memories of the classic case of William James Sidis. At the age of two Sidis could read and at four he could use the typewriter, writing in English and French. Upon entering the first grade, he passed through seven grades in six months. At the age of eight, already an accomplished mathematician, he was able to devise a new logarithmic table based on the number 12 instead of ten. At the age of nine he passed the entrance examinations at Harvard, but was not allowed to matriculate until the age of eleven.

But William James Sidis' precocity did not become widely known until 1910 when he lectured at age eleven to a mathematical society of Harvard professors on the fourth dimension. This feat, in itself not nearly so outstanding as many of his earlier accomplishments, captured the imagination of reporters and scarcely an editorial page in the country escaped some mention of the "Sidis boy."

The reason that "the boy prodigy of Harvard" is remembered is not so much for his accomplishments, and the tragic aftermath of his outstanding college career, but instead for the training which his father gave him. Professor Sidis, a physician and psychologist colleague of William James, believed that the boy's ability was not the result of heredity or of any "abnormality of the child's brain." The results achieved, according to Professor Sidis, were "due wholly to the methods of training pursued."

There were those who believed that Professor Sidis had demonstrated William James' theory that "hidden springs of energy and achievement could be uncovered in the individual by certain types of training (2)." One editorial clearly stated, "A case like this Sidis boy does not mean precocity, but good education (3)." It would be difficult to find anyone today who would put as much faith in education.

The father, in 1910, explained in some detail the procedure followed in educating his son (4). Paraphrasing the report, the following steps appear to be the more pertinent ones:

1. Begin a child's education as soon as he displays any power to think.
2. Keep alive the quickening power of curiosity.
3. Do not repress him, but answer his questions in a manner which he can understand.
4. Teach him to draw upon his "reserve mental energy," more popularly called "second wind." When this can be controlled at will, it is possible to "accomplish daily and regularly what we can all do under stress of circumstances."
5. Teach the child to observe accurately, to analyze and synthesize and make sound deductions.
6. Never use baby talk or foolish gestures.

7. Since the child's first interest is in sounds, using alphabet blocks, teach him to identify the elements of sounds. (The Sidis boy could read and spell by this method by the time he was two.)
8. When he discovers that typewriting is easier, his natural eagerness will lead him to master the typewriter.
9. Using the same letter blocks, teach the child to count.
10. Give the child a calendar as an infant and teach him its use.
11. Allow his own interests to lead his education further. (The Sidis boy discovered a skeleton belonging to his father and by matching each bone with pictures of the bones, he was able to identify all the bones of the body before he was six.)
12. Using a child's interest in words, teach him foreign languages. (The Sidis boy went from English to Russian, French, German, Latin and Greek.)

While these suggestions seem harmless enough, the degree to which they must have been carried in this particular case is appalling. The conclusions which one must reach from this single case are that the Sidis boy possessed a truly remarkable mind, undoubtedly stimulated to a high level of performance by the pressures placed upon him by his father.

Three observations about the education of all remarkable children were noted at this time by Stephen Colvin. He states that, without exception, the known child prodigies of that era received a similar type of training.

1. They were educated by men and women of high intelligence and ability.
2. The instruction was individual and suited to the interests and abilities of the children.
3. The children were educated from the very first months of their lives (5).

The question Can giftedness be developed? cannot be answered with any certainty. Under certain conditions, and with particular children, the answer may be "yes," although there is no assurance that the consequence of such efforts will meet with the kind of success parents want for their children.

EDUCATIONAL PLANNING FOR THE GIFTED

The disagreements over establishing special classes or providing for the gifted child in the regular classroom seem periodically to reoccur. The concept that all men were created equal prevailed until about 1920, without any acceptance of the obvious fact that not only were all men not equal in their innate mental abilities, but that not all men would use their innate ability equally well. The furor of the twenties over special classes extended into the thirties, although by this time the opposition had formed a somewhat solid front and many of the "experimental" programs were being dropped in favor of a return to the regular program. The war years of 1941–1945 saw the end of almost all programs of special classes, the notable exception being the Major Work Program in Cleveland, Ohio; but this might have been expected for there were certainly no efforts to provide for any particular groups when the main goal of the country was to win a war. The planning for the future would have to wait.

The appearance of Lewis Terman's, *The Gifted Child Grows Up*, in 1947 gave new impetus to the cause of the gifted. In 1951 the American Association for the Gifted's contribution, *The Gifted Child*, assured the continued interest in this phase of special education. But in 1957, the entrance into the space age by a power other than the United States assured a continued interest in the gifted for some time. With perhaps no other motive than survival, the general public is demanding that something be done. And so, to what Leta Hollingworth would believe was a contemporary debate in the 1920's, we return to a discussion of the relative values of how we can best provide for gifted children in the public schools.

Have we solved none of the problems of educating gifted children since 1925? Are we again to go through the trial and error method, only to discard educational provisions for the gifted when public apathy sets in? Must we always strike out on our own, without benefiting from the experiences of others? Is it not enough to say that we are educating children as well today as we did twenty-five years ago? We must begin using the results of educational experiments, and begin profiting by the mistakes of others. Only when we do this will it be possible to educate all gifted children adequately.

As is so often true in the field of education, the terms which have come to apply to particular methods or procedures often do not help in the understanding of what is meant, but actually confuse the issues. The term *gifted child* is used differently by many educators themselves, and so it becomes necessary to accept multiple definitions of such concepts as *enrichment, acceleration,* and *special classes.*

Remarkable adjustments are being made in the curriculum in order to provide better for gifted children. The notion of special classes for the gifted, so long held in disrepute by educators and the lay public, is back in vogue. Acceleration, so widely practiced in the 1920's, is again being used extensively. Enrichment in the regular classroom, the only real hope for the big majority of gifted children who attend schools where special classes are impractical either because of the small number of gifted children or the attitude within the community toward anything "special" for any particular group of children is gaining in popularity. This places the responsibility upon the classroom teacher to provide for all types of children. For the classroom teacher to do the job, however, smaller classes are an absolute necessity; adequate supplies are vitally important; and assistance in planning is needed.

DEVELOPING EMOTIONAL ATTITUDES OF GIFTED STUDENTS

The development of proper attitudes is a major responsibility of the counselor, teacher, and parent of a gifted child. A study (6) by Badt on the attitudes of university students toward exceptional children and special education indicated that "many students failed to see a problem existing with respect to the gifted." In a list of seven types of exceptionality, the students ranked the gifted third as "most in need of service," and first as "least in need of service." This indicates that in each ranking there was no great degree of agreement as to which area really needed service the most. They ranked the gifted third in the category entitled "most like to teach," and third in "least like to teach." This indicates that the gifted aroused strong feelings both positively and negatively, as this category was rated at one extreme or the other by most students.

In spite of numerous articles decrying the lack of attention to the gifted, as is so true in education, there is now the movement which is saying that the gifted are being adequately provided for and all of this hubbub is nothing more than the old "wolf, wolf" cry. Hoppock, in "Gifted Children—An Examination of Some Current Assumptions," presents a convincing argument that must make us remember that "all children are gifted, in a sense."

> Everybody says we are neglecting our gifted children. . . . I have never found out who "everybody" is.
> Exceptionally able children have the same basic needs as all children do.
> A defensible curriculum for all children is by nature rich. If it is not we want to make it so in the interests of learning at all levels (7).

The only conclusion that can be reached from all of the uncertainty about gifted children is that, as adults, we do not know exactly what attitude to take toward gifted children. Should we recognize their gifts, or should we instead emphasize those areas in which they are like others? Only when we reach decisions on such questions as these can we hope to develop properly the attitudes of the children themselves.

It does not seem too much to ask, however, both of the gifted children themselves and from society in general, that there be more acceptance of one another. The antagonism and actual bitterness displayed by society in general toward anyone who dares to be different in any fashion hardly reflects credit upon the intellectual level of the masses. And by the very same measure, the lack of understanding displayed by many gifted individuals toward the general population does not speak well of the gifted group itself.

This is not meant to be the rigid drawing of a line between the two groups, but is instead a plea for more common understanding of the ways in which the two groups are alike. The terms *egg head, high brow,* and *long hair* are used in just as derogatory a sense as are the terms *stupid, dumb* and *nitwit.* The goal of counseling must therefore be the development of attitudes which will not be negative but from which will come more tolerance of individuals unlike oneself.

Hollingworth repeats this plea for more tolerance, both for and by the gifted, through her writings. She states that "failure to learn to tolerate in a reasonable fashion the foolishness of others leads to bitterness, disillusionment, and misanthropy (8)." Her belief was that gifted children should "learn to suffer fools gladly." Interpreting this to be a plea for more tolerance of those less capable is fine. The advisability of using these exact words, however, is certainly questionable because of the unfortunate use of the word "fools." This was demonstrated so clearly in an instance in which some gifted children in a special class discovered a mistake in an encyclopedia. Being very provoked at the idea that this could ever have happened, the children decided to write a letter to the editor telling him how terrible they thought his encyclopedia was. Leta Hollingworth, seeing here a chance to teach tolerance, said, "No, you must learn to suffer fools gladly." At this, a delighted fourth grade boy spoke up enthusiastically and said, "That's it, make them suffer. Roll rocks on them (9)."

Hollingworth further states that "particularly deplorable are the struggles of these gifted children against dull or otherwise unworthy adults in authority (10)." This must certainly be recognized as a major problem, but only points out that the counselor's role is not only to develop attitudes of gifted children toward others, but also to develop the attitudes of others toward the gifted.

In a most interesting series of discussions prepared by Ruth Strang for the American Association for Gifted Children the one entitled, "Guideposts for the Gifted Children Themselves," makes the following suggestions:

Can You Resist The "Tyranny of the Group"?

It is fine to have a feeling of belonging to a group and of being accepted by them. But what price conformity? Sometimes the price is too high. It is too high when it prevents you from realizing your potential ability and being a real person in your own right.

Do You "Maintain Your Ego Courteously"?

Some children and young people do this successfully. They do not push themselves forward; they do not brag about their high marks; they do not try to answer all the questions raised in a discussion, even though they know the answers; they show appreciation for the contributions of others; they help other, less able students to succeed (11).

It would be wise if more of this type of material could be written to help bright children develop proper attitudes, and to help counselors better understand the types of attitudes which are desirable for bright children. Counselors must also accept the responsibility of helping parents of gifted children. Ruth Strang states: "It is also important for parents to understand their own feelings and the reasons why they behave as they do toward their gifted children. Thus they will avoid the two extremes: exploiting their gifted children, or neglecting to give them the education and encouragement they need (12)."

The Science Research Associates Life Adjustment Booklets (13) have many valuable suggestions. *You and Your Mental Abilities, Making the Most of Your Intelligence,* and *Improve Your Learning Ability* are titles which would be particularly valuable for both a counselor and a gifted child himself.

HELPING THE GIFTED CHILD ADJUST

In addition to developing attitudes of gifted children, it is also necessary for the counselor to recognize that gifted children have some unique adjustment problems peculiar to the gifted group alone. Hollingworth must again be referred to, for she alone has devoted extensive study to this particular problem. "A lesson which many gifted persons never learn as long as they live is that human beings in general are inherently very different from themselves in thought, in action, in general intention, and in interests (14)."

This must lead us then to a basic principle in counseling gifted children. Gifted children must learn to accept themselves as they are. This implies, of course, full recognition that in many ways they are different and in many ways they are like other children their own age. It means recognizing that even though their mental abilities are far beyond their actual chronological age, they are not adults in a child's body. They are still children, and must be provided for as such in many ways.

In learning to accept themselves as they are, gifted children will have to know both their mental and physical strengths and weaknesses. This necessitates an adequate testing program, far beyond the usual score obtained on a group measure of mental ability. It means at least a Stanford-Binet intelligence test, with a careful analysis of such vitally important factors as the basal age level, the range of responses, and the particular strengths and weaknesses indicated on the test. Further intelligence testing on the Wechsler Intelligence Scale for Children would be strongly recommended, with other types of special abilities tests, interest inventories and observational reports being added to the picture of the child's make-up.

In addition to the important intellectual traits in their make-up, the adjustment problems they are likely to face should be examined. In spite of the fact that "highly intelligent children are more stable emotionally than are children in general (15)," teachers' reports show that they are often more "restless" and show more "lack of interest" than other children. These are traits which might easily be explained by the fact that gifted children are not always motivated by what occurs in the regular classroom, but since they are a part of our society and must conform to some degree, they can be just as great a problem to the teacher as the slow learning child.

It would be expected that gifted children are never faced with problems of inferiority, for certainly their superior ability should lead them in exactly the opposite direction. Such is not always the case, however. In an effort, which is not always successful, to be accepted by his peer group, the gifted child will sometimes discover that he is inadequate in meeting the problems of being different in some ways and yet so much alike in other ways. In such instances the gifted child must be given the help of the counselor before the problem becomes so great that it is a life pattern which the gifted child neither knows how to change nor even wants to change.

The problems of adjustment increase as the child's intelligence becomes a great deal higher. The 130 to 150 range seems to do quite well in finding its own solution to the problems of living in an "average" world. Over 150 or 160 the problems seem to become too great and the tendency of the group is to become isolated from average children. Counseling problems are not different from those for all gifted children, but there are strong reasons to believe that the need for counseling in this higher group is even more imperative.

DETERMINING EMOTIONAL ADJUSTMENTS OF THE GIFTED

Just how the emotional makeup of the gifted can best be determined is not known. There are indications that projective techniques may provide more answers in the study of the gifted than the more traditional types of standardized tests (16).

Ruth Strang, in an article (17), "Gifted Adolescents' Views of Growing Up," reports on the attitudes of gifted children as obtained from compositions which they had written. Compositions of 241 children with I.Q.'s over 120 were compared with compositions wirtten by another group of children with a 95 I.Q. average. Generally speaking, she found the expressed problems not too dissimilar between the gifted group and the average group. This would indicate that the problems of the gifted adolescent are not particularly unlike those of the average student, that the gifted individual has at least as many adjustment problems, and that both the gifted and the average group need help in the solution of these problems.

"The Adjustment of Gifted Children in the Regular Classroom," by Gallagher and Crowder (18) reports on research to "discover to what extent highly intelligent children are having difficulty in adjusting to the regular classroom situation academically, intellectually, socially, and emotionally." Teachers' ratings were obtained on the following aspects of behavior and personality:

1. academic ability	6. enjoyment
2. contributions to class	7. social abilities
3. creativity	8. behavior disorders
4. leadership	9. fears
5. persistence	

The somewhat alarming discovery was that teachers generally rated the children, all of whose I.Q.'s were 150 or above, high in all areas except creativity and leadership. Examining the list, one would expect a group of highly gifted students to rate highest particularly in these two areas.

Some light is thrown on the adjustment problem area, however, by the following discovery by Gallagher and Crowder:

One of the more striking observations to be made was that the problems that exist in these children were generally of the non-irritating variety. They were not anti-socially aggressive. They were not academic problems. They did not generally have emotional problems of sufficient magnitude to disturb their teacher, parents, or peer group. In short, their problems were not ones of commission, but omission (19).

This finding may well explain the reason why there has been so much apathy toward providing counseling for the gifted. It is very clear, as Gallagher and Crowder state, that the gifted child's problems are of the "non-irritating" variety.

The counselor must recognize that since the problems are often of the "non-irritating" variety, they will not come to the attention of the teacher or parent as readily. This means, then, that teacher or parent referral must not be depended upon solely. Even depending upon self-referral may not reach the gifted child, although it will perhaps be more effective than depending upon other methods. A systematic plan of providing counseling, both individual and group, for all gifted students is probably the only real solution.

HOW MUCH SHOULD THE GIFTED CHILD CONFORM?

One of the greatest adjustment problems facing gifted children is the need to be accepted by others and at the same time the equally important need for expressing his own individuality. Because gifted children are different, must they conform to the average to be accepted? Or should they be nonconformists?

It is certainly not the goal of education to develop every child into a stereotyped pattern; but neither is it the goal of education to see how differently children can be developed. Criticism has been directed toward the schools for attempting to make all children alike, and it has been claimed that television is succeeding in doing this where the schools failed.

In counseling with gifted students, this is the most commonly mentioned area of difficulty. The gifted child's interests are different from his age group's, but to admit that he is not interested in their activities is interpreted as just another indication of his conceit. If the gifted child turns to older children for his friendships, he is frequently treated as an inferior because he is smaller in physical size.

There can be no real solution to this problem, because to some extent conformity will be necessary. Perhaps the important thing to remember is that conformity is not bad until it hinders the development of the individual or society itself. The counselor must assist the gifted individual in understanding the reasons for the group's behavior; and he must also assist the gifted child in learning how to conform when he wants to. The real tragedy is when a gifted child wants to take part in the activities of the group, wants to conform, but does not know how to do so.

Training for leadership also implies training in how to follow. The gifted child must learn both roles. Learning the role of the follower may be more difficult for some gifted children, but it is important that they learn it and learn it well, for the majority of their life will be spent in this role. If this role is not learned well, their role as a leader will be greatly handicapped.

REFERENCES

1. Fine, Benjamin, "How To Raise Your Child's I.Q.," *Coronet*, Vol. 38, No. 6 (October, 1955), pp. 62-66. (Reprinted from *Coronet*, October, 1955, © 1955 by Esquire, Inc.)
2. Maazel, Marvin, "What to do about the Child Prodigy?" *Etude*, Vol. 68, No. 8 (August, 1950), p. 12.
3. Editorial, "The Sidis Boy," *The Independent*, Vol. 68 (January 20, 1910), p. 162.
4. Wheeler, Edward J., editor, "The Boy Prodigy of Harvard," *Current Literature*, Vol. 48 (March, 1910), pp. 291-293.
5. Colvin, Stephen, "What Infant Prodigies Teach Educators," *Illustrated World*, Vol. 24 (September, 1915), pp. 47-52.
6. Badt, Margit, "Attitudes of University Students Toward Exceptional Children and Special Education," *Exceptional Children*, Vol. 23, No. 7 (April, 1957), pp. 286-290, 336.
7. Hoppock, Anne, "Gifted Children—An Examination of Some Current Assumptions," *Education Digest*, Vol. 23, No. 2 (October, 1957), pp. 4-6.

8. Hollingworth, Leta, *Gifted Children.* New York: The Macmillan Company, 1926, p. 260.
9. *Ibid.*
10. *Ibid.*
11. Strang, Ruth, "Guideposts for Gifted Children Themselves." (Written for the American Association for Gifted Children, 15 Gramercy Park, New York 3, N.Y.), p. 2.
12. Strang, Ruth, "Guideposts for Parents of Gifted Children." (Written for the American Association for Gifted Children, 15 Gramercy Park, New York 3, N.Y.), p. 3.
13. Life Adjustment Booklets. Chicago, Ill.: Science Research Associates. (57 West Grande Avenue, Chicago, Illinois.)
14. Hollingworth, Leta, *Children Above 180 I.Q.* New York: Harcourt, Brace & World, Inc., 1942, p. 254.
15. *Ibid.*
16. Mensh, I. N., "Rorschach Study of the Gifted Child," *Journal of Exceptional Children,* Vol. 17, No. 1 (October, 1950), pp. 8-15.
17. Strang, Ruth, "Gifted Adolescents' Views of Growing Up," *Exceptional Children,* Vol. 23, No. 1 (October, 1956), pp. 10-15, 20.
18. Gallagher, James and Crowder, Thora, "The Adjustment of Gifted Children in the Regular Classroom," *Exceptional Children,* Vol. 23, No. 7 (April, 1957), pp. 306-312, 317-319.
19. *Ibid.,* p. 318.

9 | EDUCATING THE GIFTED

Major Issues in the Education
of Gifted Children

LEWIS M. TERMAN
MELITA H. ODEN

Of the many unresolved issues in the education of gifted children, we have chosen five for brief discussion in this symposium. These are: (1) democracy and the IQ, (2) the educational lockstep, (3) early identification of the gifted, (4) educational opportunities that are feasible, and (5) needed guidance and counseling.

Democracy and the IQ. This is a very old issue, but it was the late Professor Bagley who first brought it to the fore and who did more than anyone else to prejudice the minds of educators against offering any kind of special opportunities for the gifted. He wrote with particular scorn of training the gifted for leadership, and proposed instead that the important thing was to teach the average people when and where to tell their would-be leaders to get off. To argue, as Bagley did, that all children should have the same kind of school training, at least through the grades, seems to us no less absurd than to argue that all children should have the same kind of medical treatment. Yet the Bagley point of view not only survives; it is in fact fairly widespread, though it is losing ground.

The Educational Lockstep. This refers to the belief that for the sake of normal social adjustment the gifted child should be kept with others of his own age, and that only such opportunities should be provided for him as are possible under this limitation. The doctrine is based on the belief that the social maladjustment caused by acceleration outweighs any of its advantages. The truth is that the evidence from every serious investigation of the problem shows this view to be largely false. Our data show there is a marked tendency for children of very superior IQ to be

Reprinted from *Journal of Teacher Education,* Vol. 5, No. 3 (September, 1954), pp. 230-232. By permission of the publisher.

more mature both socially and physically than children of average ability. This is not to say that every child should complete high school and college as early as his IQ would permit. The gifted child who is already maladjusted or exceptionally immature socially should be allowed little acceleration or none, but the facts obtained in the thirty-year follow-up of our large gifted group prove conclusively that children of 135 IQ or higher who are accelerated one, two, or even three years are usually more successful in later life than equally bright children who are held in the lockstep. If you don't believe it, see chapter 20 in *The Gifted Child Grows Up*. Acceleration is especially desirable for those who plan to enter a profession that calls for years of graduate study. Other advantages are that the accelerated find their school work more challenging and that earlier graduation enables them to marry earlier (which, on the average, they do).

Early Identification of the Gifted. Thirty years ago if you wanted to know who was the brightest child in a classroom, your best single chance of finding out was not to ask the teacher but to take the name of the youngest child in the room. But in these days when tests of intelligence and school achievement are so easily available, one might suppose that nearly all of the gifted would be identified at an early age. Such is not the case. There are still millions of children who leave school without ever having had any kind of standardized test. Even where tests are used their results are so frequently misinterpreted that some of the gifted are likely to be overlooked. One reason why early identification is important is that acceleration by grade skipping is most feasible in the lower grades. Another reason is that the earlier the gifted child is identified the better his later education can be planned for.

Educational Opportunities That Are Feasible. Under current conditions of teacher shortage and overcrowded classrooms, about the only kinds of special opportunity that are readily feasible for the gifted are three: (a) segregation in special classes; (b) parallel classes for fast, medium, and slow learners, and (c) acceleration.

The pros and cons of segregation have long been debated. Our belief is that segregated classes at their best are very good indeed, but that they are rarely at their best. Parallel classes are a great help, but they are possible only in the larger schools. Acceleration, on the other hand, is always possible and in the majority of cases is desirable whatever other special provision may be made. As for the curriculum enrichment that is so often praised as the ideal solution for the gifted, it is indeed fine in theory but it is very difficult in practice. Under the conditions that presently prevail it can hardly be regarded as a panacea. We believe, nevertheless, that teachers should be alerted to the desirability of special assignments for the gifted in their classes and that they should be instructed by school supervisors and principals in the kinds of enrichment that are possible.

Needed Guidance and Counseling. In 1953 the National Manpower Council, composed of twenty nationally eminent persons, reported after extensive investigation that 40 per cent of the young men and women in the United States who are potentially good college material either do not enter college or, if they enter, do not continue to graduation. What causes are responsible for this appalling wastage of brainpower at a time when there is an acute shortage of well trained minds in nearly every field of science, teaching, scholarship, and business?

There are doubtless many causes, but we believe that two of the most important are: (1) frequent failure to identify the gifted, and (2) when they *are* identified, failure to provide the kind of counseling service that is so badly needed in high schools and colleges. Of the more than 1,450 members of our gifted group (all of them in the top 1 per cent in general intelligence), nearly 15 per cent did not enter college and 30 per cent did not graduate. It is true that the schooling of some was cut short by the great depression, which began shortly before or shortly after most of them reached college age. We are quite certain, however, that many more of them would have gone to college if there had been adequate counseling service in the high schools they attended. As a matter of fact there was little or none at all in most of the schools. The result was that nearly two hundred did not enter college and more than four hundred did not graduate. The situation has improved in the last twenty years, especially in the educationally more progressive cities, but we are reliably informed that in both amount and quality the counseling available in most high schools is far below what is needed.

Counseling at the high school level is not only necessary to insure that more of the brighter students will get the amount of training they should have, but also to insure that each will get the kind of training best adapted to prepare him for later specialization. This means *vocational* counseling, not for the purpose of encouraging the student to choose once and for all the occupation he will enter, but rather to discover the broad general fields where his abilities and interests lie. One of the most valuable single tools for this purpose is Strong's Vocational Interest Test, especially the form designed for men. This test reveals more clearly and accurately than any other what the student's patterns of interest are like; for example, whether they resemble most closely the interest patterns of successful men in the physical sciences, engineering, medicine, law, architecture, journalism, or some of the thirty other occupations for which the test can be scored. The thing that counts is not so much the score in a particular occupation but rather the patterns of interest that are disclosed. To interpret the great variety of patterns that are found calls for skill and experience, but when properly used the test is so valuable that every boy should be given a chance to take it before the end of his senior year. If the Strong test had been available and could have been taken by all the men in our gifted group when they were in high school, at least 10 to 20 per cent might have made a better choice of career.

Education for a Classless Society:
The Jeffersonian Tradition

JAMES BRYANT CONANT

The United States was once proclaimed as the land of the free. Now we are more often reminded that it has been the profitable home of an acquisitive society. Greed and 'lust for money,' we are told, determined the course of development of even the first years of the republic.

Yet, as early as 1800 a potent but silent ferment was at work which had nothing to do with the almighty dollar. In describing conditions at the beginning of Jefferson's administration, Henry Adams writes as follows: 'European travelers who passed through America noticed that everywhere, in the White House at Washington and in log cabins beyond the Alleghenies, except for a few Federalists, every American, from Jefferson and Gallatin down to the poorest squatter, seemed to nourish an idea that he was doing what he could to overthrow the tyranny which the past had fastened on the human mind.' This idea so widely disseminated among the citizens of the raw republic of sixteen states seems to me one of the most essential and continuing elements in the development of American education. I have ventured to associate with this passion for freedom of the mind two other closely allied elements—namely, a belief in careers open to all through higher education, and a faith in universal schooling. I have labeled the whole with Jefferson's name. I trust that neither his shade nor American historians will be unduly offended by my terminology.

In his brief autobiographical sketch Jefferson wrote that he deemed it essential to a well-ordered republic to annul hereditary privilege. He proposed 'instead of an aristocracy of wealth, of more harm and danger, than benefit, to society, to make an opening for the aristocracy of virtue and talent, which nature has wisely provided for the direction of the

Reprinted from *Atlantic Monthly*, Vol. 165, No. 5 (May, 1940), pp. 593-602. By permission of the author and publisher.

interests of society, and scattered with equal hand through all its conditions. . . .' Elsewhere, in describing his new educational scheme for Virginia, he speaks of that part of his plan which called for 'the selection of the youths of genius from among the classes of the poor.' He declared, 'We hope to avail the State of those talents which nature has sown as liberally among the poor as the rich, but which perish without use, if not sought for and cultivated.' These quotations sum up for me the second component in the Jeffersonian tradition in education—a sincere belief in the paramount importance of careers freely open to all the talented.

Most important for its effect on the development of American educational practice was the third element of the tradition—Jefferson's devotion to the principle of universal schooling. This doctrine naturally has had more general popular appeal throughout the years than either concern for freedom of the mind or desire for opportunity through higher education. For here was a proposition which directly affected every family in the land. To quote from the proposal for Virginia, 'The ultimate result of the whole scheme of education would be the teaching of *all* the children of the State reading, writing and common arithmetic. . . .' These words of Jefferson may now seem to us to describe a degree of general education so small as to be negligible. But when they were written they expressed a revolutionary doctrine—a belief that every potential citizen in a democratic republic should receive at least a minimum of formal instruction. The campaign against illiteracy had begun in earnest.

As a recent biographer has said, Jefferson believed that any boy or girl was capable of benefiting from the rudiments of education and would be made a better citizen by acquiring them. He believed in keeping open the door of further opportunity to the extent that a poor boy of ability should not be debarred from continuing his education. 'To have gone farther and made a higher education compulsory on all,' suggests this biographer, 'would have seemed as absurd to him as to have decreed that every crop on his farm, whether tobacco, potatoes, rye, corn, or what not, must be treated and cultivated in precisely the same way as every other. . . . In terms of the citizen, he believed in the maximum of equality of opportunity. In terms of the state, he believed in the minimum of compulsion and interference compatible with the training of all its citizens as citizens to the maximum of the capacity of each.'

To understand the bearing of Jefferson's ideas on the development of American schools and colleges we must realize, of course, that they represented only one aspect of a wider social philosophy. As this philosophy was understood by large numbers of the citizens of the young republic, it included the following points: a belligerent belief in individual freedom; complete confidence in the powers of man's intelligence to overcome all obstacles; the assumption of a society without hereditary classes, without an aristocracy; a differentiation of labors with a corresponding

differentiation in the types of education (but no ruling caste, no hereditary educational privileges, everyone to be 'as good as everyone else');
widespread education for all citizens so that political decisions might be
'rational.' Dominating all was the doctrine of the maximum independence
of the individual, the minimum of social control by organized society.

I

Some such set of ideas as I have grouped together under Jefferson's
name would have been widely recognized, I believe, as 'American ideals'
in every period of our national history. To understand their significance
for the future let us examine one by one the three components of the
Jeffersonian tradition in American education.

Hatred of tyranny in general and a desire to overthrow the tyranny
which the past had fastened on the human mind went hand in hand in
the early years of the nineteenth century, for the intellectual leaders of
the Jeffersonian tradition were steeped in eighteenth-century rationalism.
The liberal faith of the Age of Reason was a product of a cultural evolution intimately associated with economic and political change, on the
one hand, and the great triumphs of late seventeenth-century science on
the other. Newton was one of its heroes, and John Locke a major prophet.
The bill of rights and the laws of celestial mechanics are lasting monu-
ments to its glory. All who live in a land of free institutions and enjoy
the benefits of applied science have reason to be grateful to the liberal
leaders of the eighteenth and nineteenth centuries.

Our gratitude cannot blind us to the fact, however, that these rational-
ists greatly overestimated the rôle of reason in human affairs. They were
much too optimistic in their expectation of the practical consequences
which would follow the liberation of the human mind from the tyrannies
they so despised. Can anyone doubt that if Jefferson and Franklin should
return today they would be amazed and disappointed? Science, to be
sure, has developed far beyond their expectations; the material conquest
of an untamed continent has exceeded their wildest dreams. But the
tyrannies which control our minds remain defiant and largely unsubdued.
We can imagine how shocked these eighteenth-century statesmen would
be to find after one hundred and fifty years the survival of emotional
reactions which they fondly supposed were founded only on ignorance
or superstition. Inanimate nature has proved more yielding than they
imagined, human nature more stubborn and barbarous than they supposed.

Today we live in a period of reaction. The optimistic tide has ebbed.
To many the failure of the 'war to end war' and the terrifying international scene may be sufficient reason for discouragement. But I believe
the cause lies deeper. Are we not to a large measure suffering from the
consequences which must result whenever human beings base their hopes

on fallacious premises? Our intellectual ancestors were wrong on many fundamental points. The complexities of both the inanimate and the animate world were greater than they dreamed. Their errors, however, in physics, chemistry, and biology do not trouble us. The impossibility of perpetual motion, of navigation to the moon, of the manufacture of an elixir of life, we accept as a matter of course. But the contrast between their hopes concerning the behavior of human beings and the realities of the present has shattered many a modern soul.

The contemporaries of Jefferson idolized freedom of the mind. They placed one ideal upon a pedestal and depicted a new era when humanity would bow down before this shrine. In so doing they passed on to their descendants a bondage to the hopes their prophecies engendered—utopian hopes of reforming man as a social animal. In reality, a belief in a new form of magic came upon the scene. The goddess Reason was to wave a wand and all mankind would be prosperous and at peace. In the twentieth century we find the spell has failed. Or so I read the past. And if I am right, then widespread enthusiasm for intellectual freedom can be rekindled only when a sufficient number of men and women readjust their expectations. Only then will the whole country strain to unleash once more the potentialities of the human mind. When that time comes a new sense of humility will reflect an altered mood. No easy faith in the inevitability of progress will cheer us on. Instead, courage will flow from a determination to face the problem of evil, not from a skill in hiding it.

Scientists appear to agree that we must now modify even those modes of thought which concern inanimate nature. The scientific point of view of the late nineteenth century is already out of date. This is but another step in the progress of a healthy skepticism. It is a recognition that we cannot settle many questions we once thought solvable. It is a recognition that our scientific theories are only models—models that help us formulate those empirical observations which we generalize into scientific laws. It may even be necessary, as in the case of light, to employ two theories which once appeared to be mutually contradictory. The physicist has learned to like this situation, perhaps even to love the apparent contradiction involved in employing a wave theory for explaining one set of optical phenomena, a corpuscular theory for another. Parenthetically one may remark that those who teach the elements of the subject have not had their task made easier!

The impact of these new modes of thinking about the sciences will eventually have repercussions on all our ways of thought. In the annual report of the Rockefeller Foundation for 1938 the President writes as follows: 'The physical sciences have centuries of experimentation behind them; the social sciences are just emerging from *a priori* and deductive methods. Even today a good deal that masquerades under the name of social science is metaphysics, as obsolete in its approach as was Francesco Sizzi's logic against Galileo's discovery of the satellites of Jupiter. "The satellites are invisible to the naked eye," he said, "and therefore can have no influence on the earth, and therefore would be useless, and therefore do not exist." This same logical method, long outmoded in the physical sciences, is traceable in some weighty books on economics and political science written as late as 1938.'

This statement of Dr. Raymond B. Fosdick is indicative of a new critical approach to vital problems. A reassessment of the realities of individual behavior and the nature of society is in progress along several lines. Some look to a fruitful combination of the work of the social anthropologist and psychologist. Some believe that the new line of march should parallel that followed so successfully in the development of modern experimental medicine by clinicians. From many quarters come reports that a new strategy is now developing. Once this is formulated and accepted there will be a rush of able pioneers to exploit the field. Confidence in our intellectual leaders will again surge upward. The Jeffersonian tradition will move forward; American thought will change its orientation and American education will feel a quickening of the pace.

II

I venture, then, to look forward to a renaissance of the vitality of the first element in the Jeffersonian tradition in education—freedom of the mind. I am equally optimistic about the second—equality of opportunity. I plead guilty at once to wishful thinking. Furthermore, I admit cheerfully that I propose to indulge in dangerous prophecy. But can anyone discuss the future with a neutral mind?

Until fairly recently it was taken for granted that the American republic could be described as classless. For a century and a half Americans have been saying with pride, 'This is a free country. There are no classes in the United States.' Note these words carefully, for the denial of classes in America is the denial of hereditary classes, not the denial of temporary groupings based on economic differences. 'Caste' and 'class' are equated by the average American, and I shall follow this usage. 'This is a free country. There are no classes in the United States.' The number of times these two sentences have been sincerely spoken could be recorded only by a figure of astronomical magnitude. Were they ever an approximately accurate description of typical American society? My answer would be yes. Have they today sufficient vitality and validity to be the basis for a continuation of Jefferson's educational program? A crystal gazer alone could tell. But I think the chance is good enough to demand our careful consideration of the possibility. For my own part, I risk with enthusiasm an affirmative answer and stand on the hope of our reconstituting a free and classless nation.

Phrases descriptive of a free, casteless, or classless society have not only represented an American belief of great potency in the past, but have described actual conditions in many sections of this republic. As compared with the situation in even such free countries as England and France, this country was unique in being without hereditary classes. The importance of this fact, I believe, has not been fully emphasized. But, I hasten to add, the social changes which have altered the situation during the last fifty years have all too often been ignored.

American society in some localities has always been organized on definite class lines; money and power have been passed on from father to son. The different strata have been relatively rigid and impenetrable. But until recently such situations were the exception rather than the rule. Now we see in progress the rapid extension of such stratification over the whole land. We see throughout the country the development of a hereditary aristocracy of wealth. The coming of modern industrialism and the passing of the frontier with cheap lands mark the change. Ruthless and greedy exploitation of both natural and human resources by a small privileged class founded on recently acquired ownership of property has hardened the social strata and threatens to provide explosive material beneath.

Let us not shut our eyes to the realities. The vanishing of free lands, the spread of large-scale manufacturing units, the growth of cities and their slums, the multiplication of tenant farmers and despairing migratory laborers, are signs of the passage from one type of social order to another. The existence of vast unemployment only emphasizes the evil significance of an unwelcome change. Have we reached a point where the ideal of a peculiar American society, classless and free, must be regarded as of only historical significance?

Our friends on the Left will, I imagine, say yes. A class struggle is inevitable, they declare. Forget the dreams of a pioneer civilization, the early American town or farm, and face the modern capitalistic world, they urge. From their viewpoint no discussion of present problems which refuses to fit every fact into the framework of a class struggle can be realistic. The extremists will add, at least to themselves, that the outcome of the struggle is also inevitable—a classless society, not of the early American type, but on the Russian model.

On the extreme Right we may find an equally clear renunciation of the ideal—equally clear, but not, as a rule, equally outspoken, for the underlying assumptions here are often entirely unconscious. Throughout the history of this republic there has been among a small group undue admiration for the educational system of England, a system built largely on class lines. Among such people Jefferson's idea of careers open to all the talented has evoked little enthusiasm. There has been little concern with recruiting the professions from every economic level. The ideal has been education of a ruling caste rather than a selective system of training leaders.

Yet the unique character of the American way of life has been repeatedly emphasized since Jefferson's time. Lincoln in his first message to Congress declared that 'the leading object of the Government for whose existence we contend' is 'to elevate the condition of men; to lift artificial weights from all shoulders; to clear the paths of laudable pursuit for all; to afford all an unfettered start and a fair chance in the race of life.' The historian, F. J. Turner, writing at the beginning of the present century, summed up the case as follows: 'Western democracy through the whole of its earlier period tended to the production of a society of which the most distinctive fact was freedom of the individual to rise under conditions of social mobility. . . .'

Let me pause a moment to examine the phrase 'social mobility,' for this is the heart of my argument. A high degree of social mobility is the essence of the American ideal of a classless society. If large numbers of young people can develop their own capacities irrespective of the economic status of their parents, then social mobility is high. If, on the other hand, the future of a young man or woman is determined almost entirely by inherited privilege or the lack of it, social mobility is nonexistent. You are all familiar with the old American adage, 'Three generations from shirt sleeves to shirt sleeves.' This implies a high degree of social mobility, both up and down. It implies that sons and daughters must and can seek their own level, obtain their own economic rewards, engage in any occupation irrespective of what their parents might have done.

Contrast this adage with a statement of the aristocratic tradition—namely, that it takes three generations to educate a gentleman. Fifty years ago the contrast between these two statements would have been proclaimed by many intelligent Americans as the epitome of the difference between the New World and the Old. The possibility that each generation may start life afresh and that hard work and ability would find their just rewards was once an exciting new doctrine. Is it outworn? In short, has the second component of the Jeffersonian tradition in education still vitality? Can a relatively high degree of social mobility be realized in this modern world?

The distinction between a stratified class system and one with a high degree of social mobility is apparent only when at least two generations are passed in review. A class, as I am using the word, is perpetuated by virtue of inherited position. For one generation, at least, and perhaps two, considerable differences in economic status as well as extreme differentiation of employment may exist without the formation of classes. Uniform distribution of the world's goods is not necessary for a classless society. If anyone doubts this statement, let him examine the social situation of many small communities in different parts of this country during the early stages of their development. Continuous perpetuation from generation to generation of even small differences, however, soon produces class consciousness. Extremes of wealth or poverty accelerate the process.

It is not within my province to consider what political measures should be taken if we reject the idea of an inevitable stratification of society. It is not for me to say what legislation is in order if we desire to implement the ideal of a free classless society. My unwillingness to discuss this important aspect of the problem is not to be taken as a measure of my dissatisfaction with the rapidly growing social and economic differentiation of the United States. On the contrary, if the American ideal is not to be an illusion, the citizens of this republic must not shrink from drastic action. The requirement, however, is not a radical equalization of wealth at any given moment; it is rather a continuous process by which power and privilege may be automatically redistributed at the end of each generation. The aim is a more equitable distribution of opportunity for all the children of the land. The reality of our national life must be made a sufficiently close approximation to our ideal to vitalize a belief in the possibility of the envisaged goal.

I am wary of definitions—even in expounding the exact sciences to an elementary class. It is often more profitable to explain the nature of a concept by illustration than to attempt a definition. Both the words 'free' and 'classless,' as I am employing them, have a relative, not an absolute, meaning. They are useful, I believe, even in a rough quantitative sense, in contrasting different types of social organizations which have existed in the last few centuries in the Western World. It is easy to imagine a small segment of any country where one would be hard put to it to say whether the society in question was free and classless, or the contrary. To pass a judgment on larger social units is even more difficult, but I should not hesitate to say that Russia today is classless, but not free; England free, but not classless; Germany neither free nor classless.

To contrast the social history of the United States and that of even so closely related a country as Great Britain is illuminating. If we examine, for example, the recent history by G. D. H. Cole entitled *The British Common People, 1746–1938*, we shall see portrayed the evolution of one type of political democracy within a highly stratified caste system. Compare this picture with the history of the growth of this republic by expansion through the frontier in the last one hundred years—a history in which social castes can be ignored; a history where, by and large, opportunity awaited the able and daring youths of each new generation.

This fundamental difference between the United States and England has been blurred by similarities in our political and legal systems and by our common literary culture. Failure to give due weight to the differences between a casteless society and a stratified society has had unfortunate consequences for our thinking. I have already suggested that many of our friends on the Right have had their educational views distorted by too ardent contemplation of the English public schools (so-called) and English universities. Similarly, I believe that in the last few decades our friends on the Left, who look towards a collectivist society, have suffered from overexposure to British views—views emanating in this case not from the ruling class but from the left-wing intellectuals of the Labor Party. It seems to me that in this century, as in a much earlier period of our history, an imported social philosophy has strongly influenced radical thought. I am not referring to orthodox Marxism, but rather to the general slant of mind inevitable among English and Continental reformers whose basis of reference is a society organized on hard-and-fast class lines. The original American radical tradition has been given a twist by the impact of these alien ideas. As far as the rôle of government is concerned, the political reformer has swung completely round the circle. On this issue, Jefferson with his almost anarchistic views would find difficulty, indeed, in comprehending his modern political heirs.

Native American radicalism has all but disappeared. Our young people now seem forced to choose between potential Bourbons and latent Bolsheviks. But without a restoration of the earlier type of radical the Jeffersonian tradition in education will soon die. Obviously it cannot long survive a victory of the socialistic Left—there is no place for such ideas in a classless society on the Russian model. And it will likewise disappear automatically unless a high degree of social mobility is once again restored. To keep society fluid, the honest and sincere radical is an all-important element. Those in positions of power and privilege (including college presidents) need to be under constant vigilant scrutiny and from time to time must be the objects of attack. Tyrannies of ownership and management spring up all too readily. In order to ensure that the malignant growths of the body politic will be destroyed by radiations from the Left, much abuse of healthy and sound tissue must be endured. Reformers and even fanatical radicals we must have. But if the unique type of American society is to continue, those who would better conditions must look in the direction of the progressive or liberal movements of an earlier period. The Left must consider returning to the aim of checking tyranny and restoring social mobility. Reformers must examine every action lest they end by placing in power the greatest tyrant of all—organized society.

III

There are probably some who feel that I am indulging in nostalgic fancy when I hope for the evolution of a less stratified and more fluid society. You may say that the modern world of large cities, vast industries, and scientific methods of communication has made the America of a hundred years ago as irrelevant as the Middle Ages. You may argue that a way of life which was possible in the 1840's is impossible in the 1940's; that in the near future we shall all of us have to move in a quite contrary direction. You may contend that soon we shall have to take sides in a bitter class struggle and choose between an American brand of Fascism and an American brand of Socialism.

I know that many believe this to be inevitable. I venture to disagree. And here is the reason for my rash dissent. In my opinion, our newly erected system of public education has potentialities of which we little dream. In this century we have erected a new type of social instrument. Our secondary-school system is a vast engine which we are only beginning to understand. We are learning only slowly how to operate it for the public good. But I have hope that it will aid us in recapturing social flexibility, in regaining that great gift to each succeeding generation—opportunity, a gift that once was the promise of the frontier.

Let me explain. Today some six million boys and girls attend our secondary schools, ten times the number enrolled a half century ago. Today nearly three quarters of those of high-school age are enrolled as pupils; fifty years ago schooling at this level was a privilege of less than ten per cent of those who might attend. Opportunity can be evaluated only in terms of personal capacity. What is opportunity for one young man is a blind alley for another. In rapidly expanding pioneer communities, openings for capabilities of all sorts automatically appeared. Only doctors, lawyers, and ministers needed an extensive education. Opportunities were ready at hand for all other types of talent. In our highly industrialized, relatively static society, the situation is otherwise. The personal problem of each boy or girl is much more difficult. Abilities must be assessed, talents must be developed, ambitions guided. This is the task for our public schools. All the future citizens pass through these institutions. They must be educated as members of a political democracy, but, more important still, they must be equipped to step on to the first rung of whatever ladder of opportunity seems most appropriate. And an appropriate ladder must be found for each one of a diverse group of students. This may seem an overwhelming burden to put upon our educational system. But is it not possible that our public schools, particularly our high schools, can be reconstructed for this specific purpose?

Jefferson thought of universal schooling of younger children chiefly in terms of educating potential voters. His selective process for higher studies was conceived in terms of intellectual pursuits—of preparation for the learned professions such as law and medicine. To continue the tradition he started, we must expand both of his ideas today. The roads which lead to those careers which depend on aptitude for 'book learning' still run through the universities. We must fight to keep them open. State-supported universities have blazed the way. But the task is far from done.

In many localities the opportunities for the children of the really poor are lamentable indeed. Outside of metropolitan areas and college towns, the privileges of a professional training are hard to win. An expanded scholarship policy in our privately endowed universities is imperative. Wisely administered student aid will go far to right the balance. Perhaps this device merits more attention even by institutions supported by the state.

The changes required to provide adequately for the intellectually gifted are relatively slight. The real problems of reconstruction of our schools and colleges do not lie in this area. The real difficulties are with the careers of a different sort. Our schools must be concerned with educating for a useful life a great variety of boys and girls. They must be concerned not only with the able scholar, but with the artist and the craftsman. They must nourish those whose eye or ear or manual dexterity is their greatest asset. They must educate others whose gifts lie in an ability to understand and lead their fellow men. The school curricula must include programs for developing the capacities of many who possess intuitive judgment on practical affairs but have little or no aptitude for learning through the printed page.

It has been a natural consequence of our history that many false values now permeate the entire educational system. 'Book learning' is placed too high in the scale of social ratings by some; too low by others who profess to scoff at 'brains.' That type of ability which can handle easily the old-fashioned subjects of the curriculum is often glorified by being equated with 'intelligence' by educational snobs. On the other hand, the same ability often suffers from lack of stimulation when there is failure to maintain high standards. As a result, we have a great deal of make-believe in our schools and colleges—too many feeble attempts at tasks which are proper only for a restricted type of individual; too many failures to explore talents which fall outside orthodox academic bounds. Jefferson in the simpler society of his day naturally thought of only a few avenues of opportunity open through education. Today we must recognize the existence of many and strive for the social equality of all.

Parents who expect miracles worked upon their children must be reminded of the limitations imposed by nature. In athletics, at least, the coaches are expected to develop only promising material. No one complains if his undersized son with awkward legs does not become a football hero. Some fathers, however, seem to demand the intellectual equivalent of such a miracle. We expect our college health departments to direct each student into that form of sport which is suited to his physique and power. We need a parallel form of educational guidance in both schools and colleges to assist the development of the skills of brain and hands.

But again I venture to be optimistic. I see signs everywhere of enormous strides forward in such matters. Our educational pattern is becoming daily more diversified; a recognition of the need for a radically different type of education is growing. We look forward to the opening of many channels which lead to a variety of attractive goals; we can envisage the building up of more than one 'élite.'

Of course, in any realistic discussion of these problems we cannot neglect the social and economic factors. As long as the shadow of unemployment is upon the land, some method of providing food and clothing for the children of many families must be found. For even free schools offer little real opportunity to famished youngsters; public education is only theoretically available to those in rags. Providing food and clothing for those to whom assistance is essential is clearly necessary for a satisfactory functioning of the entire educational system. Many a talented youth is lost by dropping out of the competition, for financial reasons, during the high-school years. In short, we must explore every method of developing the individual capacity of each future citizen for useful labor based on individual initiative.

Political and economic changes must go hand in hand with educational innovations—the revision of methods of perpetuating control of many large industries, the overthrow of nepotism and patronage wherever possible, the stimulation of small enterprises, the spreading of private ownership. All this and more is needed if a free classless society is to become once again an ideal which affects our lives.

IV

Freedom of the mind, social mobility through education, universal schooling—these, let me repeat, are the three fundamentals of the Jeffersonian tradition. They have represented the aspirations and desires of a free people embarked on a new experiment, the perpetuation of a casteless nation. Popular enthusiasm for enlightenment, for overturning dogmas, for intellectual exploration, has temporarily waned. I have given my reasons for hoping that the black reaction of these years is only a passing phase. The ideal of a free republic without classes has likewise suffered an eclipse. To many of the present college generation the phrase 'equality of opportunity' seems a mockery, a trite collection of idle words. In this I see the major challenge to our educational system, a challenge which can be met only by a radical reconstruction. If the nation wants to bend its efforts to have as free and classless a society *as possible,* then for those of us concerned with schools and colleges our course is clearly plotted.

So it seems to me. If we as educators accept the American ideal, then this acceptance must be the major premise for all our thinking. Without neglecting the older roads designed for those of academic brilliance, we must construct many new approaches to adult life, and we must do so very soon. Extreme differentiation of school programs seems essential—

differentiation of instruction, but not necessarily a division into separate schools. From this it follows that rapid improvement in our testing methods must be forthcoming; a much more conscientious and discriminating form of educational guidance must be developed soon if we are not to fail. In short, a horde of heterogeneous students has descended on our secondary schools; on our ability to handle all types intelligently depends in large measure the future of this country.

Is it too late—too late for our schools to revitalize the idea of a classless nation? Can we complete the necessary major readjustments in our educational system in time to prevent the extinction of the Jeffersonian tradition? I believe we can, if we make haste. I predict at least another century of vigor for the American ideal. I envisage a further trial on this continent for many generations of our unique type of social order. I look forward to a future American society in which social mobility is sufficient to keep the nation in essence casteless—a society in which the ideals of both personal liberty and social justice can be maintained—a society which through a system of public education resists the distorting pressures of urbanized, industrial life. I have faith in the continuation of a republic composed of citizens each prepared to shoulder the responsibility for his own destiny. And if at each step in the educational journey opportunity truly beckons, will not each student rejoice in the struggle to develop his own capacities? Will he not be proud of the continuing American tradition and find in contemplation of our national history ample courage to face those risks and hazards that come to all who would be free?

Teaching the Gifted–A New Frame of Reference

WALTER B. BARBE
EDWARD C. FRIERSON

Concern for the gifted in the twentieth century may be traced through three distinct periods. Beginning with the work of Lewis Terman and Leta Hollingworth, emphasis was primarily upon the identification of individuals with superior mental abilities in an attempt to discover those characteristics which were unique to these individuals. Although Terman and Hollingworth considered the implications of their findings for education, their major contributions were to dispel false preconceived ideas and to arouse widespread interest in gifted children.

Terman and Oden's twenty-five-year follow-up study in 1947 clearly indicated that in addition to identification there was a need for specific educational programs for the gifted. The Educational Policies Commission and the American Association for Gifted Children followed Terman and Oden's report with publications that laid the groundwork for special educational planning. Interest in providing for gifted children became of national concern with the unexpected launching of man's first earth satellite.

Through these three stages educators have been primarily concerned with developing identification procedures and administrative provisions for the gifted. Extensive programming, which is the characteristic of the current stage, has brought with it the need for the development of teaching techniques designed specifically for the gifted.

There is a belated awareness today that teaching the gifted does not mean merely exposure to more work or the expectation of completing the same work in a shorter period of time. Administrative provisions have been successful in many situations, but except in the case of individual teachers there has been no consideration of the possibility that the learning pattern followed by the gifted child is different from that of the average child.

If this is true, the teacher of the gifted must not be satisfied only to teach more, or more rapidly, but must teach differently.

Reprinted from the April, 1926, issue of *Education* by permission of The Bobbs-Merrill Co., Inc., Indianapolis, Indiana.

PRODUCT OR PROCESS?

Traditionally the teacher has been concerned with the product of learning rather than the process, the possession of knowledge rather than the projection of knowledge. Emphasis upon end-results fostered a teaching approach which called for the presentation of subject matter in a logical progression. Usually this meant simple to complex, concrete to abstract, cause to effect, singular to plural, and whenever possible in chronological order.

It is a credit to gifted students that they have been able to adjust themselves to this pattern of teaching. Underachievement might be only an indication of some gifted students' inability to fit themselves satisfactorily into this pattern of learning.

The process-oriented teacher, as opposed to the product-oriented teacher, is concerned with how gifted students learn, rather than how the material is learned by most students. Emphasis upon the learning pattern of the gifted fosters a teaching approach which calls for the introduction of material at the exploratory level.

The exploratory level is the point toward which the product-oriented teacher is working, but it is the beginning point of the process-oriented teacher. The exact point of the exploratory level can be defined by the process-oriented teacher no more clearly than the point at which the product-oriented teacher can say with assurance that the child "understands."

DIFFERENT ROLES FOR TEACHERS

The role of the teacher in the product-oriented concept of teaching necessitates (1) mastery of the material to be taught in the course, (2) experience in teaching the subject in order that emphasis can be put on those areas which have proved to be difficult, (3) pre-planning to avoid confusion or interruption of the thought processes of the students, (4) sequential presentation of material and (5) quantitative measurement of how much was learned. Since the average student needs this structure in order to retain the vast amount of information to which he is being exposed, he learns best under the leadership of such a teacher.

The product-oriented classroom requires a teacher who is a leader-participant. This teacher must be able either to answer students' questions or direct them to the answer.

The product-oriented teacher is primarily concerned with how much and how rapidly each child has learned. Therefore her effectiveness is measured in terms of how much progress the students have made on an achievement test.

The role of the teacher in the process-oriented concept of teaching is different. It necessitates (1) mastery of a teaching approach that introduces students to material at the exploratory level, (2) experience which manifests itself in the continuing pursuit of knowledge, (3) pre-planning to insure presentation of materials at the exploratory level, (4) intentional interruption of the "lock-step" sequential development of ideas and (5) teacher involvement in the learning process to the extent that there is an awareness of individual students' involvement.

The process-oriented approach requires a teacher who is a learner-participant. She must involve herself skillfully in the learning process itself, teaching by example the pursuit of knowledge. The absence of predetermined goals allows her to use her experience of the learning process to involve the students in the process. The evaluation of the involvement of the student becomes not only the function of the teacher-participant, but also the function of the student himself.

DIRECTION OF LEARNING

As has been pointed out, in the product-oriented pattern of teaching, the direction of learning is the same for all students. In process-oriented teaching for the gifted direction is determined by each student for himself.

The material is presented at the exploratory level, but the direction which the learning process takes is then determined by the student and not the teacher. Some students may work in the direction of established facts, while others may work toward the discovery of novel solutions or applications.

Creativity, about which there is so much concern today, can result from either product-oriented or process-oriented teaching. Since process-oriented teaching encourages individual direction, however, creative pursuits are more likely in this type of teaching. The very absence of rigidity in teaching will encourage creativity.

EXISTENCE OF "CONTENT BOUNDS"

In both product-oriented and process-oriented teaching there are "content bounds." In product-oriented teaching these bounds evolve from resources the teacher has at her disposal. They may be bounds or limitations imposed by textbooks, library facilities, curriculum guides, school policies, the teacher's educational background, or any number of other things which might be called teachers' resources.

In process-oriented teaching the bounds are also present, but they evolve not from predetermined teachers' resources but instead from students' resources. The age of the students, their experiences both real and vicarious, their interests and a variety of other individual student char-

acteristics establish these bounds. The important point is that the bounds
are determined by characteristics of the students, not of the teacher or
the school.

SUMMARY

It must be recognized that teaching gifted children effectively requires
a different concept of teaching. This results in a different perspective and
role as well as different teaching techniques and evaluative emphases.

The differences in emphasis of these two types of teaching, product-
oriented teaching and process-oriented teaching, can best be demonstrated as follows.

Product-Oriented Teaching for the Average	*Process-Oriented Teaching for the Gifted*
Emphasis on end-result (product)	Emphasis on learning pattern (process)
Leader-participant teacher	Learner-participant teacher
Predetermined learning direction	Learning direction is determined by each student for himself.
Content-bounds evolve from teachers' recources.	Content-bounds evolve from students' resources.
Teacher is evaluated and evaluates students on the basis of quantitative measurement of the end-result (product).	Teacher is evaluated and evaluates students on their involvement in the learning process.

10 | ISSUES IN MOTIVATING AND DEVELOPING TALENT

Conditions Favorable and Detrimental to the Development of Talent

ROBERT J. HAVIGHURST

How many of the gifted children found in the schools will realize their potentialities and become distinguished persons, contributing in an outstanding way to the welfare of their society and gaining for themselves the satisfactions of excellent performance? Under present conditions, certainly less than half of them will do so.

Even this, however, is not a bad situation when compared with what other societies have done for their gifted children. Probably no other society has done as well as the United States in this respect. Even Athens at the height of her creativity in the fifth century, B.C., or Florence in the Renaissance, or England in the sixteenth century, reached these peaks without having utilized the latent talent of the great mass of the people, who were submerged in slavery or grinding poverty. It is only when the facts of the development of talent in present-day America are compared with what might be and what the democratic ideal suggests they ought to be that the record looks inadequate.

Americans generally believe in the unique value of the individual and in the desirability of his developing his abilities, whatever they are, along socially valuable directions. The development of ability requires education, and Americans have great faith in the power of education to bring out the latent excellence of a person.

Then, too, there is the American discovery that the poor and downtrodden produce many children who have remarkable talents. It is understood that these talents cannot flourish in a non-supportive family or a barren community environment. As people have come to recognize the importance of the environment in developing talent, the attitude has

Reprinted from *School Review*, Vol. 65, No. 1 (March, 1957), pp. 20-26. By permission of the author and publisher.

gained ground that society should seek to discover and to help the talented but underprivileged child or youth.

These positive attitudes toward the use of education to develop gifted children are balanced by some negative attitudes. There has been the belief that "talent will out" in the American environment; that, if it is real talent, it will be irrepressible; that it will follow a natural course of development; that it should not be rewarded until it has fully proved its worth in competition. Coupled with this has been the Puritan attitude that nothing good should come easily, that a person should work slavishly, especially while young. He should sell newspapers on cold street corners, memorize long lists of spelling words, work all the problems in the geometry book, wait on tables in the fraternity house, wash beakers in the chemistry laboratory. To complicate the situation further, Americans tend to distrust the talented person who is somewhat "queer." If a child has a remarkable aptitude in mathematics, or music, or poetry, especially if he does well in these areas without apparent effort, he is regarded as psychologically abnormal, with the unfavorable nuances that are part of abnormality in American thought. As a result of these attitudes, there is an American tendency to discourage the development of special gifts in children and to encourage them to become "well-rounded" superior persons rather than somewhat eccentric geniuses.

This emphasis upon social and emotional adjustment has been buttressed by a corresponding emphasis in society as a whole on security and conformity at the expense of freedom. Children and adults are taught the virtues of co-operation, of being a smoothworking part of a team, or group, or corporation. In this situation an outstanding individual success may cut one off from the group, and this may be such a severe threat to a student that he will deliberately do less than his best, "reduce output," so as not to get better marks than most of his fellows. The aloneness of creative achievement cannot always compete with the need to be a part of the group.

Under these circumstances, despite the relatively large educational opportunities in America, a great deal of talent remains undiscovered, undeveloped, and unrewarded. By any ordinary definition of talent, at least half of the talent of American youth suffers this fate. Thus it seems that the gifted child is favored by the abstract American ideals of opportunity and of the desirability of developing the individual to his maximum but that specific attitudes penalize him. In school and community the gifted child may be treated in ways which make him content with a performance and a developmental level definitely under his capacity or which may even discourage his attempts at spontaneity and individual excellence.

With the public's ambivalent attitudes toward gifted children, the American school system also operates both to encourage and to discourage the development of talent. By offering educational opportunity at the secondary-school and college levels to a higher proportion of youth than does any other country, the American schools act to discover and develop talent, especially of the intellectual variety. On the other hand, the fact that the schools are non-selective means, in effect, that the average high-school student body consists mainly of boys and girls with ability just average or slightly above or below average. The proportion of gifted youth can hardly exceed 25 per cent in the ordinary comprehensive high school. (This estimate is based on the assumption that the top 20 per cent of the population may be regarded as gifted intellectually, artistically, or socially. Since a few of the slower pupils drop out of high school, the proportion of gifted in the high school will be somewhat greater than it is in the general population.)

Thus the gifted youth are likely to be outnumbered in the high school and college classes as well as in the elementary school. Unless the teaching is remarkably skilful and clearly directed toward stimulating gifted students, such students tend, when outnumbered, to adopt the learning pace and the attitudes toward learning of their average age mates. This is particularly likely to happen in America where the pressure of the peer group to conform to peer standards is greater and more effective than it is in any other country that has been studied in this connection.

While conditions in the schools are ambiguous with respect to the development of talent, there is no such ambiguity about the demand for talent in the adult world. The American economy is desperately short of highly trained minds. This pressing, immediate need has been well publicized in recent years. What is less well understood is the present crisis in world civilization as a whole. Civilization is rapidly approaching the point in its development where it must achieve new levels in the utilization of the resources of the world or forever fail to develop them. The burden of making such advance in controlling and developing the environment falls largely on the shoulders of the gifted.

Social conditions may favor or discourage the development of gifted people. In exploring the influence of such conditions, it is necessary to distinguish between the production of highly specialized talent, such as artists or musicians, and the production of superior persons with adequate training to do work that requires a high level of skill and knowledge but does not necessarily require creativity.

Conditions favoring the appearance of productive genius may not be the same as conditions favoring the appearance in large numbers of superior craftsmen of the mind and the market place. One such condition has already been mentioned: the demand for well-trained superior people. Another condition is economic prosperity. With economic prosperity there is money that can be spent by parents and by philanthropy on the training of young people. There is also money to spend on art, music, literature, and the theatre and thus to support the work of people in the arts. Less tangible, but certainly important in the making of an environment favorable to the development of gifted children, is the belief that everyone should attempt to achieve in relation to his capacity. "From each according to his ability" is a generally accepted American attitude.

In general, because the economic situation is favorable and because the attitudinal climate is at least partially favorable, children with superior potential abilities are in a relatively good position to receive help in developing their potential abilities into real existing abilities. The society expects education to give this help. It is as clear a mandate from society as any the schools are likely to receive.

If only about half of the ablest 20 per cent of gifted children actually develop their abilities to a point where they make an important contribution to society, who are the other half, and why do they not develop their talents more fully? The general answer to this question is that those with undeveloped talent are persons whose environments have been least favorable to the production of high-level ability.

Girls, and children from families of low socioeconomic status, form the two large groups of persons with potentially high ability whose environment has not provided stimulation for the development of talent. Children from low-status families fail to develop their abilities because of lack of opportunity and stimulation—a lack commencing in their earliest years. Their families do not encourage them to read, to learn music, to draw pictures, to develop scientific hobbies, or to do any of the things that can bring budding talent into flower. Many of them live on subsistence farms, where the family simply struggles to survive. Lack of stimulation is, in general, characteristic of low socioeconomic families, but there are exceptions in which a working-class family does as well by a gifted child as does a family with more means. However, when the child of a lower-status family reaches high school, he often feels a pressure to get out and earn money, and he seldom gets the kind of financial support, from home or through scholarship aid, which will carry him through college or through a program of special training.

The true importance of the factor of socioeconomic background has not always been recognized because until quite recent decades the notion has prevailed in Europe and America that high ability was to be found almost entirely in the upper classes and was inherited according to simple laws of heredity. The modern view is that a large amount of potential ability remains under-developed because of lack of environmental stimulation and that most of this under-developed ability is to be found in people of lower socioeconomic status and in women of all social levels.

Women as a group do not develop their abilities to as high a degree as men because society does not expect them to do so. Girls, however, show fully as much talent as boys do. In fact, girls excel boys in achievement tests and in artistic, musical, and writing ability. They hold their own with boys in social leadership up into the high-school years. In adolescence the pressures of society make them want to adopt feminine rather than masculine roles. The feminine roles stress tenderness, tranquility, submissiveness, in contrast to the ambitiousness, productivity, and aggressiveness which are stressed in the masculine roles.

Even though the twentieth century gives women a wider variety of acceptable roles than did the nineteenth, the social pressures still operate to suppress the high-level development of talent in most women in favor of motherhood, homemaking, and emotional support of a husband. Thus, although there are excellent women novelists and poets and singers, there are no women musical composers of note; no orchestra conductors; few famous performers on musical instruments; relatively few women college presidents, artists, lawyers, doctors, or scientists.

Most of the children of both sexes who exhibit giftedness come from middle-class homes, although the majority of all children enrolled in the schools come from working-class homes. These facts are illustrated by the results of a program of discovery of talent in the seventh grade in the public schools of Quincy, Illinois. Fifteen schools were ranked on the basis of the average socioeconomic status of the children attending them. The school in the high-status neighborhood enrolled a relatively high proportion of the children who, at the age of twelve or thirteen, showed high-level ability, while the school in the slum neighborhood enrolled almost no gifted children. Still, a considerable number of boys and girls showing talent at this age came from working-class and lower-middle-class families (1). It is in this group that lack of financial ability and lack of family expectation will operate most heavily to prevent the development of latent talent through education or special training.

From another part of the country there is further evidence of the effect of low socioeconomic status in suppressing the development of talent. Boys in the second and third years of public high schools of the Boston metropolitan area were studied. The highest 20 per cent in intellectual ability were asked whether they expected to go to college (2). Those whose fathers had high-status occupations generally expected to go to college, while boys whose fathers had low-status occupations generally did not expect to go to college.

Estimates of the educational progress of the ablest youth in the population of the entire country show that most children of upper- and upper-middle-class families go to college if they are in the upper quarter of the population in intellectual ability. On the other hand, while 45 per cent of the ablest quarter of youth come from homes of manual workers, less than one-fourth of this group graduate from college (3). While the factors of environmental stimulation and of financial ability both operate to reduce the numbers of able youth who develop their abilities through higher education, there has been great progress in the past fifty years in recognizing the potentialities of these youth and in giving them educational opportunities. Compared to the nineteenth century, the present century is more favorable to the discovery and development of talent in children of lower socioeconomic status and also in girls.

REFERENCES

1. Paul H. Bowman and Others, *Mobilizing Community Resources for Youth,* pp. 20, 21. Supplementary Educational Monographs, No. 85. Chicago: University of Chicago Press, 1956.
2. Joseph A. Kahl, "Educational and Occupational Aspirations of 'Common Man' Boys," *Harvard Educational Review,* XXIII (Summer, 1953), 186-203.
3. Robert J. Havighurst and Bernice Neugarten, *Society and Education,* chap. x. New York: Allyn & Bacon, 1957.

The Utilization of High Level Talent in Lower Socioeconomic Groups

HARRY BEILIN

There are a number of observers of the contemporary economic scene who maintain the country is faced with serious manpower shortages particularly in the technical and scientific occupations. Some others observe that the shortages, if any, are of top quality creative people and there never have been and there may never be enough of these.

Whether either or both these positions are valid, it is evident that top-level talent will be in constant and possibly increasing demand.

The principal thesis of this paper is that to solve the present shortage of high level talent will require the recruitment of larger numbers of highly capable youth from the lower socioeconomic groups particularly into college programs. Accomplishing this will necessitate an examination and understanding of the factors involved in social mobility and application of this understanding to manpower policy.

Having exhausted to some extent the "usual" sources of such talent it becomes necessary to tap those that have been relatively unexplored. The colleges traditionally have been the primary source of technical and scien-

Reprinted from *Personnel and Guidance Journal,* Vol. 35, No. 3 (November, 1956), pp. 175-178. By permission of the author and publisher.

tific workers. Although college enrollment is increasing, it still appears (2) that an astonishing proportion of those with exceptional intellectual potential do not attend. Many of these persons are in lower socioeconomic groups. Although these groups contain *proportionately* fewer persons with top IQ's, because of their numbers they become a prime source in the development of a recruiting program. It is here that the largest *number* of persons with high level ability exist but where proportionately the smallest number go on to college. If a reasonable percentage of those from the lower class groups who do not now attend college were to do so we would come a long way toward meeting present and future needs for scientific and technical personnel.

The crucial question remains as to how this can be achieved. In this case, guidance and educational programs can be of help and can facilitate the process of upward mobility from the lower socioeconomic groups.

SCHOLARSHIP PROGRAMS

A technique that has been in use for a long time and which seems to be getting major emphasis and support in present attempts to encourage college attendance is the scholarship program for able youth. Undoubtedly it is having some of the desired effect, but it is necessary to ask whether scholarship programs are achieving what they have intended to achieve. The essential questions concern how many of these scholarships actually bring to college those who *would not* have attended without financial aid, and to what extent these programs merely entice into engineering, for example, those who might intend to become physicians or teachers of high school science. In other words, are these programs merely acting to channel the placement of such talent rather than facilitate potentially unused talent to be utilized more adequately?

SOCIAL MOBILITY AS A FACTOR IN
RECRUITMENT OF CAPABLE YOUTH

Important as scholarship programs may be and as significant as good occupational information might be in helping to create or channel interests in many crucial occupations these considerations are essentially secondary to the principal obstacle to mobility—the person himself.

There are a number of reasons why lower status youth who have ability may not go to college. These appear, for the most part, organized about the attitude that education is not important; the way of life it presents essentially alien; the rewards at the end of the line not worthwhile or not worth the effort, and the goals not achievable. The educational system is seen as hostile and, at the least, offers the minimum of rewards. It comes as no news that the school itself offers little solace to these youngsters, and age mates of different social backgrounds are usually none too friendly. As a result one sees, as Hollingshead has shown (3), that the school remains a middle-class institution in which lower class youngsters get little reward and participate in school activities to a minimum. In essence these youngsters show up as lacking in "drive" (achievement motivation, in McClelland's terms), the necessary values that go with middle class living (for example, the postponement of immediate gratifi- cations for future reward), and the kinds of habits and personality pat- terns that go along with middle class success in our society ("manners" and "personality"). These are the very characteristics, however, which lower class youth who are upwardly mobile do possess (1) and this leads to the thesis that if upward mobility is to be achieved (and college at- tendance thereby facilitated) these values have to become a part of the personalities of these youths.

Before a lower class youngster can be expected to go on to college and succeed, there must be some kind of psychological preparation for it. In some cases parents will have oriented him to the upward climb. For most lower class youngsters this will not have been the case, however, and preparation must come from the youngster's peers and/or the school. The school does do a great deal to introduce lower class youth to the values of middle class culture, but often as not it serves only to antag- onize them and generate a feeling of being different. It is not usually made clear how achievement is possible within this framework except by exhortation. What is required, if larger numbers of lower class young- sters are to go on to college is a clear cut attempt to change the lower class values, make faith in them less certain and substitute middle class goals for those relinquished. But most of all the youngster must be given the feeling that he is capable of rising in the social scale by his own ef- forts, and this not by such slogans as "everyone who applies himself can get ahead," even though it is true that the only way to get ahead is to apply onself. Having ambition and working hard provides no guarantees, particularly without the accoutrements that go with upward mobility. In regard to these secondary aspects guidance programs can and do help, too. Learning some of the social graces is a necessity for successful up- ward mobility and making such learning possible in school will facilitate easier integration into a new social group. When youth come to be aware of the relevance of this training to the rest of their preparation some of the antagonism encountered among lower class youth should be dissi- pated. It is in regard to this that the non-vocational elements of the school guidance program have as much relevance to the general problem of search for high level talent as more direct vocational guidance.

The most difficult aspect of the program suggested here involves gener- ating the "drive" necessary to make the hard task before each youth worthy of sustained effort. An important possible way of generating the drive is by developing values and setting up goals (*e.g.,* occupational goals) which by their very nature will be stimulating to drive. This only begs the question, of course, because one must then ask how one develops these values and goals. Secondary reinforcement of the satisfactions derived from the activities which go along with scholastic achievement may facilitate value acquisition. With good teaching available it should not be too difficult to create intellectual curiosity and thereby satisfaction from the acquisition of knowledge itself. This in turn will make college attendance itself desirable. The stimulation from an intellectually challenging curriculum will, with stimulating and challenging teachers, do much for the ambitions of lower class youth and all able youth for that matter.

Another important method of creating the desire to go on is through identification with persons who can serve as role models and create the desire to be like these persons. Many a boy who has "gotten ahead" can cite the important influence of a teacher or others upon his decision to achieve. The school can do more to encourage this. Leaders in the community in a wide variety of professions for example might be induced to come into the school for an hour or two a week to act as leaders or resource persons in clubs, in addressing assemblies, in meeting and talking with young persons in school, encouraging them, providing them with information and intellectual challenge. Many guidance workers can (and of course in many instances do) play a vital role in initiating such programs. The social program of the school itself might be examined to find ways to interest lower class youths to participate in extra-curricular social and athletic activities. Many schools delude themselves by thinking they have no problem with respect to limitations upon participation of lower class youth in these programs.

Working with individual youngsters in this complex of changes is important but what would facilitate and strengthen the process even more would be working with groups of such lower class youngsters. The rationale for this lies in the fact that a youngster needs psychological support outside the school, particularly among his peers should his home be hostile to his upward aspirations. He needs the support of other youngsters who are also upwardly mobile. They can be a source of intellectual and social stimulation through the years of discovery and achievement. The effect or potential effect of the armed forces experience upon most lower class youths should not be overlooked. The services, with extensive educational and training programs exert a powerful influence upon such young people. Sometimes the rise to higher levels will come as a direct result of military occupational training, in other cases the effect of service experience may be to motivate one to get additional education subsequent to the military. What the services can do to accelerate or further this trend has hardly been explored.

INHIBITORS TO SOCIAL MOBILITY

Interestingly enough there are some aspects of the educational system which may act as inhibitors to social mobility. One of these is the system of specialized vocational education at the high school level.

For some youths of low socioeconomic status an education in a trade school may actually provide a means of upward mobility by giving him the skills to enter skilled occupations as has been implied before. One fact, however, not established by controlled research is that those who obtain vocational education are actually better off occupationally, that is, have achieved more highly, than those who obtained a similar level of education but did *not* obtain the specialized education. It might even be questioned whether a larger number entered the occupations they were trained for than those who desired to enter these occupations and did not get the specialized training.

For the lad with high level ability who becomes enrolled in one of these vocational education programs, obtaining a measure of it may make moving from the field to another kind of training (*e.g.*, college) extremely difficult. Many a lad so trained has discovered after leaving a vocational school program that he does not have the requisite qualifications for college entrance and at that point becomes discouraged at the prospect of obtaining them. Forcing early choice, involving a commitment the consequences of which may be difficult to reverse, contributes to these difficulties. Counselors should therefore be quite cautious in working with youth who so wish to commit themselves. The least a counselor can do under such circumstances is provide information concerning the consequences of such choices and discuss the possibility of alternatives, should the desire to change one's course of action subsequently materialize. One of the National Manpower Council's recommendations is cogent; that vocational school students be given two years of general education prior to undertaking a specialized vocational program (4). This would help the vocational student to go on educationally should he desire and be intellectually capable of doing so.

Another limitation to social mobility may be the necessity of being *geographically* mobile. This applies particularly in rural areas and small towns. Most of these communities cannot provide the opportunities for professional employment at the time the youth is ready to obtain training or enter a professional occupation. For most such occupations there may be no opportunity for employment at all in the local community. In such cases the youth has to be prepared for moving from his place of birth or early education. For some this may not be easy and real emotional conflicts may result. In other cases of course, getting training away from home may be just the excuse the youth is looking for to get away from his community.

In any case, the counselor may provide a real service in preparing youth and their parents early in the process for the prospect of moving from such communities.

As a corollary, counselors should be well informed as to the occupational opportunities available in their own communities for reasons which by now should be fairly evident.

SUMMARY

It is the thesis of this paper that to solve the present and anticipated shortages of high level talent larger numbers of highly capable youth from lower socioeconomic groups be motivated to attend college.

The role of scholarship programs should be examined to determine the extent to which they encourage youth to attend college who would ordinarily not do so.

It is suggested that an understanding of the bases for social mobility be applied to manpower policy to stimulate college attendance by able persons in these groups.

Some factors important to social mobility and ways the school and guidance programs can respond to these are discussed.

REFERENCES

1. Beilin, H., The Pattern of Postponability and Its Relation to Social Class Mobility. *J. Social Psychol.* In press.
2. Berdie, R. F., *After High School—What?* Minneapolis: Univ. of Minnesota Press, 1954.
3. Hollingshead, A. B., *Elmtown's Youth.* New York: John Wiley & Sons, Inc., 1949.
4. National Manpower Council, *A Policy for Skilled Manpower.* New York: Columbia University Press, 1954.
5. Wolfle, D., *America's Resources of Specialized Talent.* New York: Harper and Bros., 1954.

The Underachieving Gifted Child— a Problem for Everyone

J. C. GOWAN

One of the greatest social wastes in our culture is that presented by the gifted child or young person who either can not or will not work up to his ability. Moreover, this situation often leads to undesirable social or personal behavior as an outward indication of the power within which is seeking some outlet. Counseling and rehabilitating these young people presents a challenging and important problem for teachers and personnel workers.

DEFINITIONS AND POPULATION

The present study uses *gifted child* to mean a youngster two or more standard deviations from the mean in general intelligence, within approximately the top 2 per cent of the population, equivalent to an intelligence quotient above 129 on the Stanford Binet. Recognizing that practically all gifted children are underachievers to some extent, we define *underachievement* in general as performance which places the individual 30 percentiles or more below his ability standing in the same group. Applying this concept to gifted children, we shall call them *underachievers* when they fall in the middle third in scholastic rank, and *severe underachievers* when they fall in the lowest third.

Some of the best work in surveying the problems of gifted underachievers has been done by teachers, counselors, supervisors, and principals in the field. All of the research referred to in this article presents unpublished projects undertaken by experienced school personnel in the writer's classes as listed in the bibliography which follows.

First, let us see what percentage of gifted children are underachievers as represented by the previous definitions. Alter (1) found that in a high socioeconomic area, one suburban high school enrolling 1162 students had 74 or 7 per cent of students with intelligence quotients of 130 or more on the California Test of Mental Maturity. Among the 45 of these who were in senior high school, 19 or 42 per cent were under-

Reprinted from *Exceptional Children*, Vol. 21, No. 7 (April, 1955), pp. 247-249, 270-271. By permission of the author and publisher.

achievers, and three or 6 per cent were severe underachievers. In similar research in an independent boarding school enrolling 485 boys of whom 57 or 12 per cent showed 130 IQ or above on the Terman-McNemar, the writer found that only five of the 57 or 9 per cent were underachievers and none to be severe underachievers. This lower number of underachievers probably reflects greater 24-hour control as well as differential attrition factors. Wilbar (5) discovered that in a representative suburban high school, 31 or nine per cent of the students had intelligence quotients of over 130 on the California Test of Mental Maturity, and of these 5, or 16 per cent, were underachievers and one, or 3 per cent, was a severe underachiever.

It seems evident that, while the percentage of underachievers and severe underachievers is a function of the program of the school, its location, the control it has over its students, and student interests, there are in all cases significant numbers of underachievers among the highly gifted. These students merit special attention.

STUDIES OF UNDERACHIEVERS

Robert (4) found that of 587 cases of maladjusted youngsters handled by a clinic in a large metropolitan area, 38 or 6.5 per cent had intelligence quotients of 130 or above on the Stanford Binet almost evenly divided between boys and girls. The majority of these children like school and their problems centered around the home situation. Those who were school problems stated their reasons as follows:

> Not interested
> Didn't like the teacher
> Work was too easy
> Didn't have any friends and couldn't make any
> Liked to stay home with mother (4:4)

Only one child was proud of her school record, and only one had been accelerated. All indicated that they could do better work if they tried.

The major disturbances characteristic of the group (some children, of course, had more than one) were noted in clinic records as follows:

> 27 felt insecure
> 17 had poor social adjustment
> 15 had enuresis
> 14 were intolerant of parental authority
> 13 were fearful
> 7 were jealous
> 9 had no identification with parents
> 6 were poor sleepers

5 were nail biters
5 were poor eaters
9 had miscellaneous behavior disturbances (4:5)

The basic causes for the children's behavior as diagnosed by the clinic staff were:

1. Disagreement between the parents, and of the parents with their parents, over methods of rearing the child.
2. Transference of problems of parents to the child,
3. Overanxiety or overprotectiveness on the part of parent,
4. Fears of parents regarding child's health or safety,
5. Divorces or separations of parents,
6. Parents failure to prepare child for the birth of a new baby.

Landstrom and Natvig (3) conducted a provocative survey of four groups of 25 students each in a metropolitan senior high school. All were scored on the California Test of Mental Maturity. Group I consisted of gifted students who were high achievers with IQs ranging from 125 to 150 with a median of 131. Group II consisted of gifted students who were underachievers ranging similarly from 125 to 150 in IQ with a median of 130. Group III consisted of overachieving students who were not gifted, whose school marks matched those for Group I but whose IQs ranged from 86 to 112 with a median at 103. General biographical data including material concerning home relationships were then secured from each individual.

Table I indicated that the gifted achievers and underachievers in this study differed significantly (at the 5 per cent level of confidence or better) in that the underachievers were predominantly boys, had parents who took little part in church activities, had fewer books in their homes, had less often received private lessons, and expressed a desire in choosing a vocation for working away from the parental family. In general, the pattern that emerges is one of indifference and rejection on the part of the parent, or at least of behavior which is significantly more often interpreted in this manner by the underachiever. In addition, it is interesting to note that while the underachiever does less studying, he also has less time for other activities. Clearly, one of his problems is handling his time. He seems to lack ability to handle himself well in social interaction and to make easy adjustments to the societal structure.

In an earlier study (2) the writer found that when a secondary school population of 485 boys was analyzed for underachievement and overachievement as previously defined, 16 per cent of the *total* group were underachievers, and 11 per cent were overachievers. The overachievers asserted much more leadership than did the underachievers. The underachievers were significantly less sociable as measured by the

TABLE I. Home Background and Extra-Curricular Activities of High School Students by Categories of Ability and Achievement

	I Gifted Achievers	II Gifted Non-Achievers	III Over-Achievers	IV Average Controls
Number in group	25	25	25	25
Scholarship grades	A	C	A	C
Median IQ	131	130	107	103
Number of boys	12	19*	3**	6
Number of parents deceased	1	3	5	0
Father in professions	11	8	5	5
Mother a housewife	12	13	17	20
Parents divorced	2	3	4	6
Family attends church	14	6*	15	10
Foreign language in home	11	12	6	8
Favorite subject, Mathematics	13	7*	1**	0
High school major is Mathematics	16	15	4**	1
Skipped grades	15	10	4	4
Hours per week homework	8.4†	5.5	11.0	6.9
Number with time for other work	21	11*	16	14
Private lessons, training	20	12*	16	14
Total number of awards	50†	20	42	20
Activities or offices	134†	65	145	50
Number with 100 books or more	15	6*	6	7
Part time job	13	7	9	15
Vocational choice, profession	25	21	13**	5
Preference for working with people	20	16	18	21
Preference for working near family	19	10*	11	11

The minimal difference between columns to make the activity discriminate at the 5 per cent level is seven.

† Means the response is in units as given but the significance of the difference was not computed.

* Indicates a difference between columns I and II significant at the 5 per cent level.

** Indicates a difference between both columns I and II and column III at the 5 per cent level.

sociability scale of the Bernreuter. The conclusion was that the genesis of underachievement lay in self-sufficiency, and that, in general, underachievement in academic work and underachievement in leadership tended to appear together and to be connected with high unsociability ratings.

RESEARCH FINDINGS

Summing up the experience of these and other researchers, it may be said that counseling gifted underachievers offers a number of problems:

1. The gifted underachiever tends to be *self-sufficient* and unsociable. He is, therefore, harder to reach, and harder to interest in social activities. He learns less from exposure to the normal socializing effects of his peers because he has less contact with them.
2. The gifted underachiever has identified less with his parents, who themselves seem to be less active than parents of overachievers and less supporting of him and of his increased needs.
3. Because the gifted underachiever is less sociable, and because most teachers are overachievers, he tends to find fewer surrogate parental models among his teachers. This added lack of identification with an adult model makes his behavior still more difficult to influence.
4. The gifted underachiever seems to have fewer salable skills, either to offer for part time jobs, to bolster his economic situation, or to gain eligibility for college scholarship.

Employment is limited because he participates less and hence is less well adjusted; college is lost because of his poor scholastic showing. As a result it is harder for him to become independent of an unsatisfactory family situation, harder for him to gain a sense of worth and participation through his job, and harder for him to keep going in college. The combination tends to push him out of school into an economic market where he has only marginal skills and into situations where he derives little if any job satisfaction.

SUGGESTIONS FOR COUNSELORS

The following suggestions are offered for working with gifted underachievers.

1. Make a survey of the percentage of underachievers in your school. If it runs much higher than 15 per cent, there may be problems of morale, antisocial trends, or other factors in the school which should receive special attention.
2. Since gifted underachievers are usually boys by a ratio of two to one, make an effort to assign counselors who are most capable of reaching them; a male counselor may often be more effective than a woman with such boys.
3. Give attention to building up the gifted underachiever in the area where he has a real chance of outstanding success, whether this is athletics, music, a hobby, or an academic course. The real and enduring interest of some strong adult model figure with whom the young person can easily relate should be secured.
4. Give attention to the anxieties which plague boys at this period. These

stresses may include economic dependence on a hostile home figure, ignorance about sex, worry about the draft, concern with how a mediocre record can be brought up to college standards, anxiety over the rejecting attitudes of a fussy stick-to-the-rules type of teacher, and many others. If the manifold social roles which the adolescent male is called upon to play in our culture can be gradually and easily assumed, much anxiety and frustration can be prevented. Above all, the boy should sense that the counselor *has time for him.* He should be encouraged to go on with college plans.

5. Try to find membership roles for the gifted underachiever in clubs, activities, and student leadership. He should be engaged in responsibilities which will enlarge his social ability as much as possible.

6. Because this type of young person feels insecure and is likely to lack a real peer group, attempt group therapy with a number of gifted underachievers if at all feasible. This may at least lead to confidences and possibly friendships among these people, leading ultimately to improved social adjustment. It may also help to establish stronger worth-while personal attitudes.

SUMMARY

This article has attempted to bring together some recent unpublished research in the special problems of the gifted underachiever. Because of the nature of the needs of this type of young person the material has been organized around a counseling situation, and suggestions for such counseling which have been indicated by experience are listed. It would seem that no other group in high school is potentially capable of making greater personal and social gains than this one as a response to wise and sympathetic guidance.

REFERENCES

1. Alter, H. M., "A Study of High School Students with Scores of 130 and Above on the California Test of Mental Maturity." Unpublished paper. 1953.
2. Gowan, J. C., "The Analysis of Leadership in a Military School." Unpublished Ed. D. dissertation. University of California, Los Angeles, 1952.
3. Landstrom, F. M. and Natvig, A. M., "Biographical Study of Gifted Achievers and Non-Achievers Compared with Over-Achievers and Central Groups." Unpublished paper. 1954.
4. Robert, Lucille, "Findings from Clinical Reports on the Behavior Problems of Gifted Children." Unpublished paper. 1952.
5. Wilbar, Mildred, "High School Evaluation Study of the Program for Gifted Students." Unpublished paper. 1954.

Emotional Problems of Gifted Students

GLADYS H. WATSON

Among the many patterns of college life deserving classification and study is that of the gifted student whose performance lags behind his aptitude. The problems bearing on such a student's behavior may not in themselves be unique, but his reactions to common problems tend to separate him from other students of different intellectual endowments. The easy judgment, unhappily too common to faculty members, that reference to personal and emotional problems is merely a shield for failure avoids a grave situation by denying its existence. Reluctance to investigate and, consequently, to discriminate personal problems leads to the summary attitude expressed in, "Why coddle the unfit? These students are just not college material; they should never have been admitted." The implications of such comments demand examination.

STUDY POPULATION

How does the superior student react to emotional problems? To what extent is his potential achievement modified by emotional problems? What kinds of personal problems are most likely to beset the superior student? In an attempt to answer these questions for one college, the present survey is offered. It is based upon the records of all Brooklyn College students of high academic promise who came for personal counseling during the academic years 1956–1957 and 1958–1959. The criteria for inclusion are: (1) high scholastic aptitude as evidenced by the attainment of entrance examination scores which placed the student at or above the 65th percentile in his class at Brooklyn College in academic aptitude, or by graduation with honors; (2) referral of the student for personal counseling because of emotional problems; (3) termination of attendance at the College before the fall of 1959.

The group under study totaled 308 students. Of these, 232 had graduated and 76 had either withdrawn or had been dismissed for poor scholarship. Of the 232 graduates, 100, or slightly more than 43 per cent, ranked at the time of admission in the top one-third of their class in aca-

Reprinted from *Personnel and Guidance Journal,* Vol. 39, No. 2 (October, 1960), pp. 98-105. By permission of the author and publisher.

demic aptitude. Among this 100, 57 ranked in the top one-fifth of their class, 30 in the top tenth, and 5 in the top one-hundredth of their class. (See Tables 1 and 2 below.) Of the 76 who had not graduated, but who

TABLE 1. Comparison of Selected Group with Total Group,
Entrance Examinations Scores
Brooklyn College Norms

	Whole Group	Test Scores 65%ile or Higher	Per Cent of Total with High Score
Graduated	232	100	43
Not in attendance	76	23	30
TOTAL	308	123	40

TABLE 2. Entrance Test Scores of 100 Graduates
Brooklyn College Norms

Percentile Rating	Number in Group
65–79	43
80–89	27
90–98	25
99–100	5

were no longer in attendance, 23, or about 30 per cent, were in the top one-third of their class at entrance. Sixteen of these 23 had been dismissed for poor scholarship or had withdrawn under an academic deficit. Of the remaining seven, three had left college because of a serious psychiatric condition, one had transferred to another college, one had married, and two had given no reason for their withdrawal. These seven are not included in the study.

Three distinct groups emerged from the total, an honors group, a middle group undistinguished by either excellence or failure, and a low performance group.

The honors group contains 25 students classified as high scoring and 10 others whose entrance scores were unavailable or below the criterion, but who had graduated with honors. The middle group contains 46 students. The low performance group contains 45 students. Twenty-nine of these graduated in spite of academic difficulties ranging from limited probation to the danger of temporary suspension, to actual dismissal from the College for poor scholarship. Twenty-one students had been dismissed or had withdrawn because of poor scholarship. Of these, five had been readmitted with non-matriculated status, had earned their way back to matriculation and eventual graduation.

FAMILY BACKGROUND

For the group as a whole, family background seems to represent a cross section of the College population. In 40 per cent of the families, both parents were born abroad; in 40 per cent both parents were born in the United States; in 16 per cent the father alone and in 4 per cent the mother alone was foreign born. It may be of interest to note that of the 128 foreign born parents, 106 came from Iron Curtain countries, and nine others from Germany or Austria. Occupations of the fathers similarly represent a cross section of the College. Nineteen are professional men, 27 own their own businesses, 29 are white-collar workers, 38 are skilled workmen, and 13 semi-skilled.

If the family background of each subgroup is studied independently a somewhat different picture emerges. It now appears that 51 per cent of those who graduated with honors had both parents born abroad, that 46 per cent of those who had academic difficulty had both parents born in the United States. In both groups the largest number of fathers were skilled workers, but in the honors group only 6 per cent of the fathers were professional men while in the low performance group, 22 per cent were in that class. On the whole the fathers in the low performance group were of a higher occupational status than those of the honors group. (See Tables 3 and 4.)

TABLE 3.   Comparison Among Honors, Average, and Low
Performance Students
Birthplace of Parents

PARENTS BORN	Honors	%	Average	%	Low Perform- ance	%	TOTAL
Both in U.S.	9	26	17	37	21	46	47
Father U.S., mother non-U.S.	2	6	3	7	3	7	8
Mother U.S., father non-U.S.	6	17	9	19	7	16	22
Neither U.S.	18	51	17	37	14	31	49
TOTAL	35	100	46	100	45	100	126

TABLE 4. Comparison Among Honors, Average, and Low
Performance Students
Paternal Occupation

FATHER'S OCCUPATION	Honors	%	Average	%	Low Perform- ance	%	TOTAL
Professional	2	6	7	15	10	22	19
Business, managerial	4	11	14	30	9	20	27
White collar	9	26	12	26	8	18	29
Skilled worker	14	40	9	19	15	33	38
Semi-skilled	6	17	4	9	3	7	13

A rather striking sex difference appears. Of the 35 honors students, 23, or nearly two-thirds, are women; of the low performance group, 32, or more than two-thirds, are men. (See Table 5.)

TABLE 5. Sex Distribution in Honors, Average, and Low
Performance Groups

SEX	Honors	Average	Low Perform- ance	TOTAL
Male	12	19	32	63
Female	23	27	13	63
TOTAL	35	46	45	126

The majority of students come from two-child families, and family position appears to have relatively little effect on scholastic achievement. For both the honors and the low performance groups, life is equally difficult whether one is first or last born. The exception may be in the average group, where the oldest child seems to be in a somewhat favored position.

TIME OF REFERRAL

It has sometimes been suggested that counseling during the first two years of college life will so prepare a student that he will need little or no help during the final two years. For this group at least, that suggestion seems not to be true. Seventy-six or 60 per cent of the referrals were made during the last two years of college. Almost a third of all referrals

TABLE 6. Class Status at Time of Referral: Honors, Average, and Low Performance Groups

CLASS	Honors	Average	Low Performance	TOTAL
Freshman	3	9	13	25
Sophomore	7	11	10	28
Junior	15	15	15	45
Senior	10	11	7	28
TOTAL	35	46	45	126

occurred during the junior year. (Table 6.) If we take seriously the notion that one of the functions of the liberal arts college is to enable the student to know himself, it seems reasonable to suppose that the more advanced student might be more aware of questions about his full identity, than the freshman or the sophomore. A large part of college teaching is designed to raise just such questions. Many, probably the majority of students, can find answers within themselves or in the process of free discussion with their peers in and out of the classroom. A minority, and this apparently includes some of our most gifted students, have more difficulty and feel the need for some individual counseling in this area. In *The Student and Mental Health* it is noted that in liberal arts colleges where instruction is individualized and where students are encouraged to question their values, identity crises occur more frequently than in larger more impersonal colleges (1). In the same book, one of the student participants comments, "It appears to me that the 10 or 20 per cent of the students seen in the college mental health clinic are perhaps, the most fortunate students in the college, because college has disturbed them enough to pull the rug out from under their feet (4)."

In a large number of instances the student had first asked for career counseling but had soon discovered that his questions were not so much "What shall I do?" "What opportunities are there for people with my qualifications?" "How shall I prepare for a given profession?" as "Who am I?" "What kind of a person am I?" There is certainly a place for vocational counseling of the pragmatic information-giving type, counseling which will help to answer questions of the first kind. But to confuse this with counseling which is concerned with helping a young person discover his identity in the world is to try to answer the wrong question at the wrong time, never helpful to students nor rewarding to counselors. The choice of a career can only be made wisely after the student has answered the primary questions about himself. Career counseling is tangential in such instances, and this fact should be clearly recognized by both student and counselor.

SCHOLARSHIP RECORD

In a group selected for high academic potential, graduation with honors would be expected. Actually of the 100 graduates of known high capability, only 25 earned honors. When we remember that 30 in the group were in the top 10 per cent of their class, the number is disappointingly small. Twenty-four graduated *cum laude,* nine *magna cum laude,* and two *summa cum laude.* Departmental honors were earned by 17; five in Humanities, four in Social Science, four in Natural Science, and five in Education. Among graduation awards were two National Science Foundation Fellowships, one Woodrow Wilson Award, one Fulbright Research Grant, and one Regents College Teaching Fellowship. On the other hand, among the 100 graduates with known high entrance scores, 24 had scholarship difficulties ranging from "danger of dismissal" to "plus probation." An additional five were actually dismissed for poor scholarship, but had earned their way back into college and to graduation.

PRESENTING PROBLEMS: THE HONORS GROUP

The composite picture of the honors group shows a tense, driven individual with a compulsive need to achieve which excludes almost everything else. He has few or no friends, seems unable to relate to anyone, and feels valued only in proportion to his ability to bring home high grades. Fear tends to be his dominant emotion; fear of failure, fear of water, fear of meeting his peers. There is frequently a notation of schizoid tendencies. The important parent is likely to be the father, who is seen as stern, demanding, often distant, sometimes uninterested except for the constant pressure for high achievement. Parents in general are seen as over-protective and infantilizing. For both men and women the area of sex is a fearful and largely unexplored one. For a number, the problem of identity has never been recognized. The comment of the counselor, "You are a man, you now have to make your own life, your own choices" may come as a revelation.

In general, the honors group tends to be fearful, obedient, to have introjected the demands of the parents, to have repressed many of their natural cravings. This is in marked contrast to the low achievement group which tends to be resistant, rebellious, and "acting-out." Since two-thirds of the first group are women and of the second, men, it is possible that there is here a sex difference which reflects differing cultural expectations for men and women. The expression of aggression is considered more acceptable in a boy than in a girl. Female rebellion is generally more quickly and more decisively repressed. Girls tend to be more docile than boys, possibly more able to accept the demands of parents as reasonable and justified, more willing to work very hard for parental approval. Moreover, the demands on the girl are not so great as those on the boy. Of course she must not disgrace the family by failure, but equally of course she will eventually marry and be supported by her husband. The boy has no such refuge. From the beginning it is clear that he must support a family. Often there is also the expectation that he will do better than his father. When this is coupled with the unspoken admonition not to undermine his father's authority by surpassing him, there seems to be no way out of the dilemma. At home the boy must be passive and obedient; outside the home he must be aggressive and dominating. The girl does not face so many conflicting demands. It is possible, even praiseworthy, for her to be submissive and passive both at home and abroad; there is no requirement that she equal or surpass her father. The girl, allowed less freedom than the boy, may be more influenced by parental values; the boy, spending more time outside the home, may be more responsive to peer values. The girl tries to fulfill the feminine role as she sees it by obedience and study; the boy tries to fulfill the masculine role as he perceives it by rebellion and refusal to conform.

In this study, honors students come largely from homes in which both parents were born abroad, in which the father is a skilled workman. Low performance students come largely from homes in which both parents were born in the United States and in which the father is a business or professional man. Possibly where both parents are foreign born there is a greater strength and cohesiveness in cultural background than there is among the first generation Americans. Father may be distant, stern, dominating; mother meek and submissive, but everyone accepts that pattern as the right and normal one; although as the child moves through high school and college, he may come to question the eternal fitness of this arrangement. In those families where both parents were born in the United States, father, especially if he is a successful business or professional man, may be trying to perpetuate the old pattern in opposition to mother. The fact that neither may be conscious of the problem may lead to the destructive in-fighting which is disastrous to the children.

The cultural conflict includes more than the struggle for the emancipation of women and a more democratic way of living. There is also the question of religion, for this predominantly Jewish group a very serious one. As has often been pointed out, the child who rejects his parent may reject all that his parent stands for. This may mean rejection of the parent's religion. As one young man said, "I'm not Jewish! I refuse to be Jewish! Oh, yes, I know my parents are Jewish, but I'm talking about the Jewish religion. I simply *am not Jewish!* (But if not Jewish, what am I?)"

Or there may be the demand of the child to choose his own friends, his own marriage partner, even though friends and mate are of a religion different from the parent.

The cultural gap between the lives of the parents and the lives that the children as college graduates will lead is sometimes so wide that it is not surprising that the young people quail before it. One young man said, "But it's presumptuous for me to think of being a college teacher! My father can't read or write, can hardly speak English. And I should be a college teacher? That might be for my son, not for me." Another, who had graduated *summa cum laude,* with departmental honors, decided to be a post office clerk. It looked safer and easier than trying to become a professional man. Many others will settle for lives of quiet mediocrity. This does not mean that they will not become bitter frustrated men who may vent their frustrations on their families. It may mean that their sons, like so many of the young men in this sample, will regard their fathers as poor weaklings, people to be despised and pitied.

Margaret Mead has observed that "college presents a hazard . . . the alienation of one's children from one's own way of life (3)." Too often the parents do not realize this until it is too late. The fear of this alienation is often back of the unspoken demand not to surpass the parent. It may find expression in a mother's command to her daughter not to "go out with a Ph.D. because he would be too good for you." Whether it is expressed or not, the fear is often with the parent as with the child. The danger is perhaps greater for this very gifted group, or perhaps they are more aware of it. The nearer they are to graduation, the more frightening is the prospect of leaving the well-known and safe world of the parents and venturing into the unknown and frightening world which may be theirs.

THE AVERAGE GROUP

This is a group with a wide variety of problems of relationships with parents, problems of growing up, of discovering one's own identity, of relationships with authority figures. Fear, anxiety, depression, hostility are all reported. Men in the group tend to feel inadequate, to fear they will not be able to fulfill the masculine role in society. Three of them have had acute psychotic episodes. Both men and women report difficulty in relating to people, inability to make decisions, jealous of siblings. There is some evidence of retarded heterosexual development. One man in this group, and one woman in the honors group, were distressed at their resort to alcohol as an escape. Those with parents born in the United States generally report that their mothers are over-demanding, overprotective. Depression, anxiety, hostility are characteristic, together with feelings of worthlessness, of lack of a sense of personal identity. Those with one or both parents foreign born generally report that they have distant and domineering fathers, and that they have considerable difficulty with authority relationships.

Standing between the honors and the low achievement group in academic achievement, they occupy this relative position in other respects. So far as birthplace of parents and occupation of father are concerned, they are nearer to the low achievement group. They also tend to show more hostility and aggression and less fear. Here again they resemble the low achievers. Perhaps this is not surprising in view of the fact that for young people of this degree of ability their record, while not one of failure, does not correspond to their potential.

Students in this group are more concerned with problems of personal identity and less with failure to relate to others than are those in either of the other groups. Many of them are student leaders, some of them very successful ones who have won awards for campus citizenship. Possibly they are trying to atone for academic failure by developing interpersonal relationships; possibly they have refused to compete with siblings in the academic area and have chosen another field of interest. Whatever the reason for choice, they tend to be dissatisfied with their achievements and to be searching for a better way of living than they have found.

Here, as in the honors group, women predominate, 27 to 19.

THE LOW ACHIEVEMENT GROUP

These students often come from home situations that are described as brutalizing, over-powering, extremely destructive. Parents may openly reject the child or may more subtly reject him by over-protecting or making too great demands on him. In some instances there is no father in the home, only a malicious, hostile mother, often one who because of her own failures hates all men. It is not clear why more boys than girls should come from homes like this. Possibly it is a result of admissions policy, though it seems more likely that girls from this kind of vicious background never get to college. They have not the strength to survive in an academic world. Possibly too, the girls in families like this are more often forced to leave school and go to work, since after all, "the education of a woman is not important." Perhaps more of them escape into marriage. Whatever the reason, fewer of them come to Brooklyn College.

A few students in this group have reacted by retreat and withdrawal. They find safety in hiding. They find it difficult to speak in class. They avoid competition by refusing to try. It is more bearable to such a student to fail in an examination because he did not study, than to study and get a poor grade; more bearable to have no friends, than to try to find a friend and risk a rebuff. The men tend to be effeminate, passive, dependent. In a sense, these students are committed to failure; they await it with the passivity of the defeated.

The other, and larger, part of this group has reacted with rebellion and resistance. They are committed to the opposition. Their rebellion is as overdetermined as the failure of the first group. They are compelled to resist, to see all authority, even their own, if they are student teachers, as dangerous, inimical, destructive. They find it difficult, if not impossible, to suppose that an adult might be friendly, might have any reason other than hostility or innate perversity for the requests or demands that he makes. Ironically, it is from this group that some of our best known student leaders come. It is satisfying to be aggressive and defiant in class, but infinitely more so to act out one's rebellion on a larger stage. With guidance and help such students may become winners of gold or silver keys for campus citizenship; without such guidance, they may become disruptive forces. Instances of both kinds are to be found in this sample.

No matter which course they choose, the young people in this group are unsure of themselves and are seeking to discover their identity. They are trying out possible roles for the world of adults. If the young man who is trying failure as a way of life is accepted by others as a failure, he may adopt that role permanently. If the young woman who adopts resistance and opposition as a role is accepted by others and labelled a rebel, she may carry that role through life. The one who refuses to grow up, who clings to childhood as the only safe refuge, may spend his life seeking protection and security.

Here are to be found the anxious and depressed young people who unconsciously seek their own destruction, sometimes to punish parents, sometimes to agree despairingly with what they feel to be the adult judgment of their worthlessness. It is here that the largest number of frank psychoses are found. In a group of 45, three have been hospitalized, and four others are said to be possibly or probably pre-psychotic. Others who are clearly too neurotic to be treated on campus need to be helped to seek off-campus therapy. Still others, not yet fixed in their roles, have enough ego strength and resiliency so that even short-term counseling can help them to adopt new and more satisfying ways of living. Those who fear failure so desperately can be helped to succeed, modestly at first, but so that they can have a taste of success instead of the bitter one of failure. Those who must rebel can be helped to forget the straw men and to use their rebellion for constructive purposes. Both can be helped to realize that they are no longer helpless children in a world of angry giants, but men and women in a world of other men and women who have difficulties much like their own; and that even parents and teachers are only people.

SUMMARY AND CONCLUSIONS

An analysis has been made of the records of 126 students who, having been referred for personal counseling, had entrance examination scores or achievement records that placed them in the top one-third of their class, and who have terminated their work at the College. Of 232 who had been referred for counseling and who had graduated, 110 or nearly 48 per cent were in the high ability group as defined by this study. An additional 16 students who had been dismissed or had withdrawn from college because of serious academic difficulty were in the high ability group. In the group of 126, 27 per cent graduated with honors, 37 per cent graduated without distinction, and 36 per cent had academic difficulties, in some cases so serious that they were dismissed before graduation.

Two-thirds of the honors group were women; two-thirds of the low achievement group were men. Descent from foreign born parents of the working class seemed to be associated with the achievement of honors; even as descent from United States born parents of the professional or business class seemed to be associated with low achievement. The honors students tended to be compulsive, driven people, with few or no satisfactory interpersonal relationships. The low achievers tended to be rebellious and resistant, unable to achieve well in any area. The average group tended to be more concerned about personal identity than about interpersonal relationships, to be less driven and repressed than the honors group, somewhat less rebellious than the low achievers. For the men, there is some evidence that the presence of a dominating father is accompanied by rebellion against authority, and by expressions of hostility and aggression; and that the presence of a driving dominating mother is attended by feelings of personal worthlessness and hopelessness.

There is no evidence that the students in the group were using the presence of emotional problems as an excuse for not doing well in college work, nor is there evidence that they were not "college material." There is considerable evidence that distress interferes with, if it does not prevent, effective study; and that moreover, distress is detrimental to happy interpersonal relationships and to achieving an effective maturity. In the words of Malleson,

> The university has to take the growing senior boy and act upon him in such a way that he matures into a well-balanced man. . . . To do this, the university must employ a variety of means far wider than those of the lecture room. . . . Personal problems, inherent in the process of growing up, inhibit the student from making full use of the university. Hence, counseling him about his personal difficulties and helping him over his periods of distress is as germane to the whole process of education as lectures, seminars, preparing essays, etc. (2).

REFERENCES

1. Funkenstein, D. H. (Ed.), *The Student and Mental Health*. New York: The Riverside Press, 1956.
2. Malleson, M., Ecological Concept in Student Health Services. In Funkenstein, D. H. (Ed.), *The Student and Mental Health*. New York: The Riverside Press, 1956.
3. Mead, M., Cultural Change and the Student. In Funkenstein, D. H. (Ed.), *The Student and Mental Health*. New York: The Riverside Press, 1956.
4. Wilkie, G. H., A Student View of Mental Health. In Funkenstein, D. H. (Ed.), *The Student and Mental Health*. New York: The Riverside Press, 1956.

11 | PROMOTING GOOD ADJUSTMENT

Hazards of the High I.Q.

DOUGLAS A. THOM
NANCY NEWELL

Very little recognition has been given to the fact that extremely high intelligence is as far from normal as is mental deficiency and that it creates problems of its own that may be as acute, though not as depressing, as the problems of inferior intelligence. In psychological theory, the range of normal intelligence runs from the dull, border-line mentality, at 70 I.Q., to the very superior level of 130 I.Q., or thirty points of divergence from 100 I.Q., which represents the average performance of children at given age levels.

An eight-year-old child with an I.Q. of 70 may be normal in size and appearance, and be mannerly if he has been well trained. He has, however, the mentality of five-and-one-half years and is hardly ready to learn to read. If he is placed in Grade I, he may be embarrassed by his size and be subjected to teasing and to the humiliation of failure. He cannot hold his own with children of his own age and may become quarrelsome, or take refuge with adults who give him special consideration.

On the other hand, the eight-year-old child with an I.Q. of 130 may also be normal in size and appearance, but he has the mentality of ten-and-one-half years, which throws his adjustment to his group also out of balance. He learns his lessons quickly, is bored with the activities of Grade III, and may work off his excess energy in unprofitable mischief. He attracts attention by his clever remarks and develops a desire for the center of the stage. He bosses children of his own age, but is rejected by older and larger children whose interests fascinate him and challenge his ability to compete with them. He is still only eight years old in physical skills, in dependence upon parents, in emotional experience, and in a certain naïveté, which is charming, but which may be a dangerous pitfall if he tries to capitalize it.

Reprinted from "Hazards of the High I.Q.," *Mental Hygiene,* Vol. 29, No. 1 (January, 1945), pp. 61-77. By permission of the publisher.

Children of high intelligence who develop personality problems are reported to be less likely to retain their problems than children of lower intelligence. In the course of time, their intelligence enables them to recognize the advantages of conformity to established custom, and they discard undesirable forms of behavior which they see are going to be unprofitable to them. Nevertheless, disturbances of personality are deep-rooted; early environmental experiences leave their mark in conditioned reactions which, by repetition, become permanent traits.

In an effort to examine the interplay of high intelligence with personality factors, the authors, through the Massachusetts Division of Mental Hygiene, made a follow-up study of 43 children of I.Q.'s above 130 who had been seen in the child-guidance clinics between 1927 and 1934. The interval of time between the first contact and the follow-up averaged eleven years. The children came to the clinics because of some problem of management or educational placement which was sufficiently troublesome for the parents to seek advice.

The objects of the study were to check the correctness of the original diagnosis and treatment; to learn what methods of training the parents had used; to find out how the children had reacted to the problem of their own superiority; to discover what factors had contributed to success or failure in their adjustment to their life situation.

THE HIGH I.Q. PERSISTS

Thirty-eight of the 43 children were available for reëxamination and tests were selected which corresponded as closely as possible to the original Stanford-Binet (1916 revision) which had been given when the children's ages ranged from two to ten years. Their I.Q.'s on this test had ranged from 130 to 166, with the mean or average for the group at I.Q. 139. The results of the reëxamination were unexpectedly consistent. The children at this time were from ten to twenty years of age, their I.Q.'s ranged from 106 to 161, but only one, a boy who had been twenty-three months of age at the time of the first test, fell below 120. The average for the group was 135 I.Q. on the Stanford-Binet (1937 revision) and 125 I.Q. on the Wechsler-Bellevue test. This decrease in average I.Q. was not significant in view of the advanced ages of the children and the well-known inadequacies of tests to measure the abilities of older adolescents.

Particularly interesting was the discovery that the I.Q.'s of 24 children who had been under school age at the time of the first examination fulfilled the predictions of superiority as satisfactorily as the I.Q.'s of children of school age, for whom intelligence tests are considered to be best adapted. Although intelligence tests may be unreliable in discriminating within the middle range of very young children, nevertheless, a child who shows exceptional ability in these early years may be expected to maintain superiority as he grows older. . . .

THE HOMES OF THE CHILDREN

The parents of these children were, in most cases, interested and willing to discuss problems of family life and to give information that would show what sort of homes produced these superior children. Were they prosperous homes, with advantages of leisure and luxury? Were they happy homes? Were the prosperous families happier than those with precarious incomes?

In 24 homes, there had been security and comfort, with varying degrees of luxury and expensive advantages for the children. In 19 homes, the incomes had been irregular or marginal, requiring careful economy; while in five homes there had been periods of actual dependency during the depression.

Twenty-seven homes had had an harmonious family life, with unity of aims and sharing of interests and privileges. In 16 homes, there had been indifference, selfishness, or conflict, which in five cases had resulted in divorce.

The question naturally suggested itself as to whether there was any correlation between the 24 families with comfortable incomes and the 27 homes in which there was solidarity or harmony, and whether there was any relationship between parental conflict and economic stress. Interestingly, there appeared to be no correlation between economic level and family solidarity, as harmony was found in 15 of the 24 prosperous homes and in 12 of the 19 precarious homes. In the latter group, the parents had compensated for financial restrictions by intelligent planning of family activities through the use of facilities that did not involve much expense. The planning of projects and the sharing of privation had contributed to the unity and happiness of the families. However, in those homes of the precarious group in which the parents were not harmonious, the conflict had been aggravated by financial stress.

In conclusion, it appears that the children of the study came chiefly from families of moderate degrees of both economic security and economic stress, and that financial status bears little relationship to the ability of parents to provide happy homes and to make satisfactory family adjustments.

THE PARENTS

One is inclined to expect high intelligence and advanced education in the parents of very brilliant children, so it was surprising to find an educational level that was moderately, but not exceptionally high. Approximately one-half of both fathers and mothers were graduates of high schools; eight fathers and nine mothers were graduates of colleges; four fathers and six mothers had not progressed beyond the elementary grades; and the remainder of the parents had had a smattering of high-school education.

Six fathers were practicing in professions; 14 others held positions of responsibility; the remaining fathers who were living held various minor positions. Of the mothers, 22 had been engaged in business, 13 had practiced minor professions, two had been factory workers, and six had never been employed.

It was interesting that 41 mothers professed definite religious affiliations. In only three cases was there conflict in religious matters. More than half of the children were actively interested in church affairs and several were seriously concerned. The weight and quality of religious background was definitely high.

Nine fathers and 10 mothers were from foreign-speaking nations. Seventeen fathers and 20 mothers had foreign-born parents, many of whom had emigrated to escape poverty or persecution. Among the families of foreign extraction, there had been great effort to improve the status of the family, to take advantage of educational opportunities, and to prepare for vocational success. This was most marked among the seven Jewish families, some of whose forebears were uneducated according to American standards, but had had a thorough training in Hebrew culture and were religious leaders.

There were four families with Indian blood, and the precocious infant had a mixture of French, German, Negro, and Indian inheritance.

Individual ancestors provided some interesting material, which can be reported only briefly. Three families were descendants of prosperous Tories who fled to Canada during the American Revolution. All three families had brilliant and talented members. One boy was fathered by a descendant of a famous inventor whose genius revolutionized the textile industry in England; collateral relatives were active in Colonial affairs, and there have been professional men in the family through four generations. The mother of this boy was descended from a Dutch pioneer who founded a religious settlement in America and traveled through the colonies teaching the art of grafting trees. This family includes a prominent politician and a nationally known philanthropist.

Other interesting forebears were the president of a college, the president of a large bank, a mathematical genius, several noted artists and musicians, two state governors, a celebrated actress, and several famous novelists.

Unfavorable tendencies occurred in 17 families. There were seven neurotic and four unstable mothers, two neurotic fathers, and two alcoholic and delinquent fathers, one of whom was "the black sheep" of a good family. Among grandparents, there were two cases of alcoholism and three cases of mental disease.

PARENTAL PERPLEXITIES

There was a good deal of bewilderment among the comfortably intelligent parents who had unexpectedly produced exceptional offsprings. Their attitudes varied between the extreme conceit of the couple who were convinced of the genius of their child from the moment of birth, to the scepticism of the mother who would not admit any superiority in her daughter.

Seven parents had gratified their own vanity by boasting about their children and exploiting their cleverness at every opportunity. Eleven had pushed and overstimulated their children beyond their capacity to maintain a balanced adjustment. Fifteen had been possessive and overprotective to such a degree that the children had become seclusive, bookish, or abnormally shy. Seven parents were deferential to, or actually afraid of, the ability of their offspring to outwit or circumvent them. Seven parents, who had attempted forcibly to repress the effervescent precocity of their children, had become involved in an undeclared war in which mutiny, conflict, and antagonism were the order of the day.

Problems of discipline were much more in evidence at the time of the first contact when the children were younger. Twenty-two children were being handled with inconsistent methods because the parents or other relatives were operating on differing theories of management, or because the mother was at times overlenient and at other times oversevere. Seventeen children were being subjected to corporal punishment, and 10 were contemptuous of authority. Most of these early disciplinary problems were resolved under the guidance of the clinic, and the cases were closed as improved or recovered.

During the years intervening between the first and the second contacts, problems of behavior had practically disappeared, but, in some cases, had been replaced by problems of personality and undesirable attitudes. Twenty-eight children were being managed easily by reasoning, while 12 remained difficult or defiant, and three had continued to rule tyrannically in the home. In general, the early misbehavior may be attributed to the aggressiveness and the self-assertion of the brilliant child who is testing his wit and will against the forces of his environment. With increasing maturity and understanding, he recognizes the value of social adaptation and turns his aggressiveness into acceptable channels, which lead to satisfying achievements and worth-while pleasures.

No child in the group was without love from one parent or the other. Only fifteen of the 43 children had received wise management, which had given freedom of activity within suitable limits so that they were able gradually to assume responsibility for their personal affairs.

HEALTH OF THE CHILDREN

At the time of the follow-up study, all of the 43 children were in good health. All but one had been full-term pregnancies. Thirty-six were first-born and, although 22 had had instrumental deliveries, only four had been injured. Eleven were "only children" and families were small, averaging 2.3 children per family. Fourteen children had had serious diseases and 12 had suffered from various chronic complaints previous to adolescence. There were 12 cases of poor vision requiring lenses.

Fifteen children were left-handed or ambidextrous; six of them had been trained to use the right hand, four had speech difficulties, and six were extremely poor writers.

SCHOOL HISTORIES

The educational history of the group was relatively disappointing. Twenty-four of the 43 children had attended kindergarten and 15 had learned to read before entering Grade I. At the time of the first contact, 12 had skipped a grade or had entered school a year early. At the time of the second contact, 34 had received high marks, 19 had been honor students, and nine had won awards, varying from prizes to college scholarships. Sixteen had graduated from high school, three from vocational schools, and four from colleges. Of 20 pupils remaining in school, 14 were a year or more advanced in grade placement. Nine children had disliked school, and five had done poor work.

Although these attainments appear to be gratifying, they seem to have been achieved principally through the energy and initiative of the children themselves. The schools had little to offer them in the way of special opportunities. In many instances, superior ability had not been recognized, particularly in pupils who were competing in an older group. In only five cases had any enrichment of program been provided.

One boy had been penalized by poor marks for lack of effort. He tossed off his lessons without effort and then relieved his boredom by attempting to run the class, which annoyed the teacher and provided him with some interesting diversion. Several boys were so antagonistic that they refused to do well lest they outshine their classmates. The boy of remarkable ancestry, whose psychological rating was close to genius, was submerged in a large high school. He was doing well in a college preparatory class, but, because of his retiring disposition, he was completely overlooked as an intellectual rarity. Three other children, who had made poor records in public school, blossomed into high accomplishment when transferred to private schools, where their potentialities and emotional adjustment were given individual attention. A bright girl from an impoverished home had been placed in a domestic-science course, which fitted her neither for further education nor for earning a living commensurate with her ability.

On the other hand, two children, whose parents had tried to impose scholastic advantages beyond their social and emotional maturity, had become so maladjusted that their education was a complete failure and they were unfitted to go on with the higher education which had been planned for them.

The boy who obtained the highest psychological rating was normally placed in school for his age in Grade V. The clinic recommended that he remain there for the present because he was very small for his age and the school had nothing to offer other than double promotion. He was supplying his own enrichment by reading formidable literature which he preferred to playing childish games. In school, he monopolized prizes and honors without effort, and he lacked the stabilizing influence of wholesome competition.

The children whose abilities had been recognized at school were those who had been aggressive and socially well adjusted, and who had striven for honors and awards. The more retiring students had often been overlooked and, from the clinical point of view, had lacked guidance in utilizing their abilities and in making personal adjustments.

PERSONALITY PROBLEMS

The problems for which these children originally attended the clinic were chiefly the normal problems of childhood in connection with eating, sleeping, elimination, and discipline. The clinic looks upon such manifestations as symptoms indicative of emotional maladjustment and tries to correct or to modify the conditions that produced the symptoms instead of treating the symptoms themselves. As previously suggested, most of the immediate difficulties were eliminated under clinic therapy.

The personalities of the children were discussed with the parents on the basis of 36 character traits. The traits that appeared most frequently were happiness, energy, generosity, independence, and persistence. The traits that appeared least frequently were selfishness, dependence, and jealousy.

During the interval between the first and second contacts, there was an increase of confidence, conscientiousness, coöperation, and ambition, while a marked decrease appeared in the undesirable traits of stubbornness, defiance, negativism, and a tendency to "show off." The group as a whole gave a delightful impression of vitality, exuberant spirits, and worth-while interests.

The social adjustment of these precocious children was difficult. The very young children, at the time of the first contact, were amusing themselves with imaginative play and with comradeship or conflict with their mothers. As they grew older, there was a tendency to prefer older playmates and to seek the companionship of adults. The discrepancy between intellectual and social development led to preoccupation with lonely pursuits, so that in some cases the parents were obliged to force the children to join groups at play. Some of the children who were leaders in school had few companions outside of school hours. Fifteen children, however, had developed qualities of leadership and were making an excellent adjustment in all sorts of activities.

In an attempt to analyze the factors that had contributed to the excellent development of some of the superior children, and to the less satisfactory developments of others, a division of the children was made into two groups on criteria not only of scholastic achievement, but also of personality factors and present adjustment to life situations. Half of the children (21 cases) had attained a high level of development and had fulfilled the potentialities that were found in the early contacts. The other half (22 cases) had achieved only mediocre success or were definitely maladjusted or unhappy.

TWENTY-ONE SUCCESSFUL CASES

In the group of successful cases, home conditions were predominantly good or had improved during the interval between first and second contacts. Fifteen children had had economic security, and 16 had had harmonious homes.

Fourteen children had received wise and beneficial guidance. Training had been consistent in early childhood, and punishment had taken the form of penalties rather than of chastisement. Several mothers had profited by the advice of the clinic in avoiding the interference of relatives and in adopting less emotional attitudes toward childish self-assertion. These 14 children were so active and happy, and their lives so filled with engrossing interests, that they were refreshingly unconcerned with their superiority. The parents had made a special effort to preserve normality and to uphold good standards of conduct.

One outstanding girl, an only child, had been taught by her invalid mother to make decisions for herself, to use her gifts for the benefit of others, and to accept humbly the honors and admiration that were heaped upon her. Graduating from college at twenty, she was popular and gay, thoughtful of her parents, but not restricted even by the invalidism of her mother and eager to specialize in a profession in which she could render her best service.

Another girl, who also was graduating from college at twenty, had been guided and encouraged by a stepmother who had assumed the care of four small neglected children after the death of an intellectual, but highly impractical mother. As the home was in a poor neighborhood, the girl had no suitable friends until she went to college. With her stepmother's help, however, she made a good adjustment, was prominent in college activities, and served as an assistant instructor. Her three brothers also made enviable records.

An interesting adopted girl, now in high school, has been so much more agile mentally than her adoptive parents that they have had their bewildering moments, but with patience and love they have guided her through some trying episodes and have been rewarded by her increasing stability and good achievement.

In the other seven successful cases, early training had been lax and inconsistent, or there had been antagonism and friction in the home, but these children eventually rose above these handicaps and, with increasing independence of family influences, were able to make satisfactory adaptation. In this group was the boy who deliberately flunked Latin School, but he was more effective than his parents in controlling his unruly younger brothers, and was a respected leader among his friends. Here also was the arrogant boy whose lack of effort had been penalized by his teacher. He was later entered in one of the larger private preparatory schools, where his desire for prestige may be both satisfied and curtailed.

A girl, now eleven years old, had been monopolized by her mother to compensate for the indifference of the husband, but in spite of over-possessive and indulgent training, she showed promise of well-balanced development.

Another girl, who had been set on a pedestal as her father's favorite, was so upset by loss of prestige to her equally bright sisters that she failed miserably in a large high school, thereby further alienating her father. When she was transferred to a private school, she regained her confidence, took her college examinations against the advice of the school, and passed them "with flying colors." She felt herself restored to favor and gained self-reliance from the experience.

A boy, who had been taken by an elderly grandmother because his home had been broken by divorce, and who had languished in effeminacy and loneliness in a city school, blossomed into honors and leadership in a suburban town under the care of an intelligent young stepmother.

A twenty-year-old boy of exceptional ancestry had been bandied about among relatives as a result of the unfortunate marriage of his spoiled and willful mother, who had treated him with alternate over-indulgence and cruelty. Escaping from his predicament at last by enlistment in the army, he earned rapid advancement in the artillery by his mathematical ability. His patience and generosity to his mother indicated a high quality of character.

In this group of 21 successful children, wise guidance and favorable circumstances contributed to the development of 14 of the cases, whereas the remaining seven overcame various handicaps by means of their own initiative and personal qualities.

TWENTY-TWO LESS SUCCESSFUL CASES

In the group of cases that showed only moderate success or actual failure, home conditions had been less favorable. Only nine families had had economic security, and 13 had suffered financial distress. Twelve homes had been the scene of domestic conflict, and only one child had had security, harmony, and good training. This boy had been adopted to fill a woman's emotional need, had received devoted care, and had never been told of his adoption. His personality was charming, but his school work was only fair and he displayed no unusual ability.

In the 21 remaining cases of the less successful group, there was a greater degree of nervous instability among the parents or grandparents which may have affected the children either by inheritance or by association. Of the 17 families in which unfavorable familial tendencies had occurred, 13 were included in this group, whereas among the successful children only four instances were found.

The parents of the less successful children reflected a greater degree of vanity and more dissatisfaction when their children did not make a spectacular showing. Seven children had been overstimulated, and had reacted with a good deal of antagonism or fear of failure. Nine mothers had used corporal punishment, and three were still whipping boys who were from ten to fourteen years of age. Seven children had been overprotected, and in 16 cases marked favoritism had been shown for the child by one parent or the other. On the other hand, six mothers had rejected our clients in favor of a brother or sister. One such girl had transferred her affection to a brilliant and capable aunt, with unpleasant consequences in the household. She defied parental restraint, escaped to the aunt, and filled her time with expensive and erratic pursuits.

The child whose parents expected her to be a genius lived in a haphazard household where every one was allowed full liberty of self-development. At the age of eight, she had been removed from school after a quarrel about her placement, and had been irregularly instructed by tutors. At the age of sixteen, she had not completed the requirements of the eighth grade, but talked fluently and superficially on philosophy, psychology, and the arts. She was desperately trying to find a short cut to a profession that she considered worthy of her genius, and was becoming pathetically aware of her plight as she began to see the inadequacy of her preparation.

Two boys had been idolized and exploited by overdevoted mothers. One was submissive, seclusive, and unhappy. The other, the former "quiz kid," was so maladjusted scholastically that he was sent to a private school to be brought up to standards in subjects that he disliked and had neglected.

Another disturbed boy had been in bitter conflict with a stepmother who had taken him from a doting grandmother in order to give him the discipline that she thought he needed. With her he adopted the attitude of a "whipped dog," but he retaliated by committing all sorts of petty misdemeanors in the community and by doing little else at school than read and rate high in psychological tests. He flunked college after winning a scholarship. Finally he enlisted in the army and made a fine record in the air force. He adjusted well to the impersonal type of discipline, but was homesick. From the distance that lends enchantment, he expressed appreciation of his stepmother's efforts to bring him up properly.

Another boy, the only son in an ambitious family, had been forced ahead in various private schools at an early age. He had managed to evade fundamental courses and was not equipped for college, but he had developed dramatic and artistic talent and wanted to become an actor. No doubt the stage seemed to offer him publicly the recognition he had failed to obtain from his family. He finally specialized in accounting, to please his father, and astonished every one by an excellent record. He hoped, in spite of poor vision, to be accepted for war service, where he could use his mathematical ability.

A girl, who originally came to the clinic because of nightmares about fire, had been overexcited by a neurotic and timid mother, and favored by a clever and charming father. When he remarried after the mother's death, the daughter and stepmother engaged in a relentless duel which kept the home and the younger children in an uproar until the girl finally graduated from high school—where she had been a model of deportment—and became self-supporting. She was successful in her job, but was lonely and resentful, and continued to harass her family at long range.

A Jewish girl, who had been overawed by a tyrannical older brother, gained self-confidence away from home at a junior college. She was determined to defend herself, and the conflict resulted in a nervous breakdown in the mother.

Another girl, who had been suppressed by a dominating mother, found release for her abilities and expansion of her personality in the profession of nursing.

Three girls in this less successful group had been left fatherless by death or desertion, and had been casually supervised while their mothers took up the economic struggle. Two of them became headstrong and willful, refusing to be advised or restrained. They preferred to learn the lessons of life the hard way and were employed at very ordinary jobs. The third girl, who had been overprotected and indulged during her father's life, found uncongenial work in a factory. She insisted that because she was Jewish she was handicapped by racial discrimination, and used this as an excuse for her failure to make an effort to improve her position.

In this group of cases, emotional instability, false standards of the parents, and poor methods of training, as well as individual misfortunes and adverse circumstances, prevented the best development of the children, although psychological tests showed a persistence of their superior ability.

CONCLUSIONS

Although the number of children included in this study was small and an evaluation of the interplay of intangible factors was baffling in prospect, nevertheless, in the actual process of study, certain elements that had contributed to success or failure projected themselves in sharp relief.

The consistency of the later examinations indicated that the early psychological tests were reliable and predictive of continuing ability. The success or failure of the individual child, however, depended upon factors other than his numerical intelligence quotient.

Economic advantages above the low level of distress had little effect upon success or failure, but a happy and harmonious home life was definitely favorable to good development. Some children, however, were able to overcome adverse factors of home life as they approached maturity and were able to use their intelligence in the solution of their own problems.

Probably the most definite contribution to success was consistent and reasonable training in the very early years, because it accustomed the children to orderly and useful habits and attitudes. The acceptance of regulations that are for the good of all precluded the unfortunate philosophy so frequently observed among children that one must be naughty to have fun and that an audience must be secured at any price.

The children who had been kept in normal relationship in family and social life made the best adjustments as they matured; those who failed in fulfillment had been hampered by family instability or unfortunate environmental conditions.

From a clinical point of view, a need was revealed for a closer relationship of schools with social and clinical services in order to relieve emotional pressures and to help individual children to overcome their difficulties. Otherwise, they cannot utilize their abilities to the best advantage.

Public schools have, on the whole, offered little in the way of specialized opportunities for superior children because this group gets along creditably in the program geared to the average child. Handicapped and retarded pupils, who are unable to adjust to regular classes, have been provided with various types of special classes. For the superior group, there is no emotional appeal to pity or protection such as has been used to obtain appropriations for the education of the handicapped and retarded group.

It is time for the public to awaken to a realization of the neglect of a national asset that can be of inestimable value in the solution of the difficult civic problems that loom ahead. In a democracy, where many intelligent leaders are urgently needed, unusual abilities should not be allowed to go to waste, but should be developed for clear thinking and sound judgment, and should be directed toward goals of human service rather than those of self-aggrandizement.

REFERENCES

1. See "The Child of Very Superior Intelligence as a Special Problem in Social Development," by Leta Hollingworth (*Mental Hygiene*, Vol. 15, pp. 3-16, January, 1931). See also "Time as a Factor in the Solution of Delinquency," by D. A. Thom and F. S. Johnston (*Mental Hygiene*, Vol. 25, pp. 269, 37, April, 1941).

Social Values and Individual Motives: The Dilemma of the Gifted

J. W. GETZELS

Exceptional children are coming to be looked upon, not as individuals of special abilities to be given freedom and opportunity for their own self-realization, but as a source of *manpower*—manpower that is fair game for training, stockpiling, and directing, if not conscripting, into the service of efficiency and production. To be sure, this attitude is frequently expressed as the establishment of "early career lines." But Karl T. Compton, of the Massachusetts Institute of Technology, expressed the point of view more bluntly when he said: "Do we have, or can we get, the engineers we need? The problem is . . . just as important to the national safety as the stockpile of critical materials."

In response to this type of exhortation, there has been a notable increase in the direct and indirect pressures on our gifted to undertake *training* in a specific discipline, most frequently science and engineering, rather than *learning* in the broad fields of human wisdom. Most recently this pressure has been exerted not only at the graduate, but at the undergraduate, level as well. The New York State Board of Regents, for example, in 1956 inaugurated a program of five hundred scholarships of $500 each for high-school graduates who chose to enter the fields of science or engineering. No similar program was inaugurated for equally gifted students who chose the field of literature, say, or philosophy. In fact, one condition of the scholarship as it now stands is that a student who changes his major from engineering or scientific studies may forfeit the scholarship. One may properly ask: Is there not a danger that such unequal distribution of scholarship funds and pressures may seduce our gifted into the technologies, not because they want technology, but because they need the money if they are to enter and remain in college at all?

Indeed, there are those who would maintain that the "training" rather than "learning" emphasis into which we may be drifting (an emphasis which is only one symptom of what we may call the "Manpower concept of education") is indenturing our best brains to drafting-rooms and

Reprinted from *School Review*, Vol. 65, No. 1 (March, 1957), pp. 60-63. By permission of the author and publisher.

to research and development time clocks without considering the consequences of such *occupational segregation* on the gifted individuals themselves and on our culture. To be sure, we are not conscripting our gifted into particular disciplines by force, as an authoritarian people might do, but, in a sense, we are conscripting them by other pressures, including money.

It is no accident that the concept of Manpower applied to education should bring to my mind a military image. In December, 1945, the United States was host to 370,000 prisoners of war of authoritarian ideology. The problem was raised in the Prisoner of War Special Projects Division as to what was the single most significant fact to tell these prisoners of war regarding democracy, not as a political system, but as a way of life and a pattern of values different from the one to which they were accustomed. Here is what the Special Projects Division came up with: " 'The Democratic Way of Life' assumes as its basic postulate that all men can, and in the long run will, voluntarily choose those courses of action that are most advantageous to them individually and collectively, if all are given full opportunity to choose" (2).

This concept of the human being as a free agent, the lord of society and not its slave, stands in sharp contrast to the Manpower concept. As Kenneth Boulding says:

[The Manpower concept] contemplates society as having a single well-defined end which is to be pursued with *efficiency*. Society is conceived as a great machine, feeding Manpower in at one end and grinding out maximum quantities of the Single Well-defined End . . . at the other. . . .

Man as Manpower is all very well for a slave society, where man is a domestic animal, to be used for ends which are alien to him. But in a free society man is not manpower. . . . He is a free being, the lord of society and not its slave (3).

It is a tragic paradox that, ten years after having made the distinction between Man and Manpower clear to our prisoners of war and to the world at large, and having pointed out vividly the moral and practical superiority of the concept of Man over the concept of Manpower, we now find ourselves in the dilemma of applying the concept Manpower to the self-realization of man in our own society. This paradox cannot be understood outside the value framework of present-day America. For the motives of an individual in a society cannot be understood outside the value system of that society.

It is in the context of what is occurring in our value system that our present concern with the gifted and the nature of the proposed solutions to the problem take on special meaning. As I have tried to show elsewhere, perhaps the most significant feature of our life today is the rapidly changing character of our operating values. And I am arguing that one aspect of this transformation is the subtle shift in our attitude toward the individual from the concept of Man to the concept of Manpower.

This shift in values, these values in flux, places all of us (but especially the gifted person) in an anomalous position. If the gifted individual is to be productive and innovative, the culture must encourage, or at least be receptive to, personal independence and autonomy. But our emerging values tend to reward conformity and cheerful compliance with the status quo. If the gifted person is to realize his endowment and potentialities, he must be motivated to work hard and sacrifice present ease for future achievement. But our values tend to prize sociability and hedonistic present-time criteria of worth. If he is to express his exceptional talents (and, by definition, the gifted person is exceptional), he must be able to maintain firm commitment to his own standards and to his own beliefs. But again our emerging values are quite opposed to this; they tend instead to hold in esteem relativistic attitudes without strong personal commitments.

To be sure, talented people have always disturbed the statistical equilibrium of normalcy and have themselves been confounded, in turn, by the conventional standards of their culture. I suspect that by the very nature of things this is inevitable up to a point. But the dilemma of the gifted in our time seems to me especially critical. For one thing, the discrepancy between the individual motives necessary for exceptional behavior and the social values that might support such behavior appears to be steadily increasing. For another, this discrepancy is in a fair way of being exacerbated by the very measures we are taking to alleviate it. We appear to be drifting to a Manpower concept of the individual and a Manpower concept of education, at least where the gifted are concerned. We are attempting to implement the paradox of applying the concept of Manpower to the self-realization of man. Early career lines, orderly training in narrow disciplines, stockpiles and stockpiles of engineers—these may give us a comfortable sense of neatness and security. But, last time out, the concept of the individual as Manpower got quite a licking from the concept of the individual as Man. I like to think that thus it ought to be, and thus it always will be. And so whether it be education in general or education of the gifted, I prefer to say with Kenneth Boulding: not Manpower, but Men—men in their infinite variety and complex personalities, in the unfolding of their desires and the unfettered expression of their *own* talents and of *all* their talents.

REFERENCES

1. K. T. Compton, "Engineers," *Scientific American*, CLXXXV (September, 1951), 9-12.

2. E. Casady, "The Basic Assumptions of Democracy as Presented to German POW's," in *Conflicts of Power in Modern Culture: Seventh Symposium of the Conference on Science, Philosophy and Religion.* Edited by L. Bryson and Others. New York: Harper & Bros., 1947.
3. K. E. Boulding, "An Economist's View of the Manpower Concept," in National Manpower Council, *Proceedings of a Conference on the Utilization of Scientific and Professional Manpower,* pp. 11-26. New York: Columbia University Press, 1954.

Personal and Social Adjustment of Intellectually Gifted Accelerants and Non-Accelerants in Junior High Schools

JOSEPH JUSTMAN

Various devices have been adopted throughout the United States to enable the gifted pupil to progress through the grades more rapidly. The most widely used plan, and the most simple to utilize from an administrative point of view, is double promotion, or grade-skipping. Many communities have instituted multiple-track programs, while others have installed modifications of the Dalton and Winnetka plans as a means of providing for the very superior child. In New York City, as one way of meeting the challenge presented by such children, we have formed special classes in which intellectually gifted pupils complete the normal span of junior high school work in two, rather than three, years. Such classes enroll children with intelligence quotients of 130 and over who show superior academic achievement. Pupils selected for admission must also possess personal characteristics of initiative, enthusiasm, willingness to work, reliability, regular attendance, and capacity for sustained work.

Underlying the introduction of such special-progress classes in the New York City schools is the assumption that homogeneous groups constitute a better approach to providing a school program which will meet the needs of intellectually gifted pupils than do the more common heterogeneous groups. It has been felt not only that the special class will serve as a medium for stimulating pupils to better academic achievement but that the formation of such groups will make it possible for the school to

Reprinted from *School Review,* Vol. 61, No. 8 (November, 1953), pp. 468-478. By permission of the author and publisher.

stimulate the development by pupils of a broad range of interests and to foster the inculcation of sound civic and social attitudes.

Another reason advanced for the organization of special classes grows out of the school's increasing concern with helping pupils to attain better personal and social adjustment. It has been felt that the very superior child, who functions on a level so much higher than that of his less intelligent classmates, will find it difficult to enter into the normal give-and-take of the usual classroom. The gifted child, the argument runs, will find the climate of a special class composed of his intellectual peers more conducive to the development of personal and social adequacy.

The present study seeks to assess the part that the special-progress class plays in furthering the personal and social adjustment of intellectually gifted pupils. To be sure, a complete evaluation of the role of such classes in fostering personal and social adjustment would entail a thorough clinical study, requiring a considerable investment in time and psychological personnel. The large number of pupils included in this study made it impossible to undertake a comprehensive evaluation of the adjustment of each child. Rather, group measures of personal and social adjustment, including a standardized group test of personality and a series of sociometric measures, were used.

SUBJECTS OF THE STUDY

Many pupils with intelligence quotients of 130 or higher were denied admission to the special-progress groups because they did not show the necessary academic attainment or because, in the judgment of their teachers, they did not possess the required personal characteristics. In some instances poor attendance, and in others parental disapproval of a program of acceleration, resulted in retention of otherwise acceptable special-progress candidates in normal-progress classes. Thus, it was possible to identify pupils in normal-progress classes who met some or all of the standards set for admission to special-progress groups.

The basic approach utilized in this study involved a comparison of matched pairs of intellectually gifted pupils drawn from special-progress and from normal-progress classes. Pupils were matched on the following bases: school attended, grade, sex, chronological age, mental age, and intelligence quotient. The Pintner General Ability Test, Intermediate Test, Form B, was utilized as the measure of intellectual status. Groups of ninety-five matched pairs of special-progress and normal-progress pupils were formed, drawn from eleven special-progress and eleven normal-progress classes in nine junior high schools located in comparable middle-class neighborhoods in New York City.

The mean chronological age of the matched pupil pairs in the special-progress and normal-progress groups was 11 years and 10 months. The mean mental ages for the two groups were 15 years and 10.9 months and 15 years and 9.8 months, respectively; the mean intelligence quotients, 134.4 and 134.1, respectively. The differences between the two groups were extremely small, and none was statistically significant.

APPRAISAL INSTRUMENTS

Sociometric techniques lend themselves readily to the determination of pupil status and interrelations in the classroom situation. Three sociometric approaches were utilized in the present study.

1. A Friendship Nomination technique, in which each pupil was asked to select the three classmates he liked best and the three he liked least.

2. A modified form of the Ohio Social Acceptance Scale, Advanced Series. This approach asked each pupil to rate his classmates on a five-point scale, in which the following scale values were to be used to designate ratings: 1—Very, very best friends; 2—Good friends; 3—Not friends, but okay; 4—Don't know them; 5—Not okay. Experience has indicated that the values assigned to pupils in a class may be looked upon as points on a continuum.

3. "Casting Characters for Class Plays," a variant of the "Guess Who" test, in which each pupil in the classes surveyed was asked to select a classmate to act a given role in a class play. Twelve characters were described, and the pupil was asked to indicate "the one classmate you think is best suited for each part because he (or she) is just that way naturally." In actuality, the descriptions given could be classified as representing positive or negative traits:

"Someone who is always in good humor, who smiles or laughs a good deal; who makes others happy."

"Someone who is snobbish and conceited; who feels superior to others; who likes to order others around."

Six positive characterizations (happy, cooperative, leader, dependable, friendly, and outstanding) and six negative characterizations (shy, snobbish, poor loser, bookworm, unhappy, and "show-off") were developed to comprise the total scale.

In order to secure a measure of the personal functioning of the matched groups, the California Test of Personality, Intermediate Series, was used. This test is divided into two sections: Section I, Self Adjustment, purports to indicate how the pupil feels about himself—his self-reliance, his estimate of his own personal worth, his sense of personal freedom, and his feeling of belonging. In addition, an attempt is made to determine the pupil's freedom from withdrawing tendencies and nervous symptoms. Section II, Social Adjustment, seeks to indicate how the pupil functions as a social being—his knowledge of social standards; his social skills; his freedom from antisocial tendencies; and his family, school, and community relations.

FINDINGS

Two groups of 95 intellectually gifted pupils, one drawn from a total group of 418 pupils enrolled in 11 "special-progress classes," and one drawn from a total group of 397 pupils enrolled in 11 "normal-progress classes," were compared by means of sociometric techniques. In the discussion which follows, the first of these groups is referred to as the "special-progress in-group," while the second is referred to as the "normal-progress in-group." The remaining pupils comprising the total group are referred to as the "special-progress out-group" and the "normal-progress out-group," respectively. Through comparing the responses of these four groups, insights can be developed concerning the adjustment of intellectually gifted pupils enrolled in special-progress classes composed of their intellectual peers as contrasted with the adjustment of similar pupils attending normal-progress classes, which enroll a large number of less gifted children.

1. *Friendship Nominations.* One of the questions that might be raised concerning the social adjustment of intellectually gifted pupils is: "Will intellectually gifted pupils be accepted by classmates more readily when attending classes composed of their intellectual peers than they will be in classes enrolling, for the most part, normal-progress pupils?"

The Friendship Nominations made by the pupils in both types of classes provide a partial answer to the question. Table 1 presents a summary of the number and per cent of "best-liked" and "least-liked" choices directed to in-group pupils enrolled in special-progress and in normal-progress classes.

The per cent of choices, both as "best-liked" and "least-liked," directed to the in-groups enrolled in normal-progress classes is generally slightly higher than that of choices directed to the in-groups attending special-progress classes. Statistical analysis reveals that the small difference in per cent of "best-liked" choices directed to the in-groups drawn from special-progress and normal-progress classes is not significant. However, the per cent of "least-liked" choices directed to the in-group drawn from normal-progress classes by members of the total group proves to be significantly greater than that directed to the in-group drawn from special-progress classes. This significant difference may be attributed, in large measure, to the choices made by members of the out-group. The indications are, then, that pupils who meet the intelligence-test standards for admission to special-progress classes and who remain in normal-progress classes are somewhat less acceptable to their classmates than their matched pairs who are placed in special-progress groups. Moreover, it appears that this lower degree of acceptability is determined by the

TABLE 1. Number and Per Cent of "Best-Liked" and "Least-Liked" Choices Directed to In-Groups in Special-Progress and in Normal-Progress Classes (Friendship Nominations)

| GROUP AND CHOICES | BEST-LIKED CHOICES | | | | LEAST-LIKED CHOICES | | | |
| | Special-Progress Classes | | Normal-Progress Classes | | Special-Progress Classes | | Normal-Progress Classes | |
	Number	Per Cent	Number	Per Cent	Number	Per Cent	Number	Per Cent
Pupils in total group	418	100.0	397	100.0	418	100.0	397	100.0
Pupils in in-group	95	22.7	95	23.9	95	22.7	95	23.9
Possible choices, total group	1,254	100.0	1,191	100.0	1,254	100.0	1,191	100.0
Choices directed to in-group by total group	274	21.9	278	23.3	213	17.0	259	21.7*
Possible choices, out-group	969	100.0	906	100.0	969	100.0	906	100.0
Choices directed to in-group by out-group	212	21.9	217	24.0	174	18.0	203	22.4†
Possible choices, in-group	285	100.0	285	100.0	285	100.0	285	100.0
Choices directed to in-group by in-group	62	21.8	61	21.4	39	13.7	56	19.7

* Significantly different from paired per cent at .01 level.
† Significantly different from paired per cent at .05 level.

greater rejection of such potential special-progress class members on the part of their less intelligent classmates.[1]

Further evidence concerning the relative acceptance of special-progress pupils grows out of a consideration of the mutual choices and rejections noted in the special-progress in-group as compared with those in evidence in the normal-progress in-group. Table 2 presents a summary of the number and per cent of mutual choices and rejections in which members of the in-groups drawn from both types of classes participate. In addition, the table presents the number and per cent of such mutual choices and rejections in which two in-group members choose or reject each other.

[1] It should be noted that this analysis is based upon the use of the usual formula for the standard error of the difference of two proportions, which is not rigorously correct in this situation since the ratings involved are not experimentally independent but are made by a common group of raters and of a common group of raters. A more appropriate statistic is not available at the present time.

TABLE 2. Number and Per Cent of Mutual Choices and Rejections in Which Members of In-Group in Special-Progress and in Normal-Progress Classes Participate

CHOICES AND GROUP	Special-Progress Classes		Normal-Progress Classes	
	Number	Per Cent	Number	Per Cent
Mutual choices:				
Total group	248	100.0	222	100.0
Out-group choosing in-group	86	34.7	86	38.7
In-group choosing in-group	8	3.2	14	6.3
Mutual rejections:				
Total group	84	100.0	75	100.0
Out-group rejecting in-group	28	33.3	32	42.7
In-group rejecting in-group	1	1.2	3	4.0

The per cents of both mutual choices and rejections directed to members of the in-group drawn from normal-progress classes are greater than those observed in special-progress classes. None of the obtained differences, however, is statistically significant. Although in-group members drawn from normal-progress classes tend to select each other more frequently and tend to be rejected by and to reject, out-group members to a greater degree than their counterparts enrolled in special-progress classes, the weight of the evidence is not conclusive.

A third approach which may be utilized in determining the relative acceptability of intellectually gifted children enrolled in special-progress and normal-progress classes makes use of the ability of the Friendship Nomination technique to delineate the formation of cliques, which are readily identified through the development of a sociogram charting pupil choices. Table 3 summarizes the data resulting from a consideration of the clique identified in the classes studied.

At first glance, it would seem the children who meet the intelligence test standards for admission to special-progress classes but who remain in normal-progress classes do find it somewhat more difficult than their counterparts in special-progress classes to enter into the closely knit social framework which constitutes a clique and that, when such pupils are accepted as clique members, they manifest a greater tendency to select their intellectual peers as clique partners. However, differences between the special-progress and normal-progress classes are generally rather small and do not reach a statistically significant level.

2. *Ohio Social Acceptance Scale.* The Ohio Social Acceptance Scale provides another approach to evaluation of the social adjustment of the pupils. The average rating received by each pupil may be looked upon

TABLE 3. Number and Per Cent of Cliques Observed in In-Groups in Special-Progress and in Normal-Progress Classes

	Special-Progress Classes		Normal-Progress Classes	
	Number	Per Cent	Number	Per Cent
Pupils in total group	418	100.0	397	100.0
Pupils in cliques	179	42.8	161	40.6
Cliques	49	100.0	43	100.0
Cliques enrolling in-group members	31	63.3	28	65.1
Cliques enrolling more than one in-group member	10	20.4	11	25.6
In-group members	95	100.0	95	100.0
In-group members in cliques	43	45.3	39	41.1

as a quantitative expression of the pupil's status within the group of which he is a member. Table 4 presents the mean status scores received by members of the in-group and out-group, when rated by in-group and out-group members, respectively, in both special-progress and normal-progress classes.

TABLE 4. Mean Status Scores of In-Group and Out-Group Members Drawn from Special-Progress and Normal-Progress Classes When Rated by In-Group and Out-Group Members

GROUP RATED	Special-Progress Classes		Normal-Progress Classes	
	Mean	Standard Deviation	Mean	Standard Deviation
In-group by in-group	2.91	.65	2.92	.64
In-group by out-group	2.81	.47	2.86	.56
Out-group by in-group	2.95	.59	3.00	.65
Out-group by out-group	2.91	.50	2.90	.53

The mean status of in-group members rated by out-group members is slightly higher in the case of groups drawn from special-progress (2.81) rather than from normal-progress (2.86) classes. Moreover, the mean status score of out-group members rated by in-group members enrolled in special-progress (2.95) classes is also somewhat higher than that observed in groups drawn from normal-progress (3.00) classes. However, no significant difference appears between mean status scores of in-group and out-group members in special-progress and in normal-progress classes, when such status scores are the result of ratings by out-group and in-group members, respectively. Thus, although the obtained scores point to a slightly higher degree of mutual acceptability of in-group and out-group members in special-progress classes, no definitive difference can be established between groups drawn from special-progress and from normal-progress classes.

3. *"Casting Characters."* The use of the "Casting Characters for Class Plays" technique provides a third approach to the assessment of social adjustment. It will be remembered that the scale designates six positive and six negative roles for which each pupil is to select a classmate. Table 5 presents a summary of the number and per cent of choices for positive

TABLE 5. Number and Per Cent of Choices for Positive and Negative Roles Directed to In-Groups in Special-Progress and Normal-Progress Classes

CHOICES	POSITIVE ROLES				NEGATIVE ROLES			
	Special-Progress Classes		Normal-Progress Classes		Special-Progress Classes		Normal-Progress Classes	
	Number	Per Cent	Number	Per Cent	Number	Per Cent	Number	Per Cent
Made by total group	2,229	100.0	2,268	100.0	2,155	100.0	2,196	100.0
Directed to in-group	529	23.7	599	26.4*	488	22.6	457	20.8
Made by out-group	1,658	100.0	1,734	100.0	1,613	100.0	1,683	100.0
Directed to in-group	401	24.2	465	26.8	360	22.3	362	21.5
Made by in-group	571	100.0	534	100.0	542	100.0	513	100.0
Directed to in-group	128	22.4	134	25.1	88	16.2	95	18.5

* Significantly different from paired per cent at .05 level.

and negative roles directed to in-group pupils enrolled in both types of classes.

The per cent of positive choices directed to members of the in-group by the total group of which it is a part is smaller in the group of pupils enrolled in special-progress classes than it is in the group drawn from normal-progress classes. Moreover, the per cent of choices to play positive roles which is directed to special-progress in-group members by both in-group and out-group members is smaller than that directed to in-group members enrolled in normal-progress classes. When choices to play positive roles are used as a criterion, the more favorable picture is noted in normal-progress rather than in special-progress classes.

When choices to portray negative roles are considered, minor differences appear in the per cent of choices directed to members of the in-groups by the total group of special-progress or of normal-progress pupils. However, the per cent of choices to play negative roles which is directed to in-group members by out-group members is slightly smaller in the normal-progress rather than in the special-progress classes, while the per cent of such choices directed to in-group members is greater in the group of pupils drawn from normal-progress rather than from special-progress classes. Therefore, when choices to play negative roles are used as a criterion, the group of normal-progress pupils is again placed in the more favorable light.

In order to test the generalizations advanced, the observed differences between special-progress groups and normal-progress groups were examined for statistical significance. Only one of the observed differences proved to be significant. Thus, the per cent of choices to play positive roles directed to in-group members drawn from normal-progress classes by the total group of which it is a part is significantly greater than that directed to in-group members attending special-progress classes. In some measure, this difference may be looked upon as the outgrowth of differences in choices directed to in-group members on the part of their respective out-groups. No significant differences appear when choices to play negative roles are considered. The results of this analysis may be offered as partial confirmation of the generalization advanced above: when the "Casting Characters" approach is used as a criterion, intellectually gifted children attending normal-progress classes tend to show better social adjustment than their counterparts enrolled in special-progress classes.

In order to cast further light upon the differences between the two groups, the number and per cent of choices for *each* positive and negative role directed to in-group members enrolled in special-progress and in normal-progress classes was determined. The differences between groups were found to be rather small. Only four of the obtained differences between groups (all found for negative roles) proved to reach a statistically significant level. Although the per cent of total choices to play positive roles directed to normal-progress in-group members by the total group of which it is a part was significantly greater than the per cent directed to special-progress in-group members, this difference cannot be attributed to a consistent tendency to select in-group members to play a given role in one type of class as opposed to another.

The total choices for negative roles failed to give rise to significant differences between groups. Two significant differences appeared when individual roles were considered. Thus, in comparison to choices of pupils in normal-progress groups, a significantly larger per cent of the choices of total groups attending special-progress classes (4.17) in comparison with choices of pupils in normal-progress classes (2.68) characterize in-group members as "shy." A significantly larger per cent of the choices of the total groups attending normal-progress classes (4.78) designate in-group members as "bookworms" as compared with the corresponding per cent of special-progress classes (3.15). In both instances, the significant differences could be attributed to the choices made by the respective out-groups.

4. *The California Test of Personality.* For the most part, there was little difference in the functioning of the two groups as revealed by an analysis of the results obtained by seventy-nine matched special-progress and normal-progress pupils on the California Test of Personality. In only one subsection of the test did a significant difference appear. The mean score of pupils enrolled in normal-progress classes (12.95) proved to be significantly higher than that of their counterparts enrolled in special-progress classes (12.29) on the section of the test purporting to measure adjustment in community relations. Since this subsection of the test contains only fifteen items and the obtained difference is less than one raw-score unit, the psychological significance of the obtained difference may well be questioned. It is quite evident that similarities in functioning of pupils on the test in question far outweigh such minor differences as do appear and that, for all practical purposes, the personal adjustment of the two groups of pupils may be considered equivalent.

It was felt that an examination of the individual items of the test should be undertaken in order to determine whether additional insights concerning the functioning of the two groups might be developed. The per cent of each group of pupils giving a "favorable" (well-adjusted) response to each item of the test was determined. In general, differences in the per cents of pupils in each group responding favorably to the separate items were relatively small. Actually, the differences reached a statistically significant level in only 17 of the 180 items comprising the total test. In four instances, items to which a significantly larger per cent of normal-progress pupils responded favorably deal with community relations. Three additional discriminating items, all of which tended to favor the normal-progress group, centered in the sense of personal freedom which the pupils have developed.

Another approach to the assessment of the personal adjustment of the pupils made use of sociometric instruments in conjunction with the California Test of Personality. Previous experience with the measures has indicated that low scores on the latter test, combined with rejection as a friend by other classmates and with the nomination to serve as one or more of the less desirable characters in the class play is diagnostic of maladjustment (1). In order to identify the specific pupils who might be considered maladjusted, the following criteria were applied:

1. A score on the California Test of Personality below the fiftieth percentile.
2. Rejection by more than three classmates on the Friendship Nomination technique.

3. An average score of 3.50 or higher on the Ohio Social Acceptance Scale.
4. Being chosen as an undesirable character in "Casting Characters for Class Plays" in two or more instances.

Table 6 presents a summary of the number and per cent of pupils in the special-progress and normal-progress groups who would be considered maladjusted if the first criterion were applied singly and if it were applied in combination with the other three criteria. When any one of

TABLE 6. Number and Per Cent of Maladjusted Pupils Among Seventy-nine Matched Pairs in Special-Progress and Normal-Progress Classes

CRITERION	Special-Progress Classes		Normal-Progress Classes	
	Number	Per Cent	Number	Per Cent
California Test of Personality	22	27.8	19	24.1
California Test plus:				
Friendship Nominations	4	5.1	6	7.6
Ohio Social Acceptance Scale	8	10.1	8	10.1
Casting Characters for Class Play	6	7.6	2	2.5
Two other criteria	4	5.1	5	6.3

the comparisons is considered, differences between the two groups are relatively small. Upon analysis, it is evident that the minor differences between the two groups may be attributed to chance factors. If the approach utilized may be looked upon as an adequate measure of personal adjustment, it is safe to say that the two groups show approximately equivalent functioning.

DISCUSSION OF RESULTS

The results obtained through the use of the sociometric instruments prove to be inconclusive of differences in functioning and adjustment of pupils in special-progress and in normal-progress groups. In only a few instances do the obtained differences between the contrasted groups reach a statistically significant level. Thus, intellectually gifted children attending normal-progress classes are chosen as "least-liked" to a significantly greater extent than their matched pairs enrolled in special-progress groups. Moreover, this lower degree of acceptability is determined by the greater rejection of such potential special-progress class members on the part of their less intelligent classmates. On the other hand, the per cent of choices to play positive roles depicted in the "Casting Characters" instrument which are directed to intellectually gifted children enrolled in normal-progress classes by the total normal-progress group is significantly greater than that directed to matched pairs drawn from special-progress groups.

In spite of this difference, however, there appears to be no consistent tendency to select intellectually gifted children to play a given positive role in normal-progress classes. Rather, the term "bookworm" is applied to such children by their less able classmates to a greater degree than it is to a group of matched pupils enrolled in special-progress classes by their intellectual peers. Apparently, then, the lower degree of acceptability characteristic of the group of intellectually gifted pupils enrolled in normal-progress classes may be attributed, in some measure, to their greater preoccupation with what their less intelligent classmates feel are bookish pursuits.

This finding leads a person to wonder what the role of the teacher of such heterogeneous groups has been. Has he tended, through his organization of learning activities in the classroom, to emphasize just those aspects of the gifted child's equipment which will cause him to lose face among his classmates? Has he stressed individual achievement to such a degree that he has lost sight of the importance of developing a sound group feeling?

One must be careful, however, not to belabor these differences between the two groups unduly. It must be emphasized that similarity in functioning on the part of the two groups of pupils is far more characteristic than difference. In general, there appears to be little difference in the personal and social adjustment of matched groups of intellectually gifted pupils drawn from special-progress and from normal-progress classes. The indications are, then, that failure to place gifted pupils in homogeneously organized groups will not be reflected in less adequate personal and social adjustment, nor will such placement be associated with greater personal and social adequacy.

REFERENCES

1. Wrightstone, J. Wayne, "Assessing Pupil Adjustment by Self-descriptive and Sociometric Technics," *Growing Points in Educational Research*, pp. 330-335, Official Report of the American Educational Research Association, 1949. Washington 6: American Educational Research Association, 1949.

12 | PLANNING FOR THE GIFTED— ELEMENTARY SCHOOL

Program Organization and Implementation

VIRGIL S. WARD

A. INTRODUCTION

Radical departure from the customary and conventional must characterize the organizational forms of programs for the gifted as well as their curricula. Procedures which govern the deployment of gifted students and their teachers, and which control the rate of movement of students through the graded sequence, must be related to the unusual abilities and needs of these students. Practices which can be shown by reason or research to be specifically appropriate for the gifted must replace those which have developed to meet the needs of average students.

This section of the report focuses on areas of administrative practice which have particular applicability to program organization and implementation for the gifted—especially ability grouping, acceleration, and independent study. Descriptions of the many forms of ability grouping and acceleration are available at large in the literature, as are discussions of the pros and cons of these practices. No comprehensive treatment of this easily obtainable normative material will be provided in this *Manual*. The present purpose, rather, is to discuss the process qualities inherent in these procedures, and to indicate a number of general observations regarding these and other administrative matters, which indications comprise guidelines to practice.

Reprinted from *The Gifted Student: A Manual For Program Improvement*. A Report of the Southern Regional Project For Education of the Gifted, 1962, pp. 71-78. By permission of the author and publisher.

It should be recognized that ability grouping, acceleration, and independent study, alone or in combination, do not constitute an adequate program for the gifted. They are merely administrative procedures which allow and facilitate the development of known characteristics of gifted students and which support curriculum development of the kind outlined in the preceding section of this report.

The various methods of acceleration, for instance, constitute administrative recognition that gifted students accomplish standard learning tasks more rapidly than average students. Actually the school does not accelerate the student, who may enter the first grade already reading as well as the average third or fourth grader; rather, it accelerates instruction to keep pace with the student. The gifted student's learning ability does not lend itself to the neat sequential ordering of tasks according to grade levels. The school must acknowledge this and adjust itself to keep pace with him, sometimes making it possible for him to move ahead rapidly on one front while "marking time," or progressing slowly on another.

Grouping students according to selective ability patterns for all or part of their instruction is a practice which parallels the gifted student's ability to function in the classroom situation at intellectual levels not attainable by those of average ability. Only through ability grouping can the gifted student engage in stimulating discourse—discussion and debate— with his intellectual peers. This needed high level engagement of like minds cannot be carried on effectively or efficiently in the typically heterogeneous classroom.

Other characteristics of gifted children are recognized by the intellectual and behavioral involvements inherent in independent study. The value of independent study has already been noted in the preceding section where the concept of "reversed ratios" of teaching and learning was introduced. Independent study, as a recognized and formally adopted administrative procedure, makes possible learning of the nearly unlimited depth and breadth demanded by the wide range of interests and abilities of gifted students, and by the increasing amount and complexity of the body of man's knowledge.

Each administrative procedure employed in the program for the gifted thus embodies certain detailed mental processes of which this identified group of pupils are capable. These techniques are not merely grafted on to the educational program, but rather they grow naturally out of the needs and abilities of these students in the same manner that special curricular provisions are rooted in these needs and abilities.

The remainder of this section of the report will be devoted to further discussion of administrative procedures in the organization and implementation of programs for the gifted. The discussion will take the form of a limited number of generalizations which have been distilled from the total Project experience.

B. ABILITY GROUPING

The Desirability of Grouping. Observers of special programs come quickly to the conviction that grouping of students according to ability for at least pertinent portions of their school experience is eminently desirable at every grade level. The mere grouping of pupils does not make a program, nor does absence of grouping necessarily mean that a program is absolutely ineffective. Nevertheless, ability grouping greatly increases the school's power to effect a marked improvement in the process of education for gifted students.

Ability grouping *makes possible* many teaching and learning experiences which cannot be accomplished in the typical classroom. This can be seen again and again in specially composed classes in all parts of the country. There is an electric quality, an aura of purposefulness, about such a class—whether it contains the remarkable five and six year olds of the Colfax School in Pittsburgh, lucid, earnest, and intensively engaged in making research reports or the 12th grade social studies students in Portland, Oregon, arguing political theory as though they were the Franklins, Paines, and Jeffersons of their generation. The kinds of intellectual activity that can be engaged in by a group of gifted children under the guidance of a carefully selected and specifically trained teacher simply cannot go on in the typical classroom, regardless of the kind of "enrichment" attempted.

Ability Grouping and the Teacher. Perhaps the most important and yet the least controllable variable in the grouping situation is the teacher. Ability grouping is of no particular value when teachers do not or cannot capitalize on the fact that they are working with children who have special capabilities and needs. In many classrooms in schools renowned for their programs for the gifted, teachers can be observed using the same plodding, pedestrian techniques that are so often necessary in the typical classroom where students are slow to grasp even elementary facts and concepts—with frustration and boredom as the end products, instead of intellectual excitement and challenge. Whether or not the potential value inherent in ability grouping is realized is to a considerable extent the teacher's responsibility. If the teacher does not recognize these potentialities and fails to modify his or her approach to the teaching-learning situation, the potential value of ability grouping is lost. Too often, one suspects, this is why research data fail to show significant differences between the results of grouping and the results of "enrichment" in the regular classroom.

One common source of failure to translate well-conceived programs into good classroom practice is the administrative procedure of rotating the task of teaching gifted groups through the entire teaching staff of given grades. In many school systems staff members are required to take turns teaching the bright groups regardless of interest in or ability to work with such children. Teachers should be selected for work with gifted groups on the basis of ability and interest. There can be no doubt that some teachers are better teachers for gifted children than others, just as some teachers are better fitted through training, temperament, experience, and interest to teach retarded children. Teaching each type of student requires the development of skills and knowledge which can best be achieved by special training and by continuous experience of some duration. It is difficult to see what is to be gained by assigning a teacher whose real forte is teaching the gifted to a retarded group one year and an average group the next.

It is a matter of interest to note that in numbers of school systems with a successful pattern of experiences for the gifted, it is established practice to allow teachers of gifted classes additional time for preparation. Effective teaching of gifted children is a demanding task, more so than teaching average children whose range of interests is narrower and for whom drastic departures from standard curriculum and teaching methods already reasonably well developed need not be made.

Reducing the class loads of teachers of gifted classes need not be destructive of staff morale, provided the whole staff has been led to understand the purposes and the processes integral to this complicated task. *All* teachers should be involved in the planning and development of the gifted program, and the program itself should, of course, be thought of as a part of the total school program. The importance of this approach to program development has already been emphasized.

The Feasibility of Ability Grouping. Some form of ability grouping appears to be feasible (as well as desirable) for any school system regardless of size, wealth, or location. The kinds of grouping practices most suitable for any given system or school will, of course, depend on many factors such as the number of gifted children at various age levels, the number of schools in proximity to each other, and the availability of funds for compensating the factor of reduced teacher-pupil ratios. A sufficient number of "models" are described in the literature so that any school system—those in large, medium, or small cities, and those in suburban or in rural locations—should find help in planning and developing suitable ability grouping procedures. Practically every successful school in this particular has incorporated ability grouping of some kind into its program for the gifted, the forms varying from the massive complex of specialized high schools in New York City to the weekly seminars for general intellectual stimulation in rural Lewis County, New York. Everywhere the salutary effects of ability grouping upon motivation, achievement, and morale of able students is readily noticeable. There is little evidence in the experience of these school systems to substantiate the fears of those who believe that snobbishness and "elitism" are the inevitable by-products of ability grouping. Nor have they found grading of students in special groups to be an unmanageable problem. The collective experience of teachers and administrators who have worked in the midst of this kind of provision indicates that the common arguments against ability grouping are unfounded in fact.

C. ACCELERATION

Acceleration a Neglected Practice. Despite the fact that research evidence supporting acceleration is unquestionably greater than that supporting ability grouping, systematic acceleration appears to be less often a formal feature of present programs for the gifted. Certain types of acceleration, especially advanced placement, are being increasingly practiced and seem to be gaining in acceptance. Others, such as early admission to first grade, early admission to college, and the "non-graded" primary are less frequently encountered. There seem to be several reasons for this widespread failure of the schools to adopt proven methods of acceleration. State laws prevent early admission to the first grade in some communities. Simple ignorance of existing research findings may account for some of the delay in adopting this and other practices where there are no laws to prevent such action.

Schools that deny, or fail to provide acceleration, frequently operate upon the now discredited belief that "social maladjustment" is the inevitable result of even moderate acceleration. It is not unlikely, however, that much of the reluctance to adopt certain techniques of acceleration may be correctly attributed to administrative inertia—unwillingness to sacrifice the convenience of the chronological age "lockstep" for flexible procedures which more adequately reflect known facts about individual differences in ability and total developmental readiness. Doubtless many gifted five year olds are refused admission to school not because they are not ready in every way but because a flexible admission policy would tend to create administrative "headaches" in the form of parental pressures to admit unqualified children. Such sacrifice of sound procedure to considerations of expediency is indefensible.

Acceleration a Desirable Practice. Acceleration, like ability grouping, should be a part of every school program for the gifted. There is nothing startling about this obesrvation, of course. Terman strongly suggested that many able students should be promoted sufficiently to allow them to enter college at age seventeen at the latest, and he claimed that many were ready at sixteen. *Any school system* can make such progress possible for its gifted students and the experience of those school systems which do practice moderate acceleration indicates that the benefits derived accrue not only to the gifted students but to the school as a whole. Teachers have found that a flexible promotion policy can help to reduce the range of variability within the classroom, and at the same time help to lessen the boredom and dissatisfaction of bright students. The anticipated administrative difficulties sometimes do not arise, and in any case they are outweighed by the positive gains derived from elimination of the "lockstep." Finally, and in addition to the benefits of acceleration for students and teachers, it should be pointed out again that society stands to benefit from the earlier entry into productive citizenship of its most able citizens. It seems unlikely that American schools can much longer ignore the compelling logic and impressive empirical evidence that can be marshalled in favor of moderately accelerated progress through the educational system for those who are capable of such progress.

Acceleration Alone not a Program. It is perhaps unnecessary to point out again that acceleration alone, as with grouping, does not constitute an adequate program for the gifted. This fact is not universally comprehended, however. All too frequently administrators unblushingly talk of "programs" that consist solely of advanced placement classes at the twelfth grade level. While advanced placement is in many ways a useful concept, those who offer it as a "program" hold an impoverished concept of special education for the gifted. Acceleration is an administrative procedure which should be a part of every program for the gifted, but it does not obviate other modifications of the standard school routine, especially in the area of curriculum content and organization.

D. INDEPENDENT STUDY

The Promise of Independent Study. It was suggested in the preceding section of this report that the unique characteristics of gifted children make possible a "reversed ratio" of teaching to learning; i.e., gifted students are capable of much learning with relatively little teaching. For this reason independent (individual) study is particularly suited to the needs of gifted students.

The Trump Commission prophesies that in the secondary school of the future even average students will spend perhaps forty per cent of their in-school time in individual study. How much American schools must change in order to make that prediction come true is apparent to observers who have like the SRPEG participants visited in school after school noting the frequency of given practices. Independent study as a formally recognized procedure, i.e., by inclusion into the administrative plan of the school of independent study courses for which credit is given, is quite rare. While it is true, of course, that teachers everywhere often make individual assignments which involve some degree of independent study, it is doubtful that the true potentialities of this method have been generally recognized. Understanding and acceptance of independent study as a salutary administrative procedure will greatly improve educational opportunity for gifted students. It will mark another step in the direction away from the rigid lock-step procedures still characteristic of American education and toward true individualization of education.

E.   OTHER ADMINISTRATIVE CONSIDERATIONS

Articulation. The necessity of assuring continuity in the gifted student's school learning experiences was emphasized in the preceding discussion of curriculum development. Administrative innovations such as ability grouping and acceleration can disrupt established continuity and therefore the administrator must consider the probable consequences for all ensuing grade levels of any administrative decision affecting a level. Problems can arise, for instance, when junior high schools fail to take account of the high level of motivation, achievement, and expectancy of gifted students entering from valid differentiated elementary school programs. Administrative liaison between levels in the system can help to eliminate or reduce such potential problems. Establishing and maintaining continuity in the gifted student's school experience is extremely important. It can be accomplished only by administrators who can keep in focus the whole school program from kindergarten to college.

Financing Special Education for the Gifted. It is impossible to say how much of a school budget should be allocated to the special education of gifted children. Obviously some provisions are far more expensive than others and may be beyond the reach of many school systems at the present time. On the other hand some provisions such as curriculum revision, most forms of acceleration, and many forms of ability grouping need add little or nothing to the budget.

There can be no question that expenditure of funds for special education of gifted students is fully justified. One of the tenets of the democratic philosophy of education is that each student should have an equal opportunity to develop his potentialities to the fullest. On this basis American schools provide special facilities and equipment for those who are athletically talented, musically promising, and for those who are blind, deaf, crippled, or mentally retarded. When the special intellectual capacities of children demand special educational provisions these should be provided whatever the cost.

F.   CONCLUSIONS

The unique abilities and needs of gifted students demand unusual administrative provisions. Traditional patterns of pupil and teacher deployment and of pupil progress through the graded sequence are inadequate. It has been suggested in this report that certain administrative procedures embody process qualities which parallel known characteristics of gifted learners. Acceleration implements the gifted learner's ability to accomplish school tasks more rapidly than average students. Ability grouping recognizes his need to engage in activities with his intellectual equals. Independent study capitalizes on his ability and motivation to learn without direct and constant teacher supervision. All of these administrative practices, plus others familiar and commonly reported to be feasible, should be part of every program for the gifted.

The overriding importance of the teacher in the implementation of programs for the gifted is an inescapable observation on the part of persons pointedly studying class upon class. In many cases programs which are outstanding from the standpoint of planning and organization are subverted in the classrooms by teachers who are unable to relate their teaching procedures to the needs and abilities of gifted students.

Ability grouping of some kind is a feature of practically every program for the gifted that has received any attention in the literature. Acceleration procedures, with the exception of advanced placement, are much less often included. The desirability of independent study as a formal administrative procedure has apparently been very largely overlooked by American schools. Thus even in schools noted for their attempts to provide differential education for the gifted there is evidence of inconsistency in philosophy and planning, poor articulation between schools, reluctance to begin special provisions in the early grades, and other evidences of inertia, lack of knowledge of research findings, and lack of imagination. The sum total of the experience of the Project participants suggests that despite the pioneering efforts of a few school systems there is still much room for improvement with respect to administrative aspects of program development for the gifted in American schools.

The Status of Acceleration or Grade Skipping as an Administrative Practice

PAUL A. WITTY
LAROY W. WILKINS

The problem of providing adequately for individual differences continues to harass educators. One method, widely proclaimed as an educational panacea, illustrates some of the limitations of most current educational palliatives. Homogeneous grouping is a shibboleth which was superficially considered and widely advocated only a decade ago by certain crusaders in education. So enthusiastic did the disciples of the movement become that one wrote that ". . . *the problem of discipline disappears* with the segregation of gifted pupils (1). . . ."

Despite the enthusiasm exhibited even now by some, others feel that the attempts to group pupils homogeneously have been futile, since relatively little has been accomplished in changing method and developing differentiated curricula during the years following the pronouncements and recommendations of Thorndike (2), McCall (3), Terman (4), *et al.*

HOMOGENEOUS GROUPING

The apathy or antagonism of school officials to the practice of grouping children according to ability, and of providing *materials and methods of instruction suited to the abilities of children* is ably illustrated by the summaries of A. H. Turney (5). Turney reviews sixty-six articles and books; he finds few experiments carefully enough carried out to warrant any real evaluation of the practice. Most of the studies "have only added evidence bearing on the nature and extent of individual differences . . . Most of the experimental attacks upon the value of ability grouping have failed to evaluate the chief claim for it, *i.e.*, the possibility of adapting content, method, or time."

Turney feels that there is fairly good evidence that "when efforts are

Reprinted from *Educational Administration and Supervision*, Vol. 19, No. 5 (May, 1933), pp. 321-346. By permission of the senior author and publisher.

made to adapt the means and materials of instruction to the needs of different levels of ability better achievement occurs in homogeneous than in heterogeneous groups." Nevertheless, Turney stresses these facts: Pupils are motivated only a little more to increase their effort when ability grouping is followed than when it is not; there is no acceptable evidence regarding the effect of grouping upon the mental hygiene of the child; inconclusive data point out that while ability grouping reduces *somewhat* the frequency of failure, it does not affect elimination from school. Indeed, most experiments do not report evaluation of *changed content and method* accompanying ability grouping. Those aspects of school work which are peripheral to effective teaching are more often considered. Obviously, "any true evaluation of ability grouping must [therefore] be deferred."

One sees clearly from the summary by Turney that homogeneous grouping, followed by differentiated instruction, has never been given a fair chance; therefore it cannot be evaluated fairly. The experimental work has been characterized by inadequate numbers of subjects, by improper control of factors, and by confused presentation of results and speculation.

Even though one grants, for a moment, that homogeneous grouping is desirable, one must admit that there is much trouble ahead for the administrator who attempts to practice grouping in his school system. First, there is the problem of selection of pupils: What measures shall be used in effecting classification? Second, there is the difficulty of developing differentiated curricula (no little task in itself). Third, there arise the problems of providing for systematic *reclassification* of entire school systems and of periodic reclassification of classes and of particular pupils (since no instruments or series of devices are now available which will identify groups which *remain homogeneous*). Fourth, there exist almost insurmountable difficulties when small school systems attempt homogeneous classification because of small numbers of pupils and consequent troubles in allocating teachers, in balancing teacher load, and so forth. These, among many others, indicate the nature and the scope of administrative problems which attend the practice of homogeneous grouping.

PRESENT-DAY EMPHASIS UPON INDIVIDUAL DIFFERENCES

Nevertheless, the school administrator is obliged to face anew the task of differentiating instruction so as to tax the disparate abilities and interests of school children. Educational workers and theorists have sharply criticized our school leaders for their failure to recognize individual differences, and for their dilatoriness in providing educational reform. Psychologists have done much in recent years in illuminating the nature and needs of deviates in general mental ability. Possibilities for somewhat general change have emerged from the work in experimental schools, wherein much has been accomplished in activity programs based upon dependable motivating drives which attend the maturation of the child. This work, although inchoate, is promising. More directly applicable in practical school administration appears the educational endeavor with, and the curricula for, the extreme mental deviate. The efforts of Goddard, Hollingworth, Wallin, and Terman illuminate to no small degree a direction which public education might well follow in adapting school enterprise to individual needs. Terman's "Genetic Studies of Genius" has done much to reanimate child study and to direct attention sharply to a type of deviate who has received scant attention, one who has had restricted opportunity in the prevailing educational lockstep (6).

INDIVIDUALIZATION OF INSTRUCTION

Some methods have been advanced to care for the gifted child. One method, complete individualization of instruction, originated perhaps by Montessori (and publicized and adapted to particular school situations by Burk, Washburne, and Parkhurst), has been recommended as an appropriate method of giving the much-needed opportunity to the deviate (as well as to all others). The writers will not discuss the merits or the weaknesses of Washburne's plan: Kilpatrick has evaluated the scheme to some extent at least in, "An Attempt at Appraisal (7)." Washburne's own presentation demonstrates the failure of the method to tax the abilities of gifted children (in his study of three groups of elementary school children) (8). The gifted group consisted of children of IQ 123–166; the middle group of IQ 100–122; the low group of IQ 60–100. All of the children were in grades four to seven of the Winnetka schools, and all had been in the system not less than two years. He concludes:

There is a wide range in the rate of progress of gifted children—so wide that the lower half of them actually progress less rapidly than an equal number of children from the top and middle group . . . Gifted children not only differ in average rate of progress, but in the subjects in which they excel. Consequently, any attempt to treat gifted children as a homogeneous group will defeat its own purpose, which is the adaptation of the school work to gifted children (9).

Gifted children, Washburne believes, must not be treated *en masse* but in the light of their varying abilities for progress in the many school subjects. Nevertheless, the results of Washburne's analysis suggest that complete individualization of instruction fails to bring large returns in the way of educational growth for *gifted children*. The results secured by Stedman (10) and by Goddard (11) with classes of gifted children indicate that *general superiority and attainment* usually characterize gifted children. And Gray and Hollingworth (12) show that somewhat *general* superiority characterizes the unsegregated as well as the segregated gifted (if results from the Stanford Achievement Examination *sample* fairly well the general attainment of children in the elementary school).

Data are available also from the work of Spearman, who emphasizes the *g* factor, and from that of Thorndike, who advocates the *c* factor, to show that Burk's and Washburne's concept of specific abilities is doubtless gratuitous when it is used in the manner exemplified in Washburne's statement.

SPECIAL NEEDS OF GIFTED CHILDREN

Particularly essential is it that something more be done for the gifted children than to provide regular class work or to essay "enrichment" of the usual type. Almost all work with the gifted shows that the educational attainment of the gifted (unsegregated) falls far short of sensible expectation based upon calculations from intelligence measures. Terman and DeVoss report:

The average progress quotient for our entire group (gifted children) is 114, which here means that the typical gifted child is accelerated fourteen per cent of his age beyond the norm for the cities in which they attend . . . In mental age, however, they average forty-eight per cent above the norm. The mean educational quotient is 135. *That is, the typical gifted child has already mastered the subject matter thirty-five per cent (of his age) beyond the norm for his age* (13).

The studies of Terman have been corroborated by the work of Witty (14) and by the report of Freeman (15). Freeman studied the data available in 1923 and concluded: ". . . that exceptional ability should be given special treatment is supplemented by the inference that the progress which exceptional children make in school does not comport with their superiority in intellectual capacity. It has usually been found that the subject quotients are somewhat lower than the intelligence quotients in the case of superior pupils (16)."

HOMOGENEOUS GROUPING FOR GIFTED CHILDREN

We have already pointed out that unsegregated gifted children usually exhibit educational attainment somewhat below that which would appear to be consonant with their ability. We refer of course to that small group of deviates who possess unusual ability to a degree such that the term "potential genius" has been used by one worker to describe a section of them. In terms of IQ they have been designated as above 125 (Rugg), above 130 (Hollingworth), or above 140 (Terman). Certainly the education of these children presents a great challenge, as well as an opportunity.

The *Twenty-third Yearbook* of the National Society for the Study of Education, Part I, contained many accounts of the nature and needs of the gifted. The consensus of competent thought expressed therein seemed to favor the forming of special classes to provide enrichment for these children in the elementary school. It will be well, therefore, to ask: What do we know concerning the relative success of gifted children in special classes and of gifted children not in such classes?

Benson compared a class of gifted children with a "regular" class. The average chronological age of the gifted was 8 years, 5 months; of the "regular" 9 years, 8 months. The gifted did the work of three grades in two. The saving in time is evident, but the educational value of the special class was not clearly demonstrated (17). Freeman points out in his summary and conclusions that when pupils are chosen from Benson's two groups, on the basis of IQ and age, they are found to be practically equal in educational attainment (18).

Engel compared the school marks of special class children with those of unselected mentally superior children (19). Despite the similarity of the marks of the two groups, the control (unsegregated) was somewhat higher in five subjects; the special class group in one (English). The small number of cases (only thirty-eight pupils had IQ's above 120) makes the report of doubtful significance. These children in a special group were treated, not in a single class *for gifted*, but in the advanced classes—the upper division of the familiar X.Y.Z. classification.

Cook reported a study of 495 unsegregated and segregated high school pupils who were taking English, history, and geography (20). The experimenter concludes that:

. . . while the mere device of grouping according to ability, from the evidence shown in this investigation, does not show strong enough or consistent enough advantages in any subject to justify the time and work which is required to classify pupils in this manner, it is quite possible that with a special method of instruction, adapted to each of these groups according to its needs, such a plan of grouping might show positive results.

Another report in the *Yearbook* is that of E. L. Moyer (21), who studied classes grouped according to results on the National Intelligence tests. Superior and average pupils seemed to benefit academically in algebra and Latin (not greatly, however); dull pupils did not profit by the segregation.

Several facts should be noted concerning these rather curious experiments:

1. The familiar three-track plan is used in almost every report concerning "segregating" the gifted. This kind of segregation provides for the upper ten to twenty per cent in mental ability or educational achievement. Obviously this is not segregation of the gifted (despite the title of the *Yearbook*).
2. Results are based in several of the studies upon scholastic attainment evidenced only by teachers' marks. Informal tests were used, however, in Cook's study; and the Hotz Algebra, and the Henmon Latin tests were employed in Moyer's study. The inadequacy of all the testing programs is conspicuous.
3. In no experiment were content and method modified greatly. Indeed, no report indicates either the nature or the scope of curricular changes. Attempts to ascertain educational gains following merely upon the adoption of an administrative device must be conceived in a spirit of optimism and ingenuousness.
4. Social adaptation, mental hygiene, and physical development were overlooked or inadequately treated in the reports.

It must be clear therefore, from these reports, that no true evaluation of segregation or of homogeneous grouping for gifted children can follow. Certainly the differences in educational attainment between homogeneously grouped and unselected children of superior ability appear negligible, if the results of these several experiments be considered in composite.

Nevertheless the studies of the gifted published in 1924 probably helped to reanimate child study and to bring about effort to provide more adequately for the gifted.

Several studies of special classes have been published recently. Stedman described the projects and activities provided for the enrichment of the curriculum in an opportunity room for gifted children. Sixteen detailed case histories present vividly the nature of superiority and point to the desirability of individual study of *every gifted child,* as well as to the desirability of enriching experience for each. There is no way to evaluate truly this interesting report, since no data are presented for a control group (unsegregated). The methods employed by Miss Stedman might be utilized with profit with mentally normal children of the same intellectual status as that of the gifted. Stedman's report includes for the most part opportunities which, in our opinion, should be given every normal child (22).

An attempt to provide enrichment for gifted children in a complete city system is set forth by Goddard (23). Most of the special classes in Cleveland include children from three grades: For example, first, second, and third. "Some of the classes have some children with an IQ lower than 120. . . ." The children are, as groups, distinctly superior in mental ability.

Enrichment is that which the teacher does when he has more time (according to Goddard); the teachers of the special classes have more time because the grades are not skipped, and the regular curriculum materials are completed by the gifted in one-half the time usually allotted to them. Goddard does not believe that gifted children should be rushed through the grades, because, ". . . this latter alternative we have found to be detrimental to the child because it brings him into high school and college while he is still too immature to profit by his opportunity." In Cleveland not much of the enrichment is prescribed. "Most of it is left to the judgment of the teacher, the principal, and the supervisor. French, however, is one of the required enrichments." Goddard believes that the enrichment programs *really enrich*. No concrete evidence is brought out to substantiate this view (although Goddard states in his preface that, to make the book useful for teachers, he will leave out statistical treatment of results); in this presentation he depends upon illustrative material to make his point. He gives abundant, interesting material in the form of teacher programs and children's products. This presentation is indicative of *good* teaching. The results, we believe, differ in no essential way from those which accrue from good teaching anywhere.

One bit of statistical evidence is set forth. Results of the Stanford Achievement Examination of bright children in a special high IQ class are compared with those of bright children in other junior high schools not in such classes. Group A (IQ range 111–147), Group B (IQ range 115–150), and Group C (IQ range 115–139) "show only slight differences." Group A is a special class; B and C are made up of unsegregated children. Says Goddard, ". . . although some of the pupils in Groups B and C are good students, for the most part they are lazy and do not apply themselves." No data are introduced, apart from teachers' reports to support this. The book as a whole is a eulogy to the pupils and teachers of the special classes in Cleveland. Since no experimental data are introduced, it is impossible to evaluate the special class work.

Similarly unconvincing, if it is used to propagandize ability grouping, is the excellent work of Hollingworth and her associates with a special class followed for seven years in New York City. This gifted group from Public School 165 had three years of rich and varied experience in a special class. They entered high school very young, since *acceleration and enrichment* characterized their elementary school work. Their adjustment in high school has been carefully surveyed by Lamson (24). Miss Lamson found that the gifted group excelled "the controls" in every item taken into consideration. Noteworthy is it that the gifted participated more frequently than "the controls" in extra-curricular activities, and that, "The gifted group appears not to have suffered in health as a result of entering high school two years younger than the generality of their classmates, on the average." Hollingworth's contribution seems significant: The adjustment of an acceleration-enrichment class, followed through high school, does not appear to have been jeopardized in any measurable way by the special provision made in the elementary school. This study does not, however, support strongly the pleas for "special classes," since no data are presented for comparable gifted children in high school, who had not been in a special class. The desirable adjustment of the *young* children leads one to doubt the undocumented statement of Goddard, to the effect that young gifted children are too immature to adjust to the secondary school environs.

Two studies of the value of enrichment programs for gifted children are included in the report of the White House Conference (25). Woods compared two groups of children: The first was made up of three hundred forty children (Average IQ 136) who had been in special class for gifted children, the second, of three hundred seventy-three children (Average IQ 137) who had not been segregated. Each child in each group was rated by the teacher and by the principal on the following traits: Leadership, self-assurance, desire for attention, seclusiveness, helpfulness, respect for self, respect for school authority, sympathy for misfortune, and independence. The results of the rating are not given, but the experimenter is quoted as saying that segregation into special classes does not affect any of the traits mentioned, since no significant differences were found between the two groups. In this study, as in so many eulogizing enrichment programs, no measurable differences are reported, but "It was the universal opinion of the teachers that the groups that had been segregated for two or three years were superior in general educational performance to the other group (26)."

Danielson, in the other study, reduced to grade points the school marks of two hundred forty-eight children who had been in special classes for gifted children and treated similarly the marks of three hundred eighty-one children of equal IQ who had not been in special classes. "An outstanding advantage" in favor of the children who had been in the special classes is reported.

The recent studies, as well as those reported in the *Twenty-third Yearbook* permit no generalization concerning the efficacy of enrichment or of special classwork for the gifted.

METHODS FOR SELECTING THE GIFTED

The superior advantage of special classes for gifted has clearly not been established. But the advisability of providing in some way for the gifted is brought out clearly by consideration of the education retardation of the gifted (Terman and DeVoss) and by the fact that social gains of no small order may accrue from appropriate education of a great national asset—gifted children. Therefore it becomes apparent that effort should be directed toward discerning appropriate means for selection as well as toward developing sane educational policies for this group.

Rugg emphasized the need of broadening our understanding of talent, recognizing abstract, social, mechanical, and aesthetic types of intelligence; he stressed also the obligation of the school to give opportunity for the development of these different phases of personality (27). The identification of gifted children is, therefore, a difficult and complex task.

Baldwin raised a plea for classification of mentally superior school children; he urged enhancing the concept of "superiority" to posit comprehensive development taking into consideration the complete personality of the child, including physical, mental, social, moral, and educational development, and in addition, he pointed out the necessity of attending to the relative development of special gifts or abilities in any of these types of growth (28).

The relative importance of various indexes in identification and classification of school children is as yet unknown; some significant data are available. That mental age, indicated by the Binet test, is a relatively meagre, inadequate, and incomplete picture of the total unit of personality is generally granted by careful workers in the field of child study. Physiological maturity has been proposed as a major factor in promotion and therefore as an important consideration in classification. Gates has revealed that, when the factor of chronological age is eliminated, physiological age as measured by the development of the wrist bones, yields a coefficient of correlation with mental age so low as to make this measurement of no value in classifying school children.

Mere physical status or maturity, then, however adequately measured, apparently does by no means gauge mental, educational, social, or emotional maturity satisfactorily. Classification of pupils alike in general physical status will not result in a satisfactory classification on any other basis. They will be alike physically provided enough physical measurements are made, but they may be quite unlike in mental, social, scholastic, and emotional maturity (29).

Social maturity has been advanced also as an important consideration in identification and classification of the superior child. The knowledge of the relationship between social maturity and success in school is scant. One may reasonably assume that desirable social adjustments are conditioned to a considerable degree by mental development and therefore bear some relationship to mental age. By "social intelligence" some mean the ability to "get on" with one's fellows. The basis of this ability, it seems reasonable to suppose, lies in the capacity to foresee consequences of acts, and in the varied responses which facilitate quick and suitable adjustment. This description includes reactions similar to those which are grouped under the rubric: abstract intelligence (adaptation). The assumption that social adjustments are dependent in some measure upon general *mental ability* posits accelerated growth in social adjustments with rapid growth in mental age (30). There is some evidence to support this. Very dull children play with children younger in chronological age than they, and superior children choose as their companions children older than they. Nevertheless, the efforts to measure social intelligence or social adaptability have proved rather unsuccessful (31). Until reliable, quantitative measures possessing some validity are available, the administrator must rely primarily upon his judgment and upon that of teachers for estimating this very significant type of growth (32). Obvious is it, therefore, that precise measures of social intelligence can not be employed at the present time in classifying school children.

The general all-around adjustment of gifted children is intimately associated with variabilities in physical and social growth. It has been shown that gifted children are *superior* to children of their own ages in physical maturity. And social maturity may be inferred to depend in part upon physical growth as well as upon mental maturity.

PEDAGOGICAL ACCELERATION—CONSIDERED AND RECOMMENDED

How, then, can we best provide for variation in the physical and in the social maturity of the gifted? May it not be that curricular adjustments to develop social adaptability and physical adjustment are *at present* most successfully wrought in supplementary and extracurricular activities: Therefore measures of social adjustment and physical growth may not affect directly our basic classification for purposes of classroom instruction? Adjustments in play groups and in gymnastic work might accomplish the necessary aims in providing salutary social and physical development. "The class organized for work in the three R's and other scholastic work need not be kept intact for athletic, social, mechanical, artistic, and other pursuits. For each activity, an appropriate group may be sifted from several scholastic levels (33)."

After recognizing and considering the difficulties in obtaining valid indexes for selecting gifted children, and after thinking carefully regarding the difficulties in modifying curricula, Freeman defends acceleration as a general educational policy. He emphasizes the fact that acceleration as a means of adjustment has advantages not generally accredited to it; that grade skipping as a systematic practice is not as detrimental as we have been inclined to think. He states:

We have in the past emphasized the distinction between acceleration and enrichment. In so doing we have made a false distinction. The real distinction is between the adjustment which merely aims at saving time and the adjustment which aims at securing for the gifted an opportunity to do work at a higher intellectual level. We have further assumed that enrichment implies keeping the pupil engaged in work in which the pupil of average classification of the same age is engaged. This assumption is, I believe, incorrect. Acceleration actually provides enrichment. The work of the advanced grades is intellectually superior because the method which is pursued and the content are superior to those of the lower grades. From the point of view of intellectual adjustment, then, acceleration accomplishes both the saving of time and the enrichment of the instruction. The difficulties with this mode of adjustment are not of an intellectual nature but of a social nature. These difficulties may be met by proper forms of organization and they are being progressively diminished by the very increase in the frequency of acceleration itself (34).

Gates also has made a suggestion similar in character to that quoted above. These suggestions should be given serious consideration since we now have fairly accurate and reliable devices for estimating mental and educational status; therefore we can identify with some precision the gifted, promising youth. Indeed, one writer states: "The new knowledge thus accumulated, and the new tests invented in the twentieth century, afford us the modern approach to the study of the gifted. We can now study gifted children and learn eventually all we care to know about extraordinarily able persons, their education, and their place in civilization (35)." Of course Hollingworth's statement reflects unusual optimism; nevertheless we agree with her in one respect: Gifted children can be *identified* with a considerable degree of accuracy. Decision concerning their future must await the presentation of empirical evidence resulting from long-continued genetic studies. After identification of the deviates has occurred the problem arises: What shall be the direction of our efforts in providing for them? One method, acceleration, has been proposed *as a necessary expedient,* by Gates and by Freeman. Freeman has recommended the method in taxing the abilities of academically superior children as well as of gifted children.

Unequivocal data are not available concerning the relationship of pedagogical acceleration to educational adjustment, to social development, and to physical well-being. It is expedient therefore that we examine critically those studies which have already been made of under-age and accelerated school children. The writers will review many experimental studies, and they will attempt therefrom to arrive at an evaluation of pedagogical acceleration both as a general practice and as a means of caring for superior children. This is one way of ascertaining the validity of the common-sense suggestions of Freeman and of Gates.

STUDIES OF PEDAGOGICAL ACCELERATION AMONG ELEMENTARY AND JUNIOR HIGH SCHOOL CHILDREN

One of the pioneer studies was that of E. E. Jones in 1912 (36). Jones studied two hundred fifty-seven pedagogically accelerated children, using a questionnaire to secure teacher ratings of various abilities and traits. These ratings pointed clearly to the superiority of precocious children in the several abilities and traits. Since the study was highly subjective, and since no control group was utilized, it is impossible to evaluate it and to estimate its reliability.

In Milton, Massachusetts, children are admitted to the kindergarten and to the first grade when their mental ages suffice. Of two hundred fifty-eight children, whose chronological ages at admittance were below the average age at which children are usually admitted, sixty-two per cent were in the upper half of their classes (according to teachers' judgments and marks), and thirty-three per cent were in the first quarter of their classes, while only twelve per cent were in the lowest quarter of their classes. Of those in the lowest quartile two-thirds had been in school less than four months. Educational adjustment of the children was increasingly satisfactory as length of residence in school increased. Of those in school a year or more, only seven and one-half per cent were in the lowest quarter of their classes. These under-age children had been admitted over a period of five years. "These findings reveal that under-age children are successful to a degree somewhat above the average for their school grade, and that their ability to excel becomes more noticeable as they progress through the grades (37)."

Lincoln carried on an extended experiment in Massachusetts to determine the scholastic achievements of children who were admitted at ages younger than school regulations permitted (38). Children too young to enter the first grade were given a mental test and those whose mental age rating indicated sufficient mental ability to carry the work were admitted. Progress was checked at the end of the first grade, and at the end of the third and fourth grades, and at the end of the seventh and eighth grades. Of seventy-two children, four had dropped behind (one because of parents' wishes, a second because of protracted illness, a third because of attending only sixty-nine and one-half days of one year, and the fourth at the parents' insistence and against the advice of principal and teacher). The other children were distinctly superior: "The findings of the three studies which have been made on the later performance of these under-aged children all point to the conclusion that children admitted on the basis of mental age are not only able to maintain their scholastic accomplishment on equal terms with their classmates, but are decidedly superior in some phases of the work."

A recent study of elementary school pupils is reported by McElwee (39). In Public School 208, Brooklyn, teachers of the second, third, and fourth grades were asked to check a miscellany of traits indicating which of the traits described each pupil in their classes. Groups of one hundred accelerated, one hundred regularly promoted, and one hundred retarded children were selected from the entire enrollment in these grades. There were fifty boys and fifty girls in each group: Equal amounts of acceleration for boys and for girls had occurred. A child was designated "retarded," if he had been left back one or more terms. The amount of retardation ranged from one to five terms. An accelerated child was one who had been doubly promoted one or more terms: The range was one to three terms.

Since seven of the fourteen traits were deemed desirable and seven undesirable, McElwee assumed that desirable and undesirable adjustment is revealed merely by reference to the frequency with which traits were checked for the children in the three groups. The accelerated children possessed all of the desirable traits (with the exception of attentiveness) to a greater degree, and all the undesirable traits to a smaller degree than did the other groups.

Case studies of three accelerated children are given by Dougherty, who reports that the academic attainment and general physical and social status of the accelerates were *improved* after grade skipping had occurred (40). The small number of cases renders this report of little value in an attempt at evaluation of acceleration. Nevertheless, the careful case study technique probably insures greater validity than do the methods usually employed in preparing reports concerning acceleration.

Gist has stated the case for increased acceleration from studies made in Seattle (41). "At the B. F. Day School of Seattle, Washington, as high a percentage of the total school population as ten may be promoted in a single year." (This means extra promotion.) Gist does not emphasize the educational implications, but cites the tremendous saving to the community when the apt pupil is allowed to progress through the school at a rapid rate. Ayres pointed out the same fact years ago in an early Russell Sage pamphlet (42), when he estimated that some school systems could save eleven per cent of school expenses by accelerating certain pupils whose academic records warranted grade-skipping.

Candee describes the selection of pupils for the rapid advancement classes of New York City junior high schools (43). The New York school system provides "that any child whose school record warrants it, at the time he enters junior high school, may be recommended by the principal of the elementary school which he is leaving for rapid work . . . Fifteen per cent of the children in the system are supposed to carry this double program."

Candee shows the folly of the supposition that every school will have fifteen per cent of its pupils capable of acceleration and suggests the use of more thorough and more reliable mental tests to supplement teachers' judgments in selecting pupils for the rapid advancement classes.

At the Whittier School, Denver, Colorado, bright pupils are accelerated by being taught in a special room for one-half semester until they have caught up with the class immediately above (44). They then join this class. Pupils are chosen for acceleration on the basis of (1) class standing, (2) mental age (Stanford-Binet), (3) effort, (4) physical condition. The originator of this plan warns that chronological age is an unreliable factor for consideration when promoting a child—for it accelerates the subnormal and retards the gifted. "Experience in this room has proved that a child is capable of acceleration until he has reached the grade corresponding to his mental age (45)." He concludes,

This room has been run on this plan continuously for the past twelve years and has demonstrated its usefulness in the lives of nearly one thousand different children, by putting them creditably through the grades from a half to two years earlier than they otherwise would have been. Many of these children have gone on through high school and college, never missing a single promotion throughout their school career (46).

In Fond du Lac, Wisconsin, a study was made of a selected group which finished the seventh and eighth grades in one year. This group was compared with another group which utilized the conventional two years. Both groups demonstrated conspicuously similar educational attainment in the ninth grade. The author of this report concludes that acceleration should be practiced after the probable ages and grades when children are to leave school are carefully considered. If children's future plans show clearly that they are to enter professional schools, the practice is recommended (47).

Moeser reports certain characteristics of one hundred most accelerated pupils in the eighth and ninth grades of a junior high school in East St. Louis, Illinois (48). This experiment seems to be one of the most carefully carried out in the entire literature. From the thirty youngest boys and the thirty youngest girls in each grade were selected the fifty boys and the fifty girls with the highest progress quotients. Scholastic achievement was reckoned by comparing the average of the school marks of the accelerated group with the average of the school marks of a carefully selected control group (of unaccelerated pupils). In the semester grades of all the pupils in the accelerated group there were only three failing marks. The average grade for the accelerates was 86.37; the average grade for the non-accelerates was 82.23. (This difference is statistically significant.) On the Stanford Achievement Examination (Form V) EQ's of the accelerated pupils ranged from 86 to 132 (with a mean of 110.48, SD of 10.46). Of seventeen pupils who had EQ's below 100, more than half also had IQ's below 100. Apparently some of these pupils were accelerated despite low intelligence quotients. All were achieving close to their capacities, if AQ is any index of a pupil's working up to capacity. A seven point rating scale was used to reveal the degree of social adjustment. Sixty-seven of the pupils were rated good or superior. The accelerated pupils rated above average in industry, self-confidence, coöperation, dependability, ambition, honesty, perseverance; but rated below average in leadership and originality. In the eighth grade the accelerated pupils read almost twice as much as did the non-accelerates. Accelerates showed a greater versatility of interest in activities outside of school. When age and height were taken into account, the accelerates were closer to the norms in weight than were ordinary pupils. "Acceleration, therefore, appears to maintain these junior high school children on a relatively high level of scholastic achievement, to result in satisfactory social adjustments, and to be favorable to many social activities. It appears also to have no injurious effect upon the child physically. Accelerated pupils are likely to be the superior pupils in their school (49)."

STUDIES OF ACCELERATED PUPILS IN THE SECONDARY SCHOOL

Alltucker studied the one hundred thirty-five most accelerated children in the senior high school in Berkeley, California (50). No child was found to be below average in IQ and only eight per cent were average. Over sixty-eight per cent were distinctly above average, ranging in IQ from 115–154. The scholarship was clearly superior among the accelerates: Seventy-seven per cent were designated as thoroughly satisfactory or excellent in this respect (51).

Interesting is Alltucker's study of the social adjustment of these young children. Faculty advisers (teachers) rated students in leadership, stated attitudes of other students toward them, and estimated whether these students were socially adapted to the groups with which they were associated. Alltucker's comment concerning leadership follows: "(1) The percentage of pedagogically accelerated girls who are above average is approximately twice as great as the percentage of pedagogically accelerated boys who are above average; (2) the percentage of boys rating below average is approximately the same as the percentage of girls rating above average; (3) the ratings for both boys and girls give a fairly normal curve of distribution."

The teachers report that, from their observation of the children, over seventy-five per cent of the accelerates are liked or admired by their fellow students; that most (seventy-eight per cent) are "socially adapted"; that over twenty-seven per cent obtain unusual recognition in special appointments (class officers and other appointments). The accelerated child obtains recognition in being selected as a class officer more frequently than the non-accelerated. One notable exception occurs: That special "plum," class president, usually goes to that conspicuous athlete, the football captain. For this position, the accelerated child obviously has no chance because of physical immaturity. Nevertheless, the accelerate obtains recognition in every other phase of school and extra-school life more frequently than the non-accelerate.

C. H. Sackett, at the Blewett junior high school of St. Louis, Missouri, compared the success of pupils who had completed a three-year course in two years with that of pupils who had spent three years in the same junior high school. Both groups were pupils of superior intelligence. He found that the differences in their scholastic achievements were negligible, although the accelerated group was eight months younger in chronological age, and seven points lower in intelligence quotients than the non-accelerated group. He reports also that the accelerates are more likely to be successful in the senior high school if they are selected on the basis of mental, social and physical qualities rather than if they are selected solely because of mental superiority. This group selected for concentrated work during the junior high school did hold its own scholastically in senior high school—even when they were compared with older children of similar IQ. The method of grouping was presented by Ryan in 1923 (52); *The School Review* referred to Sackett's study in 1927 (53), and Sackett reported further progress in 1929 (54).

STUDIES OF ACCELERATED PUPILS IN COLLEGE (55)

An experiment with four hundred ninety-one students who entered college at seventeen and one-half years of age or younger is reported by Silverman and Jones (56). The experimenters collected the views of these students about things such as difficulties in adjusting to the college situation, scholastic demands, and social life. They were asked whether they would have preferred to enter college later in life, and if so what they would have liked to do with the time saved. In general, those who entered college late thought that others should not enter early. About seven per cent of the early entrants would have preferred to spend more time in the elementary school. Seventeen per cent would have been amenable to devoting much more time to high school. About nine per cent indicated that more time spent in junior college would have been desirable. Those remaining (sixty-seven per cent) were satisfied with the time allotment given to college preparation.

Four to seven per cent felt that because of their age, they were at a disadvantage in social life, in opportunities for leadership, and in athletics. Of older college entrants only two to four per cent reported this. One-third of those who entered college at seventeen or younger felt they were at a disadvantage in discussions of social, economic, sociological, and philosophical problems, whereas only one-sixth of older groups reported a consciousness of such a disadvantage. In educational achievement the young students show no inferiority upon an extensive test; the scores of young students were superior to those of older ones on the College Achievement Test.

This experiment suffers from the obvious limitations of the questionnaire, but it appears to indicate rather clearly that young college students are well-adjusted educationally, and they are happy socially. The acceleration has not been attended by feelings of inferiority or their opposite.

Dean Holmes studied the academic records of 5769 Harvard students (57). The frequency of maladjustment among the youngest men was ascertained by study of the scholarship records, and by the frequency of disciplinary difficulties.

The college gets better average results, with less friction, from younger men than from older men (58).

Youth in itself is not an active cause, which will operate independently to produce honor men. Good students come to college young because they are brilliant; they are not brilliant because they come to college young . . . But negatively the figures give us a very valuable guarantee. They prove that youth, in itself considered, is no bar to a creditable college career. They prove that college conditions do not put young men to a fatal disadvantage (59).

Dean Holmes' study, while dealing principally with the fact that the youngest men in college cause the dean's office no trouble, brings out the fact that, other things being equal, the younger a man enters Harvard the more likelihood he has of graduating *cum laude, magna cum laude,* or *maxima cum laude.*

EXTENT OF PROVISION FOR THE GIFTED

Many studies have been made of the extent to which gifted children are identified, and of the frequency with which differentiated instruction is employed to challenge their abilities. Witmer, in 1919 concluded that a negligible amount of provision was made (60) in the *Twenty-third Yearbook* Baldwin stated that "the schools of the country at large have hardly made a beginning in their provisions for gifted children (61)"; and in 1932, Kramer (62) reported that even though gifted children be segregated for instructional purposes, the curriculum usually remains the same, the basic textbooks are employed, and enrichment takes the form generally of added work of the same type as that followed by children in the regular classes. Noticeable indeed in Kramer's report is the fact that special classes for gifted children are now found only in a few large cities.

HAS ACCELERATION BEEN GIVEN A FAIR TRIAL?

Almost every educator has *an opinion* about the value of acceleration, but in an attempt at evaluation, one must turn to experimental studies which employed relatively small groups, since extremely small frequencies of acceleration are generally found; this fact precludes large-scale evaluation. At this point, mention should be made of the apparent success of *seven year elementary schools* (replacing the eight year schedule) which save time for all children. Especial notice should be made of the progress of the Kansas City, Missouri, schools. Superintendent George Melcher's evaluations seem to point to the efficacy of this work. This type of reorganization, while saving time and money, does not necessarily provide special adjustment for the child whose mental or educational growth is decidedly accelerated.

There is without doubt some small gain for the gifted child who, with others, has been allowed to complete the eight-year program in seven years. There is, however, no evidence to lead to the supposition that, in the school systems (notably in the South) where the elementary school period is shortened, the deviates are given special opportunity, and that rapid advancement classes or enrichment classes are found with greater frequency than in communities having the conventional eight-year elementary school program. Nevertheless, the White House Conference report, in its conclusions relating to the education of gifted children includes these statements:

1. Rapid promotion has been more or less the policy of our schools for sixty years, and has never solved the problem of the so-called gifted child;
2. Special classes for rapid progress have been more or less in vogue since 1900, and in thirty years have never solved the problem of the gifted child, nor made sufficient appeal to educators to produce any important development in them (63).

Several criticisms of these conclusions might be made:

Our present concept of the *gifted child* is not something which goes back sixty years. We had no way accurately to identify the gifted child until reliable intelligence tests enabled us to do so. These tests have been developed and used during the twentieth century.

The statement that rapid promotion has been *"more or less"* the policy of our schools could be emended to read simply "less." Examinations of pertinent records reveal no emphasis on general acceleration policies in the past. Scrutiny of surveys beginning with the Cleveland survey in 1916 and continuing on to include the Chicago survey of 1932, shows that acceleration has been tried out only infrequently and probably in many instances with a few pupils who were too bright or too difficult for the teacher to handle. Estimates of under-ageness and of rapid progress are none too reliable, but they certainly do not support strongly the conclusions drawn by the White House Conference. One real attempt to set up standards in this regard has been made recently by Mort and Featherstone (64). An examination of these national figures shows the inaccuracy of the conference's report. Differences exist in the amount of acceleration practiced in schools which follow exclusively the annual promotion practice as well as in schools which promote semi-annually. In the sixth grade (the last grade of the elementary school) only *four* per cent of the pupils in annual promotion schools are accelerated; in semi-annual promotion schools only 7.9 per cent are accelerated. Evidently acceleration is not as widely practiced in the elementary school as the conference workers thought! Of pupils completing ninth grade (the last grade of the junior high school) only 2.1 per cent in annual promotion schools make rapid progress; only two per cent of those in schools promoting semi-annually make rapid progress. And this in spite of the fact that one of the reasons for the institution of the junior high school was the saving of time for the bright pupil! In the twelfth grade (the last grade of the senior high school) 1.7 per cent of the pupils in annual promotion schools make rapid progress; 8.9 per cent of those in schools promoting semi-annually make rapid progress. Interesting data on the incidence of under-ageness (as distinguished from rapid progress) are contained in the recent publication by Mort and Featherstone.

The only conclusion to be drawn from these data is that acceleration as a device for taking care of the gifted has not yet been adequately tried. Only a few studies are reported (most are redacted in this report) and every one of these seems to indicate that acceleration, when practiced wisely—that is, when a sufficient number of factors (65) is taken into consideration, does alleviate somewhat the problem of the gifted child.

COMMENTS

This summary contains a somewhat impartial overview of experiments dealing with acceleration in the elementary and secondary schools, and in college. The experiments are fragmentary, and, in many instances, they are poorly conceived, inadequately controlled, and vaguely reported.

Nevertheless, most reports show clearly that acceleration, when practiced, is associated with desirable adjustment in *all* types of development for which data have been assembled. A truly scientific evaluation of acceleration as a general educational procedure must await the presentation of more valid data, and we must at present rely for practice in part upon a theoretical subjective estimate.

Homogeneous grouping may also be defended by theoretical considerations. This has been done innumerable times. The latest defense which has come to our attention is that of A. S. Otis who asserts, among other things, that success in work at one's mental level is a salutary preparation for later living, and that, where ability grouping prevails, the curriculum is almost automatically modified (66). The first of these points is an argument which can be made for the value of acceleration as well as for the worth of special classes. Perhaps the fact that children are permitted to work for tangible goals which require at least a modicum of intellectual competition and an expenditure of intense effort is one of the reasons for the general success of accelerates. Otis' second point is not corroborated by the review of A. H. Turney, nor by the analysis of the literature herein reported.

We have directed our attention in this report particularly to the affect of acceleration upon the gifted child in the light of our steadily increasing amount of data regarding gifted children, and in terms of the problem of *educational* adjustment which the gifted present.

More widespread adoption of acceleration in dealing with the gifted seems desirable since the gifted child is typically somewhat above the average in physical development and in general health. It seems also that we must, at present, rely upon acceleration primarily in meeting the problem of classification of the gifted for the following reasons:

1. The frequency of the gifted child is not sufficiently large in sparsely populated districts to permit the formation of special classes.
2. Limitations in administrative facilities in many schools present insurmountable obstacles to the formation of special classes. Particularly vital from an administrative point of view is the problem of providing adequately trained teachers for special classes.
3. Where organization is successfully wrought in the grades, there remains the problem of reorganizing junior and senior high school curricula. The detailed development of a workable scheme requires time, and demands administrative measures which are impossible in many schools.

More general adoption of acceleration is urged also as a feasible measure in a sane attempt to care more adequately for the mentally and educationally superior child who is superior to the average but who is not "gifted." Acceleration should be essayed only after a careful study has been made of each child. This should include estimates of physical, mental, and educational growth, and the emotional stability and the social maturity of the child should be evaluated to the best of our ability. Class placement should be determined primarily, however, by the mental and educational maturity of the child. Athletic and social activities might well be taken care of by sifting from several scholastic levels groups to participate in these activities. This latter type of adjustment appears necessary; however, the increase in the frequency of acceleration will alleviate somewhat the problem of making adjustments for the social-physical needs of young children, since widespread adoption of acceleration will automatically increase the frequencies of young children in various grades. Thus, the young bright child will have, in his own class, companions of similar chronological age and possibly of similar social development.

This recommendation favoring widespread use of pedagogical acceleration is made after careful consideration has been given to the claims for the value of homogeneous grouping. The failure of homogeneous grouping thus far to justify the claims made for it arises in part from the lack of agreement over the validity (and consequent selection) of devices to provide homogeneity. The apparent failure of the classes actually established is to be attributed no doubt in large measure to the neglect or to the inability of educators: To provide workable methods for the segregated, to modify curricula, and to define and practice enrichment.

True indeed is it that enrichment classes have never been given a fair chance. Let us have some experimentation to disclose the true status of the practice when method and curricula are altered appreciably. In the meantime, the schools must (should) go on. Let us recognize the integrity of every child's personality, and try to provide sensibly for his best interests. Acceleration has proved a rather effective aid in taking care of superior students in the elementary school, and in the secondary school. From the data at hand, it appears that most students who have been accelerated in the elementary and secondary schools exhibit no maladjustment during their college or university careers. Unmistakable and general have been the educational gains for many children who have been accelerated. Results and theory therefore seem to favor our recommendation.

REFERENCES AND NOTES

1. Davis, Helen, *Twenty-third Yearbook*, National Society for the Study of Education, Part I, p. 134.
2. Thorndike, E. L., *Twenty-first Yearbook*, National Society for the Study of Education, pp. 1-9.
3. McCall, Wm. A., "How to Measure in Education," pp. 19-66.
4. Terman, L. M., "The Measurement of Intelligence," pp. 78-104.
5. Turney, A. H., The Status of Ability Grouping, *Educational Administration and Supervision*, Vol. XVII, 1931, pp. 21-42, 110-127.
6. Terman, L. M. and others, "Genetic Studies of Genius," Volumes I and III. Stanford University Press, 1925 and 1931.
7. *Twenty-fourth Yearbook*, National Society for the Study of Education, Part II, pp. 273-286.
8. Washburne, C., *Twenty-third Yearbook*, National Society for the Study of Education, Part I, pp. 247-261.
9. Washburne, C., *Op. cit.*, p. 260.
10. Stedman, L. M., "Education of Gifted Children." New York: World Book Co., 1924.

11. Goddard, H. H., "School Training of Gifted Children." New York: World Book Co., 1928.

12. Gray, Howard A. and Hollingworth, L. S., The Achievement of Gifted Children Enrolled and Not Enrolled in Special Opportunity Classes. *Journal of Educational Research*, Vol. XXIV, Nov., 1931, pp. 255-261.

13. Terman, L. M. and DeVoss, J. C., The Educational Achievements of Gifted Children. *Twenty-third Yearbook*, National Society for the Study of Education, Part I, pp. 169-184, especially pages 169-170.

14. Witty, P. A., A Study of 100 Gifted Children. *Bulletin of the School of Education*. University of Kansas, Lawrence, Kansas, 1930, p. 42.

15. Freeman, F. N., *Twenty-third Yearbook*, National Society for the Study of Education, Part I, p. 209.

16. *Ibid.*, p. 213.

17. Benson, J. R., A Comparison of Selected Groups with Mixed Classes. *Twenty-third Yearbook*, National Society for the Study of Education, pp. 290-296.

18. Freeman, F. N., *Twenty-third Yearbook*, pp. 214-215.

19. Engel, A. M., Comparison of Class Ratings of Pupils in Special Advanced Classes with Accelerated Pupils in Regular Classes in the Detroit Public Schools. *Twenty-third Yearbook*, pp. 297-301.

20. Cook, R. R., A Study of the Results of Homogeneous Grouping of Abilities in High School Classes. *Twenty-third Yearbook*, pp. 302-312.

21. Moyer, E. L., A Study of the Effects of Classification by Intelligence Tests. *Twenty-third Yearbook*, pp. 313-322.

22. Stedman, L. M., "Education of Gifted Children." New York: World Book Co., 1924, pp. viii-192.

23. Goddard, H. H., "School Training of Gifted Children." New York: World Book Co., 1928, pp. x-226.

24. Lamson, E. E., "A Study of Young Gifted Children in High School." Bureau of Publications, Teachers College, Columbia University, New York, 1930.

25. White House Conference on Child Health and Protection, Section III. Education and Training. "Special Education: The Handicapped and the Gifted." New York: Century, 1931, pp. 546-548.

26. *Ibid.*, p. 547.

27. Rugg, H. O., The Curriculum for Gifted Children. *Twenty-third Yearbook*, National Society for the Study of Education. Part I, pp. 91-121.

28. Baldwin, B. T., Methods of Selecting Superior or Gifted Children. *Twenty-third Yearbook*, National Society for the Study of Education, Part I, pp. 25-47.

29. Gates, A. I., The Nature and Educational Significance of Physical Status and of Mental, Physiological, Social, and Emotional Maturity. *Journal of Educational Psychology*, Vol. XV, 1924, pp. 329-358. Especially p. 352.

30. Coefficients of correlation between MA and sociability or social adjustment are usually very low, often insignificant; however, the various measures of social development are occasionally specious, usually unreliable.

31. For a summary see Witty, P. A., The Measurement of Sociability. *Religious Education*, Vol. XXVII, March, 1932, pp. 255-260.

32. Certainly, the cautious will refrain from using the present array of so-called character tests until evidence concerning the validity of these measures is presented.

33. Gates, A. I., *Op. cit.*, p. 358.

34. Freeman, F. N., The Treatment of the Gifted Child in the Light of Sci-

entific Evidence. *Elementary School Journal*, Vol. XXIV, May, 1924, pp. 652-661.

35. Hollingworth, L. S., "Gifted Children: Their Nature and Nurture," p. 40.
36. Jones, E. E., "Suggestions from Cases of Unusually Rapid or Irregular Progress in Public Schools." *Proceedings* of the National Education Association for 1912, pp. 640-645.
37. Study of the Progress of Under-age Pupils at Milton, Massachusetts. *American School Board Journal*, Vol. LXXXIII, November, 1931, pp. 34.
38. Lincoln, Edward A., The Later Performance of Under-aged Children Admitted to School on the Basis of Mental Age. *Journal of Educational Research*, Vol. XIX, January, 1929, pp. 22-30.
39. McElwee, E. W., A Comparison of the Personality Traits of 300 Accelerated, Normal, and Retarded Children. *Journal of Educational Research*, Vol. XXVI, September, 1932, pp. 31-34.
40. Dougherty, M. L., School Acceleration. *The Educational Clinic of the Department of Education*, The Johns Hopkins University, pp. 42-51.
41. Gist, A. S., Acceleration of Pupils. *School and Society*, Vol. V, January 27, 1917, pp. 116-118.
42. Ayres, L. P., Money Cost of Repetition versus the Money Saving through Acceleration. *Division of Education*, Russell Sage Foundation, Bulletin No. 111.
43. Candee, Beatrice, The Use of Tests in the Selection of Pupils for Rapid Advancement. *Psychological Clinic*, Vol. XIX, December, 1930, pp. 210-213.
44. Zirkle, H. W., Taking Care of the Gifted Child. *Bulletin* of the Department of Elementary School Principals. *Eighth Yearbook* (reprint of the *first yearbook*), pp. 429-434.
45. *Ibid.*, p. 430.
46. *Ibid.*, p. 434.
47. Unzicker, S. P., A Study of Accelerates in the Junior High School. *School Review*, Vol. XL, May, 1932, pp. 346-356.
48. Moeser, G., "A Study of One Hundred Accelerated Pupils in a Junior High School." Unpublished master's thesis. Northwestern University, 1932.
49. Moeser, G., *Op. cit.*, p. 26.
50. Out of eighteen hundred students at Berkeley, California one hundred thirty-five were accelerated as follows:

Amount of acceleration		Per cent
Nine months to	eleven months	38.5
One year to	one year six months	43.7
One year seven months to	two years	12.6
Two years one month to	two years nine months	5.2

51. Alltucker, M. M., Is the Pedagogically Accelerated Child a Misfit in School? *School Review*, Vol. XXXII, March, 1924, pp. 193-202.
52. Ryan, H. H., Grouping Pupils for Acceleration. *Elementary School Journal*, Vol. XXIV, September, 1923, pp. 50-53.
53. *School Review*, Vol. XXXV, March, 1927, pp. 170-172.
54. Sackett, C. H., The Later Success of Accelerated Pupils. *Junior-Senior High School Clearing House*, Vol. IV, September, 1929, pp. 22-27.

55. For a critical review of studies not mentioned here see Gray, H. A., "Some Factors in the Undergraduate Careers of Young College Students." Teachers College, Columbia University, Contributions to Education No. 437.
56. Silverman, Y., and Jones, Vernon, A Study of Early Entrance to College. *The Journal of Educational Psychology*, Vol. XXIII, January, 1932, pp. 58-72.
57. Holmes, H. W., Youth and the Dean: The Relation Between Academic Discipline, Scholarship, and Age of Entrance to College. *Harvard Graduates Magazine*, Vol. CXXI, June, 1913, pp. 599-610.
58. *Ibid.*, p. 604.
59. *Ibid.*, p. 607.
60. Witmer, L., The Training of Very Bright Children. *Psychological Clinic*, Vol. XIII, December, 1919, pp. 88-96.
61. Baldwin, B. T., *Op. cit.*, p. 28.
62. Kramer, H. J., "Present Practices in Training for Gifted Children in Selected Cities of the United States." Master's thesis, School of Education, Northwestern University, 1932.
63. Mort, P. R. and Featherstone, W. B., "Entrance and Promotion Practices in City School Systems: Standards and Accounting Procedures." Bureau of Publications, Teachers College, Columbia University, 1932.
64. "White House Conference on Child Health and Protection. Section III, Education and Training: Special Education: The Handicapped and the Gifted." New York: Century, p. 548.
65. Such as health, intelligence, achievement, social maturity, emotional stability, and whether the intervening work which is to be skipped will be adequately covered.
66. Otis, A. S., Ability Grouping. *School and Society*, Vol. XXXVI, July 23, 1932, pp. 116-118.

A New Look at "Acceleration"

SIDNEY L. PRESSEY

A few years ago, acceleration was commonly viewed with distrust by teachers and school administrators, but now attitudes are changing and for reasons to be looked at shortly. As a recent NEA report has stated, "The research testimony as to the advantages of acceleration is weighty, consistent, and continuous over several decades" (1). But first, *what is acceleration?* It is going through an educational program more rapidly, or at a younger age, than is usual for the average child. That child starts school at the age of six, progresses a grade each year, and so enters the

Reprinted from *Acceleration and the Gifted* (Columbus, Ohio: Ohio State Department of Education, 1963), pp. 1-4. By permission of the author and publisher.

seventh grade at the age of twelve. If a child enters at the age of five or completes the first six grades in five years so as to enter the seventh grade at the age of eleven, he might be considered a bit accelerated.

However, some children are already reading and seem ready for the first grade at five; and their number is probably increasing because more homes now have favorable conditions for growth, and also much reading matter and both radio and television to stimulate abilities and the beginnings of reading. And some children develop mentally, physically and socially, sufficiently more rapidly than the average child during the elementary school period, that it is in accord with their real rate of growth that they cover the first six grades in five years. To hold them back to the rate of the average child would be really to retard them.

Why not "keep them with their age group" but give them an "enriched" program? But many such children, really physically and socially as well as intellectually more mature than children of their own chronological age, prefer to play with older children. The best way to enrich their education may be to let them go ahead. Another consideration is becoming increasingly important for bright children. Most of them should go on to college; and a majority of the graduates of most colleges now go on to some more advanced work—to medical school or law school or some other type of graduate training and may not finish their education until they are near thirty or over (9). If they can somewhere along the line "accelerate" a little, they may complete their educations and begin their careers a little earlier—with less postponement of marriage and establishment in adult life. An able young physician may begin practice at 29 instead of 30 because he was allowed to complete the first six grades in five years!

Is there not, however, risk of social maladjustment in putting a young child in with a group of older children? Probably every teacher has known an instance where such an accelerate became shy and withdrawn and the older pupils resented his being moved in with them. Perhaps their parents did too. The important factor here is how the acceleration is brought about.

METHODS OF ACCELERATION

Formerly the most common method of acceleration was by double-promotion, and it is usually the worst method. An occasional bright child is moved from third to fifth grade, skipping the fourth, or at least skipping a half-grade. He thus not only misses the work in the grade or half-grade skipped; he is moved from a class in which he is acquainted into one where he is a stranger and may be resented as apparently given a special favor. If there is to be skipping, it may come most easily when a child moves from one school to another, or goes from elementary school to junior high and so is going into a largely new group anyway. But usually there are better methods than grade-skipping.

One has been mentioned already: starting a bright child to school before his sixth birthday, even though he has not quite reached the age required by the school system for school entrance. Many investigations have shown that bright youngsters, thus admitted a few months earlier than the strict letter of the law would bring about, have done well in their school work and have gotten along well with the other children. Follow-ups, even to the eighth grade, have shown these initial accelerates continuing to do excellently (12). If the law is rigidly enforced, it is sometimes possible to start a very bright and well-adjusted child, who has already begun to read, in the second grade. Little second graders do not usually note or resent such a skipping over the first grade.

Probably the best opportunity for bright youngsters to progress more rapidly than the average child comes in non-graded schools (5). Children in the first three grades may be thrown together in a "primary pool." The teacher of such a group will have the largest portion of her group with her for three years; however, some will be ready to move into the fourth grade after only two years and the slow pupils stay there four. There are enough "fast" and also "slow" pupils that neither group feels conspicuous. The children who do get ready for the fourth grade in two years do not skip any work; they are simply helped by the teacher to progress more rapidly. It is probably desirable that grades 4–6, or the entire elementary school, be similarly dealt with.

In a large junior high school there may be rapid progress sections made up of carefully selected, bright, well-adjusted youngsters. These groups may cover the three years of junior high school in two years, or two years and a summer session. There may be similar rapid-progress sections in senior high school. Such sections do not skip any work but only cover it more rapidly, and the members are not isolated since they provide their own companionship—and are also with other youngsters in athletic, musical and other activities, as well as some classes. Follow-ups of such junior high school rapid progress sections have shown that they do as well in senior high school as youngsters equally bright who spent the regular three years in junior high, and also get along well in senior high with the other students (3, 8). Similarly, rapid progress pupils in senior high have been found to do well in college. There they also seem to get along well with the other students. Most often instead of behaving immaturely they tend, in the more mature group and with greater responsibilities put upon them, to take on a greater maturity and responsibility than would have been the case if they had remained another year in high school—as parents often testified.

Of course, in junior or senior high school, a student may "accelerate" in only one or two subjects—may do advanced work in science, for instance. But he may then be able to pass a special college entrance examination which will give him advanced credit in that subject if he goes to college. Some able students obtain enough such credit that they enter as sophomores, or can, with a little extra work, graduate from college in three years (4, 6, 11). Once more there is evidence that such students do well in college. And if they can thus get ahead, saving time and money, they are more likely to be able to go on into some form of advanced training, as into medicine, law, or graduate school.

In short, there are many ways by which a bright ambitious youngster may move ahead in his school work. Most do not involve missing or skipping any needed schooling. Most involve little hazard of emotional maladjustment or social isolation. The bright accelerate is one of a group which is moving more rapidly than the average child, and as acceleration becomes more common, these accelerated groups will become larger and more numerous and more accepted. Obviously there should be careful selection and guidance. Perhaps the greatest danger is that ambitious parents will urge that a child not very able or physically vigorous be put in a rapid progress section, and an occasional bright child may have problems of health or social maladjustment which make acceleration unwise. But mostly it is natural and healthy for bright vigorous youngsters to move along more rapidly than the "lock step" pace of a grade a year, which has been planned so that the child of only average ability can manage it. There should be careful selection taking account not only of ability and school work to date but also health, social adjustment, and both educational and vocational plans. A girl who plans to drop out of school after high school graduation and a boy headed for medical school are obviously in very different positions as regards desirability of acceleration. Guidance and school organization should be such that a youngster who attempts to accelerate and then thinks differently can easily shift back to an average pace and group. The attitude in school and community should be such that each child should go at his own rate, a good many faster than average and a good many slower, so that neither the accelerate nor the slow developer will feel conspicuous or subject to criticism or jealousy for his rate of progress.

How many should accelerate? The answer obviously involves the proportion of superior pupils in a school and their educational plans, also the extent that the school has guidance personnel and an organization facilitating progress at different rates, and the attitude of the community. In a suburb with most of the youngsters planning to go to college, there should be many accelerates, especially, if there is a local junior college or other institution to which young high school graduates can go while still living at home. *Won't the cost of guidance personnel, and of teachers for rapid progress sections or non-graded classes be prohibitive?* If children finish school a year or two sooner than average, that *saves* the school money! And it can afford to spend something on helping bright pupils progress more rapidly than the lock step. The net effect of a good program for acceleration is to save the school money and relieve congestion by getting children through sooner—no justification in itself—but a welcome bonus, if as indicated, acceleration is justified in benefits to the child.

OUTCOMES OF ACCELERATION

As already mentioned, bright children who begin school a little early have been found thereafter to do well both in school work and relations with other children. So have such children who do the first six grades in five years, or finish junior or senior high school in two years instead of three. Moreover, students who graduate from high school young have in many investigations been found more likely to go on to college and there do well both academically and in relations with other students. Students graduating from college young are more likely to go on for some form of advanced training—now so much needed by this country, in the cold war. *Why should this be?* Obviously a bright boy who graduates from high school at sixteen is less likely, than if graduating at eighteen, to drop school for a job or marriage. One little-mentioned value of acceleration is that it tends to break up the "going steady with one's age group" which may lead to too early marriage. It has also been repeatedly found that those who finish college or advanced training early are more likely to be successful in their career. *Why this?* Probably because they then begin their career in the full flush of young manhood—healthy, vigorous, enthusiastic, still within those young adult ages when, as has repeatedly been shown, men do their very best creative work (7).

SUMMARY

Acceleration may be defined as going through an educational program more rapidly, or at a younger age, than the average child. Acceleration is now being regarded more favorably than formerly, because ways of accelerating have been developed that are less likely to cause social and emotional maladjustment than grade-skipping. The greatly lengthened training now needed in occupations commonly sought by bright youngsters, and the demands of the "cold war" for people with advanced training, make time-saving often desirable.

School entrance before the sixth birthday, non-graded elementary schools, summer sessions, rapid-progress sections in secondary schools, opportunities to earn advanced credit for college entrance, all facilitate progress without the educational gaps of grade-skipping, and with minimal danger of maladjustment. Much research evidence shows that these methods work well, and make it possible for more students to accelerate than formerly, with savings to them in time and often money, and savings also to the schools.

Wise acceleration has been found to save time and money for all concerned with no educational loss. Accelerated youngsters have been found more likely to go on to college and advanced training, and more likely to succeed in a career, than equally bright youngsters proceeding at the "lock step" pace.

It is thus very timely that experiments in acceleration are being undertaken in Ohio schools. It is hoped that those reported in this bulletin will be the beginning of both further research and an increased use of acceleration in Ohio.

REFERENCES

1. Anderson, K. E. (ed) *Research on the Academically Talented Student,* Washington: National Education Association, 1961, p. 60.
2. Flesher, Marie and Pressey, S. L., "War-time Accelerates Ten Years After," *Journal of Educational Psychology,* 1955, 46, 228-238.
3. French, J. L. (ed) *Educating the Gifted.* New York: Holt-Dryden, 1959, pp. 555.
4. *Fund for the Advancement of Education, Bridging the Gap Between School and College.* New York: The Fund, 1953, pp. 127.
5. Goodlad, J. L. and Anderson, R. H., *The Non-graded Elementary School,* Harcourt Brace, 1959, pp. 248.
6. Jones, E. S. and Ortner, Gloria, *College Credit by Examination,* University of Buffalo Studies, Vol. 21, No. 3, January, 1934.
7. Lehman, H., *Age and Achievement.* Princeton, N.J.: Princeton University Press, 1953, pp. 358.
8. Pressey, S. L., *Educational Acceleration: Appraisals and Basic Problems,* Columbus, Ohio: Ohio State University Press, 1949, pp. 153.
9. Pressey, S. L., "Age and the Doctorate—Then and Now," *Journal of Higher Education,* Vol. 33, 153-160.
10. Terman, L. M. and Oden, Melita H., *Genetic Studies of Genius, IV: The Gifted Child Grows Up,* Stanford, California: Stanford University Press, 1947, pp. 448.
11. Wilcox, E. T. A., *Report to the Faculty of Art and Sciences on the Program of Advanced Standing.* Cambridge, Massachusetts: Harvard University, 1962, pp. 16.
12. Worcester, D. A., *The Education of Children of Above-Average Mentality,* Lincoln, Nebraska: University of Nebraska Press, 1956, pp. 68.

Early School Admission for Mentally Advanced Children

JACK W. BIRCH

This is a report on the adjustment and progress of 43 mentally advanced children who were accelerated one full year in school age-grade placement by early admission to first grade. The minimum age of entrance to first grade in Pennsylvania is five years and seven months as of the first day of September of the year of admission. A special case under regulation of the State Council of Education permits admission of children less than five years and seven months but over five years of age if recommended by a public school psychologist. In order to ascertain the effects of early entrance, periodic follow-up inquiries were made regarding children admitted early in September, 1951, September, 1952, and September, 1953. In 1951, in the Pittsburgh school system, six boys and eight girls were admitted early; in 1952, four boys and thirteen girls; in 1953, four boys and eight girls making the total of 43 children whose adjustment is studied here.

It is apparent that girls outnumber boys in this sample, although there is no obvious reason why this should be the case from the manner in which the sample was drawn. The newspapers gave wide publicity to the fact that parents could apply for examination for early admission consideration for their children. No applications for consideration were denied. Approximately nine times as many children were examined as were recommended for early admission. There seemed to be no considerable social or economic factor limiting the sample; the 43 early admissions recommended involved 27 different elementary schools representing all parts of the city. It may be that the important factors were that girls tend in general to develop verbal abilities earlier than boys and that bright girls tend to manifest their brightness to their parents earlier than do bright boys.

None of the children admitted early were very much younger than five years and seven months. Information on the children's ages as of the first day of September of the year of first grade admission follows:

Reprinted from *Exceptional Children*, Vol. 21, No. 3 (December, 1954), pp. 84-87. By permission of the author and publisher.

Age at First Grade Admission (Below minimum general admission age of 5 years, 7 months)	No. of Children
1 to 15 days	8
16 to 30 days	11
31 to 45 days	4
46 to 60 days	16
61 to 75 days	4
76 to 90 days	1
91 to 105 days	1
TOTAL	43

The youngest child admitted early was five years, three months, and twenty-two days old, and the oldest child admitted early was just one day short of being old enough to be admitted without special examination.

The psychologists who made the examinations interviewed each child and at least one of the child's parents. In some cases the application forms which came to the psychologists contained comments by the principal of the school in the elementary district of the child's residence. These comments were particularly helpful in cases where the child had attended kindergarten for a period of time and the comments could include observations of the kindergarten teacher. However, not all children being considered for early admission had attended kindergarten, and there was not sufficient data to evaluate the possible effects of kindergarten attendance on later adjustment of children admitted early.

The information used by the psychologists in determining whether early admission should be recommended included the following:

1. Evidence from the interviews or other data of superior social maturity for the child's age.
2. Evidence from the interviews or other data of superior emotional maturity for the child's age.
3. Evidence from observation, interview, and other data of reasonably normal height and weight and robust physical health.
4. Evidence of superior reading aptitude from objective individual examinations of reading readiness.
5. Evidence of superior mental capacity from objective individual examinations of intelligence (mental age of seven years or higher and intelligence quotient of 130 or higher were considered advisable, although not required in every case).
6. Knowledge of the general characteristics of the first grade population and instructional program of the school the child would attend.

Where it was feasible, two psychologists took part in examining the child, each doing a share of the examination separately, and then the psychologists pooled their judgments. When a decision either to admit or not to admit early had been reached, either by pooled judgments or where one psychologist did the complete evaluation, the decision was given to the parent at the time in an interpretive interview.

The interviews tended to follow one of three patterns. In about one out of 10 cases the psychologist recommended early admission, told the parent generally what to expect from the child, pointed out some considerations in preparing the child for first grade, and answered the parents' questions about the child and the school. Second, in about one out of 40 cases the psychologist did not recommend early admission, but did not recommend against it. These were questionable cases, where a clear-cut decision was not easy to make. In such cases the psychologist explained the findings to the parent, presented both sides of the case, the factors which seemed to favor early admission and the factors which caused misgivings, and offered the choice to the parent. This usually occasioned discussion which resulted in a decision shared by the psychologist and the parent. The third pattern of interview, occurring in approximately nine out of 10 cases was that in which the psychologist recommended against early admission and explained why that decision had been reached. It seems appropriate to point out in this connection that the interviews in which early admission was refused did not present anything like the number of difficulties that might have been anticipated. No doubt there were a number of reasons for this, and certainly one of the most important was the skill of the psychologists involved. In addition, however, school principals and other school personnel had carefully informed many of the parents at the time they applied for consideration that the odds were heavily against a recommendation for early admission. Suggestions for dealing with this matter had been made to principals in an administrative letter. The local press, too, had proved a major aid by carrying accurate and informative articles about the early admission process. In the judgments of the psychologists involved, the examinations and interviews had positive values for most of the parents and children whether early admission was recommended or refused as well as positive values to the school from the data still useful when the children who were not recommended entered under the general age regulations a year later. At least one child each year was found whose mental development was retarded enough to justify the opposite of early admission—postponement of school admission even the following year. The early identification of both bright and dull children was an outcome of the process.

After the mentally advanced children were entered in school, a follow-up process began. Twice each year, winter and spring, a letter was addressed to the principal of each school. This letter listed the

names of the children who had been admitted early to that school and
asked the principal to offer such information about the adjustment of
the children as might prove helpful in giving guidance to future policy
and practice on early admission. For some of the children admitted in
1951 there are five follow-up comments, involving reaction from several
teachers. These children are now in the second semester of the third
grade. Some of the children were lost through moves out of the school
system after one or more follow-ups. The total number of follow-up
comments on all 43 cases is 116.

For the purpose of this report, the comments concerning the children
have been classified into four kinds.

1. *Positive:* the report indicates that the child is making satisfactory or better
   school adjustment in all areas, academic, social, emotional, and physical.
2. *Positive–Questionable:* the report indicates that the child is making satisfactory or better school adjustment in all areas with the possible exception
   of one.
3. *Negative–Questionable:* the report indicates that the child, while not fail-
   in school, is definitely not making satisfactory or better school adjustment
   in one or two areas.
4. *Negative:* the report indicates that the child, while not failing in school,
   definitely shows evidence that early admission has contributed to current
   maladjustments.

Below are examples of statements.

Positive:

Marilyn has adjusted to first grade very satisfactorily. She is a superior child,
mentally. Her social adjustment has been very good. Personality and attendance in kindergarten are contributing factors to this. I am not in favor of
early entrance to first grade. It should be discouraged rather than encouraged.
The majority of children under age will make better progress if they stay in
kindergarten full time. Marilyn is the exceptional child, one in a hundred.

Positive–Questionable:

Carol is doing very well in reading and number work. She is alert and very
intelligent. Socially she is shy and needs to be stimulated to associate with
other children. She keeps busy at all times, but much to herself. Her attendance has been very irregular this first semester. She had chickenpox and has
been out several times with colds. Altogether she was absent 33½ days. With
an attendance of this sort, she has rated a B rating.

Negative–Questionable:

George is an easy-going child who lets nothing disturb him. He has shown
no interest so far in achieving. His attention span is exceptionally short, even
during development of a new lesson. George must be constantly reminded
to finish the task to be done; without prompting he does nothing, but his
work is correct when he does do it. His rating is high average, but he must

be prompted to do each page. As a whole, George is still very immature in many ways, even to his size. Although he will learn to read I believe he would have profited more if he had remained in kindergarten another semester. He reads with the third (low) group.

Negative:

Wanda is a lovely child, but is so easily frustrated she cries often. Wanda's reading achievement is due largely to her learning to read with an older sister. She is not capable of reading independently or thinking for herself. At the first sign of difficulty she cries to go to her sister. It takes much reassurance to understand she must work alone. Although her mother wants her to be in first grade, she does not want her to do any work which presents any difficulty or upsets her. She reads with the second group, and seems to be able to tell about the coming lesson, although she cannot recognize the words. In my opinion Wanda definitely should have had more kindergarten.

TABLE 1. Proportions and Number of Comments

Number of Children	Number of Comments	Proportions
30	64	100% Positive
1	3	75% Positive
	1	25% Positive–Questionable
1	4	80% Positive
	1	20% Negative
1	3	75% Positive
	1	25% Negative
1	2	66% Positive
	1	33% Positive–Questionable
2	6	60% Positive
	4	40% Positive–Questionable
2	6	60% Positive
	4	40% Negative
1	1	50% Positive
	1	50% Positive–Questionable
1	1	33% Positive
	2	66% Positive–Questionable
1	1	20% Positive
	2	40% Positive–Questionable
	1	20% Negative–Questionable
	1	20% Negative
1	1	20% Positive
	2	40% Positive–Questionable
	2	40% Negative
1	1	100% Positive–Questionable
43	116	

It should be pointed out that Marilyn, Carol, George and Wanda are all doing quite well in school now. George is still rather happy-go-lucky, and Wanda is still somewhat dependent; but their present teachers find these characteristics well within the normal range for all children.

The responses were classified so that a more objective evaluation could be made of the results of early admission. Table 1 shows the number of comments made on all the children in each category and the proportion of each classification of comments made regarding the children.

The data in Table 1 indicate that an overwhelming majority of the children admitted early to first grade were making satisfactory school adjustments in all areas, academic, social, emotional and physical. The data also indicate that the preponderance of all ratings was on the combined Positive and Positive—Questionable side for all children, and no child had a majority of ratings on the Negative and Negative—Questionable side.

While the data in Table 1 do not illustrate this further finding, it was apparent by inspection that where some Negative and Negative—Questionable evaluations were given, these tended to be the ones given during the first year of school and that later evaluations of the same child, usually in second or third grade, swung toward the Positive side.

SUMMARY, CONCLUSIONS, AND IMPLICATIONS

Forty-three children identified as mentally advanced were admitted early to first grade. The practice was evaluated by follow-up statements from their principals and teachers. The following conclusions can be drawn from the investigation:

1. Early admission of mentally advanced children to first grade is a very promising educational procedure in the general category of provisions for acceleration in age-grade placement, if it is practiced in accord with the procedures followed for the children in this investigation.

2. Further objective evaluation is advisable through follow-up of the same children and also of other children admitted at earlier ages to determine the practical limits on age of early admission.

Some of the implications of this report which appear of major importance are:

1. The early identification of mentally advanced children for optimum educational planning requires that all children have psychological examinations prior to first grade admission. Although only 1.1%

of the five-year-olds would be eligible for early admission by State Council of Education early admission standards in Pennsylvania, examination of almost all children is necessary to locate that group.

2. It is crucial that the opportunity for early admission to first grade occurs only once in a child's lifetime. Individual psychological study of each apparently precocious child is essential in the pre-school years if this opportunity is not to be lost.

3. In formal school situations involving no kindergarten provisions, early admission to first grade is the earliest step, chronologically, that can be taken to adjust the prevailing public educational program to the gifted child's needs. Certainly it is not the only move, and it may not be the most important, but it is the first possible action of its kind in the child's school career.

4. Early admission to first grade seems to combine most of the favorable features associated with acceleration and to minimize the unfavorable features. It paves the way for such advantages as earlier entrance into post-college training and earlier marriage, while it does not require that a child start school with one group of children and then find himself forced to adjust socially with a new group after acceleration.

5. Six full years of education in the elementary school, rather than the five which usually result in cases of acceleration, are provided by early admissions to first grade. Not only need there be much less concern over gaps in skill sequences brought about by "skipping," but with a full six years of elementary education there is more time for the activities which are usually grouped under the much maligned, but valid, concept of enrichment.

6. If early admission and enrichment for bright children should become a prevailing practice in the early grades in public schools, success in the practice will depend in a large measure on the readiness of primary school professional personnel to provide the school learning program and the understanding needed by such children. Where there is reluctance to accept these younger children into first grade, and where there is the feeling that the children admitted early should begin immediately to behave like "geniuses," the implication regarding professional training, both pre-service and in-service, is evident.

7. Perhaps the most general implication of acceleration by early admission to first grade lies in the need which is pointed up for integration of educational practices regarding mentally advanced children at all levels in the school program. Acceleration at first grade entrance modifies the conditions under which attendance in special classes or later acceleration may operate. The same is true for any other special educational adjustment or combination of adjustments.

8. Finally, the systematic procedures presented in this paper for

evaluating children referred for consideration for acceleration at the pre-first grade stage, with an attempt to objectify the evidence on how satisfactorily the procedures worked, should be thought of as indicative of the pressing need to develop and assess, by bona fide research techniques, the value of such procedures at all levels where acceleration or any other type of educational adjustment is to be attempted with mentally gifted children and youth.

Homogeneous Grouping for Gifted Children

WALTER B. BARBE

The need for attention to the education of gifted children has long been recognized. The development of provisions for this, however, has not kept pace with the research findings on the nature and needs of the gifted. To only a limited extent have special provisions been made for them. Acceleration, enrichment and homogeneous grouping are the major types of provisions. Few programs have been based solely upon only one of these. Enrichment has come to be an essential part of any provision for the gifted, while homogeneous grouping is practiced to some extent in every class.

But there are those who believe that formal provisions are necessary if the gifted child is to be adequately provided for. There is much evidence to prove that the gifted child frequently is neglected (1).

Recognizing this need for special attention to gifted children, in 1920 Cleveland, Ohio, began a program of special classes for gifted children. This, known as the Major Work Program, was the beginning of a slow and spasmodic increase in the belief that gifted children can best be provided for in special classes (2).

The program of providing for gifted children in the schools of New York City was started in 1922 by Leta Hollingworth. Even though Public Schools No. 64 and 11 had reported grouping rapid learners shortly before this time, "they did not carry with them the scientific research and evaluation begun by Hollingworth in No. 165 (3)." These classes, known as Special Opportunity Classes, were given partial financial support by the Carnegie Corporation of New York.

Reprinted from *Educational Leadership*, Vol. 13, No. 4 (January, 1956), pp. 225-229. By permission of the copyright © owner, The Association for Supervision and Curriculum Development.

In an article in *Ungraded* (4), Hollingworth, Cobb and others stated that the purposes of the program were: "First, the particular children in it must be educated—the class exists for them; but secondly, they must be studied—our knowledge of such children must be increased, for we have, after all, very little information to guide us in differentiating their schooling."

These early classes were entirely of an experimental nature and continued for a period of three years. Two groups of children were selected to be in the experiment. Group A was formed with children of 150 I.Q. and above, while Group B consisted of children with I.Q.'s between 135 and 154. All of the children were between the ages of 7½ and 9½ years and were accelerated in their school grade placement.

At the end of the three-year experiment, comparisons were made of achievement of the experimental groups and control groups of children who were of equal intellectual capacity but not in special classes. It was found that there was no great difference in the achievement scores of the segregated and non-segregated groups. In the evaluation, it was concluded that: "The advantages to be hoped for from the homogeneous grouping of gifted children lie not so much in the expectation of greater achievement in the tool subjects of reading, arithmetic and spelling as in an enrichment of scholastic experience (5)."

Hildreth recently reported on another attempt at special schools in New York. In 1940, Hunter College in New York City received authorization from the Board of Education to organize an elementary school for gifted pupils. Children from the ages of 3 to 11 who test above 130 I.Q. and "show other evidence of being mentally gifted and having other favorable traits (6)" are eligible for these classes.

Admission to the school is limited to those children living within a limited area of the Borough of Manhattan who meet the necessary mental and social qualifications. There is no tuition charge. An effort is made to keep the number of boys and girls as nearly equal as possible. Because of the enormous number of applicants, the staff believes that admission on the basis of objective tests is a fair method. An interesting point which Hildreth makes is that "the range [in I.Q.] . . . was around 60 points; the groups were seldom more homogeneous than in other schools except that the minimum rating was not below 130."

In telling of the children in the Hunter program, Hildreth describes them as having attractive personalities and possessing vitality and vivacity.

The parents of the Hunter group are a cross sampling of the population. Their occupations vary from day laborer to business executive. The majority of the parents have had some college, were born in New York, and would be ranked in the high-middle income bracket.

At the present time there are 22 classes for gifted elementary children.

In addition to the one regular teacher for each class, there are five full-time special teachers. All of the teachers have the M.A. degree. The physical plant is, in itself, unique. All facilities for which a teacher could ask are available.

The goals of the educational program as outlined by Gertrude Hildreth are:

1. Mental health and adjustment.
2. Health and physical education.
3. Learning to become an economically efficient citizen, both as producer and as consumer.
4. Acquiring skill in social relationships.
5. Learning about one's role as an enlightened and active world citizen.
6. Education for initiative and originality (7).

Oliver (8) reports that an entire school is set aside in Baltimore for gifted junior high school students, while Allentown, Pennsylvania, brings superior students from all over the city to one school for "opportunity classes." A division within a school is described and the Cleveland Major Work Program is mentioned briefly as an example of this type. He mentions the differentiated high school programs in most cities where the college preparatory course, which is essentially for the gifted students, is offered to some, while a commercial curriculum is offered to others.

Colfax School in Pittsburgh, Pennsylvania, operates a partial segregation plan to "provide for better living conditions for its mentally superior children." The entire school, from the third grade on, is on the platoon plan. It is described by Pregler as a "workshop" plan: "The plan provides the maximum opportunity for group acceptance of the individual child, it encourages the pupil to work to capacity, and it makes it possible for superior children to work with and be challenged by their mental peers. Furthermore, it has enabled the school to develop special methods and materials well suited to the teaching of gifted children (9)."

The gifted children at Colfax School are segregated in the skill subjects and mix with their regular home room in the special subjects. Pregler points out that by use of the workshop plan, the gifted child still remains a part of the regular class. When he leaves the regular class, it is just as if a child in the typical school would go to orchestra practice. Actually, it amounts to segregation for half of the day. All of the skill subjects are taught either in the morning or afternoon, and the gifted child leaves his regular group for this period of time.

Baker (10) describes the program in Detroit for mentally superior children. Generally, he says, Detroit has a "mild amount of extra promotion." At the elementary school level, most schools follow the platoon plan of departmentalizing subjects. At the junior high level, the screening of gifted children is done by means of weighted formula. Five points are given for intelligence, four for school achievement, and two for chronological age. Children are then segregated according to the total points which they have. At the high school level, Baker says, the program consists of little more than the customary college preparatory courses.

Interest in provisions for the gifted has been outstanding throughout California. This is perhaps due to Terman's study (11) of gifted California youth.

A program described by Cora Lee Danielson, former supervisor of this work (12) was in operation for over twenty years. Los Angeles no longer has special classes but is attempting to meet the needs of the gifted through various other means.

In considering the merits of special classes, Goddard says that this is the best method by which the school can keep "the child happily employed with work that is educative, both because it is interesting to him and because it challenges his capabilities by calling for his best efforts continually (13)." The Educational Policies Commission says that in its broader sense, enrichment is a policy rather than a plan, and that special classes for the gifted have little justification if they do not provide enrichment. Activities especially appropriate for the gifted involve creative expression, ample opportunity for out-of-school contacts, and a chance for each child to learn more about his fields of special interest and to express his particular talents (14). Witty quotes Schwartz as saying:

> The real purpose of the special class seems to lie in the assignment of tasks which challenge the child's interest and capacity, the enrichment of the curriculum to include a wide variety of experiences which are not possible in a regular class, the opportunity to think and to discuss with other children of equal ability the problems of life within their grasp, the development of initiative and independence of thought, and last, but not least, the realization of responsibility to the community, looking toward the use of their powers for the benefit of mankind (15).

Carroll presents a strong argument for special education of the gifted: ". . . each child must receive the education best suited to his abilities and needs. To force upon all an education planned for average children, regardless of individual intellectual capacity, is to grant special privilege to the central group and to deny to the bright and the dull their rights (16)."

A larger number and greater variety of learning experiences can be had by students in a homogeneously superior class, partly because less time is required for routine drill and remedial instruction (17). The enriched curriculum keeps the child's intellectual power active in an environment affording opportunities for association with children who are mentally and physically equal (18).

To the argument that the slower child is stimulated by the bright child, Goddard answered that the slower child is not stimulated but frightened (19). Instead of the special class making the gifted child feel superior, Carroll believes that it is the regular class where this happens and not the special class. He says that in an unselected group the gifted child is constantly made conscious of the fact that he is brighter than his classmates, so that different classes eliminate one of the causes of inflated self-esteem (20). Edith Carlson agrees with this view. She says that the "smugness, feelings of superiority, and other undesirable characteristics are alleviated when bright children are placed in special classes (21)."

Pregler recognizes (22) that there are advantages and disadvantages of each method of providing for the gifted child, but she believes, as do most educators, that it should be determined by what is best for the child. She believes that the partial segregation plan is the best yet devised for the particular situation in which she is located.

In a doctoral disseration at Columbia University (23), Alice Keliher strongly opposes homogeneous grouping as a provision of caring for the gifted. Her major criticism is that segregation adversely affects society. Throughout her dissertation, however, she is careful to note that segregation, *as it exists today,* is not advisable. The dissertation, written in 1931, was aimed at the idea of complete segregation which was prevalent at that time. Today, in few programs is complete segregation followed. As is true about the Major Work Program, in Cleveland, Ohio, segregation, but not isolation, appears to be the more acceptable method.

Oliver summarizes present day thinking rather well in saying that mere segregation does not assure the gifted child of a better education. The ultimate need of the gifted child is an enriched program, whether it is in a homogeneous or heterogeneous classroom.

In discussing the criticisms of homogeneous grouping, Oliver says:

> There is considerable reason to believe that the alleged shortcomings [of special classes] are not inherent but are a matter of creating a proper environment and of establishing a proper attitude in the gifted, in the other pupils, in the teachers, and especially in the parents (24).

While no definite conclusions can be reached about the best method of providing for the gifted, it is important to recognize that the gifted child is being neglected and is in need of special attention.

REFERENCES

1. Walter B. Barbe, "Are Gifted Children Being Adequately Provided For?" *Educational Administration and Supervision,* Vol. 40, No. 7 (November 1954), pp. 405-413.
2. Walter B. Barbe and Dorothy Norris, "Special Classes for Gifted Children in Cleveland," *Exceptional Children,* Vol. 21, No. 2 (November 1954), pp. 55-57.
3. Grace Loomis, "The Education of the Gifted Child," *Curriculum Bulletin,* No. 97 (December 12, 1951), Eugene, Oregon: School of Education, p. 14.
4. Paul Witty, *The Gifted Child* (Boston: D. C. Heath, 1950), p. 55.
5. Howard A. Gray and Leta S. Hollingworth, "The Achievements of Gifted Children Enrolled and Not Enrolled in Special Opportunity Classes," *Journal of Educational Research,* Vol. XXIV (November 1931), p. 261.
6. Gertrude Hildreth, *Education of Gifted Children* (New York: Harper and Brothers, 1952), p. 40.
7. *Ibid.,* pp. 43-46.
8. Albert I. Oliver, "Administrative Problems in Educating the Gifted." *The Nations Schools,* Vol. 48, No. 5 (November 1951), pp. 44-46.
9. Hedwig O. Pregler, "Adjustment Through Partial Segregation," *National Elementary Prinicipal,* Vol. 19 (September 1952), p. 243.
10. Harry J. Baker, "Characteristics of Superior Learners and the Relative Merits of Enrichment and Acceleration for Them." Supplementary Educational Monograph, No. 69. Edited by William S. Gray. Chicago: University of Chicago Press, October 1949, p. 157.
11. Lewis M. Terman and Melita H. Oden, *The Gifted Child Grows Up.* Stanford, California: Stanford University Press, 1947.
12. From personal correspondence with Miss Cora Lee Danielson.
13. Henry H. Goddard, *School Training of Gifted Children.* Yonkers-on-Hudson, New York: World Book Co., 1928, p. 1.
14. Educational Policies Commission, *Education of the Gifted.* National Educational Association of the United States and the American Association of School Administrators. Washington, D.C., 1950, pp. 56-58.
15. Witty, *op. cit.,* p. 189.
16. Herbert Carroll, *Genius in the Making.* New York: McGraw-Hill Book Co., Inc., 1940, p. 253.
17. Educational Policies Commn., *op. cit.,* p. 53.
18. W. J. Osburn and Ben J. Rohan, *Enriching the Curriculum for Gifted Children* (New York: The Macmillan Co., 1931), p. 186.
19. Goddard, *op. cit.,* pp. 27-33.
20. Carroll, *op. cit.,* p. 213.
21. Witty, *op. cit.,* p. 188.
22. Pregler, *op. cit.,* p. 242.
23. Alice Keliher, "A Critical Study of Homogeneous Grouping." New York: Columbia University Press, 1931.
24. Oliver, *op. cit.,* p. 44.

13 | PLANNING FOR THE GIFTED— HIGH SCHOOL

The Gifted Pupil in the High School

EARL M. McWILLIAMS

The public high schools of the United States are facing the challenge of providing the best possible education for gifted American youth. Many critics of public education assert that gifted youth are neglected and constitute an underprivileged group within our schools. All of this criticism does not come from those who are obviously aiming to destroy confidence in secondary education—for it is the consensus of many supporters of our schools, both lay and professional—that the needs of gifted children have not received as much attention as they merit.

In a recent nation-wide survey of educational provisions for gifted children, the writer found an awareness of this issue in every section of the nation and at all levels of education from kindergarten through twelfth grade. Parents and patrons of our schools, as well as educators, are seeking answers to the many perplexing questions inherent in the complex problem. Are there many secondary schools meeting this challenge with a sincere effort to build a program that provides for gifted children and, at the same time, maintaining the values of our education for all American youth? The answer is an emphatic *YES*. Schools which differ greatly in size, organizational plan, philosophy, student population, and financial support are providing for the needs of the gifted in a multitude of ways. These programs are not all equally effective. However, there is an increasing number of schools endeavoring to find the ways to provide the best possible education for gifted children, and the problem is receiving a noteworthy amount of serious attention and study throughout the nation.

Every individual or group that investigates the possibility of providing for the gifted is confronted by certain troublesome aspects of the problem—definition and identification of giftedness, acceleration, segre-

Reprinted from the *Bulletin of the National Association of Secondary-School Principals*, May, 1955. Copyright: Washington, D.C. Vol. 39, No. 211, pp. 1-9. By permission of the author and publisher.

gation, and enrichment of the school program. The following paragraphs, describing some approaches to these issues, are based upon the writer's observations in the schools visited.

IDENTIFICATION

Some schools prefer to use such terms as "fast learners," "very superior," "more capable," "special progress," "rapid learners," and "talented." Giftedness is limited by some definitions to the confines of intellectual ability, while in others it is applied to any ability which a child possesses to a superior degree. The writer accepted the latter definition and sought out provisions for all types of giftedness. It is important to note at the outset that exceptional ability can usually be recognized early in the life of the child, and the responsibility for identification resides with educators at all levels, from kindergarten through high school.

Intellectual giftedness is the type most commonly recognized in setting up school programs. While the IQ rating of the individual pupil is universally recognized as a significant indicator, not one school was found to be using the IQ as the sole criterion for labeling him as gifted. Additional commonly accepted data for rating pupils are: teacher evaluations, school achievement records, opinions of counselors and parents, reading level, mathematical ability, interests, and hobbies.

Other varieties of giftedness are not as readily identified, since existing instruments for measurement and rating are not adequate. Schools which are attempting to develop the talents of pupils (other than intellectual talents) usually have to work out their own identification procedures before initiating any activity. Giftedness in children can be recognized in music, art, mechanical comprehension and skill, drama, creative writing, rhythm, and social leadership. Social leadership is not necessarily a concomitant of intellectual giftedness. Schools can build potential leadership for our democracy by early recognition and effective training of "natural born leaders."

Previous research has shown that giftedness in children does not depend upon their racial or socio-economic background. This means that gifted children are found among all races and on all socio-economic levels. These studies have further shown that children are gifted in specific directions. For a specific ability, individual children vary from practically no ability in one aspect to very superior ability if another trait is chosen. That is to say that giftedness is not a generalized characteristic. The musical prodigy, for example, is not necessarily a prodigy in whatever he attempts. However, we know a positive correlation exists generally among degrees of attributes in a randomly selected population. This principle is important to retain with respect to the gifted. Individual differences among gifted children do exist, even within the structure of a highly positive correlation.

One of the most difficult problems is that many gifted pupils are not easily identified as such. Very few schools have the resources to support the kind of activity necessary for seeking out these cases. However, the price our nation pays for failing to discover this hidden potential is both the sad waste of human resources and a high frequency of maladjustment among individuals in our society. Schools which have moved in the direction of seeking out unrevealed giftedness in pupils have discovered certain recurrent facts. Intellectually gifted pupils, especially those with emotional disturbances, are sometimes not challenged by group tests to perform to the utmost of their capacity, and they go unrecognized as superior. Also, pupils need to achieve status in their peer society and may inhibit any performance that would get them the label of "brain" or that would demonstrate their interest and superiority in an area not acceptable to the group. This factor serves to prevent some pupils from expressing themselves freely in the field of art, drama, music, rhythm, or creative writing. The social stigma attached to "vocational education" in some communities serves as a deterrent to youth seeking to develop giftedness in mechanical ability.

Learning readiness in various subject areas is a phenomenon to be found among gifted children as well as among all children. Sometimes the gifted group will show extreme examples of readiness, such as the case of the 17-year-old top-honor senior in high school who did not learn to read until he was in the fourth grade. Another, less drastic example, is the ninth-grade boy who was not at all interested in algebra, but who had recently begun to develop the hobby of amateur radio operation. His teacher wisely allowed him to ignore algebra until from the hobby activities there came a need for a knowledge of mathematics. Then the boy, who was highly gifted intellectually, rapidly brought himself up to the rest of the class in algebra achievement.

PROGRAMS FOR THE GIFTED

Acceleration. One of the earliest methods of meeting the needs of the gifted child was to shorten the time spent in school. This was accomplished either by "skipping grades" or by speeding up assignments so as to cover the required subject matter in less time than that expected of the average pupil. In only two of the cities [1] visited were there programs offering this kind of acceleration for groups of gifted pupils. Both permit selected pupils to enroll in accelerated junior high-school

---

[1] Schools with acceleration in junior high schools are located in Baltimore, Maryland, and New York City. The schools included the Lee Junior High School in Baltimore and special classes in many of the junior high schools of New York City.

programs that condense the regular three-year program into two years. These are plans that have been in operation for many years and are continued at the request of those parents who want this kind of acceleration for their children. One inevitable feature of this type of acceleration is squeezing out of the educational experience of these pupils those activities which provide for social and cultural exploration and development.

Most schools believe that acceleration should be regarded as a possible device for aiding the individual pupil and as an advisable measure only when it guarantees the maximum benefit to every aspect of his development. Careful attention must be given to the physical and social maturity of the pupil, and any suggestion for acceleration should be carefully studied in relation to development.

Within the senior high schools there are some exemplary projects providing for acceleration of the gifted within specific subject areas. There are several plans in operation which enable the gifted student to receive advanced standing in college for work done in high-school classes. This enables the individual to mature socially with his age mates at the same time that he is advancing intellectually to a degree commensurate with his abilities.

Segregation. School policy in the matter of segregation of gifted pupils reflects local educational philosophy and is the most controversial issue in any discussion of the education of the gifted. Practices observed by the writer range from complete segregation of the gifted in separate schools to absolute adherence to a policy of non-segregation. In New York, special progress classes are found in many junior high schools.

Separate public schools [2] for the gifted were found in only three cities. In each case, the school has been in existence for over fifty years and is a selective, college preparatory institution. A few schools in other cities segregate gifted children by keeping them apart from other pupils throughout the entire day's schedule. Again, this was usually a college preparatory type of curriculum for the selected children.

Some people that have had experience with segregation either in separate schools or within a school are enthusiastic about the results obtained. There are others who as strenuously support the opposite point of view.

It was noted earlier that the gifted individual is not equally talented in all possible ways. To some this seems to be the biggest stumbling block to the success of complete segregation. Pupils gifted in mathematics are not necessarily so endowed in the language arts, or *vice versa.*

[2] Segregated schools for the gifted included: Lee Junior High School of Baltimore, Maryland; Walnut Hills Junior-Senior High School of Cincinnati, Ohio; and the Boston Latin School in Boston, Massachusetts.

Many schools, profiting from later research, do some grouping in terms of particular subject area and frequently regroup for different activities.

There is truth in the principal arguments on both sides of the question of segregation of gifted pupils. When pupils of high ability work together, there is an environment which is challenging and stimulating to the individual. Such groups have produced amazing achievements in all areas of school activities. On the other hand, gifted pupils need to learn how to cope with those of lesser abilities in the areas of social problems, political affairs, religious activities, family life, and the occupational world. These are not irreconcilable points of view. It is possible to provide both types of experience for the gifted, and many schools are doing this effectively. They allow the gifted individual to share with all pupils those activities in which he will be associated with people of all levels of ability throughout his life. On the other hand, they encourage him to work alone or with his gifted peers in those activities where he can develop his analytical and creative powers. Schools which are providing both kinds of experience are producing happy educational environments in which achievement of the gifted pupil's development in citizenship and scholarship is assured.

Schools may plan programs for groups of gifted pupils, but there is the occasional one who does not fit into any group planning. This exception is the genius. When a school finds such a pupil, it must give him special attention. No set formula applies in his case. One junior high school allowed such a boy to spend part of his day "free lancing." During this time he did extensive research in astronomy.

Enrichment. The most widely accepted method of planning for gifted youth is to enrich the curriculum so as to provide the maximum educational opportunities for them. Enrichment activities provide outlets for research interests and creativity in every phase of secondary-school programs. In all sections of the nation can be found schools which provide science fairs, trips, individual research projects, outlets for creative writing, art and music activities, dramatics, school service organizations, and hobby clubs. In some schools such activities are a part of the regular class work, and in others they are extraclass activities. The need for emotionally secure teachers with imagination and breadth of background is most evident, for enrichment must not simply be "more of the same" or "busy work" for the fast learner.

Grouping of the gifted in special classes should be on the basis of common interests. It should be flexible so that the individual pupil is placed with high ability groups only in those areas where he is able to keep up with the others in the group. The writer observed special classes for the gifted at all levels of both elementary and secondary education and in such widely varied interest areas as science, creative writing, dramatics, foreign languages, human relations, business and industrial organization, current affairs, mathematics, and speech activities. Several senior high schools have seminar type activities, as well as classes which allow the gifted to advance rapidly in subject fields. At the junior high-school level, the gifted pupil can be aided in his exploration of the intellectual and cultural opportunities of his society through individual and group experiences in a variety of activities. This type of program appears in many schools, under such names as "Exploration Hour," "Special Needs Period," and "Major Interest Workshops." Schools generally provide outlets for leadership and special talents through opportunities to participate in student council activities, publications, radio programs, audio-visual crews, and social events. The invaluable assistance rendered by the library in the enrichment of the curriculum cannot be over-rated. The librarian is often one of the most effective teachers in the school. In some states, universities offer extension courses at the high-school level. This enables individuals to study subjects not offered in their schools.

Any school system which initiates a study of enrichment will discover many fine examples of effective enrichment practices being used by teachers within the system. A device used by some faculties to exchange ideas is the publication of bulletins [3] containing contributions of teachers and supervisors in which they describe successful enrichment practices from their own experience.

The most difficult method of providing enrichment for the gifted pupil is to allow him to remain in a heterogeneous class and take care of his individual needs within the framework of the class activities. The difficulty is in the lack of time and resources of the average classroom teacher to cope with a wide span of individual differences. Schools which follow this philosophy cannot leave the responsibility of providing for the gifted in the hands of the teacher alone. The teacher needs assistance of many kinds. In several cities the position of teacher-consultant has been created to fill this need. The teacher-consultant visits both teacher and gifted pupil regularly to help with methods and materials. This plan has been characterized by singular success in every instance. There are, unfortunately, only a few schools which have classes so small that teachers are able to provide for wide variations in individual ability without any unfair burden of time or effort. Consequently, some plan of help for the teacher is essential to the success of enrichment in heterogeneous classes.

[3] Such schools include the following: "Dealing with the Superior Student in Mathematics," Garrison Junior High School, Baltimore, Maryland; "The Very Able Child," Modesto City Schools, Modesto, California; "The Very Superior Child," Public Schools, Long Beach, California; also, the Huddle Junior High School, Brooklyn, New York, and the Mosholu Parkway Junior High School, Bronx, New York.

THE ROLE OF THE PRINCIPAL

Every American public high school must accept the challenge of providing for the educational needs of gifted youth. The primary responsibility for initiating and sustaining action rests with the principal. There are seven clearly defined areas wherein he must function effectively or his school will not fulfill its obligations to the gifted youth of the community it serves.

1. *School Climate.* An essential condition for worth-while educational experimentation and progress is an environment characterized by democracy and a sincere effort on the part of everyone in the school to build together the best possible program. There is no single factor in the establishment of such a school climate greater than the attitude of the principal and his relations with his staff and student body.

2. *Co-operative Planning.* The school which wishes to provide more adequately for its gifted children cannot turn to any ready-made program or even use a synthesis of "best programs." Each school must study its own needs and resources in order to develop a program which is within the limits of both. The experience of other schools can be used as a source of suggestions for activities and as an aid in avoiding pitfalls or unnecessary repetitions of experimentation. This study and planning should be carried out by the entire staff with lay personnel included in all phases. In order to avoid undue influence from pressure groups whose ideas and aims may not coincide with our concepts of child growth and development, this combined group of school staff and citizens must take the initiative in planning for and working with the program for the gifted pupil.

3. *Personnel Selection.* Principals everywhere state that the key to success of a program for gifted pupils is the wise selection of outstanding teachers to implement the plan. It is the responsibility of the principal to survey the abilities and interests of his staff so as to know what resources are available in planning for enrichment of the curriculum. Teachers for the gifted must have the ability to encourage individual creativity and research. The teacher does not have to know more than the pupil, and, indeed, cannot follow along every road that every pupil will travel. The pupil can be guided in the correct use of methods of research and supplied with adequate materials with which to work. It is especially true in the education of the gifted that the best teaching is on the level of inspiration. To prevent staff disharmony, the principal must see that undue prominence is not given to the program of the gifted or to those who participate in it. (When planning is done by the entire staff, it has been found that many teachers eliminate them-

selves from consideration for teaching gifted groups because they find
the prospect of the inevitably complex programs unattractive.)

4. *Public Relations.* In the handling of public relations can rest the
success or failure of any educational program. The administrator must
know how the patrons of his school will react to any proposals for
changing the school procedures. In many schools the inclusion of lay
representatives on all planning committees has proved to be of inestimable value in achieving rapport with school patrons. A crucial
problem in setting up programs for the gifted is the extent to which
parents should be appraised of the nature of the plans. Some schools
seek the co-operation of parents of gifted children, and in a few cases
the parents are called in for a conference with school staff members.
Other schools feel that they should take care of these needs without
labeling the pupils in any way or revealing their status to their parents.
There is another aspect of public relations in the use of community
resources for supplementing the staff and equipment of the school,
especially for gifted youth who have particular interests and abilities
for which there are no adequate outlets within the regular school program. One junior high-school boy in a western city is pursuing a deep
interest in optics by working in a local lens grinding plant. This not only
serves the boy's needs but also builds strong public relations, for principals everywhere report that people in the community are more than
willing to help such persons in both their vocational and avocational
interests.

5. *Guidance.* Since gifted pupils have such a high achievement
potential and usually evince a wide variety of interests, it is absolutely
essential that they have available at every level of their educational experience adequate guidance services. The finest schools visited were
characterized by guidance programs in which counselors and classroom
teachers had access to complete records of the individual pupil, and the
pupil was able to receive help and advice whenever the need arose.

6. *In-service Training.* Since the success of all school planning rests
eventually with the teacher and the pupils in the classroom, the primary
duty of the principal is supervision. He must maintain continuous in-
service training for his staff. Principals who excuse themselves from
accepting this responsibility on the plea that they do not have time to
serve as supervisors will find that the program for the gifted (or any
program for that matter) will degenerate into a plan on paper but without any substance. If the principal delegates this function to his assistant
or to some staff member, such as a teacher-consultant, it is still his direct
responsibility to see that the teacher is receiving all possible assistance.

7. *Continuous Evaluation.* A vital part of the operational procedure
of those schools which are most effective in their educational programs

is that they constantly examine and re-evaluate their ongoing activities. Such schools recognize the fact that education in our society can never be static and must ever be alert to constant change. In short, no single program for the gifted is ever the final answer, for next year always brings new pupils and new conditions.

SUMMARY

A final word as to the over-all picture of public education is revealed by this coast-to-coast tour of schools—the experience was rewarding and thrilling beyond all expectation. The secondary schools visited are doing an exemplary job of seeking the best way to meet the problems of the gifted. These schools were selected because they are doing outstanding work in this area, but there is evidence that countless other schools are doing as well and that schools everywhere are becoming aware of this vital need. It was the experience of the writer that, when he found a school that was doing an especially fine job of dealing with gifted pupils, that school was also meeting the needs of all pupils through a good educational program.

One of the most memorable statements heard was made by a mother who was describing the activities of her teenage, genius son. She sighed and said, "They are gifted up to a point, and then they are just children." The educator must never forget the lessons implicit in this observation, for very often the gifted child needs more help in being a child than he does in being gifted.

Some critics of public education are clamoring for us to set up the type of program for gifted pupils that would be, in effect, "education for the elite." This is in direct opposition to the ideals of American education which have made it one of the unifying forces of our democracy. The best way to meet such unsound proposals is to demonstrate that we can provide for the gifted within the existing school set-up and in a way that is compatible with our educational philosophy. The responsibility for achieving this rests with the principals of our high schools. It is the fervent hope of this observer that each will accept the challenge and give public secondary education the opportunity to help gifted pupils grow into the kind of citizens our democracy requires for its survival and progress.

How Fare the Talented in Our High Schools?

A. HARRY PASSOW
ABRAHAM TANNENBAUM

The stimulation for more widespread discovery and development of talent in our schools comes from at least two sources: (a) a concern that the great effort to provide educational opportunities for all youth left serious gaps in provisions for those with special potential and (b) a belief that any neglect of the talented represents a loss in manpower and leadership which we cannot afford in these critical times.

In recent years our schools have become increasingly sensitized to the crucial role they are expected to play in this stepped-up talent search. Having been made aware of the possible limits of our talent resources and of the vital need to seek out youngsters who possess outstanding and desirable abilities, schools throughout the nation are facing up to the challenge. Reports from schools indicate increasing attention to and services for the talented. Supplementing these is the interest of many professional and community groups as evidenced by their literature, research, and special meetings in this area. Despite this swell, the task of designing curriculum to develop potential talent remains a difficult one with a high priority.

How schools determine the kinds of talents that ought to be nurtured is most clearly reflected by the instruments and procedures they use in screening for exceptionally able students. Tests of general intelligence are still highly popular in gauging potential. This attraction to the high IQ was probably inspired by Terman's (1) now-famous studies of some 1,500 children with Stanford-Binet scores of 140 and above. His researches shed light on the mental, physical, and social attributes of these children as well as their outstanding achievement in adulthood (2). He indicated the high predictive validity of the intelligence test in uncovering potential success in academic endeavors. Since our schools had traditionally committed their aims mainly toward development of academic abilities and interests, their search for talent in terms of high IQ could indeed be expected.

Reprinted from the *Bulletin of the National Association of Secondary-School Principals,* May, 1955. Copyright: Washington, D.C. Vol. 39, No. 211, pp. 10-15. By permission of the senior author and publisher.

BROADENED CONCEPTION OF TALENT

But in the thirty years since Terman initiated his studies, we have been broadening our conception of school curriculum to include other than intellectual learnings. At the same time there have been intensive studies of intelligence tests to re-assess the kinds of mental abilities they do reveal. Some research suggests, for example, that present tests do not measure the nonverbal potential of children of lower socio-economic levels.

Paralleling an expanding view of the curriculum, there has developed a more complex characterization of talent in educational theory and practice. Witty summarized such an approach when he advised that we "broaden our definition of *gifted* and consider any child gifted whose performance, in any potentially valuable line of human ability, is consistently remarkable (3)." He would include in his definition not only individuals of high intellectual ability but also those who exhibit any number of socially useful abilities which may not necessarily be associated with high IQ. This more inclusive definition is seen in some of the current programs involving identification and development of talented youth. Havighurst in the Community Youth Development Program, for example, screened for children with special abilities and talents of social value, including:

1. High intelligence
2. Talent in creative fields, such as art, music, and writing
3. Special abilities in a variety of socially useful areas, such as mechanics, science, dramatics, athletics, human relations, social organization
4. Creative talent, or the ability to make new and novel solutions to problems (4).

Bringing more and more talents into the classroom for proper recognition and nurture raises many problems and issues for curriculum planners. The task is further complicated by the absence, as yet, of an accepted comprehensive theory of the nature of talent. We still need a well-developed framework to guide experimentation and program development efforts. Some schools, in earnest attempts to meet their responsibilities, have begun to modify programs and produce materials without any clear notions of what they are planning for; others have begun by refining identification instruments and procedures. Long recognized is the practical value of applying good screening methods early in the child's education so that teachers have ample opportunity to guide the youngster wisely. However, schools still must come to grips with some fundamental problems regarding the discovery of talents if effective educational programs are to be developed. Even though a particular faculty feels it cannot provide conclusive answers to these questions, unless they are given adequate consideration in planning, real progress seems unlikely.

WHAT IS TALENT?

The first basic question is: What is the nature of talent? What are the biological, cultural, and psychological factors contributing to superior attainment? Despite voluminous literature, we are provided relatively little insight into what we are dealing with when we attempt to provide for "the talented."

Frequently school planning begins with a decision to give more attention to the "gifted" or "talented," and it then proceeds to set criteria for the selection of students to be included in a particular program. Screening procedures often take on exaggerated importance as they are allowed to master the idea, rather than *vice versa*. To the testing instruments goes the function of determining which talents are worthy of being revealed and developed. The assumption is made that, by meeting certain criteria on tests or other devices, a student reveals talent. Such criteria are usually descriptive rather than explanatory. They provide bases for selecting students, but do not begin to explain the nature of these talents or how they can best be nurtured. While these procedures have undoubtedly altered the learning experiences of some youngsters, they contribute little to deepen our understandings of the underlying components of aptitude and fulfillment. We know little, for example, about where or how these talents originate; whether we are dealing with one or a cluster of factors; what relationships exist among specific or general potentials; or how we can be sure that promise will be channeled toward fulfillment.

For every leader in almost any area of human endeavor, there are untold numbers who, at some point in their development, have demonstrated similar potential in existing screening procedures but whose attainment is comparatively negligible. Only half of those capable of acquiring a college degree enter college; about two fifths of those who start are not graduated, and for every high-school student who eventually earns a doctoral degree there are twenty-five others, just as able, who do not (5). While finances account for some of these losses, we know there are other important reasons. Research like that of Ausubel (6) seems to unearth at least one clue in relating the motivation of personal recognition and prestige to achievement. Work sponsored by the Social Science Research Council on various socio-cultural, personal and situational determinants of academic and social achievement may shed additional light on why youngsters who show promise in schools do or do not achieve later.

WHAT TALENTS DO WE NEED?

Another fundamental question is: what kinds of talent are needed in our era for advancing our culture and civilization? If we look beyond the school world boundaries into the vast mosaic of superior human abilities and note how strongly each contributes to progress, we can begin to see our talent needs in their deepest, most significant context. Society in each age continually modifies its demands for skilled leadership and, as Terman pointed out, "will decide, by the rewards it gives or withholds, what talents will come to flower (7)." Highest rewards have not necessarily gone to those who satisfy society's profoundest needs, however; these often go to persons who fill immediate, ephemeral wants.

The literature today sounds its most sonorous plea for scientific talent and urges schools to give greatest attention to recruiting and training future scientists. When we consider the vital part science plays in the protection and advancement of our way of life, there is logic behind this plea. Yet this current emphasis can overwhelm and distort our perspective in selecting the areas of learning in which talents deserve more careful development. In his analysis of our manpower needs, deKiewiet observed that the "greatest skills we need are not in science or engineering, but in human relations (8)." Those who would have us believe that schools can best cure humanity's ills by furnishing us with more and better scientists cannot blot out the equal importance of other talents for which the cry is presently not so great. We cannot decide what our talent needs are solely on the basis of the loudest shouts in the literature nor can we neglect in our considerations the needs of the child and his ability to attain self-fulfillment.

Closely related to our talent needs is the question: How can the social attributes vital to potential leaders be identified and developed? At best, our popular mental tests, for example, tell us something about the child's capacity to learn, but nothing about whether he will use his abilities to benefit humanity or to confound it. We need to understand more about ways of guiding learning into socially positive channels.

The school then has the job of bringing into focus and perspective the talent needs of our generation and of judging the extent to which it can relate its objectives to their discovery and development. Many difficult value judgments will have to be made as we examine the needs and potentials of our youth and the needs and wants of society in terms of the goals and resources of our schools. In which of several possible directions should we guide youngsters who indicate exceptional abilities in a number of areas? On what basis should we make a decision? Some educators cling to the notion that only training in verbal skills is important enough for schools to consider. Others go to the opposite extreme and take a view that the school can and should nurture an endless variety of human skills. Neither of these two positions suggests a clear demarcation of the school's function in society.

As the school's role is better defined, each of various social institutions will find its areas of responsibility for filling our talent needs. Obviously the home, community, and church influence talent—but how much or how? We do not yet know.

PLANNING FOR OUR TALENTED

Although these basic questions—What is talent? What talents do we need?—have been raised for the past two or three decades, there are significant differences in our approach today which are promising and which may provide us with better insights for educating our talented youth. First, our secondary schools are recognizing the need for making special provisions for talented youth and are not willing to leave these either to chance or to the ingenuity of the youngsters. "Don't worry about the talented, they'll take care of themselves" is an approach which is neither acceptable nor accepted. Secondly, while many psychological and social blocks still exist, the search for the talented is no longer viewed as looking for the "queer" or the "odd." Although talented youngsters are exceptional in terms of potential, we know they can and do make normal personal and social adjustments. Lack of opportunity to develop potential abilities may cause these youth to escape either into mediocrity or unusual behavior. As we look at what is happening in our schools, these approaches seem promising:

a. Faculties should begin to probe into the nature of talent more deeply. Instead of beginning with a superficial tinkering with practices, some groups have begun asking such questions as: What do we know about the talented? What do we need to know if we are to build an effective program in our own situation? Rather then engage in endless debate and argument about the advantages and disadvantages of segregation, acceleration, or enrichment, school groups should examine alternative possibilities in terms of the goals they want to achieve. When they make changes, these should be made as hypotheses to be tested to attain particular objectives in a specific situation.

b. Faculties should try to understand what the general objectives of their schools mean when tailored to fit children with special abilities and potentials. The objectives in educating the talented are essentially the same as those for all youth—maximum development of the individual in society. What is there that is different about these goals when applied to the talented? Groups must begin to examine existing programs to see possible adjustments which may help attain these newly interpreted goals. Instead of adding a specific course or altering existing requirements of another, faculties are experimenting with changes which fit into a more comprehensive school philosophy.

c. Faculties should analyze existing traditions and administrative procedures to test their validity in practice. Must a child take a year of algebra if he can meet present requirements in far less time? If not, what kinds of provisions need to be made which will make optimum use of this time in terms of our goals for these youth?

d. Faculties should attempt total school planning for talented youth rather than indulge in isolated efforts. In considering special provisions, the resources of the entire school should be examined and analyzed for possible contribution to educating these youngsters. Those responsible for extraclass activities, special services, administration, and supervision must all be involved with classroom teachers in studying existing programs and available resources.

e. Faculties should try to increase their sensitivity to the impact of peers, parents, teachers, and community on talented youth and *vice versa*. For example, we recognize that there are teachers who feel insecure and inadequate in working with talented youth who should be provided with the in-service and supervisory assistance needed to meet the challenge of providing educational opportunities for these youngsters. If understanding of the talent is to be increased and all available resources made available, there will have to be continuous co-operation and co-ordination among teachers, parents, and community.

f. Faculties should recognize the enormity of planning for every conceivable talent. Before determining screening procedures, for example, they must define which areas they wish to give attention and what it is they want to achieve. Staffs which have begun with objectives and aims and then utilized or developed identification instruments have shown evidence of more creative approaches to providing for the talented. The possibility that there are many kinds of talents which may be identified and developed in different ways at various age and developmental levels suggests that faculties should explore continuous identification procedures.

These are some guides in the work of providing better educational opportunities for talented youth, some of which have been considered and implemented by individual schools. There is no need to urge school groups to give attention to making special provisions for the talented. There is, however, a real need to urge faculties to use a sound approach as they meet this challenge. No shortage exists in "testimonials" about programs and practices, but there is a real dearth of experimental evidence of the effectiveness of these programs. As schools begin to provide such data which emerge from research in local situations and these are coupled with researches from other disciplines, we will begin to gain a deeper understanding about the nature of talent which will enable us to do an even better job in meeting the needs of these youngsters and our democratic society.

REFERENCES

1. Lewis M. Terman and others, *Genetic Studies of Genius*. Three volumes. Stanford, California: Stanford University Press, 1925.
2. Lewis M. Terman and Melita H. Oden, *The Gifted Child Grows Up. Genetic Studies of Genius*, Vol. IV. Stanford, California: Stanford University Press, 1947. 448 pages.
3. Miriam C. Pritchard, "Total School Planning of the Gifted Child," *Exceptional Children*, 18:109, January, 1952.
4. Robert J. Havighurst and others, *A Community Youth Development Program*. Chicago: University of Chicago Press, 1952, p. 2.
5. National Manpower Council, *Science*, 117:617-622, June 5, 1953.
6. David P. Ausubel. *Prestige Motivation of Gifted Children*. New York: Teachers College, Columbia University, 1950. 112 pages. (Unpublished Doctoral Dissertation.)
7. Lewis M. Terman, "The Discovery and Encouragement of Exceptional Talent," *The American Psychologist*, 9:227, June, 1954.
8. Cornelis W. deKiewiet, "Education for Survival," *Scientific Monthly*, 76:61, February, 1953.

Enriching High-School Subjects for Intellectually Gifted Students

JULIAN C. STANLEY

Most ways of helping bright children get extra stimulation do not require expenditures far beyond those normally made by a first-class school system. "Enrichment" within classrooms is no exception; it calls for more finesse than finance.

The intellectually gifted student is *mentally* hungry. He needs a diet that will satisfy his cerebral cravings. Do we give a hungry man water and a thirsty one food? Of course not. But, for instance, we are sometimes prone to force upon a mathematically brilliant pupil experiences that, though worth while in general, do not meet his special needs.

I refer especially to the misuse, in the name of added enrichment, of such highly important activities as music, art, social studies, and training for classroom leadership, which, though desirable in themselves, are irrelevant to the special abilities and interests of many intellectually gifted children. Herein lies the danger in most *programs* of enrichment.

Reprinted from *School and Society*, Vol. 87, No. 2151 (April 11, 1959), pp. 170-171. By permission of the author and publisher.

Even more obvious abuses of the term "enrichment" occur frequently. A student who completes class work quickly and accurately may merely be assigned more of the same type at the same level. No wonder he is not challenged by this "busy work"!

Also, there are many modern equivalents of the traditional eraser-dusting and message-carrying that result in physical rather than mental activity. Even letting the ablest pupil tutor the slowest one or insisting that a boy whose interest is primarily theoretical construct some object has obvious limitations when used as enrichment.

Intellectually gifted youth can function at higher levels of difficulty, abstractness, and complexity than their classmates. They can learn the fundamentals of a subject quickly and then apply this knowledge effectively for generalizing, problem-solving, comparing and contrasting, analyzing, synthesizing, evaluating, and appreciating.

Possibilities for "enriching" a given subject with respect to the intellectually gifted within regular classes are restricted only by the ingenuity, resourcefulness, and especially the energy of the teacher and his colleagues. Causing students to think rather than merely to memorize is the key concept. While departing from rote learning would enliven most classes, it is doubly important for the brightest pupils.

Comparing and contrasting several literary selections for mood, author's intent, and various literary devices, for example, are higher-level undertakings than merely learning the names of the characters in each selection or outlining the plots. Devising original experiments in chemistry requires more use of a pupil's mental equipment than does following the directions in a typical laboratory manual. Evaluating presidents of the United States in accordance with explicit external criteria calls into play far more judgment than just memorizing their names. Inferring the meaning of the term "Mardi Gras" demands, of course, greater mental acumen than simply learning that this event occurs annually in New Orleans.

Books and articles concerning gifted children say very little about how to "enrich" courses at the secondary level. Perhaps their authors hope —unduly optimistically, it would seem—that the intelligent high-school teacher who knows his field well will have sound ideas as soon as he realizes what types of added intellectual stimulation are needed.

A senior-high teacher can get considerable help from the book describing the Advanced Placement Program of the College Entrance Examination Board, which illustrates types of content and mental processes suitable for superior high-school students in 12 subjects: American history, biology, chemistry, English composition, European history, French, German, Latin, literature, mathematics, physics, and Spanish.

Teachers at all grade levels should derive considerable benefit from the "Taxonomy of Educational Objectives," which contains illustrative educational objectives and test items for six levels of complexity: knowledge, comprehension, application, analysis, synthesis, and evaluation (1).

Science teachers should find the Dressel-Nelson folio of 13,000 specimen test items for senior high-school and college science courses suggestive of levels and content (2). These questions are classified according to the six major categories and the subcategories of the above "Taxonomy."

Teachers from Grade 3 onward may want to inspect the new Sequential Tests of Educational Progress (abbreviated STEP and pronounced "step"), which are separate tests of listening, mathematics, reading, science, social studies, and writing that have higher level items than the usual achievement battery (3).

Besides the things a teacher can do in his own classes, there are many administrative arrangements that will facilitate the education of gifted youngsters. For example, the ablest students might be allowed to elect an extra subject every year. They might be encouraged to choose the academically most demanding subjects in the school or by correspondence. Some might even get permission to enroll as special students in local colleges and extension centers to take regular college courses during the year or in the summer. A really bright student should profit more from a beginning college course in chemistry than from a well-taught high-school course, for example, and by getting college credit he could avoid the considerable overlap that probably would result if he took the course both in high school and in college.

Let me close with two warnings. The finest way to defeat plans to meet some of the special needs of intellectually gifted students is to argue that anything good for them must be valuable for typical students, too. Some youth are a lot brighter than others in their own grade. They think faster and at higher levels of abstraction, complexity, and difficulty. To a great extent, their intellectual needs are more like those of pupils several grades further along than they resemble the mental processes of their own classmates. This is one of the most solidly established facts in psychology. Stepping up requirements for *all* the pupils in a given class is *not* enrichment in the sense that we have been considering that word here.

Little "enrichment" for the gifted actually goes on in most regular classes. It does take the time of the teacher for a small number of students, and other members of the group may not benefit much. Few, if any, schools can afford to rely solely or even mainly upon this deceptively alluring procedure. Many other approaches, including several types of acceleration, also must be employed in order to provide effectively for the diverse mental and emotional needs of intellectually gifted students.

V

Issues and
Research

THE NEW INTEREST in gifted children which began in the early 1950's is now of sufficient age that its influence has been felt on all phases of American life. Some of the earlier problems have been resolved, and in some instances new problems have arisen. Many of the issues discussed with such furor in the 1950's have become part of the generally accepted philosophy of American education in the 1960's. The trend toward accepting responsibility for the education of all children, whether they have mental or physical gifts or limitations, continues.

Justification of special education for the gifted and the slow learner alike comes not only from the benefits which result for the child who is exceptional, but also from the benefits to the child in the regular class. Concern for one group, at the expense of the other, cannot be justified.

SOME PROBLEMS TO BE RESOLVED

Two distinct problems must be resolved if all of our gifted are to be adequately provided for in the public school system. We have no great surplus of mental superiority, and neglecting to utilize this "greatest of our natural resources" can only lead to disaster. The major problems to be resolved concerning the gifted, now that the all important problem of changing the attitude has been resolved in such an earth-shaking manner, have many ramifications, but basically they deal with (1) inequality of education, and (2) inequality of opportunity to use a particular gift.

The inequality of education is much greater than would ever be imagined. Only occasionally is there any definite evidence that children in a particular situation are not given the same opportunities as are children in other areas, but when such evidence does appear it usually shocks those in the underdeveloped areas of the country at the same time it strengthens the complacency of those in the more developed areas.

Writing about the Science Talent Search for the Westinghouse Science Scholarships, Morgan (1) points out that in the first thirteen years of its operation, "in 18 states the difference between the number of winners expected on a population basis and the actual number of winners exceeds 100 percent." (This list excludes states where the population is less than a million: Florida, Georgia, Iowa, Kentucky, Louisiana, Maryland, Michigan, Mississippi, Tennessee, Texas, Virginia and Washington.) Morgan points out that it is not that these states have less interest in science, for nine of these states have science searches of their own, and Oregon and New York, where the greatest percentage of winners occur, do not have. Other studies have clearly indicated that the number of scientists from a particular region is in direct proportion to the annual expenditure per pupil. At a recent national meeting it was noted that in only one high school in the nation were students licensed to handle cobalt, and yet in that same state there were high schools that did not yet have running water.

Of course, the problem is not entirely one of the shortage of money. Added expenditure would undoubtedly alleviate the problem somewhat, but there are other factors which also play a part. Racial and religious discrimination, in which separate but unequal schools have existed, have contributed to the problem. For the most part, however, those states which appear to have been most negligent about providing a high level of education have actually spent a larger percentage of their income on education than have the wealthier states. While this may seem to be a weak excuse to those living in highly developed areas, it is nevertheless a national problem and not just a local one.

The solution to the inequality of education must not be standardization of requirements, teaching procedures, or even teacher certification. Perhaps part of the solution could be achieved by accrediting students, rather than schools or courses, as Lewis Terman suggested many years ago (2). Standardization itself, by means of tests or course requirements, accomplishes little other than place a minimum level on particular courses. This may or may not be valuable for the average student, but it definitely produces little for the gifted. It may actually hinder the enrichment program for the gifted student, for he obviously can go far beyond the usual course requirements if he is given the freedom to do so without being held back by a specific course guide which must be followed by all students.

Even equal spending by school systems will not assure equality of education. It must be recognized, however, that when one school system can spend three times as much per child per year as another school system, the children in the school where more money is being spent will in most instances receive a better education. It is definitely a fact that some school systems get more for the money they spend than others, so that merely comparing the expenditure per child is not a definite measure of the type of education which the children are receiving.

The second problem, which is equally as important as the first, is the inequality of opportunity given all gifted individuals to use their gifts. Of particular concern is the role which gifted women are expected to play in our society. While the woman's role as wife and mother has changed somewhat, there are still many professions into which women are either not expected to enter or, if they are allowed to enter, the number is intentionally kept at a minimum.

Studies repeatedly show that of the large group of gifted children who do not go to college, women are the greatest number. The attitude is not uncommon that a girl will marry and therefore her college education will be wasted. The number of gifted individuals in any society is greatly limited and no country can afford to immediately cut the number in half by a notion that somehow women are either unwilling or incapable of assuming creative and productive lives beyond that of motherhood.

Women have been allowed to assume roles of leadership in the fine arts, but participation in scientific fields has been frowned upon and actually worked against. High school counselors have told girls that advanced mathematics classes are for boys, science classes may include a few girls, but they should not devote too much effort to these "impractical for a girl" fields. This advice is assuming that we have enough gifted individuals to waste half of the potential giftedness available. Exactly the opposite is true, but the advice of the counselor is unfortunately wise. Girls in advanced mathematics or scientific fields have limited choices of jobs, and may actually be unable to find any employment at all. So, in the change of attitudes toward gifted individuals, the American public must be made to realize that there is no such thing as a superiority in one field or another merely because of the sex of the individual. Cultural factors have somehow placed the woman in a superior role in the verbal areas, while men are supposed to be superior in nonverbal areas. The influence of these cultural factors result in waste of human talent to such a great extent that no time can be lost in changing the attitudes which cause such waste.

To what extent the gifted woman should be expected to produce has never been decided. Her most important role must, necessarily, be that of wife and mother. In this present day of automation, however, there is sufficient time to allow her to produce in a creative fashion beyond this limited role. College attendance for the gifted woman is essential for her own personal satisfaction as well as to prepare her for the life she should lead as a mother and a creative individual. We cannot afford to cross from the creative list half of our gifted population because of the notion that the mother's place is in the home. The gifted woman has a responsibility to society just as important as that of the gifted man.

Of great importance is the inequality of opportunity for racial and religious groups somehow based upon the assumption that giftedness is the special advantage of only the majority group. The very shortage of potential talent itself demands that we not waste this resource.

Both of these problems, the inequality of education and the inequality of opportunity, have many other facets than those discussed. Essentially the solution to both must first be a change in attitudes. Society's responsibility to the gifted is to provide the type of education which will develop to the limit those particular areas of strength in each individual. The responsibility of the gifted person is then to produce at the highest possible level for the benefit of mankind. If either is not done, and in far too many instances neither is being done, future generations will suffer because of our neglect.

REFERENCES

1. Morgan, Antonia B., "Identification and Guidance of Gifted Children," *Scientific Monthly,* Vol. 80, No. 3 (March, 1955), p. 172.
2. Cited in Stedman, Edith, *The Gifted Student and Student Personnel Programs in Colleges and Universities,* Pasadena, Calif.: Western Personnel Institute, 1956, p. 3.

14 | ISSUES

Creativity

J. P. GUILFORD

I discuss the subject of creativity with considerable hesitation, for it represents an area in which psychologists generally, whether they be angels or not, have feared to tread. It has been one of my long-standing ambitions, however, to undertake an investigation of creativity. Circumstances have just recently made possible the realization of that ambition. But the work has been started only within the past year. Consequently, if you are expecting answers based upon new empirical research you will be disappointed. What I can do at this time is to describe the plans for that research and to report the results of considerable thinking, including the hypotheses at which my students and I have arrived after a survey of the field and its problems. The research design, although not essentially new, should be of some interest. I will also point out some implications of the problems of creativity in vocational and educational practices.

SOME DEFINITIONS AND QUESTIONS

In its narrow sense, creativity refers to the abilities that are most characteristic of creative people. Creative abilities determine whether the individual has the power to exhibit creative behavior to a noteworthy degree. Whether or not the individual who has the requisite abilities will actually produce results of a creative nature will depend upon his motivational and temperamental traits. To the psychologist, the problem is as broad as the qualities that contribute significantly to creative productivity. In other words, the psychologist's problem is that of creative personality.

In defining personality, as well as other concepts preparatory to an

Reprinted from *American Psychologist*, Vol. 5, No. 9 (September, 1950), pp. 444-454. By permission of the author and the American Psychological Association.

investigation, definitions of an operational type are much to be preferred. I have often defined an individual's personality as his unique pattern of traits. A trait is any relatively enduring way in which persons differ from one another. The psychologist is particularly interested in those traits that are manifested in performance; in other words, in behavior traits. Behavior traits come under the broad categories of aptitudes, interests, attitudes, and temperamental qualities. By aptitude we ordinarily mean a person's readiness to learn to do certain types of things. There is no necessary implication in this statement as to the source of the degree of readiness. It could be brought about through hereditary determination or through environmental determination; usually, if not always, by an interaction of the two. By interest we usually mean the person's inclination or urge to engage in some type of activity. By attitude we mean his tendency to favor or not to favor (as shown objectively by approach-withdrawal behavior) some type of object or situation. Temperamental qualities describe a person's general emotional disposition: for example, his optimism, his moodiness, his self-confidence, or his nervousness.

Creative personality is then a matter of those patterns of traits that are characteristic of creative persons. A creative pattern is manifest in creative behavior, which includes such activities as inventing, designing, contriving, composing, and planning. People who exhibit these types of behavior to a marked degree are recognized as being creative.

There are certain aspects of creative genius that have aroused questions in the minds of those who have reflected much about the matter. Why is creative productivity a relatively infrequent phenomenon? Of all the people who have lived in historical times, it has been estimated that only about two in a million have become really distinguished (5). Why do so many geniuses spring from parents who are themselves very far from distinguished? Why is there so little apparent correlation between education and creative productiveness? Why do we not produce a larger number of creative geniuses than we do, under supposedly enlightened, modern educational practices? These are serious questions for thought and investigation. The more immediate and more explorable problem is a double one: (*a*) How can we discover creative promise in our children and our youth? and (*b*) How can we promote the development of creative personalities?

NEGLECT OF THE STUDY OF CREATIVITY

The neglect of this subject by psychologists is appalling. The evidences of neglect are so obvious that I need not give proof. But the extent of the neglect I had not realized until recently. To obtain a more tangible idea of the situation, I examined the index of the *Psychological Abstracts* for each year since its origin. Of approximately 121,000 titles listed in the past 23 years, only 186 were indexed as definitely bearing on the subject of creativity. The topics under which such references are listed include creativity, imagination, originality, thinking, and tests in these areas. In other words, less than two-tenths of one per cent of the books and articles indexed in the *Abstracts* for approximately the past quarter century bear directly on this subject. Few of these advance our understanding or control of creative activity very much. Of the large number of textbooks on general psychology, only two have devoted separate chapters to the subject during the same period.

Hutchinson, reviewing the publications on the process of creative thinking to the year 1931, concluded that the subject had hardly been touched by anyone (7). Markey, reviewing the subject of imagination four years later, reported very little more in the way of a fundamental contribution to the subject (9).

Some of you will undoubtedly feel that the subject of creative genius has not been as badly neglected as I have indicated, because of the common belief that genius is largely a matter of intelligence and the IQ. Certainly, that subject has not been neglected. But, for reasons which will be developed later, I believe that creativity and creative productivity extend well beyond the domain of intelligence.

Another important reason for the neglect, of course, is the difficulty of the problems themselves. A practical criterion of creativity is difficult to establish because creative acts of an unquestioned order of excellence are extremely rare. In this respect, the situation is much like that of a criterion for accident proneness which calls for the actual occurrence of accidents. The accidental nature of many discoveries and inventions is well recognized. This is partly due to the inequality of stimulus or opportunity, which is largely a function of the environment rather than of individuals. But if environmental occasions were equal, there would still be great differences in creative productivity among individuals.

There are, however, greater possibilities of observing individual differences in creative performance if we revise our standards, accepting examples of lower degrees of distinction. Such instances are more numerous. But even if we can detect and accept as creative certain acts of lower degrees of excellence, there are other difficulties. Creative people differ considerably in performance from time to time. Some writers on the subject even speak of rhythms of creativity. This means that any criterion, and probably any tests of creativity as well, would show considerable error variance due to function fluctuation. Reliabilities of tests of creative abilities and of creative criteria will probably be generally low. There are ways of meeting such difficulties, however. We should not permit them to force us to keep foot outside the domain.

Another reason for the oversight of problems of creativity is a methodological one. Tests designed to measure intelligence have fallen into certain stereotyped patterns, under the demands for objectivity and for scoring convenience. I do not now see how *some* of the creative abilities, at least, can be measured by means of anything but completion tests of some kind. To provide the creator with the finished product, as in a multiple-choice item, may prevent him from showing precisely what we want him to show: his own creation. I am not opposed to the use of the multiple-choice or other objectively scorable types of test items in their proper places. What I am saying is that the quest for easily objectifiable testing and scoring has directed us away from the attempt to measure some of the most precious qualities of individuals and hence to ignore those qualities.

Still another reason for the neglect of the problems of creativity is to be found in certain emphases we have given to the investigations of learning. For one thing, much learning research has been done with lower animals in which signs of creativity are almost nonexistent. For another thing, learning theory has been generally formulated to cover those phenomena that are easiest to order in logical schema. Learning theorists have had considerable difficulty with the behavior known as insight, to which creative behavior shows much apparent relationship (15). It is proper to say that a creative act is an instance of learning, for it represents a change in behavior that is due to stimulation and/or response. A comprehensive learning theory must take into account both insight and creative activity.

THE SOCIAL IMPORTANCE OF CREATIVITY

There is general recognition, on the part of those outside the academic fold, at least, of the importance of the quest for knowledge about creative disposition. I can cite recent evidences of the general interest in the discovery and development of creative talent. Large industries that employ many research scientists and engineers have held serious meetings and have had symposia written about the subject (9). There is much questioning into the reasons why graduates from the same institutions of higher learning, with high scholastic records and with strong recommendations, differ so widely in output of new ideas. The enormous economic value of new ideas is generally recognized. One scientist or engineer discovers a new principle or develops a new process that revolutionizes an industry, while dozens of others merely do a passable job on the routine tasks assigned to them.

Various branches of the government, as you all know, are now among the largest employers of scientific and technical personnel. These employers, also, are asking how to recognize the individuals who have inventive potentialities. The most common complaint I have heard concerning our college graduates in these positions is that while they can do assigned tasks with a show of mastery of the techniques they have learned, they are much too helpless when called upon to solve a problem where new paths are demanded.

Both industry and governmental agencies are also looking for leaders. Men of good judgment, planning ability, and inspiring vision are in great demand. How can leaders with imagination and vision be discovered? Can such qualities be developed? If those qualities can be promoted by educational procedures, what are those procedures?

We hear much these days about the remarkable new thinking machines. We are told that these machines can be made to take over much of men's thinking and that the routine thinking of many industries will eventually be done without the employment of human brains. We are told that this will entail an industrial revolution that will pale into insignificance the first industrial revolution. The first one made man's muscles relatively useless; the second one is expected to make man's brain also relatively useless. There are several implications in these possibilities that bear upon the importance of creative thinking. In the first place, it would be necessary to develop an economic order in which sufficient employment and wage earning would still be available. This would require creative thinking of an unusual order and speed. In the second place, eventually about the only economic value of brains left would be in the creative thinking of which they are capable. Presumably, there would still be need for human brains to operate the machines and to invent better ones.

SOME GENERAL THEORIES OF THE NATURE OF CREATIVITY

It is probably only a layman's idea that the creative person is peculiarly gifted with a certain quality that ordinary people do not have. This conception can be dismissed by psychologists, very likely by common consent. The general psychological conviction seems to be that all individuals possess to some degree all abilities, except for the occurrence of pathologies. Creative acts can therefore be expected, no matter how feeble or how infrequent, of almost all individuals. The important consideration here is the concept of continuity. Whatever the nature of creative talent may be, those persons who are recognized as creative merely have more of what all of us have. It is this principle of continuity that makes possible the investigation of creativity in people who are not necessarily distinguished.

The conception that creativity is bound up with intelligence has many followers among psychologists. Creative acts are expected from those of high IQ and not expected from those of low IQ. The term "genius," which was developed to describe people who distinguish themselves because of creative productivity, has been adopted to describe the child with ex-

ceptionally high IQ. Many regard this as unfortunate, but the custom
seems to have prevailed.

There is much evidence of substantial, positive correlations between
IQ as measured by an intelligence test and certain creative talents, but
the extent of the correlations is unknown. The work of Terman and his
associates is the best source of evidence of these correlations; and yet,
this evidence is not decisive. Although it was found that distinguished
men of history generally had high estimated IQ's, it is not certain that
indicators in the form of creative behavior have not entered into those
estimations (2). It would be much more crucial to know what the same
individuals would have done on intelligence tests when they were children. Terman's study of the thousand children of exceptionally high IQ's
who have now reached maturity does not throw much light on this theory.
Among the group there is plenty of indication of superior educational
attainment and of superior vocational and social adjustment. On the other
hand, there seems to be as yet little promise of a Darwin, an Edison, or a
Eugene O'Neill, although the members of the group have reached the
age level that has come to be recognized as the "most creative years."
The writers on that study recognize this fact and account for it on the
basis of the extreme rarity of individuals of the calibre of those whom I
have mentioned (11). It is hoped that further follow-up studies will give
due attention to criteria of a more specifically creative character.

When we look into the nature of intelligence tests, we encounter many
doubts concerning their coverage of creative abilities. It should be remembered that from the time of Binet to the present, the chief practical
criterion used in the validation of tests of intellect has been achievement
in school. For children, this has meant largely achievement in reading and
arithmetic. This fact has generally determined the nature of our intelligence tests. Operationally, then, intelligence has been the ability (or complex of abilities) to master reading and arithmetic and similar subjects.
These subjects are not conspicuously demanding of creative talent.

Examination of the content of intelligence tests reveals very little that
is of an obviously creative nature. Binet did include a few items of this
character in his scale because he regarded creative imagination as one
of the important higher mental functions that should be included. Revisions of the Binet scale have retained such items, but they represent only
a small minority. Group tests of intelligence have generally omitted such
items entirely.

The third general theory about creativity is, in fact, a theory of the
entire personality, *including* intelligence. I have defined personality as a
unique pattern of traits, and traits as a matter of individual differences.
There are thousands of observable traits. The scientific urge for rational
order and for economy in the description of persons directs us to look

for a small number of descriptive categories. In describing mental abilities, this economy drive has been grossly overdone when we limit ourselves to the single concept of intelligence. Furthermore, the term "intelligence" has by no means achieved logical or operational invariance and so does not satisfy the demand for rational order.

We do not need the thousands of descriptive terms because they are much interrelated, both positively and negatively. By intercorrelation procedures it is possible to determine the threads of consistency that run throughout the categories describing abilities, interests, and temperament variables. I am, of course, referring to the factorial conception of personality. From this point of view, personality is conceived geometrically as a hypersphere of n dimensions, each dimension being a dependable, convenient reference variable or concept. If the idea of applying this type of description to a living, breathing individual is distasteful, remember that this geometric picture is merely a conceptual model designed to encompass the multitude of observable facts, and to do it in a rational, communicable, and economical manner.

With this frame of reference, many of the findings and issues become clarified. The reason that different intelligence tests do not intercorrelate perfectly, even when errors of measurement have been taken into account, is that each test emphasizes a different pattern of primary abilities. If the correlations between intelligence-test scores and many types of creative performance are only moderate or low, and I predict that such correlations will be found, it is because the primary abilities represented in those tests are not all important for creative behavior. It is also because some of the primary abilities important for creative behavior are not represented in the test at all. It is probably safe to say that the typical intelligence test measures to a significant degree not more than a half-dozen of the intellectual factors (8). There are surely more intellectual factors than that. Some of the abilities contributing to creative success are probably non-intellectual; for example, some of them are perceptual. Probably, some of the factors most crucial to creative performance have not yet been discovered in any type of test. In other words, we must look well beyond the boundaries of the IQ if we are to fathom the domain of creativity.

DEVELOPMENT OF CREATIVITY

Before referring to the experimental design and to more specific hypotheses concerning the nature of creativity, I will venture one or two opinions on the general problem of the development of creativity. For I believe that much can be done to encourage its development. This development might be in the nature of actual strengthening of the functions involved or it might mean the better utilization of what resources the individual possesses, or both. In any case, a knowledge of the functions is important.

We frequently hear the charge that under present-day mass-education methods, the development of creative personality is seriously discouraged. The child is under pressure to conform for the sake of economy and for the sake of satisfying prescribed standards. We are told by the philosophers who have given thought to the problem that the unfolding of a creative personality is a highly individual matter which stresses uniqueness and shuns conformity. Actually, the unfolding of the individual along the lines of his own inclinations is generally frowned upon. We are told, also, that the emphasis upon the memorizing of facts sets the wrong kind of goal for the student. How serious these charges are no one actually knows. We have very little experimental evidence that is decisive one way or the other and such evidence is hard to obtain.

Charles Kettering one time commented upon a survey in which it was found that a person with engineering or scientific training had only half the probability of making an invention compared with others. His comment was that an inventor should be defined as "a fellow who doesn't take his education too seriously" (9). If the results of that survey represent the actual situation, either creative individuals do not seek higher education in engineering and science, or that kind of education has negative transfer effects with respect to inventiveness.

Many of us teachers assert that it is our main objective to teach students how to think, and this means also to think constructively. Certainly, if we succeeded in this objective, there should be much evidence of creativeness in the end product. I am convinced that we do teach some students to think, but I sometimes marvel that we do as well as we do. In the first place, we have only vague ideas as to the nature of thinking. We have little actual knowledge of what specific steps should be taken in order to teach students to think. Our methods are shotgun methods, just as our intelligence tests have been shotgun tests. It is time that we discarded shotguns in favor of rifles.

We all know teachers who pride themselves on teaching students to think and yet who give examinations that are almost entirely a matter of knowledge of facts. Please do not misunderstand me. I have a strong appreciation of knowledge of facts. No creative person can get along without previous experiences or facts; he never creates in a vacuum or with a vacuum. There is a definite place for the learning of facts in our educational system. But let us keep our educational objectives straight. Let us recognize where facts are important and where they are not. Let us remember, too, that the kinds of examinations we give really set the objectives for the students, no matter what objectives we may have stated.

The confusion of objectives is illustrated by the following incident. The story was told by a former dean of a leading Midwestern University. An old, experienced teacher and scholar said that he tried to encourage originality in his students. In a graduate course, he told the class that the term paper would be graded in terms of the amount of originality shown. One school teacher in the class was especially concerned about getting a high mark in the course. She took verbatim notes, continuously and assiduously, of what the learned professor said in class. Her term paper, the story goes, was essentially a stringing together of her transcribed lecture notes, in which the professor's pet ideas were given prominent place. It is reported that the professor read the term papers himself. When the school teacher's paper was returned, the professor's mark was an A, with the added comment, "This is one of the most original papers I have ever read."

Before we make substantial improvement in teaching students to think, in my opinion we will have to make some changes in our conceptions of the process of learning. The ancient faculty psychology taught that mental faculties grow strong by virtue of the exercise of those faculties. We all know from the many experiments on practice in memorizing that exercises in memorizing are not necessarily followed by improvement of memory in general. We all know that exercises in perceptual discriminations of certain kinds are not followed by improvement of perceptual discriminations in general (13). Thorndike and others concluded that the study of courses in high-school curricula did not necessarily result in a general improvement in intellect, but that the increases in test scores could be attributed to learning of a more specific nature (1, 12). Following this series of experiments the conclusion has often been that learning consists of the development of specific habits and that only very similar skills will be affected favorably by the learning process.

In view of the newer findings concerning primary abilities, the problems of formal discipline take on new meaning, and many of the experiments on the transfer of training will have to be reexamined and perhaps repeated with revised conditions. The experiments just cited do justify the rejection of the concepts of a general memory power, a general perceptual-discrimination power, and perhaps, also, rejection of the concept of a single power called intellect. These findings are in harmony with factorial theory. But the other alternative to the idea of formal discipline is not necessarily a theory of specific learning from specific practice.

There is certainly enough evidence of transfer effects. Experiments should be aimed to determine whether the instances of positive, zero, and negative transfer effects conform in a meaningful way to the outlines of the primary abilities. The work of Thorndike and others that I have just cited does, in fact, actually throw some light on this question. Although this aspect of their findings is usually not mentioned, they reported that high-school students' experiences in numerical, verbal, and spatial types of courses—arithmetic and bookkeeping, Latin and French, and manual training—were associated with relatively greater gains in numerical, verbal, and spatial types of tests, respectively.

A general theory to be seriously tested is that some primary abilities can be improved with practice of various kinds and that positive transfer effects will be evident in tasks depending upon those abilities. At the present time some experiments of this type are going on in the Chicago schools under the direction of Thelma Gwinn Thurstone (14). In one sense, these investigations have returned to the idea of formal discipline. The new aspect of the disciplinary approach is that the presumed functions that are being "exercised" have been indicated by empirical research.

FACTORIAL RESEARCH DESIGN

The general outline of the design for a factor-analysis investigation is familiar to many of you. It has been described before but needs to be emphasized again (14). The complete design involves a number of steps, not all of which are essential but all of which are highly desirable if the investigator is to make the most efficient use of his time and to achieve results of maximum value. The major steps will be mentioned first, then more details concerning some of them.

One first chooses the domain of his investigation. It may be the domain of memory abilities, visual-perceptual abilities, reasoning abilities, or the domain of introversion-extraversion.

One next sets up hypotheses as to the factors he expects to find in that domain. His preparatory task of hypothesis formation goes further. It includes the framing of several alternative hypotheses as to the more precise nature of each factor. This is necessary as the basis for transforming each factor hypothesis into the operational terms of test ideas. He then constructs tests which he thinks will measure individual differences in the kind of ability, or other quality, he thinks the factor to be. He will want to include in the test battery some reference tests that measure already known factors. One reason for this is that the new tests will almost inevitably also measure to some extent factors that have previously been established, such as verbal comprehension, number facility, and visualization. If such variance is probably going to appear in more than one new test in the battery, it is best to have that variance clearly brought out and readily identifiable. Another reason is that it is possible, after all, that one or more of the hypothesized factors will turn out to be identifiable with one or more of the known factors. The possibility of this identification must be provided for by having the suspected, known factors represented in the battery.

The test battery is administered to a sample of adequate size from a population of appropriate qualifications. Certain kinds of populations are

better for bringing out variances in some common factors and other kinds
are more suitable for other purposes. There should be relative homogeneity in certain features that might be correlated with the factors, such
as sex, age, education, and other conditions. Some thought should be
given to whether tests should be speed tests or power tests or something
between the two. Some consideration should also be given to the most
appropriate type of score for each test.

Factors are extracted and their reference axes are rotated into positions that are compelling because of the nature of the configuration of
test vectors in the hyperspace. The psychological nature of each factor
is surmised by virtue of the kinds of tests that have substantial variance
attributable to that factor in contrast to tests which lack that variance.

In many respects, the complete factor-analysis design has properties
parallel to those of a good experiment. In both, we begin with hypotheses. In both, some conditions are held constant while others are varied.
In both, the measured outcomes point toward or away from the hypotheses. One important difference is the possibility of a statistical test of significance of the measured result for the experiment but not for the factor
analysis. Confidence in the latter case depends upon the compellingness
of the factor structure and the repeated verification of a result.

As an illustration of this analogy to an experiment, I will cite the factorial study of the well-known figure-analogies test. In the Army Air
Forces research results, the figure-analogies test exhibited variances in
three factors denoted as reasoning I, II, and III (6). They were thus
designated because they were peculiar to a number of reasoning tests,
but their more precise natures were obscure. Examination of what one
does in solving a figure-analogies item suggests several possible psychological functions or activities. First, one has to grasp correctly the relation
between figure one and figure two. This suggests an ability to see a relationship between two objects. Second, one must observe the properties
of the third figure. Then, one has to see what kind of a fourth figure it
takes to satisfy the same relationship between figure three and figure four.
Having decided upon the kind of figure needed, one has to find it among
four or five that are supplied in the multiple-choice item. This is a kind
of classifying act. There is still another possibility. The mislead responses
may be so reasonable that considerable discrimination may be needed to
select the best figure for the purpose. Considering the figure-analogies
item from a more holistic point of view, there may be a primary ability
involved in seeing that there is an identity of two relationships when the
elements related are different. Or, there may be a general reasoning-by-
analogy ability. Transposability of relations may be a key function here.
Thus, we have several hypotheses as to the functions involved. There
could be others. For every one of them we also have the further question
as to whether the ability implied is restricted to the visual perception of

figures or whether it is more general, extending to word meanings, numbers, and sounds. And if it is general, what are its limits?

To seek answers by factorial methods, one would construct special tests, each limited, if possible, to one kind of act implied by each hypothesis. One would also vary the kind of material in each type of test to explore the scope of generality. The answers to the hypotheses (for each hypothesis is in reality a question) would be to find that the loading for each factor would rise with some of the variations and fall with others as compared to its loading in the traditional figure-analogies test. We would hope to find the changes in factor loadings so marked that we would not feel seriously the lack of t tests or F tests.

The question of the sources of factor hypotheses calls for some comment. In a domain in which there have already been factorial studies, the previous results are always suggestive. This makes it appear that the factorist merely moves from hypotheses to hypotheses. This is quite true. It is a fundamental truth of all scientists, no matter what their methods. Some hypotheses are merely better supported and more generally accepted than others at the time. There is enough uncertainty left in many a hypothesis to invite further investigation. That is what makes science interesting. That is what I think Kettering meant when he stated that the inventor is one who does not take his education (or knowledge) too seriously.

In a personality domain in which there has been little previous illumination of the underlying variables, other sources of hypotheses must be sought. The critical-incident technique of Flanagan would be one useful exploratory approach (4). Incidentally, one might say that this method has been used informally in connection with creative people from the "Eureka" episode of Archimedes down to modern times. The literature includes many descriptions of creative events. It would be more correct to refer to these historical reports as anecdotes, however, rather than critical incidents, since they suffer from most of the weaknesses of anecdotes. Where modern writers have attempted to interpret them psychologically, the interpretations have been quite superficial. They abound with vague concepts such as "genius," "intuition," "imagination," "reflection," and "inspiration," none of which leads univocally to test ideas. In the writings of those who have attempted to give a generalized picture of creative behavior, there is considerable agreement that the complete creative act involves four important steps.

According to this picture, the creator begins with a period of preparation, devoted to an inspection of his problem and a collection of information or material. There follows a period of incubation during which there seems to be little progress in the direction of fulfillment. But, we are told, there *is* activity, only it is mostly unconscious. There eventually comes the big moment of inspiration, with a final, or semi-final, solution, often accompanied by strong emotion. There usually follows a period of evaluation or verification, in which the creator tests the solution or examines the product for its fitness or value. Little or much "touching up" may be done to the product.

Such an analysis is very superficial from the psychological point of view. It is more dramatic than it is suggestive of testable hypotheses. It tells us almost nothing about the mental operations that actually occur. The concepts do not lead directly to test ideas. In attempting to distinguish between persons with different degrees of creative talent, shall we say, for example, that some individuals are better incubators than others? And how would one go about testing for incubating ability? The belief that the process of incubation is carried on in a region of the mind called the unconscious is of no help. It merely chases the problem out of sight and thereby the chaser feels excused from the necessity of continuing the chase further.

It is not incubation itself that we find of great interest. It is the nature of the processes that occur during the latent period of incubation, as well as before it and after it. It is individual differences in the efficiency of those processes that will be found important for identifying the potentially creative. The nature of those processes or functions will have to be inferred from performances of the individuals who have been presented with problems, even though the creator is largely unaware of them.

SPECIFIC HYPOTHESES CONCERNING CREATIVE ABILITIES

The hypotheses that follow concerning the nature of creative thinking have been derived with certain types of creative people in mind: the scientist and the technologist, including the inventor. The consensus of the philosophers seems to have been that creativity is the same wherever you find it. To this idea I do not subscribe. Within the factorial frame of reference there is much room for different types of creative abilities. What it takes to make the inventor, the writer, the artist, and the composer creative may have some factors in common, but there is much room for variation of pattern of abilities. Some of the hypotheses mentioned here may apply also to areas of creative endeavor other than science, technology, and invention, but others may not. Included in the list of primary abilities that may contribute to creative efforts of these special groups are the reasoning factors, but I shall restrict mention here to other possible thinking factors that are more obviously creative in character.

First, there are probably individual differences in a variable that may be called *sensitivity to problems*. How this variation among individuals may come about will not concern us at this time. Whether it is best regarded as an ability or as a temperament trait will not concern us, either.

The fact remains that in a certain situation one person will see that several problems exist while another will be oblivious to them.

Two scientists look over a research report. There are generally acceptable conclusions, but there is one minor discrepancy in the results. One scientist attributes the discrepancy to "experimental error." The other feels uneasy about the discrepancy; it piques his curiosity; it challenges him for an explanation. His further thinking about the matter develops into a new research project from which highly important findings result. Such an incident was reported by Flanagan (4); it could be found duplicated many times.

There are questions as to the generality of such a variable. Is the supposed sensitivity restricted to a certain kind of situation or a certain kind of problem? Is it a perceptual quality as well as a thought quality? Could it be a general impressionability to the environment? Is it our old friend "curiosity" under a new name? Is it an ability to ask questions? Is it a general inhibition against closure? There may be other hypotheses just as pertinent. Each one suggests possible tests of individual differences.

Examples of possible tests follow. One might present the examinee with a short paragraph of expository material and instruct him to ask as many questions as he can that are suggested by the statements, with relatively liberal time allowed. A large part of the scientist's success depends upon his ability to ask questions, and, of course, to ask the right questions. In another test, one might name common household appliances, such as a toaster, or articles of clothing, such as trousers, and ask the examinee to list things that he thinks are wrong or could be improved. As a perceptual test, one might present pictures of objects or forms that are conventional and regular except for minor irregularities. Can the examinee detect the unusual features or will he overlook them? A third possibility is in the form of what we have called a "frustration test," merely because it is somewhat frustrating to many who have tried it. Contrary to the usual test practice, no task instruction is given: only items, and the very general instruction "do something with each item; whatever you think should be done." Each item is of a different type. One or two examinees have refused to do anything with the test.

There is very likely a *fluency* factor, or there are a number of fluency factors, in creative talent. Not that all creators must work under pressure of time and must produce rapidly or not at all. It is rather that the person who is capable of producing a large number of ideas per unit of time, other things being equal, has a greater chance of having significant ideas. There have been previous results yielding several verbal-fluency factors but I have insufficient time to acknowledge those studies properly here. It is probable that there are a number of fluency factors, nonverbal as well as verbal, yet undiscovered. There is a general problem to be investigated, apart from creativity, whether many of the primary thinking abilities have both a power and a speed aspect somewhat independent of each other. Some work of Davidson and Carroll (3) suggests this in a result with regard to one of the reasoning factors.

One kind of fluency test would consist of asking the examinee to name as many objects as he can in a given time, the objects having some specified property; for example, things round, things red, or things to eat. In another test, the ideas might be more complex, as in naming a list of appropriate titles for a picture or for a short story. Still more demanding and also more restricting would be the task of naming exceptions to a given statement. Fluency of inferences may be tested by providing a hypothetical statement to which the examinee is to state as many consequences or implications as he can in a limited time. The statement might be: A new invention makes it unnecessary for people to eat; what will the consequences be? This type of test has been previously proposed by several investigators.

The creative person has *novel* ideas. The degree of novelty of which the person is capable, or which he habitually exhibits, is pertinent to our study. This can be tested in terms of the frequency of uncommon, yet acceptable, responses to items. The tendency to give remote verbal associations in a word-association test; to give remote similarities in a similes test; and to give connotative synonyms for words, are examples of indications of novelty of ideas in the category of verbal tests.

The individual's *flexibility* of mind, the ease with which he changes set, can possibly be indicated in several ways by means of tests. Although there have been disappointments in the attempt to establish a common factor of this type (6), the concept of flexibility and of its probable opposite, rigidity will not be downed. In conjunction with some of the fluency tests, there may be opportunities to obtain some indications concerning flexibility. Does the examinee tend to stay in a rut or does he branch out readily into new channels of thought? Tests whose items cannot be correctly answered by adhering to old methods but require new approaches, in opposition to old habits of thinking, would be pertinent here. Certain types of puzzles fit this requirement fairly well, for example, a problem in which the examinee cannot succeed without folding the paper on which he writes, and the idea of doing so must come from him.

Much creative thinking requires the organizing of ideas into larger, more inclusive patterns. For this reason, we have hypothesized a *synthesizing ability*. As a counterpart to this, one might well expect an *analyzing ability*. Symbolic structures must often be broken down before new ones can be built. It is desirable to explore many kinds of both synthesizing and analyzing activities, in both perceptual and conceptual problems, in order to determine the existence of such factors and their numbers and whether they cut across both perceptual and conceptual areas.

From Gestalt psychology comes the idea that there may be a factor involving *reorganization* or *redefinition* of organized wholes (15). Many inventions have been in the nature of a transformation of an existing object into one of different design, function, or use. It may be that this activity involves a combination of flexibility, analysis and synthesis, and that no additional hypothesis of redefinition is really needed, but the possibility must be investigated.

There is a possibility of a dimension of ability that has to do with the degree of *complexity* or of intricacy of conceptual structure of which the individual is capable. How many interrelated ideas can the person manipulate at the same time? The scientist must often keep in mind several variables, conditions, or relationships as he thinks out a problem. Some individuals become confused readily; they can keep only one or two items of structure delineated and properly related. Others have a higher resistance to confusion—a greater span of this type. Such an ability might be identifiable with the hypothesized synthesizing factor, but the study should make possible a separation of the two if the distinction is real.

Creative work that is to be realistic or accepted must be done under some degree of evaluative restraint. Too much restraint, of course, is fatal to the birth of new ideas. The selection of surviving ideas, however, requires some *evaluation*. In this direction there must be a factor or two. The evaluations are conceivably of different kinds, consequently the kinds of possible tests are numerous. In a paragraph of exposition, we may ask the examinee to say whether every underlined statement is best classified as a fact, a definition, or a hypothesis. He will, to be sure, need some preliminary instruction in these distinctions. In another test, we can present him with a stated problem, then ask him which of several items are relevant to its solution and which ones are not. In still another test, we can give a problem and several alternative solutions, all correct. The examinee is to rank the solutions in the order of degree of excellence or fitness.

The hypotheses mentioned, as was stated earlier, refer more specifically to a limited domain of creative thinking more characteristic of the scientist and technologist. Even so, this entails a factorial study of substantial proportions. Similar studies will need to be made in the domains of planning abilities, in order to anticipate abilities more characteristic of the economic, the political, and the military leader. Still other restricted domains will need to be investigated to take care of the writer, the graphic artist, and the musical composer.

The question will inevitably arise, "How do you know your tests are valid?" There are two answers to this question. The first is that the factorial study of the tests is in itself one kind of validation. It will determine which tests measure each factor and to what extent. That is a matter of internal validity or factorial validity. It answers the question, "What does the test measure?" The second answer will be in terms of which factors are related to the creative productivity of people in everyday life. That calls for the correlation of factor measures with practical criteria. I feel very strongly that only after we have determined the promising factors and how to measure them are we justified in taking up the time of creative people with tests. If a certain factor we discover turns out not to be related to creative production, we have made a bad guess, but we will have discovered a new factor that may have some other practical validity. If a certain factor is not related to the criteria of creative productivity, the tests which measure it uniquely will also prove to be invalid for predicting these criteria. It is better to fail in the validation of a single factor measure than to fail in the validation of a half-dozen tests. If we make a study of the practical validity of every creative test we can think of before it is analyzed, we are bound to exert considerable wasted effort of our own and of our examinees. This statement, incidentally, applies to the validation study of any test.

Creative productivity in everyday life is undoubtedly dependent upon primary traits other than abilities. Motivational factors (interests and attitudes) as well as temperament factors must be significant contributors. Hypotheses concerning these factors in connection with creative people might be fruitful starting points for factorial investigations. The design of the research would be much the same as that described for creative abilities.

SUMMARY AND CONCLUSIONS

By way of summary, it can be said that psychologists have seriously neglected the study of the creative aspects of personality. On the other hand, the social importance of the subject is very great. Many believe that creative talent is to be accounted for in terms of high intelligence or IQ. This conception is not only inadequate but has been largely responsible for the lack of progress in the understanding of creative people.

The factorial conception of personality leads to a new way of thinking about creativity and creative productivity. According to this point of view, creativity represents patterns of primary abilities, patterns which can vary with different spheres of creative activity. Each primary ability is a variable along which individuals differ in a continuous manner. Consequently, the nature of these abilities can be studied in people who are not necessarily distinguished for creative reasons. Productivity depends upon other primary traits, including interests, attitudes, and temperamental variables.

It is proposed that a fruitful exploratory approach to the domain of creativity is through a complete application of factor analysis, which would begin with carefully constructed hypotheses concerning the primary abilities and their properties. It is suggested that certain kinds of factors will be found, including sensitivity to problems, ideational fluency, flexibility of set, ideational novelty, synthesizing ability, analyzing ability, reorganizing or redefining ability, span of ideational structure, and evaluating ability. Each one of these hypotheses may be found to refer to more than one factor. Some hypothesized abilities may prove to be identical with others or accounted for in terms of others. At any rate, these hypotheses lead to the construction of tests of quite novel types, which is a promising condition for the discovery of new factors. The relation of such factors to practical criteria of creative performance will need to be established. It is likely that the tests have been aimed in the right direction.

Once the factors have been established as describing the domain of creativity, we have a basis for the means of selecting the individuals with creative potentialities. We also should know enough about the properties of the primary abilities to do something in the way of education to improve them and to increase their utilization. These ends certainly justify our best efforts.

REFERENCES

1. Broyler, C. R., Thorndike, E. L., and Woodyard, E., A Second Study of Mental Discipline in High Schools. *J. Educ. Psychol.*, 1927, **18**, 377-404.
2. Cox, C. M., *Genetic Studies of Genius*, Vol. II. Stanford, California: Stanford University Press, 1926.
3. Davidson, W. M., and Carroll, J. B., Speed and Level Components in Time-Limit Scores. *Educ. & Psychol. Meas.*, 1945, **5**, 411-435.
4. Flanagan, J. C., et al., *Critical Requirements for Research Personnel*. Pittsburgh: American Institute for Research, 1949.
5. Giddings, F. H., *Elements of Sociology*. New York: Macmillan Co., 1907.
6. Guilford, J. P. (Ed.), *Printed Classification Tests*, Army Air Forces Aviation Psychology Research Program, Report No. 5. Washington, D. C.: Government Printing Office, 1947.
7. Hutchinson, E. D., Materials for the Study of Creative Thinking. *Psychol. Bull.*, 1931, **28**, 392-410.
8. Jones, L. V., A Factor Analysis of the Stanford-Binet at Four Age Levels. *Psychom.*, 1949, **14**, 299-331.
9. Kettering, C. F., How Can We Develop Inventors? In a Symposium on *Creative Engineering*. New York: American Society of Mechanical Engineers, 1944.
10. Markey, F. V., Imagination. *Psychol. Bull.*, 1935, **32**, 212-236.
11. Terman, L. M., and Oden, M. H., *The Gifted Child Grows Up*. Stanford, California: Stanford University Press, 1947.
12. Thorndike, E. L., Mental Discipline in High School Studies. *J. Educ. Psychol.*, 1924, **15**, 1-22, 83-98.
13. Thorndike, E. L., and Woodworth, R. S., The Influence of Improvement in One Mental Function upon the Efficiency of Other Functions. *Psychol. Rev.*, 1901, 8, 247-261, 384-395, 553-564.
14. Thurstone, L. L., Implications of Factor Analysis. *Amer. Psychologist*, 1948, 3, 402-408.
15. Wertheimer, M., *Productive Thinking*. New York: Harper & Bros., 1945.

Opposition to Education of the Gifted in the United States

G. Z. F. BEREDAY

When the mid-fifties became the scene of the long-overdue revival of interest in the education of the highly talented, it became fashionable to say that this revival would stumble upon the resistance of 'democratic purists' in the United States. A number of very thoughtful writers, among them John Gardner, President of the Carnegie Corporation, in his recent book *Excellence*, have condemned the cult of the average, and the suspicion of intellectual *élitism* flourishing among many groups of people, and inhibiting the care for the gifted in the schools. There is no doubt, to use Whitehead's concept of inert ideas, that the original grand design of education for all has in countless schools been replaced by atrophied forms which see safety for the individual only in sticking to the middle of the group and in adjusting to it. On the other hand, the new recognition of the importance of the maximum development of talent can be similarly wrecked by fads and band wagons that propose enthusiastically without knowing what it is that they are proposing. Some of the criticisms of the current emphasis on the gifted has been of the thoughtful, responsible kind. This article is an attempt to present the tenor of these criticisms. They should be respectively examined before Americans proceed, as they must, with the development of programmes for the highly talented.

Opponents of the current proposals can roughly be said to concentrate on three issues: who are the gifted; must they be separated from the mainstream of their classmates; and how are they to be separated? Because the second question raises the more philosophical issue it will be discussed after the more practical first and third query have been accounted for.

WHO ARE THE GIFTED?

Which children precisely are 'gifted'? The critics point out that some agreement should be reached as to what constitutes gifts before pro-

Reprinted from *Concepts of Excellence in Education*. The Yearbook of Education, 1961, pp. 352-367. By permission of the author, Evans Brothers, Ltd., and Harcourt, Brace & World, Inc.

grammes of teaching them are launched. Much has been written on the subject, but visible marks of such agreement have as yet to appear. John Deeb's unpublished Columbia University dissertation, for instance, investigated most U.S. books and articles on the gifted for the years between 1945 and 1955, only to find that "there is no common feeling as to who the gifted student is, nor is there a definition written in the literature to which most writers would subscribe," yet "no other category shows such tremendous increase in literature as . . . the writings on various school programs used and suggested to meet the problems of gifted pupils." So long as nobody seems to know who the gifted pupils are it will seem legitimate to view with misgiving those who jump on the band wagon to do something for them.

Some psychologists argue that the gifted are the persons of inherited general ability, a cognitive facility that makes them develop early, grow taller and stronger and excel in all fields. There seem to be many difficulties when this psychological principle, be it true or not, is converted into pedagogical practice. Proponents of general ability themselves admit that every able man in the end focuses on and distinguishes himself in one particular, even if accidentally chosen field, thus rendering the notion of general ability largely theoretical. There is also some uncertainty about what the general ability precisely represents and thus how to cater for it. Its admitted correlation with high socioeconomic status of parents casts a shadow of doubt on its purely hereditary derivation. In the group followed through by Terman, for instance, Jews and Scotsmen represented twice as high a proportion as in the general population. The rabbinical tradition of learning among the former, and the parish-school-derived seriousness about intellect in the latter, could go far to explain their success, perhaps as far as any appeal to heredity. Again, persons selected by Terman owed at least part of their subsequent rise merely to the bonus conferred by the label of 'Terman's geniuses.' The theory of general ability is also pedagogically weakened by the fact that in English selective schools, no less than in American mass schools, such ability has been found to be consistently under-developed. An unstructured environment seems to aid the flourishing of such ability, but all structures deter it. Thus the usefulness of the concept for the proper scheduling of school activities is plainly limited.

Several psychologists have, in fact, reacted from the concept of general ability by postulating series of special gifts. They would have the schools serve the cause of such endowments by early detection and special tutoring. But in so far as they want to cater for all gifts, including the artistic, the athletic, and the social, their lessons for America are few. In American schools, far more than in the schools of any other country, such gifts have been well catered for. Moreover, since these are coupled in pairs and threesomes in different pupils, it is difficult to determine precisely how they should be grouped homogeneously. The school programme geared to all gifts would simply have to mean a *better* school programme for *all* students. No one can deny this to be the perennial task of education. Continuous attention to, and search for, better ways to serve all talent is the essence of good schooling.

But most writers, intellectual or pseudo, educators or laymen, really think only of intellectual gifts no matter what they profess in public. Sometimes they recognize the great need for such gifts in the future science-run society. Sometimes they project into the recommendations of public policy the image of themselves and how they would like that image to be treated. Whatever their motives, even in the area of relatively clear-cut intellectual gifts, some problems remain unsolved. For instance, the separate identification of the scientific and the literary talents has not been well worked out anywhere. Precedents for such division exist in European schools. But enough misplacing occurs there to undermine confidence.

The uncertainty about the merits of selections stems from the question: How and when does one measure whatever one decides to measure? The usual practice is to provide no more than a rather crude sorting of students by subject-matter examinations, intelligence tests, and references of teachers. Each of these three ways, especially when applied separately, raises as many problems as it solves.

The critics of examinations, for instance, recall the wave of indignation that swept France three years ago when the *concours de sixième,* the entrance examination to the *lycées* and *colleges,* contained improbable assignments: a rather perverse story of André Gide, a request for definition of 'abnegation,' and intricate arithmetic speculations. This examination for 11-year-olds has now been entirely replaced by teachers' references. Similar outcries are being heard in England. The publication of specimen questions by Paul Tanfield, for instance, in the *Daily Mail* a few years ago, was greeted by a wave of protests. A few English counties have already abolished selection examinations and new national agitation against them flares up each time they are held. In the Soviet Union, too, several school and university examinations have been cut or modified. It is argued that subject-matter examinations often tend to degenerate into devices successful only in promoting large-scale frustration of parents and children. They cast a heavy shadow of exacting, but sometimes meaningless and premature effort, over the schools that must prepare for them. To some unknown degree they are an unfair measure of ability. They reflect the early culture of the home and confer upon the examining boards unfair powers to act as social reception committees. Examinations test memory, writing style, power of reasoning, and above all, fast performance under duress. But as a general index of talent they are deemed by many to be unacceptable.

Intelligence tests are considered by critics only a little better. They point out that those who use tests are usually much surer of their validity than those who devise them. Even as staunch a supporter of IQ testing as Philip Vernon, in England, usually goes through a veritable gamut of reservations before pronouncing the tests best suited for assessing the aptitudes of young children. But even if the tests are valid predictors, it has never been made clear where to set the cut-off point of giftedness. Suppose one selects all children over an IQ of 130? What about those with IQ's of 129 or 128 or 127? An additional uncertainty was supplied by Philip Vernon himself. He found that simply by a few hours' coaching, IQ performance can be permanently improved by as many as 15 points.

In addition, there is the unfinished quest for tests that would really be culture free. No known test of intelligence can fully offset the disadvantages of home background, low initial literacy, or lack of training in abstract thinking. Consider, for instance, a test which asks for a definition of the word *fast* and scores *flirtatious* as the correct answer. Such result would favour the amorous, but penalize the religious to whom the word *fast* has quite a different connotation. Little can be expected from such measurements. At the very best they favour the quicker to the disadvantage of the slower, less spectacular minds. They tell little about depth, or creativity, or persistence, or moral commitment, none of which can be ignored in the selection of future leaders.

American education, on advice of its psychologists, is deemed to be suffering in addition from the belief in the efficacy of testing at an early age. It is not unusual for elementary schools to run classes for the IGC's (Intellectually Gifted Children). But in Europe, in no country does selection occur before the age of 11. Moreover, even so early an age as 11 has provoked continued and increasing opposition. In England, schools operate under a regulation that provides (at least in theory) for a corrective reshuffling at 13 after the initial 11+ ordeal. In France, the law just passed plans for a *cycle d'orientation* between the ages of 11 and 13, the actual selection to occur at the latter age. In Germany, a similar *Förderstufe* has just been proposed in the *Rahmenplan*. In all other countries of Europe the expansion of the 'middle schools' does something further to bridge the gap between the old elementary school and the old *Gymnasia*. The principle of comprehensive education (as against selective training) now accepted for young children almost everywhere is relentlessly creeping upwards to include adolescents. Such precedents seem to the critics to afford little comparative justification for the unqualified use of tests for the identification and separation of intellectually gifted children. Before the usual age of separation for college preparatory, commercial, trade, and general courses, the tests, it is argued, should only be used as supplementary to other records.

Anybody who has graded term papers knows that teachers' references, though perhaps most accurate of the three methods suggested, are also not accurate enough as predictors of talent. Teachers are people and bring their own human weaknesses into their scales of judgment. Class feelings, ethnic and racial positions, interests and foibles, all project into grading. In addition, different teachers bring out different qualities in their charges. Somewhere in the world there is a teacher capable of triggering off the *best* qualities even in the worst pupils. But even in best circumstances, a teacher's reference translates itself only with difficulty into accurate means of the assessment of talent. How securely is an A— record divided from a B+? Does the teacher believe in abstract immanent standards or is he grading on a curve, a pernicious habit which truly victimizes the highly talented groups? Is the student aggressive and thus known to the teacher, or quiet and self-effacing and thus classed as sluggish? There is some force behind the arguments of those who claim that neither examinations, nor tests, nor teachers give the measure of genius or true ability.

The best measuring tools, even when applied all at once, do not satisfy the opponents of the present proposals for the gifted as good enough to assign permanently young children to diverse careers, let alone to label them invidiously. For every one talented child which the methods of selection identify and assist, they, by their very operation, ignore or vitiate the education of another. Labelling not only identifies, but also encourages and discourages. Every right choice may thus be offset by a mistake. It is understandably hard to accept the present methods of selection as reliable. There is a quip that under such methods Einstein, an undistinguished performer at school, would have flunked out of American gifted classes while Marilyn Monroe would have been accelerated. Such results might not be advantageous to anyone concerned. As one writer in the *New York Sunday Times Magazine* put it, with all due respect to Miss Monroe's admitted brilliance, it is generally agreed that her major gifts are in quite other areas.

Nor is the enlargement of the talent pool always tantamount to emergence of great genius. As Spencer Brown once put it in an article in *Commentary:*

> Society's eager misunderstanding of the question was illustrated to me not long ago at a lecture by a prominent educator who was lamenting the waste of our nation and the world caused by our failure to use fully the powers of our gifted children. In a rhetorical flight, he invoked Mozart: if only our schools could do their job, they would turn out Mozarts every year. Everybody nodded

in approval. But this was nonsense. We may lose a Mozart once a century, but no more; that's all there are.

Promotion of ability is also said to be complicated by the fact that the concepts of talent vary with geography. In Europe, an old culture with long tradition of cultivation and delicacy, educators are still commonly referring to the innate frailty of the gifted. "Natural ability is not a piece of good fortune like good health," said Lord Hailsham, at the time the British Minister of Education, in a speech reported in *The Times Educational Supplement:*

> The gifted on the whole find life more difficult than the relatively uncomplicated. They are more easily hurt. They often go wrong more easily. They hurt themselves and others far more dangerously when they do go wrong. In order to use and develop their gifts they require much higher standards of courage, integrity, and persistence than other people. They are not generally popular, and because they have that in them which reaches out for perfection they are far more conscious of failure when they fall.

In Europe, the intellectually gifted tend to be regarded by all except the more expert of psychologists as more vulnerable than the average. Logically enough, the educational system is designed to accord them special protection. But in the United States the gifted are claimed to be not frailer but more robust. It is amusing to note how our frontier has contributed the proof that our notions of excellence are seldom culture-free. In the United States, from Terman onwards, the strong, not the weak traits of character of the gifted were persistently emphasized. "The stereotype of the intellectual giant, all brain with puny wizened frame, is contrary to fact," wrote Charles C. Cole in *Encouraging Scientific Talent:* "Although their physical characteristics are less distinguished than their mental ones, the intellectually gifted group generally also get superior ratings for their non-intellectual qualities. Furthermore, contrary to popular opinion, this group is apparently less likely to experience nervous breakdowns or to have difficulty making emotional adjustment."

In an activist go-getting culture, not the gentle and fragile qualities and sensitive insight but all-around healthy energy geared to the conquest of the environment is considered a 'gift.' Hence, European intellectuals often have a hard time understanding their American counterparts, sometimes to the point of being unable to accept them as *bona fide* intellectuals at all. And hence, also, the programmes proposed to rear gifted Americans tend to emphasize quantity rather than quality, speeding up the rhythm of education rather than slowing it down. With such concepts of 'giftedness,' the critics fear, American education is likely to produce better educated salesmen; it will still be short on poets, theoretical scientists, and philosophers.

HOW BEST TO TREAT THE GIFTED?

So many unanswered questions about what qualities are gifts and who are the people that possess them should make it difficult to venture into the field of practical policies. But everybody agrees that one can sense without any precise definition when an outstanding child appears on the scene. One can see, or imagines one can see, or sees in terms of what one likes to see, in other people, the flash of talent that dazzles and enchants and elicits enthusiastic encouragement. It is precisely these discoveries and this enthusiasm that makes the sometimes monotonous and always repetitive task of teaching worthwhile. It is this power to mould the future that makes teaching a vocation.

There is thus excellent moral and professional foundation for wanting to do something for the exceptionally talented. But the disparity between what the gifted might need and deserve and what is proposed for them instead presents a new set of perplexities to some uneasy observers.

Nowhere, perhaps, as much as in the area of oustanding talent can one better establish the axiom that children are different from one another. A given group of talented, even when narrowed to the most minutely homogeneous classification such as, for instance, good mathematicians, still exhibits differences in aptitude, in temperament, in speed of learning, in personality, that would probably be much more important than their basic similarity. Thus in legislating programmes for the gifted, it should be especially important to avoid 'group think.' Yet it is feared that it is precisely planning for *type* instead of planning for *individuals* that the advocates of gifted programmes seem to be proposing.

It is often assumed, for instance, light-heartedly that what the gifted children need most in education is 'challenge.' One is exhorted to isolate them with children of similar tested aptitudes and give them the best teachers so that they may be challenged. To be sure, placing high demands on people 'stretches' them to fulfil the expectations. But most children with outstanding talents already know that they possess them. From early childhood, their precocity and repeated success gives them the awareness of their strength and the necessary motivation. For such children school organization can provide only a minimum of support, a minimum that consists of a maximum commitment to learning and of the *availability* of facilities. The library, the laboratories, the contact with teachers; these the gifted can use to cultivate their best interests. *More* organization, *more* routine, *more* scheduling can aid the wavering or the slothful. But upon the gifted, the truly sensitive, it most likely has a contrary, inhibiting impact. Institutional, systematic 'challenge,' if only slightly off focus, may throw out of balance and up-set the delicate mechanism of a first-rate brain. Talented people often want to spend time pursuing their own sometimes erratic ways, ex-ploring the by-ways and pathways, spending time on irrelevancies. Above all, as every truly creative man knows, they passionately desire freedom to be their own intellectual masters. To quote Spencer Brown again, the gifted need to make "peace with and a place in a slow-witted world." Instead, object the critics, well represented in this instance by Bruno Bettelheim's article in *Commentary*, it is proposed that the schools should clamp upon them the new-fangled regime of more courses and a faster pace.

The systematization of the programmes for the gifted, because of the inertia inherent in all institutions, is said thus actually to discourage instead of challenging the gifted. At the same time the opposite assump-tion that it is the heterogeneous grouping that has this adverse effect on them has been a subject of critical discussion.

It is one of the most frequent arguments in favour of the programmes for the gifted that the public schools doomed to large heterogeneous classes neglect and even discourage the intellectually able pupils. But even this simple and too often true proposition is pronounced 'loaded' with assumptions that require elucidation. The critics ask whether it is the largeness or the heterogeneity that is at the root of the problem. Are the gifted discouraged because they are forced to take their educa-tion by the side of the less able, or because they are lost in the vast throng of children foisted upon a single teacher for simultaneous at-tention?

The neglect of the gifted might be simply due to the overlarge size of classes. The experience of the American private schools proves how well the gifted fare in small, though nonetheless heterogeneous classes. The vogue for the separation of the gifted in public schools should not get under way before the experience of such small classrooms has been thoroughly examined. The critics argue that the favourable effects of greater individual attention which such classrooms supply might go far towards meeting the charges of neglect of talent.

But if haphazard heterogeneity rather than size of classes is at fault, one should still have to ask whether limited heterogeneity might not supply the needed solution. It would be madness to put a lame boy into a football team. The question remains whether a team of top-flight half-backs is the only alternative. A narrower IQ range or group-ing by reading readiness, or, for that matter, even selection by height and health, might, it is argued, ensure the desired optimum without resort to separation.

There is also an important moral principle involved in the public attitude towards the gifted programmes. Suppose it is true that even in *small* classes the gifted would continue to receive less than their due in education. After all, it is true that for social, rather than educational reasons, the intellectually gifted children are often unpopular with their schoolmates and uncatered for by their teachers. It is claimed, with justice, that brilliant children are forced by their average contemporaries to conceal their talents. Girls in particular, in search of dates and husbands, are likely to be deterred from showing mental brilliance. "You can't get a Romeo with a Smith diploma: you can't get a man with your brain," runs one class song. Isolation with their peers, the proponents of the gifted argue, is their guarantee of freedom from victimization.

The critics retort that there is something perversely confusing in stating the situation in this way. If men are so stupid as to require girls to conceal their intelligence, they deserve stupid spouses. Nor are the girls who conceal their brains to get husbands really as intelligent as they were pronounced to be by the original definition. The critics also point out that such discouragement cannot alone be blamed for creating conformity. On the contrary, an attempt to cure the faults of mass education by separating the gifted in the name of nonconformity is said to be an evasion of teachers' responsibility. It is, in fact, an accentuation of the malady. For it is proposed to save the gifted from anti-intellectual *conformity* prevailing in the heterogeneous classrooms by subjecting them instead to intellectually oriented *conformity* in the separate classrooms. Rather than have them conform to the average, the argument runs, separation will cause them to conform to each other. Courage to defy the tyranny of the mass and the tolerance for the ignorant born of the sense of duty patiently to uplift them, these characteristics of leadership, the capacity to stand alone, which the gifted might learn in common schools, are, it is claimed, too highly relinquished in an effort to breed specialized brains in isolation.

A somewhat similar answer can be given to the argument that in a heterogeneous classroom the gifted are frustrated and bored. Special treatment and separation is thus recommended as a means of stimulating their interest and performance. Everyone performs better in an atmosphere of intellectual stimulation and excitement. But the presence of normal though less gifted children does not necessarily mean boredom, nor does the presence of intellectually sharp children remove the danger. Human gifts are sufficiently diverse and erratic to defy such a simple classification.

This writer himself, for example, recently watched a gifted class in arithmetic engaged in doing division sums. This class had quickly become a race to do the problems the fastest. It had degenerated into a contest between the four brightest children. As soon as the teacher put the figures on the blackboard, these were hastily scribbled on any nearest piece of paper and quickly divided. There was no care and attention paid to setting down the figures in symmetrical columns, no pause to survey the work done; everything was overshadowed by the feverish contest to be the first ready with solutions. And most important of all, there was nothing but boredom and apathy for the rest of the children, all selected for brightness, as time after time failure to make the first four places brought to them the realization that in this game they must forever remain beaten. The decision as to whether it is better for these children to be first men in villages or second men in Rome depends on the situation and the children involved.

Some students, in particular if weak, timid, or myopic, benefit most by being grouped with their intellectual equals. Others might benefit more by being given responsibility at the helm of less gifted groups. Some might need both experiences as part of their school time. There might also be other cases. Abnormally snobbish children might have to be kept in a general grouping even against their intellectual interests. Average but physically small children might have to be separated. Partial selection, even if only for body characteristics, is not farfetched. An intellectual child, in particular if small, might incur some form of victimization from more average but physically stronger classmates, a point which the proponents of acceleration seem to neglect. It is also the first obligation of society to give its ablest people a sense of confidence, not only in their mental but also in their physical proficiency. Those who worship Greek intellectual precedents are being reminded by the critics that the Greeks would recoil with horror from a genius brain mounted on a puny body. Yet, it is pointed out, the majority of best intellects in America do not take adequate care of their health and physical fitness. Partial control of heterogeneity, on mental, or even on physical grounds, does not seem at all ridiculous. Obviously no two situations are alike, and what is needed is not doctrinaire programmes but simple flexibility. There is a whole range of alternatives before the drastic remedy of a separate Bronx High School of Science, or even separate programmes for the whole science stream, are unavoidable. In these matters teachers must be allowed to play by ear. Multiple and varied human situations must be met by multiple and varied adaptations.

But to say this, the critics of the gifted programmes argue, is precisely to put forward an argument for heterogeneity, however circumscribed. Only in a flexible situation, in a situation in which one can count on a physical availability of all types of children can one adjust the groupings and the programme to the needs of the moment. To impose upon the schools the straight-jacket of preconceived, rigid classifications unrelated to the available opportunities and to the nature of the children involved, is to satisfy a pedantic mind but not to answer the problem of the neglect of the gifted.

And certainly, whatever action is taken it need not be accompanied by invidious labelling. The universities operate degree programmes and curricula suited to people with different aptitudes. Yet nowhere does such a policy include an advertisement of this fact. In schools one should similarly avoid 'typing' the ablest pupils. There are three or four companies in an army battalion and three or four platoons in a company because three or four sub-units make a tactically manageable unit. But the school is not an army. Children do not act and learn in three ways, but rather in as many different ways as there are persons involved in each situation. Individual differences are legion. To think of 'fast,' 'mediocre,' and 'slow' learners can never take care of all human situations. When educators allow themselves to say that people are bright or dull instead of different, they impose uniformities of type where diversity ought to flourish.

Thus, in a final analysis the thoughtful critics of the programmes for the gifted do not advocate the abandonment of the special experimentation in this area. They only plead for the treatment of this problem within the appropriate broader social context. The gifted child programme to them has no separate life of its own for the sake of which individual lives must be moulded and sacrificed. The concern for the gifted should instead be in terms of what represents the normal, healthy, desirable development of young children. American research energies should be overwhelmingly directed to this great, and as yet unanswered, question: What makes children learn and grow at different ages and in varying conditions? The special provisions for talent, as for any other special cases, are pedagogically justifiable only within this frame of reference.

THE VALUE OF THE GIFTED

The greatest argument on the subject of the gifted centres, however, not on methods of their identification or handling but on the ethical and functional justification of an equalitarian as against the *élite* society. In the 1957 catalogue of publications of the Association of University Presses, for instance, an announcement of a book on *The Education of Children of Above Average Mentality* began with a sentence: "Our most valuable national resource is the above average child." This at once prompted the critics to raise an eye-brow. Valuable, certainly—but why *most* valuable? Why in a democracy where "all men are created equal" and possess certain inalienable rights, where all are called upon to cast intelligent votes, where the government is a system of checks and balances depending solely on the will and vigilance of *all* its citizens, why in such a society are *some* more valuable than others? Equalitarians point out that the American society has been the one society to hold as irrelevant the accidental differences of birth, wealth, race, religion, and nationality. Why are differences of brain, an equal accident of birth, not irrelevant? Why are they to be a privilege, a bonus that entitles their holders to special regard and not an obligation, a condition of duty? The equalitarians complain that it is almost by an unconscious slip of the tongue that the words 'better children' are substituted for the word 'gifted.'

It is obvious that rights of individuals demand that talent should find proper opportunities. Gifted children with aptitude and liking for intellectual professions must thus be given all proper help to reach these professions. It is equally obvious that the nature of professional work requires that its practitioners enjoy respect and thus be provided for financially in sufficiency. Men who must wonder how to pay next month's bills are likely to do this at the expense of thorough absorption in their professional work. On the other hand, it has been argued that after an allowance for rare skills, intellectuals are not really entitled to any favouritism in salary policies or social prestige.

"There is something eugenically wrong here and now, without waiting for ultimate consequences," wrote Lord Stamp in 1931, "when a first-class honours graduate lecturing on chemistry, or doing research work, is getting little more than the man who cleans the laboratory windows or minds the building." Several equalitarians have wondered what it is that is so eugenically wrong with such a proposition. They reflect that from the point of view of welfare, the drudgery of the window cleaner, undertaken presumably through economic necessity, would seem to merit larger rewards than the work of an intellectual worker. After all, the latter follows an occupation which, by virtue of his inclination, is interesting to him, and which enables him to postpone the entry into productive market during several years of training while others of his generation already contribute their services to society. An intellectual, is not an athlete. He must be indebted to society for furnishing him with the accumulated heritage of knowledge without which he could not become intellectual at all. The great dependence of intellectuals upon their heritage is a debt they must pay, by the benefits and services which the society derives from them. Why, then, ask the critics, are intellectuals "the most valuable resource," more valuable than other members of society which sustain them?

It has also been argued that a near-genius who decides to become a fisherman in Maine cannot be forced, and perhaps ought not even be coaxed, into intellectual work. Last summer this writer had an occasion to visit briefly a class of gifted 11-year-olds. Culled from the ablest children of that age in Manhattan, this class, under the guidance of an able teacher, was spending a sunny morning indoors at Teachers College, Columbia, discussing the meaning of force in the writings of

Rousseau. It was an excellent lesson. But, ask those hostile to the project, why should our 11-year-olds, genius or not, spend their summer discussing the meaning of force in Rousseau? Why is this a better use of summer-time for young children than the Tanglewood Music Festival would be, or, for that matter, a swimming pool?

Nor is this question meant to be anti-intellectual in character. Recently a 14-year-old girl from California made the American Olympic swimming team. To achieve this, she must have been kept in water from the age of 3. But is it right and good, the critics ask, to keep a girl in water from the age of 3, so that we may have the vicarious thrill of seeing our flag from the winner's mast in the Olympics? Is it even good for her as a young person to have this 'thrill,' to be applauded, famous at the age of 14?

An academically over-specialized gifted child, to quote David Riesman, "is exploited dangerously by the curriculum in the same way that a boy who is good at football or basketball might be exploited by the coach and the community." The question of early intellectual specialization is no different from the question of early physical specialization. The point of those who advocate caution is this: Is the insistence on early excellence really in any way different from early child labour? We have by law and custom pronounced our younger teenagers unsuited for factory work, for matrimony, and for adult movies. Yet no one protests when, after *Lolita*, scores of 10-year-old girls model flimsy negligées in degenerate magazine advertisements. Nor does anyone seem to protest when, for reasons that are pedagogically dubious, adults work off their various frustrations by insisting on over-ambitious programmes which interfere with the natural growth of children.

Abuses notwithstanding, the most sensible and the most usually advanced rationalization for early attention to the gifted is, of course, that they are indispensable to our civilization. The pressure for programmes for the gifted is built upon the argument that the waste of talent affects adversely the quality of our life. In the words of Havighurst and DeHaan:

> Civilization is rapidly approaching the point in its development where it much achieve new levels in the utilization of the resources of the world or forever fail to develop them. The burden of making such advances towards controlling them and developing our environment falls largely on the shoulders of the gifted. For the two hundred out of a thousand who have superior ability, there is, therefore, a great demand. The demand will continue into the foreseeable future. Since only half of these two hundred develop their talent to a point where it is highly useful, the demand is not being met and everyone is the loser.

There is no doubt that talented people render great services to the enrichment and expansion of our civilization, answer the critics. But such talent will not be elicited if we fail to provide the spontaneous *total* upgrading through which the many intangible, immeasurable, and unsuspected human talents can find true fulfilment. How many Mozarts can we hope to find if six-tenths of the children of the world have never seen or heard a piano? Where is the much needed Miltiades to come from in the hour of need, if six out of ten children are illiterate or rachitic? If eliciting of high talent is to be the goal of education its achievement, according to the equalitarians, depends upon an advanced schooling for all.

Furthermore, equalitarians maintain that emphasis on the highly talented *alone* cannot be a sufficient condition of progress. The history of the last hundred years differs from that of previous centuries not in the education of talented but in the process of galvanization by which the masses are now affected. Excitement, growth, and participation of all, or at least of a considerably larger number, is said to cause our time to stand out in comparison with other epochs. It is the general level of culture that makes comprehension and consumption possible on a scale hitherto unparalleled. It is the mass that creates the market for the talented. To neglect to educate the mass is to spell the doom of our culture no matter how well one caters for the talented. It is pointed out that the economic successes of the United States, U.S.S.R., and the miraculous post war rebirth of Germany and Japan, are due to these countries' systems of mass education.

Such opinions cause many Americans to regard public schools as improper places for the training of leaders. Their basic function, it is claimed, is that of levelling all upward towards the basic ideals of humanity and knowledge. No one is trained for a position of leader in a true democracy. All are trained to exercise qualities of leadership, if and when fate demands it, and to subordinate such urges and to offer co-operation when circumstances require.

Leadership in a democratic society is too complex a process to be regulated by schools. It involves so much more besides intellectual prowess—a sense of timing, ability to handle people, courage, and perseverance. Leadership responsibilities come also by pure chance. Hundreds of young professors at any time are equally well suited to be President of Harvard, but only one chosen for personality, background, education, matrimonial alliances, administrative record, and, last but not least, his age at the time the incumbent retires achieves this coveted academic post. Leadership even in the academic field has little to do with what the school does for talent. The school must do most for all. Only life can tell whether what it has done was worth doing.

The care for the finding and development of talent is the very heartbeat of all education. But that concern forever implies the opportunity for children to have access to alternative choices. The school is a broad waterfront on which each talent should finally be able from a storm-tossed sea to come to a peaceful mooring. This must be a mooring of his own choice, albeit selected with the advice of the harbour master. Plethora of courses, multiplicity of incentives, variety of stimuli, these are deemed to be indispensable educational conditions in which the American society and schools should pioneer.

The public schools are by now traditionally places of mass education. They are a public service, and, like a public utility, supply a free subway ride and not an expense account limousine. Concern with basic skills and virtues needed by all is the basis of public education. The public schools offer to all the irreducible minimum. Such philosophy implies that everybody has gifts. In the whole range of his activities there is something he does *best*. This *best* should be encouraged and cultivated. It is only an accident of residence and grouping that determines whether this *best* is better than other people's *best*. Every teacher knows that this *best* will be even better if encouragement and incentives condition their possessors to work hard and to seek richness of learning.

In a free society, argue the equalitarians, the schools point the way towards this ideal. The ideal that all individuals are of infinite worth covers the needs of the gifted. An attempt to prove that a different formalized breeding process is necessary to obtain good service from them has little pedagogical substantiation.

Schools are also defined on ethical grounds as places where all children should be trained to be persons, not items on a giant conveyor-belt supplying talent into the slots of national interest. This national interest has no meaning without a reference to persons. The first condition of true mass education is that all people are people. They may not be separated into sheep and goats; they are *not* sheep and goats. Such separation is indefensible ethically and intellectually.

This, then, for the sake of the record, is the opinion of dissenters from current enthusiasm for education of the gifted. It is hard to tell whether they are in the majority or minority. There is less doubt that their voice is now drowned by their more vocal opponents. But the power alignment of to-day is not the balance of to-morrow. We may expect the educational development of the future to be a function of both the dissenter opinion and of the enthusiastic persons who now concentrate on the highly talented.

Creative Thinking and Teacher Effectiveness: A Review

KAORU YAMAMOTO

The past decade has seen an upsurge in interest in creative thinking variously defined and variously interpreted. In school situations, many teachers and administrators have reacted to this new interest either with enthusiasm or with anxious aversion, while counselors have been exhorted to find, protect, and encourage creative talents among students. In the face of this, rather faddish, atmosphere, we might justifiably ask two simple questions: how does creative thinking affect a teacher's performance in her classroom and what personality characteristics does a creative teacher show? This paper presents a brief review of the present status of our knowledge concerning these two questions, teacher effectiveness and personality characteristics in relation to creative thinking.

CHARACTERISTICS OF EFFECTIVE TEACHERS

The personality aspects of the problem of teacher effectiveness have received some amount of attention in recent years from research workers (McClusky, 1949; Hunt, 1956; Strang, 1960) but, in general, "efforts to identify personality differences between superior and inferior school personnel, to isolate a 'teacher personality,' or to predict either competence or effectiveness of student teachers by means of psychometric or projective instruments led to limited results" (Hunt, 1956, p. 507).

Hunt (1956) went on further to point out the possibility that several kinds of personality make-up and role behaviors in students, teachers and their judges interact to result in various kinds or types of "competence" and "effectiveness" being tapped by various studies. So far, our understanding is too limited to answer the question, "What precisely is the form and extent of these interactions?"

Two studies quoted in McClusky (1949) are worth being noted here. The first of these (Anderson, Brewer, & Reed, 1946) revealed that certain personality characteristics of teachers persisted into the year suc-

Reprinted from *Gifted Child Quarterly*, Vol. 7, No. 2 (Summer, 1963), pp. 66-71. By permission of the author and publisher.

ceeding that in which subjects had had direct contact with these particular teachers, and that children's behavior tended largely to change with different teachers. Integrative behavior on the part of teachers tended to decrease conflicts among children, while dominative behavior tended to lead to unhappiness and frustration among pupils. Pupils of the dominating teacher tended more to the extremes of resistance and conformity and they displayed less spontaneity and less courtesy.

The second (Barker, 1946) study showed a high relationship between efficiency in teaching and teacher's adjustment to pupils, administrators, and associates, as well as the teacher's possession of a philosophy of life.

Borow (1959), after having pointed out the fact that much of the research in mental-health education has been of an informal, exploratory character, commented on the role of our school in facilitation of mental health as follows: "School contributes to the formation of positive student attitudes and effective personal interactions not alone by direct and deliberate teaching about human behavior but also by creating and maintaining a stable social microcosm in which wholesale human relations are the accepted order" (p. 223).

It is, therefore, expected that teacher attitudes "sharply influence the personal and social behavior of the student" in this microcosm.

Replication of the well-known Wickman study (1928) has been made from time to time by various workers and the results show that "all are in essential agreement that modern teachers have moved toward a clearer understanding and acceptance of behavior but still tend to emphasize as most serious those problems which transgress their moral sensibilities or frustrate them in their classroom duties (Hunt, 1956, p. 510). Beilin (1959) pointed out, however, that there is no reason to regard mental hygienists' or clinicians' attitudes as an ideal criterion against which to measure teachers' attitudes, since the observed difference is largely due to differences in roles of these two groups of workers and not alone to teachers' ignorance nor to their insecurity. The teacher's role remains primarily task-oriented, while the clinician's is more adjustment-oriented. Thus, it is unrealistic to expect one and the same reaction to children's behavior problems from these two groups.

CREATIVE THINKING AS A FACTOR

Now, creative thinking ability of a teacher as a variable in teacher effectiveness has not received enough attention as yet. This is apparently because of the recency of careful research in this particular area.

Knoell (1953) administered six tests of verbal fluency to 112 undergraduate students and followed up one year later 38 of them who began teaching in secondary schools. Three independent fluency factors identified earlier by Calvin Taylor, word fluency, verbal versatility, and ideational fluency, were represented in these tests and three types of independent ratings were collected from observers, superintendents, and/or principals. When these were correlated with each other, it was found that correlations between two measures of ideational fluency and various ratings were significant ($r = .30 - .40$). The author concluded: "It appears that ideational fluency is significantly correlated with teaching success."

The position which ideational fluency occupies in creative thinking has been repeatedly pointed out by many workers (e.g., Guilford, 1959). It must, however, be admitted that a teacher could be rated as "acceptable" or "successful" by her principal or supervisor while she is not affecting her pupils in any favorable fashion at all. Verbal facility is an important factor in interpersonal relations of adults' and it could therefore be overemphasized by observers in their evaluation of teachers.

Chorness and Nottleman (1956) administered a Guilford-type battery of creative thinking ability to 52 students (Air Force personnel). Nine tests representing six factors identified by Guilford, associational fluency, ideational fluency, spontaneous flexibility, originality, problem sensitivity, and redefinition, were included in the battery. The subjects were then observed individually as they conducted lecture-discussion sessions and rated on a nine-criterion, nine-point scale as for observable characteristics of instructor performance. By factor analysis, five factors were identified for the rating scores. These are: audience reaction, native ideation, problem sensitivity, originality, and spontaneity. The "best" single predictor in the creativity battery was the test measuring associational fluency ($r = .11 - .32$), the poorest, the one measuring redefinition ($r = .01 - .16$). Intelligence index obtained from Airman Classification Battery correlated .21-.34 with criterion rating scores. Exclusion of this index from multiple correlation tended to decrease the size of coefficients but these were still significant ($r = .19 - .48$). When two or three creativity tests are combined, they seem to predict the criterion equally as well as does the intelligence measure and little was gained by including both the measure of intelligence and the measure of creativity in a single multiple correlation.

The size of the multiple correlation found in this study seems to leave much to be desired. It is clear that creative thinking abilities measured here were, in and of themselves, not sufficient to explain a major portion of the variances of the performance ratings.

Torrance, in his preliminary report (1960) on an analysis of the evaluative thinking of effective and ineffective teachers of experimental mathematical courses, gave data collected from 163 teachers from grades six through twelve by achievement tests, aptitude tests, and daily logs recorded and submitted by teachers themselves. The results, though tentative, suggest that the most effective teachers do more "thinking" activities (convergent, divergent, and evaluative thinking) than the least effective ones, while the former tend to report proportionately fewer cognitive and memory activities compared to the latter. In addition, the most effective teachers, when they evaluate, do a "troubleshooting" or hypothesis-making kind of evaluation rather than straightforward positive or negative evaluation. The measure of effectiveness used in identifying the most and least effective teachers in this study is the regression coefficient of the post-test (in May) achievement scores of their pupils on the pre-test (in September) achievement and aptitude scores. The author stresses the need for developing new instruments better adapted to new concepts.

The use of daily logs is an interesting venture in the study of teacher behavior but this also presents some technical problems. What teachers say they do does not necessarily correspond to what they actually do in classrooms. In addition, the study does not allow us to answer the question whether certain kinds of teacher thinking are always correlated with teacher effectiveness in terms of pupil performance, regardless of the nature of pupils, of the method of teaching, or of the characteristics of teachers.

Sommers, in his Ph.D. dissertation (1961), presented a hypothesis to the effect that some specific teaching methods could be devised which, at one and the same time, accelerates subject matter learning (Freehand Drawing: a laboratory type course in industrial education) and general creative thinking ability. To test this hypothesis, a group of college freshmen was randomly divided into experimental and control sections of this required course and the former was subjected to "creative learning" activities emphasizing brain-storming or divergent thinking types of learning activities, while the latter received "traditional" teaching treatment. Analysis of covariance technique was applied to adjust for pre-test differences in creative thinking abilities and subject matter knowledge and the adjusted pre-post test gain was used as the criterion measure. The results revealed that the experimental teaching methods were not equally effective for various aspects of creative thinking ability, although they brought forth greater gains in subject matter understanding among experimental subjects than they did among control subjects.

It is one thing to show that certain divergent thinking activities add to students' scores on tests of creative thinking ability (e.g., Torrance, 1959) and it is another to show that such activities add to students' achievement defined and measured within the scope of our traditional curriculum and its underlying philosophy. Unless we revise or improve our curriculum to suit our enlarged knowledge about and understanding of the human mind, it would seem rather difficult to expect that learning activities specifically designed for creative thinking add materially to students' academic achievement measured on traditional scales depending heavily upon convergent thinking, cognition, and memory aspects of human intellect. If they do, then we should suspect some kind of incipient contamination on criterion effected through investigator's or instructor's knowledge about the enlarged concept of human intellect. The use of a subjective test on course work constructed by the investigator himself (e.g., Sommers in his study) had better be avoided to guard against such contamination.

Yamamoto (1963) studied the relationships between creative thinking abilities of fifth-grade teachers and academic achievement and personal-social adjustment of their pupils in a suburban school system. Results were based upon 19 teachers and 461 pupils and it was shown that high creativity level among teachers and pupils does *not* usually result in better pupil achievement and favorable pupil adjustment, when both of these variables are considered in terms of the adjusted post-test means. Obviously, the role of creative thinking in real educational settings is not a simple, clear-cut one and further research and re-examination of values are urgently needed before any extensive changes in educational practices are proposed in regard to creative thinking.

PERSONALITY CORRELATES OF CREATIVE THINKING ABILITIES

Few or no studies have been reported on personality correlates of creative teachers, while several studies have dealt with general personality characteristics of highly creative or highly effective people.

In the study cited above, Yamamoto (1963) observed that highly creative teachers show a significantly stronger *theoretical orientation* than that shown by less creative teachers. In addition, there was a fairly strong indication that the former group show a tendency to perceive and react to the more *complex* aspects of their environment when compared with the latter group. The two groups of teachers did not differ in their *aesthetic orientation*. Further, the two groups did not show any significant difference in their classroom behavior measured on five observation scales, Teacher Individual Activities, Teacher Grouping Activities, Pupil Class Activities, Pupil Disruptive Behaviors, and Classroom Emotional Climate.

MacKinnon (1960), in his discussion of highly effective individuals, enumerated the following characteristics as qualities related to creativity: (1) self-assertive, dominant, and high energetic, (2) high intelligence, (3) relative absence of repression and suppression, (4) concern with meanings and implications rather than with facts and details, (5) cognitive flexibility and verbal skills, (6) emphasis on theoretical and aesthetic values, (7) expression of the opposite-sex traits, (8) independence in thought and action.

MacKinnon (1960, 1962) describes a creative person as someone open to new experiences who struggles with the opposites in his nature and strives ever for a more effective reconciliation of them. He seeks to tolerate increasingly large quantities of tension as he strives for a creative solution to ever more difficult problems which are not set for him but which he sets for himself. What we see here, it might be said, is not a person of passive orientation who merely tries to attain a balance but an active person who spontaneously disturbs his present balance to attain a higher state of balance, or who strives to attain an equilibrium in the true dynamic sense of the word.

Torrance and his colleagues (Torrance, DeYoung, Ghei, and Michie, 1958) conducted a study to find out about the differentiating personality traits between graduate students who turned out creative projects in a personality development and mental hygiene course and those who did not on this score. With subjects amounting to 167 in number, they found that the more creative subjects differed significantly from the less creative subjects in the following five ways: (1) less authoritarian and rigid, (2) more creative or curious, (3) more sensitive to interpersonal relations, (4) more acceptable, dominant, nurturant, affiliative, succorant (less autonomous), and acceptant of needs, (5) more skilled in perceiving analogies.

Difference in personality measures used and lack of uniformity in semantics make it difficult to obtain an integrated picture of a creative person from various studies. Nevertheless, it seems to this writer that an adequate combination of both strong, able characteristics and skillful interpersonal qualities is a necessary prerequisite for a "socially effective" creative person.

Such an observation is partially confirmed by a study reported by Radig (1959). Earlier, Torrance and his associates had experimented on a 100 true-false item inventory, called Personal-Social Motivation Inventory, which yields eight subscores. Three of these eight were hypothesized as representing three fundamental attitudes conducive to successful creative work: creative attitude characterized by aggressive, divergent thinking; defect sensitivity characterized by critical, evaluative thinking; and self-confidence. The remaining five represent five attitudes hypothesized to be inimical to creative work. These are: excessive quest for certainty, excessive quest for power, excessive quest for meaning, excessive quest for social relations, and rejection of social relations.

Radig took two of these eight scales, creative attitude and excessive quest for power, as his measures and reported a correlation coefficient of −.68 between them. In addition, the interaction between these two measures was found significant and it was observed that a high power drive accompanied by a high creative drive seems to interfere with the quality of ideas produced by 105 (mostly graduate) students in a mental hygiene course at a college of education, whereas a high power drive accompanied by a low creative drive seems to provide a boost necessary for the production of original ideas of high quality. The best performance was observed among those with a high creative drive and a low power drive.

The results obtained here are quite interesting. It seems necessary, however, first to validate the various scales in the inventory before we start formulating hypotheses to be tested in future studies.

Rivlin recently reported a study (1959) of the relationships between creativity and self-attitudes and sociability among high school students. She used teacher nomination to identify creative students and equally able non-creative students among her 126 subjects of the tenth and eleventh grades and compared these two groups on various measures. There were no significant differences in self-attitude between these two groups, but, on social confidence, the creative group was significantly higher than the non-creative group. No grade or sex differences were found in this regard. Both achievement measured on the Iowa Tests of Educational Development and intelligence on the Pintner General Ability Test revealed significant differences between the sexes and between the creative and non-creative students. The boys scored much higher on both the achievement and intelligence tests. The creative boys' performance on both of the tests was the major source of differences between the creative group and the non-creative group, for the creative girls did not score much higher than the non-creative girls. No difference in parental occupation level was found. However, the creative students' parents reached a significantly higher level of education. Rivlin concluded that, in the case of high school students, two factors associated with creativity appeared to be social confidence and parents who had attained a somewhat higher educational level.

This study, somewhat handicapped by its exclusive dependence upon teacher nominations in identifying creative students, nevertheless suggests the need for further careful research on the relationships among intelligence, creativity, and achievement, and on the possible family background factors in creativity.

Flanders, Anderson, and Amidon (1960) and Flanders, Amidon, Clarke (1961) have reported some of the results of their study on dependence-proneness responses in the classroom by a 45-item pencil-and-paper test. Their subjects are several hundred eighth-grade students in Minneapolis-St. Paul public schools. They suggest that students showing low dependence proneness might show a stronger tendency toward creativity and, at the same time, be less restricted by teacher influence. Compared with students in general, on the other hand, dependent-prone students are apparently more sensitive to the influence pattern of a teacher.

In this study, however, no more than an educated guess is presented as for the possible relationships between certain attitudes of students and their creative thinking abilities.

SUMMARY

In summary, then, inquiry about the role of creative thinking abilities in social-personal effectiveness has been short in its history and narrow in its scope. Few or no studies exist, to the writer's knowledge, of the relationship between the creative ability of adults and their differential effectiveness as teachers with students who themselves differ in their creativeness. There are, however, some indications that creative teachers (or people in general) show certain characteristic reaction patterns toward the world within and around themselves and, hence, affect their pupils (or people with whom they associate) in a different way than that of their less creative colleagues. More studies along this line are definitely in order to throw more light upon this important factor in interpersonal relations and to generate hunches and hypotheses on its nature and functions.

REFERENCES

1. Anderson, H. H., Brewer, J. E., and Reed, M. F., "Studies of Teachers' Classroom Personalities: III. Follow-up Studies of the Effects of Dominative and Integrative Contacts on Children's Behavior." *Applied Psychology Monograph*, 1946, No. 11.
2. Barker, M. E., *Personality Adjustment of Teacher Related to Efficiency in Teaching*. New York: Teachers College, Columbia University, 1946.
3. Beilin, H., "Teachers' and Clinicians' Attitudes Toward the Behavior Problems of Children: A Reappraisal." *Child Development*, 1959, 30, 9-26.
4. Borow, H., "Frontiers of Personnel Research in Education: Part I. Modern Perspectives in Personnel Research." In N. B. Henry (Ed.), *Personnel Services in Education: Fifty-eighth Yearbook of the National Society for the Study of Education, Part II*. Chicago: University of Chicago Press, 1959, pp. 210-230.
5. Chorness, M. H., and Nottelmann, D. A., *The Predictability of Creative Expression in Teaching*. Lackland Air Force Base, San Antonio, Texas: Air Force Personnel and Training Research Center, 1956. (AFPTRC-TN-56-130, ASTIA Document No. 098905.)
6. Flanders, N. A., Amidon, E., and Clarke, P., *Studies of Classroom Interaction and Influence*. Minneapolis: Bureau of Educational Research, University of Minnesota, 1961.
7. Flanders, N. A., Anderson, J. P., and Amidon, E. J., *Measuring Depend-*

ence Proneness in the Classroom. Minneapolis: Bureau of Educational Research, University of Minnesota, 1960.

8. Guilford, J. P., *Personality*. New York: McGraw-Hill, 1959.
9. Hunt, J. T., "School Personnel and Mental Health." *Review of Educational Research*, 1956, 26, 502-521.
10. Knoell, D. M., "The Prediction of Teaching Success from Word Fluency Data." *Journal of Educational Research*, 1953, 46, 673-683.
11. MacKinnon, D. W., "The Highly Effective Individual." *Teachers College Record*, 1960, 61, 367-378.
12. MacKinnon, D. W., "The Nature and Nurture of Creative Talent." *American Psychologist*, 1962, 17, 484-495.
13. McClusky, H. Y., "Mental Health in Schools and Colleges," *Review of Educational Research*, 1949, 19, 405-412.
14. Radig, H. J., "Creative Attitudes, Quest for Power, and Creative Ideas of Educators." In E. P. Torrance (Ed.), *Creativity: Proceedings of the Second Minnesota Conference on Gifted Children*. Minneapolis: Center for Continuation Study, University of Minnesota, 1959, pp. 130-135.
15. Rivlin, Leanne G., "Creativity and the Self-attitudes and Sociability of High School Students." *Journal of Educational Psychology*, 1959, 50, 147-152.
16. Sommers, W. S., The Influence of Selected Teaching Methods on the Development of Creative Thinking. Unpublished Doctoral Dissertation, University of Minnesota, 1961.
17. Strang, Ruth, "Mental Health." In C. W. Harris and M. R. Liba (Eds.), *Encyclopedia of Educational Research* (3rd ed.). New York: Macmillan, 1960, pp. 823-833.
18. Torrance, E. P., *Explorations in Creative Thinking in the Early School Years: II. An Experiment in Training and Motivation*. Minneapolis: Bureau of Educational Research, University of Minnesota, 1959.
19. Torrance, E. P., *A Preliminary Analysis of the Evaluative Thinking of Effective and Ineffective Teachers of Experimental Mathematical Courses*. Minneapolis: Bureau of Educational Research, University of Minnesota, 1960.
20. Torrance, E. P., DeYoung, K. N., Ghei, S. N., and Michie, H. W., *Explorations in Creative Thinking in Mental Hygiene: II. Some Characteristics of the More Creative Individuals*. Minneapolis: Bureau of Educational Research, University of Minnesota, 1958.
21. Wickman, E. W., *Children's Behavior and Teacher's Attitudes*. New York: Commonwealth Fund, 1928.
22. Yamamoto, K., "Relationships Between Creative Thinking Abilities of Teachers and Achievement and Adjustment of Pupils." *Journal of Experimental Education*, 1963, 32, 3-25.

15 | RESEARCH

Evaluation of Some Research on the Education of Academically Gifted Children

PAUL WITTY

In spite of growing and relatively widespread efforts to offer improved educational opportunities for gifted pupils, there are few programs based upon research. Many of the published accounts are largely descriptive. There is a great need for research designed especially to evaluate current practice in the education of gifted children.

Several summaries of research on superior and gifted pupils have appeared; for example, one by Miriam L. Goldberg (1), another by T. Ernest Newland (2), and a third by Louis A. Fliegler and Charles E. Bish (3). The summary by Fliegler and Bish cites 251 studies, many of which deal with pupils of high IQ. Included also is a treatment of creativity and related topics.

There are in addition a rather large number of recently published books dealing with the gifted. Among them are volumes by Bruce Shertzer (editor), *Working with Superior Students: Theories and Practices* (4); the John Dewey Society's Yearbook, *Programs for the Gifted*, edited by Samuel Everett (5); and Maurice Freehill's *Gifted Children: Their Psychology and Education* (6). Several books addressed to parents have also appeared; e.g., Florence Brumbaugh and Bernard Rasho's *Your Gifted Child* (7), Ruth Strang's *Helping Your Gifted Child* (8) and Willard Abraham's *Common Sense about Gifted Children* (9).

Of special interest in connection with the present topic are the following publications: *Planning for Talented Youth* (10) by A. Harry Passow and others, Jack Kough's *Practical Programs for the Gifted* (11), and

Reprinted from *Educating Tomorrow's Leaders* (Columbus, Ohio: State Department of Education, 1962), pp. 43-63.

James J. Gallagher's *Analysis of Research on the Education of Gifted Children* (12). The comprehensive volume by Gallagher offers the most useful analysis of current practice in the education of gifted pupils.

TERMINOLOGY EMPLOYED IN DESIGNATING SUPERIOR PUPILS—A PERSISTENT PROBLEM

Until recently, a high intelligence test-rating was the criterion usually employed in identifying the gifted child. Concerning this psychometric approach J. W. Getzels and P. W. Jackson pointed out that despite its longevity, it is only "an historical happenstance." They indicate that "if the context of learning involved the production of novelty rather than the remembrance of things known, then creativity as well as IQ might become the appropriate defining quality of giftedness (13)." Within the last few years we have seen the introduction of new terms and broader concepts. Some writers continue to refer to pupils as gifted when ratings on intelligence tests are high (the pupils in the special class or school for the gifted); others may designate as "gifted" pupils who demonstrate very high educational attainment (the Merit "scholars"): some use the term "gifted" to include the "academically talented" (the upper 15 to 20 per cent scholastically of secondary school pupils); and still others treat among the gifted, pupils having aptitude in a special area such as science, writing, music, or art (as in the Portland experiment).

Several writers have attempted to make their definitions specific. For example, James J. Gallagher includes three groups which fall along a continuum of general intellectual superiority. The lowest level can be referred to as the *academically talented;* it constitutes about 15-20 per cent of the general school population . . . the Stanford-Binet reference point of IQ 116 and above would delineate this particular group. The second group can be labeled *gifted* and represents about 2-4 per cent of the general school population . . . their Binet IQ reference point is 132 and over.

The third group can be labeled *highly gifted.* It represents about one-tenth of 1 per cent of the general population, or about one child in 1000 . . . This group can be represented by a Binet IQ of 148 and above (14) . . .

Another definition of the gifted was implied by Fliegler and Bish who state:

For purposes of this review, the term *gifted* encompasses these children who possess a superior intellectual potential and functional ability to achieve academically in the top 15 to 20 per cent of the school population; and/or talent of a high order in such special areas as mathematics, mechanics, science, expressive arts, creative writing, music, and social leadership; and a unique creative ability to deal with their environment (15).

Still another definition appears in the *Fifty-seventh Yearbook of the National Society for the Study of Education.* Thus, the chairman states:

. . . The talented or gifted child is one who shows consistently remarkable performance in any worth-while line of endeavor. Thus, we shall include not only the intellectually gifted but also those who show promise in music, the graphic arts, creative writing, dramatics, mechanical skills, and social leadership. Although most of the attention of educators has been directed toward the intellectually gifted . . . we think of such special attention to the intellectually gifted as a weakness or shortcoming in the kind of program for gifted children that we should like to see in existence (16).

The following statement illustrates a very flexible approach to the selection of superior students in a project cooperatively undertaken by the Reed College faculty and the Portland school officials. This project includes not only

the intellectually gifted and academically skillful but also those with high capacity in art, music, dramatics, dancing, creative writing, mechanical skill and comprehension, and social leadership. Moreover, the Reed faculty advisers to the project and the co-operating public school teachers have concentrated attention on personality characteristics such as drive, self-direction, creativity, curiosity, and some sixteen more. Students who rate high on these are identified as gifted, even though their scores on intelligence tests are ordinary. When identified and grouped by fields, these high-school students are given seminars, many of them participated in by Reed instructors (17).

The foregoing variations in the use of terms suggest not only the need for clarification generally but also the need for specificity in a paper of this nature. We have been asked at this session to discuss research on the education of the "academically gifted." We have seen that the term "gifted" is used to refer to various types and degrees of superiority. Accordingly, we have found it necessary to restrict our discussion and have decided to discuss only the following groups: (a) the "verbally gifted" as indicated by high IQ such as that required for the Major Work Classes, (b) the "academically talented" as indicating the upper 15-20 per cent of the high school population in ability to pursue rewardingly subjects frequently regarded as college preparatory, and (c) students of very high academic attainment who are offered scholarships and awards. Procedures employed in providing for the various types of pupils will be presented; e.g., special classes, enrichment, and acceleration. Brief analyses or evaluations of each procedure will follow. Finally, a persistent problem will be cited and briefly discussed; namely the relationship of high intelligence to creativity.

SPECIAL CLASSES FOR THE VERBALLY GIFTED
ELEMENTARY SCHOOL PUPIL

During the past ten years a strong interest in special classes for the gifted has emerged, and programs are being initiated in which gifted pupils are placed in such classes. Of course, much of this work is influenced by the earlier contributions from cities such as Cleveland, Ohio; Los Angeles, California; Allentown, Pennsylvania; and New York City.

Two of the best known efforts to provide special opportunities for the gifted have taken place in Cleveland with its Major Work Classes (18), and in New York City in the Hunter College Elementary School (19). A diversified curriculum is offered in both programs. One of the characteristics of the Cleveland project is the emphasis given to social development and adjustment. Similarly in the Hunter College Elementary School, careful planning assures the well-balanced growth of each child.

In Indianapolis pupils who have an intelligence quotient of 130 or above are considered for special classes. Gifted pupils complete the work in the regular course of study, but their program is enriched and expanded. It is believed that "this program of enrichment has many advantages over the practice of acceleration or 'skipping' grades." For example:

> The gifted child's study program is designed to increase his knowledge, power, skill, alertness, and efficiency beyond what could be done in a regular classroom. This is accomplished through additional work in literature, history, science, and social studies. Regular subject matter is expanded through teacher-pupil conferences, educational excursions into the community, special research projects, and individualized instruction . . .
>
> The study of French begins in the fifth grade and the fundamentals of typing are taught in the seventh and eighth grades. Many other special skills are developed by pupils and teachers working together (20).

Another type of program that has received much attention is characterized as "partial segregation." In the Colfax Elementary School of Pittsburgh, "partial segregation" enables the gifted pupils (IQ 130+) to spend half the school day in a "workshop" designed to extend worthwhile interests and foster academic programs (21). Here children plan, discuss their projects, and learn to work together. Among special opportunities are the study of German and the stimulation and extension of various interests through research. Hedwig O. Pregler, principal of the school, states:

> . . . In the primary grades all children spend the first half of the morning with their regular classes, at which time they have their social activities, sharing of experiences, music, games, safety and character education, and similar

things normally done by an entire group. Midway through the morning the children move into their skill subjects, at which time the mentally superior children leave for their workshops.

In the upper grades the school is run on the platoon plan. The gifted children leave class when the group goes to the academic teacher and rejoin it for the special subjects like art, music, and physical education (22).

COMMENTS ON GROUPING IN THE ELEMENTARY SCHOOL

Since the advent of the special classes for the gifted there have been a number of efforts to evaluate this form of grouping. Some of these efforts have been concerned with the Major Work Classes of Cleveland because of their outstanding character and longevity. Thus, as early as 1928, H. H. Goddard (23) published a book about these classes and the progress made by children in them. In 1941, a book by Merle Sumption (24) described 300 pupils from the Major Work Classes.

Among the recent efforts to evaluate the Major Work Classes, the writing of Dorothy Norris and Walter Barbe (25) is noteworthy. The questionnaire approach was used by Barbe who found that the attitudes on the part of the respondents were generally favorable and that the later educational attainment of pupils from the Major Work Classes was superior. In New York City W. P. Schwartz (26) compared 200 gifted pupils in a special class program with 200 pupils in the regular program and showed superiority for the segregated groups.

Several other studies have sought to determine the effects of grouping upon the gifted. One of these, made with elementary school pupils, has been reported by Vera Miller for Evanston, Illinois children (27). Some pupils of high IQ were placed in special classes; others were "partially segregated"; and still others were given additional kinds of special opportunities. Comparisons were then made of the various groups, and the following conclusion was drawn: "While it appears that there are no great advantages to any particular plan, academically speaking, as measured by the usual achievement tests, any effort to help these pupils use their potential wisely undoubtedly pays real dividends."

Horace Mann (28) questioned whether partial segregation changed the friendship or academic clusters of the gifted. He studied acceptance and rejection patterns of children in the Colfax Elementary School of Pittsburgh and found that gifted children tended to choose gifted children as friends and for companions in academic endeavor in both segregated and unsegregated groups.

James J. Gallagher, in a brilliant discussion of the problem of evaluating programs for the gifted, points to the need for controls and stresses the difficulty in providing them, the dangers in employing subjective evaluations, and the hazards in the use of norms for comparative purposes (29). He suggests, too, some effective research designs. Gallagher states:

> Evaluation of these special elementary programs for the gifted have been sparse. The evidence seems to suggest that favorable results are obtained through special planning especially in the areas of motivation and creative expression. Changes in achievement test data are less definitive. There is some suggestion that the goal of "enrichment of gifted children in the regular classroom," while admirable in concept, falls short in actual practice. The classroom teacher has limited time available and more important, lacks knowledge of curriculum enrichment skills and content information that would be necessary to carry out such a program. Most of the programs now in existence have found it necessary to add specially trained personnel with specialized talents and training in order to make such a program effective (30).

PROGRAMS, CLASSES, AND SCHOOLS FOR SUPERIOR HIGH SCHOOL STUDENTS

One result of the renewed emphasis on the role of superiority is found in increased attention to the needs of the college-bound high school student. A conference was called in Washington in February, 1958 to discuss this problem. James B. Conant, who served as chairman, made these recommendations in a report which appeared in *School and Society,* May 10, 1958:

> . . . Throughout the conference we used the phrase, "academically talented" to refer to that 15 to 20 per cent of an age group who have the ability to study—effectively and rewardingly—advanced mathematics, foreign language, physics and chemistry. Obviously the gifted would be included in this broader definition . . . Throughout the conference it was taken for granted that the academically talented would be educated in the same secondary school as others less talented. The assumption was that such a general high school can offer a good educational program to a wide variety of pupils who benefit from the social experience of participating in a common enterprise with pupils of different backgrounds and abilities (31).

It was recommended that a comprehensive program for "academically talented" students be established at the high school level. This program would include as requirements for such students: (a) four years of the study of English; (b) four years of one modern language; (c) one year of physical science, and one year of a biological science; (d) one year of American history, one year of history other than American, and one additional year of some other aspect of social science; and (e) three years of mathematics.

The current interest in the gifted has brought not only increased attention to the curriculum of the secondary school, but also to the provision of special curricula within the various fields, particularly in science. Morris Meister, principal of the High School of Science, New York, stresses the fact that the High School of Science is a school in which science is being used as one of the tools by which a more liberal education is obtained (32). The high school is organized "around a purpose that is meaningful and attractive to the students."

The writer, in collaboration with Samuel W. Bloom has described some programs in science for the rapid learning pupil (33). The programs include the outstanding endeavor in the Bronx High School of Science, the Forest High School, the Monroe High School (Rochester), and the Evanston (Illinois) Township High School. Included also are descriptions of the work in Baltimore, in New York, in Phoenix, and in Los Angeles and other California cities.

Various other plans for grouping high school students have been developed such as the "honor classes" and "honor schools" which have been employed in New York City for many years. Recently, the "honor class" has gained in popularity.

COMMENTS ON GROUPING IN THE SECONDARY SCHOOL AND ON THE COMPREHENSIVE HIGH SCHOOL

There are relatively few reports on efforts to evaluate various types of grouping secondary school students. Perhaps this is because of the recency of the movement to care for the gifted at this level. In the 1946 *Manual of Child Psychology,* Catherine Cox Miles wrote: "The gifted, the potential leaders, discoverers, and creators, however, are usually left to develop their own skills in their own way, and in terms of personal initiative alone (34)."

David A. Abramson reported one study to ascertain the relative effectiveness of various types of grouping of superior high school students. The college achievements of 192 students who were graduates of the 1955 classes in four high schools were compared. Superior attainment in college was not found for the students who had been enrolled in the special high school, "the honor school," or the "honor-class programs" as compared with those who were graduates of a comprehensive high school practicing heterogeneous grouping. Abramson concluded: "The over-all achievement of students, as indicated by grade-point averages and honors, is associated with their level of intelligence rather than with the particular high school they attended (35)."

Joseph Justman evaluated the results of homogeneous grouping at the junior high school level. His investigations led him to recommend grouping and acceleration at this level. He concludes:

The segregation of intellectually gifted pupils in a special class is generally accompanied by academic achievement superior to that normally attained by equally gifted pupils who remain in normal progress groups. To be sure, in several of the areas to which attention is here directed, the better attainment which special-progress pupils manifest must be attributed in part, to the greater amount of course work which they complete and to the selection, for such classes, of pupils who show greater initial mastery of reading skills. However, these two factors, operating independently or jointly, do not wholly account for the superiority of the special-progress group. The indications are that some of the advantage is associated with pupil enrollment in a special-progress group.

The acceleration of intellectually gifted pupils by a period of one year on the junior high school level is not accompanied by loss in those areas to which the program of appraisal was directed. On the contrary, a concomitant gain in academic achievement may be noted. On the basis of the evidence resulting from this study, it is clear that the segregation of intellectually gifted pupils in homogeneous special-progress groups on the junior high school level has some value (36).

Several studies have sought to ascertain the effects of grouping upon the attitudes of pupils. The following comment is made in *Administration: Procedures and School Practices for the Academically Talented Student in the Secondary School* (37):

> Contrary to the idea that grouping makes the gifted student conceited, he is likely to be less so when competing with students with like abilities rather than with others over whom he excels by a large margin with relatively little effort. The real competition which gifted students meet in special sections makes it less likely that they will become egotistical about their superiority. The Talented Youth Project (38) has indicated that special grouping of superior students causes their self-estimates to go down (they are now comparing themselves with their real intellectual peers, and they find they must work like everyone else); thus, "the gap between their perception of their present status and of their wished-for status increased . . . leaving more psychological space for improvement."

It has frequently been pointed out that the provisions recommended for the "academically talented" student in the comprehensive high school are insufficient to challenge the very superior pupil. A. Harry Passow has cited some of these charges and has stressed the fact that "secondary schools fail to get many of the brightest youth." He indicates too that attention to motivation is often inadequate. Consequently, many capable students fail to go on to college. Moreover, critics have said that the "comprehensive high school program is watered down, fragmentized, and incohesive." However, he cites some of the values of the comprehensive high school and describes areas of need.

> The daily press and professional journals alike clamor about shortages of scientists and engineers . . . Perhaps our most frightening shortages are not in the general supply of scientists but in those rare persons with imagination,

creativity, motivation, competence, and education who can contribute something fresh and basic to our understanding of man's relations with man (39).

ACCELERATION AS A METHOD OF CARING FOR THE GIFTED

As early as 1933, W. L. Wilkins and Paul Witty summarized the literature on acceleration and stated that moderate amounts of acceleration seemed justifiable for the gifted (40). J. W. Trusler later recommended more frequent grade-skipping for pupils of IQ 125 and above (41). This recommendation seems to be in accord with suggestions drawn from genetic studies which show that acceleration in the elementary school up to two full grades is not associated with undesirable later adjustment in the gifted. A summary of studies in this field has been prepared by Dean A. Worcester, who stresses the values of acceleration (42).

The School-College Plan (Ford Foundation), involving Andover, Exeter, Lawrenceville, Harvard, Yale and Princeton, was developed to avoid course duplication and repetition of instruction. As a result of study and investigation, it was recommended that superior students of good emotional control, health, and social adjustment be permitted to take the normal eight years of high school and college in seven years. A Ford-sponsored project, the Program for Early Admission to College, involved four hundred twenty young students admitted in September, 1951, to twelve colleges prior to their graduation from high school. Four hundred forty more were admitted in September, 1952. Additional grants in 1953 and 1954 brought the total to 1350 (43).

Another related plan encouraged by the Ford Foundation involves the provision of college-level work in high school. This experimental program—the Advanced Standing Program—is now sponsored by the College Entrance Examination Board, which provides high schools with descriptions of college courses in twelve fields and prepares examinations in them. Students who pass the examinations may apply for college credit. In 1953–1954, the first year of the program, eighteen secondary schools and 532 students participated; many more students took part the following year (44).

It has long been recognized that lack of motivation is an important reason for the failure of academically gifted pupils to realize their promise. Acceleration seems to be associated with enhanced motivation and consequent success in academic endeavor. In fact, the students who have gone to college early have proved to be generally successful in their academic work. It has been pointed out, too, that these students are assuming leadership in school activities and are causing instructors to raise their standards and goals (45). These findings seem to be in accord with results reported by S. L. Pressey, after studying the relationship of acceleration to success in college: "The evidence was practically unanimous that younger entrants were more likely to graduate, had the best academic records, won the most honors, and presented the lowest disciplinary difficulties (46)." Additional studies were summarized by Gallagher who states: "It is very difficult to find any study which has reported on balance, any negative effects of acceleration when the acceleration is done as part of a planned program and is limited to reducing the student's total educational program one or two years (47)."

Many administrators have inquired concerning the most appropriate times to practice acceleration. The following provocative suggestions are made by Worcester:

. . . Whether the acceleration be done individually, by special groups, or by subjects, will depend upon the size and facilities of the school. The school entrance age, the fifth grade, and the senior high school years are especially critical periods for the development and maintenance of high motivation. A policy which encourages the setting aside of customary rules in order to care for the needs of the individual child at any time when these needs appear will save many gifted minds from disinterest and defeat. A policy which allows bright high school students to carry heavier loads not only saves their time but allows for higher scholarships as well (48).

SCHOLARSHIPS AND AWARDS FOR THE GIFTED

A very important source of motivation for the gifted pupil is associated with the availability of scholarships and awards. Several programs, such as that of the Westinghouse Science Talent Search have long offered substantial help to qualified students. In 1956 the National Merit Scholarship Corporation conducted its first screening program with the objective of granting 556 four-year scholarships to talented high school students.

As a first step, 58,158 high school seniors ranking in the top five per cent of their class were nominated as participants by high school principals throughout the United States including Alaska, Hawaii, and Puerto Rico. This sample was given a preliminary screening test measuring verbal and mathematical aptitudes. Next, a sample of 5,078 students or finalists was secured from the large participant sample by selecting the highest scoring students on this test from each state in proportion to the size of the high school senior population for that state . . . Last, a selection committee composed of eight educators made the selection of 556 students from the sample of 5,078 (49).

Recent studies have shown that in many ways these "scholars" resemble the "gifted" adolescents of earlier studies. The number of four-year scholarships has been greatly increased. Thus, in the *Fourth Annual Report of the Corporation*, we find that:

By the end of the Corporation's fourth year, more than 3,000 students with Merit Scholarships, sponsored by NMSC and participating corporations and foundations, had entered college. Twenty-six had already been graduated—almost all with honors—completing their college work in less than four years, some in as little as two.

In the fourth program, completed in 1959, the Corporation provided qualifying examinations to 478,991 students in 14,454 participating secondary schools —the largest number of participants in any one year until that time. From these examinees it selected 10,334 semifinalists from 4,101 schools, chose 920 of the most outstanding as Scholars, and awarded them Merit Scholarships (50).

COMMENTS ON SOME VALUES OF OFFERING AWARDS

Students who have been given scholarships and awards have generally been successful in college. Thus, in the 1960 Report of the National Merit Scholarship Corporation, a statistical profile of the first class is given, "The first class of 555 Merit Scholars entered college in 1956." It is of interest to note that: "Of these 555, as of August 31, 1960, 461 have been graduated, 37 of them in less than four years and 424 on schedule." Of the 461 graduates:

Almost 80 per cent were graduated with academic honors. More than 60 per cent were elected to one or more national academic honor societies.

Nearly one in five won national or campus honors for leadership in student organizations and extracurricular activities.

One hundred nine (about one out of three of the women and one out of five of the men) married while in college or soon after graduation.

Three out of four entered graduate or professional schools in the fall of 1960 (51).

THE RELATIONSHIP OF HIGH VERBAL ABILITY TO CREATIVITY

The tendency to equate high IQ with creativity is of long standing. Even before 1930, the writer indicated the fallacy of referring to a child of IQ 140 plus as a "genius" or "near-genius (52)." He warned too against accepting the widely-held view that "only the gifted can create!" With Harvey C. Lehman he prepared a series of articles on "drive" and other factors . . . neglected traits in the study of the gifted (53). However, the tendency to equate IQ with creative ability persisted and still may be noted. Thus, J. W. Getzels and P. W. Jackson state:

Although few would argue that the terms "creative" and "intelligent" refer to independent classes of phenomena, still fewer would seriously propose that the two terms are synonymous. Despite this recognition of relative independence at the theoretical level, when turning to practical problems involving

the assessment of the two qualities, one finds that the well-established intelligence test is most frequently used as *the* indicator of creativity. Individuals
are grouped by IQ, and generally there is disappointment if the high-IQ person is not also creative. Sometimes he is not. There is also bewilderment when
the creative individual has a relatively low IQ as is often the case (54).

There is underway a much needed antidote to the foregoing tendency,
which is finding expression in a number of outstanding studies of
creativity. Among the significant reports are those of Viktor Lowenfeld
and J. P. Guilford. Concerning these efforts, Lowenfeld states:

We have been trying to find criteria which may significantly differentiate
between creative and less- or non-creative people in the arts. Our efforts to
find measurable criteria responsible for creativeness were not made for the
purpose of testing people or categorizing them, but mainly in order to find
means which could more effectively promote creativeness especially on the
adolescent or postadolescent level.

While we were conducting our experiments, we came across an entirely
independent study which J. P. Guilford and his staff were conducting at the
University of Southern California in an effort to find measurable criteria of
creativeness in the exact and applied sciences.

The significant factor of the two entirely independent studies (testing the
same phenomena but for different purposes) is that both investigators, after
exploring numerous possible criteria, arrived at almost exactly the same eight
criteria of creativity which significantly differentiate between creative people
and those who are less- or non-creative.

Since we were not positive that the two tests measuring these criteria actually tested the same attributes, Kenneth Beittel of my staff conducted a
study to correlate the two batteries of tests. He found that there is a highly
significant correlation (.454 and .541 in two studies) between the attributes
tested in both investigations. This would, then, as far as our data are concerned, establish that *creativeness in the arts has common attributes with
creativeness in the sciences* (55).

Lowenfeld lists the following eight criteria of creativity:

1. Sensitivity to Problems
2. Fluency of Idea
3. Flexibility
4. Originality
5. Redefinition and the Ability to Rearrange
6. Analysis or the Ability to Abstract
7. Synthesis and Closure
8. Coherence of Organization

J. P. Guilford and his associates have set forth forty components of
intellect (56). With tests based on such studies, Jacob W. Getzels and
Philip W. Jackson (57) have experimented further. They conducted a

number of investigations to identify the creative child by use of the following measures:

a. Word associations, the ability to attach varied definitions to single words.
b. Uses for things, the ability to find different uses for things having stereotyped functions and to categorize them.
c. Hidden shapes, the ability to discover a hidden geometric form within complex patterns.
d. Fables, the ability to complete fables with a concern for appropriate and original endings.
e. Make-up problems, the ability to make up many problems from given information.

A group of pupils in the top 20 per cent in creativeness but not in the top 20 per cent in IQ were selected for comparison with a group in the top 20 per cent in IQ but not in the top 20 per cent in creativeness. The results of comparisons between the highly creative and the highly intelligent adolescent are summarized as follows:

First, with respect to school achievement, despite a difference of twenty-three points between the mean IQ's of the two groups, they were *equally* superior in school achievement to the student population as a whole. *Second,* when asked to rate the children on the degree to which they would like to have them in class, the teachers exhibited a clear-cut preference for the high IQ child . . . *Third,* comparing the personal aspirations of the children as reflected in the personal qualities they would like to possess, we find that the creative child rates high marks, IQ, pep and energy, character, and goal directedness *lower* than do members of the highly intelligent group, and that he rates wide range of interests, emotional stability, and sense of humor higher than do members of the highly intelligent group . . . *Fourth,* the groups show distinct differences in the degree to which they aspire for "success" in adult life. The high IQ child desires to possess those qualities *now* which he believes will lead to success in adult life; the creative child does not seem to use this remote goal as criterion in the selection of his present aspirations. *Fifth,* the relationship between the child's own personal aspirations and those qualities which he believes teachers prefer is quite different for the two groups. The high IQ child holds to a self-ideal which is consonant with one he believes teachers will most readily approve; the self-ideal of the creative child is not only not consonant with what he believes to be the teacher approved model, but shows slight negative correlation with such a model. *Sixth,* and finally in their written responses to our six stimulus pictures, the creative students exhibited a degree of imagination and originality unmatched by the high IQ students (58).

Getzels and Jackson comment further as follows:

The high IQ's tend to converge on stereotyped meanings, to perceive success by conventional standards, to move toward the model provided by teachers, to seek out careers that conform to what is expected of them. The high creatives tend to diverge from stereotyped meanings, to produce original fantasies, to perceive personal success by unconventional standards, to seek out careers that do not conform to what is expected of them (59).

TECHNIQUES FOR THE IDENTIFICATION OF CREATIVE STUDENTS

Few reliable measures are now available to identify the gifted in art and other forms of creative expression. Hence, observation and subjective judgment may be employed in identifying pupils whose performance in these areas is consistently or repeatedly remarkable. From performance, the possession of a gift is inferred. Ruth Strang comments on this approach which is designated "work sample" technique:

Creativity is probably best appraised by the "work sample" technique: the individual is given a task involving inventiveness and imagination. His production is then judged by experts in the field. This is a more direct way of appraising creativity than the elaborate inventories that have been developed (60).

Several techniques are being used successfully to detect consistently remarkable performance in the arts. For example, the symbolic and imaginative film *The Hunter in the Forest*, photographed by the distinguished cameraman, Arne Sucksdorff, was shown in about 80 classrooms in forty schools located in thirty-four cities (61). This eight-minute motion picture is not accompanied by narration or dialogue. But it has a musical score with sound effects which accompany the appearance of birds and animals. The subtitle "A Story Without Words" is used to provide an introduction to the pupils who are invited to write their own stories about the film. A film guide, is available for teachers who may suggest related language experiences.

More than two thousand compositions composed by the children after viewing the film were judged according to the extent to which the writing disclosed creativity and reflected: (a) genuine feeling; (b) sensitivity to the value of particular words, phrases, and larger units in expressing their reactions; (c) recognition of the film-maker's intent and the significance of his use of symbolic presentations; and (d) correct and appropriate use of English. About 10 per cent of the total number of compositions were judged to be outstanding and to suggest potential creative ability on the part of the writers. Many of these compositions were written by pupils whose IQ's varied from 115 to 130. An investigation is now being conducted at Northwestern University to explore further the relation of IQ to creativity in writing.

The increased interest in creativity may be noted in the comparatively large number of recent studies cited in summaries and in the attention given to the topics in *Yearbooks*. Thus, Frank Wilson in a chapter on "Creativity" in *Education for the Gifted* discusses experimental work on the creative process and includes suggestions for fostering the components indicated by research (62). Another evidence of the present interest in creativity is found in conferences devoted to various aspects of this topic. C. W. Taylor has reported the work of two research conferences on the identification of creative scientific talent (63). Another phase of the topic—creative thinking in the early years—is being explored by E. P. Torrance and his associates (64). Related topics are also being studied by J. C. Gowan whose comprehensive analyses of various studies are adding to our understanding of the dynamics of underachievement and of achievement as well (65).

CONCLUDING STATEMENT

We have reviewed some recent studies on the education of the gifted. In these studies we may note significant trends. One of these is reflected by the greatly increased interest in providing more stimulating programs for verbally or academically gifted students. Many of these programs are new and have not been evaluated carefully. Another trend reflects a concern for identification in terms of a criterion larger than that which regards giftedness as revealed solely or primarily by high IQ. Another significant trend centers in the study of the creative process and of creativity. In these and other areas more extensive research may now be undertaken since clearer concepts have transpired and more effective measuring instruments are being devised. The promise for widespread research on gifted and creative persons is indeed great. The importance of such an effort was indicated by L. M. Terman who wrote:

The current *Zeitgeist*, under the influence of the cold war, is pointing up the need for many more scientists and engineers than we have, with the result that a desperate effort is being made to increase their number. Granted the great need for such increase, that fact should not lead to the neglect of other kinds of talent. What I propose is that education of the gifted should be planned not merely to satisfy the felt needs of a given time but also to prepare the way for future appreciation of needs not yet recognized. By encouraging the development of all kinds of special talent and of aptitude for every kind of leadership and scholarly achievement, the *Zeitgeist* itself would, in time, be molded along more liberal lines and to the appreciation of whatever enlarges the spirit of men (66).

REFERENCES

1. Miriam L. Goldberg, "Recent Research on the Talented," *Teachers College Record*, LX, No. 3, December, 1958.
2. T. Ernest Newland, "The Gifted"—*Review of Educational Research*, XXIII, December, 1953.

3. Louis A. Fliegler and Charles E. Bish, "Summary of Research on the Academically Talented Student," *Review of Educational Research*, XXIX, No. 5, December, 1959.

4. Bruce Shertzer (editor), *Working with Superior Students*. Chicago: Science Research Associates, 1960.

5. Samuel Everett (editor), *Programs for the Gifted*. New York: Harpers, 1961.

6. Maurice Freehill, *Gifted Children: Their Psychology and Education*. New York: The Macmillan Company, 1961.

7. Florence M. Brumbaugh and Bernard Rasho, *Your Gifted Child*. New York: Henry Holt, 1959.

8. Ruth Strang, *Helping Your Gifted Child*. New York: E. P. Dutton and Company, Inc., 1960.

9. Willard Abraham, *Common Sense about Gifted Children*. New York: Harper and Brothers, 1958.

10. A. Harry Passow (with Miriam Goldberg, Abraham Tannenbaum, and William French), *Planning for Talented Youth*. New York: Bureau of Publications, Teachers College, Columbia University, 1955.

11. Jack Kough, *Practical Programs for the Gifted*. Chicago: Science Research Associates, 1960.

12. James J. Gallagher, *Analysis of Research on the Education of Gifted Children*, Springfield, Illinois: Office of the Superintendent of Public Instruction, 1960.

13. J. W. Getzels and P. W. Jackson, "The Social Context of Giftedness—a Multidimensional Approach to Definition and Method." Paper read at the Sociological Society meetings. Seattle, Washington, August 1958.

14. James J. Gallagher, *op. cit.*, pp. 5-6.

15. Louis A. Fliegler and Charles E. Bish, *op. cit.*, p. 409.

16. Robert J. Havighurst, "The Meaning of Giftedness," in *Education for the Gifted*, the Fifty-seventh Yearbook of the National Society for the Study of Education, Robert J. Havighurst (chairman). Part II, Chicago: University of Chicago Press, 1958, p. 19.

17. Malcolm S. MacLean and Robert B. Carlson, "College and University Programs for the Gifted," in *Education for the Gifted*, *op. cit.*, chapter XIII, p. 325.

18. Theodore Hall, *Gifted Children: The Cleveland Story*. Cleveland: The World Publishing Company, 1956.

19. Gertrude H. Hildreth, in collaboration with Florence M. Brumbaugh and Frank T. Wilson, *Educating Gifted Children in Hunter College Elementary School*. New York: Harper and Brothers, 1952.

20. "The Gifted Child in the Indianapolis Public Schools." Brochure, published by the Board of School Commissioners of the City of Indianapolis.

21. Hedwig O. Pregler, "Adjustment through Partial Segregation," *National Elementary Principal*, Vol. 32 (September, 1952), pp. 241-246.

22. Hedwig O. Pregler, Principal, Colfax School, Beechwood Boulevard, Pittsburgh. Quoted in Robert J. Havighurst, Eugene Stivers, and Robert F. DeHaan, *A Survey of the Education of Gifted Children*. Chicago: The University of Chicago Press, Supplementary Educational Monographs, No. 83, November, 1956, p. 95.

23. H. H. Goddard, *School Training of Gifted Children*. Yonkers-on-Hudson, New York: World Book Company, 1928.

24. Merle R. Sumption, *Three Hundred Gifted Children*. Yonkers-on-Hudson, New York: World Book Company, 1941.

25. Walter B. Barbe, "Evaluation of Special Classes for Gifted Children." *Exceptional Children,* November, 1955, Vol. 22, pp. 60-62. Walter B. Barbe and Dorothy E. Norris, "Special Classes for Gifted Children in Cleveland," *Exceptional Children,* November 1954, Vol. 21, pp. 55-57.
26. W. P. Schwartz, "The Effects of Homogeneous Classifications on the Scholastic Achievement and Personality Development of Gifted Pupils in Elementary and Junior High Schools." Unpublished Ph.D. Dissertation, New York University, 1943. Reported by J. J. Gallagher, *op. cit.*
27. Vera Miller, "Education of the Gifted." *American School Board Journal,* September, 1959, p. 66.
28. Horace Mann, "How Real Are Friendships of Gifted and Typical Children in a Program of Partial Segregation?" *Exceptional Children,* Vol. XXIII, February, 1957, pp. 199-201.
29. James J. Gallagher, *op. cit.,* pp. 60-63.
30. James J. Gallagher, *op. cit.,* p. 84.
31. James B. Conant, "Education of the Academically Talented," *School and Society,* May 10, 1958.
32. Morris Meister, "A High School of Science for Gifted Students," in Paul Witty (editor), *The Gifted Child, op. cit.,* p. 215. See also Morris Meister, "Bronx High School of Science, New York 68, N.Y.," in *A Survey of the Education of Gifted Children* by R. Havighurst, E. Stivers, and R. De-Haan, *op. cit.,* pp. 74-76.
33. Paul Witty and Samuel W. Bloom, "Science Provisions for the Gifted," *Exceptional Children,* Vol. XX, March, 1954, pp. 244-250, 262.
34. Catherine Cox Miles, "Gifted Children," in *Manual of Child Psychology,* L. Carmichael (editor). New York: John Wiley and Sons, Inc., 1946.
35. David A. Abramson, "The Effectiveness of Grouping for Students of High Ability," *Educational Research Bulletin,* Vol. XXXVIII, October 14, 1959, pp. 169-182.
36. Joseph Justman, "Academic Achievement of Intellectually Gifted Accelerants and Non-accelerants in Junior High School." *School Review,* Vol. 62, March, 1954, pp. 140-150.
37. *Administration: Procedures and School Practices for the Academically Talented Student in the Secondary School.* Project on the Academically Talented Student and National Association of Secondary School Principals. Washington, D. C.: *National Education Association,* 1960, p. 80.
38. *Talented Youth Project. Horace Mann–Lincoln Institute of School Experimentation.* Teachers College, Columbia University. Current Research Projects (unpublished).
39. A. Harry Passow, "The Comprehensive High School and Gifted Youth," *Teachers College Record,* Vol. 58, December, 1956, pp. 144-152.
40. Paul Witty and W. Laroy Wilkins, "The Status of Acceleration or Grade-skipping as an Administrative Practice," *Educational Administration and Supervision,* XIX, May, 1933, pp. 321-346.
41. J. W. Trusler, "Pupil Acceleration in the Elementary Schools," *Grade Teacher,* LXVII, October, 1949, pp. 96-98.
42. Dean A. Worcester, *The Education of Children of Above-Average Mentality.* Lincoln, Nebraska: University of Nebraska Press, 1955, p. 36.
43. Morris Meister, "Ford Foundation Experiments: Their Implications for the Science Education of High-Ability Youth." *Science Teacher,* XX, April, 1953, pp. 107-110.
44. William H. Cornog, "School and College Study of Admission with Advanced Standing," *Bulletin of Information,* November, 1952, pp. 1-17.

220 Wilford Building, Philadelphia 4, Pa. See also Fund for the Advancement of Education: *Bridging the Gap Between High School and College,* Evaluation Report for the Advancement of Education, 1957.

45. Elbert Fretwell, "Challenge of the Gifted," *Journal of Higher Education,* June, 1957.

46. S. L. Pressey, *Educational Acceleration: Appraisals and Basic Problems,* Bureau of Education Research Monographs, No. 31, Columbus, Ohio: Ohio State University, 1949.

47. James A. Gallagher, *op. cit.,* p. 113.

48. D. A. Worcester, "Methods of Acceleration," *The American School Board Journal,* Vol. 140, June 1960, p. 51.

49. John L. Holland and Ruth C. Stalnaker, "A Descriptive Study of Talented High School Seniors, National Merit Scholars." *The Bulletin of the National Assn. of Secondary School Principals,* Vol. 42, March, 1958, pp. 9-21.

50. *Recognizing Exceptional Ability Among America's Young People.* Fourth Annual Report, National Merit Scholarship Corporation, for the Year Ending June 30, 1959.

51. *A Pledge to the Future.* National Merit Scholarship Corp., Annual Report, 1960.

52. Paul Witty, *A Study of One Hundred Gifted Children.* Lawrence, Kansas: *University of Kansas Bulletin of Education,* Vol. II, No. 7, 1930.

53. Paul Witty and Harvey C. Lehman, "Drive—A Neglected Trait in the Study of the Gifted." *Psychological Review,* Vol. XXXIV, 1927; see also Witty and Lehman, "Ability Versus Effective Ability," *Psychological Review,* Vol. XXXV, 1928.

54. J. W. Getzels and P. W. Jackson, "The Study of Giftedness: A Multidimensional Approach," in *The Gifted Student,* Cooperative Research Monograph, No. 2, p. 6, United States Department of Health, Education and Welfare, Office of Education, Washington, D.C., 1960.

55. Viktor Lowenfeld, "Current Research on Creativity," *National Education Association Journal,* Vol. XLVII, No. 8, November, 1958, pp. 538-540.

56. J. P. Guilford, *op. cit.*

57. Jacob W. Getzels and Philip W. Jackson, "The Highly Creative and the Highly Intelligent Adolescent: An Attempt at Differentiation," paper presented at the American Psychological Association Convention in Washington, D.C., August 28, 1958.

58. Jacob W. Getzels and Philip W. Jackson, "The Meaning of Giftedness: An Examination of an Expanding Concept," *Phi Delta Kappan,* Vol. XL, November, 1958, pp. 75-77.

59. J. W. Getzels and Philip W. Jackson, "The Highly Intelligent and the Highly Creative Adolescent: A Summary of Some Research Findings." (Mimeographed).

60. Ruth Strang, "Developing Creative Powers of Gifted Children," in *Creativity* by Paul Witty, James B. Conant and Ruth Strang. New York: Bureau of Publications, Teachers College, Columbia University, 1959, p. 23.

61. Paul Witty, "The Use of Films in Stimulating Creative Expression and in Identifying Talented Pupils," *Elementary English,* October, 1956. See also Paul Witty and William Martin, "An Analysis of Children's Compositions Written in Response to a Film," *Elementary English,* March, 1957.

62. Frank Wilson, "Creativity," Chapter VI in *Education for the Gifted, op. cit.,* pp. 108-126.

63. C. W. Taylor, *Research Conference on the Identification of Creative Scientific Talent.* Salt Lake City: University of Utah Press, 1956. See also C. W. Taylor (same title), 1958.
64. E. P. Torrance and others, "Minnesota Studies of Creative Thinking in the Early Years," University of Minnesota, 1960. (Mimeographed)
65. J. C. Gowan, "The Present State of Research on the Able." *Exceptional Children,* Vol. XXVII, September, 1960. See also J. C. Gowan, "The Underachieving Child—A Problem for Everyone." *Exceptional Children,* Vol. XXI, April, 1955.
66. L. M. Terman in *Education for the Gifted, op. cit.,* p. 17.

Needed Research on Gifted Children

DIVISION 16 SUBCOMMITTEE
ON NEEDED RESEARCH ON
GIFTED CHILDREN

APA Division of School Psychologists,
Subcommittee on Needed Research
on Gifted Children:

GERTRUDE HILDRETH
GEORGE MYER
LEE MEYERSON
PAUL WITTY
HARRIET E. O'SHEA, *Chairman*

Many social scientists are concerned with the welfare and development of gifted individuals. There has been much research on retarded children and on children with behavior problems but relatively little is known about the gifted child. It is the conviction of the Subcommittee on Needed Research on Gifted Children that society cannot afford to block or damage the functioning of gifted children; if they function at their optimal level, they undoubtedly constitute one of the major reservoirs of real wealth in the country.

The Subcommittee has endeavored to locate and formulate troublesome, unanswered questions about gifted children, questions for which the lack of experimental answers is probably directly interfering with such children's receiving optimum guidance in homes, schools, and the community. Each psychologist who is interested in gifted children will

Reprinted from *American Psychologist,* Vol. 9, No. 2 (February, 1954), pp. 77-78. By permission of the American Psychological Association.

undoubtedly make additions to this list of important and puzzling questions. The Subcommittee has studiously avoided shaping any experimental designs to explore these questions. Each experimenter's design will be his own. This report has been approved by Division 16's Committee on the Gifted, by its Executive Committee, and by the entire Division of School Psychologists. It is the hope of the Division that activities devoted to the developmental progress of gifted children and to their education may be lifted rapidly out of areas of uncertainty and controversy by way of an increasingly solid foundation of pertinent experimentation.

By gifted children, the Subcommittee means children whose rate of mental growth is 1.4 or 1.5 mental years per calendar year or faster.

The Subcommittee hereby submits questions concerning gifted children that in its judgment are urgently in need of research exploration. The experimental design and procedure are conceived of as being the province of the research worker to determine. It is anticipated that each of the questions listed below will prove to encompass a family of research projects.

1. Educational administrative procedures.
   A. What are the relative merits (emotional, social, and intellectual effects) of various administrative plans for the gifted such as the following?
      a. Keeping the child with his chronological age group and "enriching the curriculum."
      b. Locating the individual close to his mental age level in school class with chronologically older children.
      c. Retaining the child in his chronological age group for some subjects and advancing him in others.
      d. Establishing special classes for children who have high rates of mental growth.
      e. Utilizing no special administrative plan for the gifted.
   B. What preceding or concomitant conditions can be recognized that are correlated with varying results from a given administrative plan such as any of the foregoing or any combination of such plans?
   C. Which of these administrative procedures (or others not listed or any combination of procedures) has the best over-all results for the gifted child?

2. What is the effect (emotional, social, and intellectual) upon the gifted child of organizing his school work:
   A. In terms of greater quantity of work of the same level of difficulty as that which he has been doing?
   B. In terms of introducing additional new subject matter (both in classroom and extramural)?
   C. In terms of advancing to higher levels of organization and abstraction in whatever experience is provided for him?

3. Relationship between ability and performance.
   A. To what extent is there "concealed failure" among gifted children; that is, are they operating below their appropriate achievement level although not failing by the school's standards?
   B. What personality correlates are there to such "concealed failure"?
   C. What factors have contributed to such "concealed failure"?
   D. What are the over-all effects of various procedures intended to raise the gifted child's performance to its optimum level?

4. What is the teacher's distinctive role in training the gifted?
   A. What effects upon a gifted child result from various characteristics of his teacher?
   B. Are special qualifications necessary in the teacher of the gifted and if so, what are they?

5. Life work.
   A. Is it desirable or undesirable to explore vocational interests and aptitudes earlier in the life of the gifted child than in the life of other children?
   B. What are the effects of beginning vocational planning and vocational preparation at various times in the life of the gifted child?

6. Personal relationships.
   A. Do close personal relationships become established between children of widely different mental age?
   B. Does the gifted child have to have companions at or close to his mental age in order to experience close personal relationships?

7. Special frustrations.
   A. Are there special frustrations that impinge upon the gifted child that less often affect other children:
      a. in his family,
      b. in his neighborhood,
      c. in the classroom,
      d. in extracurricular activities,
      e. in job placement?

8. Special satisfactions.
   A. Does the gifted child experience special satisfactions?
   B. If so, what are they and what are their effects upon the gifted child?

9. What factors account for any undesirable personality traits that may be found among the gifted?

10. Status as a group.
    A. Do the gifted in effect constitute a minority group receiving some of the typical hostilities directed toward such a group?
    B. What are the effects upon the gifted of such treatment when it does occur?

   C. Are there recognizable elements in a community that attack gifted children?

   D. What are the effects of various procedures instituted to make favorable changes in attitudes toward gifted children?

11. Does the gifted child have special needs with respect to his ultimately developing desirable citizenship traits, needs either in terms of the subject matter or in terms of the age at which subject matter (classroom and extramural) is introduced?

How Research on Intellectually Gifted Children Can Be Done

JAMES R. HOBSON
WILLIAM ITKIN
TOM A. LAMKE
HARRIET E. O'SHEA

Educational research is frequently difficult and complex. Results are often not definitive. Because these things are true, many present practices in education are based on opinion rather than on objective evidence.

It is clear, however, that to be sure of improving school practice educators rely on evidence when evidence can be obtained. It is more certain that progress has been made when evidence indicates progress than when nothing but informed opinion supports it.

At a minimum, in a school setting, research-oriented procedure may involve nothing more than an awareness that, prior to change, consideration should be given to the possible results of the change. Even these minimum requisites are not always present in a developing and expanding school program. The purpose of this discussion is to encourage research orientation for school programs as they make provision for the academically talented.

Felt needs and demands for research activities concerning gifted school children arise from many different sources. Research arising within the school system includes (a) the planned, long-term, comprehensive investigation initiated by the professional staff in guiding or carrying out school policy, (b) the smaller-scale inquiry into a specific

Reprinted from *University of Kansas Bulletin of Education*, Vol. 16, No. 3 (Spring Issue, May, 1962), pp. 107-116. By permission of the senior author and publisher.

problem in her own classes by a classroom teacher, or (c) an attempt to answer the "what" and "how" questions arising from immediate community needs.

Other starting points for research in the field of gifted adolescents are college and university departments of education, psychology, and sociology, through Masters' and Doctors' problems and theses as well as through more far-reaching projects involving college faculty personnel. Cooperation in research at this level and under these auspices may be looked upon as a professional responsibility for education and as a privilege to participate in enterprises which add to existing knowledge. Such cooperation is not a one-way street, and schools should expect a return in terms of assistance with their special research problems, adjustment to their convenience, and such reports from the projects as may be of information or perhaps of long-term assistance to the schools' operations.

Research demands or opportunities come also from national professional organizations and private or quasi-public foundations and from State Departments of Education. Many of these activities are purely fact collecting in nature on the part of the school.

The role of the top school administrator in educational leadership has been well recognized, and it appears in research as well as elsewhere. Manifest interest in gifted children on the part of a general superintendent can be the greatest impetus to the development of programs for gifted children. This was dramatically illustrated in one of the nation's largest cities by an increase in programs for gifted children from 109 programs existing in 1955, as a result of all the preceding years' efforts, up to 339 programs operating in 1958, following the superintendent's surveys of 1956 and 1958 (1). Leadership from top administrators who have the vision and the courage to evaluate instructional programs is much needed to place the art of education upon a sound scientific basis.

In undertaking research studies of significant questions and problems, the school staff will find itself operating somewhat differently with projects of different origins and, of course, with different questions that are being studied. Various sources of research projects and their operational implications are suggested below.

I. PLANNED CHANGES IN PROCEDURES (MATERIALS, METHODS, GROUPING, SELECTION OF STUDENTS, AND THE LIKE)

A. Projects Originating at the Administrative or General Teaching Staff Level. (Here the clearest and most comprehensive use of research techniques are in order.)

1. A survey of research literature (2) must be made to determine what is already known in the area of concern and to locate available measuring instruments that would be best suited to uncover the facts to be studied (or to disclose the absence of appropriate instruments, necessitating the development of new ones).
2. It is essential to formulate clearly the main question to be answered and as many sub-questions as may be desired. Generally, such formulations are the result of a continued process of discussion and rediscussion, resulting in many reformulations until a satisfying position has been established.
3. Ideas can be greatly expanded and clear choices effectively promoted through consultation with available experts in educational and psychological research and in statistical procedure, experts either within the school system or in nearby colleges or universities, in appropriate consulting firms, or wherever they may be found.
4. A clear plan for the experiment must be established (the experimental design). Such a plan will involve the following essential elements:

    a. The individuals or groups to be used for the experimental procedure must be selected and a decision made as to how many subjects will be used.
    b. A control group must be selected, matched with the experimental group in characteristics that are considered to be likely to have an effect on the traits or performances to be measured, such as: age, sex, socio-economic status, ethnic background, type of community lived in, prior education, known performance in the area in question, and the like.
    c. It is to be noted that when certain conditions are met, statistical procedures can be employed which are, in effect, the equivalent of a control group, if for some reason a control group cannot be established.
    d. As an integral part of the experimental plan, the final statistical procedures to be used in analyzing the data obtained must be decided upon in the beginning. The way in which data is collected will determine and limit the statistical operations which can finally be performed and the conclusions that can be drawn; therefore, all of the major statistical operations to be employed must be foreseen and provided for in advance.

5. When the experimental plan is fully developed, then both groups of children can be given the same initial measurement

at approximately the same time under the same circumstances; and a predetermined, satisfactory system for handling and preserving records must be put into operation.

6. The experimental conditions may then be applied to the experimental group for the agreed upon length of time, and simultaneously, the control group will go along under its usual pre-existing conditions with no essential change in these conditions.

7. At the conclusion of the experimental period, both groups (experimental and control) will be given, at as nearly the same time as possible and under the same conditions, the same final set of measurements.

8. When the data are in, statistical analysis will be undertaken and conclusions can be drawn as to the desirability or the lack of desirability of the procedures tested.

An example of an experiment carried on in a school system follows:

In the New York City School system (3) a question was raised as to how the achievement of homogeneously grouped, intellectually gifted pupils who completed the junior high school (7th, 8th, and 9th grades) in two years would compare with that of normal-progress, intellectually gifted pupils who completed junior high school in three years. This was the type of study indicated above in IA, "Planned changes in procedures: projects originating at the administrative or general teaching staff level." Specific questions were asked as to how the two groups would compare in achievement in mathematics, in science, in the social studies, and in creative writing. In addition, it was desired to know what would be the work-study skills of such pupils.

The experimental group, 95 pupils, were chosen with intelligence quotients of 130 or higher who already showed "superior academic achievement and the personal characteristics of initiative, enthusiasm, willingness to work, reliability, regular attendance, and the capacity for sustained work." They were enrolled in 11 special-progress classes in 9 junior high schools.

The control group consisted of 95 junior high school pupils in normal-progress classes matched with the experimental pupils on: the school attended, grade, chronological age, mental age, and intelligence quotient. The Pintner General Ability Test, Intermediate Test, Form B was used as the measure of intellectual status. The normal-progress pupils attended 11 normal-progress classes in 9 junior high schools located in comparable middle-class schools in New York City.

Of the 95 pairs of pupils, between 70 and 83 matched pairs were available for testing with the various final post-testing instruments.

According to plan, the experimental pupils completed the junior high school work in two years, and the control pupils completed the work in the usual three years.

On the final testing, the X Forms of the Cooperative Tests for Grades 7, 8, and 9 were used as measures of pupil performance; the Iowa Every-Pupil test of Basic Skills, Test B: Work Study Skills, Advanced Battery Form N was used to test work-study skills; and an assignment to write an original poem to be titled "The Stranger" and to write a story about a picture which was shown to all were used to measure creative writing. (The rating of the poems and the stories was done by specially-trained judges using an arranged analysis.)

On the tests of subject matter, the special-progress pupils exceeded the normal-progress pupils with a statistically significant difference in mathematics, science, and social studies. When those items on the Co-operative Test which applied to ninth grade material were removed and the two groups were compared only on the subject matter extending through the eighth grade, the special-progress pupils exceeded the normal-progress pupils to a statistically reliable amount in mathematics and in science. The difference in the social studies did not reach a statistically reliable difference, although the difference found was in favor of the special-progress pupils.

On the Work-Study Skills Test, the special-progress pupils were significantly higher than the normal-progress pupils on three of the sub-tests and on the total test. The remaining two sub-tests did not reach a statistically significant difference, but were in favor of the special-progress groups. An additional statistical study was made of the work-study skills to determine whether there was a relationship between reading skills and the score on the Work-Study Skills Test. It was found that there was a significant relationship, which meant that the special-progress pupils were probably helped in their work-study skills by their superior reading achievement.

When matched pairs were compared on their creative writing productions, the special-progress pupils were superior to normal-progress pupils both in their stories and in their selection and development of basic poetic themes as well as in their mastery of all the more technical aspects of literary creativity.

The findings of the study justified the author's conclusion, "On the basis of the evidence resulting from this study it is clear that the segregation of intellectually gifted pupils in homogeneous special-progress groups on the junior high school level has some value."

B. Teacher Originated, or "Grass-Roots" Research

With the ability and training represented by the more capable class-room teachers of today, it is to be expected that many questions about gifted teenagers and their instruction will arise together with the desire to answer these questions at the grass-roots level. Such questions ordinarily concern instructional techniques and materials, criteria, and methods of intra-class grouping, or the behavior and motivation of the gifted.

While the research steps to be taken would more or less follow the paterns outlined above, two pre-steps to be added at the beginning would include presentation of the problem to the teacher's immediate superior officer with whatever information and suggestions this might bring forth, followed by consultation with colleagues who may have the same problem and who might be happy to join in making the research a cooperative or team project.

The process of drawing an informed conclusion or of making an intelligent decision is the same whether it is arrived at through individual or small group effort or through long-term, complex, large-scale research.

C. The Researcher as a Member of a Wider Community

The research worker is not merely a member of his school faculty. He is also a member of the teaching profession, of the world of other research workers, of the community of children and youth and their families, of the city, the state, and the nation. No matter how small the research question dealt with, or how large, the research worker can help his many communities through reporting his findings—perhaps in mimeographed form, perhaps in a newsletter, perhaps at a meeting, perhaps in a journal. Other workers will be assisted by knowing what he has found. Publication in any form is both a friendly service and a professional obligation.

II. CHANGES IN PROCEDURES WITH GIFTED ADOLESCENTS INSTITUTED IN RESPONSE TO IMMEDIATE COMMUNITY NEEDS

When the impetus for changes in organization, in program, or in materials of instruction of the gifted do not originate with the professional staff, and when immediate action is expected, it is not possible to plan a long-range research project with an appropriate research design. In such an instance it is of the utmost importance that the school executive in charge of instituting the expected changes become a consumer of research for such guidance in his decisions as he can get through reviewing the research literature on the subject, followed by such small scale research as time and opportunity permit, which may consist only of specific inquiries in selected, similar communities.

In such cases, pre-testing may be impossible, but there may be data on hand in the school files about the children in question which might be usable in place of planned pre-testing, and it is possible to plan for continued evaluation ex-post-facto, followed by reconsideration and re-evaluation.

III. COOPERATION IN RESEARCH BETWEEN SCHOOL AND UNIVERSITY

When a university asks for permission to engage in some research within a school or within a school system, to grant the request may provide an important in-service training opportunity for the specialized school personnel who participate with the research workers in their project. Such a project may also help to sensitize participating teachers and principals to instructional problems, and it may improve their instructional methods and broaden their knowledge of instructional materials.

Participation in such university originated projects may contribute knowledge to the field which may have important ultimate applications. At the same time, participation in large-scale or longitudinal research projects may or may not yield immediate returns. Examples of investigations of wide scope would be: the development of improved tests to measure intellectual and creative ability; follow-up studies of the effectiveness of special provisions for gifted students with respect to their post-school contributions to society. Schools and school systems may make significant research contributions by supplying a few cases for a carefully selected sample as well as by doing smaller studies of their own.

IV. THE SCHOOL AS A PSYCHOLOGICAL LABORATORY

There are special responsibilities which inhere in a psychologist's being allowed to operate in a school system which have been well presented by a psychologist who is one of the assistant superintendents of schools in one of the nation's largest cities. In this connection Dr. Mullen has said:

The doors of the school are by no means wide open to the psychologist and his student trainee at this time. There are several reasons why this is true, and why it will remain true unless there are basic changes of attitudes both in the universities and in the schools. First, the university staff must realize that psychological work in the schools requires thoughtful preparation, not merely of the individual would-be experimenter or observer, but of his supervisors or advisors on the university staff. Urgently needed are an appreciation of the magnitude and of the endless ramifications of the task of the schools, a respect for the profession of education and for the individual teacher, insight into and interest in group as well as individual dynamics.

Secondly, the university psychologist who hopes to make use of the boundless laboratory opportunities of the schools must realize that he, or at least the psychologists in the schools as a group whom the teachers and administrators identify with the profession, must be prepared to give as much as they get. Psychology must sell its wares to skeptical if not openly hostile teachers and administrators, tired of being given advice on all subjects by persons who could not last a day in a tough school. In most clinics, if the family will not cooperate, the case can be closed and staff time given to some one more responsive. The public school has no such alternative. If the school psychologist makes elaborate diagnoses in language of no use to the teacher, or suggestions that do not work, or no suggestions at all, he comes back to that same school next week or next month to be faced with the failure of his work. The school psychologist has to be willing to get in and dig on the problems that are bothering the school. He has to be a member of the team, not an outsider who makes recommendations and washes his hands of the matter if the school teacher cannot make those recommendations work. He has to make as accurate and scientific a diagnosis as his profession gives him the tools to make; he has to bring his theoretical concepts and his basic principles to bear in achieving understanding. But, in addition, he must be willing to add his empirical judgments, his intuition, his imaginative suggestions for procedures to those of the teacher, principal, counselor, attendance officer, policeman, nurse, or whoever else is working on the case, admitting that he has no magic nostrums, admitting failures and gaps in knowledge, but working with the child or the family or the police officer, keeping on trying. Such therapy may not be scientific, but it can be grounded in sound concepts, with the gaps filled by inspiration and perspiration. It can be carried on in a perpetual state of intellectual curiosity as to why one child responds and the next one does not. In such a working climate, some successes will be achieved, some failures will be accepted as inevitable. The school psychologist will be accepted and trusted and used. When this happens, the profession of psychology will have an entree into the schools not otherwise available.

Thirdly, psychologists must drop their supercilious attitude toward some of the basic tasks of school psychology. Articles on school psychology too frequently contain belittling references to "routine psychometrics for placement in special classes." If the differential diagnosis of mental retardation, emotional disturbance, specific and localized kinds of brain damage, cultural deprivation or depravity is routine psychometrics, then a lot of lobbyists have been selling a bill of goods to state legislatures from New York to California. Such differentiations are not only the bread and butter of the financial life of school psychological services; they are or should be complex and challenging professional tasks. Certainly this is not all there is to school psychology. Psychologists should be used in re-education of the emotionally disturbed child or parent, in consultation on personnel and curriculum and administrative aspects of the school, in a thousand other ways. But that is not to belittle what is still a basic and significant task. If special class placement is routine psychometrics, let us teach the technique of the Binet to the kindergarten teacher, as many a school superintendent has suggested. If it is not, let us train psychologists to look upon it as the challenge that it is, lest many a youngster be harmed and psychology itself be sold short (4).

V. RESEARCH INITIATED BY A STATE DEPARTMENT OF EDUCATION

In carrying on state-wide studies, or studies of state-wide significance through selected samples, a State Department of Education may need the following kinds of cooperation from a school, or similar kinds of participation: (a) identification of subjects who fit specified sampling needs (children or teachers), (b) administration of a battery of tests, (c) information from existing school records to be entered in a questionaire, (d) release of teacher or pupil time for participation in experimentation, (e) space made available for experimental procedures, (f) consultation in planning experiments or studies.

Since education in these United States is a state function, it is in the interest of all schools to participate in research inquiries or projects at the state level. An example of a large scale state project follows.

The California Project on Programs for Gifted Pupils (5) is a current example of research on intellectually gifted children initiated by a State Legislature. The project was set up to determine costs of special programs for gifted children, special administrative problems of such programs, and benefits that might accrue from them. The specific objectives of this study were to enable the State Department of Education to formulate recommended programs for gifted pupils adapted to schools and school districts of different sizes and types. The study was carried on in three centers within the state, representing rural, semi-urban, and urban areas, and different geographic locations and socio-economic groups.

Three general classifications of programs were studied in the California project: (1) planned programs of enrichment accompanied by teacher consultant service; (2) advanced educational placement with accompanying special help to the pupil; and (3) full or part-time special grouping.

An in-service training program for teachers was an integral part of the California Project, although not part of the experiment to measure the effects on pupils of the different procedures. Teachers participating in this program have had the benefit of consultation with curriculum specialists and other consultants in orientation meetings and in summer workshops.

The advanced placement programs included several different plans. One group of children was accelerated in grade placement. A second kind of grouping involved gradual acceleration in ungraded classrooms. A third grouping consisted of junior high school pupils who completed the junior high school program in two years through summer session attendance. High school seniors who took junior college or university courses along with their usual fourth year work constituted a fourth advanced placement grouping.

Several different plans of special groupings were also provided for. These included "clusters" of pupils placed together within a regular structure, part-time interest groups, and planned contacts between pupils and community resource personnel who shared their special interests.

Pupils in the study were matched with control groups in terms of chronological age, mental age, educational achievement, and socio-economic status. Plans for evaluation included both subjective appraisals by participating teachers and objective data on scholastic and extra-curricular interests, on personal-social adjustment, and on intellectual and academic status.

The three school systems used in the project participated in one or all of the ways indicated above by which teachers, schools, or school systems can participate in experiments initiated at the state level, either by the State Department of Education, or, as in this case, by the State Legislature.

One interesting development of the California study was the impetus it has given other schools and school systems not directly involved in the study to initiate programs of their own utilizing the state materials and procedures.

VI. RESEARCH OF NATIONAL SCOPE

Research studies of national scope may arise in governmental agencies. Participation in such studies is apt to take the form of staff time to reply to questionnaires together with whatever assembling of records may be needed to answer the questions involved. There may also be an opportunity for a staff to formulate studies which it would like to see done on a national basis and to request that such studies be done.

From time to time, national associations may also have nation-wide studies underway which require the cooperation of local schools for their completion. To respond to such requests may be to contribute to new knowledge which may be beneficial to school communities or which may add to the general understanding of gifted children and youth and of what contributes to their sound development or what hinders it. Here, again, it may be possible for the school to request research to be done on selected questions of immediate interest to the school.

REFERENCES

1. Benjamin C. Willis, "A Second Look at the Program for the Gifted." Chicago Board of Education, Chicago, Illinois, 1958.
2. Aids in discovering information such as the following will be found useful: *Encyclopedia of Educational Research,* The Macmillan Company, New

York; *The Education Index,* The H. W. Wilson Company, New York; *Review of Educational Research,* American Educational Research Association, 1201 Sixteenth Street, N.W., Washington 6, D.C.; *Psychological Abstracts,* American Psychological Association, 1333 Sixteenth Street, N.W., Washington 6, D.C.; *Child Development Abstracts and Bibliography,* Society for Research in Child Development, Purdue University, Lafayette, Indiana; *Dissertation Abstracts,* University Microfilms, Ann Arbor, Michigan; *Masters Theses in Education,* Iowa State Teachers College, Cedar Falls, Iowa; *Mental Measurements Yearbook,* Buros, O. K., Editor, The Gryphon Press, Highland Park, New Jersey.

3. Joseph Justman, "Academic Achievement of Intellectually Gifted Accelerants and Non-accelerants in Junior High School." *School Review,* 62 (March, 1954) 143-150.

4. Frances A. Mullen, "The School as a Psychological Laboratory." *American Psychologist,* 14 (January, 1959) 55-56.

5. Simpson, Roy E. and Martinson, Ruth E., "Educational Programs for Gifted Pupils." California State Department of Education, Sacramento, California, 1961.

AUTHOR INDEX

529